THE PHILIPPINES READER

The Philippines Reader

A History of Colonialism, Neocolonialism, Dictatorship, and Resistance

Edited by
Daniel B. Schirmer &
Stephen Rosskamm Shalom

South End Press
Boston

———

Production by South End Press, USA
Manufactured in the USA
First edition, first printing

———

Cover by Jeff Smith

Library of Congress Cataloging-in-Publication Data

The Philippines reader.

Bibliography: p.
Includes index.
1. Philippines—History—1898-1946.   2. Philippines—History—
1946-   I. Schirmer, Daniel B.   II. Shalom, Stephen Rosskamm.

DS679.P63 1983   959.9'03   86-14637

ISBN 0-89608-276-8
ISBN 0-89608-275-X (pbk.)

———

South End Press 116 St. Botolph St Boston MA 02115 617-266-0629

PERMISSIONS

"The Philippine-American War" by Luzviminda Francisco, reprinted by permission of the author. "The Conception and Gestation of a Neocolony" by Daniel B. Schirmer and "Counter-Insurgency in the Philippines" by Stephen R. Shalom, both (c) by *The Journal of Contemporary Asia*, reprinted by permission of *The Journal of Contemporary Asia*. "The Miseducation of the Filipino" by Renato Constantino, reprinted by permission of the author. "The Independence Lobby" by Shirley Jenkins reprinted by permission of Stanford University Press. "Anti-Filipino Race Riots" by Emory S. Bogardus, reprinted by permission of the UCLA Asian American Studies Center and Ruth Bogardus Allen. "Struggle of the 1930s" by Luis Taruc, reprinted by permission of International Publishers Co. "Philippine Collaboration in World War II" by David Joel Steinberg, from David Joel Steinberg, *Philippine Collaboration in World War II*. Copyright (c) 1967 by The University of Michigan. Used by permission of The University of Michigan Press. "Roxas Violates the Constitution" by Ramon Diokno reprinted by permission of Jose W. Diokno. "Inequality in Development" by the International Labour Office, reprinted by permission of the International Labour Organisation, from *Sharing in Development: A Programme of Employment, Equity and Growth for the Philippines*, copyright 1974, International Labour Organisation, Geneva. "U.S. Investment in the Philippines" reprinted by permission of the Interfaith Center for Corporate Responsibility. "The CIA in the Philippines" by James Burkholder Smith, reprinted by permission of the Putnam Publishing Group from *Portrait of a Cold Warrior*, by James Burkholder Smith, copyright (c) 1976 by James Burkholder Smith. "Against U.S. Military Bases" by Claro M. Recto, reprinted by permission of Renato Constantino. "The Folklore of Colonialism" by Lorenzo M. Tañada, reprinted by permission of the author and Teodoro V. Agoncillo III from *History of the Filipino People*, ed. Teodoro A. Agoncillo and Milagros C. Guerrero, copyright 1971. "Protest Movement in the Philippines Widening Rapidly" by Philip Shabecoff, (c) 1970 by the New York Times Company. Reprinted by permission. "Agrarian Reform in the Philippines" by the Rand Corporation, reprinted by permission. "Tourism Promotion and Prostitution" by A. Lin Neumann, reprinted by permission of the author. "1975 Mission to the Philippines" and "1981 Mission to the Philippines" by Amnesty International, reprinted by permission of Amnesty International. "The Muslim Insurgency" by Lela Noble, reprinted by permission of the author and *Southeast Asia Chronicle*. "National Minorities" by Sally Swenson, reprinted by permission of the Anthropology Resource Center. "Church Opposition to Martial Law" by Robert Youngblood, (c) 1978 by The Regents of the University of California. Reprinted from *Asian Survey*, vol. 18, no. 5, May 1978, pp. 505-520, by permission of the Regents and the author. "Philippine Women and Transnational Corporations" by Sr. Mary Soledad Perpiñan, from "Women and TNCs: The Philippine Experience," *Access to Justice: The Struggle for Human Rights in Southeast Asia*, ed. Harry M. Scoble and Laurie S. Wiseberg, Zed Press, 57 Caledonian Road, London N1 9BU, reprinted by permission of Zed Press and the author. "The Amended Military Base Agreement" reprinted from *Malaya*, by permission. "The Logistics of Repression" by Walden Bello and Severina Rivera, reprinted by permission of the authors. "Aid to the Philippines: Who Benefits?" by Jim Morrell, reprinted by permission of the Center for International Policy. "The International Monetary Fund in the Philippines" by Walden Bello and Robin Broad, reprinted by permission of the authors. "Reagan's Advice" by Steve Psinakis, reprinted by permission of the author. "Majority Report, Agrava Commission," "The Convenors' Statement," and "U.S. Policy Towards Marcos, National Security Directive" reprinted by permission of the *Philippine News*. "Post-Assassination Economic Crisis" by Gerald Sussman, David O'Connor, and Charles Lindsey, reprinted by permission of Gerald Sussman and Charles Lindsey. "Growth of the Labor Movement" by Karin Aguilar-San Juan, reprinted by permission of Resist. "Hunger in the Countryside" by Kathy McAfee, reprinted by permission of Oxfam America and the author. "A Woman's Place Is In the Struggle" by Brenda J. Stoltzfus, reprinted by permis-

TABLE OF CONTENTS

ACKNOWLEDGMENTS

We would like to thank the following people for help they gave us in the preparation of this book: Delia Aguiar, Michael Bedford, Walden Bello, Jonathan Best, Gene Bruskin, Renato Constantino, Becky Cunningham, Doug Cunningham, Marites Danguilan-Vitug, Randolf David, Maria Socorro Diokno, Doreen Fernandez, Willie Fernandez, Joseph Gerson, Todd Jailer, Charles W. Lindsey, Mariandre Louis-Ferdinand, Tim McGloin, Helen Mendoza, John Miller, Baboo Mondonedo, Francisco Nemenzo, Lin Neumann, Connie Ozawa, John Pankowicz, Dr. Mita Pardo de Tavera, Charito Planas, Lorna Porras, Linda K. Richter, Severina Rivera, Joel Rocamora, Robert C. Rosen, Vivian Rosskamm, Lydia Sargent, Jennifer Schirmer, Peggy Schirmer, Chris Schmiedhauser, Evelyn R. Shalom, John Silva, Dante Simbulan, Roland Simbulan, Gerald Sussman, Ed Tadem, Edward Tawil, Robert Youngblood, and Sr. Aurora Zambrano.

GLOSSARY

AFP	Armed Forces of the Philippines
AMT	League of Poor Laborers, pre-World War II union in Central Luzon
barrio	village
Batasang Pambansa	National Assembly (1978-86)
BMLO	Bangsa Liberation Organization, Muslim guerilla group, rival of the MNLF
bolo	Philippine machete used for farming or as weapon
cacique	landowner
CAO	Civil Affairs Office of the Philippine Armed Forces
carabao	water buffalo
cavan	unit of dry measure; 44 kilograms of rice
CIA	U.S. Central Intelligence Agency
CIC	Counter-Intelligence Corps, U.S. Army
compadre	sponsor at a baptism, confirmation, or wedding
comprador	Filipino manager working for foreign capitalist
copra	the dried, oil-bearing meat of a coconut
CPP	new Communist Party of the Philippines, founded 1968
dato (also datu)	village leader in the pre-Spanish Philippines
hacendero	owner of a landed estate
hacienda	landed estate
hectare	unit of land area equal to 2.47 acres
Huks	Philippines guerilla organization. Technically, the Hukbalahap was the People's Anti-Japanese Army during World War II and the HMB was the People's Liberation Army which fought the Philippine government in the late 1940s and early 1950s
Igorots	largest grouping of tribal minorities in the Philippines, located in northern Luzon
ilustrados	indigenous Philippine intelligentsia in late 19th century

IMF	International Monetary Fund
JUSMAG	Joint U.S. Military Advisory Group
Katipunan	Philippine revolutionary movement of 1896
KBL	"The New Society Movement," Marcos's political party, created to contest the 1978 election
KMP	Union of Philippine Peasants, founded 1985
KMU	May First Movement, militant trade union organization founded in 1980
Malacañang	Philippine Presidential Palace
MAP	U.S. Military Assistance Program
mestizo	a person of mixed Filipino and Spanish or Chinese blood
Moro	term used for Philippine Muslims
MNLF	Moro National Libertaion Front, guerilla organization of Philippine Muslim led by Nur Misuari
MSA	U.S. Mutual Security Administration
NDF	National Democratic Front
Negritos	one of the Philippines' upland tribal minorities
nipa	palm leaves from which Philippine huts are frequently made
NPA	New People's Army
NSC	U.S. National Security Council
P	symbol for peso (see peso below)
PANAMIN	Philippine Presidential Assistant on National Minorities
peso	unit of Philippine currency; for many years equal to $.50, currently about $.06; 1 peso equals 100 centavos
PKP	Communist Party of the Philippines, founded 1930
RAM	Reform the Armed Forces Movement, formed February 1985
reconcentrado	policy of concentrating the population to facilitate counter-insurgency operations; used by Spanish and U.S. in Philippines at turn of the century
sugar central	mill for processing sugar
tao	common person; a peasant

xiv

TFD, TFDP	Task Force Detainees (Philippines)
TUCP	Trade Union Congress of the Philippines, established by Marcos government in 1977
USAFFE	U.S. Armed Forces in the Far East during World War II and the guerillas who served with them

CHRONOLOGY

1565		Spain colonizes Philippines
1896	Aug. 26	Philippine Revolution against Spain
1897	Dec.	Pact of Biak-na-bato temporarily suspends fighting between Filipinos and Spanish
1898	May 1	Admiral Dewey defeats Spanish in Manila Bay
1898	June 12	Emilio Aguinaldo declares Philippine independence
1899	Jan. 23	Aguinaldo declares Philippine Republic
1899	Feb. 4	Fighting breaks out between U.S. and Filipino forces
1899	Feb. 6	U.S. Senate votes to annex Philippines
1901	Mar. 23	Aguinaldo captured
1901	July 4	Pres. McKinley establishes civil government under appointed Philippine Commission headed by William Howard Taft
1902	July 1	Congressional legislation provides for colonial administration in the Philippines (First Organic Act)
1907	Oct. 16	First meeting of elected lower House; Osmeña elected Speaker
1909	Aug.	Payne-Aldrich tariff establishes free trade between U.S. and Philippines
1916	Aug. 29	Jones Law promises Philippines ultimate independence; elected Senate replaces appointed Commission
1934	Mar.	Tydings-McDuffie Act sets Philippine independence after 10-year Commonwealth period
1935	Nov. 15	Philippine Commonwealth established with Manuel Quezon as president and Sergio Osmeña as vice-president
1941	Dec. 7	Japanese attack Pearl Harbor and Clark Airfield in the Philippines
1942	Jan.	Prominent Philippine politicians organized by Japanese into Philippine Executive Commission
1942	Mar. 29	People's Anti-Japanese Army set up (Hukbalahap or Huks)
1942	May	Last U.S. forces in Philippines surrender to Japanese
1943	Oct.	Japanese establish puppet "Philippine Republic" and grant it "independence"
1944	Oct. 20	U.S. forces under General MacArthur return to Philippine island of Leyte
1944	Oct. 23	Philippine Commonwealth re-established with Osmeña as president

1945	Feb.	Manila cleared of Japanese troops
1946	Apr. 23	Manuel Roxas defeats Osmeña for presidency
1946	May-June	Opposition legislators ousted from Philippine Congress
1946	July 2	Philippine Congress accepts Bell Trade Act
1946	July 4	Philippines given independence
1946	Sep. 18	Philippine Congress passes "parity" amendment to Philippine constitution, granting special rights to U.S. investors
1947	Mar. 11	"Parity" amendment ratified in plebiscite
1947	Mar. 14	Military Bases agreement signed with U.S. for 99 year term
1947	Mar. 21	Military Assistance agreement signed with U.S.
1948	Jan. 28	Collaborators with Japanese pardoned
1948	Mar. 6	Huks declared illegal organization
1948	Apr. 16	Roxas dies in office; succeeded by Elpidio Quirino
1949	Nov. 8	Quirino re-elected president
1950	Oct. 1	U.S. economic survey mission finds situation in Philippines desperate
1950	Nov. 9	U.S. National Security Council authorizes all necessary steps to defeat insurgency
1951	Aug. 30	U.S.-Philippine Mutual Defense Treaty signed
1953	Nov. 10	Ramon Magsaysay defeats Quirino for the presidency
1954	Sept. 8	Southeast Asia Treaty Organization (SEATO) established in Manila
1955	Sept. 6	Bell Trade Act replaced with the Laurel-Langley agreement
1957	Mar. 17	Magsaysay dies in plane crash; succeeded by Carlos Garcia
1957	Nov. 12	Garcia re-elected president, defeating his traditional opponent, and nationalist Clara Recto
1959	Oct. 12	Bohlen-Serrano agreement on military bases: U.S. agrees to consult before using bases for non-SEATO or non-Philippine defense combat operations or before deploying long range missiles in the Philippines
1961	Nov. 14	Garcia defeated for presidency by Diosdado Macapagal
1962	Jan. 21	Macapagal removes import controls
1962	June 12	This date declared new Philippine independence day
1965	Nov. 9	Ferdinand Marcos defeats Macapagal for presidency; Marcos, going back on campaign promise, backs sending civic action unit (PHILCAG) to support U.S. war in Vietnam

1966	Sept. 16	Rusk-Ramos agreement: fixed term of military bases agreement changed to expire in 1991
1969	Nov. 11	Marcos re-elected
1970	Jan-Mar.	"First-quarter storm": massive student demonstrations in Manila against Marcos and U.S. government
1971	Aug. 21	Grenades thrown at speakers' platform of Marcos's political opponents; perpetrators never caught; writ of habeas corpus suspended (restored Jan. 11, 1972)
1972	Sept. 21	Marcos signs declaration of martial law
1973	Jan.	New constitution ratified by village assemblies, voting by show of hands
1974	July 4	"Parity" amendment expires
1976	Dec. 23	Tripoli Agreement signed to end fighting between government and Muslim guerillas
1978	Apr. 7	Elections for Interim National Assembly held, generally regarded as fraudulent
1979	Jan. 7	U.S. bases agreement amended: Philippine flag to fly over bases, but U.S. guaranteed "unhampered" military use
1980	Nov. 4	Ronald Reagan elected president of the U.S.
1981	Jan. 17	Marcos "lifts" martial law, but retains most martial law powers
1981	June 16	Marcos elected president in elections boycotted by most of his opponents
1982	Sept.	Marcos on state visit to U.S.
1983	Aug. 22	Former Senator Benigno Aquino Jr. assassinated at Manila airport as he returns from exile in U.S.
1984	Apr. 14	National Assembly elections; some oppositionists participate but fraud minimizes the number of seats they win
1984	Oct. 24	Agrava Commission finds there was a military conspiracy to assassinate Aquino
1984	Nov.	Secret U.S. National Security Study Directive finds Marcos part of the problem and part of the solution
1985	May	CIA chief William Casey meet with Marcos in Manila
1985	Oct. 16	Reagan friend of Sen. Paul Laxalt meets with Marcos in Manila
1985	Nov. 3	Marcos announces snap election

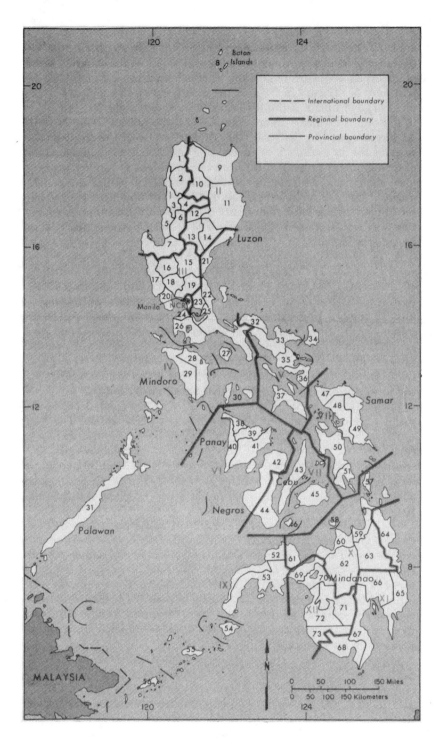

Classification of Provinces by Geographic Regions

NCR NATIONAL CAPITAL REGION

I ILOCOS
  1 Ilocos Norte
  2 Abra
  3 Ilocos Sur
  4 Mountain
  5 La Union
  6 Benguet
  7 Pangasinan

II CAGAYAN VALLEY
  8 Batanes
  9 Cagayan
  10 Kalinga-Apayao
  11 Isabela
  12 Ifugao
  13 Nueva Vizcaya
  14 Quirino

III CENTRAL LUZON
  15 Nueva Ecija
  16 Tarlac
  17 Zambales
  18 Pampanga
  19 Bulacan
  20 Bataan

IV SOUTHERN TAGALOG
  21 Aurora
  22 Quezon
  23 Rizal
  24 Cavite
  25 Laguna
  26 Batangas
  27 Marinduque
  28 Mindoro Oriental
  29 Mindoro Occidental
  30 Romblon
  31 Palawan

V BICOL
  32 Camarines Norte
  33 Camarines Sur
  34 Catanduanes
  35 Albay
  36 Sorsogon
  37 Masbate

VI WESTERN VISAYAS
  38 Aklan
  39 Capiz
  40 Antique
  41 Iloilo
  42 Negros Occidental

VII CENTRAL VISAYAS
  43 Cebu
  44 Negros Oriental
  45 Bohol
  46 Siquijor

VIII EASTERN VISAYAS
  47 Northern Samar
  48 Samar
  49 Eastern Samar
  50 Leyte
  51 Southern Leyte

IX WESTERN MINDANAO
  52 Zamboanga del Norte
  53 Zamboanga del Sur
  54 Basilan
  55 Sulu
  56 Tawitawi

X NORTHERN MINDANAO
  57 Surigao del Norte
  58 Camiguin
  59 Agusan del Norte
  60 Misamis Oriental
  61 Misamis Occidental
  62 Bukidnon
  63 Agusan del Sur

XI SOUTHERN MINDANAO
  64 Surigao del Sur
  65 Davao Oriental
  66 Davao
  67 Davao del Sur
  68 South Cotabato

XII CENTRAL MINDANAO
  69 Lanao del Norte
  70 Lanao del Sur
  71 North Cotabato
  72 Maguindanao
  73 Sultan Kudarat

Source: U.S. Dept. of State, **Background Notes: Philippines,** August 1986.

Source: Frederica M. Bunge (ed.), **Philippines: A Country Study** (Washington DC: U.S. Government Printing Office, 1984), pp. 190-91.

GENERAL INTRODUCTION

More than four hundred years ago, on the Philippine island of Mactan, the European explorer Ferdinand Magellan was killed by a tribal chieftain, Lapu-Lapu. Filipinos at this time lived in many separate communities, linked by a well-developed system of trade and some loose political compacts, with widespread literacy. Little of the written record from this period survives, however, for the later Spanish authorities determined to expunge all pagan writings.

A few decades after Magellan's death, Spanish conquerers returned in force and colonized the Philippine archipelago, but throughout the next three centuries the new rulers had to deal with uprisings from the native population that were increasingly frequent and increasingly more large scale. Although suffused with heavy religious and millenarian overtones, Filipino resistance to foreign domination was a constant theme of these years. But resistance was not universal. Some Filipinos found that they could secure privileges for themselves by cooperating with the colonizers. And the popular uprisings were often directed as much at this domestic elite as at the Spanish.

At the end of the nineteenth century, Philippine resistance coalesced for the first time into a national struggle: the Revolution of 1896. Sidetracked for a while in 1897, fighting resumed a year later, but as the revolutionaries delivered the final blow to their Spanish masters, a new colonial ruler appeared: the United States. Filipinos fought valiantly for their independence, but the superior arms of the U.S. troops and the insurgents' own political weaknesses made the result a foregone conclusion.

The attitude toward the U.S.-Philippine War was unanimous in neither country. In the Philippines, while many gave their lives to repel the foreign colonizer, others collaborated with the U.S. against their compatriots. Generally these were the same elite individuals who had just a short time before served the Spanish. In the United States, while much of the population was roused to the jingoism of colonial conquest, a powerful minority spoke out eloquently for Philippine freedom.

During World War II, the Japanese conquered the Philippines from the United States and once again Filipinos fought back. And also once again, some Filipinos—by and large the same elite—collaborated with the foreign ruler. When the U.S. forces returned, the elite switched sides again.

In 1946, Washington granted the Philippines independence, keeping a long-standing promise in good part as a result of pressure from U.S. domestic economic interests. But although colonialism was thus coming to an end, Filipinos were not to be truly sovereign. U.S. economic and military domination of the Philippines would continue though the country was now nominally independent. The peasantry of the Central Luzon region of the country, many the veterans of the anti-Japanese struggle, opposed this "neocolonial" situation. And they opposed even more strongly the exploitation they suffered at the hands of their landlords. Resentment and repression eventually led to a new guerilla war, the Huk rebellion. The United States stepped in to help the Philippine elite defeat the Huks, thereby preserving U.S. interests and elite privilege.

Two decades later, resistance to the status quo was revived as students, peasants, and workers pressed for an end to foreign domination and the crushing inequities of wealth and power. The government of Philippine President Ferdinand Marcos responded by declaring martial law. Washington, then waging a war in Vietnam, supported the dictatorship so as to protect its military bases and foreign investments. As Filipinos' living standards declined, resistance resumed; and when the resistance was met with repression, the resistance grew even stronger. Neither U.S. weapons nor cosmetic changes in the dictatorship could tame the popular upsurge. And within the United States, an anti-interventionist movement pressed to cut off U.S. backing for Marcos.

Finally, after the murder of his leading political opponent, Benigno Aquino, Marcos became so discredited that his chief props of support—the army and the rich, internally, and the United States, externally—ultimately abandoned him to protect themselves. A surge of people's power ousted the dictator and Corazon Aquino took over the presidency. The struggle of Filipinos for genuine independence and social justice had not ended, but it had at least reached a new level. This book seeks to bring together a collection of documents and articles that tell the story of that struggle, from the turn of the century when the United States became the chief foreign power in the Philippines, and continuing up to the present day. We do not cover in this volume the pre-Spanish Philippines nor the period of Spanish colonial rule.

In selecting readings, we have tried to provide a mixture of first-hand accounts, in which the participants in this history speak for themselves, and survey articles that illuminate particular issues or events. We have attempted to strike a balance between journalistic accounts, academic pieces, manifestos, and government documents, both public pronouncements and internal reports. We have sought to represent both Filipino and U.S. writers and as many different viewpoints as possible.*

We do not claim to have constructed a "neutral" book. Our interpretation of U.S.-Philippine relations has obviously influenced what we have chosen to include in this volume: which issues and perspectives we considered important, given the limitations of space. Our interpretations are reflected as well in the introductions we have written to each of the chapters and selections. But we are convinced that the best way to present the history of colonialism, neocolonialism, dictatorship, and resistance in the Philippines is to let the

---

*Our aim of including a full range of selections has meant that we have often had to shorten articles and documents. In general, for considerations of space we have deleted most footnotes from the selections. Interested readers can refer to the original sources.

reader experience some of the range of material that exists, from Aguinaldo to Aquino, from McKinley to Reagan, from the CIA to the Communist Party of the Philippines.

We hope this book will prove useful to those who seek to understand the background to the current situation in the Philippines. Given the historic and ongoing role of the United States in the Philippines, such an understanding is particularly important for U.S. citizens. And, indeed, more than understanding is required: as Filipinos continue their efforts to achieve justice and national sovereignty, people in the United States will have to try to prevent their government from intervening—not an easy task, but a crucial one.

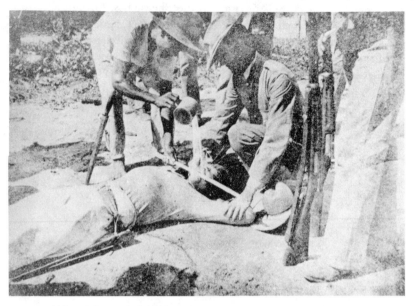

U.S. soldiers administering the torture technique known as the "water-cure."

CHAPTER 1: CONQUEST

Introduction

Integral to the history of the Philippines in the 20th century has been its relation to the United States. From its very beginning in the closing years of the 19th century this relationship has been marked by contention between those Filipinos who desired their country's full independence and sovereignty and those in the United States who favored a policy of intervention in Philippine affairs to further U.S. interests.

In the second half of the 19th century, the United States emerged from the Civil War as a powerful industrial and commercial nation, whose economic strength was increasingly expressed in great corporations and monopolies. In 1897, for example, the United States became the foremost producer of pig iron in the world, and in 1900 the largest corporation the country had ever seen, the U.S. Steel Company, was formed. Released from their domestic preoccupation with the struggle against the Southern slave-owners, the Northern business elite, aided and abetted by the political leadership of the country, gave their attention to securing a place for the United States among its commercial rivals that more nearly coincided with the nation's outstanding industrial strength.

The first important manifestation of the U.S. bid for supremacy over its economic rivals occurred in South America, a traditional field of operations for U.S. merchants, manufacturers, and bankers. Here, in 1895, a Venezuelan boundary dispute gave rise to a confrontation between the United States and Great Britain that was in effect an expression of their competition for predominance in that part of the world. Threatened with war by the Democratic administration of Grover Cleveland, Great Britain backed down.

In nearly coming to blows with Great Britain in South America, the United States was in fact joining the great scramble of the leading commercial and financial powers of Europe in the closing decades of the 19th century to divide what is now called the Third World into colonies and spheres of influence among themselves, so as to acquire new markets, investment opportunities, and raw materials. In the 1880s all of Africa was being swallowed up by Great Britain, France, Germany, and others. In the 1890s these same powers, with Czarist Russia included, began to carve up China, hoping to secure the markets and resources of that vast country for their own nationals. This did not go unnoticed in the United States.

Besides the activities of their international rivals, what gave a special impetus to the drive of the U.S. business community to secure increased control over world markets was the outbreak of a severe economic crisis in 1893. This paralyzed industry, threw thousands out of work, and bankrupted agriculture. A consensus developed in the ranks of the U.S. business and political elite that the way out of this depression lay in the expansion of foreign markets for U.S. manufactured goods, since the crisis was widely regarded as one of overproduction in relation to the domestic market.

As the commercial and political leaders of the United States looked overseas for new foreign markets (and new military and naval positions abroad from which to support the drive for foreign trade), colonies of a weak and decrepit rival, imperial Spain, presented themselves as suitable acquisitions. It happened that, at this time, Cuban nationalists had risen in revolt against their Spanish colonial masters. Proclaiming the intention of helping to free Cuba from Spanish rule, the Republican administration of William McKinley, closely identified with big business, made war on Spain. The United States won the war, and, by the terms of the Treaty of Paris, stripped Spain of valuable colonial possessions.

As part of the war, U.S. Commodore George Dewey had sailed to Spain's colony of the Philippines and destroyed the Spanish fleet in Manila Bay. Dewey's presence was soon reinforced by the arrival of U.S. infantry detachments. These troops found themselves facing what was a relatively new feature in Philippine life and society: the armed forces of Philippine nationalism.

For, in the last quarter of the 19th century as the economic and social forces of overseas expansion were maturing in the United States, a movement of nationalist resistance to Spanish rule had been emerging in the Philippines (as in Cuba). While spontaneous revolts against Spain had been erupting for three centuries, now Philippine resistance to Spain began to take conscious form in what was known as the Propaganda Movement. This was, as its name implied, a movement for the development and propagation of nationalist ideas. At the root of this new movement were the sons of the wealthy Filipino landed elite who were sent for higher education to Spain and other countries of Europe where they absorbed the democratic and nationalistic ideas of the French revolution. They returned to find that their educational and economic status did not earn them political or social equality with the Spanish. They agitated for reforms, but Spain responded with harsh repression. The leader of this initial period of ideological preparation was a talented Philippine intellectual, Jose Rizal, who in 1896 was executed by Spain.

In the last decade of the 19th century Philippine nationalism entered a new phase, that of armed resistance to Spanish rule. The organized movement changed from reformist propaganda and education, to fostering armed revolt through an organization called the Katipunan, founded by Andres Bonifacio, a working class disciple of Rizal.

Internal divisions within the revolutionary movement led to the replacement of Bonifacio by Emilio Aguinaldo, a small landowner. The Filipinos by their own military efforts broke the back of Spanish rule in the Philippines and established an independent and republican form of government for themselves. This happened just after Dewey took up his position in Manila Bay.

By the summer of 1898, on the main island of Luzon, Philippine troops had driven the Spanish colonialists out of the countryside into the capital city of Manila, where they laid their former rulers under siege. U.S. forces under Dewey, however, arranged to have the Spanish surrender to them, took over Manila, and did not allow the Filipinos to enter their capital city. So two armies—that of the U.S. interventionists and that of the Philippine national-ists—confronted each other uneasily at the turn of the century.

When in February 1899 the U.S. military started to move beyond Manila to conquer and colonize the Philippines, Aguinaldo and the Philippine nationalists resisted and a war ensued. Thus it turned out that the essential starting point for U.S.-Philippine relations in modern times was a war of conquest waged by the United States against the Filipinos. This lasted offi-cially for three years, unofficially for at least twice that long. The war destroyed a fledgling Philippine republic and turned that country into a U.S. colony bereft of the independence it had newly won from Spain [see selection 1.1].

According to its proponents, the U.S. war effort had two main aims: to secure the Philippines as a market and source of raw materials for U.S. industry, and to secure the Philippines as a military strong-point from which to penetrate the markets of China [see selections 1.3, 1.5, 1.9]. The supporters of conquest gave other reasons for this policy as well, notably the need to civilize and uplift the Filipinos [see selection 1.4].

The last motive was closely related to feelings and theories of racial superiority that permeated the U.S. war effort. Racial prejudice appears to have accentuated the cruel and brutal character of the U.S. war of conquest, marked as it was by the use of torture, the killing of prisoners, and genocidal tendencies [see selections 1.1, 1.8].

For the Philippine side the war was one of defense of national independ-ence [see selection 1.2]. It was led for the first two years by Emilio Aguinaldo, the small landowner who typified the elite officer class of the Philippine army. But the bulk of the armed resistance to U.S. colonial conquest was provided by Philippine tenant farmers, agricultural laborers, and urban working people whose long-standing economic grievances at the hands of the Spanish led them to militant support of the nationalist cause. Outgunned from the start by the U.S. military, the army of the Philippine republic broke up after several months of fighting and the Philippine nationalist resistance turned to guerilla warfare until its final defeat. To isolate the guerilla fighters from their support in the countryside the U.S. army adopted a policy of driving the Philippine rural population from the land they tilled into concentration camps where hunger and disease took their toll [see selection 1.1].

The war of conquest in the Philippines was not a popular one in the United States, and a massive movement of opposition developed, led by an organization called the Anti-Imperialist League. (The terms "imperialism" and "imperialist" were commonly used at the time by both opponents and supporters of McKinley's Philippine policy.) The League had a membership of 30,000 and it influenced the political thinking of millions [see selections 1.6, 1.7, 1.8]. The treaty to annex the Philippines passed the Senate by only one vote and William Jennings Bryan, the Democratic presidential candidate in 1900, declared imperialism to be the paramount issue of the campaign.

The anti-imperialists, however, did not have sufficient strength to halt the U.S. war in the Philippines, and the superior military might of the U.S. government eventually defeated the Philippine nationalists and turned their country into a U.S. colony. The goals of the war were thus fulfilled; the Philippines became an important market for U.S. manufactured goods, and in 1900 provided the base from which the McKinley administration sent U.S. troops to China to put down an uprising of Chinese nationalists, the Boxers, who would have closed China to penetration from foreign capital and manufacture [see selection 1.9].

For the Philippine people, the war was a disaster. It snatched national independence from their grasp and left hundreds of thousands of Filipinos dead from war or war-related causes. Arising out of a U.S. war with Spain that had the appearance of a democratic war to free Cuba, the Philippine war was one of colonial conquest. As such it revealed the entire military process, in both its Spanish and Philippine phases, for what it was in fact: an exercise in imperial politics on the part of the United States. Its consequences have been lasting. The war and subsequent colonization established a pattern of U.S. intervention in Philippine affairs to further U.S. economic and military interests that remains unbroken to the present day.

Selection 1.1: The Philippine-American War, Luzviminda Francisco

Editors' Introduction

When Emilio Aguinaldo, from a small landlord background, took over command from Andres Bonifacio, it signified new influence for the Philippine elite in the leadership of the armed Philippine resistance to Spanish rule. This influence brought with it a long-standing tendency on the part of the elite to further their own interests at the expense of the struggle for national independence and in this way to compromise with alien rule. Aguinaldo took command in 1897, and in the same year the leadership of the resistance entered into negotiations with the Spanish colonialists, agreeing to halt the fighting in what was called the Pact of Biak-na-bato

(named for the location of Aguinaldo's headquarters); the Spanish, for their part, promised a large sum of money to the Aguinaldo leadership and certain reforms, including elite access to additional political office under Spanish rule.

At this point Aguinaldo left the Philippines for Hong Kong and Singapore. There, later on, representatives of Admiral Dewey met with him and brought him back to the Philippines on a U.S. naval vessel with verbal assurances of U.S. assistance to the Philippine struggle for independence. Before Aguinaldo's return, however, the nationalists started to fight again, the reforms promised by the Spaniards having failed to materialize. The result of this Philippine offensive was the siege of the Spanish forces in Manila.

In August 1898 the Spanish command in Manila and U.S. officers representing Admiral Dewey conferred behind the backs of Aguinaldo and his men in their positions outside Manila. An agreement was reached that, after a sham battle, the Spanish would surrender to the U.S. military, on the condition that the Philippine nationalists be excluded from Manila. To this condition U.S. officials readily agreed. After the mock battle took place as planned the U.S. military took over Manila from the Spanish and came into direct confrontation with the Filipinos. In February 1899 U.S. troops were ordered to move through the Philippine lines, and the war began.

For many years the Philippine war has been a forgotten war in the United States. History textbooks have typically devoted pages to the Spanish-American War and only a paragraph or two to the Philippine conflict. But the Spanish-American War was much shorter and much less costly in lives and money. Further, it was less significant historically, since it merely re-asserted a pre-existing U.S. hegemony in Central and South America, whereas the Philippine-American War established the U.S. as an Asian power for the first time.

Nations, like individuals, have a way of putting out of sight and mind past behavior that is embarrassing or negates the preferred self-image. The Spanish-American War, which resulted in a semblance, at least, of freedom for Cuba, has been well remembered; the Philippine-American War, which resulted in U.S. colonial rule, has virtually disappeared.

Perhaps it is also no accident that the Philippine scholar, Luzviminda Francisco, wrote her penetrating account of the U.S. war in the Philippines in 1973, at a time when the U.S. was engaged in another war of intervention in Southeast Asia. The Vietnam War led many to question and re-examine the foreign policy of the United States, both past and present, particularly in relation to Third World countries.

Source: Luzviminda Francisco, "The First Vietnam: The Philippine-American War, 1899-1902," in *The Philippines: End of an Illusion,* London: AREAS, 1973.

By autumn 1898 it was clear that the Americans intended to retain the Philippines as a Pacific colony. American troop strength was increasing and Admiral Dewey showed no sign of weighing anchor. Battle lines around Manila continued to be drawn roughly as they had remained at the end of the mock battle against the Spanish in the previous August. The Americans held the city and had trenches along its perimeter, facing Filipino trenches along a semi-circle of several miles.

The Treaty of Paris, designed to end the war with Spain and to cede the Philippines to the U.S., was signed in December and awaited confirmation in the U.S. Senate, which required a two-thirds majority vote as necessitated by the Constitution. When Congress reconvened in January 1899, the pro-annexationist faction in the Senate held a clear majority, but were one or two votes shy of the required two-thirds majority they needed to ratify the treaty. Voting on the treaty was scheduled for Monday, February 6, and during the week preceding it seemed fairly clear to most observers that the McKinley Administration was not likely to rally enough support in the Senate to win ratification. By implication, this put American retention of the Philippines in jeopardy.

In the Philippines, insults—and occasionally shots—were being traded across the trenches by the two opposing armies throughout the month of January. But war did not come until the evening of February 4, 1899, when general fighting erupted all along the line. The American command in Manila claimed at the time that the Filipinos initiated the fighting, but there seems little doubt that the Americans themselves started the war and as much was later admitted by U.S. commanders. That the outbreak of the war was carefully orchestrated to influence the outcome of the treaty vote in the Senate seems almost beyond question. . . .

The news of the fighting—and the false information as to its instigation—was wired to Washington and its dramatic effect persuaded the Senate to ratify the treaty by a margin of one vote.

The First Battle

From the very beginning, superior American firepower had a telling effect, and although the Filipino troops bravely stood their ground, weaponry ensured the one-sidedness of the conflict. Dewey steamed up the Pasig River and fired 500-pound shells into the Filipino trenches at close range with pulverizing effectiveness. The first battle was so one-sided that the American troops jokingly referred to it as a "quail shoot" and dead Filipinos were piled so high that the Americans used the bodies for breastworks. . . .

For the Filipino patriots, the opening battle in what proved to be one of the longest and bloodiest wars in the sorry history of imperial aggression produced two sharp lessons. It was clear that the Filipinos could not hope to survive by fighting on American terms of fixed position, set-piece battles in the classical military tradition. The Philippine Army was quickly forced to resort to mobile warfare where their superior knowledge of the terrain and the universal support they enjoyed among the people could be utilized to their advantage. Although an overt policy of guerilla war was not specifically enunciated until the following November, guerilla tactics were employed out of necessity immediately after the initial rout at Manila. The first battle also indicated to the Filipinos that they were faced with a foe which gave no quarter and which was prepared to disregard the fundamental rules of warfare. The Americans were contemptuous of Filipinos generally and they had little respect for the fighting ability of the Philippine Army. They referred to the Filipino as "niggers," "barbarians," and "savages," reflecting both the racist and imperialist attitudes of American society at large.

The Americans were elated by their initial success and their commander, the rather wooden and unimaginative Gen. Elwell Otis, confidently predicted that the war would be ended in a matter of weeks. Otis had convinced himself that the opposition to U.S. rule came only from the Tagalog "tribe," which (it was claimed) was only one of eighty or so "tribes" in the Philippines. This theme, which was trotted out by domestic U.S. annexationists at every opportunity, gave the impression that the war in the Philippines was but a slight variation of the familiar Indian wars of the American West.

After the devastating first battle, the Filipino Army retreated into Central Luzon, fighting rear-guard actions as it went. Malolos, capital of the Philippine Republic, quickly fell and within the conventional framework within which he was operating, Otis equated this event with the fall of the Philippine Government, which in turn would mean the surrender of the Philippine Army. Or so he hoped. . . .

It was with a growing sense of uneasiness that the American command began to realize that the further they were drawn into Central Luzon and the more they had to disperse their forces, the more difficult it became to defend themselves against counter-attack, ambush, and harassment by the highly mobile Philippine Army, which was itself free of the need for the ponderous supply chain required by the Americans. The odds, which were so disastrously against the Filipinos in early February, began to even up.

There was another—and to the more perceptive American commanders, rather more disturbing—character to the fighting. It gradually dawned on the Americans that the reason the Filipino troops could move around so easily without concern for a supply base, and the reason information and advice were so difficult to elicit from the native population, were due to the fact that the Aguinaldo government and the Philippine nationalist cause had the total support of the Philippine masses. They slowly began to realize that their major foe was not really the formally constituted, but in many ways ineffectual, Philippine Army; rather, it was the Filipino people, who, having finally gotten rid of the Spanish, were unrelentingly and implacably hostile to American imperialist designs. The implications of this understanding were fully realized only later and in the bloodiest manner imaginable. But as early as April 1899, General Shafter gave grisly portent to the future conduct of the war: "It may be necessary to kill half of the Filipinos in order that the remaining half of the population may be advanced to a higher plane of life than their present semi-barbarous state affords."

The American command had presumably been taken in by its own press releases. Gen. Arthur MacArthur, Otis's subordinate (and later replacement) commented, " . . . I believed that Aguinaldo's troops represented only a faction. I did not like to believe that the whole population of Luzon—the native population, that is—was opposed to us . . . " But this he was "reluctantly compelled" to believe because the "unique system of warfare" employed by the Filipino Army " . . . depended upon almost complete unity of action of the entire native population."

With the approach of summer and with victory still beyond their grasp, the War Department began to suggest to Otis that he might need more troops. Embarrassed by his earlier confident predictions and even more so by his growing inability to produce tangible results, he at first declined the offer, but then he reversed himself and surprised the Department by asking for 60,000 more troops. Otis was limited by his textbook approach to war and failed to realize that American "victories" in which the Filipinos were "scattered" or "routed" were next to meaningless.

By October all the American reinforcements had arrived and it was decided that the best way to terminate the war was to capture Aguinaldo and his staff. An ambitious three-pronged encirclement campaign, encompassing the whole of Central Luzon, was decided upon. One column went north from Manila along the rail line, another went by sea to the Lingayen Gulf port of Dagupan, and a third went north from Manila along the eastern rim of the Central Luzon plain in a giant pincer movement. The idea was to prevent Aguinaldo's escape into the mountains of northern Luzon.

Aguinaldo did manage to escape, however, and from mountain headquarters he issued orders to formally adopt the guerilla policy . . .

The Filipinos began to realize that although outright military victory was unlikely at best, simply by keeping their forces intact they preserved the possibility of an ultimate political victory.

The Filipinos had some knowledge of the divisions being created in American society by the McKinley Administration's imperialist policy. The Anti-Imperialist League was strongly condemning the war and the opposition Democrats were taking a position against the retention of the Philippines. It appeared likely, even a year before the event, that the November 1900 presidential election would be fought on the issue of McKinley's colonial policy. This held out some hope at least for a political settlement of the war favorable to the Philippines.

The war took on a somewhat new character after the completion of the Central Luzon campaign. From November 1899, the U.S. considered the entire Philippines to be occupied territory—as indeed it was—and the American command set about establishing garrisons throughout Luzon and the rest of the country. Filipino guerillas were no longer treated as soldiers of an opposing army but were considered to be bandits and common criminals (ladrones). When captured they were treated as such. With the break-up of the Philippine Army, Otis once again felt he had victory within his grasp. . . .

First, the fighting simply continued. Chasing Aguinaldo into the mountains had made no difference, breaking up the Filipino Army made no difference, and garrisoning the archipelago simply invited guerilla attacks on isolated outposts. Secondly, as the Americans spread their forces and their garrisons to other areas of Luzon and to other islands, they found they were confronted with exactly the same kind of public hostility and guerilla opposition which characterized the situation in Central Luzon. . . .

Settling In for a Long War

The war, far from being over, had entered a new and far more difficult phase for the Americans. The enemy was now no longer simply the Philippine Army, the remnants of which had been scattered over the whole of Luzon in any case. Now the Americans found themselves harassed and attacked throughout the Islands by poorly trained and poorly organized but fanatically determined peasant irregulars. MacArthur observed: " . . . all regular and systematic tactical operations ceased; but as hostile contact was established throughout the entire zone of activity an infinite number of minor affairs resulted, some of which reached the dignity of combats."

A major problem for the Americans resulted from their inability to penetrate the guerilla infrastructure. They soon began to realize, to their dismay, that the whole underground network of dual government loyal to the guerillas existed, even in areas considered thoroughly "pacified." When a town was occupied the stars and stripes flew, and gratifying expressions of loyalty and support for the American cause were publicly proclaimed by town officials. But reliable information about the guerillas was almost never forthcoming, supplies and equipment were forever disappearing, and occasionally an American soldier would stray too far from camp and be found the next day hacked to pieces by bolo. . . .

It was becoming clear that the entire Islands would have to be "pacified." Moreover, guerilla activity was both increasing and becoming increasingly effective. Being incessantly ambushed, boloed and betrayed was nerve-wracking and the Americans began to exercise their mounting frustration on the population at large. All the "niggers" were enemies, whether or not they bore arms. Patrols sent to fight the guerillas usually had difficulty locating the enemy and often simply resorted to burning barrios in their path. Village officials were often forced at bayonet point to lead American patrols, and non-combatants began to be held responsible for the actions of the guerillas. Any form of resistance to American objectives subjected the perpetrator to a charge of treason.

Press censorship was so effective that few Americans actually knew the difficulties being experienced in the Philippines—or, in fact, that there were 70,000 U.S. troops in the Islands. In early 1900 the first whiff of scandal reached American shores. . . .

Reports of the burning of villages, the killing of non-combatants and the application of the "water cure" to elicit information began to filter back to the U.S. Often this information was contained in letters written by U.S. soldiers to their families which found their way into local newspapers. A typical example: "On Thursday, March 29th [1900] . . . eighteen of my company killed seventy-five nigger bolomen and ten of the nigger gunners. . . . When we find one who is not dead, we have bayonets". . . .

Such atrocities were systematically denied by the War Department. When the evidence was irrefutable, they were minimized and countered with examples of Filipino "barbarity." A standard response was that "harsh" methods had to be employed against "savages". . . .

With one eye on the upcoming November election, McKinley also sent a federal judge, William Howard Taft, to Manila with instructions to establish a "civilian" government in the Islands no later than September 1, 1900. The move was purely a public relations venture designed to trick the American voters into thinking all was progressing smoothly in the Philippines. Taft was densely ignorant about the Philippines, but he knew enough about class society to detect a certain amount of pliability in the upper-class elements in the country. This group, composed largely of mestizo landlords and export agriculture interests, had been largely ignored by the U.S. military command, but Taft set out to woo them, appealing to their economic interests by offering protected markets for agricultural products in the U.S. The effort bore fruit insofar as Taft was able—on cue—to establish his Civil Government on September 1. . . .

Lack of firearms indeed continued to be perhaps the single most pressing problem for the Filipinos. By mid-1900 they had at most 20,000 rifles, meaning that only one partisan in four was actually armed. The American naval blockade made it all but impossible to obtain arms and supplies from abroad and although efforts were made to manufacture gunpowder locally, cartridge shells had to be used over and over to the point of uselessness. The Filipinos had to adapt to their limitations as best they could. They stood up to the heavily armed Americans with spears, darts, the ubiquitous bolo, and even stones, prompting General Lawton to remark, " . . . they are the bravest men I have ever seen". . . .

Otis was clearly unsuited for his job. His frequent pronouncements of victory and his incompetent handling of the war were proving to be an embarrassment to the McKinley Administration, which was nervously anticipating the forthcoming presidential election. Accordingly, Otis resigned "for pressing personal reasons" and was replaced by General MacArthur. MacArthur had had experience in the American Indian wars and he, more than anyone on Otis's staff, understood the wide-ranging implications of the problems then confronting the American expeditionary force in the Philippines. A convinced imperialist, he was also a realist. He openly admitted that the Filipinos hated the Americans and he did not flinch from estimating that it would take "ten years of bayonet treatment" to subdue the Filipino people—a prescient observation, as it turned out.

With the nomination of William Jennings Bryan as the Democratic presidential candidate, the question of American colonialism and continued military intervention appeared likely to become a major issue in the 1900 campaign. The Filipinos hoped to topple the "imperialist party" of McKinley by launching an offensive just before the election, and September and October saw some of the sharpest fighting of the war. In spite of these efforts the question of the Philippines never became the issue it might have been. Aided by heavy press censorship and the inability to obtain independent information on the Philippine situation, McKinley predictably pointed to the Taft Government as proof that all was going well in the Islands. Bryan, moreover, was a rank political opportunist. . . .

When he began to see that his anti-colonial position was hurting his campaign rather than helping, he back-pedaled furiously and quickly compromised himself, arguing for a vaguely defined American "protectorate" for the Philippines. . . .

Predictably perhaps, McKinley was an easy victor. The result was a crushing blow for the Filipino guerilla leaders who had counted heavily—too heavily—on a Bryan victory. Indeed, the guerilla leadership began to falter badly after November and the surrender of several commanders (with men and guns) was a sharp blow to the Filipino cause. . . .

The class divisions within the Filipino forces began now to emerge. The officers, like Aguinaldo himself, were usually fairly well educated and came largely from middle-class backgrounds; the ranks were invariably filled by men of peasant origins. The American command played upon these class divisions and treated surrendering commanders with the respect due to fellow "officers and gentlemen," sometimes dangling choice of civil service positions as inducement for officers to defect. . . .

. . . in the autumn of 1900 there was a perceptible alteration in American tactics. Tired of being chronically harassed and boloed by the Filipinos and finding it difficult to pin the guerillas down in the kind of conventional firefight they so urgently desired, the Americans began to resort to revanchist attitudes and policies. . . .

If the people supported the guerillas then the people must also be classified as the enemy. The grim implications of such an evaluation were beginning to emerge, although the fiction that wide-spread public support for the U.S. existed in the Islands was maintained for domestic U.S. consumption. . . .

"Pacification" Begins In Earnest

In December 1900, with the election safely out of the way, martial law was declared and the pretense of civil government was scrapped. American operations were extended to southern Luzon and to the Visayan islands of Leyte, Samar, Panay, Negros and Cebu. As far as the American command was concerned there were no longer any neutrals. Everyone was now considered an active guerilla or a guerilla supporter. Thus in the Visayas campaign the Navy felt free to shell the coastal villages with its gunboats prior to invasion. In January and February 1901, the entire population of Marinduque Island (pop. 51,000) was ordered into five concentration camps set up by Americans. All those who did not comply with the order " . . . would be considered as acting in sympathy with the insurgent forces and treated accordingly." This was to be the first of many instances of the application of the *reconcentrado* policy in the Philippines. . . .

In April 1901 major operations began in northern Luzon. The frequent examples of American terror tactics which had heretofore occurred were, arguably, the acts of individual units in at least technical violation of overall U.S. policy. With the advent of the northern Luzon campaign such pretensions and qualifications could no longer be maintained. If the people sympathized with and supported the guerillas, and if, indeed, this was a "people's war," then the only solution was war against the people. The American Governor of Abra Province described the "depopulation campaign" in the following terms: "Whole villages had been burned, storehouses and crops had been destroyed and the entire province was as devoid of food products as was the valley of Shenandoah after Sheridan's raid during the Civil War." An American congressman who visited the Philippines, and who preferred to remain anonymous, spoke frankly about the results of the campaign: "You never hear of any disturbances in Northern Luzon," he reported, "because there isn't anybody there to rebel . . . . The good Lord in heaven only knows the number of Filipinos that were put under ground. Our soldiers took no prisoners, they kept no records; they simply swept the country and wherever and whenever they could get hold of a Filipino they killed him". . . .

Also in April 1901, Aguinaldo was finally captured. The Americans had been so unsuccessful at trying to catch him that for a long period they simply gave up the effort. But an intercepted message resulted in a daring raid by Brig. Gen. Frederick Funston and Aguinaldo's capture. The Americans were delighted with the news, which made banner headlines in the U.S. Taft felt the war was as good as over, especially after he persuaded Aguinaldo to sign an oath of allegiance and a proclamation calling upon his erstwhile comrades to give up the struggle. . . .

. . . the Americans were dismayed to discover that his capture and surrender appeal made no perceptible difference in the fighting, which continued unabated. This was too much for MacArthur, who resigned and was replaced by Maj. Gen. Adna Chaffee.

By mid-summer 1901, the focus of the war started to shift south of Manila. Some of the guerilla leaders of northern and Central Luzon who were close to Aguinaldo began to surrender. Others held out, however, and Gen. Miguel Malvar, operating in Batangas, was proving to be every bit as difficult for the Americans as Aguinaldo had been. . . .

On the eve of the Samar campaign, the war was clearly degenerating into mass slaughter. It was hardly precise to call it "war" any longer. The Americans were simply chasing ragged, poorly armed bands of guerillas and, failing to catch them, were inflicting the severest punishment on those they could catch—the people of the villages and barrios of the theater of operation

In late September, in the town of Balangiga, Samar, American troops had for some time been abusing the townspeople by packing them into open wooden pens at night where they were forced to sleep standing in the rain. Several score of guerilla General Vincent Lukban's bolomen infiltrated the town and on the morning of September 28, while the Americans were eating their breakfast, Lukban's men suddenly fell upon them. Heads dropped into breakfast dishes. Fifty-four Americans were boloed to death, and few of the eighteen survivors escaped serious injury.

The Balangiga massacre initiated a reign of terror the likes of which had not yet been seen in this war. General ["Howlin' Jake"] Smith, fresh from his "victories" in northern Luzon and Panay, was chosen to lead the American mission of revenge. Smith's order to his men embarking upon the Samar campaign could not have been more explicit: "Kill and burn, kill and burn, the more you kill and the more you burn the more you please me." It was, said Smith, "no time to take prisoners." War was to be waged "in the sharpest and most decisive manner possible." When asked to define the age limit for killing, Smith gave his infamous reply: "Everything over ten." Smith ordered Samar to be turned into a "howling wilderness" so that "even the birds could not live there." It was boasted that " . . . what fire and water [i.e., water torture] . . . had done in Panay, water and fire would do in Samar." The now-familiar pattern of operations began once again. All inhabitants of the island (pop. 266,000) were ordered to present themselves to detention camps in several of the larger coastal towns. Those who did not (or those who did not make it their business to learn the existence of the order), and were found outside the detention camp perimeter, would be shot, "and no questions asked." Few reporters covered the carnage; one who did noted: "During my stay in Samar the only prisoners that were made . . . were taken by Waller's command; and I heard this act criticized by the highest officers as a mistake . . . .The truth is, the struggle in Samar is one of extermination". . . .

In the face of mounting and irrefutable evidence of the true conduct of the war, the War Department resorted to by-now-standard procedure—deny, minimize, obliterate charges and criticism with a blizzard of rhetorical over-kill. Secretary Root : " . . . the warfare has been conducted with marked humanity and magnanimity on the part of the U.S.". . . .

The Batangas Campaign

As Smith ravaged Samar, General Malvar and his men carried on the guerilla struggle in Batangas, Tayabas, Laguna and Cavite. With General Smith already occupied, command of the Batangas campaign was given to Maj. Gen. J. Franklin Bell. By word and by deed, Bell made it clear that he was not going to be put in the shade by his brother officer when it came to slaughtering Filipinos. Even before he took command, Bell made his feelings known in unmistakable terms. "All consideration and regard for the inhabitants of this place cease from the day I become commander," he said. "I have the force and authority to do whatever seems to me good and especially to humiliate those in the Province who have any pride. . . ."

Beginning in early December 1901, and continuing for the rest of the month, Bell issued a frightening series of orders. On December 8 he began setting up his concentration camps. The people of Batangas had two week in which to move into the garrisons. Everything lying outside the perimeter of the camps was subject to confiscation or destruction. Anyone found there would automatically be considered an "insurgent." Neutrality was not to be entertained. Everyone "should either be an active friend or classified as an enemy." How did one become an "active friend"? "The only acceptable and convincing evidence of the real sentiments of either individuals or town councils should be such acts publicly performed as must inevitably commit them irrevocably to the side of the Americans by arousing the animosity and opposition of the insurgent element." How did one arouse the animosity and opposition of the "insurgent element"? By guiding troops to the camps of the enemy, by publicly identifying "insurgents," by accompanying troops in operations against the guerillas, by denouncing the "enemy" publicly, and by identifying secret guerilla supporters. Suspicion of aiding the guerillas in any way was sufficient cause for arrest without charge and incarceration for an indefinite period of time. "It is not necessary to wait for sufficient evidence to lead to a conviction by a court". . . .

Beginning January 1, 1901, as promised, Batangas was indeed thoroughly searched and devastated, as were the neighboring provinces. Bell assembled 2,500 men in columns of 50 and the hunt for Malvar was on. Expecting to destroy everything, Bell was at least as ruthless as Smith had been in the preceding extermination campaigns. The details of the concentration camp policy were, by now, depressingly familiar. Filipinos were rounded up and herded into detention camps where overcrowded conditions and lack of proper food and clothing resulted in the predictable spread of infectious diseases. Malaria, beriberi and dengue fever took their toll. One correspondent described the prisoners as " . . . a miserable-looking lot of little brown rats . . . utterly spiritless."

In the "zone of death" outside the camp "dead line," "all rendered themselves liable," according to Bell. All property was destroyed, all houses put to the torch and the country was made a "desert waste . . . of death and desolation." According to statistics compiled by U.S. Government officials, by the time Bell was finished at least 100,000 people had been killed or had died in Batangas alone as a direct result of the scorched-earth policies, and the enormous dent in the population of the province (which was reduced by a third) is reflected in the census figures. American policy was so brutal that even some of the U.S. government personnel became apprehensive. The American civil governor of Tayabas noted in his official report that killing, burning, torture and other harsh treatment was "sowing the seeds for a perpetual revolution. If these things need be done, they had best be done by native troops so that the people of the U.S. will not be credited therewith."

With Malvar's surrender in April 1902, the Americans at long last felt the war was finally over. . . .

President Roosevelt proclaimed the war to be over on July 4, 1902. . . .

Declaring it over did not make it so. A sullen, hostile people, the victims of three and a half years of the most savage aggression, simply refused to give up.

Malvar may have surrendered, but many of his men had not, and fighting in Batangas continued. Elsewhere, new leaders such as Sakay, Ricarte, Ola and

Bulan emerged to carry on the struggle in places previously considered pacified. Others, such as Felipe Salvador and "Papa" Isio, both of whom had been fighting the Spanish for many years prior to 1898, simply kept on fighting. Not all of them were principled men; many were without ideology and fought simply out of fanatical hatred of the occupying power; some interjected a confusing welter of reactionary religious dogma to their often ill-defined and unsophisticated response to (ill-defined and unsophisticated) colonialism. Moreover, there were depressing tendencies toward blind revanchism, dead-end millenarianism, and the development of personality cults which paralleled similar "primitive rebellions" in other areas of the world at the time. Having noted this, the point cannot be overemphasized that these movements represented the collective will of the vast majority of the Filipino people who—however imperfectly they understood the phenomenon—simply refused to submit to imperial aggression.

The Cost of the War

How many Filipinos died resisting American aggression? It is doubtful if historians will ever agree on a figure that is anything more than a guess. The figure of 250,000 crops up in various works; one suspects it is chosen and repeated in ignorance and in the absence of hard evidence to the contrary. Records of the killing were not kept and the Americans were anxious to suppress true awareness of the extent of the slaughter in any case, in order to avoid fueling domestic anti- imperialist protest. How many died of disease and the effects of concentration camp life is even more difficult to assess. General Bell, who, one imagines might be in as good a position to judge such matters as anyone, estimated in a *New York Times* interview that over 600,000 people in Luzon alone had been killed or had died of disease as a result of the war. The estimate, given in May 1901, means that Bell did not include the effect of the Panay campaign, the Samar campaign, or his own bloodthirsty Batangas campaign (where at least 100,000 died), all of which occurred after his 1901 interview. Nor could it include the "post-war" period, which saw the confinement of 300,000 people in Albay, wanton slaughter in Mindanao, and astonishing death rates in Bilibid Prison, to name but three instances where killing continued.

    A million deaths? One does not happily contemplate such carnage of innocent people who fought with extraordinary bravery in a cause which was just but is now all but forgotten. Such an estimate, however, might conceivably err on the side of understatment. To again quote the anonymous [U.S.] Congressman, "They never rebel in Luzon anymore because there isn't anybody left to rebel."

Selection 1.2: To the Philippine People, President Emilio Aguinaldo

Editors' Introduction

On February 4, 1899, U.S. troops began to move out of Manila and opened fire on the Philippine nationalists ringing the city, thus starting the Philippine-American War. The next day, Emilio Aguinaldo, President of the Philippine Republic, issued a proclamation to the Philippine people announcing that the fighting had begun. His proclamation may have suggested a reluctance to give up the attempt to negotiate a way out of the U.S.-Philippine confrontation as he had earlier done with the Spanish at Biak-na-bato [see introduction to selection 1.1 above]. But the Philippine leader placed the war now begun very clearly before his people as a war for national independence and urged their full support.

Source: Major-General E. S. Otis, *Report on Military Operations and Civil Affairs in the Philippine Islands, 1899*, Washington: Government Printing Office, 1899, pp. 95-96.

By my proclamation of yesterday I have published the outbreak of hostilities between the Philippine forces and the American forces of occupation in Manila, unjustly and unexpectedly provoked by the latter.

In my manifest of January 8 last I published the grievances suffered by the Philippine forces at the hands of the army of occupation. The constant outrages and taunts, which have caused the misery of the people of Manila, and, finally the useless conferences and the contempt shown the Philippine government prove the premeditated transgression of justice and liberty.

I know that war has always produced great losses; I know that the Philippine people have not yet recovered from past losses and are not in the condition to endure others. But I also know by experience how bitter is slavery, and by experience I know that we should sacrifice all on the altar of our honor and of the national integrity so unjustly attacked.

I have tried to avoid, as far as it has been possible for me to do so, armed conflict, in my endeavors to assure our independence by pacific means and to avoid more costly sacrifices. But all my efforts have been useless against the measureless pride of the American Government and of its representatives in these islands, who have treated me as a rebel because I defend the sacred interests of my country and do not make myself an instrument of their dastardly intentions.

Past campaigns will have convinced you that the people are strong when they wish to be so. Without arms we have driven from our beloved country our ancient masters, and without arms we can repulse the foreign invasion as long as we wish to do so. Providence always has means in reserve and prompt help for the weak in order that they may not be annihilated by the strong; that justice may be done and humanity progress.

Be not discouraged. Our independence has been watered by the generous blood of our martyrs. Blood which may be shed in the future will strengthen it. Nature has never despised generous sacrifices.

But remember that in order that our efforts may not be wasted, that our vows may be listened to, that our ends may be gained, it is indispensable that we adjust our actions to the rules of law and of right, learning to triumph over our enemies and to conquer our own evil passions.

—Emilio Aguinaldo, President of the Philippine Republic
Malolos, February 5, 1899

Selection 1.3: Interview with President McKinley, Senator Henry Cabot Lodge

Editors' Introduction

When Senator Lodge, a leader of the imperialist-minded group in the U.S. Senate, accompanied by his fellow imperialist Senator Elkins, visited President McKinley in May 1898 and urged him to hold the Philippines as a U.S. colony; he appealed to McKinley as one who had previously identified himself with U.S. business interests through his support of high tariffs. (McKinley's presidential campaign of 1896 had been the first in the history of the country in which the big corporations had intervened with massive financial support.) Now, Lodge told the President in the interview below, the protected domestic market was not enough, and McKinley should sustain his identification with U.S. business providing it with an additional market in the Philippines. "From this theory the President expressed no dissent."

Source: "Lincoln" [Robert L. O'Brien], Washington correspondent, *Boston Evening Transcript,* June 3, 1898.

A few days ago Senators Lodge and Elkins went to see the President, and among other things presented this argument to him. "You have stood," they said in substance, addressing Mr. McKinley, "for the great American doctrine of protection to American industries, thus insuring the possession of the home market for our manufactures. So far so good. But the time has now come when this market is not enough for our teeming industries, and the great demand of the day is an outlet for our products. We cannot secure that outlet from other protective countries, for they are committed to the same policy of exclusion that we are, and so our only chance is to extend our American market by acquiring more trade territory. With our protective tariff wall around the Philippine Islands, its ten million inhabitants, as they advance in civilization, would have to buy our goods, and we should have so much additional market for our home manufactures. As a natural and logical sequence of the protective system, if for no other reason, we should now acquire these islands and whatever other outlying territories seem desirable." From this theory the President expressed no dissent.

Selection 1.4: Remarks to Methodist Delegation, President William McKinley

Editors' Introduction

On November 21, 1899, to a visiting delegation of Methodist church leaders, President McKinley explained how he came to colonize the Philippines. The President's story illustrates the peculiar and characteristic combination of piety and commercialism that some voters apparently found irresistible, others repellent [see William James letter, selection 1.6].

Source: General James Rusling, "Interview with President William McKinley," *The Christian Advocate* [New York], January 22, 1903, p. 17.

"Hold a moment longer! Not quite yet, gentlemen! Before you go I would like to say just a word about the Philippine business. I have been criticized a good deal about the Philippines, but don't deserve it. The truth is I didn't want the Philippines, and when they came to us, as a gift from the gods, I did not know what to do with them. When the Spanish War broke out Dewey was at Hongkong, and I ordered him to go to Manila and to capture or destroy the Spanish fleet, and he had to; because, if defeated, he had no place to refit on that side of the globe, and if the Dons were victorious they would likely cross the Pacific and ravage our Oregon and California coasts. And so he had to destroy the Spanish fleet, and did it! But that was as far as I thought then.

"When I next realized that the Philippines had dropped into our laps I confess I did not know what to do with them. I sought counsel from all sides—Democrats as well as Republicans—but got little help. I thought first we would take only Manila; then Luzon; then other islands perhaps also. I walked the floor of the White House night after night until midnight; and I am not ashamed to tell you, gentlemen, that I went down on my knees and prayed Almighty God for light and guidance more than one night. And one night late it came to me this way—I don't know how it was, but it came: (1) That we could not give them back to Spain—that would be cowardly and dishonorable; (2) that we could not turn them over to France and Germany—our commercial rivals in the Orient—that would be bad business and discreditable; (3) that we could not leave them to themselves—they were unfit for self-government—and they would soon have anarchy and misrule over there worse than Spain's was; and (4) that there was nothing left for us to do but to take them all, and to educate the Filipinos, and uplift and civilize and Christianize them, and by God's grace do the very best we could by them, as our fellow-men for whom Christ also died. And then I went to bed, and went to sleep, and slept soundly, and the next morning I sent for the chief engineer of the War Department (our map-maker), and I told him to put the Philippines on the map of the United States (pointing to a large map on the wall of his office), and there they are, and there they will stay while I am President!"

Selection 1.5: Our Philippine Policy, Senator Alfred J. Beveridge

Editors' Introduction

Senator Beveridge's speech comes close to being a definitive statement of U.S. war aims in the Philippines, embracing all the main themes: the drive for markets, raw materials, and military strongpoints, the rivalry with other commercial powers, the racist morality of white Anglo-Saxon supremacy. It was Beveridge's first Senate speech and had been very carefully prepared. Coming forward as a champion of the U.S. imperialism then emerging in the Philippines, and with strong support from the Indianapolis business community, Beveridge had won election to the U.S. Senate from Indiana in 1899. Before assuming his Senate seat, however,

Beveridge's zeal for imperial policy had led him to visit the Philippines and U.S. battle-fronts there, so that his testimony was first-hand and of unique authority and received special attention. Delivered in January 1900 the speech came at a difficult time for the imperialists; with the U.S. war in the Philippines still inconclusive and with the anti-imperialist drum beat of opposition strong and steady, a certain alienation was to be seen even in the ranks of McKinley's supporters. Beveridge's powerful speech was a rallying cry to close ranks and get on with the war. It created a sensation in Washington and the country at large.

Source: *Congressional Record*, Senate, Jan. 9, 1900, pp. 704-711.

Mr. President, the times call for candor. The Philippines are ours forever, "territory belonging to the United States," as the Constitution calls them. And just beyond the Philippines are China's illimitable markets. We will not retreat from either. We will not repudiate our duty in the archipelago. We will not abandon our opportunity in the Orient. We will not renounce our part in the mission of our race, trustee under God, of the civilization of the world. And we will move forward to our work, not howling out regrets like slaves whipped to their burdens, but with gratitude for a task worthy of our strength, and thanksgiving to Almighty God that He has marked us as His chosen people, henceforth to lead in the regeneration of the world.

This island empire is the last land left in all the oceans. If it should prove a mistake to abandon it, the blunder once made would be irretrievable. If it proves a mistake to hold it, the error can be corrected when we will. Every other progressive nation stands ready to relieve us.

But to hold it will be no mistake. Our largest trade henceforth must be with Asia. The Pacific is our ocean. More and more Europe will manufacture the most it needs, secure from its colonies the most it consumes. Where shall we turn for consumers of our surplus? Geography answers the question. China is our natural customer. She is nearer to us than to England, Germany, or Russia, the commercial powers of the present and the future. They have moved nearer to China by securing permanent bases on her borders. The Philippines give us a base at the door of all the East.

Lines of navigation from our ports to the Orient and Australia; from the Isthmian Canal to Asia; from all Oriental ports to Australia, converge at and separate from the Philippines. They are a self-supporting, dividend-paying fleet, permanently anchored at a spot selected by the strategy of Providence, commanding the Pacific. And the Pacific is the ocean of the commerce of the future. Most future wars will be conflicts for commerce. The power that rules the Pacific, therefore, is the power that rules the world. And, with the Philippines, that power is and will forever be the American Republic.

China's trade is the mightiest commercial fact in our future. Her foreign commerce was $285,738,300 in 1897, of which we, her neighbor, had less than 9 per cent, of which only a little more than half was merchandise sold to China by us. We ought to have 50 per cent, and we will. And China's foreign commerce is only beginning. Her resources, her possibilities, her wants, all are undeveloped. She has only 340 miles of railway. I have seen trains loaded with natives and all the activities of modern life already appearing along the line. But she needs, and in fifty years will have, 20,000 miles of railway.

Who can estimate her commerce then? That statesman commits a crime against American trade—against the American grower of cotton and wheat and tobacco, the American manufacturer of machinery and clothing—who fails to put America where she may command that trade. Germany's Chinese trade is increasing like magic. She has established ship lines and secured a tangible foothold on China's very soil. Russia's Chinese trade is growing beyond belief. She is spending the revenues of the Empire to finish her railroad into Pekin itself, and she is in physical possession of the imperial province of Manchuria. Japan's Chinese trade is multiplying in volume and value. She is bending her energy to her merchant marine, and is located along China's very coast; but Manila is nearer China than Yokohama is. The Philippines command the commercial situation of the entire East. . . . And yet American statesmen plan to surrender this commercial throne of the orient where Providence and our soldiers' lives have placed us. When history comes to write the story of that suggested treason to American supremacy and therefore to the spread of American civilization, let her in mercy write that those who so proposed were merely blind and nothing more.

But if they did not command China, India, the Orient, the whole Pacific for purposes of offense, defense, and trade, the Philippines are so valuable in themselves that we should hold them. I have cruised more than 2,000 miles through the archipelago, every moment a surprise at its loveliness and wealth.

I have ridden hundreds of miles on the islands, every foot of the way a revelation of vegetable and mineral riches.

No land in America surpasses in fertility the plains and valleys of Luzon. Rice and coffee, sugar and coconuts, hemp and tobacco, and many products of the temperate as well as the tropic zone grow in various sections of the archipelago . . . . The wood of the Philippines can supply the furniture of the world for a century to come. At Cebu the best informed man in the island told me that 40 miles of Cebu's mountain chain are practically mountains of coal. . . .

I have a nugget of pure gold picked up in its present form on the banks of a Philippine creek. I have gold dust washed out by crude processes of careless natives from the sands of a Philippine stream. Both indicate great deposits at the source from which they come. . . .

And the wood, hemp, copra, and other products of the Philippines supply what we need and can not ourselves produce. And the markets they will themselves afford will be immense. Spain's export and import trade, with the islands undeveloped, was $11,534,731 annually. Ultimately our trade, when the islands shall be developed, will be $125,000,000 annually, for who believes that we can not do ten times as well as Spain? . . .

It will be hard for Americans who have not studied them to understand the people. They are a barbarous race, modified by three centuries of contact with a decadent race. The Filipino is the South Sea Malay, put through a process of three hundred years of superstition in religion, dishonesty in dealing, disorder in habits of industry, and cruelty, caprice, and corruption in government. It is barely possible that 1,000 men in all the archipelago are capable of self-government in the Anglo-Saxon sense.

My own belief is that there are not 100 men among them who comprehend what Anglo-Saxon self-government even means, and there are over 5,000,000 people to be governed. . . .

Mr. President, reluctantly and only from a sense of duty am I forced to say that American opposition to the war has been the chief factor prolonging it. Had Aguinaldo not understood that in America, even in the American Congress, even here in the Senate, he and his cause were supported; had he not known that it was proclaimed on the stump and in the press of a faction in the United States that every shot his misguided followers fired into the breasts of American soldiers was like the volleys fired by Washington's men against the soldiers of King George his insurrection would have dissolved before it entirely crystallized. . . .

But, Senators, it would be better to abandon this combined garden and Gibraltar of the Pacific, and count our blood and treasure already spent a profitable loss, than to apply any academic arrangement of self-government to these children. They are not capable of self-government. How could they be? They are not of a self-governing race. They are Orientals, Malays, instructed by Spaniards in the latter's worst estate.

. . . What alchemy will change the oriental quality of their blood and set the self-governing currents of the American pouring through their Malay veins? How shall they, in the twinkling of an eye, be exalted to the heights of self-governing peoples which required a thousand years for us to reach, Anglo-Saxons though we are? . . .

. . . The Declaration [of Independence] applies only to people capable of self-government. How dare any man prostitute this expression of the very elect of self-governing peoples to a race of Malay children of barbarism, schooled in Spanish methods and ideas? And you, who say the Declaration applies to all men, how dare you deny its application to the American Indian? And if you deny it to the Indian at home, how dare you grant it to the Malay abroad? . . .

. . . the archipelago is a base for the commerce of the East. It is a base for military and naval operations against the only powers with whom conflict is possible; a fortress thrown up in the Pacific, defending our Western coast, commanding the waters of the Orient, and giving us a point from which we can instantly strike and seize the possessions of any possible foe. . . .

Mr. President, this question is deeper than any question of party politics; deeper than any question of the isolated policy of our country even; deeper even than any question of constitutional power. It is elemental. It is racial. God has not been preparing the English-speaking and Teutonic peoples for a thousand years for nothing but vain and idle self-contemplation and self-admiration. No! He has made us the master organizers of the world to establish system where chaos reigns. He has given us the spirit of progress to overwhelm the forces of reaction throughout the earth. He has made us adept in government that we may administer government among savage and senile peoples. Were it not for such a force as this the world would relapse into barbarism and night. And of all our race He has marked the American people as his chosen nation to finally lead in the regeneration of the world. This is the divine mission of America, and it holds for us all the profit, all the glory, all the happiness possible to man. We are trustees of the world's progress, guardians of its righteous peace. The judgment of the Master is upon us: "Ye have been faithful over a few things; I will make you rule over many things."

Selection 1.6: Letter to *Boston Evening Transcript*, William James

Editors' Introduction

The Anti-Imperialist League won the adherence of many outstanding intellectuals like Jane Addams, Mark Twain, and William James. On March 1, 1899, James, nationally known as a psychologist and philosopher, published a letter in the *Boston Evening Transcript*. The letter was, and still is, an eloquent expression of

anti-imperialist opposition to the Philippine War. It was a response to a speech President McKinley gave defending his Philippine policy at a great banquet in Boston of the Home Market Club, an association of leading manufacturers. James was for a time Vice-President of the Anti-Imperialist League, and his letter reflects the shock and resistance of the best of the anti-imperialists to the unprecedented social and political reality that confronted them: the explosion of militarism, chauvinism, and racism that seemed to have been set off by the new dominance of huge monopolies over the economic life of the country. It reflects the anti-imperialist nostalgia for an earlier day when, as they recalled, such tendencies had not run rampant over U.S. society and government. Above all,

James's letter was a call to his contemporaries to speak out against the Philippine War, to bring it to an end. Perhaps its intensity of tone is best explained by Ralph Barton Perry, a friend and biographer, who wrote: "The political issue which stirred James most and exacted from him the greatest time and effort was that of imperialism."

Source: *Boston Evening Transcript,* March 1, 1899.

... Our treatment of the Aguinaldo movement at Manila and at Iloilo is piracy positive and absolute, and the American people appear as pirates pure and simple, as day by day the real facts of the situation are coming to the light.

What was only vaguely apprehended is now clear with a definiteness that is startling indeed. Here was a people towards whom we felt no ill-will, against whom we had not even a slanderous rumor to bring; a people for whose tenacious struggle against their Spanish oppressors we have for years past spoken (so far as we spoke of them at all) with nothing but admiration and sympathy. Here was a leader who, as the Spanish lies about him, on which we were fed so long, drop off, and as the truth gets more and more known, appears as an exceptionally fine specimen of the patriot and national hero; not only daring, but honest; not only a fighter, but a governor and organizer of extraordinary power. Here were the precious beginnings of an indigenous national life, with which, if we had any responsibilities to these islands at all, it was our first duty to have squared ourselves. Aguinaldo's movement was, and evidently deserved to be, an ideal popular movement, which as far as it had had time to exist was showing itself "fit" to survive and likely to become a healthy piece of national self-development. It was all we had to build on, at any rate, so far—if we had any desire not to succeed to the Spaniard's inheritance of native execration.

And what did our Administration do? So far as facts have leaked out, it issued instructions to the commanders on the ground simply to freeze Aguinaldo out, as a dangerous rival, with whom all compromising entanglement was sedulously to be avoided by the great Yankee business concern. We were not to "recognize" him, we were to deny him all account of our intentions; and in general to refuse any account of our intentions to anybody, except to declare in abstract terms their "benevolence," until the inhabitants, without a pledge of any sort from us, should turn over their country into our hands. Our President's bouffe-proclamation was the only thing vouchsafed: "We are here for your own good; therefore unconditionally surrender to our tender mercies, or we'll blow you into kingdom come."

But that small concern, Aguinaldo, apparently not having the proper American business education, and being uninstructed on the irresistible character of our Republican party combine, neither offered to sell out nor to give up. So the Administration had to show its hand without disguise. It did so at last. We are now openly engaged in crushing out the sacredest thing in this great human world—the attempt of a people long enslaved to attain to the possession of itself, to organize its laws and government, to be free to follow its internal destinies according to its own ideals. War, said Moltke, aims at destruction, and at nothing else. And splendidly are we carrying out war's ideal. We are destroying the lives of these islanders by the thousand, their villages and their cities; for surely it is we who are solely responsible for all the incidental burnings that our operations entail. But these destructions are the smallest part of our sins. We are destroying down to the root every germ of a healthy national life in these unfortunate people, and we are surely helping to destroy for one generation at least their faith in God and man. No life shall you have, we say, except as a gift from our philanthropy after your unconditional submission to our will. So as they seem to be "slow pay" in the matter of submission, our yellow journals have abundant time in which to raise new monuments of capitals to the victories of Old Glory, and in which to extol the unrestrainable eagerness of our brave soldiers to rush into battles that remind them so much of rabbit hunts on Western plains.

It is horrible, simply horrible. Surely there cannot be many born and bred Americans who, when they look at the bare fact of what we are doing, the fact taken all by itself, do not feel this, and do not blush with burning shame at the unspeakable meanness and ignominy of the trick?

Why, then, do we go on? First, the war fever; and then the pride which always refuses to back down when under fire. But these are passions that interfere with the reasonable settlement of any affair; and in this affair we have to deal with a factor altogether peculiar with our belief, namely, in a national destiny which must be "big" at any cost, and which for some inscrutable reason it has become infamous for us to disbelieve in or refuse. We are to be missionaries of civilization, and to bear the white man's burden, painful as it often is. We must sow our ideals, plant our order, impose our God. The individual lives are nothing. Our duty and our destiny call, and civilization must go on.

Could there be a more damning indictment of that whole blasted idol termed "modern civilization" than this amounts to? Civilization is, then, the big, hollow, resounding, corrupting, sophisticating, confusing torrent of mere brutal momentum and irrationality that brings forth fruits like this! . . .

. . . there was a horribly suspicious look about the performance. On its face it reeked of the infernal adroitness of the great department store, which has reached perfect expertness in the art of killing silently and with no public squealing or commotion the neighboring small concern.

. . . The issue is perfectly plain at last. We are cold-bloodedly, wantonly and abominably destroying the soul of a people who never did us an atom of harm in their lives. It is bald, brutal piracy, impossible to dish up any longer in the cold potgrease of President McKinley's cant at the recent Boston banquet—surely as shamefully evasive a speech, considering the right of the public to know definite facts, as can often have fallen even from a professional politician's lips. The worst of our imperialists is that they do not themselves know where sincerity ends and insincerity begins. Their state of consciousness is so new, so mixed of primitively human passions and, in political circles, of calculations that are anything but primitively human; so at variance, moreover, with their former mental habits; and so empty of definite data and contents; that they face various ways at once, and their portraits should be taken with a squint. One reads the President's speech with a strange feeling— as if the very words were squinting on the page.

The impotence of the private individual, with imperialism under full headway as it is, is deplorable indeed. But every American has a voice or a pen, and may use it. So, impelled by my own sense of duty, I write these present words. One by one we shall creep from cover, and the opposition will organize itself. If the Filipinos hold out long enough, there is a good chance (the canting game being already pretty well played out, and the piracy having to show itself henceforward naked) of the older American beliefs and sentiments coming to their rights again, and of the Administration being terrified into a conciliatory policy towards the native government.

The programme for the opposition should, it seems to me, be radical. The infamy and iniquity of a war of conquest must stop. A "protectorate," of course, if they will have it, though after this they would probably rather welcome any European Power; and as regards the inner state of the island, freedom, "fit" or "unfit," that is, home rule without humbugging phrases, and whatever anarchy may go with it until the Filipinos learn from each other, not from us, how to govern themselves. . . . Until the opposition newspapers seriously begin, and the mass meetings are held, let every American who still wishes his country to possess its ancient soul—soul a thousand times more dear than ever, now that it seems in danger of perdition—do what little he can in the way of open speech and writing, and above all let him give his representatives and senators in Washington a positive piece of his mind.

Selection 1.7: Platform, American Anti-Imperialist League, 1899

Editors' Introduction

The Anti-Imperialist League was first organized in Boston in November 1898 by a group of individuals who had been active in the anti-slavery struggle. (The platform, reprinted here, with its reference to 1861 and Abraham Lincoln, reflects this previous experience.) Spreading rapidly throughout the country, the League held a conference in Chicago in October 1899, became a national organization, and adopted the platform below. In the course of its short life the Anti-Imperialist League conducted four campaigns which won massive public support: it opposed the Senate passage of the treaty to annex the Philippines; it opposed the Philippine-American War; it opposed McKinley in the election of 1900; and, finally, it carried on a campaign against U.S. military atrocities in the Philippines that in 1902 resulted in a Senate investigation. As the Philippine nationalist movement subsided in defeat, the mass following of the Anti-Imperialist League fell off, never to be regained. But in their prime, the anti-imperialists' opposition to the Philippine war caused difficulties for the U.S. imperialists and was an expression of solidarity with the Philippine people as they fought for independence.

Source: *Speeches, Correspondence and Political Papers of Carl Schurz*, ed. Frederic Bancroft, New York: G. P. Putnam's Sons, 1913, vol. VI, note, pp. 77-79.

We hold that the policy known as imperialism is hostile to liberty and tends towards militarism, an evil from which it has been our glory to be free. We regret that it has become necessary in the land of Washington and Lincoln to reaffirm that all men, of whatever race or color, are entitled to life, liberty and the pursuit of happiness. We maintain that governments derive their just powers from the consent of the governed. We insist that the subjugation of any people is "criminal aggression" and open disloyalty to the distinctive principles of our government.

We earnestly condemn the policy of the present National Administration in the Philippines. It seeks to extinguish the spirit of 1776 in those islands. We deplore the sacrifice of our soldiers and sailors, whose bravery deserves admiration even in an unjust war. We denounce the slaughter of the Filipinos as a needless horror. We protest against the extension of American sovereignty by Spanish methods.

We demand the immediate cessation of the war against liberty, begun by Spain and continued by us. We urge that Congress be promptly convened to announce to the Filipinos our purpose to concede to them the independence for which they have so long fought and which of right is theirs.

The United States have always protested against the doctrine of international law which permits the subjugation of the weak by the strong. A self-governing state cannot accept sovereignty over an unwilling people. The United States cannot act upon the ancient heresy that might makes right.

Imperialists assume that with the destruction of self-government in the Philippines by American hands, all opposition here will cease. This is a grievous error. Much as we abhor the war of "criminal aggression" in the Philippines, greatly as we regret that the blood of the Filipinos is on American hands, we more deeply resent the betrayal of American institutions at home. The real firing line is not in the suburbs of Manila. The foe is of our own household. The attempt of 1861 was to divide the country. That of 1899 is to destroy its fundamental principles and noblest ideals.

Whether the ruthless slaughter of the Filipinos shall end next month or next year is but an incident in a contest that must go on until the Declaration of Independence and the Constitution of the United States are rescued from the hands of their betrayers. Those who dispute about standards of value while the Republic is undermined will be listened to as little as those who would wrangle about the small economies of the household while the household is on fire. The training of a great people for a century, the aspiration for liberty of a vast immigration are forces that will hurl aside those who in the delirium of conquest seek to destroy the character of our institutions.

We deny that the obligation of all citizens to support their Government in times of grave National peril applies to the present situation. If an Administration may with impunity ignore the issues upon which it was chosen, deliberately create a condition of war anywhere on the face of the globe, debauch the civil service for spoils to promote the adventure, organize a truth-repressing censorship and demand of all citizens a suspension of judgment and their unanimous support while it chooses to continue the fighting, representative government itself is imperiled.

We propose to contribute to the defeat of any person or party that stands for the forcible subjugation of any people. We shall oppose for reelection all who in the White House or in Congress betray American liberty in pursuit of un-American ends. We still hope that both of our great political parties will support and defend the Declaration of Independence in the closing campaign of the century.

We hold, with Abraham Lincoln, that "no man is good enough to govern another without that man's consent. When the white man governs himself, that is self-government, but when he governs himself and also governs another man, that is more than self-government—this is despotism." "Our reliance is in the love of liberty which God has planted in us. Our defense is in the spirit which prizes liberty as the heritage of all men in all lands. Those who deny freedom to others deserve it not for themselves, and under a just God cannot long retain it."

We cordially invite the cooperation of all men and women who remain loyal to the Declaration of Independence and the Constitution of the United States.

Selection 1.8: Anti-Imperialist Resolutions, Black Citizens of Boston

Editors' Introduction

White middle class professionals provided the main leadership of the anti-imperialist movement, but it gained support from farmers (for whom William Jennings Bryan especially spoke), from labor, from recent immigrant groups notably the Irish and the Germans, and from blacks. Of all these, perhaps it was the black anti-imperialists who identified most closely with the Filipinos. They saw themselves like the Filipinos as victims of U.S. racism and racist policies. Evidence of this sympathy was to be seen in the opposition of most of the black press to McKinley's Philippine policies and in the unusual rate of desertion of black troops serving in the Philippines, some of whom went over to fight on the Filipino side. On July 17, 1899, in anticipation of the coming presidential election, a meeting of Boston blacks was held to further the influence and organization of anti-imperialist sentiment in the black communities of the nation. This meeting adopted the following resolutions.

Source: *The Boston Post*, July 18, 1899.

Resolved, That the colored people of Boston in meeting assembled desire to enter their solemn protest against the present unjustified invasion by American soldiers in the Philippine Islands.

Resolved, That, while the rights of colored citizens in the South, sacredly guaranteed them by the amendment of the Constitution, are shamefully disregarded; and, while the frequent lynchings of negroes who are denied a civilized trial are a reproach to Republican government, the duty of the President and country is to reform these crying domestic wrongs and not to attempt the civilization of alien peoples by powder and shot.

Resolved, That a copy of these resolutions be sent to the President of the United States and to the press.

Selection 1.9: Remember Pekin! Leaflet of the Republican Club of Massachusetts

Editors' Introduction

Senator Beveridge had hailed the Philippines as a "base for military and naval operations . . . a point from which we can instantly strike and seize the possessions of any possible foe." Six months later McKinley first used the Philippine base in this way when he ordered U.S. troops in the Philippines to intervene in China in concert with Japan, Britain, Russia, and other imperial powers to put down a nationalist uprising of Chinese Boxers. In the course of this intervention U.S. troops rescued U.S. citizens held hostage by the Boxers in Peking ("Pekin"). To take votes from William Jennings Bryan, the Democratic opponent of McKinley's Philippine policies in the election of 1900, the Republican Club of Massachusetts (of which Senator Lodge was a leader) issued a leaflet citing the advantage of the Philippines as a jumping off point for U.S. intervention. What follows is the text of this leaflet.

Source: Campaign leaflet.

Isn't Every American

Proud of the part that American soldiers bore in the relief of Pekin? But that would have been impossible if our flag had not been in the Philippines.

Gen. Chaffee led two infantry regiments, the Ninth and the Fourteenth, and one battery of the Fifth Artillery to Pekin. They did not come direct from the United States; there was not time. The Sixth Cavalry, which was despatched from San Francisco, failed to catch the relief column. The Ninth, the Fourteenth and Reilley's battery, CAME UP FROM MANILA FROM GEN. MAC-ARTHUR'S ARMY.

But for these men and the marines from Manila barracks, Minister Conger and his American comrades in the besieged legation would not have seen their country's flag, and would OWE THEIR RELIEF TO BRITISH, JAPANESE AND RUSSIANS.

When Mr. Bryan tells you that the Philippines are worth nothing to America, you tell him to

"REMEMBER PEKIN!"

U.S. colonial administrator (and later president) William Howard Taft.

CHAPTER 2: COLONIZATION

Introduction

In the years following the Philippine-American War, the United States government consolidated and stabilized the foremost result of that war—U.S. colonial rule in the Philippines.

The most striking feature of the process of colonization was the grant by the U.S. empire-builders of formal political concessions to Philippine nationalism, in policies that appeared democratic when contrasted to those of the Spanish colonists. As was evidently intended, these concessions diffused both the Philippine and domestic opposition to U.S. imperial policy in such a way as to improve the hold of this policy on the governments of both countries. While reducing direct and formal U.S. rule in the Philippines, these concessions strengthened U.S. controlling mechanisms, economic and cultural, and so foreshadowed the policy that is known today as neocolonialism [see selection 2.1].

The first and most obvious of these concessions was the opening up of the colonial government to the Philippine economic elite, the wealthy landowners in particular. While these had formerly served as a social base for Spanish rule, the Spanish had denied them and all other Filipinos access to political office above the municipal level. In 1902 the U.S. Congress passed legislation to open a lower house to Philippine representation, and in 1907 the first elections were held for this body, within the limits of a strict property qualification for voting. Besides elective offices, positions in the colonial administrative bureaucracy and civil service were increasingly opened to the Philippine elite and middle class. These concessions were made in the name of preparing the Philippines for eventual self-rule. So in virtually unprecedented manner the U.S. government established colonial rule in the Philippines with the declared purpose of self-liquidation of that rule, and enlisted the collaboration of the Philippine elite to this end. This promise of eventual independence took on the force of law with the passage of the Jones Bill in 1916 that conceded a Philippine upper house or Senate. The preamble to this legislation declared it to be "the purpose of the people of the United States to withdraw their sovereignty over the Philippine Islands and to recognize their independence as soon as a stable government can be established therein."

Particularly to win influence with the mass of the Philippine people the U.S. government developed a program of free and universal public education, conducted in the English language. The Spanish, on the other hand, had made little effort to educate the population; their efforts in this quarter being largely confined to religious instruction. The effect of this educational policy was to bolster the hold of the U.S. government on the popular mind in the Philippines, to undermine the influence of Philippine nationalism, and to inculcate ideas of white superiority [see selections 2.1 and 2.2]. The official insistence that instruction be based on the English language was a particularly formidable blow to Philippine national identity, as the historian Renato Constantino indicates [see selection 2.2]. For these reasons 1901, the year that brought the first massive influx of U.S. school teachers to the Philippines, must be regarded as one of the seminal dates in the process of U.S. colonization.

Policies of concession, or "attraction" as it was called, had the desired effect of consolidating a social base for U.S. rule in the ranks of the Philippine elite. Political office was not the only reward the Philippine elite got in exchange for acquiescence in the loss of Philippine sovereignty. In 1909 the passage of the Payne-Aldrich tariff law opened the markets of the U.S. to wealthy Philippine landowners so that henceforth they prospered from the sale of the raw products of their plantations (sugar, hemp, tobacco, coconut oil) in tariff-free U.S. markets.

The effect of these policies was a complete success in the case of the Filipino elite, winning them over solidly to U.S. rule, but their effect on the mass of the Filipino people seems to have been more mixed. Even in the heyday of the U.S. colonial regime there remained in popular ranks a strong nationalist tendency, forcing the elite to give lip-service to the demand for independence when they ran for the offices proffered by the U.S. government [see selections 2.3 and 2.4].

In the United States, too, these policies of concession weakened the opposition. Since the anti-imperialist movement was above all an anti-war movement, the subsiding of the war did much to deflate it. But the distinctive features of the U.S. colonizing process (the implied support for ultimate independence, the opening of the colonial government to the Philippine elite, the push for education) also helped to appease those U.S. voters who, war or no war, objected to imperialism as a policy of colonial domination.

Only the initial Boston group, the most thoroughgoing and principled anti-imperialists, seemed to sense what was happening. In 1901 Congress passed the Platt Amendment which granted formal independence to Cuba while preserving U.S. domination there. While many of the former supporters of the anti-imperialist movement endorsed the Platt Amendment and even called for a similar arrangement for the Philippines, the Boston anti-imperialists warned that such policies were leading to a new form of imperialism, to empire without colonies, to imperial control over other nations in the guise of aiding and assisting them [see selections 2.1 and 2.5].

By this time, however, those who gave the warning were losing their public influence. This, indeed, was the period in which the war of conquest began to be forgotten in the United States, screened as it was by the establishment of civil government in the Philippines and the new policies that accompanied it.

For two decades Philippine landowners prospered under the free-trade relationship. Then the outbreak of the worldwide economic crisis in 1929 put an end to this profitable arrangement, as it reactivated forces in the United States demanding that the Philippines be given its independence. With the moral force of the anti-imperialist movement long-since dissipated by the neocolonial posture of the U.S. government in the Philippines, the political thrust for Philippine independence was, at this time, more or less reduced to its long-standing economic base: the U.S. agricultural interests that had from the beginning opposed Philippine annexation for fear of competition from Philippine agricultural produce. Blaming their economic troubles on Philippine competition, they demanded that Congress free the Philippines so that tariffs could be erected to protect them from Philippine farm products [see selection 2.6]. Racial riots against Filipino farm workers on the West Coast in the Depression years also contributed to the demand for Philippine independence legislation [see selection 2.7], as was reflected in the strict limits on Philippine immigration the legislation was to include. After the election of Franklin Delano Roosevelt to the presidency, the Tydings-McDuffie Act of 1934 was passed granting the Philippines independence after a ten year transition period of Commonwealth status.

The colonial period brought wealth to Philippine landowners from the free-trade relationship, but it brought no such benefit to the majority of the Philippine people, who lived in the countryside as tenant farmers and farm laborers. As the Philippine historian Teodoro Agoncillo has written:

Free-trade reinforced the backward feudal agrarian system carried over from the Spanish regime and . . . increased the suffering of the growing numbers of exploited farmers and workers in the country. The big landlords, in their desire to reap astronomical profits, continued to practice exploitative techniques they had learned from their Spanish masters on the hapless peasantry. . . . The result was poor living conditions, agrarian unrest, and periodic peasant uprisings and laborers' strikes in the 1920s and 1930s. [See selection 2.8.]

At the turn of the century, the misery and suffering of the Filipino peasantry had provided an essential impulse and mass base for the armed nationalist struggle against both Spain and the United States. The repetition of these conditions of peasant life under U.S. colonial rule some decades later was to have a similar result: the emergence of an armed Filipino guerilla resistance of nationalist inspiration, especially in Central Luzon, during and after World War II.

Those in the United States who sponsored and organized the colonization of the Philippines realized two achievements with far-reaching impact: they helped form a Filipino elite that was for years to come a reliable social and political base for the exercise of U.S. influence, and they helped to create a neocolonial psychology that affected both the Filipino elite and the mass of the Filipino people, bringing with it enduring attitudes of subservience to the United States. So the weight of U.S. dominance would be preserved even after independence was declared and the formal trappings of colonial rule removed.

Selection 2.1.: The Conception and Gestation of a Neocolony, Daniel B. Schirmer

Editors' Introduction

Although actual combat between U.S. troops and Philippine guerillas did not come to an end until some six years later, President McKinley in 1901 established a civil government in the Philippines (the Philippine Commission) under the leadership of William Howard Taft. The article below describes the dynamics and the distinctive characteristics of the colonizing process initiated by Taft.

This selection illuminates a special feature that has colored U.S.-Philippine relationships for many years to the advantage of the United States government. The United States came to the Philippines as an imperial conqueror and by a war of unremitting harshness and brutality robbed the Filipino people of the beginnings of national sovereignty that they had just won for themselves; but this is not the perception of events that has lingered in the popular consciousness, either in the United States or in the Philippines. What remains in the public memory is the official United States version of the origins of the U.S.-Philippine relationship, namely that the United States came to the Philippines on a mission of benevolence and generosity, intent on nothing else so much as to teach the Philippines the benefits of democracy and self-government.

The manner in which U.S. officials established a colonial government in the Philippine does much to explain the success with which this historical fraud has been perpetrated upon the public both in the Philippines and in the United States.

Source: *The Journal of Contemporary Asia,* vol. 5, no. 1, 1975.

Describing a form of colonial domination that sprang into international prominence after World War II, neocolonialism is characterized, on the part of the imperial powers, by the exercise of indirect rather than direct, control over subject nations. In 1919 almost 70% of the world's population was in colonies, but in 1968, due to the post-war growth of national liberation movements, considerably less than 1% remained so, and many imperial states were forced to make their influence felt (where able to do so) in former colonial areas by indirect or neo-colonial means.

In the second half of the 19th century, while the European powers were busy establishing colonies in Africa and Asia, United States imperialism was expanding its influence in South America by economic penetration rather than by colonial acquisition. Then, in connection with the Spanish-American War and Spain's defeat in 1898, U.S. imperialism annexed Hawaii, Puerto Rico, and the Philippines. This colonial venture was brief however, for by 1900 the experience gained in it had turned U.S. empire builders back to a primary reliance on indirect methods of expansion.

There were two factors that especially brought about this shift in policy.

The first was the armed resistance of the Philippine people to U.S. conquest. . . .

The second was the U.S. domestic opposition to Philippine annexation. . . .

Two men were decisive in directing this shift in U.S. policy, Elihu Root and William Howard Taft. Root, as McKinley's Secretary of War, had overall responsibility for policy towards Spain's former colonies coming under U.S. influence after the Spanish-American War, and William Howard Taft, as first civil administrator of the Philippines, was responsible for detailed development of the U.S. policy toward that country. Both men were conscious of the need to adjust U.S. policy to the pressing realities of the moment.

Root's special concern at this time was Cuba, and here the problem he faced arose from the fact that, although Congress had earlier passed the Teller Amendment promising Cuban independence, strong imperialist pressure had since developed to disregard that pledge and impose, there too, a conventional colonial rule. In 1903 Root spoke before a Senate Committee and told its members how he had seen the situation three years before:

> There were not a dozen men in Cuba who believed that the United States was going to keep faith with them, not a dozen men in Cuba believed that we were going to carry out your resolution, Senator [Teller], and we were daily on the verge of the same sort of thing that happened to us in the Philippines of having those people, who had fought for their independence for years and who believed that we were going to hold them in subjection the same way that Spain had held them, take to the woods and begin another insurrection. And I can tell you that I had an uneasy life for a long time with the apprehension that the morning paper when I looked at it any morning might contain news of American troops firing on Cubans.

While Root considered "A Philippine war in Cuba . . . too disastrous to contemplate," he also was highly sensitive to the domestic opposition aroused by the Administration's colonial policy in the Philippines. In May 1900, for example, he wrote President Eliot of Harvard, who had spoken out against Philippine annexation, "We are trying to give the Cuban people just as fair and favorable a start in governing themselves as possible."

Such were the pressures upon Root that induced him to go against those imperialists advocating the colonial annexation of Cuba and to propose, instead, the Platt Amendment. This allowed for formal Cuban independence, but gave the United States control of Cuban foreign affairs and finances, the right to military bases on Cuban soil, and to military intervention in Cuban affairs. U.S. imperial hegemony over Cuba would be preserved by indirect, rather than direct means.

In Taft's case these same pressures operated even more immediately as determinants of policy. In 1907 Taft described the conditions he had faced when he set about his work in the Philippines:

The Civil Government was inaugurated in 1901 before the close of a war between the forces of the United States and the controlling elements of the Philippine people. It had sufficient popular support to overawe many of those whose disposition was friendly to the Americans. In various provinces the war continued intermittently for a year after the appointment of a Civil Governor in July 1901. This was not an auspicious beginning for an organization of a people into a peaceful community acknowledging allegiance to an alien power.

Secondly there was in the United States a strong minority party that lost no opportunity to denounce the policy of the Government and to express sympathy with those arrayed in arms against it, and declared in party platform and in other ways its intention, should it come to power to turn the islands over to an independent government of the people.

These factors produced an effect upon U.S. Philippine policy similar to their effect on Cuban policy. The U.S. switch away from a traditional colonialist posture was to be seen not only in the Platt Amendment, but also in the policies adopted to set up a colonial administration in the Philippines. What you had here was nothing less than the establishment of a colony in a neocolonial manner.

President McKinley gave the signal for this development when he said in 1900 that the goal of U.S. policy in the Philippines was to "guide the Filipinos to self-development." But it was Taft, with the general support of Root, who was responsible for the elaboration of this policy in its concrete applications to the military, political, economic and educational spheres.

Since the Taft approach was new in many ways, it aroused opposition from U.S. imperialists who favored traditional methods. But there was a matter of ideology which Taft, with his neo-colonialist leanings, shared with the traditionalists. This was the assumption that the colored citizens of the Philippines were inferior to the white citizens of the Unites States, and that, therefore, white Americans were bound to run the affairs of the Filipinos for them, to one degree or another. . . .

Taft said, more than once, that the Filipinos as he found them were incapable of self-government, but he expressed this white supremacist attitude in a new way, combining military suppression with friendly condescension and patronizing guidance. This new emphasis brought him into conflict with old-style imperialists, particularly those in the U.S. military, who were accustomed to giving vent to racism in hostile and discriminatory ways alone.

Taft's insistence on checking open racist hostility and discrimination, at least towards friendly Filipinos of the upper class, was made necessary by the fundamental thrust of his policy. Seeing that a colonial administration had to be established in the face of Philippine nationalist resistance and domestic anti-imperialist opposition, Taft sought to find a social and political base for this regime in those elements in the Philippine population willing to collaborate with the Americans: the rich, the conservative, the large landowners, and the well-educated, that group known as ilustrados. In this way Philippine participation in the colonial administration could be secured, "self-government" encouraged and displayed, Philippine nationalists and U.S. anti-imperialists divided among themselves and mollified.

Shortly after his arrival in the Philippines in the early summer of 1900 Taft had a dispute with General Arthur MacArthur (in charge of the U.S. military) about Taft's proposal to inaugurate a Filipino constabulatory and militia (to be officered, of course, mainly by Americans). MacArthur was reluctant to trust any Filipinos at all and looked forward to the maintenance of U.S. power in the Philippines by large-scale military occupation over an indefinite period. On the other hand Taft and the members of his Commission (the administrative body he led) developed arguments that touched on all their concerns: a Filipino militia and constabulary, knowing the language, terrain and the people, would be more effective fighting guerillas than would U.S. troops; such forces would "have a very healthy effect upon the people because it will show them that they are to take part in the government"; the enlistment of Filipinos was essential because it would send U.S. troops home and quiet protest there. . . .

In his dispute with MacArthur, Taft won on all counts. Root (who felt domestic pressure to "bring the boys home") recommended the enlistment of a Filipino militia to Congress in January 1901; the formation of a Philippine constabulary came six months later. . . .

It was of course, in the field of politics, rather than the military, that the neocolonial aspects of Washington's Philippine policy showed up most characteristically. Here, the declared purpose of preparing the Filipinos for self-government took main form. The Spanish had denied the ilustrados representation in the colonial administration above the municipal level. Taft soon made it clear that the United States meant to change this, in both elective and appointive posts. He opened place to the ilustrados as provincial governors, as members of his Commission, as delegate-observers to the U.S. Congress in Washington, in addition to maintaining their access to municipal office. He found those in the Filipino elite who were willing to compromise their nation's sovereignty in exchange for office.

That such was to be the nature of the bargain was indicated by McKinley's instructions to the Philippine Commission (authored by Root) which stated categorically that "an indispensable qualification for all offices and positions of trust and authority in the Islands must be absolute and unconditional loyalty to the United States." The U.S. authorities offered public office to the ilustrados in the first place as a means of quelling the armed resistance (for many in this class served in the insurgent command), and Taft's Commission soon issued a ruling that any Filipino still fighting by April 1901 would be disenfranchised and therefore ineligible for political office or appointment.

While Taft encouraged Filipino participation in government, he did this, however, within the framework of ultimate U.S. control. The municipal governments, though completely Filipino, were under the supervision of the provincial government. The provincial governor, who might be Filipino, could be outvoted by the two other members of the provincial board, the treasurer and supervisor, who were to be U.S. citizens.

Perhaps Taft's purposes in promoting Filipino participation in the government came into sharpest focus around the proposal for a Philippine popular or elected assembly. One scholar calls this "the most important provision of the Philippine Bill of 1902" (the U.S. legislation that provided for a permanent Philippine colonial administration) and notes that "it represented a radical departure from prevailing colonial practice." The U.S. Senate at first voted against the assembly, and its imperial opponents included none other than the ardent expansionist Senator Albert J. Beveridge. To counter Congressional opposition Taft wrote Senator Henry Cabot Lodge that granting an assembly would have a "good effect" in the United States as well as in the Philippines. Calming the fears of his fellow-imperialists, Taft told Lodge, "I think we shall always be able to control a majority of the Popular Assembly."

If it is a characteristic of neocolonial policy to appease nationalist consciousness while it secures imperialist control, then it would seem evident that Taft was quite deliberately establishing a colonial administration in the Philippines with very marked neo-colonial features. He told Root that his Commission would have completed most of the legislation decisive to the establishment of the new colonial regime before the assembly met, but, Taft emphasized, the assembly would perform a very important service:

> Vesting it with the power to initiate legislation, to have discussions, to pass laws—some of which would doubtless be approved, would not only practice the people in insular government, but would give them the feeling that they were actually taking part in it.

Taft saw his policy as giving the Filipinos a feeling of participation, the Americans, control.

Taft sought to secure support for U.S sovereignty in the Philippines from wealthy Filipinos by offering them economic advantage as well as political office. Taft chose Jose R. de Luzuriaga, the millionaire sugar planter from Negros, as one of the first three Filipino members of the Civil Commission, and it was for the wealthy sugar growers like Luzuriaga, and for the tobacco planters (with a crop second to sugar in the Philippine export trade), that Taft sought free entry into the U.S. domestic market.

While a 25 percent reduction on Philippine goods under the Dingley tariff was achieved in 1901, this did little to help Filipino planters. U.S. sugar and tobacco growers offered resistance to tariff reduction, and it was not until 1909, as Taft became President, that free trade was established between the United States and the Philippines and Filipino sugar and tobacco entered the U.S. market duty free.

Since the 1909 arrangement also allowed U.S. manufactured goods free entry to the Philippine market (in contrast to the duties paid by other nations), one of the goals sought in U.S. colonization by imperialists like Senator Henry Cabot Lodge was thereby fulfilled. . . .

On August 18, 1900, he (Taft) wrote Root that "an independent government of the Filipinos would produce a condition worse than in Hayti" (the all-black republic much condemned by the imperialists at the time); "capital would be driven from the islands," a "fact", he explained, "which itself requires us to stay here". . . .

So it was that, in the very first place, Taft believed the neocolonial policies he was developing to be a necessary adjunct to the investment of U.S. capital in the Philippines. In Taft's eyes, the security of U.S. investment capital in the Philippines not only precluded that country's independence at the moment, it also made necessary the policy of "attraction," or Filipino participation in the government. Taft complained to Root of those American capitalists who were in favor of ignoring "Filipino prejudices, Filipino interests, and Filipino rights," who urged the policy of the "strong hand." In Taft's opinion it was:

> . . . entirely possible to permit the lucrative investment of American capital here without outraging the feelings of the Filipinos and without giving them the impression that we are here merely to exploit their country without respect to their welfare, but if the methods which are pressed upon us were adopted they would cause a great deal of trouble.

In this light, his policy of "The Philippines for the Filipinos" derived its importance because it made the Philippines safe for U.S. investors, avoiding the trouble bound to result from "the strong hand". . . .

. . . Taft's program was such as to encourage a threefold economic dependence of the Philippines upon the United States: first as a market for Philippine export goods, then as a source of manufactured goods, and finally as a source of investment capital. Moreover under the policies Taft inaugurated these economic ties were to grow at the same time that the participation of the Filipinos in their government was to grow. A firm economic base for the indirect exercise of U.S. political control was to be established at the same time that formal and direct U.S. rule was being minimized.

In developing neocolonial techniques for the treatment of their Philippine colony, U.S. imperialists did not rely on economic power alone to buttress their rule. They quickly turned to ideological influence as another base from which to secure political control by indirect means. Popular education, the organization of a public school system in the Philippines, became the chief focus of this effort. . . .

Since the U.S. imperialists' outlook was marked by racism, their sponsorship of public education in the Philippines meant exposing the mass of the Filipino people to white supremacist attitudes in an organized way. Fred W. Atkinson was the U.S. citizen who served as the first General Superintendent of Education in the Philippines and he put his ideas about the U.S. role in the Philippines on record:

> The Filipino people, taken as a body, are children, and childlike, do not know what is best for them. . . . In the ideal spirit of preparing them for the work of governing themselves finally, their American

guardianship has begun . . . by the very fact of our superiority of civilization and our greater capacity for industrial activity we are bound to exercise over them a profound social influence.

The white supremacist attitude expressed by the first General Superintendent of Education was influenced by the dominant neocolonial approach, so that the harsh master-servant relationship of the traditional colonial mode blurred softly into that of guardian and ward. But, if Superintendent Atkinson's ideas were at all representative, U.S. educators taught Filipinos that they were inferior, the Americans, superior; they cultivated in their pupils a colonial mentality, however new their approach to this task. . . .

In 1904 Elihu Root told the Republican National Convention:

. . . there seems to be no reasonable doubt that under the policy already effectively inaugurated, the institutions already begun in the Philippine Islands . . . the Philippine people will . . . come to bear substantially such relations to the people of the United States as do now the people of Cuba.

If the conditions surrounding its independence in 1946 are examined [see chapter 4], in particular the military and economic restrictions, a strong case can be made that the Philippine colony at that time became a neocolony as Cuba had been under the Platt Amendment. From this viewpoint, the military, political, economic and educational institutions and relationships that Root and Taft originated led to the outcome that Root, in 1904, predicted, i.e., the neocolonial features that the U.S. imperialists gave their Philippine colony did, indeed, pave the way for its transformation to a neocolony.

Both Root and Taft were aware that their Philippine policy represented a break with conventional imperial rule, a new colonial departure. Writing in 1913, Root said, ". . . our work in the Philippines . . .has differed from all other colonial experiments that I know anything about in following consistently . . . the purpose to fit the Filipinos themselves for self-government." Writing earlier, while Root and he were still hammering out these policies, Taft noted that, "The English student of colonial government is fixed in his view that we have pursued a wrong course in the Philippine Islands by conferring upon the people much more popular control than was wise."

An Asian national liberation movement and a domestic anti-imperialist movement, both advanced for their time, combined to force the U.S. imperialists to develop a new colonial policy that only later became the general rule for the maintenance of world empire.

Selection 2.2: The Miseducation of the Filipino, Renato Constantino

Editors' Introduction

Renato Constantino is a leading Philippine historian, whose writings have been an important influence on the current generation of Philippine nationalists. "The Miseducation of the Filipino" is one of the most famous of his works. The topic of this extract is the early system of public education inaugurated in the Philippines by the U.S. colonists, a system that seemed to be the physical manifestation of their proclaimed intent to teach democracy and self-government to Filipi-

nos. Constantino describes this system as a powerful instrument whereby Washington taught millions of Filipinos to accept the image of the United States as a generous benefactor and to forget the nationalist heroes and struggles of their past. What might also be noted is that this system helped pacify domestic opposition to U.S. Philippine policy.

Source: Renato Constantino, *The Filipinos in the Philippines and Other Essays*, Quezon City: Malaya Books, 1966, pp. 39-65.

... The molding of men's minds is the best means of conquest. Education, therefore, serves as a weapon in wars of colonial conquest. This singular fact was well appreciated by the American military commander in the Philippines during the Filipino-American war. . . .

General Arthur MacArthur, in recommending a large appropriation for school purposes, said:

> This appropriation is recommended primarily and exclusively as an adjunct to military operations calculated to pacify the people and to procure and expedite the restoration of tranquility throughout the archipelago.

Beginning of Colonial Education

Thus, from its inception, the educational system of the Philippines was a means of pacifying a people who were defending their newly-won freedom from an invader who had posed as an ally. The education of the Filipino under American sovereignty was an instrument of colonial policy. The Filipino had to be educated as a good colonial. Young minds had to be shaped to conform to American ideas. Indigenous Filipino ideals were slowly eroded in order to remove the last vestiges of resistance. Education served to attract the people to the new masters and at the same time to dilute their nationalism which had just succeeded in overthrowing a foreign power. The introduction of the American educational system was a subtle means of defeating a triumphant nationalism. As Charles Burke Elliott said in his book, *The Philippines*:

> To most Americans it seemed absurd to propose that any other language than English should be used in schools over which their

flag floated. . . .

Of course such a system of education as the Americans contemplated could be successful only under the direction of American teachers, as the Filipino teachers who had been trained in Spanish methods were ignorant of the English language . . .

Arrangements were promptly made for enlisting a small army of teachers in the United States. At first they came in companies, but soon in battalions. The transport *Thomas* was fitted up for their accommodation and in July 1901, it sailed from San Francisco with six hundred teachers—a second army of occupation—surely the most remarkable cargo ever carried to an Oriental colony.

The American Vice-Governor

The importance of education as a colonial tool was never under-estimated by the Americans. This may be clearly seen in the provision of the Jones Act which granted the Filipinos more autonomy. Although the government services were Filipinized, although the Filipinos were being prepared for self-government, the department of education was never entrusted to any Filipino. Americans always headed this department. This was assured by Article 23 of the Jones Act which provided:

> That there shall be appointed by the President, by and with the advice and consent of the Senate of the United States, a vice-governor of the Philippine Islands, who shall have all the powers of the governor-general in the case of a vacancy or temporary removal, resignation or disability of the Governor-General, or in case of his temporary absence; and the said vice-governor shall be the head of the executive department known as the department of Public Instruction, which shall include the bureau of education and the bureau of health, and he may be assigned such other executive duties as the Governor-General may designate.

Up to 1935, therefore, the head of this department was an American. And when a Filipino took over under the Commonwealth, a new generation of "Filipino-Americans" had already been produced. There was no longer any need for American overseers in this field because a captive generation had already come of age, thinking and acting like little Americans.

This does not mean, however, that nothing that was taught was of any value. We became literate in English to a certain extent.

In exchange for a smattering of English, we yielded our souls. The stories of George Washington and Abraham Lincoln made us forget our own nationalism. The American view of our history turned our heroes into brigands in our own eyes, distorted our vision of our future. The surrender of the Katipuneros [the revolutionaries of the Katipunan] was nothing compared to this final surrender, this levelling down of our last defenses. Dr. Chester Hunt characterizes this surrender well in these words:

The programme of cultural assimilation combined with a fairly rapid yielding of control resulted in the fairly general acceptance of American culture as the goal of Filipino society with the corollary that individual Americans were given a status of respect.

This, in a nutshell, was (and to a great extent still is) the happy result of early educational policy because, within the framework of American colonialism, whenever there was a conflict between American and Filipino goals and interests, the schools guided us toward action and thought which could forward American interests.

Goals of American Education

The educational system established by the Americans could not have been for the sole purpose of saving the Filipinos from illiteracy and ignorance. Given the economic and political purposes of American occupation, education had to be consistent with these broad purposes of American colonial policy. The Filipinos had to be trained as citizens of an American colony.

. . . Philippine education was shaped by the overriding factor of preserving and expanding American control. To achieve this, all separatist tendencies were discouraged. Nay, they had to be condemned as subversive. With this as the pervasive factor in the grand design of conquering a people, the pattern of education, consciously or unconsciously, fostered and established certain attitudes on the part of the governed. These attitudes conformed to the purposes of American occupation.

An Uprooted Race

The first and perhaps the master stroke in the plan to use education as an instrument of colonial policy was the decision to use English as the medium of instruction. English became the wedge that separated the Filipinos from their past and later was to separate educated Filipinos from the masses of their countrymen. English introduced the Filipinos to a strange, new world. With American textbooks, Filipinos started learning not only a new language but also a new way of life, alien to their traditions and yet a caricature of their model. This was the beginning of their miseducation, for they learned no longer as Filipinos but as colonials. They had to be disoriented from their nationalist goals because they had to become good colonials. The ideal colonial was the carbon copy of his conqueror, the conformist follower of the new dispensation. He had to forget his past and unlearn the nationalist virtues in order to live peacefully, if not comfortably, under the colonial order. The new Filipino generation learned of the lives of American heroes, sang American songs, and dreamt of snow and Santa Claus. The nationalist resistance leaders exemplified by Sakay were regarded as brigands and outlaws. The lives of Philippine heroes were taught but their nationalist teachings were glossed over. Spain was the villain, America was the savior. To this day, our histories still gloss over the atrocities committed by American occupation troops such as the water cure and reconcentration camps.

Economic Attitudes

Control of the economic life of a colony is basic to colonial control. Some imperial nations do it harshly but the United States could be cited for the subtlety and uniqueness of its approach. For example, free trade was offered as a generous gift of American altruism. Concomitantly, the educational policy had to support this view and to soften the effects of the slowly tightening noose around the necks of the Filipinos. The economic motivations of the Americans in coming to the Philippines were not at all admitted to the Filipinos. As a matter of fact, from the first school-days under the soldier-teachers to the present, Philippine history books have portrayed America as a benevolent nation who came here only to save us from Spain and to spread amongst us the boons of liberty and democracy. The almost complete lack of understanding at present of those economic motivations and of the presence of American interests in the Philippines are the most eloquent testimony to the success of the education for colonials which we have undergone. What economic attitudes were fostered by American education?

It is interesting to note that during the times that the school attempts to inculcate an appreciation for things Philippine, the picture that is presented for the child's admiration is an idealized picture of a rural Philippines, as pretty and as unreal as an Amorsolo [Philippine artist noted for idyllic rural scenes] painting with its carabao, its smiling healthy farmer, the winsome barrio lass in the bright clean *patadyong* [native shirt], and the sweet little nipa hut. That is the portrait of the Filipino that our education leaves in the minds of the young and it hurts the country in two ways.

First, it strengthens the belief (and we see this in adults) that the Philippines is essentially meant to be an agricultural country and we can not and should not change that. The result is an apathy toward industrialization. It is an idea they have not met in school. There is further, a fear, born out of that early stereotype of this country as an agricultural heaven, that industrialization is not good for us, that our national environment is not suited for an industrial economy, and that it will only bring social evils which will destroy the idyllic farm life.

Second, this idealized picture of farm life never emphasizes the poverty, the disease, the cultural vacuum, the sheer boredom, the superstition and ignorance of backward farm communities. . . .

With American education, the Filipinos were not only learning a new language; they were not only forgetting their own language; they were starting to become a new type of American. American ways were slowly being adopted. Our consumption habits were molded by the influx of cheap American goods that came in duty-free. The pastoral economy was extolled because this conformed with the colonial economy that was being fostered. Our books extolled the Western nations as peopled by superior beings because they were capable of manufacturing things that we never thought we were capable of producing. We were pleased by the fact that our raw material exports could pay for the American consumption goods that we had to import. We now are used to these types of goods, and it is a habit we find hard to break, to the detriment of our own economy. We never thought that we too could industrialize because in school we were taught that we were primarily an agricultural country by geographical location and by the innate potentiality of our people. . . .

The pathetic result of this failure of Philippine education is a citizenry amazingly naive and trusting in its relations with foreigners, devoid of the capacity to feel indignation even in the face of insults to the nation, ready to acquiesce and even to help aliens in the despoliation of our natural wealth. Why are the great majority of our people so complaisant about alien economic control? Much of the blame must be laid at the door of colonial education. Colonial education has not provided us with a realistic attitude toward other nations, especially Spain and the United States. The emphasis in our study of history has been on the great gifts that our conquerors have bestowed upon us. A mask of benevolence was used to hide the cruelties and deceit of early American occupation. The noble sentiments expressed by McKinley were emphasized rather than the ulterior motives of conquest. The myth of friendship and special relations is even now continually invoked to camouflage the continuing iniquities in our relationship. Nurtured in this kind of education, the Filipino mind has come to regard centuries of colonial status as a grace from above rather than as a scourge. Is it any wonder then that having regained our independence we have forgotten how to defend it? It is any wonder that when leaders like Claro M. Recto try to teach us how to be free, the majority of the people find it difficult to grasp those nationalistic principles that are the staple food of other Asian minds? The American architects of our colonial education really labored shrewdly and well.

Selection 2.3: Taft's Terms of Probation, *El Renacimiento*

Editors' Introduction

While U.S. control of public education did much to blunt the force of nationalist sentiment in the Philippines during the colonial period, such sentiment continued to have a hold, especially among the mass of the Philippine people. Giving voice to Philippine nationalism was the Manila journal *El Renacimiento*, described by the U.S. Governor General of the Philippines, W. Cameron Forbes, as "a mean sheet trying all the time to stir up trouble for the government between the two races." In its issue of October 30, 1908, *El Renacimiento* published an editorial "Birds of Prey" accusing a U.S. official of using his office for private gain. The official brought suit for libel that was sustained by the U.S. Supreme Court, and the editors, under jail sentence and heavy fines, were forced to close the paper down in 1910. The editorial printed below, "Taft's Term of Probation" of November 30, 1908, expresses impatience with the postponement of Philippine independence, a position urged by William Howard Taft, who was then President-elect of the United States. Other Philippine journals took up the nationalist cause after *El Renacimiento*'s demise.

Source: Reprint in handbill by the Boston Anti-Imperialist League.

Why should the Filipinos not be masters of their own destiny and arbiters of their own fate? Thus spake America, through the mouth of its leading statesmen, after having favorably decided the same question concerning the Cubans in the Gulf of Mexico. But this nation, free by tradition and by nature, this generous deliverer, found an answer in the discovery that we were incapable of self-government, and, since, according to oft-repeated and solemn statements, its object was to assist us in the realization of our national aspirations, it could only suggest that we might be granted our independence when we became capable of governing ourselves—the sovereign nation undertaking to prepare us suitably for such a condition!

Ten long years passed in this preparation, ten years of guardianship, ten years of painful experience, ten years of bitter deception, and as yet the problem remains unsolved. Very small indeed has been the progress made in this respect. Our advance is very slow; at least such is the opinion of Mr. Taft.

This old assertion of our incapacity is the stock argument of the smart imperialist politicians who clamor for American expansion. Among the most prominent of these is the President-elect of the United States. With what ingenuity does he evade the responsibilities of the situation!

In his report after enumerating the failures of the Filipinos in municipal government, which he calls the essence of self-government, Mr. Taft says:

> The result does not show that the Filipinos are capable of complete self-government, but it does not show, either, that they cannot reach a condition of capacity therefore and finally arrive at absolute self-government by means of the gradual extension of a partial self-government, extended as they gradually grow more and more capable of enjoying it.

Such is the manner in which Mr. Taft defines our political aptitude.

Incapable at present, yet endowed with qualities to attain final capacity by means of a slow preparation—so slow as to be simply disheartening.

Is this all the result realized by the Philippine nation in ten years of submission to a foreign guardianship? Sad destiny indeed for the Filipinos!

Furthermore, the sincerity of Taft may be doubted. In the imperialistic designs which betray themselves in the stronghold of genuine democracy the Philippine archipelago looms up as a most valuable prize, the open gate to China—the key of the Pacific—a strategical basis—a naval station—an inexhaustible source of coal and wood. Of course, therefore, ours must needs be a nation incapable for self-government for generations yet to come!

Let no one say that those who feel such sad presentiments and distrust are only the radicals—the theorists,—the demagogues among us; no, far from it; the most conservative Filipinos, the friends of the government, those who have been ardent partisans of the American sovereignty, do not hide their fear now lest the dominating element today will before long be the owner of the entire country, and they do not hesitate to denounce the educational period of two generations which Taft has indicated.

The Philippine nation aspires more ardently with every passing day to be independent.

Selection 2.4: Interview with Manuel Quezon, General Frank McIntyre

Editors' Introduction

In the colonial period, Manuel Quezon and Sergio Osmeña were the two foremost leaders of the Philippine ruling elite. In December 1913, Quezon had an interview with General Frank McIntyre, Chief of the U.S. War Department's Bureau of Insular Affairs, a supervisory agency for U.S. colonial possessions. McIntyre's memorandum of the interview, quoted from below, represents Quezon as saying, in confidence, that both he and Osmeña privately opposed early Philippine independence.

(In public, of course, Quezon and Osmeña were enthusiastic proponents of independence.) In this interview Quezon places the fear of future Japanese expansion as a reason for opposing independence. Though not stated here, the prospect of the loss of the colonial free-trade access to the U.S. domestic market was perhaps an even more immediate concern.

Source: General Frank McIntyre, "Memorandum No. 1-1913," Dec. 29, 1913, National Archives, Washington, DC, pp. 2-3.

Quezon then brought up the question of policy with reference to the Philippine Islands. He wanted to know what the policy of the President Woodrow Wilson, [Democrat] was.

I told him that I had only the few public statements, including the statement of Governor [Francis Burton] Harrison, [U.S. Governor General of the Philippines, 1913-1921, appointed by Wilson] quoting the President and the President's message to Congress, on which to base an opinion, and that I thought that those statements gave very accurately the policy of the President. He said that there was a fear in the Philippine Islands that they contemplated a very early grant of independence; that this worried greatly the Americans and others with interests in the Islands, and that he himself thought it would be a mistake.

He said that he wished to advocate an elective Senate with an appointive Governor with a veto not absolute but absolute unless two-thirds of both

Houses should vote to override it, and that this two-thirds vote should have the effect of submitting the acts for the consideration of the Secretary of War, whose opinion thereon would be final. He said that the thought that the Governor might be prejudiced by some local condition and that a presentation of the case to the Secretary of War, with the pros and cons, would get a better result.

He said that he was prepared to advocate a new organic act along this line and believed this would settle the question of the relations between the Philippine Islands and the United States for at least twenty-five years, when it would become a matter of interest to their successors rather than to those people now living. He said that there would perhaps be a little more difficulty in getting an agreement to this now than there would have been a few years ago, in that independence had now acquired an attractive sound to the ear of the Filipinos.

He expressed his fears of independence in the near future, basing his fears largely on the conduct of Japan. He said that on this trip for the first time he became convinced that the Japanese had designs on the Philippine Islands; that he had been approached in a way to indicate this and that he believed if the Japanese became convinced that independence would come in the near future there would be an immediate beginning of officially assisted emigration of Japanese to the Philippine Islands, and the Japanese would remain Japanese and would not be assimilated by the Philippine people. . . . He said, however, that before he would advocate anything short of independence or short of what he had been talking for heretofore, he would like to feel that it would meet the approval of the administration in that it would necessarily lose him all of his old friends, the extreme anti-imperialists, and he would not like to go ahead without feeling that he would have the backing of some part of the community.

I suggested to him that he might talk to the Secretary of War. I asked him if he had explained this view to Mr. Osmeña. He said that he had, and that he thought Osmeña would be all right.

I asked him if he had spoken of it to Governor Harrison. He said: "My God, no. I think he believes in independence. He thinks he can turn us loose in about four years," and he repeated: "He believes in it."

Selection 2.5: Free America, Free Cuba, Free Philippines, George S. Boutwell

Editors' Introduction

The granting of political office to the Philippine elite, the introduction of a universal public education, the promise of eventual independence: all these new and unusual aspects of U.S. policy in the Philippines can be linked to the U.S. grant of independence to Cuba under the restrictive terms of the Platt Amendment. Both the Philippine and Cuban policies illustrated one important historical fact: the United States in the first years of this century was moving away from the colonial to neo-colonial forms of imperial rule, from direct to indirect control over other nations, the better to stabilize the dominance of U.S. imperial policy both abroad and at home.

On March 30, 1901, under the slogan "Free America, Free Cuba, Free Philippines," the Boston anti-imperialists held a meeting which in effect gave notice that they had an understanding of the shift in U.S. imperial policy and of its domestic and foreign implications. George S. Boutwell, the president of the Anti-Imperialist League (who as an anti-slavery Republican had been appointed first Commissioner of Internal Revenue by President Lincoln), gave the main address. The conditions governing Cuban independence advocated by General Leonard Wood (then U.S. military governor of Cuba), and roundly denounced by Boutwell, later became the substance of the Platt Amendment for Cuba. Like Secretary of War Elihu Root (author of the Platt Amendment), Boutwell foresaw the day in which the United States government would treat the Philippines like Cuba under the Platt Amendment. Unlike Root (and some former supporters of the anti-imperialist movement), however, he condemned such an eventuality as a sign that the United States "will have taken on, irretrievably taken on, all the characteristics of an empire." Having opposed the policy of imperialism with colonies, the Boston anti-imperialists now declared that they opposed as well the policy of imperialism without colonies, to which the U.S. government was turning. Justifiably worried about the effect on public opinion of this change in policy, Boston anti-imperialist leader Erving Winslow wrote New York's Carl Schurz in May 1901: "I am afraid adversity is the only thing which will bring the American people to a sense of the danger which menaces them in this new departure."

Source: Pamphlet "Free America, Free Cuba, Free Philippines," issued in Boston 1901 by the New England Anti-Imperialist League, in collection of Widener Library, Harvard University.

We commemorated the nineteenth of April, 1898, as a day of freedom in the annals of America, and on the twentieth we volunteered a tender of independence and unqualified sovereignty to Cuba, whose freedom from the dominion of Spain we had proclaimed. In that pledge of freedom to Cuba the President and the Congress united, and with the general approval of the American people. We are now redeeming that pledge, and by what process? We demand concessions that are inconsistent with our pledge of independence and sovereignty. Let me read the demands as made by the administration through General Wood on Washington's birthday anniversary, 1901.

First. No government organized under the constitution shall be deemed to have authority to enter upon any treaty or engagement with any foreign power which may tend to impair the independence of Cuba or confer upon any such power any special right or privilege without the consent of the United States.

Second. No government organized under the constitution shall have the power to assume or contract any public debt except to the capacity of the ordinary revenues of the island after defraying current expenses and paying interest.

Third. Upon the transfer of Cuba to the government organized under the constitution, Cuba consents that the United States shall retain the right to intervene for the preservation of Cuban independence, the maintenance of a stable government, adequately protecting property and individual liberty, and discharging the obligations with respect to Cuba, imposed by the treaty of Paris upon the United States, now assumed by the government of Cuba.

Fourth. All acts of the military government, and all rights acquired thereunder, shall be valid and shall be maintained and protected.

Fifth. To facilitate the performance by the United States of such duties as devolve under the foregoing provisions, and for its own defense, the United States may acquire and hold land for naval stations and maintain the same.

With these concessions yielded or extorted, will not Cuba have become a vassal state? By the first article its foreign trade will be in the hands of the United States. In the exercise of that power the United States may create or it may destroy industries; it may give value to labor or it may make labor valueless; it may enhance or it may cripple the resources of the country; and without much delay Cuba will be subjected to a Congress in which it will not be represented.

Thus will Cuba have been made powerless for valid negotiations abroad, and for defense at home. Next, Cuba cannot enter upon any expenditure in excess of its ordinary resources, without the consent of the United States. How are railways to be built, public buildings to be erected, water systems to be created: how are towns and cities to be lighted and drained; in fine, how is Cuba to possess the advantages of modern civilization if the power to create a debt is denied? The answer of the administration is always the same: The United States will do what is right. Do you doubt your own government? By the third article we reserve the right to intervene, whenever, in our opinion, the government is not stable, whenever liberty and property are not protected, or whenever, in our opinion, Cuban independence shall be threatened.

If such a power of supervision and intervention existed in our Congress over the States of this Union there would remain not even a shadow of that sovereignty which was once claimed for them. Under the third article the limits of the authority of the United States could be found only in the discretion of the government of the United States; in other words, in the policy and purposes of the party in power.

Under Article 5 the government of the United States may set up naval stations on any land that it may acquire. Under this provision it may acquire heights and other strategic points by which the cities and ports of the island can be brought under our control. Thus and in this manner are we keeping our pledge of 1898—a pledge of unconditional independence and full sovereignty to Cuba. Having thus violated the pledge that we made in April, 1898, the President may expect Cuba to accept as good coin his new promise that all these powers will be exercised in moderation, and that gratitude for what America has done for Cuba should be recognized by unlimited confidence in the good purposes of America. . . .

. . . Thus does the administration subvert a policy of freedom and sovereignty in states into a policy by which strong states may tyrannize over the weaker ones upon the pretext of aiding and defending them. And thus is the administration struggling to become a world power by alliances with the strong, as in the case of China, and by usurpations over the weak, as in Hawaii, Puerto Rico, Cuba, and the Philippines. . . .

The demand has been made in Congress and in the country that the Philippines should be put upon the basis of Cuba. If the terms named can be imposed upon Cuba with the approval of Congress and the consent of the country the President may accept like terms for the Philippines. Thus, upon the theory of the President, the Republic will have been far advanced as a world power, and thus the Republic will have taken on, irretrievably taken on, all the characteristics of an empire.

Selection 2.6: The Independence Lobby, Shirley Jenkins

Editors' Introduction

In March 1934, the U.S. Congress passed the Tydings-McDuffie Act providing for Philippine independence after a ten year Commonwealth period. The grant of independence to the Philippines by the United States has been the subject of varied interpretations. To many, both in the Philippines and the United States, it has been seen as the crowning act of U.S. generosity and benevolence, in which that nation fulfilled its promise to give the Philippines self-government and so to liquidate any imperial ties. To others, especially to increasing numbers of Philippine nationalists who have become uneasy with the military and economic restrictions that accompanied and followed the grant of independence, it has seemed merely to mark the exchange of a formal dependency on the United States for an informal dependency, the shift from a colonial to a neo-colonial status.

The first interpretation (proclaimed by the U.S. government and echoed at the time by most of the Philippine elite) seems to obscure the basic motivations for the independence legislation, in particular the pressure from the U.S. farm lobby to lessen what it saw as the injurious competition of Philippine agricultural products on the domestic market.

At the time of the independence legislation, as at the time of conquest and colonization, official proclamations of benevolence and generosity coupled with measures of formal democracy cloaked the selfish motives of powerful interests in the United States, and a psychological advantage again went to those who wished to maintain the dominance of U.S. influence in Philippine affairs under new conditions.

Shirley Jenkins, in the excerpt below from her larger study of U.S.-Philippine economic relations, points to pressures from the agricultural interests of the United States as the dominant force in the granting of independence to the Philippines.

Source: Shirley Jenkins, *American Economic Policy Toward the Philippines,* Stanford: Stanford University Press, 1954, pp. 34-37.

In the United States the move to grant independence to the Philippines was supported by interest groups with varying motives. Philippine independence had been a plank of successive Democratic party platforms, although the formulation became more vague as the years went on. American labor took an anti-imperialist position in general. Specific concern was voiced by the American Federation of Labor over the supposed threat of competition from cheap labor in Asia and from Oriental immigration to the United States. There was a determined Filipino group in this country which repeatedly urged an independent status for its homeland. But while all these were important, the major pressure for action on the independence issue came from the American farm lobby, whose members saw in continued Philippine preferences a threat to domestic agricultural production.

In a revealing study of the farm groups supporting Philippine independence, [*Philippine Independence* (New York: 1936)] Dr. Grayson Kirk analyzed the experience of American agricultural producers in the nineteen-twenties, when, coincidentally, imports from the Philippines rose substantially and American agricultural prices fell year after year. American agriculture did not share in the industrial expansion which followed World War I. Preferring to seek an external explanation, rather than to look at the inner workings of the domestic economy, these farm groups put the blame on Philippine competition. It should be recalled that, over these years, American tariff walls rose steadily and Philippine products were placed in an increasingly favorable position. For the decade 1920-30 Philippine sugar exports to the United States rose by 450 percent, coconut oil exports (including copra) by 223 percent, and cordage by over 500 percent. But, as Dr. Kirk pointed out, no causal relationship between these increases and the lowering of domestic prices has been shown.

The anti-Philippine group flourished, however, supported by the dairy organizations, general farm groups, domestic sugar producers, and cordage manufacturers, with the moral backing, at least, of the Cuban sugar lobby. The Tariff Defense Committee of American Producers of Oils and Fats was formed. Representative Harold Knutson of Minnesota included as part of his remarks in Congress, on December 14, 1929, a letter he had written to the editor of the St. Paul *Pioneer Press,* which stated, "It is generally agreed that the Philippine Islands today constitute the greatest single menace to our dairy industry because of their huge exports to our country." Failing to secure what they considered adequate protection in the form of quotas and duties from the Smoot-Hawley Tariff of 1929, these groups gave their wholehearted support to the move to cut the Philippines loose from the American free-trade bloc.

From 1930 to 1932 various Philippine independence bills were discussed in Congress, and finally the Hare-Hawes-Cutting Bill was approved. Agreement was reached on provisions for a ten-year transitional period of free trade, for imposition of quotas on Philippine products, for immigration restrictions allowing fifty Filipinos a year entry to the United States, and for special American rights in the Islands. The bill received a decisive veto in January 1933 by President Herbert Hoover, who stated that the readjustment period was too short, and insufficient security was provided for the Islands. It was, however, promptly repassed by Congress over the President's veto. Congressional support for the bill arose in response to the desperate domestic agricultural situation. The drop in farm incomes in the depression years sent legislators grasping at any tariff or quota straws to protect American products from overseas competition. When the American election of 1930 resulted in a shift of power to a slim Democratic majority in the House, some action on Philippine affairs was bound to occur.

The Hare-Hawes-Cutting Act created a storm of dispute in the Philippines, and resulted in a factional fight within the leading political party. President Quezon opposed the act, while both Sergio Osmeña and Manuel Roxas were in favor of accepting it. President Quezon was finally able to secure the passage of a resolution against the measure in the Philippine legislature on October 17, 1933. Four main objections were listed: the trade provisions, the immigration restrictions, the allocation of indefinite powers to the High Commissioner, and the military and naval restrictions, which were considered to be "inconsistent with true independence."

President Franklin D. Roosevelt, who took office in March 1933, recommended to Congress that the measure be modified by eliminating provisions for permanent military bases, except naval stations. The Tydings-McDuffie Act was speedily enacted, and became effective on March 24, 1934. It was accepted by the Filipinos, primarily because it was considered to be the best that could be secured at the time, and also because there was implied a promise of later review. This was apparent in the resolution of the Philippine legislature which, in accepting the act, quoted from President Roosevelt's message to Congress, which declared, "Where imperfections or inequalities exist, I am confident that they can be corrected after proper hearing and in fairness to both peoples." This statement, according to the Filipino legislators, "gives to the Filipino people reasonable assurance of further hearing and due consideration of their views."

The Tydings-McDuffie Act included both political and economic provisions. On the political side, it defined the steps toward independence. The Philippine legislature was authorized to arrange for a constitutional convention to result in a document "republican in form" and including a bill of rights.

Also stipulated for inclusion in the framework of the interim government were a number of provisions defining American sovereignty in the Islands for the ten-year transitional period. Thus no foreign Philippine loans could be made without the approval of the President of the United States; the United States retained control of Philippine foreign affairs; all decisions of Philippine courts could be reviewed by the United States Supreme Court; and American citizens were to have equal rights with Filipino citizens in the Islands. Filipino immigration to the United States was limited to the minimum quota of fifty a year. Most of these restrictions applied only in the transitional Commonwealth period. On July 4 of the independence year the President of the United States was to surrender all sovereignty and recognize the independence of the Philippines.

Major portions of Tydings-McDuffie Act were devoted to defining economic relationships between the two countries. Free trade was to be continued from 1935 to 1940, but the quantities of products entering the United States duty-free were restricted to 850,000 long tons of sugar, 200,000 tons of coconut oil, and 3 million pounds of cordage each year. Imports in excess of these quotas were to pay full duty. There were no restrictions on United States products entering the Philippines. In the period 1941-46 products receiving preferential treatment were to be subject to a Philippine export tax of an initial 5 percent, increasing annually by 5 percent to 25 percent in 1946. Full United States tariffs were to be paid after July 4, 1946, the independence date. Tariff revenues before independence were to be applied to liquidate the bonded indebtedness of the Commonwealth. . . .

Commenting on the events of 1934, Dr. Kirk said:

> . . . the Seventy-third Congress closed its Philippine account. It had offered independence to the Islands and that independence had been accepted. But whatever nobility there may possibly have been in the gesture was completely overshadowed by an appalling indifference to Philippine welfare. Statesmanship had surrendered openly and callously to the dictates of lobbyists.

Selection 2.7: Anti-Filipino Race Riots, Emory S. Bogardus

Editors' Introduction

Another form of political pressure underlay the grant of Philippine independence: the call to limit Philippine immigration to the U.S. Opposition to Philippine immigration was inflamed by anti-Filipino race riots that occurred on the West Coast in the late 1920s and early 1930s.

The most publicized of these riots took place in Watsonville, California, in January 1930. Emory S. Bogardus investigated this incident and shortly thereafter reported his findings in a talk—excerpted below—to the Ingram Institute of Social Science in San Diego.

White racist antagonism to brown-skinned Filipinos had been an element in the anti-imperialist movement opposing colonization at the time of the U.S. conquest; this was particularly strong at the time among the Democratic politicians of the South, who also reflected agrarian opposition to colonization. So it is not surprising that racist antagonism to those Filipinos who had emigrated in the colonial period to the United States as farm laborers should play a part in the final grant of independence. The essentially conservative nature of this act on the part of the United States government is indicated by the chauvinist and conservative nature of its leading proponents: white racists, and agricultural entrepreneurs opposing foreign competition, the most backward and least principled elements of the earlier anti-imperialist opposition to Philippine colonization.

Source: *Letters in Exile, An Introductory Reader on the History of Pilipinos in America,* A Project of Resource Development and Publications, UCLA Asian American Studies Center, Copyright 1976 by the Regents of the University of California, pp. 51-57.

Before an analysis is attempted of the riots, an account will be given of antecedent factors. . . .

(1) A few cases of Filipinos had been brought into court of the justices of peace of Pajaro township, and into the county court at Salinas (of Filipinos living in the Watsonville district). The offenses were usually "reckless driving" of automobiles.

(2) On January 10, 1930, there appeared newspaper accounts of a set of Resolutions passed in Pajaro (adjoining Watsonville) by the Northern Monterey Chamber of Commerce and written it is stated by the justice of peace of Pajaro township. The article in the *Pajaronian,* appeared under a double column, first page headline which read: "Resolution Flaying Filipinos Drawn by Judge D. W. Rohrback." The article began as follows:

> Coming out square-toed and flat-footed in an expression on the Filipino question, the Northern Monterey Chamber of Commerce adopted a resolution Wednesday night (January 8) designating the Filipino population of this district with being undesirable and of possessing unhealthy habits and destructive of the wage scale of other nationalities in agricultural and industrial pursuits.

The article continued:

> When interviewed this morning Judge Rohrback said the move of the Monterey Chamber of Commerce was but the beginning of an investigation of a situation that will eventually lead to the exclusion of the Filipinos or the deterioration of the white race in the state of California.

The charges made against the Filipinos in this Resolution were as follows: (1) Economic. They accept, it is alleged, lower wages than the American standards allow. The new immigrants coming in each month increase the labor supply and hold wages down. They live on fish and rice, and a dozen may occupy one or two rooms only. The cost of living is very low, hence, Americans cannot compete with them. (2) Health. Some Filipinos bring in meningitis, and other dangerous diseases. Some live unhealthily. Sometimes fifteen or more sleep in one or two rooms. (3) Intermarriage. A few have married white girls. Others will. "If the present state of affairs continues there will be 40,000 half-breed in California before ten years have passed,"—is the dire prediction.

The Resolutions included the following statement about sending the Filipinos home.

> We do not advocate violence but we do feel that the United States should give the Filipinos their liberty and send those unwelcome inhabitants from our shores that the white people who have inherited this country for themselves and their offspring might live.

It is evident that the Northern Monterey Chamber of Commerce did not speak for other Chambers of Commerce for the Resolutions contained the following challenge:

> Other Chambers of Commerce have probably passed resolutions endorsing the use of Filipino labor as being indispensable. If that is true, better that the fields of the Salinas Valley should grow into weed patches and our wonderful forests be blackened.

These and similar statements speak for themselves regarding the impassioned tone of the Resolutions.

Upon the publication of the Resolutions sensitive Filipino leaders promptly replied. A four-page pamphlet entitled "The Torch" appeared within a few days from Salinas. It contained a detailed reply to the Resolutions, by a member of the editorial staff of the *Three Stars*, Stockton, California. It questions vigorously the truth of a number of statements in the Resolutions and replies sharply to the insinuations of others. . . .

A few days later, January 19, a mass meeting of 300 Filipinos was held in a hall at Palm Beach, a few miles west of Watsonville, according to a half page paid advertisement in the Watsonville evening newspaper. As indicated by the statements in this article the reactions of the Filipinos to the Pajaro Resolutions had now reached the state of formal group action. . . .

On January 11, 1930, a new angle to the race situation in and around Watsonville developed. A small Filipino club leased a dance hall from two Americans at Palm Beach (four or five miles west of Watsonville), imported nine white dance hall girls, and set up a taxi dance hall for the Filipino members. Definite rules of propriety were apparently maintained. The American owners of the property stated that the Filipinos conducted their dances in more orderly fashion than did many American groups who had leased the dance hall property. But the idea of Filipinos dancing with white girls (no matter who the latter were) incensed white young men of Watsonville, and they determined to break up the procedure. As one white person said to the writer:

Taxi dance halls where white girls dance with Orientals may be all right in San Francisco or Los Angeles but not in our community. We are a small city and have had nothing of the kind before. We won't stand for anything of the kind.

On Sunday, the 19th, the anti-Filipino demonstrations began and lasted until the early hours of Thursday morning, the 23rd. Early Sunday afternoon it is said "that several machine loads of American youths went out to the resort (the dance hall at Palm Beach), but were barred by deputies hired to guard the place." Later that evening several fights occurred on the streets of Watsonville between Americans and Filipinos. On Monday evening, the 20th, the disturbances continued. "Possibly 200 Americans formed Filipino hunting parties, running in groups from 25 to over 100 persons." On Tuesday evening, the 21st, "a mob (of white men and boys) attempted to storm the Palm Beach premises. Word had been passed among the boys of the town that a mass meeting of the Filipinos was to be held at Palm Beach. The boys were aware that several white girls were living on the premises and working in the dance hall there. This fact infuriated them and at eleven o'clock last night full thirty machines, filled with flaming youth," went to Palm Beach, but were met by the owners of the beach resort who held them at bay with guns until "shortly after midnight" when the sheriff, deputies, and constables arrived and "made short work of the mob." Before the arrival of the officers there was some shooting but no one was seriously hurt.

On Wednesday evening, the 22nd, the rioting reached its climax. Violence developed into destroying property, beating Filipinos, and finally one Filipino was killed.

> Forty-six terror-stricken Filipinos beaten and bruised, cowered in the City Council room . . . . after being rescued from a mob of 500 infuriated men and boys who, being robbed of their prey, shattered windows and wrecked the interior of the brown men's dwellings.

Further light on the rioting is given:

> To the accompaniment of pistol shots, clubbings and general disorder. . . it is believed that 700 trouble-seekers, armed with clubs and some firearms, attacked Filipino dwellings, destroyed property, and jeopardized lives. The most serious rioting occurred on the San Juan road in Pajaro about 10 o'clock . . . when a mob estimated at 250 men entered several Filipino dwellings and clubbed the occupants.

Then came the fatal shot, and the ending of the rioting. A headline and an opening sentence tell the story tersely: "Wild Rioters Murder Filipino in Fourth Night of Mob Terror," and "Mob Violence in Watsonville Is Ended." A published account reads:

> Near midnight a carload of rowdies drove to the ranch (Murphy) and began firing into it. The unfortunate men (or boys) trapped

like rats were forced into a closet where they huddled and prayed.

One of the Filipino boys, Fermin Tober, did not follow the others. The next morning, "it was discovered that a heavy bullet, tearing through the walls and a door of the bunkhouse had pierced Tober's heart". . . .

Somewhat belatedly the leading citizens of Watsonville came to the rescue of the reputation of the city, and of the Filipinos. The headline in the *Evening Pajaronian* summed up part of the reactions: "Volunteer Deputies Bring Welcome Peace to Turbulent Town." The American Legion, the Rotary, the Kiwanis, and other organizations took action in support of law and order, and of protection of the Filipinos.

The *Evening Pajaronian* of the 24th reports that seven (white) boys were brought into the court of the justice of the peace of Pajaro township for preliminary hearing on the charge of rioting. At the hearing a total of eight boys were bound over to the Superior Court of Monterey County. The justice is quoted as stating that he hoped "with all his heart that the judge of the superior court would be lenient in handling their cases as he did not consider them criminals." On February 17, six of the eight youths pleaded guilty at Salinas for attacking Filipinos. On February 25th, the eight were sentenced to serve two years in the county jail. Probation was granted four. The other four were sent to the county jail for thirty days; then put on probation for two years, during which time they must keep away from pool halls, abstain from intoxicating liquors; they must never molest Filipinos and on the other hand they are to lead sober, industrious lives. At the inquest over the body of Fermin Tober it was decided that the person who had fired the fatal shot was unknown.

Selection 2.8: Struggles of the 1930s, Luis Taruc

Editors' Introduction

The economic benefits and political privileges of U.S. colonial rule left the Philippine elite prone to accept the status quo and U.S. domination. The political parties of the elite during the colonial period—all more or less identical variants of the leading party, the Nacionalistas—reflected these attitudes and interests, while at the same time declaring for independence because of public pressure.

On the other hand U.S. colonial rule did nothing to change the poverty of the mass of the Filipino people, with a consequent unrest that became particularly acute in Central Luzon, the country-side around Manila, during the 1920s and 1930s. The organization of the working people in the cities and rural areas, their strikes and other militant activities, led to the formation of a different type of political party: the Socialist Party in 1929 and the Communist Party in 1930. In addition to urging independence, both these parties declared their intention to represent the needs and interests of the working population in town and country: tenant farmers, farm laborers, and urban workers. In his memoirs, *Born of the People,* the peasant-born Luis Taruc describes the struggles in which he participated as a Socialist Party leader in Central Luzon.

It was the organization and struggle of the peasantry in Central Luzon during these decades that laid the basis for the nationalist resistance of the Hukbalahap guerillas, or the Huks, first in the early 1940s against the Japanese occupation [see selection 3.1 below], then in the post-war years against the Philippine govern-ment and U.S. dominance [see selection 5.2 below]. In fact, Taruc wrote his book (in collaboration with the U.S. Communist William Pomeroy) while both were "in the hills" taking part in the Huk resistance after World War II. Later captured and imprisoned for many years, Taruc was finally released as he gave support to Marcos's martial law.

Source: Luis Taruc, *Born of the People,* New York: International Publishers, 1953, pp. 26-51.

The waters ran deep in Central Luzon. The problems were ages old. The people were land hungry. The land was there, but it did not belong to them. Sometime in the past there had been land for everybody. Now it was in the hands of a few. The few were fabulously rich; the many were incredibly poor.

It had been that way under the Spanish regime for centuries. When the Americans came they made boasts about having brought democracy to the Philippines, but the feudal agrarian system was preserved intact.

On the haciendas there were laborers who were paid less than ten centavos a day. Thousands more earned less than twice that much. From ten thousand miles away the Spreckles sugar interests in California reached into the sugar centrals of Pampanga and took their fortune from the sweat of Filipino labor. . . .

The old hopeless method of peasants with a grievance going one by one to a court and being defeated each time by a legal machine, operating in the interests of the ruling class, was now completely changed. Now in Pampanga there was a union, AMT—*Aguman ding Maldang Talapagobra,* the League of Poor Laborers—which met the landlords head-on with strikes and mass demonstrations, and there was a political party, the Socialist Party, which represented the many instead of the few. The single peasant humbly seeking justice was now the mass demanding justice. . . .

Throughout 1936 and 1937 the AMT grew and became a part of the people. We had many weaknesses. Our organization was loose and slow. Our leadership did not always function as a unit. We made blunders and mistakes that the labor movement in other countries would have considered infantile; we learned as we went along. Not enough attention was paid to mass education, which made the organization top-heavy; if all the leaders had been arrested or killed, the movement would have withered and died. We did not understand yet that the people needed to be developed so that new leaders would spring up at once to replace those who had fallen.

But, if its leaders were untrained and sometimes fell into error, the AMT's members were developing in the appropriate way—in the arena of struggle. . . .

The years 1936 and 1937 were marked by an ever-increasing number of strikes. . . . There were two types of strikes among the peasants. If conditions were intolerable, the peasants would present a petition to the landlords. We demanded a 50-50 sharing of the crop. At that time the shares favored the landlord 70-30. We demanded an end to usury. At that time if a tenant borrowed one cavan of rice, he had to pay back three or even five. We called for an end to serfdom under which the peasant's wife had to go each week to the landlord's house to clean it, and the peasant had to bring one cartload of wood each week to the landlord.

If the landlord rejected the petition, it was followed by a strike. A red flag on a stick was set up in the corner of a field on strike. We used the carabao horn, the sound of which carried a far distance, to summon workers from the fields. Picket lines were set up in the fields to stop the scabs hired by the landlords. The landlords called on the Philippine Constabulary (PC) for aid. They came with clubs and often beat the strikers. Sometimes they shot unarmed peasants. We tried to propagandize both the scabs and the PC. The landlords had a weakness: they had to hire from the people to fight the people. Sometimes we could turn their weakness against them, by winning over their tools.

The other type of strike was defensive. The landlords and the capitalists had been used to dealing with phony labor unions, which they subsidized themselves, and whose leadership danced to their tune. Now they were confronted with an organization which sprang from the people, and they tried to break it. When the landlords heard of their tenants joining the AMT, they tried intimidation, threatening to evict them. Some tenants bowed to such pressure, losing sight of their rights in anxiety to provide for their families. Others who were more militant refused to be evicted and called for help from the AMT. Then a strike of all the landlord's tenants would protest the eviction. The landlords called the PC to carry out the eviction, or used their own private armies, such as the Special Police of the Baluyots, one of the biggest landowning families and an old political power in the province. When we had to, we fought the Special Police and the PC.

Gradually the people saw the need for unity. In the barrios they began to boycott peasants who refused to join the AMT. The non-members were isolated, not spoken to, nor were they helped when they had a house to build, or when they had a burial. This treatment improved the warm, close-knit community of barrio life. . . .

The union entered the lives of the people. Union club houses were built. A cultural group presented entertainment. . . .

Women's auxiliaries made the barrio wives and daughters militant, and the women often joined their husbands in struggle. Sometimes, when workers were arrested, their wives followed them into prison, shouting: "If my husband is arrested, arrest me, too!"

The landlords retaliated with increasingly harsh methods. A big strike occurred in the fish pond district of Masantol. Landlords eagerly grasping for more land were closing the river, shutting off the water for their private fish ponds. They planted mangroves along the river. The silt built up the land and shut off the flow of water. The workers cut the trees to open the river. When the landlords brought in the PC, a tenant strike spread across the whole district. The PC shot and killed three strikers. The tension was very high.

The leaders of the strike were Zacharias Viray and Halves and Manabat, of the AMT. Zacharias Viray was a man of great honor and principle. He believed that workers, above all, should be incorruptible. He concentrated his efforts to influence the overseers on plantations, to prevent the use of what he called "the tools of the oppressor within the ranks of the oppressed." He had a saying: "To die on Monday and to die on Wednesday is the same. It is just as well to die on Monday as long as you remain loyal to your principles."

During the Masantol strike Viray was called into the town to confer with the chief of police. In the municipal building he was shot and murdered by paid agents of the landlords. After he was dead a gun was placed in his hand, for a frame-up; he was then accused of attacking the police. The people were not deceived. . . .

The years preceding the outbreak of the war [World War II] were hectic. We entrenched our organization in the barrios, in the sugar centrals, in transportation, on the railroad, wherever there were workers. We did it through mass action and through legal court tests.

Unlike other labor movements at that time in the Philippines, we knitted together both peasants and factory workers in the same organization. In Arayat, again, in February 1938, there was a dramatic example of peasant-worker unity during a strike in the town's sugar central. . . .

The laborers in the central had set a strike date. The PC came and deployed in the compound. There was a tense moment as the great wheel of the central slowed and stopped, and the noise died to silence. The workers came out on strike, and the PC closed in on them. Then the sound of carabao horns could be heard from all directions and columns of peasants came out of the fields from all points of the compass, converging on the central. There were over 2,000 peasants and strikers. The PC were frightened and shrank into a corner of the compound. For two days there were demonstrations in the town. We held programs with music and dancing. Always we tried to turn our strikes into public manifestations as an expression of unity. After two days the strikers were victorious. It was the peasant support that had achieved it.

A unified peasant movement had spread further across Central Luzon by 1938, when a coordinating committee was set up between the AMT and the KPMP—*Kapisanang Pambansa ng Magbubukid sa Pilipinas*, the National Peasants Union—from Nueva Ecija. The KPMP had an even longer existence than the AMT, its leaders were more experienced, and its organization extended down into the Southern Luzon provinces. . . .

On November 7, 1938, this unity was made even more solid by the merger of the Socialist Party and the Communist Party of the Philippines. . . .

In the AMT alone we had approximately 70,000 members. . . .

The tide that reached Pampanga was now sweeping the whole world. It was the anti-fascist spirit of the people. Filipino peasants and workers, as well as the industrial workers of other nations, were awake to the menace of fascism. From our fields we had watched the Spanish people in their heroic single-handed struggle to the death against Hitler, Mussolini and Franco, and the unquenchable struggle of the Chinese people against the Japanese aggressors. . . .

Labor struggles in Central Luzon had abated somewhat by 1941, although strikes continued to occur in the sugar centrals, among the tenants, and in the Pambusco (Pampanga Bus Co.). Many demands had been won by the peasants. In 1940 eight Socialist mayors had been elected in Pampanga (in Angeles, San Fernando, Arayat, Mabalacat, San Simon, Floridablanca, Candaba, and Mexico). In addition there were Socialist or Communist mayors and councilors in Tarlac, Concepcion, La Paz, and Victoria, in Tarlac province; in Cabiao, Nueva Ecija; and in Guagua, Pampanga, where a provincial board member was also elected.

Our victory had deeper roots than the success of our movement in fighting for better wages and living conditions for the workers. The Nacionalista Party that had dominated Philippine politics for thirty years was tied completely to American imperialism. It was the party of the compradores as well as the party of the landlords, the political tool with which another nation ruled our people. The people were as tired of lip-service to independence as they were of exploitation. They voted Socialist in 1940 in Pampanga. . . .

The menace of invasion, however, caused much tension in the towns and barrios of Central Luzon. . . .

In October 1941, in an informal discussion in the AMT office, we speculated on the possibilities of guerilla war in the event of invasion. We based our conclusions on what had happened in Spain and in China. At the end of October we sent a circular to all branches of our membership, suggesting the formation of a military type of organization. Our advice was that branches should divide into squads of twelve each, with a sergeant and a commander. The preparation of communications and of a food supply was suggested, as well as an attempt to acquire some arms. There was no clear-cut policy on this matter, so the circular was never really followed up, although it did serve to alert our membership.

Japanese forces conquer Philippines, May 1942.

CHAPTER 3: WAR, COLLABORATION, AND RESISTANCE

Introduction

Under the terms of the Tydings-McDuffie Act of 1934, the Philippine Commonwealth was scheduled to obtain its independence in 1946. But in December 1941, Japan attacked Pearl Harbor and, simultaneously, struck at the Philippines, a U.S. colony and military base.

By April 1942, the last U.S. and Filipino forces holding out against the Japanese onslaught surrendered at Bataan. Just as the United States had done at the turn of the century, Japan was able to obtain the cooperation of the majority of the elite. Even four months before the fall of Bataan, leading Philippine politicians were organized by the Japanese into a Provisional Council of State. And in October 1943, when the Japanese established a totally subservient but nominally independent "Philippine Republic," they again obtained the cooperation of much of the elite. Some collaborated economically, helping to provide the Japanese with war materials and other needed goods.

There were of course many motives for collaboration. Coercion was a consideration in only a small minority of cases. Some collaborators were attracted by Japan's slogan "Asia for the Asians," an appealing concept for colonial peoples, though in practice it meant "Asia for the Japanese." Some claimed that they collaborated in order to protect their compatriots from the depredations of direct Japanese rule, but at the same time they facilitated the Japanese administration and pacification of the country. For much of the elite, collaboration with the new conquerors provided—as it had with the previous conquerors four decades earlier [see chapter 2]—a means of maintaining their political and economic power.

But just as the United States had found in 1899 that while some Filipinos collaborated many others resisted U.S. efforts at colonization, so too did the Japanese have to contend with massive resistance, as large numbers of Filipinos became guerillas. Many of the guerilla groups were recognized by the United States Army Forces in the Far East and became known as USAFFE guerillas; they were led by U.S. officers who had evaded capture or by members of the Filipino elite. Thus, as nationalist historians Renato and Letizia Constantino have cogently argued, many in the resistance rejected collaboration with one colonial power, Japan, only to embrace the other colonial power, the United States [*The Philippines: The Continuing Past* (Quezon City: Foundation for Nationalist Studies, 1978)]. But Japanese brutality made this the choice of many Filipinos.

The most significant autonomous guerilla movement developed in Central Luzon, an area of intense peasant radicalism before the war [see section 2.8 above]. In March 1942, left-wing labor and peasant leaders and intellectuals established a People's Anti-Japanese Army, the Hukbalahap (Huks for short), which grew to a strength of some 10,000 members with a mass base many times larger [see selection 3.1].

By 1944 the tide of war had turned. In October of that year, United States forces under General Douglas MacArthur began their reconquest of the Philippines. (MacArthur had close personal ties to members of the pre-war Philippine elite, ties sweetened by a half million dollar gift from Quezon just before MacArthur had left the islands in 1942.) When the U.S. Armed Forces returned to Central Luzon in early 1945, the Huks assisted them in fighting the Japanese. Nevertheless, as the Japanese troops surrendered, the United States proceeded to disarm the Huks, arrest their leaders, and dismantle the local governments they had established. In their place, the U.S. installed reliably pro-American officials from the pre-war elite, some of whom had served the Japanese.

Manuel Roxas, an elite politician who had played both sides during the war, was promptly exonerated by General MacArthur—a pre-war friend—bypassing any formal proceeding. Roxas became the champion of the upper-class collaborationists, and the re-established Congress—most of whose members had themselves been collaborators—elected him as its leader.

Sergio Osmeña, the president of the Commonwealth government-in-exile, had spent the war years in the United States and had lost control of the levers of political influence; Roxas announced that he would contest the presidency in the upcoming April election. The Huks and their peasant and left-wing supporters formed an organization called the Democratic Alliance which decided, reluctantly, to back Osmeña. Roxas was favored by U.S. officials in the Philippines while Osmeña had none of the usual advantages of incumbency—neither patronage (Roxas was able to block Osmeña's appointments) nor pork-barrel (the Philippine government had no funds to dispense); and Roxas had at least as much money and muscle as Osmeña. The latter ran a lackluster campaign and Roxas was elected president. Although some Democratic Alliance candidates won seats from Central Luzon, by and large Congress was dominated by the wealthy, intent on promoting their own economic interests and preventing punishment for collaboration. Thus, the pre-war elite, many of whom had served the Japanese while their compatriots were in the hills fighting back, was firmly in control as the Philippines was about to achieve its independence [see selection 3.2].

Selection 3.1: The Hukbalahaps, U.S. Department of State

Editors' Introduction

The next excerpt is taken from a confidential U.S. State Department document on the Huks. It provides background on agrarian radicalism [see also selection 2.8 below], and describes the wartime origin of the Huks, the sources of conflict with other

guerilla groups, and relations with
the returning U.S. armed forces in
1945.

Source: U.S. Department of

State, Office of Intelligence Research,
The Hukbalahaps, OIR Report No.
5209, September 27, 1950, pp. 1-19.

Peasant agitation in the Philippines is firmly grounded in the peasantry's long-standing and legitimate grievances. The basis of current peasant problems dates back to the quasi-feudal system that prevailed long before the Spanish arrived in the Philippines. Even then the society was divided into two classes: a small minority of landholding chiefs and aristocrats (*datos*) and a large majority of landless peasants (*taos*).

Under the Spanish, the king gave tremendous land grants to nobles and to friars for their monasteries and religious activities. Consequently, most of the land continued to be held by a relatively small group consisting of the native landed aristocracy, the Roman Catholic Church, and the Spanish nobility. Relations between the landowning and landless classes were governed by tradition. The peasant shared his harvest with the landlord; the tenant kept, at most, half the crop and less if the landowner supplied implements and work animals. Only in rare cases did the peasant rent a plot of land and retain the entire yield himself.

These arrangements kept the tenant's standard of living at a low level. In addition, the plots were so small and the methods of cultivation so primitive that the average tenant could not earn enough to sustain himself and his family from one harvest to the next. The situation was especially critical in Central Luzon, where population pressures were greatest. Peasants were forced to borrow from the only available sources—the landlords or the money lenders—at usurious rates of interest. Peasant debts grew to great proportions and were inherited by succeeding generations. Consequently, the peasant was bound to the *hacienda*. This system, however, bred little active and organized discontent. As long as the landlord lived on his hacienda, he practiced a paternalism that gave the peasant the security that the peasant's own resources could not supply.

The growth of absentee landlordism vitiated this feudal relationship and led to intensified resentment. Resentment first grew on the great estates of the Church. But the writings of such patriots as Rizal aroused Filipinos of all classes to turn against institutions they had once trusted, respected, and followed. This widespread dissatisfaction was instrumental in causing the uprising of 1896, in the course of which the Malolos government confiscated all the friar estates.

When the Americans took control of the Philippines in 1898, they inherited the problem of the friar lands. Since the United States Government had agreed in the Treaty of Paris to protect the property interests of the friars, it bought the estates, paying for them largely out of money raised from the sale of Philippine Government bonds. The land was to be sold to the landless peasantry. However, many of the estates were bought by the *caciques* [wealthy landowners] and by the middle class elements that originated during the American occupation, with the result that the peasantry derived little benefit from the sale of the friar lands.

The old relations between the *caciques* and the peasants changed under the Americans. Although the Americans set out to improve living conditions in the Islands generally, the benefits to education, public health, self-government, and national income actually only occasionally reached the peasantry. In the words of the fifth annual report of the American High Commissioner: "The bulk of the newly created income has gone to the government, the landlords and to urban areas, and has served but little to ameliorate living conditions among the almost feudal peasantry and tenantry."

As markets for Philippine products opened in America, the effects of capitalism on the feudal agrarian society of the Philippines sharpened. Production of cash crops on large tenant-operated estates increased. As the *caciques* became richer, they aspired to a more luxurious way of life. As the Americans gradually enlarged the sphere of local government, the landlords gave more time to politics and public life, participated in the government, and gradually acquired a near monopoly of political power.

These changes caused the old system to disintegrate. The landlords spent most of their time in Manila or in one of the provincial capitals. The running of the *hacienda* was left to hired plantation managers, who took a strictly business attitude toward the peasants, pressing them for repayment of loans, charging them for services rendered, and demanding more labor from them. The managers substituted an impersonal efficiency for the easygoing paternalism that had previously leavened peasant discontent. Tenants, as a rule, did not share in the political emancipation of the country. They did not enjoy freedom of speech and assemblage, could not join organizations of their own choosing, and were compelled to vote according to the political affiliation of the landowner. In the division of crops and the settlement of disputes, the peasant was defenseless against the landlord. Tenants were forced to buy all supplies from the estate stores, which charged exorbitant prices and often used fraudulent weights and measures.

The gap between the masses and the small governing class was widened still further by the tendency of the landowners to acquire large, modern homes, adopt Western-style dress, and discard established customs while the peasants continued to live in their huts in the same manner as they had for centuries.

Consequently, a new attitude developed on both sides. The *caciques* became indifferent to the welfare of their tenants. They regarded the peasants with suspicion and began to exploit their own political power to suppress the peasant's demands for improved conditions. They hired civilian guards to protect themselves and their property and enforce the crop-sharing arrangements. Attempts by the government to alleviate the plight of the peasants were largely ineffective; the *caciques*, as legislators, executives, and judges were in a position to maintain the *status quo*.

The tenants, on the other hand, began to regard the landlords with increasing resentment and distrust. By the late 1920s, they were ready to rally in open rebellion behind those who gave them hope of improving their economic and social position. . . .

Socialist and Communist Parties

Before World War II there was little room for minority parties in Philippine national politics, since the Nacionalista Party thoroughly dominated the picture. The Socialist Party, led by Pedro Abad Santos, was one of the few minority parties in existence.

The stronghold of the Socialist Party was in Santos' home province of Pampanga. In the early 1920s Santos gathered around himself many young men, especially the better educated and more intelligent of the peasant stock such as Luis Taruc, who eventually became Santos' secretary. This group accepted Santos' program for the outright expropriation of church estates and all private plantations. As a result of their activities, Pampanga was frequently the scene of agrarian disturbances and the party was a cause of constant worry and irritation to the large landholders in the province.

The Socialist Party made a particularly strong showing in the 1940 election. Santos, the party's candidate for governor, came close to winning—a showing that is particularly impressive in view of the fact that about 50 percent of his followers were disqualified from voting because of illiteracy. Although he was condemned as a Communist by his opponents, he refused to compromise his position as spokesman for the peasants and did not slacken his denunciations of the central government or his agitation for improvement of the peasants' lot.

On November 7, 1930 the Communist Party of the Philippines was formally organized, on the Stalinist tenet that a period of political agitation should precede armed revolution. It presumably had the support of Santos and the Socialist Party. The party was declared illegal by the Supreme Court of the Philippines on October 26, 1932 for violating the law of illegal association. Among those convicted were the party's top leaders, Mariano Balgos and Guillermo Capadocia. In the same year the Supreme Court also considered six cases of inciting to sedition and rebellion involving the Communist Party. The years from 1932 to 1938 were spent in clandestine activities. In 1938 the Communist Party emerged again as the Communist Party of the Philippines, a merger of the Communist and Socialist Parties. The chairman of the revived party was Crisanto Evangelista, Pedro Abad Santos was vice chairman; Guillermo Capadocia, general secretary. . . . The new party was declared to be affiliated with the Communist International. From its inception until the outbreak of the war, the new party encouraged the organization of various groups representing practically all aspects of social, political, cultural, and economic activities in Philippine society. With the outbreak of the Pacific war in December 1941, the Communist Party, its affiliated organizations, and individual sympathizers went underground, as did existing legal political parties and many individual patriotic Filipinos.

The War Period

Some of the landlords took advantage of the reign of terror that prevailed during the Japanese occupation to do away with "bad elements" and "breeders of discontent" through hired "guards." However, the disintegration that accompanied the occupation also gave the peasants of Central Luzon an opportunity to work off some of their pent-up bitterness. Familiar patterns were lost in the transfer of authority from the landlords and Constabulary to the invader. Once partly freed from their former oppressors, the peasants resorted to violence in pressing their advantage against both their landlords and the Japanese. This movement was "caught, fostered, and directed by a new organization, the Hukbalahap."[1]

This organization, conceived in December 1941, was formally established on March 29, 1942. Its official name was *Hukbo ng Bayang Laban Sa Hapon*, meaning "People's Army to Fight Japan." Many of its leaders had also been leaders in the Communist Party and in the Communist-dominated peasant groups. The Huks grew through their continued resistance to the Japanese and their emphasis on a program of welfare for the common people. In their activities, the Huks united Filipinos without regard to political, religious, or social differences.

The Communist leaders of the Huks were careful to direct their efforts along lines that would appeal to the masses and attract a large following. "In resisting the Japanese they were able to evoke sentiments of nationalism and patriotism among the masses. In persecuting collaborators, most of whom were members of the *cacique* class, they were able to arouse the peasants against both oppressors and betrayers. In pursuing a radical socio-economic program, they were able to win for the Hukbalahap a reputation of militancy in championing the peasant's rights."[2]

The Hukbalahap initially was merely a military force, but a civilian counterpart, the "United Front Movement," [UFM] was soon formed as the political arm of the Huks. The combined organization then consisted of military, political, and "mass" sections: the military assured the force, the political provided propaganda, and the "mass" supplied the men as well as food and money.

Military activities were under the direction of the Military Committee, whose original members were Luis Taruc, Casto Alejandrino, and Silveria Guina. . . .

The Huks were . . . in continual conflict with other guerilla forces. The anti-Huk forces, known as the USAFFE guerillas, were led by men of the *cacique* class who had taken ROTC training in the universities or had served in the United States Army Forces in the Far East. During the occupation, fierce battles took place when the Huks and the USAFFE units met.

The USAFFE guerillas favored a "lie-low" policy and concentrated on getting intelligence information for the Americans until such time as thy would be aided by the return of American forces. They felt that Huk action against the Japanese, even though reduced in scale after 1943, was likely to cause reprisals and retaliation by the Japanese against the peasantry. For their part, the Huks felt that the USAFFE guerillas did little in the way of actually fighting the Japanese. Disagreement over the "lie-low" policy was not the only cause of misunderstanding: USAFFE units resented the encroachment of Huks into their territory; the Huks claimed that military warfare was inseparable from political warfare and was, in fact, subordinate to it, and they considered their expansion and penetration to be of a political nature.

While the military branch of the Huks trained and fought, the United Front Movement was also active. Vigorous emphasis was placed on the socio-economic program of the Huks. Huk soldiers received instruction in Marxist-Leninist doctrine from the political commissars. Groups of six to ten propagandists went out to the barrios, where they called the people together by singing and dancing or with a dramatization of the feats of one of their heroes. They would tell the people what they had learned in the Huk schools in the Candaba swamps and, although the peasants did not understand "dialectical materialism," they did understand "that the masses were downtrodden, that the rich landlords had been taking advantage of them, that they had never received enough for their labor, and that taxes and interest rates were too high."[3]

Under the guidance and protection of the Huks, the Central Luzon peasant began to take action to remedy these ills. Ignoring prewar sharecropping arrangements, the peasant kept the entire harvest of the rice fields, after supplying the Huk forces, instead of supplying the Japanese as ordered by the landlords. The Huks instituted rigid price-control regulations in the towns and barrios throughout Central Luzon and were thus able to reduce profiteering to a minimum. In all these respects, the wartime activities of the Huks did much to create a political consciousness in the peasants.

Early in 1942 provisional governments were set up in thirteen of the twenty-seven municipalities of Nueva Ecija. By 1944 Pampanga, Bulacan, southern Tarlac, eastern Zambales, northern Bataan, southern Nueva Ecija, and part of Rizal were definitely under Huk-UFM control. In February 1945, eighteen municipalities under the UFM met at Cabanatuan [Nueva Ecija] to establish the structure of a provisional government. . . .

The UFM had called upon the Huks to establish law and order until 1945, when it tried to propagandize the towns and barrios directly into adopting its new-type government. The UFM lost in popularity in 1945, however, and was absorbed by new left wing opposition groups such as the Democratic Alliance, the Congress of Labor Organizations, the Peasants' Union, and the Civil Liberties Union.

Relations with the American Army

With the return of the American Army to the Huk provinces in January 1945, many Huks offered their services as guides, informants, and behind-the-line guerillas. The use made of the Huks was left up to the individual commanders. While some forces were fighting side by side with American forces, others were engaged in mopping up operations, cleaning out small Japanese pockets by-passed in the main drive. Still others were deactivated and sent home.

The liberation forces found the Huks in charge of the governments in all of Pampanga and Nueva Ecija and parts of Tarlac, Bulacan, and Bataan. In some municipalities the Japanese puppets had left in favor of the Huks; in others, there were parallel sets of officials. The Huks were prepared to take over the governments of the newly liberated areas. In fact, in most of them the Americans found the armed peasants had cleaned out the opposition and Huks were already in control of the local governments, claiming to have been elected. The Huks obviously believed that presentation of Huk control as a *fait accompli* might force American recognition and acceptance by the reestablished Commonwealth Government. However, the Army's Philippine Civil Affairs Unit replaced most of the Huk men. The Army appointees gave way in turn to appointees of the ruling Nacionalista Party, many of whom were under the cloud of collaboration during the war.

This was, of course, disappointing to the Huks, as was the policy of non-recognition of their fighting forces and later the unveiled hostility of U.S. army authorities toward their organization because of its leftist and Marxist leanings. Since the USAFFE units were the first to make contact with the landing American forces, the Huks felt these units had given the Huks a bad name and had influenced the Americans to take action against them. The resultant bitter feelings were the beginning of the present antagonism of the Huks toward Americans. This antagonism has, of course, been increased recently by the official anti-American Cominform [postwar international organization of Communist parties] line that has been infused into the movement.

A few days before the return to Leyte of the American Army, a representative of the U.S. Philippine Island Forces (USPIF) wrote to Taruc that any organization failing to cooperate would be considered unlawful. He also pointed out that the Army did not recognize any political aims or ambitions except the maintenance of the established and legally existing government. At a later date he wrote that the killing or abduction of any person, except in cases where it could be proven without a shadow of a doubt that the accused had betrayed the guerillas or attacked them with armed force, would be considered murder or kidnapping with intent to murder. Whatever its merits, this statement antagonized the Huks. Their antagonism was further sharpened when Taruc and Alejandrino were taken by the American Army and kept prisoner for about seven months in Iwahig Penal Colony. Alejandrino was finally turned over to the Commonwealth Government with oblique hints from U.S. Army authorities that vigorous action should be taken. However, Solicitor General Lorenzo Tañada found no case and released him without bail and the Army released Taruc shortly thereafter. Taruc complained of maltreatment and expressed surprise at such treatment from Americans. However, he expressed his faith in the great mass of the American people, "especially the progressive and liberal elements to whom Democracy is not a mere word."

As a result of the official American attitude toward the Huks, the treatment of Taruc and Alejandrino, and the ambush of a Huk squadron that had been disarmed and sent home, Huk soldiers again went underground.

NOTES

1. Henry Wells, "Communism in the Philippines," *American Perspectives,* Winter 1950, p.21.

2. William A. Owens, "Will the Huks Revolt?" *Asia,* Feb. 1946, p. 55.

3. Wells, p. 85.

Selection 3.2: Philippine Collaboration in World War II, David Joel Steinberg

Editors' Introduction

In the following selection from the definitive U.S. academic study of Philippine collaboration with the Japanese, David Joel Steinberg discusses the treatment of the collaboration issue after the return of the U.S. forces to the Philippines and how this was influenced by the emerging Cold War.

Source: David Joel Steinberg, *Philippine Collaboration in World War II,* Ann Arbor: University of Michigan Press, 1967, pp. 115-19, 132-33, 141-44, 162-63.

[In the spring of 1945 General Douglas MacArthur captured Manuel Roxas and other cabinet members of the Japanese-sponsored government.] The statement from MacArthur's headquarters said that "among those freed is Brigadier General Manuel Roxas, former Speaker of the Assembly. Four members [Yulo, De las Alas, Paredes, and Sison] of the Philippine collaborationist cabinet have been captured. They will be confined for the duration of the war as a matter of military security and then turned over to the government of the Philippines for trial and judgment." The hidden significance of this statement, which radically altered postwar Philippine politics, was that MacArthur had by fiat distinguished Roxas from the rest. Roxas was freed, restored to his rank of general on MacArthur's staff, and given MacArthur's personal pardon, while all the rest were summarily interned.

MacArthur claimed that he knew that Roxas was innocent, that Roxas had helped the guerilla movement, and that he personally was able to speak for Roxas' character. While this was in large measure accurate, MacArthur willfully disregarded legal procedure, leaving men like Yulo interned in a penal colony awaiting possible charges for treason. The glaring quality of Roxas' special treatment raised a chorus of protest. MacArthur's headquarters explained that, unlike all the others, Roxas alone held a commission in the United State army and was therefore an American army officer rather than a Filipino collaborationist. This justification conveniently ignored men who, like General Francisco, also had held commissions in the American army but who were interned anyway.

MacArthur must have been well aware that by freeing Roxas he was pardoning, liberating, and encouraging Osmeña's great potential rival for the presidency. MacArthur's imprimatur was a sign clearly and correctly read throughout the archipelago as signifying support for Roxas over Osmeña. Because Roxas had been a member of the oligarchy living in Manila through the war, his liberation was also seen by the rest of the oligarchy as the wedge for their own political rehabilitation. As General [Emilio] Aguinaldo expressed it, "Roxas became the hope of those who faced prosecution for treason, and among them were the most powerful political leaders [and himself]." Since Roxas was given a push toward the presidency, he would be expected to show clemency if elected, and at least force Osmeña toward a more concessionary policy if defeated. Thus, while the American Counter-Intelligence Corps, the C.I.C., was arresting some six thousand Filipinos, MacArthur's handling of this one key Filipino was vitiating effectively much of the original Washington policy. . . .

[In Washington, Harry Truman, who had just succeeded to the presidency, was too distracted to devote attention to formulating a new policy on collaboration, so he let stand the policy announced during the war that those who had served the enemy would be removed from office; Osmeña was compelled to form a government free from the taint of collaboration.] This proved to be no easy feat. The people who had proven their loyalty—the guerillas—had never had a chance to prove their ability to govern in a peacetime environment. The people who were experienced in governing were those whose loyalty was in question. On March 8, 1945, Osmeña was able to construct a cabinet which met these requirements, but at the price of bringing into high position men who had never achieved full oligarchic status in the prewar era. Osmeña was forced to weaken the monopoly of power held by the prewar elite, and, as a result, further alienated himself from his prewar peers.

While he was able to fulfill the Washington policy at the higher levels of government, he had little choice in staffing the civil-service grades of the bureaucracy. These officials, who had continued to serve throughout the war, were so vitally needed for the tasks of reconstruction that they had to be restored to their jobs. . . .

A debate which did rage . . . was when, where, and how Osmeña would call a legislature. Since MacArthur had restored civilian government immediately, Osmeña was required by the Commonwealth constitution to call Congress as soon as possible, rather than to continue to rule by Executive Order. Upon assuming control of Manila, Osmeña had called "upon all the duly elected members of our Congress who have remained steadfast in their allegiance to our Government during the period of enemy occupation, to be in readiness to meet in Manila as soon as conditions permit for the reestablishment of the legislative branch." However, the determination of the steadfastness of the members could not be determined by the chief executive. The president did not have the authority to decide upon the seating; that was a jealously guarded constitutional right of each House itself. In late 1941 a new Congress had been elected . . . but, because of the occupation, it had never been summoned and sworn in. Since this was the last valid expression of the electorate and since a new election was impossible immediately, because of the total disruption of the society, there existed the question of whether this body should be the one called into session by Osmeña.

MacArthur and the recently liberated Roxas thought that this was the best solution, especially since Roxas had been elected a senator in the 1941 election. Osmeña, attempting to fulfill Washington's purge policy, was less sure. Because of the wartime cooperation of the prewar elite, technically there would not be a quorum if the 1941 Congress were called. The C.I.C. had detained too many to permit the formation of a legislature under the Commonwealth constitution. Moreover, since MacArthur had made it quite clear that the American army would detain Filipinos only as long as the Philippines remained a war zone, there was an excellent chance that, once these wartime officials were released on bail pending civilian trial, they might have to be seated, in case Osmeña chose to call that Congress. Since Congress had the constitutional authority to determine its own membership, calling Congress would probably violate Washington's injunctions. Finally, summoning that Congress would give his arch rival, Roxas, both a major forum to attack Osmeña's administration and an independent political source of power through Congressional appropriations and patronage. . . .

[With President Franklin Roosevelt's death in April 1945,] MacArthur was the political force with which Osmeña had to live. MacArthur wanted the 1941 Congress called, and it was summoned to meet on June 9, 1945, despite technical objections. Of the ninety-eight congressmen, only seventy were present; eleven were dead and seventeen were still detained by the American army. Of the twenty-four senators, only thirteen were present; two were dead, two, Cuenco and Rama, were still out of Manila, and seven . . . were detained by the Americans. At the first meeting Roxas was elected president of the Senate. . . . Roxas also became chairman of the influential Committee on Appointments, and with this new power he began to review all the appointments Osmeña had made on an acting basis. Roxas became the second most powerful man in the country. . . .

[In September, Truman asked the Attorney General to do a study of the collaboration issue. A study was prepared by Walter Hutchinson and in January 1946] Hutchinson submitted his "confidential" preliminary report to Attorney General Tom Clark and High Commissioner [to the Philippines] Paul McNutt. The report, which was never made public, stated frankly that "the present situation is one of our [America's] own making. After liberation of the Philippines, our army and naval intelligence had . . . developed substantial cases against practically all of the collaborators. But instead of disposing of the cases in the same manner as the other United Nations, we gave the basic and gigantic problem of collaborationism over to the Commonwealth government, harassed by problems of rehabilitation and itself, not entirely free of collaborationists in its component units, its congress, its army." Hutchinson continued by urging that it was "American duty and American principle to implement the case of the American and Filipino peoples against collaborationists." Hutchinson urged that the key collaborators be brought to trial for treason to the United States, if for nothing else, and he urged that "there must not be permitted any loopholes of escape for they are America's Quislings." He felt this was an obligation to "the thousands who have died in a sacred, democratic cause."

Hutchinson's solution was legal rather than political. Unaware of the dynamics of Fil-American relations, he urged the United States "to adopt a policy to enter into and participate in the trial and disposition" of all the treason cases under one of three methods.

Most attractive to Hutchinson was a war crime tribunal which would have Filipino judges and prosecutors but which would have American support by treaty right after independence to guarantee trial of all the cases. Hutchinson felt that "this would have universal support among the Filipinos." His second alternative was "an extra-territorial court in the Philippines to commence hearings at as early a date as possible in cooperation with the officials of the Philippines . . . ." Hutchinson wanted the United States to have the rights "to investigate, arrest, prosecute, and convict persons" charged with treason. This alternative, he felt, would "have support among the rank and file of the Filipino people." His third solution was to change venue by trying all those charged with treason before American courts in the United States. Hutchinson stated that "this likewise would receive the approval of the Filipino people. . . ." He urged immediate United States legal and financial aid for [Philippine Solicitor General Lorenzo M.] Tanada and his staff. He felt that a jury system would not work and questioned whether even the three judges could be protected from political pressure.

He noted that "there appears to be little or no consideration being given to the prosecution of members of the Philippine National Congress who served under the Japanese and who now retain their position," . . . and that only the ranking members of the prewar legislature such as Recto, Yulo, Paredes, and De las Alas were still denied their seats and were out on bail with a good chance of being seated soon. He concluded that Osmeña "has not publicly taken a position that would lend strength to an all-out prosecution of collaborators; in fact, his administrative position has been described as one of appeasement."

Hutchinson reported that "the entire plan and program . . . for investigation, arrest and trial of known collaborators" bogged down because "the problem was not attacked and pursued to conclusion by the United States military forces immediately after our re-entry into the Philippines"; instead, he remarked, it was turned over to Osmeña, who was unable to handle it. He observed that the whole question had been "so discussed in the newspapers, and by politicians so as to obscure the real crime, that of committing treason, and thereby lessening in the minds of many people, including some of the present government, the enormity of the offense." Hutchinson predicted that unless the United States acted, "general amnesty will be declared by whoever wins the election thereby freeing many if not all leading collaborators. This probability is almost a certainty if Roxas is elected."

[One prominent collaborator, Teofilo Sison, was convicted by the People's Court, but the] momentum was stopped when Washington acted on the Hutchinson proposal. Despite the strong plea by Hutchinson for active intervention in the collaboration question, Truman rejected this plan and thus finally abandoned the wartime Roosevelt policy of an American-enforced purge. Truman's statement, reached after some sharp internal debate, declared "that there is no necessity for any change in our established policy of leaving the disposition of civil collaborationists in the Philippines to the civil authorities there." Truman's decision, which was influenced by "the strong recommendation of General Douglas MacArthur," was based on the changed world situation of the approaching cold war. Its net effect was to minimize the collaboration issue for Osmeña despite the Sison conviction. The Truman decision left Osmeña pursuing a collaboration policy about which he had always been ambivalent. The decision lifted some of the cloud hanging over the Roxas forces, since it meant that Washington was less hostile than before.

For Truman to pursue the Hutchinson suggestions would have been to withdraw a vital element of Philippine sovereignty just prior to independence. It would have been an open admission that the United States did not think the Filipinos were able to handle the problem, and that they could not be trusted. Moreover, to reassume jurisdiction after such a long wait would be to shift the focus from the crime of treason against the Philippines to that of treason against the United States. Philippine nationalism would inevitably seize upon this invasion of sovereignty and convert the collaboration issue into a question of national maturity. Hutchinson was naive to think that any American intervention just before a Philippine election would be welcomed. Indeed, it was most probable that American intervention would guarantee the election of those very men whose conviction the United States had originally desired.

The American opportunity to intervene was lost when the policy planners in Washington failed to evolve a strategy before Osmeña returned. A clear American policy, formulated and executed not by the local military commander but by the President in Washington, might have kept Osmeña out of the quagmire of collaboration. It would have run the risk of making national martyrs of the wartime leaders, eliminating the possibility of their implication in crimes against Philippine society. It would, however, have permitted the United States to purge them for at least a brief time. The postwar political alignment would have altered, and Osmeña's hand would have been strengthened. The United States failed to impose its solution and at the same time allowed the wartime leaders to claim effectively that they were nationalists hounded by the metropolitan power. Charging that they had been patriots who had served the Philippines at the expense of America, the collaborators altered the debate from collaboration to latent anti-Americanism.

Tensions between the Americans and Filipinos had shown a marked increase in the months after the war ended. The large number of American troops, suddenly inactive, caused constant friction. The postwar American economic concessions were considered woefully inadequate. Many Filipinos felt that America had been *walang hiya* [ungrateful] for failing to repay the debt of gratitude, the sense of *utang na loob*, [obligation] which America owed the Philippines for wartime support. The provisions of the various agreements seemed [stingy], revealing the seamier side of American economic imperialism. The blackmail threats, like those of [U.S. Secretary of Interior] Ickes, to withhold the rehabilitation funds unless the Filipinos yielded to American wishes was an affront to Filipino dignity. American mistreatment of Philippine pride and American insensitivity to the demands of the *compadre* relationship between the two countries saddened and embittered Filipinos.

Had the Hutchinson recommendations been adopted, Truman correctly saw that the Filipino-American relationship would have deteriorated even further. Having withheld economic sovereignty from the Filipinos [see chapter 4], the Truman Administration could not deny judicial sovereignty without making a complete sham of the promise of political independence. The legal problems of collaboration could not be dissociated from their political effects, as Hutchinson proposed. The Americans missed the chance to do what they thought was correct. Thereafter, they could only hope that the People's Court would come to consider the events in a way akin to their own. The Sison case gave evidence that this might occur. Truman felt that his best course would be to gamble that the Sison case was the precedent. Any other policy contained too many risks.

This decision was greatly reinforced by the changing American policy objectives throughout the world. The emergence of a major communist threat in Europe, China, and also the Philippines, coupled with the growing American concern to contain Communism everywhere, led the Truman administration to see the Philippines in a new light. The American desire to avenge by trying the collaborators receded as the United States began the cold war. The Philippines had to be America's showcase of democracy in Asia after independence as well as before it, and Truman gradually realized that the Hukbalahap threat was at the least embarrassing and at the most potentially disastrous to American power and prestige. Since the China situation was deteriorating rapidly with the effective communist insurgency throughout this period, American planners were alarmed at how ill-prepared the Philippines, with its dowry of carnage and civil war, would be for independence.

MacArthur in Japan, McNutt in Manila, and many in Washington advocated a series of measures designed to bolster the embryonic nation and to guarantee that it would not go communist. The new priority scale embodied in these measures did not put collaboration high on the list. The new policy, in fact, advocated massive support of the traditional oligarchy to enable it to restore order, to lead the fight against communism, and to assure stable leadership in independence. This required that the collaboration question—a divisive issue within the oligarchy—be allowed to fade. As in the early American era, when the United States backed the traditional order rather than the radical reformers, once again the United States supported the establishment against the radical reformers of Philippine society. Washington, considering the Hukbalahap to be the international conspiracy of communism, ignored the noncommunist, indigenous, albeit radical, quality of peasant unrest.

The American insistence upon viewing this complex movement in simplistic terms led the United States government to reverse its wartime valuation of collaboration. The oligarchy as a whole, rather than any wartime division of it, became important. American money and prestige started to flow to the very men that Roosevelt had wanted to purge only a few years earlier. Washington began to see Roxas not as the collaborationist candidate but as an economic wizard who was anticommunist and who could be depended upon to keep the Philippines staunchly on the American side in the global struggle with communism. Osmena, in turn, was distrusted more, especially after he accepted support from the Hukbalahap and the Democratic Alliance. Caught in a web by trying to fulfill Washington's policy, Osmeña, ironically, was driven into a situation in which the Americans turned against him because of his pro-American efforts. The effect of the American shift in policy, which was visibly demonstrated by the Truman statement, was to befuddle further an already befuddled collaboration question. The American concern with the communist threat silenced many of the noncommunist but antioligarchic voices in the Philippines, since the new postwar realities made a middle position untenable. It became increasingly difficult to be antiestablishment without being labeled as a sympathizer of the Hukbalahap.

This gradual change was reinforced by the behavior of the wartime oligarchs, who demanded throughout the postwar period that society restore them to power. They refused to approach the nation as humble supplicants begging forgiveness for their wartime actions. They themselves did not doubt the compelling need of society to return them to their prewar positions, maintaining, as a result, their traditional status of dominance, even under indictment. Shrewdly aware of the dynamics of Philippine social structure and of their own historic role in that structure, they denied categorically that they had committed any acts of which they need be ashamed. . . .

[In 1948, President Roxas granted amnesty to all collaborators.] Of the 5603 cases originally filed before the People's Court, only 156 had been convicted (0.27 percent), and of those, only one, Teofilo Sison, was prominent politically. . . .

. . . 0.6 percent of the wartime leadership was convicted, and 74 percent was never in court. There was no bloodbath in which the mob ruled at the end of the war, and there was no purge either internal or external. The elite remained intact, with a remarkable survival rate, considering the risks of war and the average age of the group. The war diminished neither the size nor the authority of the establishment. The ability of this group to weather the vicissitudes of belligerent occupation attests to the flexibility and perspicacity of this remarkable elite.

Subic Naval Base, one of the military bases retained by the U.S. after Philippine independence.

CHAPTER 4: INDEPENDENCE WITH STRINGS

Introduction

As the Second World War drew to a close, it was evident to government planners in Washington that the United States would emerge as the globally dominant economic and military power. In the eyes of these officials, the U.S. role in world affairs would have to be far more active than it had been in the pre-war period. In the depths of the Depression, the United States had pursued a rather limited foreign economic policy; but by 1944 U.S. officials were warning of the need to provide foreign markets for U.S. exports if a new depression was to be averted. The United States was the only source of private investment in the world, the other capital-exporting nations having been bankrupted or destroyed during the war.

To many in the U.S. military establishment in the 1930s, distant military bases—particularly in the Philippines—represented an Achilles heel rather than a strategic asset. But as the outcome of World War II became clear, U.S. officials moved to secure an elaborate network of military bases worldwide, including the Philippines. These bases would provide the means for maintaining the status quo with U.S. dominance, whether against the Soviet Union, or against Third World nationalists who did not accept the U.S. global order.

But there could be no going back on the promise of independence for the Philippines. Even the Japanese had realized that Filipinos were determined to achieve independence. And so on July 4, 1946, the United States flag was lowered and the Republic of the Philippines was declared an independent nation. But Philippine independence was heavily circumscribed. Indeed, the Philippines went from colony to neo-colony: that is, it achieved formal independence without eliminating foreign domination.

Economic relations between the new Philippine Republic and the United States were defined by the Bell Trade Act [see selection 4.1]. This agreement tied the Philippine economy to that of the U.S. by establishing a system of preferential tariffs between the two countries; it placed various restrictions on Philippine government control of its own economy and required the Filipinos to amend their constitution to give a special position to U.S. capital. The Philippine constitution had reserved the development of public utilities and the exploitation of natural resources to Filipinos or to corporations that were at least 60% Filipino-owned. Under the so-called "parity" amendment, U.S. citizens were to be given equal treatment with Filipinos. This meant that in the reserved areas U.S. citizens could have ownership up to 100%, whereas other foreign nationals could have no more than 40%. Philippine acceptance of this arrangement was partly facilitated by tying it to rehabilitation aid and by the illegal ouster by the Roxas forces of the few leftist members of Congress [see selection 4.2]. In 1955, the Bell Trade Act was replaced with a new treaty, the Laurel-Langley Agreement. This successor agreement removed some of the more blatant infringements on Philippine sovereignty and introduced a meticulous reciprocity, but in fact extended the protection accorded U.S. capital [see selection 4.3].

The United States also retained vast tracts of land for military bases in the Philippines, particularly Clark Air Base and Subic Naval Base [see selection 4.4]. In return the United States provided the Philippine elite with the military wherewithal to reassert its authority over the radicalized peasantry of Central Luzon. This aid consisted of weaponry and a permanent group of military advisers known as the Joint U.S. Military Advisory Group (JUSMAG), where "Joint" refers only to the involvement of the various branches of the U.S. military [see selection 4.5].

Selection 4.1: Summary, Bell Trade Act

Editors' Introduction

The Philippine Trade Act of 1946, also known as the Bell Trade Act after its Congressional sponsor, C. Jasper Bell, was passed by the United States Congress and then approved by the Philippine Congress on July 2, 1946, two days before independence. An Executive Agreement was signed on July 4 formalizing the trade agree-

ment. Following is a summary of the key provisions of the Trade Act.

Source: U.S. Dept. of State, *Treaties and Other International Agreements of the United States of America, 1776-1949* Charles I. Bevans [compiler], Dept. of State Publication 8728, Washington, DC: U.S. Government Printing Office, 1974, vol. 11, pp. 7-18.

[key provisions]

Article I

U.S. exports to the Philippines and Philippine exports to the U.S. (with the exception of those Philippine exports covered in Article II) shall pay no duty until July 4, 1954. Duties on these items shall then be 5% of the regular duties from July 4 to December 31, 1954; 10% during calendar year 1955; and 5% more of the regular duty each year until 1973, when the full duty shall be paid.

Article II

1. Absolute quotas are placed on the amount of sugar, cordage (rope), rice, cigars, scrap tobacco, coconut oil, and buttons of pearl or shell that can enter the U.S. from the Philippines.

2. For the cigars and buttons of pearl, the importation into the U.S. shall be duty-free until July 4, 1954 and then a decreasing percentage of the imports shall be duty-free each year until 1973, when the regular duty must be paid on the full amount imported.

3. The quotas in paragraphs 1 and 2 (for all the items except rice) shall be allocated annually by the Philippine Government to manufacturers in the Philippines proportionate to their 1940 exports of the item to the U.S. or, for sugar, to their 1931-33 production.

4. The allocated quotas in paragraph 3 may be transferred or sold.

Article III

The U.S. may establish quotas on imports of other Philippine articles imported into the U.S. if the U.S. President determines that these articles substantially compete with U.S. products. Such quotas will be set at a level not less than the amount of the article imported into the U.S. from the Philippines in the previous twelve months.

Article IV

"3. No export tax shall be imposed or collected by the United States on articles exported to the Philippines, or by the Philippines on articles exported to the United States."

Article V

"The value of Philippine currency in relation to the United States dollar shall not be changed, the convertibility of Philippine pesos into the United States dollar shall not be suspended, and no restrictions shall be imposed on the transfer of funds from the Philippines to the United States except by agreement with the President of the United States."

Article VII

"1. The disposition, exploitation, development, and utilization of all agricultural, timber, and mineral lands of the public domain, waters, minerals, coal, petroleum, and other mineral oils, all forces and sources of potential energy, and other natural resources of the Philippines, and the operation of public utilities, shall, if open to any person, be open to citizens of the United States and to all forms of business enterprise owned or controlled, directly or indirectly, by United States citizens, except that (for the period prior to the amendment of the Constitution of the Philippines referred to in Paragraph 2 of this Article) the Philippines shall not be required to comply with such part of the foregoing provisions of this sentence as are in conflict with such Constitution."

"2. The Government of the Philippines will promptly take such steps as are necessary to secure the amendment of the Constitution of the Philippines so as to permit the taking effect as laws of the Philippines of such part of the provisions of Paragraph 1 of this Article as is in conflict with such Constitution before such amendment."

Article X

"2. This Agreement shall have no effect after July 3, 1974. It may be terminated by either the United States or the Philippines at any time, upon not less than five years' written notice. If the President of the United States or the President of the Philippines determines and proclaims that the other country has adopted or applied measures or practices which would operate to nullify or impair any right or obligation provided for in this Agreement, then the Agreement may be terminated upon not less than six months' written notice.

"3. If the President of the United States determines that a reasonable time for the making of the amendment to the Constitution of the Philippines referred to in Paragraph 2 of Article VII has elapsed, but that such amendment has not been made, he shall so proclaim and this Agreement shall have no effect after the date of such proclamation."

"4. If the President of the United States determines and proclaims, after consultation with the President of the Philippines, that the Philippines or any of its political subdivisions or the Philippine Government is in any manner discriminating against citizens of the United States or any form of United States business enterprise, then the President of the United States shall have the right to suspend the effectiveness of the whole or any portion of this Agreement. If the President of the United States subsequently determines and proclaims, after consultation with the President of the Philippines, that the discrimination which was the basis for such suspension (a) has ceased, such suspension shall end; or (b) has not ceased after the lapse of a time determined by the President of the United States to be reasonable, then the President of the United States shall have the right to terminate this Agreement upon not less than six months' written notice."

Selection 4.2: Roxas Violates the Constitution, Ramon Diokno

Editors' Introduction

U.S. officials had promised Filipinos during the war that their continued loyalty to the United States would be rewarded by rehabilitation funds at the war's end. Legislation passed by the U.S. Congress, however, tied full rehabilitation aid to Philippine acceptance of the "parity" provision of the Bell Trade Act. Even with this pressure, Philippine acceptance of the Trade Act and "parity" was accomplished only by the highly questionable ejection of some opposition sena-

tors and representatives from the Philippine Congress. One of the ousted senators here describes what occurred.

Source: Ramon Diokno, "Roxas Violates the Constitution," *Amerasia*, vol. 10, no. 6, December 1946, pp. 75-78. For further details, see Stephen R. Shalom, "Philippine Acceptance of the Bell Trade Act of 1946: A Study of Manipulatory Democracy," *Pacific Historical Review*, vol. 49, no. 3, August 1980, pp. 499-517.

On June 29, 1944, the United States Congress adopted a joint resolution, signed by the President, which stated: "That the United States shall restore as quickly as possible the orderly and free democratic processes of government to the Filipino people, and thereupon establish the complete independence of the Philippine Islands as a separate and self-governing nation." Many Americans may believe that this goal was achieved on July 4, 1946. Yet what is the real situation in the Philippines today, five months after the granting of independence? Orderly and free democratic processes of government do not exist. The Philippine Constitution is being deliberately violated for the material benefit of a handful of business interests. Many of the men responsible for these violations are Filipinos that fall within the scope of President Roosevelt's directive ordering that all those that collaborated in any way with the Japanese should be removed from office. Finally, the Philippines is not a genuinely independent country, but only a "banana republic" complete with American military bases. These facts seem to me a cause for justified concern on the part of all Americans.

To begin with, it will be recalled that after the liberation of the Philippines, the Philippine Congress held a special session. One of its first actions was to pass a law appropriating some ten million pesos for the payment of the entire back pay of Congress members and their secretaries, that is, for the payment of their salaries during the three years of Japanese occupation. This measure was enacted in total disregard of the fact that during this period they did not fulfill their duties and that a majority of them collaborated with the Japanese. The completely selfish character of this action was emphasized by the fact that no similar provision was made for other officers and employees of the Philippine Government.

At this same session, the Philippine Senate was faced with the constitutional mandate that the senators shall be divided equally into three groups, "the senators of the first group to serve for a term of six years; those of the second group for four years; and those of the third group for two years." The term of the senators in the third group had already expired as of December 30, 1943. Now it is a well established rule that Congress has no authority to extend the term of office prescribed by the Constitution. The Senate, however, decided to make the division by lot, subject to the following conditions: first, that two senators who had died during the Japanese occupation be regarded as belonging to the third group, thus reducing the number of senators that would have to fall into this category; and, second, that senators in the second and third groups continue in office until the election of their successors, receiving all salaries and emoluments in the meantime. The President of the Senate under whose direction these decisions were made was Manuel Acuna Roxas, now President of the Philippines.

How Minority Legislators were Disqualified

On April 23, 1946, a general election was held to choose a President, Vice-President, sixteen senators [out of a total of 24], and the full quota of ninety-eight representatives. In the Philippines, senators are chosen at large, while representatives are chosen by districts. The law provides that those elected and certified by the Electoral Commission shall assume office on the date fixed by law and that anyone obstructing the operation of this law shall be punished. There is also a special amendment to the Philippine Constitution pertaining to the seating of elected members of Congress. In the United States, the Constitution provides that each legislative house shall be the sole judge of the elections and qualifications of their respective members, and that both the Senate and the House of Representatives shall have the power to suspend temporarily any representative or senator when they believe that there is a case of evident falsity of returns, or fraud in the elections, or lack of qualifications. A similar provision was embodied in the Philippine Constitution until 1935. But experience proved that decisions in such cases were based on political rather than judicial grounds. Therefore, a Constitutional amendment was adopted by which the authority of the legislature in this matter was transferred *in toto* to a Constitutional body named the Electoral Tribunal.

It is against this constitutional background that the events following the elections of April 1946 must be judged. The elections were won by the so-called "Liberal Party" headed by Manuel Roxas, but a considerable number of opposition senators and representatives were elected. For the Senate, the opposition groups won seven seats, which gave them a total of eleven senators out of the twenty-four, and in the House of Representatives, they hold thirty-eight of the ninety-eight seats. Though the Roxas Party won a majority of the Senate with thirteen seats, two of their senators were sick, two others had been indicted by the People's Court, and three more (one of whom had been indicted as a traitor) had forfeited their seats by accepting judicial positions.

To deal with this situation, the Roxas majority adopted the following procedure: they allowed the indicted traitors to take their seats. They refused to take action against the three senators that had forfeited their seats. And they suspended indefinitely three minority senators because of alleged irregularities in their election, namely: Justice Vera, President of the Nacionalista Party; Romero, keynoter in the Nacionalista Party Convention; and the author. The resolution for suspension of these three men was adopted by the Senate in the absence of the opposition senators, without a quorum, and in violation of the Constitution of the Philippines.

In the House of Representative, a resolution for the suspension of seven representatives of the opposition was filed simultaneously. Though this resolution was not adopted immediately, the Speaker made it effective at once by ruling that while the resolution was pending, the representatives affected could neither take their seats nor speak on the floor of the House. The resolution was then referred to a committee, where it still rests. All this took place despite the fact that the election of the senators and representatives concerned had been certified by a majority of the Electoral Commission. Subsequently, the opposition parties filed a protest with the Philippine Supreme Court but the latter, after being "reorganized" at the instigation of President Roxas, washed its hands of the whole matter.

Railroading the Philippine Trade Act

The aims that President Roxas was seeking to accomplish by these unconstitutional tactics, and the policies that his regime intended to pursue, were first demonstrated when the Philippine Trade Act came up for consideration by the Philippine Congress. The terms of this Act, as drafted by the United States Congress . . . required that the Philippine Constitution be amended in order to provide American capital with the same rights as Filipino capital in the Philippines. According to the Philippine Constitution, an amendment requires a three-fourths vote of *all* members of both Houses—not merely three-fourths of those present and voting. In other words, an amendment requires the affirmative vote of 18 senators and 73 representatives. The Roxas majority party, however, ruled that in deciding upon this amendment, the votes of those members of Congress that had been temporarily suspended would not be counted, notwithstanding the fact that the senators and representatives concerned were (and still are) receiving their salaries, and that only the Electoral Tribunal can legally deprive them of their votes. Under this arbitrary system of computation, the votes of only 16 senators and 68 representatives were needed to pass the required amendment, and thanks to the accurate planning of the Roxas majority, this was the exact number of votes cast in its favor.

To understand the significance of this maneuver, it is necessary to bear in mind the terms of the Trade Act. This Act establishes a monopoly of the principal Philippine products that favors American business interests established before the war, and thus obstructs the development of new Filipino enterprise. Under the terms of the Act, American businessmen can import products into the Philippines free of duty, quotas, and price ceilings, whereas Philippine exports to the United States are subject to quota restrictions. Futhermore, Americans are given the same privileges in the Philippines with regard to property, business, and industry as those enjoyed by Filipinos, whereas similar privileges are denied to Filipinos in the United States. Even worse from the standpoint of Philippine business is the fact that, by Executive Order of President Roxas, Filipino businessmen are forbidden to export their major products such as copra, lumber, etc., to countries other than the United States, even though these countries may offer higher prices.

This Trade Act was sponsored by Mr. Paul McNutt, former High Commissioner and now American Ambassador to the Philippines, who is an intimate friend of President Roxas. Senator Milland Tydings, one of the authors of the Philippine Independence Act of 1934, in testifying before the House Ways and Means Committee in March 1946 regarding the Philippine Trade Act, stated that: "Fundamentally, he [McNutt] is opposed to Philippine independence, and if you would ask him he would tell you so. The truth of the matter is that most of the people, outside the Filipinos, who favor this bill are fundamentally opposed to Philippine independence. Many of them have told me so. Their whole philosophy is to keep the Philippines economically even though we lose them politically." The text of the Trade Act, as finally enacted by the United States Congress, entirely confirms this view. So does the clause in the Philippine Rehabilitation Act providing that no rehabilitation funds in excess of $500 shall be granted the Philippines unless the Trade Act is accepted. The terms of the Trade and Rehabilitation Acts indicate that the official United States representative in the Philippines will have, for some time at least, a preponderant control over both the Philippine Government and the Philippine economy.

This continuance of American control, however, could not have been achieved without the solicitous assistance of the Filipinos that now rule our country. The Roxas Government, which is headed by collaborators, obviously felt that it could not survive unless it accepted the Trade Act in order to open the way for American financial and military aid. It needed money not only for material rehabilitation, but for the maintenance of an expensive governmental system. It needed military support because large numbers of Filipinos were retaining the arms that they had used so effectively against the Japanese. Lacking faith in their Government, they were convinced that to surrender these arms would be tantamount to surrendering their hard-won freedom. Confronted with this formidable opposition, the Roxas Government chose to sacrifice Philippine independence for the sake of the advantages to be gained from American political and military support. This decision was not surprising, inasmuch as these were the same Filipinos that had worked readily with the Japanese, and that would have been removed from political and economic influence if President Roosevelt's directive regarding collaborators had been carried out. Manuel Roxas himself violated his oath as a General in the United States Army by advising puppet-president Jose Laurel to declare war against the United States and its Allies during the Japanese occupation. . . .

I must leave it to the American people to decide whether the 1944 resolution adopted by the United States Congress has been fulfilled; whether the American Government has given my country a square deal; and whether the kind of government that now exists in the Philippines deserves the financial and military support of the United States.

Selection 4.3: Parity Provisions, Laurel-Langley Agreement

Editors' Introduction

The parliamentary maneuvers and U.S. pressures that had led to Philippine acceptance of the Bell Trade Act in 1946 provoked considerable op- position from Philippine nationalists. In part to mollify some of this opposition, Washington agreed to replace the Bell Trade Act with a new treaty, the Laurel-Langley Agreement, in

1955. This agreement was to govern economic relations between the two countries for the next two decades. The provisions of the old agreement pegging the value of the Philippine peso to the U.S. dollar and prohibiting the Philippines from imposing an export tariff were dropped. (These were unnecessary from the point of view of U.S. interests and only served to inflame Filipinos, according to the State Department.) The schedule of declining tariffs was revised in favor of Philippine goods. The "parity" provision of the 1946 agreement (Article VII) was recast (now as Article VI) to establish a meticulous reciprocity. Like the proverbial French law that prohibited rich and poor alike from sleeping beneath bridges, the 1955 agreement gave Philippine investors the same right to invest in the United States as U.S. investors had to invest in the Philippines. More important, a clause was added to the 1955 agreement (a new Article VII) which extended the protection given to U.S. business interests in the Philippines. U.S. investors would now be guaranteed equal treatment with Filipinos in all areas of the economy, not just in the areas of natural resources and public utilities. Articles VI and VII of the 1955 agreement are excerpted below.

Source: U.S. Department of State *Bulletin,* September 19, 1955, pp. 469-70.

Article VI

1. The disposition, exploitation, development, and utilization of all agricultural, timber, and mineral lands of the public domain, waters, minerals, coal, petroleum and other mineral oils, all forces and sources of potential energy, and other resources of either Party, and the operation of public utilities, shall, if open to any person, be open to citizens of the other Party and to all forms of business enterprise owned or controlled, directly or indirectly, by citizens of such other Party in the same manner as to and under the same conditions imposed upon citizens or corporations or associations owned or controlled by citizens of the Party granting the right. . . .

3. The United States of America reserves the rights of the several States of the United States to limit the extent to which citizens or corporations or associations owned or controlled by citizens of the Philippines may engage in the activities specified in this Article. The Republic of the Philippines reserves the power to deny any of the rights specified in this Article to citizens of the United States who are citizens of States, or to corporations or associations at least 60% of whose capital stock or capital is owned or controlled by citizens of States, which deny like rights to citizens of the Philippines, or to corporations or associations which are owned or controlled by citizens of the Philippines. The exercise of this reservation on the part of the Philippines shall not affect previously acquired rights, provided that in the event that any State of the United States of America should in the future impose restrictions which

would deny to citizens or corporations or associations owned or controlled by citizens of the Philippines the right to continue to engage in activities in which they were engaged therein at the time of the imposition of such restrictions, the Republic of the Philippines shall be free to apply like limitations to the citizens or corporations or associations owned or controlled by citizens of such States.

Article VII

1. The United States of America and the Republic of the Philippines each agree not to discriminate in any manner, with respect to their engaging in business activities, against the citizens or any form of business enterprise owned or controlled by citizens of the other and that new limitations imposed by either Party upon the extent to which aliens are accorded national treatment with respect to carrying on business activities within its territories, shall not be applied as against enterprises owned or controlled by citizens of the other Party which are engaged in such activities therein at the time such new limitations are adopted, nor shall such new limitations be applied to American citizens or corporations or associations owned or controlled by American citizens whose States do not impose like limitations on citizens or corporations or associations owned or controlled by citizens of the Republic of the Philippines.

2. The United States of America reserves the rights of the several States of the United States to limit the extent to which citizens or corporations or associations owned or controlled by citizens of the Philippines may engage in any business activities. The Republic of the Philippines reserves the power to deny any rights to engage in business activities to citizens of the United States who are citizens of States, or to corporations or associations at least 60% of the capital stock or capital of which is owned or controlled by citizens of States, which deny like rights to citizens of the Philippines. . . .

Selection 4.4: Military Bases Agreement, March 14, 1947

Editors' Introduction

The Military Bases Agreement provided the United States with extensive military facilities in the Philippines for a term of 99 years. The two major facilities, Clark Air Base and Subic Naval Base, were immense facilities. Clark covered 130,000 acres, bigger than the entire island of Grenada; Subic included a whole city—Olongapo—within its jurisdiction. The agreement prohibited the Phil-

ippines from granting base rights to any other country and placed no restrictions on the uses to which the U.S. could put the bases, nor the types of weapons that it could deploy or store there. Finally, the agreement allowed the United States to recruit Filipino volunteers into the U.S. Armed Forces.

Over the years, some of the provisions of the bases agreement have been changed. Some of the extensive base lands have been returned to the Philippine government, including the city of Olongapo, but the bases remain the largest U.S. military facilities outside of the United States. The term of the agreement was changed in 1966 to expire in 1991. In 1959, in the Bohlen-Serrano exchange of notes, the United States committed itself to consult with the Philippine government before deploying long range missiles on the bases or using the bases for combat purposes unrelated to mutual defense. The latter provision did not apply to logistic or staging activities nor to U.S. naval forces operating directly from the Philippines. In any event, however, none of these changes altered the essential use of the bases as springboards for U.S. intervention in Asia. According to U.S. officials in 1972, "nowhere in the world are we able to use our military bases with less restrictions than we do in the Philippines." Finally, it should be noted, that Filipinos continue to be recruited into the U.S. armed forces, where they typically serve as servants to top U.S. Navy officers.

For a listing of the uses to which the bases have been put, see selection 6.4. On their role in current U.S. military strategy, see selections 8.5 and 8.6. For criticisms of the bases, see selections 6.8, 8.10, 9.5, and introduction to 11.10.

Source: "Military Bases: Agreement Between the United States and the Republic of the Philippines, March 14, 1947," in U.S. Senate, *A Decade of American Foreign Policy: Basic Documents, 1941-49*, Sen. Doc. 123, 81st Congress, 1st session, 1950, pp. 869-81.

Article I: Grant of Bases

1. The Government of the Republic of the Philippines (hereinafter referred to as the Philippines) grants to the Government of the United States of America (hereinafter referred to as the United States) the right to retain the use of the bases in the Philippines listed in Annex A attached hereto.

2. The Philippines agrees to permit the United States, upon notice to the Philippines, to use such of those bases listed in Annex B as the United States determines to be required by military necessity.

3. The Philippines agrees to enter into negotiations with the United States at the latter's request, to permit the United States to expand such bases, to exchange such bases for other bases, to acquire additional bases, or relinquish rights to bases, as any of such exigencies may be required by military necessity.

Article II: Mutual Cooperation

1. It is mutually agreed that the armed forces of the Philippines may serve on United States bases and that the armed forces of the United States may serve on Philippine military establishments whenever such conditions appear beneficial as mutually determined by the armed forces of both countries.

Article III: Description of Rights

1. It is mutually agreed that the United States shall have the rights, power and authority within the bases which are necessary for the establishment, use, operation and defense thereof or appropriate for the control thereof and all the rights, power and authority within the limits of territorial waters and air space adjacent to, or in the vicinity of, the bases which are necessary to provide access to them, or appropriate for their control.

2. Such rights, power and authority shall include, *inter alia*, the right, power and authority:

(a) to construct (including dredging and filling), operate, maintain, utilize, occupy, garrison and control the bases;

(b) to improve and deepen the harbors, channels, entrances and anchorages, and to construct or maintain necessary roads and bridges affording access to the bases;

(c) to control (including the right to prohibit) in so far as may be required for the efficient operation and safety of the bases, and within the limits of military necessity, anchorages, moorings, landings, takeoffs, movements and operation of ships and waterborne craft, craft and other vehicles on water, in the air or on land comprising or in the vicinity of the bases;

(d) the right to acquire, as may be agreed between the two Governments, such rights of way, and to construct thereon, as may be required for military purpose, wire and radio communications facilities, including submarine and subterranean cables, pipe lines and spur tracks from railroads to bases, and the right, as may be agreed upon between the two Governments to construct the necessary facilities;

(e) to construct, install, maintain, and employ on any base any type of facilities, weapons, substance, device, vessel or vehicle on or under the ground, in the air or on or under the water that may be requisite or appropriate, including meteorological systems, aerial and water navigation lights, radio and radar apparatus and electronic devices of any desired power, type of emission and frequency.

Article VI: Maneuver and Other Areas

The United States shall, subject to previous agreement with the Philippines, have the right to use land and coastal sea areas of appropriate size and location for periodic maneuvers, for additional staging areas, bombing and gunnery ranges, and for such intermediate airfields as may be required for safe and efficient air operations. Operations in such areas shall be carried on with due regard and safeguards for the public safety.

Article XIII: Jurisdiction

1. The Philippines consents that the United States shall have the right to exercise jurisdiction over the following offenses:

(a) Any offense committed by any person within any base; except where the offender and the offended parties are both Philippine citizens, not members of the Armed Forces of the United States on active duty or the offense is against the security of the Philippines, and the offender is a Philippine citizen;

(b) Any offense committed outside the bases by any member of the Armed Forces of the United States in which the offended party is also a member of the Armed Forces of the United States; and

(c) Any offense committed outside the bases by any member of the Armed Forces of the United States against the security of the United States.

2. The Philippines shall have the right to exercise jurisdiction over all other offenses committed outside the bases by any member of the Armed Forces of the United States. Notwithstanding the foregoing provisions, it is mutually agreed that in time of war the United States shall have the right to exercise exclusive jurisdiction over any offenses which may be committed by the members of the Armed Forces of the United States in the Philippines.

Article XXIV: Mineral Resources

All minerals (including oil), and antiquities and all rights relating thereto and to treasure trove, under, upon, or connected with the land and water comprised in the bases or otherwise used or occupied by the United States by virtue of this Agreement, are reserved to the Government and inhabitants of the Philippines; but no rights so reserved shall be transferred to third parties, or exercised within the bases, without the consent of the United States. The United States shall negotiate with the proper Philippine authorities for the quarrying of rock and gravel necessary for construction on the bases.

Article XXV: Grant of Bases to a Third Power

1. The Philippines agrees that it shall not grant, without prior consent of the United States, any bases or any rights, power, or authority whatsoever, in or relating to bases, to any third power.

2. It is further agreed that the United States shall not, without the consent of the Philippines, assign, or underlet, or part with the possession of the whole or any part of any base, or of any right, power or authority granted by this Agreement, to any third power.

Article XXVII: Voluntary Enlistment of Philippine Citizens

It is mutually agreed that the United States shall have the right to recruit citizens of the Philippines for voluntary enlistment into the United States Armed Forces for a fixed term of years, and to train them and to exercise the same degree of control and discipline over them as is exercised in the case of other members of the United States Armed Forces. The number of such enlistments to be accepted by the Armed Forces of the United States may from time to time be limited by agreement between the two Governments.

Article XXIX: Term of Agreement

The present Agreement shall enter into force upon its acceptance by the two Governments and shall remain in force for a period of ninety-nine years subject to extension thereafter as agreed by the two Governments.

Annex "A"

Clark Field Airbase, Pampanga
Fort Stotsenberg, Pampanga
Mariveles Military Reservation, POL Terminal & Training Area, Bataan
Camp John Hay Leave and Recreation Center, Baguio
Army Communications System with the deletion of all stations in the Port of
    Manila Area.
U.S. AF Cemetery No. 2, San Francisco, Delmonte, Rizal
Angeles General Depot, Pampanga
Leyte-Samar Naval Base including shore installations and air bases
Subic Bay, No. West Shore Naval Base Zambales Province and the existing
    naval reservation at Olongapo and the existing Baguio naval reservation
Tawi Tawi Naval Anchorage and small adjacent land areas
Canacao-Sangley Point Navy Base, Cavite Province
Bagobantay Transmitter Area, Quezon City, and associated radio receiving
    and control sites, Manila Area
Tarumpitao Point (Loran Master Transmitter Station) (Palawan)
Talampulan Island, C.G. #354 (Loran) (Palawan)
Naule Point (Loran Station) (Zambales)
Castillejos, C.G. #356 (Zambales)

Annex "B"

Mactan Island Army and Navy Airbase
Florida Blanca Airbase, Pampanga
Aircraft Service Warning Net
Camp Wallace, San Fernando, La Union
Puerta Princesa Army and Navy Air Base including Navy Section Base and
    Air Warning Sites, Palawan
Tawi Tawi Naval Base, Sulu Archipelago
Aparri Naval Air Base.

Selection 4.5: Military Assistance Agreement, March 21, 1947

Editors' Introduction

In an agreement signed just a week after the Military Bases Agreement, Washington committed itself to provide military aid to the Philippine government. The specific terms of the Military Assistance Agreement provided for a U.S. military advisory group to be assigned to the Philippine Armed Forces and for Philippine military personnel to be sent to the United States for training. The agreement prohibited the Philippines from accepting military aid or advisers from any other nation without the consent of Washington.

U.S. policy makers were well aware as they approved this military aid agreement that the weapons, training, and advice it furnished were not intended for defense against foreign aggression. The only challenge to the Philippine government at the time came from its own people, in particular from the peasants of Central-Luzon who were resisting landlord efforts to restore the pre-war status quo in the countryside. The aid agreement served as the basis for U.S.

assistance against the Huks in the early 1950s [see selection 5.2], then for maintaining the position of the elite through the 1960s [see selection 6.6], and for supporting the dictatorship in the 1970s [see selection 8.7]. Today, military aid and advisers continue to be a key element of U.S. influence in the Philippines [see chapter 11].

Source: "Military Assistance to the Philippines: Agreement Between the United States and the Republic of the Philippines, March 21, 1947," in U.S. Senate, *A Decade of American Foreign Policy: Basic Documents, 1941-49,* Sen. Doc. 123, 81st Congress, 1st session, 1950, pp. 881-85.

Considering the desire of the Government of the Republic of the Philippines to obtain assistance in the training and development of its armed forces and the procurement of equipment and supplies therefor during the period immediately following the independence of the Philippines, considering the Agreement between the United States of America and the Republic of the Philippines concerning military bases, signed March 14, 1947, and in view of the mutual interest of the two Governments in matters of common defense, the President of the United States of America has authorized the rendering of military assistance to the Republic of the Philippines towards establishing and maintaining national security and towards forming a basis for participation by that Government in such defensive military operations as the future may require, and to attain these ends the Governments of the United States of America and the Republic of the Philippines have agreed as follows:

Title I: Purpose and Duration

Article 1. Subject to mutual agreements, the Government of the United States of America will furnish military assistance to the Government of the Republic of the Philippines in the training and development of armed forces and in the performance of other services essential to the fulfillment of those obligations which may devolve upon the Republic of the Philippines under its international agreements including commitments assumed under the United Nations and to the maintenance of the peace and security of the Philippines, as provided in Title II, Article 6, hereof.

Article 2. This Agreement shall continue for a period of five years from July 4, 1946 unless previously terminated or extended as hereinafter provided.

Article 3. If the Government of the Republic of the Philippines should desire that this Agreement be extended beyond the stipulated period, it shall make a written proposal to that effect at least one year before the expiration of this Agreement.

Article 4. This Agreement may be terminated before the expiration of the period of five years prescribed in Article 2, or before the expiration of an extension authorized in Article 3, by either Government, subject to three months' written notice to the other Government.

Article 5. It is agreed on the part of the Government of the Republic of the Philippines that title to all arms, vessels, aircraft, equipment and supplies, expendable items excepted, that are furnished under this Agreement on a non-reimbursable basis shall remain in the United States of America.

Title II: General

Article 6. For the purposes of this Agreement the military assistance authorized in Article 1 hereof is defined as the furnishing of arms, ammunition, equipment and supplies; certain aircraft and naval vessels, and instruction and training assistance by the Army and Navy of the United States and shall include the following:

(a) Establishing in the Philippines of a United States Military Advisory Group composed of an Army group, a Navy group and an Air group to assist and advise the Republic of the Philippines on military and naval matters;
(b) Furnishing from United States sources equipment and technical supplies for training, operations and certain maintenance of Philippine armed forces of such strength and composition as mutually agreed upon;
(c) Facilitating the procurement by the Government of the Republic of the Philippines of a military reserve of United States equipment and supplies, in such amounts as may be subsequently agreed upon;
(d) Making available selected facilities of United States Army and Navy training establishments to provide training for key personnel of the Philippine armed forces, under the conditions hereinafter described.

Title III: Military Advisory Group

Article 7. The Military Advisory Group shall consist of such number of United States military personnel as may be agreed upon by the Governments of the United States of America and the Republic of the Philippines.

Article 8. The functions of the Military Advisory Group shall be to provide such advice and assistance to the Republic of the Philippines as has been authorized by the Congress of the United States of America and as is necessary to accomplish the purposes set forth in Article 1 of this Agreement.

Article 10. Members of the Military Advisory Group shall serve under the direction of the authorities of the United States of America.

Title IV: Logistical Assistance

Article 17. The decision as to what supplies, services, facilities, equipment and naval vessels are necessary for military assistance shall be made by agreement between the appropriate authorities of the United States and the Republic of the Philippines.

Article 19. The Government of the Republic of the Philippines agrees that it will not relinquish physical possession or pass the title to any and all arms, munitions, equipment, supplies, naval vessels and aircraft furnished under this Agreement without the specific consent of the Government of the United States.

Article 20. Military equipment, supplies, and naval vessels necessary in connection with the carrying out of the full program of military assistance to the Republic of the Philippines shall be provided from United States and Philippine sources in so far as practicable and the Government of the Republic of the Philippines shall procure arms, ammunition, military equipment and naval vessels from governments or agencies other than the United States of America only on the basis of mutual agreement between the Government of the United States and the Government of the Republic of the Philippines. The Government of the Republic of the Philippines shall procure United States military equipment, supplies and naval vessels only as mutually agreed upon.

Title V: Training Assistance

Article 21. As part of the program of military assistance the Government of the Republic of the Philippines shall be permitted to send selected students to designated technical and service schools of the ground, naval and air services of the United States.

Title VI: Security

Article 23. So long as this Agreement, or any extension thereof, is in effect the Government of the Republic of the Philippines shall not engage or accept the services of any personnel of any Government other than the United States of America for duties of any nature connected with the Philippine armed forces, except by mutual agreement between the Government of the United States of America and the Government of the Republic of the Philippines.

The CIA's Edward Lansdale with Philippine Defense Minister Ramon Magsaysay.

CHAPTER 5: SUPPRESSION OF THE HUKS

Introduction

Repression by the landlords in the years following World War II, rather than taming the Huks, pushed them into open rebellion by 1949. [See selections 2.8 and 3.1 for background on the Huks.] Although the revolt was wholly indigenous, Washington panicked. The Huks after all were opposed to the Bell Trade Agreement, the "parity" amendment to the Philippine constitution, and the Military Bases Agreement; they favored a radical restructuring of Philippine society; and they were led by Communists. In these years, as the Cold War intensified internationally, particularly after the Communist victory on the Chinese mainland, U.S. policy makers were unwilling to accept the "loss" of the Philippines from the U.S. sphere of influence, and top officials were prepared to commit U.S. forces to prevent such an eventuality [see selection 5.1]. The United States undertook a massive counter-insurgency program, involving military advisers, military aid, and covert operations. This succeeded in breaking the back of the uprising without directly employing U.S. troops, but also without addressing its fundamental causes [see selection 5.2].

Selection 5.1: U.S. Policy on the Philippines, National Security Council

Editors' Introduction

NSC 84/2 was the official statement of United States policy toward the Philippines in late 1950 as expressed at the highest levels of the U.S. government. It was prepared by the National Security Council staff with input from the Department of State and the Joint Chiefs of Staff, and was approved by President Truman on November 10, 1950. The document remained classified until 1975.

Source: "A Report to the President by the National Security Council on the Position of the United States with Respect to the Philippines," November 9, 1950, in U.S. Department of State, *Foreign Relations of the United States, 1950*, Washington, DC: U.S. Government Printing Office, 1976, pp. 1514-20.

The Problem

1. To determine the position of the United States with respect to the Philippines.

Analysis

United States Interest in the Philippines

2. The relationship, the military commitments, and the moral obligations of the United States to the Philippines are unique. The United States was responsible for the creation of the Philippine state and the independence and stability of the Philippine Republic are a fundamental interest of the United States. It is implicit in the agreement of March 14, 1947 that the mutuality of interests of the U.S. and the Philippines calls for common action, if necessary, to maintain the security of the Philippines.

3. The independence of the Philippines testifies to the recognition by the United States that nationalism in Asia is a basic reality which cannot be ignored. Failure of the Philippines to maintain independence would discredit the United States in the eyes of the world and seriously decrease U.S. influence, particularly in Asia. Collapse of the present Philippine Government or any constitutional successor might immediately and probably would eventually result in a seizure of governmental power by the communists. Failure of the Philippine Government to maintain its pro-U.S. orientation would also probably result in the early seizure of governmental power by the communists. Such an eventuality would seriously increase the danger of communist control on the mainland of Southeast Asia and in Indonesia.

4. It is the policy of the United States to strengthen its position in the Pacific area, particularly with respect to the Philippines, Japan and the Ryukyus. As Japan reassumes her position as an independent Pacific nation, the United States favors the establishment of friendly political and economic relations between Japan and the Philippines and hopes that the simultaneous sound development of these two nations will contribute to the stability of the Pacific area.

U.S. Security Considerations

5. The Philippines are an essential part of the Asian off-shore island chain of bases on which the strategic position of the United States in the Far East depends. The threat of further communist encroachment in Formosa and Southeast Asia renders it imperative that the security of the Philippines be assured. The United States is committed to the external defense of the Islands and cannot permit them to be taken by aggression or internal subversion. The strategic importance of the Philippines to the United States is such as to justify the commitment of United States forces for its protection should circumstances require such action.

6. From the viewpoint of the USSR, the Philippine Islands could be the key to Soviet control of the Far East. Soviet domination of these Islands would seriously jeopardize the entire structure of anti-communist defenses in Southeast Asia and the offshore island chain, including Japan. Therefore, the situation in the Philippines cannot be viewed as a local problem since commu-

nist domination would endanger the United States military position in the Western Pacific and the Far East.

7. From the military point of view, the immediate security interests of the United States in the Philippine Islands include occupied installations, certain bases under treaty provisions not now occupied or in use, and U.S. armed forces personnel and material. In addition, there are other areas in the Islands which may be needed for operational use.

8. There is implicit in the United States-Philippine Agreement of 1947 authority for the United States to determine the garrison strength required for the local protection of United States bases in the Philippines.

9. Military intervention in the Philippine Islands would be justified only on the basis of a clear, present, and over-riding military necessity. Such a necessity cannot now be demonstrated. Although there may be some reason for concern regarding the local security of United States installations in the Philippines, strengthening of the Joint U.S. Military Advisory Group (JUS-MAG), Philippines, has been accomplished and it is expected that it will contribute to the internal security of the country and to the security of U.S. installations. Present conditions do not indicate a requirement for stationing additional Army units there.

External Security

10. External threats to the Philippines appear to be relatively remote at this time. An enemy invasion does not appear feasible at this time and, in all probability, would not be undertaken unless Formosa had first come under communist control. In view of the U.S. commitment for external defense of the Islands, a sound Philippine military policy justifies maximum emphasis on effective forces required for internal security and, under existing conditions, minimum expenditure for defense against external invaders.

Internal Security

11. The sole apparent military threat to the internal security of the Philippine Republic at present lies in the guerilla operations of the Hukbalahaps (Huks), who now call themselves "Peoples Liberation Army." Although on the basis of military factors *alone* the Huks lack the capability to acquire control of the Philippines, their continued existence, growth, and activities reflect the ineffectiveness of the Philippine armed forces and the generally unsatisfactory social, economic, and political situation in the Philippines.

12. The large Chinese minority in the Philippines is a potential source of subversion. As the influence of the Chinese communists becomes greater in Asia this important ethnic group might contribute to a situation in which an armed and militant communist minority could seize power from a corrupt and discredited regime.

13. Opposed to the Huks are some 26,000 relatively well-armed troops who are supported by the civil police. JUSMAG, Philippines, is now engaged in assisting and stimulating the Philippine armed forces. If these forces are trained, adequately equipped, and financed, they can develop the military capability for the eventual elimination of the Huks. In fact, the Philippine armed forces, in accordance with present plans, should, by aggressive and well-directed action and leadership, be able to eliminate the Huks as a serious threat within one year, provided that the Huks receive no substantial material support from outside and provided further that the political situation in the Philippines can be stabilized.

Political Considerations

14. Denial of the Philippines to communist control depends not only upon military measures but even more upon prompt vigorous political and economic action. The present situation in the Philippines is of such gravity that military assistance may prove unavailing unless solutions are found rapidly for the pressing political and economic problems now facing the country.

15. The Philippine Government has lacked the courage and initiative to take bold, vigorous measure to wipe out corruption in government, to create a stable administrative system and to encourage confidence in the government and in the future of the country on the part of the people. Leadership in the Philippine Government has been largely in the hands of a small group of individuals representing the wealthy propertied class who, except in isolated instances, have failed to appreciate the need for reform and the pressures generated among the less prosperous and more numerous groups of the population.

16. The leadership of the Philippine Government, while friendly to the United States, is extremely sensitive and suspicious of actions by the United States which would appear in Philippine eyes to be an infringement of national sovereignty. Not only Philippine public opinion but Asiatic opinion generally would prove particularly sensitive to any step by the United States which could be interpreted as implying a revocation or abridgment of Philippine independence.

Economic Considerations

17. Due to the effect of the war and the failure of the Philippine Government to take adequate measures to increase productive efficiency since the war, the economic situation in the Philippines has deteriorated to a grave degree. The basic economic problems in the Philippines are inefficient production and extremely low incomes. Although substantial recovery in production occurred after the liberation, agricultural and industrial output per capita is still below the pre-war level, government finances have become steadily worse and are now critical, and the international payments position of the country is seriously deteriorated.

18. In agriculture, the area under cultivation was brought to the pre-war level and the livestock population partially restored. However, almost nothing was done to open new lands for the increased population, to improve methods of cultivation, or to better the position of farm workers and tenants.

19. The opportunity to increase production efficiency and to raise the standard of living during the post-war period has been wasted, largely due to misdirected investment and excessive imports for consumption. Inequalities in the Philippines, always large, have become greater during the past few years while the standard of living of the mass of people has not reached the pre-war level. The profits of businessmen and the incomes of large land owners have risen considerably.

20. The deterioration of the economic system has caused a widespread feeling of disillusionment among the population. Most agricultural and industrial workers have no faith that the economic position can or will be improved. Filipino as well as foreign businessmen are fearful of the economic future of the country. The uncertainties created by these doubts are strengthened by the recent tendency toward unemployment.

21. The communist-led Hukbalahap movement has taken advantage of the deteriorating economic situation and exploited the antagonistic attitudes of the people toward the government in order to incite lawlessness and disorder.

22. The President of the United States dispatched to the Philippines an Economic Survey Mission, which has completed an exhaustive survey of the Philippine economic situation and has submitted recommendations for improvement. The Mission's recommendations contemplate governmental reforms, reorganization and improvement of agricultural and industrial production, increased rates of taxation, and more efficient collection of taxes.

23. The Mission stresses the necessity of a program of widespread social and economic reforms, which, coupled with increased production and more competent management, the Mission finds necessary to restore the elements of sound and stable government. The Mission recommends, contingent upon the institution of these reforms by the Philippine Government, a substantial program of financial assistance through loans and grants to be carried out under supervision by representatives of the United States Government.

Method of Action

24. The security interests of the United States require that the Philippines become and remain stable, anti-communist, pro-American, and an example for the rest of the world of the intention of the United States to encourage the establishment of progressive and responsible governments. This entails the reassertion of U.S. influence to the extent required to eliminate prevalent corruption, provide efficient administrative services, and restore public faith in the concept of government in the best interests of the people.

25. Owing to the extreme sensitivity of Philippine officials and the people in general on the question of their national sovereignty, the extent and manner in which the necessary influence is brought to bear on the Philippine Government to accomplish essential reforms presents to the United States Government a most difficult and delicate problem. It is not to be expected that broad social and economic reforms can be brought about quickly or easily, even with the best of intentions on the part of the Philippine Government. Extreme care must therefore be exercised in the methods used to persuade the Philippine Government to take the necessary action.

26. It would appear, however, that this Government has no choice except to attempt to help the Filipinos bring about the necessary reforms since to do nothing would result in disaster. It should be made clear that disaster can be avoided by vigorous action on the part of the Philippine Government accompanied by the economic and advisory assistance which the United States will be prepared to extend.

Conclusions

27. The United States has as its objectives in the Philippines the establishment and maintenance of:

a. An effective government which will preserve and strengthen the pro-U.S. orientation of the people.

b. A Philippine military capability [sic] of restoring and maintaining internal security.

c. A stable and self-supporting economy.

28. To accomplish the above objectives, the United States should:

a. Persuade the Philippine Government to effect political, financial, economic and agricultural reforms in order to improve the stability of the country.

b. Provide such military guidance and assistance as may be deemed advisable by the United States and acceptable to the Philippine Government.

c. Extend, under United States supervision and control, appropriate economic assistance in the degree corresponding to progress made toward creating the essential conditions of internal stability.

d. Continue to assume responsibility for the external defense of the Islands and be prepared to commit United States forces, if necessary, to prevent communist control of the Philippines.

Selection 5.2: Counter-Insurgency in the Philippines, Stephen R. Shalom

Editors' Introduction

The article below describes the steps—military, economic, and political—undertaken by the United States to defeat the Huk insurgency in the early 1950s.

Source: Stephen R. Shalom, "Counter-Insurgency in the Philippines," *Journal of Contemporary Asia*, vol. 7, no. 2, 1977, pp. 153-172.

The Setting

In the years following World War II, the Philippine Government and landlords conducted a reign of terror against the peasantry of Central Luzon in an attempt to restore the pre-war class relations in the countryside. The left-wing wartime guerilla organization, the Hukbalahap (Huks) and their affiliated peasant union, the PKM, had no intentions of trying to overthrow the government, but they were increasingly forced to take up weapons to defend themselves. The administration of President Manuel Roxas had passed legislation that it claimed guaranteed tenant farmers seventy percent of the rice crop. In reality, however, the law allowed landlords to take half of the crop, which, of course, they did. The response to the resultant peasant discontent was government-organized "anti-dissident" operations, led by such men as Napoleon Valeriano, who had earlier led armed men with skull and cross bones on their shirt sleeves against peasants. In March 1948, Roxas declared the Huks and the PKM to be illegal organizations. This was used as justification for further indiscriminate terror against the rural population.

Roxas died the next month and was succeeded in office by his Vice-President, Elpidio Quirino. Quirino tried to negotiate an amnesty with the Huks, but the efforts were deliberately sabotaged by the landlords in his administration. As a Philippine counter-insurgency specialist has remarked, the amnesty offer failed because it "was not accompanied by tangible efforts of the government to rid itself of graft and corruption, nor was it accompanied by positive steps towards removing discontentment among the masses." Another cause, he noted, "was the inability of the government to counter the Huk accusation of bad faith on the part of the administration." Quirino then reverted to the mailed-fist approach. Terror and corruption by the Philippine Constabulary (PC), however, merely encouraged further support for the Huks.

In the meantime, the Philippine elite continued its century-old practice of using political power for its personal aggrandizement. For example in 1946, Congress amended the tax laws to make the rates more regressive. In October 1946, the war profits tax was altered to exclude a major part of the war-profiteering from the coverage of the law; in any case, by April 30, 1947, of the estimated 30,000 individuals and corporations liable to file war profits tax returns, only 1,920 had done so and of these 1,440 claimed no tax liability. . . .

The last straw came in the Philippine presidential election of 1949. . . . a landmark of dishonesty. Official records estimated more than a fifth of the ballots to be spurious. The *New York Times* called it the "costliest, most violent" national election in Philippine annals. A contributor to *Reader's Digest* observed that "every device known to fraudulent elections was used. . . . Filipinos sadly wisecracked that even the birds and bees voted in some precincts."

. . . the Huks, finding parliamentary struggle useless, called for the overthrow of the Government. Gaining the support of a disillusioned peasant population, Huk strength soon reached twelve to fifteen thousand armed supporters with a mass base of from one and a half to two million. The very continuity of the Philippine state was in question: Quirino kept a motor launch moored to the Presidential Palace to evacuate him and his family should the guerillas enter Manila. . . .

The U.S. Steps In

. . . In February 1950, when Quirino came to the U.S., the State and Treasury Departments recommended that Truman "firmly advise President Quirino that no further American aid could be considered unless and until there is tangible evidence that the Philippines has taken steps to put its house in order and that it would then need and be in a position to effectively use additional aid." Specifically, Truman was to propose to Quirino that a U.S. economic survey mission be sent to the Philippines. Quirino agreed. . . .

In early 1950 JUSMAG's view was that a

> sound military policy for the Philippines at the present time justifies maximum emphasis and expenditures upon forces required for the maintenance of internal security and minimum expenditure upon forces contributing largely to national prestige or to forces and reserves designed for defense against external invaders.

JUSMAG considered its own primary objective to be one of insuring that the Philippines followed this internal security orientation. Accordingly, JUSMAG drew up recommendations that were accepted by Philippine officials for a thorough-going reorganization of the anti-dissident campaign. Responsibility for combatting Huks had rested with the Philippine Constabulary. Because the PC was under the authority of the Department of the Interior, it was easily influenced by local politics; additionally, JUSMAG felt that PC units were too small, and suffered from poor discipline, training, and leadership. Therefore, JUSMAG urged that the PC be combined with the Armed Forces of the Philippines (AFP), under the office of the Secretary of National Defense, and that this merged AFP be given the task of fighting Huks. JUSMAG further advised that rather than anti-Huk units of about 90 men, such as the PC had employed, Battalion Combat Teams be organized—

contingents of 1,170 soldiers, with artillery, capable of engaging in major offensive actions instead of police-minded static defense. In the spring of 1950, Philippine officials implemented the JUSMAG recommendations. Recruiting to augment the Philippine Army was undertaken "throughout all areas, except Central Luzon where dissidents are concentrated." To help equip the newly formed Battalion Combat Teams, deliveries of scheduled U.S. military aid were speeded up.

Also in early 1950, at the request of the Philippine Chief of Staff, JUSMAG prepared a study proposing a complete reorganization of the intelligence agencies of the Philippine Government. All of the JUSMAG recommendations were carried out. In June of 1950, U.S. and Philippine officials exchanged notes regarding the sending of a CIA agent to Manila to act as an adviser to counter-insurgency.... [I]n late June of 1950, the Korean War broke out.... Truman announced that U.S. forces would be sent to Korea. He also used this opportunity to order that aid to France's colonial war in Indochina be stepped up, that the U.S. Seventh Fleet intervene in the Chinese civil war by defending Formosa, and that "United States forces in the Philippines be strengthened, and that military assistance to the Philippine Government be accelerated." A few days later Truman announced that an economic survey mission was being sent to Manila. It was to be headed by Daniel W. Bell, president of the American Security and Trust Co. and a former Under-secretary of the Treasury. On August 1, Truman submitted a message to Congress asking for an additional $4 billion for foreign military aid. In particular, he stated:

> In view of the increased jeopardy to the Pacific area caused by the Communist aggression in Korea, it is estimated that $303,000,000 will be required to increase and accelerate military assistance to the Republic of the Philippines and to other nations in southern and eastern Asia.

$13.2 million of this money was programmed for the Philippines, bringing the total fiscal 1951 appropriation to four times the fiscal 1950 allotment. (It should be noted that, despite the implication of Truman's remarks, there was no evidence of any non-negligible outside aid to the Huks.) That same month CIA operative Edward Landsale was given orders to pack for Manila....

In the summer of 1950, U.S. officials in the Philippines moved to get their choice appointed Secretary of National Defense. The head of JUSMAG and the American ambassador, Myron M. Cowen, strongly urged Quirino to select Ramon Magsaysay to the post.... and on September 1, 1950, Magsaysay was appointed to the cabinet position.

Later mythology was to portray Magsaysay as having come from humble origins, a "man of the masses." In fact, his family was the most well-to-do in their barrio.... They owned a general merchandise shop and various farms, including one of over 1,000 acres, and they employed tenant labor. Magsaysay first worked as a mechanic at a bus line owned by a relative. He was soon made a shop superintendent and later a branch manager. His salary at the time, 1939, was higher than the average wage made by non-self-employed agricultural workers by a factor of about thirty-five. In 1940, the employees under his authority went on strike because of his harsh methods, such as arbitrary suspensions and dismissals. Magsaysay tried to organize strike-breakers, and ultimately broke the strike by getting a court to rule that the strike leaders were attempting to sabotage American military preparations by hindering transportation.

During the war, Magsaysay headed a USAFFE guerilla unit. He was appointed military governor of Zambales province by the U.S. Army when it returned to the islands. In 1946, he was elected to Congress on a platform pledging to obtain benefits from the U.S. for USAFFE guerillas and other war veterans. He was a loyal member of the Liberal Party—for example, he praised Quirino as a modern "Sir Galahad, a knight in shining armor in search of the Holy Grail of clean and honest government." He was made head of the House Defense Committee, a position which involved him in a great deal of contact with JUSMAG. In 1948 he made a trip to the U.S. to obtain veterans' benefits legislation, at which time he also established good contacts in the Pentagon. And in March 1950 he travelled to the U.S. to request additional military aid, meeting again with top American officials. Upon his return he delivered his first and only privileged speech in his four years in Congress, a speech defending the U.S. against its critics.

As Secretary of National Defense, Magsaysay was able to obtain for himself a free hand in running the armed forces: he was able to contact the Pentagon to put pressure on Quirino, using the leverage of U.S. military aid, to get his enemies removed from office.

But this does not mean that Magsaysay led the anti-Huk campaign alone. He leaned heavily for advice on Major-General Leland S. Hobbs, the head of JUSMAG. A few years later Hobbs would write to President Dwight Eisenhower, "I think I know" Magsaysay "and his innermost desires as do few Americans." In early 1951, JUSMAG secretly reported that the U.S. was "fortunate" in having as the Philippine Secretary of National Defense a person "with a genuine admiration and faith in the United States," whose cooperation with JUSMAG "has been outstanding, and its advice and assistance is constantly sought and utilized by him."

A week after Magsaysay's appointment, the CIA's Edward Lansdale arrived in Manila. Lansdale promptly set up a desk in Magsaysay's Defense office and a cot in Magsaysay's private quarters, and the two worked closely together on the problems of counter-insurgency. Lansdale viewed Magsaysay as "an intimate friend" and in private they referred to each other as "brother."

Lansdale had served with the Office of Strategic Services during World War II and then, in the Philippines, as chief of Army intelligence for the Western Pacific. At this time he befriended, among others, Magsaysay. He returned to the U.S. in 1948 to teach economic intelligence at the U.S. Air Force's Strategic Intelligence School in Denver, was transferred to Washington to work on Cold War problems with an emphasis on guerilla warfare, and in the Spring of 1950 he organized a psychological warfare seminar for, among others, Philippine military officers undergoing training in the U.S.

Under the guidance of Lansdale, Hobbs and some of their staff officers, Magsaysay was able to revitalize the armed forces. Corrupt officers were removed: though Magsaysay himself used his office to dispense patronage and pork barrel, it was no longer at a level that prevented the military from functioning. Magsaysay also increased troop morale. As two of his biographers have said, approvingly,

> Magsaysay was winning army loyalty with the human touch. Soldiers who killed Huks earned a stripe and a personal letter of praise from him.

Magsaysay initiated a policy of giving liberal "cash incentives" for Huk bodies as well as for information, citing movies of the American Wild West as his model. The first such reward paid out was for five thousand pesos—about ten times the annual wage of agricultural laborers in the Philippines. For top Huk leaders, one could make as much as P100,000.

An office of Psychological Warfare was set up directly under Magsaysay. It was soon renamed the Civil Affairs Office [CAO] though its function remained unchanged. At its head was Jose Crisol, who, as Lansdale confided, operated "mostly under my direction." The CAO undertook a massive propaganda effort against the Huks. Within two years more than thirteen million leaflets and other literature had been distributed and over 6,000 meetings were held reaching a million and a half people. Literature and films were provided by the U.S. Information Service. The USIS set up a Regional Production Center in Manila in 1950 to reproduce propaganda materials for use by American personnel throughout Asia, and it prepared leaflets, posters, and pamphlets in local Philippine dialects for use against the Huks. JUSMAG helped in the selection of targets for air drops of propaganda leaflets.

The CAO organized anti-communist forums in universities, patriotic writing contests were set up for high-school and college students, and propaganda materials were distributed in the grammar schools. The downtown headquarters of the National Student Movement was secretly subsidized by CAO. Rafael Yabut, a disc-jockey was put on the Civil Affairs payroll. Members of the press were given food, transportation, entertainment, gifts, and even salaries. Lansdale and others forged Huk documents and spread false information through the media. Magsaysay was especially cooperative with journalists who invented news stories about his exploits. . . .

Some of the psychological warfare operations involved actions as well as words. Lansdale relates the example of a psywar operation designed to get the Huks to leave a particular hill. Stories were circulated among Huk sympathizers of an *asuang* (vampire) that lived on the hill.

> Then the psywar squad set up an ambus along a trail by the Huks. When a Huk patrol came along the trail, the ambushers

silently snatched the last man of the patrol, their move unseen in the dark night. They punctured his neck with holes, vampire-fashion, held the body up by the heels, drained it of blood, and put the corpse back on the trail. When the Huks returned to look for the missing man and found their bloodless comrade, every member of the patrol believed that the *asuang* had got him and that one of them would be next if they remained on that hill. When daylight came, the whole Huk squadron moved out of the vicinity.

Another technique of the psychological warfare campaign was the exploiting of ethnic differences among Filipinos—a technique that had been used by the U.S. conquerors of the islands at the beginning of the century. As Lansdale described it at the time, a Huk commander in Laguna

> requested, and had, a private rendezvous with Magsaysay to discuss amnesty for Laguna Huks. Magsaysay gave him a counter proposal: let the Laguna Huks surrender, join the Armed Forces in hunting down the Pampanga Huks whom they dislike so, and they can thus earn a pardon and will be resettled in Mindanao. . . . Even if negotiations are not resumed, Magsaysay has planted a seed of sectionalism which can grow.

The Civil Affairs Office also undertook a campaign of covertly fomenting mass demonstrations against the Huks. In San Luis, Pampanga, the home town of Huk leader Luis Taruc, Taruc's birthday was celebrated by burning him in effigy, "supposedly as a spontaneous public action"—to use the words of a secret JUSMAG report. . . .

The most successful psychological warfare technique was the Economic Development Corps, or EDCOR. Essentially, the Army took as its own the Huk slogan of "land for the landless" and promised to resettle any recanting Huks on their own plots of land. But though the land settlements were "supposedly for Huk surrenderees," as Lansdale noted in top secret correspondence, "secretly, they will be used in part for poor tenants and other taos [common people] who are about ready to join the Huks in desperation." When the project was completed, fewer than one thousand families had been resettled, and only 246 of these were ex-Huks (some, in fact, were members of Magsaysay's armed forces). "Actually," an American land settlement adviser reported, "this project contributed little to the rehabilitation of dissidents." The lack of substantive reform, however, was more than made up for by the thorough propaganda effort: films were made, depicting rehabilitation on government-provided farm land, and shown throughout the Philippines. As the Huks themselves acknowledged, the project helped to deplete the mass base of the insurgency.

Another program in which the propaganda value far exceeded the actual reforms was the Philippine Army's offer of free legal services to poor farmers. One U.S. official later explained it this way: Magsaysay had

> made a big publicity binge, that all you've got to do is walk into any post office in any village in the Philippines and send a collect

telegram to me, Magsaysay, and within twenty-four hours I will have a team of lawyers there to take care of your grievance.

And as Magsaysay says, if they'd really challenged him on it, he didn't have that many lawyers. But a few people did do this, and he went down there you know, peasants who had land problems—he got the lawyers to them within twenty-four hours. And the word got around, and they began to believe him. He wasn't able to accomplish the social reforms, but they believed that he would. And that defeated the Hukbalahaps.

In October 1950, the anti-Huk campaign made a major breakthrough when, in what a U.S. Army historian called "a great stroke of luck," an informer provided information leading to the capture of the entire Communist politburo [top leadership] in Manila. JUSMAG assisted Philippine officials in preparing evidence for use in the trial and subsequent conviction of the politburo members. Magsaysay and JUSMAG used the Manila round-ups as the opportunity to get Quirino to suspend the writ of habeas corpus. When the writ was restored two years later more than a thousand people were being held in prison without having been charged with a crime or having received public hearings. For these people and all the others jailed for insurrection and the like, imprisonment was a grim experience; until mid-1952, according to the same U.S. Army historian, beatings were the normal procedure for extracting information from prisoners.

In the meantime, the military operations continued. JUSMAG had recommended that the Philippines "increase ground forces as rapidly as possible." In the latter half of 1950, the Army was increased from ten to sixteen Battalion Combat Teams "upon direct JUSMAG advice." And, in the first half of 1951, ten new teams were added. Total strength of the Philippine Armed Forces rose from thirty-two thousand at the beginning of 1950, to forty thousand at the start of 1951, to fifty-six thousand in late 1952. In mid-1951, Washington approved an additional grant of $10 million in military aid to the Philippines to finance the growth of the AFP.

On JUSMAG's recommendation, further organizational reforms were implemented in the AFP and in Philippine military intelligence agencies. JUSMAG wrote some Standing Operating Procedure directives for the AFP and assisted in the preparation of others. JUSMAG considered a particular directive it wrote to be "one of the most important steps taken by the Army during the past several months to strengthen military striking power." Philippine officials set up an Intelligence School which used mostly American materials and whose lectures were rehearsed in front of a JUSMAG representative before delivery.

In the summer of 1950, JUSMAG had advised Philippine military intelligence to compile an alphabetical list of all known Huks and then to initiate broad searching and screening campaigns over cordoned areas suspected of harboring Huks. In the first six months of 1951, 15,000 people were arrested under this program. Also in the summer of 1950, JUSMAG began a policy of inspecting AFP tactical units, training installations, and supply agencies. Some time later JUSMAG officers received official sanction to accompany Philippine troops on major operations as unarmed combat observers.

The Huks were fought from the air as well. The Philippine Air Force, which was of negligible value against an invader using modern jet aircraft, had as it primary mission the "support of army troops in anti-dissident operations." Between August 1, 1950 and June 30, 1952 the Philippine Air Force flew 2,600 bombing and strafing sorties, expending over a million rounds of .50 caliber ammunition and a quarter of a million pounds of explosives on Huk targets. (These are rather insignificant figures by Vietnam standards; but this was the Philippine Air Force, not the American, and the Huks did not use tunnels.) As early as November 1949, Philippine officials had asked the U.S. for napalm. The request was held up for a while because the State Department feared that napalm created more Communists than it destroyed. The Philippine Air Force tried a locally fabricated napalm imitation developed with some JUSMAG assistance, but, as JUSMAG noted, it "did not give the desired effect because of inferior burning qualities." Finally, at the end of 1951, U.S.-provided napalm arrived in the Philippines and was used against suspected Huk concentrations. Incendiary raids against Huk agriculture were also conducted, at times with clandestine support from the U.S. Air Force.

In early 1951 a proposal was aired in the Philippine Congress to attempt an amnesty with the Huks. The Philippine military reacted with public alarm, while privately the Papal Nuncio and JUSMAG indicated their firm opposition. Nothing came of the proposal.

Although the Huks did not formally concede defeat until the mid-fifties, when they announced their retreat from armed to parliamentary struggle, they were essentially beaten militarily and psychologically in the first few years of the decade. And significantly, from Washington's point of view, though U.S. policy makers had been willing to use American troops directly in the Philippines if necessary, advisers and military aid had sufficed to crush the Huk insurgency.

Economic Measures

Keeping the Philippine Government afloat required more, however, than defeating the Huks. As the National Security Council warned, "Military assistance may prove unavailing unless solutions are found rapidly for the pressing political and economic problems now facing the country." In October 1950, the U.S. Economic Survey mission headed by Daniel W. Bell delivered its report to Truman and shortly thereafter the report was released to the public. The Philippine economy, declared the report, was on the brink of collapse. The Mission concluded that the Philippines would become totally useless to American strategic and economic interests if the disastrous state of the economy was not immediately rectified. " . . . if the situation is allowed to drift," the report stated ominously, "there is no certainty that moderate remedies will suffice."

To correct this situation, the report recommended that the Philippine Government increase tax receipts, establish a tax on the sale of foreign exchange, enact a minimum wage law, undertake land reform, and improve and reorganize public administration. It further called upon the United States Government to provide the Philippines with $250 million in loans and grants over a five year period conditioned upon Philippine enactment of the recommended reforms. Control of all such aid funds, however—even those funds allocated by the Philippine Government to match U.S. aid—was to be in the hands of the U.S. Although the official U.S. propaganda line had been, in Acheson's words, "we cannot direct, we should not direct, we have not the slightest desire to direct," the reality was quite different.

. . . Acheson explained to a closed Congressional Committee hearing that the Philippines

> will accept American advisers throughout their Government. We will come up to Congress with an aid program which will be modest in dimensions but which lays the foundation for American technicians and American advisers all through their Government.

. . . the U.S. was committed to a strategy of eliminating the conditions breeding insurgency, though with . . . important limitations.

. . . the reforms must not too seriously challenge the power of the Philippine oligarchy, for U.S. economic and military interests depended upon the alliance between U.S. rulers and this Filipino elite. The best illustration of this is land reform. . . . The Bell report had noted that the land situation in 1950 "remains the same or worse than four years ago." The minor agrarian reform program that did exist simply enriched Quirino's friends. . . . Clearly no land reform would be voluntarily initiated by Philippine officials but nor were U.S. officials anxious to push too hard on this point. The Assistant Director of the U.S. Mutual Security Administration [MSA] reported from Manila in 1952 that the United States would have to use all of its influence simply to assure free elections in 1953, and "I would hate to see us use up our ammunition in what would probably be a futile attempt to get an adequate land reform program at this time." . . . Moreover, the MSA official noted, to have Quirino promise to carry out a land reform without being serious about implementing it would inflame the peasantry even more.

In 1952, Robert Hardie, an overzealous MSA land reform adviser in the Philippines, submitted a report calling for a redistribution of land. He suggested that the Philippine Government purchase land from landlords with bonds paying 4% interest and maturing over 25 years and resell small plots to tenants who would pay off their purchase over 30 years with interest. The administration of the program was to "at all times be guided by the principle of . . . Private rather than state, individual rather than collective ownership of land." The existing land tenure system, Hardie warned,

> fosters the growth of communism and harms the United States position. Unless corrected, it is easy to conceive of the situation

worsening to a point where the United States would be forced to take direct, expensive, and arbitrary steps to insure against loss of the Philippines to the Communist bloc in Asia—and would be still faced with finding a solution to the underlying problem.

But when Hardie's report was made public, he was denounced by the Speaker of the Philippine House of Representatives as a Communist, and he was recalled from Manila in August 1953. . . .

Political Measures

. . . It remained for U.S. policy to maintain the political credibility of the Philippine Government.

Before the 1951 off-year elections, a "good government" organization called NAMFREL—National Movement for Free Elections—was set up with the help of U.S. Government funds and officials. NAMFREL members conducted a mass publicity campaign urging clean elections. The Civil Affairs Office of the Philippine Armed Forces distributed leaflets exhorting the cynical population to vote. And Magsaysay used the Army and ROTC students to police the balloting and supervise an honest count. The election turned out to be one of the bloodiest in Philippine history—21 killings on election day itself and at the very least 30 election-related deaths in the weeks before. Nevertheless, since the opposition Nacionalista Party Senate slate swept the elections, the votes were generally thought to have been tallied honestly, and this served to undercut the Huk slogan of "Bullets not Ballots". The real test was yet to come, however, in the more important presidential election of 1953.

President Quirino, although his health was failing, decided to run for re-election. U.S. Ambassador Cowen had "developed an understanding relationship" with Quirino, but, nevertheless, it was clear that the corrupt and uninspiring Quirino was hardly the ideal person—from the U.S. point of view—to lead the Philippines to economic recovery and to full victory over the Huks. Moreover, Cowen considered Quirino prone to make "impulsive and ill-considered decisions and to stand by them stubbornly once they have been made public." The obvious alternative was Ramon Magsaysay—honest, dynamic, and unreservedly committed to U.S. aims—and American officials took steps to give the Defense Secretary the wide reputation that he would need to contest the presidency. Lansdale introduced Magsaysay to foreign correspondents in Manila and to visiting journalists from the U.S. Articles praising Magsaysay appeared in almost every major American periodical. Roy Q. Howard reported from Manila that

> the achievements of the defense minister were taken more or less in
> a stride by the local press until they began to attract the attention of
> American correspondents whose press dispatches, special articles
> and magazine stories soon began to glamorize the courageous but
> not overly colorful Magsaysay. . . .

The Philippine Armed Forces also contributed to the Magsaysay public relations effort. With Magsaysay's knowledge, safe conduct passes with his picture on them were dropped in areas where there were known to be no Huks. A more elaborate scheme involved having Magsaysay's own troops disguise themselves as Huks and set upon some village, in order that these "guerillas" could be repulsed by troops under Magsaysay's personal command—thus spreading the Defense Secretary's reputation as a fearless Huk fighter. . . .

Once Magsaysay decided to run for the presidency, according to one of his biographers, "which party would sponsor him was of secondary importance." On November 20, 1952, he met privately with Nacionalista Party leaders Jose P. Laurel and Claro M. Recto and signed a secret pact whereby Laurel and Recto agreed to support a Magsaysay presidential bid on their party ticket.

In October 1953, a State Department official announced that the U.S. was adhering to a policy of "absolute impartiality" with respect to the elections. "Yet as one of our major objectives is political stability, we cannot deny that we are concerned that the democratic processes function so that the people may fully express their will. The eyes of the world will follow the elections in the Philippines next month." And, on November 6, the White House released the text of an exchange of letters between former Ambassador Cowen and President Eisenhower in which both men expressed their deep concern that the upcoming Philippine elections be conducted honestly. These were all implicit warnings to Quirino to keep the election clean and free. The context for these warnings was a confidential report by a high U.S. official a year earlier that advised Washington that Quirino "cannot win if the elections are honest" and that only a strong stand by the U.S., "possibly even going so far as to threaten to cut off both economic and military assistance," could keep Quirino from stealing the election.

After Magsaysay's nomination, public relations efforts in his behalf picked up steam. Most of the Manila press—in particular the three major American-owned papers—boosted Magsaysay, and U.S. journalists continued to write glowing articles about him. Roy Q. Howard of the United Press observed that "the Magsaysay boom bears definite 'Made in America' markings". Howard asserted that these were journalistic markings "without design or premeditation," but Philippine Ambassador to the U.S. Carlos Romulo wrote privately to ex-Ambassador Cowen: "It looks as though the build-up you started for Magsaysay is giving results."

"As a practical matter," wrote Joseph Alsop in an article that ran in the *Manila Daily Bulletin* as well as in the U.S., "Magsaysay is the American candidate."

The head of the Civil Affairs Office of the Armed Forces, Jose Crisol, resigned from the Army to begin a student organization for Magsaysay which soon developed into a large Magsaysay-for-President Movement. NAMFREL, though theoretically non-partisan, secretly started working for Magsaysay's election, and a new non-partisan organization, Citizens Committee for Good Government, covertly gathered political intelligence for Magsaysay.

In June 1953, the "sugar bloc" bolted from Quirino's Liberal Party and formed a third party, the Democrata, with Carlos Romulo as their standard-bearer. The sugar barons pledged to match a peso for every dollar Romulo was able to raise from supporters in the U.S. Romulo wrote to Cowen to try to get (illegal) contributions from U.S. firms with interests in the Philippines, and even proposed code names for use in future communications regarding fund-raising. Romulo soon learned, however, that American money was backing Magsaysay and was not willing to divide the anti-Quirino forces by bankrolling Romulo. This convinced the Democratas, in August, to give up their third party effort by merging with the Nacionalistas. . . .

Traditionally, in Philippines politics, the incumbent party has the financial advantage. But once the sugar bloc joined the Nacionalistas, the Magsaysay campaign raised more money than did Quirino's. Moreover, the Nacionalista sweep in the Senate in 1951 allowed them to block the expenditure of government funds by Quirino for political purposes. Illegal contributions from U.S. business interests swelled the Nacionalista campaign chest, but the American money was particularly important before the Democrata-Nacionalista merger, when the Magsaysay forces were desperately short of funds. There were two problems with getting contributions from Americans: one, the difficulty of getting the funds from the U.S. into the Philippines, and two, preserving the anonymity of local managers of U.S. firms who wanted to give Magsaysay money but feared retaliation by Quirino. In June 1953 Lansdale confided that he could solve both these problems and that, despite instructions from Washington to avoid politicking, he might go ahead and do so. Whether this turned out to be the conduit for U.S. funds is not clear—Lansdale has denied it; but American money did flow to Magsaysay. As *Time* magazine reported,

> In spite of a Filipino law which forbids foreigners to contribute to election campaigns, U.S. business interests in the islands anted up some $250,000 at a time when Magsaysay's Nationalist Party was seriously short of funds.

Informed Filipino politicians agree that the figure for total U.S. contributions to Magsaysay was considerably higher. . . .

Shortly before the election, the Nacionalistas prepared massive arms caches and armored vehicles, including tanks, for use in the event that Quirino won the election through fraud. The plan was to seize the Presidential Palace and strategic garrisons while Magsaysay and key Nacionalista leaders sought the safety of the U.S. Naval base at Olongapo. Arrangements for this were presumably made when Magsaysay had been smuggled into Olongapo in a Navy ambulance for a meeting with the U.S. Navy Commander there.

A few days before the election, a U.S. naval flotilla paid a visit to Manila Bay. The *New York Times* reported, without attribution, that the "naval visit was purely routine." Nacionalista Senator Jose Laurel, however, confided a year later that the presence of the U.S. warships was not entirely accidental.

On election day, the JUSMAG commander deployed a couple of dozen of his officers to observe Filipino Army personnel as the latter watched the polls. The election was one of the most peaceful in Philippine history—depending on the count, ten or twenty people were killed on election day. Major fraud did not take place and Magsaysay won an overwhelming victory, capturing more than two-thirds of the votes cast. Contrary to popular mythology, Magsaysay's electoral support was correlated positively with higher socio-economic status and negatively with the rate of tenancy.

As *Time* magazine remarked in its account of the election, "it was no secret that Ramon Magsaysay was America's boy." And once in office, Magsaysay indeed performed as "America's boy," serving U.S. imperial interests wherever possible. Only as a reformer did Magsaysay fail to live up to his image: in the words of one scholar, under Magsaysay's presidency "the pace at which economic and social reforms were introduced was slowed" compared to the period 1950-53. But no matter. To U.S. policy makers what counted was defeating the Huks and propping up a pro-American regime. In these terms, Washington could congratulate itself for having accomplished for the time being a model of counter-insurgency.

Philippine nationalist Claro M. Recto.

CHAPTER 6: THE PHILIPPINE REPUBLIC TO 1972: ELITE DEMOCRACY AND NEOCOLONIALISM

Introduction

With the defeat of the Huk insurgency in the early fifties, the domination of the elite over Philippine society was unchallenged. The political system, though formally democratic, merely provided a means for contending elite factions to rotate in and out of office; the two major parties—Nacionalista and Liberal—were indistinguishable in terms of ideology; vote buying, fraud, and violence by the private armies of the elite were the key determinants of electoral success [see selection 6.1].

The living conditions of the vast majority of the population were miserable and getting worse. Real wages of skilled workers in Manila declined by a third from 1949 to 1972; sugarcane workers received less in real daily wages in 1971 than fifteen years earlier. In 1957, the bottom fifth of families were reported to receive 4.5 percent of total income; in 1971 it was down to 3.7 percent—and the reported figures likely understated the maldistribution [see selection 6.2]. Moreover, the half of the population that was female faced special problems [see selection 6.3].

If the interests of the great mass of Filipinos were suffering, the same could not be said for the interests of Washington. The two tremendous military facilities in the Philippines, Clark Air Base and Subic Naval Base, were used by the Pentagon not to defend the Philippines from foreign invasion but as springboards for U.S. intervention in Asia; in particular, the bases served as the key logistical hub for the United States war effort in Vietnam [see selection 6.4].

With the advantage of "parity" [see chapter 4], U.S. capital accounted for some 80% of the foreign-owned equity in the Philippines in 1970, a higher fraction than when the Philippines was a formal U.S. colony. U.S. investment is difficult to quantify given the complex accounting issues, but was estimated to have had a market value in 1972 of about two billion dollars [see selection 6.5].

The United States protected its military and economic privileges in the Philippines by various means. The U.S. provided Manila with military aid, without any pretense that the weaponry was directed against external foes [see selection 6.6]. Washington also provided Manila with military advisers, the Joint U.S. Military Advisory Group (JUSMAG), and trained Philippine military and police officers. And the Central Intelligence Agency continued a wide array of covert activities [see selection 6.7].

There were, however, growing challenges to the status quo. A few members of the elite were genuine nationalists and they took issue with Philippine subservience to the United States [see selections 6.8 and 6.9]. On the campuses, a large-scale student movement developed, spurred on by opposition to Philippine participation in the U.S. war effort in Vietnam. And, with worsening living conditions, peasants and workers grew increasingly radical [see selection 6.10]. Mass demonstrations were frequent, with both the Philippine and U.S. governments being denounced by the protesters, and the police responding with violence. By 1972, the country was accurately described by one newspaper as a "seething volcano."

Selection 6.1: The Philippine Political System, U.S. Central Intelligence Agency

Editors' Introduction

The following description of the Philippine political system comes from a CIA National Intelligence Survey written in 1965 but declassified (with some deletions) only in 1980.

Source: CIA, *Philippines: General Survey,* National Intelligence Survey, NIS 99, July 1965 [sanitized copy released November 1980], pp. 48-54.

Political Dynamics

1. General

The political system in the Philippines has traditionally been dominated by a small, wealthy elite, consisting of large landholders and a few powerful industrial and commercial entrepreneurs, and their lawyers. Other elements of the population have, in comparison, few channels through which they can influence the workings or policy of government. Moreover, the traditional value system of Philippine society stresses the primacy of the kinship group over all institutions, including the state. As a result, kinship and personal connections are far more important than merit or legal niceties in political, social, and business relations; this has contributed to widespread acceptance of nepotism and corruption as the normal road to political and personal advancement. A corollary to the importance of personal relations is the widespread disrespect for the impersonal rule of law, a characteristic which was strengthened by the corrosive effects on Philippine society of the violence, hatred, and lawlessness prevalent during World War II and much of the immediate post-war period.

Notwithstanding these weaknesses, there is in the Philippines a broad and ingrained popular acceptance of the idea of democratic values and practices and constitutional restraints. The concept of a two-party system is firmly established, and there is relatively little support for extremism of either the far right or left. Furthermore, there is a trend toward new types of leadership and interest groups originating in the middle and lower classes. . . .

Although the Philippine economy is predominantly agricultural, opportunities for the average farmer are limited; as a result, political and economic power is concentrated in a few hands. About 50% of the farmers are estimated to be landless tenants, and the percentage is even greater in the so-called "rice bowl" of central Luzon. Landlords have long dominated rural community leadership. Although their influence has declined over the years, a hierarchical rural society continues to exist in most areas, in which the landlords' influence often extends over the local government, the courts, and the police.

New types of leadership, however, are also developing in the country-side. The community development program and the elected barrio council system, in particular, have led to an intensification in grass-roots interest and influence in politics and government, and to greater independence from the old hierarchy on the part of the average farmer.

In urban areas industrialization is also creating new interest groups that are affecting the balance of social and political forces. The demands of new industries and businesses for managerial and technical skills is encouraging the growth of an urban middle class, especially in Manila. The Philippine middle class is already larger than any other such class in Southeast Asia. Education of the poor and entry into business of members of the wealthy landed families further extend the middle class. Although urban labor is the largest special interest group created by industrialization, the trade union movement has been unable to organize effectively and has considerably less political influence than its size would seem to warrant.

Notwithstanding the rise of new leadership and interest groups, the machinery of government tends to be controlled by a political elite which is roughly identical with the economic elite. The average man—or *tao*—still has few channels of influence, since the groups that represent him are generally weak in organization, finances and influence. The major political parties (the Nacionalistas and Liberals), ideologically identical and led by the elite, are loose coalitions of politicians allied for the moment in pursuit of power and do not present the electorate with a clear choice in alternate programs. Electoral processes are often fraudulent, and the vote is frequently controlled by political machines.

In the Philippines the growth of democratic political institutions and practices is severely hampered by a traditional system of social values which regards the family and, beyond that, the extended kinship group, as the primary focus of an individual's loyalty. As a result, the typical Filipino does not approach political life in terms of principles, institutions, and organizations, but rather in terms of personal relationships which may yield benefits to himself or his family. Since the kinship groups of the Philippines are bilateral, with the relatives of the wife and mother being considered as close and important as those of the husband and father, the Filipino has a wide range of choice in selecting his close social and political associates.

This range is further extended by the system of ritual kinship known as *compadrazgo*, in which a nonkinsman becomes a *compadre* by acting as a godparent when a child is baptized or as a sponsor at a confirmation or wedding. The relationship between the *compadre* and the child's parents involves reciprocal obligations similar to those between true kinsmen. A business or political alliance between two families is frequently cemented by this device. The person with the greatest status in the pattern of true or ritualistic kinship is the one who has the ability, financial or otherwise, to tie large numbers of kinsmen to him through the creation of debts of gratitude.

With the growth of democracy in the Philippines, this system, which originated as a social custom, became entrenched in politics. Like allegiance to kinsmen, allegiance to political leaders became dependent largely upon debts of gratitude arising from the ability and willingness of a leader to confer benefits upon his followers. Democracy, however, added a new element; the followers could discharge their debts of gratitude with their votes, along with those of whatever *compadres*, friends, or tenants they might in turn be able to influence.

The strongly mercenary basis of Philippine politics, involving the exchange of votes for favors—as well as that aspect of public administration which involves the exchange of money for favors—may be compared to Tammany Hall operations in the United States a half century ago, the main difference being that the Philippine system is rooted not in the socio-economic aspirations of immigrants but in the family system of the Filipinos.

Despite the handicaps placed on the democratic system in the Philippines, it appears relatively firmly rooted. There is broad popular acceptance of democratic values and the constitutional system and little support for changes in a more authoritarian direction. The possibility remains, however, that this attitude could change in the absence of significant action by the Philippine Government toward fulfilling the desires of the ordinary citizen for economic progress and a higher standard of living. The concentration of power in the executive has been gradually lessening by the increasing independence of Congress and judiciary, and by growing grass-roots democracy in the barrios. The traditions of free political competition and a free press are strongly rooted, and the public school system continues to spread democratic ideals. Despite the gap between the upper and lower classes, there is increasing social mobility, and relations between the classes in most of the country are marked by benevolent paternalism, leaving limited scope for the bitter class-warfare brand of politics.

The firmly established two-party system is a strong asset. The similarity of the parties, while depriving the voter of clear choices between programs, nevertheless encourages moderation, readiness to compromise, and lack of dogmatism in the political elite. The parties, moreover, in the interest of securing votes, display some sensitivity to economic discontent and through Congress often aid local politicians with "pork barrel" appropriations. They have also enacted significant social and economic reform laws, although implementation of this legislation in most instances has been deficient.

The Philippine political system, furthermore, is evolving toward a government more responsive to popular will and in which there is increasingly wider participation by middle and even lower class elements. Mass communication media are reaching more and more of the electorate, and the keen interest of most Filipinos in politics is being broadened and becoming more sophisticated. In the face of increasing voter independence, the system of hierarchal and *compadre* loyalties is weakening, local political machines are finding it more difficult to deliver the votes, and the elite leadership is forced increasingly to go directly to the people with a program to justify its continuance in power.

The foregoing encouraging considerations must, however, be tempered by factors of a less hopeful nature. There are signs of a growing popular cynicism and disillusionment with both major parties and their leaders, and a feeling that the electorate is offered no real choice between discernable alternatives. Moreover, the economically underprivileged are beginning to realize that a better life than that of the past is possible and have demonstrated a desire to improve their lot. Widespread crime and internal insecurity are, in part, symptomatic of the lack of confidence in the existing governmental system.

2. Political parties

a. Party system—The political party system in the Philippines had its beginnings during the early part of the period of U.S. control. Of the few parties that were formed at this time, however, only one, the Nacionalista, gained significant nationwide strength, and during the Commonwealth period it dominated the political scene under the leadership of Manuel Quezon and Sergio Osmeña, President and Vice President, respectively, of the Commonwealth. In October 1944, when the Philippine Government-in-Exile returned to Philippine soil, it was headed by Osmeña, Quezon having died two months earlier. Osmeña's national leadership was soon challenged, however, by Manuel Roxas, Quezon's one-time protégé who in 1946 split the Nacionalista to found the Liberal Party, the second of the two major parties. Since then other parties have been formed, but have generally been short-lived and have not constituted a serious challenge to the two-party system.

As developed in the Philippines, the party system is determined in large measure by the formidable rewards and punishments which an incumbent President and his party can dispense. Under the highly centralized governmental system, the President has extensive powers to make or break the average politician or prominent citizen. This power, for example, fundamentally influences the political attitudes of economic interest groups. Whereas a U.S. industrialist can afford to remain a Republican while the Democrats are in power without endangering his competitive position in the business world, a Filipino planter or importer who supports the Liberals when the Nacionalistas are in power does so at considerable peril to his enterprise.

Structurally, the major Philippine political parties, like the major institutions of government, bear a much closer resemblance to those of the United States than they do to the parties of western European democracies. The four outstanding characteristics of the Philippine party system—the relative importance of local party organization, the fluidity of party membership, the similarity between the two major parties, and the lack of success of third-party ventures—are all found also in the United States. Owing to many indigenous factors, however, the Philippine parties are much more alike in ideology and in the socio-economic characteristics of their supporters as well as more fluid in membership than their U.S. counterparts. They are also more heavily dominated by government officials. . . .

Philippine political parties show marked variations in strength. Switching back and forth between the parties is common among all elements from voters to senators and even Presidents (two of the five post-World War II Presidents were elected immediately after deserting their parties) . . . . The electorate, in the words of a Filipino social scientist, is for the most part "one vast floating vote." This fluidity of party membership produces a bandwagon effect. A party that gains control of the government tends, for a time at least, to obtain substantial accretions of support from voters, interest groups, and politicians formerly affiliated with the opposing party.

Since the public favors the winning party, politicians must do the same. The expense of campaigning is high and, since a substantial share must be borne by the candidate himself and few possess great independent means, running for public office is a costly gamble. Only victory and its accompanying opportunities for additional income enable him to recoup his investment, and such opportunities are greater with the majority party than with the minority. Consequently, party switching on the part of politicians is a common occurrence.

Despite the fluidity of Philippine politics and the similarity of the Nacionalistas and the Liberals, third parties have never been successful. . . .

Since the major parties are without discernible ideological differences, the ordinary voter has little reason to develop a strong, lasting attachment to one party. There are no dues or obligations, and formal party membership as distinct from attachment to particular leaders has little meaning. What is really important to the life of Philippine political parties is not rank-and-file membership but the accession or defection of barrio leaders, mayors, governors, congressmen, and senators. The Philippine parties are thus merely combinations of politicians with their followers. They make no effort to recruit and to organize a mass membership upon which they could depend for their financial needs as well as for votes.

The concept of party membership, moreover, is nearly as meaningless to the politician as it is to the ordinary citizen. Under certain conditions, even running on a Liberal ticket does not cause a Nacionalista politician to lose his party affiliation. Through the "guest candidate" device Nacionalista senators have run on the Liberal senatorial slate, been elected, and resumed their seats as Nacionalistas. . . .

4. Elections

Elections in the Philippines constitute a more important part of the political process than in most other Asian countries. They have not yet become, however, an effective means of expressing public opinion on national issues, being at present little more than a way of choosing political leadership. Only a small percentage of the electorate attempts to correlate issues and candidates. . . .

Elections are held throughout the Philippines in odd-numbered years on the second Tuesday in November. All literate citizens over 21 years of age, subject to residence requirements and certain minor qualifications, are entitled to vote, assuming they are properly registered. . . . The literacy requirement has reduced the percentage of those voting to a figure below that of most democratic nations. In the 1961 presidential contest 6.5 million persons, about 23% of the population, voted out of a total registration of about 8.5 million.

Despite safeguards established by election laws and regulations, some fraudulent election practices are common. It is difficult to prevent a voter from registering in several places, and registration lists are padded to an unknown extent. Vote buying is customary, with as many as 33% of all votes cast in an average election being purchased for cash. Coercion of voters and terrorism against precinct inspection boards are also obstacles to free and orderly elections in some areas, notably Lanao and Cotabato Provinces in Mindanao and Cavite and Ilocos Sur in Luzon.

Selection 6.2: Inequality in Development, International Labour Office

Editors' Introduction

The following reading is from an extensive study of the Philippine economy by the International Labour Organisation (ILO). The research was undertaken for the ILO by a team headed by the respected developmental economist, Gustav Rains of Yale University. For some of the human dimensions of the economic data summarized here, see selection 6.10 below.

Source: International Labour Office, *Sharing in Development: A Programme of Employment, Equity and Growth for the Philippines*, Geneva: ILO: 1974, pp. 3-13.

. . . The over-all pattern of economic growth . . . over the past quarter of a century has, on the whole, been satisfactory. However, two kinds of problem have arisen, representing an increasing threat to the system's ability to remain on its present course. One is the fact that satisfactory growth rates have been accompanied by more and more unacceptable outcomes in terms of employment and income distribution. The second is the fact that even this over-all growth is being threatened by the constraints of a rural sector that is still performing inadequately. . . .

Whatever picture the open unemployment pictures may show, a striking aspect of postwar economic growth has been the economy's failure to provide enough productive jobs in the face of a rapid population increase. During the period 1948-60 population was growing at an average rate of over 3 per cent; and, for the decade of the 1960s, population growth was still marginally above 3 per cent. Much of the rural population still lives in poverty, and many of those who move to the cities must seek meager earnings in commerce and service activities that are not directly related to the modern sector of the economy.

Since 1960 the labour force has on average grown by 2.6 per cent per year, and employment in agriculture by about 1 per cent. But instead of this sectoral shift reflecting the increasing labour demands of dynamic industrial expansion, we find employment in manufacturing growing at less than the average for the whole labour force. During the 1960s the manufacturing sector accounted for only some 12 per cent of total employment. Moreover, its contribution slightly declined during the decade. In contrast, the commerce and service sectors of the economy increased their share of employment, from 20 per cent to 30 per cent, during the same period. The quite rapid increase in output per urban industrial worker, in response to rising capital/labour ratios and labour-saving technological change, was purchased at the expense of a declining rate of labour absorption. . . .

. . . Measures of unemployment and under-employment derived from standard labour-force concepts are therefore only one relatively minor aspect of the problem we are concerned with. The difficulties attending any estimation of total unemployment based on a low income concept are equally well known. The mission's rough "guesstimate" places total unemployment (i.e. open unemployment plus an inadequate income measure of under-employment) in the vicinity of 25 per cent.

Data on the level and trend of the earnings that represent the reward for labour services, generated either through paid employment or through self-employment, are perhaps more useful and reliable. Accordingly, an economy such as that of the Philippines may show a reasonable growth rate in real GNP per head but still be failing to meet the employment challenge set for it by the growth of its labour force, because the benefits from this growth are reflected more in the growth of profits and returns to land ownership than in increases in real earnings among the working population. The groups that are especially vulnerable in such a situation are those least sheltered from the downward pressure on wages resulting from the over-all labour-surplus condition. These may be among the unskilled but they may also be among previously middle income groups who are no longer able to defend their earning differentials. Our calculations . . . show that the property share of income appears to have grown appreciably, largely because of a very large increase in undistributed corporate profits. (The share of income from self-employment, on the other hand, fell considerably.)

Just as disturbing in this context is the variety of evidence that the distribution of income in the Philippines, which was already highly unequal, has become increasingly so during the past two decades. [The table] clearly shows that the share of the lowest 20 per cent of families has declined significantly and that this decrease in the share of the poorest households has been particularly pronounced among rural families. It can be seen that the share of the bottom rural 60 per cent (which includes most of the really poor people in the Philippines) declined from 32.8 per cent of the total in 1956 to only 27.2 per cent by 1971.

Data for the urban income distribution are more difficult to interpret because, although they show some improvement since 1956, there is good reason to suspect that under-reporting was higher in 1971 than before. For instance, for the top 10 per cent of urban families, the data imply a fall of almost one-third in real incomes from 1965 to 1971, which surely is implausible.

On balance, we can safely refer to an increasing polarisation of rural incomes and to a fairly constant urban income distribution pattern. . . .

The information available on earnings shows a generalized fall in real urban earnings for most occupational groups during the 1960s. Thus the Central Bank index of common laborers' wages indicates an 8 per cent fall in real terms from 1960 to 1971. Other sources such as the Wage and Position Classification Office's surveys of unskilled workers and average payrolls from the *Annual survey of manufacturers* of the Bureau of the Census and Statistics indicate similar declines in real wages, especially in the years after 1969 when consumer price rises accelerated. The Central Bank statistics show that semi-skilled and skilled earnings fell even more than unskilled earnings and that real earnings in the public sector fell across the board during the 1960s. Probably it was only in the large private firms that clerical and professional earnings held their own.

Changes in agricultural earnings are more problematical. The Bureau's *Family income and expenditures survey* for 1971 found that real earnings of households headed by farm laborers were over 20 per cent higher than in 1965. As a result of this and of the stagnation of urban real earnings the ratio of average incomes of urban manual labour households to agricultural labour households fell from 171:100 to 132:100. Furthermore, the average gap between urban and rural household incomes fell from 2.5 over the period 1956-65 to 2.1 in 1971 [see table]. This closing of the sectoral income gap was caused partly by incomes in non-agricultural rural activities (services, craftsmen and transport workers) moving up to the urban levels and partly by changes in the internal terms of trade, with agricultural products becoming relatively more expensive.

Nevertheless, despite a narrowing *average* gap between urban and rural incomes, the worsening rural income distribution has led to a widening of the differential at the lower income levels. In 1961 incomes among the lowest 80

Indicators of income distribution: total, rural and urban, 1956, 1961, 1965 and 1971

Indicator	1956 Total	Rural	Urban	1961 Total	Rural	Urban	1965 Total	Rural	Urban	1971 Total	Rural	Urban
Quintile of families	(percentage of total family income)											
Lowest 20 per cent	4.5	7.0	4.5	4.2	5.9	3.8	3.5	5.0	3.8	3.8	4.4	4.6
Second 20 per cent	8.1	11.1	8.0	7.9	11.8	7.5	8.0	9.5	8.0	8.1	8.9	9.4
Third 20 per cent	12.4	14.7	12.2	12.1	13.5	12.5	12.8	15.3	12.0	13.2	13.9	13.4
Fourth 20 per cent	19.8	21.1	20.0	19.3	21.9	19.5	20.2	23.0	18.7	21.1	21.8	21.9
Top 20 per cent	55.1	46.1	55.3	56.4	46.9	57.1	55.4	47.2	57.5	53.9	51.0	50.7
Top 10 per cent	39.4	30.1	39.6	41.0	31.1	40.9	40.0	30.0	41.7	36.9	34.4	33.4
Top 5 per cent	27.7	*	*	29.0	*	*	28.7	*	*	24.3	22.6	22.6
Index of quintile inequality	0.44	0.34	0.44	0.46	0.36	0.46	0.45	0.38	0.47	0.40	0.41	0.41
Gini coefficient	0.48	0.38	0.49	0.50	0.40	0.52	0.51	0.42	0.53	0.49	0.46	0.45

* not available
Mission calculations. Source of basic data: Bureau of the Census and Statistics: **Family income and expenditures surveys.**

per cent of rural families were roughly equal in magnitude to the average income among the poorest 40 per cent of families in the urban areas. By 1971, incomes of the poorest 80 per cent of rural families had risen about 10 per cent, while incomes of the poorest urban 40 per cent had increased considerably more, by at least 25 per cent. . . .

Clearly, the particular growth path chosen in the past has tended to be adverse to the interests of the average worker, and still more so to that of the below-average worker. A developmental process that nurtures and sustains trends in the structure of earnings that result in steadily increasing inequality cannot expect to continue for very long, or, at any rate, to continue without profound and painful political change.

Selection 6.3: The Status of Women in the Philippines, Linda K. Richter

Editors' Introduction

In the following selection, written especially for this volume, political scientist Linda K. Richter of Kansas State University discusses the situation of women in the Philippines. She indicates that in some respects Filipinas have been more successful than their sisters in the United States, but that sexism is institutionalized in many ways and that women in the Philippines have been second-class citizens. For more specific information on the situation of women, see selection 7.5 on prostitution, 8.4 on women and transnational corporations, and 9.7 on women's struggles.

The Filipina stands out among Asian women and, in many respects, among women anywhere in the world. Her uncharacteristic spheres of control and her high visibility have provoked many observers to contend that she is in no need of "women's liberation."

She is not veiled, denied access to education because of her gender, or shunted to a narrow range of career opportunities. Women do so well in the professions that there are both formal and informal caps on their admittance to the universities, law schools, and medical schools.

In the business world, one finds female corporate leaders. Because women are stereotyped as more honest and hard-working than men, they often are the financial officers of organizations big and small. However, very seldom are they in the top status positions of president or vice-president.

Girls and women are encouraged to take an active role in the family's economic advancement. This leads to entrepreneurship at all economic levels from the poor woman selling fried bananas on the street, the female owner working in her tiny sari-sari (general) store, or the secretary selling umbrellas as a sideline. Among the upper classes it can lead to a Cory Aquino managing her family's vast economic interests while her husband languished in jail or to the highly successful careers of many women in both economic and political life.

Because politics is often an entree to economic opportunity in the Philippines, many women and men have been politically ambitious for economic as well as political goals. Women have served as governors, cabinet ministers, and members of the Congress and National Assembly, though men still fill more than 90 percent of these positions.

Evaluating the political role of women over time is complicated because of the many changes in the system of government. During the Marcos era, 1965-1986, the political system was revised numerous times to meet the personal political needs of the President. The functions of certain offices, types of elections, constituency size, and eligibility requirements were all changed several times. And, of course, being a member of the opposition severely reduced one's chances for holding office during the martial law years. Therefore, Table 1 below, which presents available data on women in politics at various points in time, cannot be used for exact comparisons among time periods. In general, however, it shows that women's political participation in the Philippines has been low, roughly equivalent to the level in Western Europe.

Despite the fact that women are well represented in the prestigious University of the Philippines Law School and the Dean of the school is a woman, Irene Cortes, within most of the Philippine judiciary women are still a distinct minority. This is illustrated in Table 2.

The pattern then is for women to be better represented in the small, specialized juvenile courts rather than in the more prestigious, better paid posts in the judiciary. Still, even these numbers seem to challenge the stereotype of Asian women as docile, downtrodden and removed from political and commercial life. Some argue that the Filipina has had a strong and visible role in Philippine society because of the pre-colonial Malay culture which allowed women status and power more nearly commensurate to that of men. If that is true—and long ago "golden ages" tend to be romanticized—then 300 years of Spanish feudalism and 80-plus years of American-induced capitalism have significantly diluted the influence.

It would be misleading, however, only to concentrate on the visibility and influence of a few women or to be diverted by the fact that Philippine women have some advantages denied women in other nations, for women in the Philippines face a daunting struggle that often goes unrecognized in too facile comparisons with the West or the rest of Asia.

The Filipina woman shares with other women the double bind of total responsibility for domestic tasks and child care as well as the need to work outside the home. Poverty and huge families, coupled with a desperate struggle for education, have only accelerated the dominant trend of rural and urban women being forced into the badly paid labor force. Their workload and their general health and living conditions crush both the spirit and the body.

That some women rose to prominence in education, the professions, and

Table 1
Local and Provincial Government Offices

Date	Number of Women	Number of Positions	Percent Female
1971:			
Mayor	44	1,488	2.96
Vice-Mayor	61	1,430	4.26
Councilor	662	11,110	5.95
1978:			
Assembly person	10	180	5.56
Sectoral Rep's			
Youth	1	6	16.67
Industrial	1	4	25.00
July 1979:			
Provincial Govt.	6	72	8.33
City Mayor	3	61	4.91
Municipal Mayor	52	1,474	3.53
Barangay Captain	1,550	39,768	3.90
January 1980:			
Governor	5	72	6.94
Vice-Governor	5	72	6.94
Sanguniang			
Panlalawigan	37	436	8.49
Mayor	80	1,309	6.11
Vice-Mayor	78	1,309	5.96
Sanguniang Bayan	868	9,988	8.69

business occurred generally not because of government policy but because of their upper class lifestyle. They have hired other women to do "their" domestic work or other females in the extended family have supplied the necessary labor. There has been no redefinition of sex roles in the family. In a study I did recently of Philippine women in higher education administration—women who were largely a product of socialization and education during the pre-1972 era—98 percent had domestic help and 50 percent lived in extended families. Without such institutional props, the number of female professionals would plummet.

Politically, women were (and are) at the mercy of government policy largely fashioned in response to the preeminent position of the Catholic Church. Divorce is illegal and abortion is outlawed. (Birth control is legal, but the Church only approves the rhythm method.) Thus, one finds widespread infidelity, but no escape from loveless marriages. There are numerous and

Table 2
Justices of Philippine Courts

	Total Number		Number of Females		Percent Female	
	1975	1980	1975	1980	1975	1980
Supreme Court	11	11	1	1	9%	9%
Court of Appeals	34	29	2	3	6%	10%
Court of First Instance	—	304	—	19	—	6%
Juvenile Court and Domestic Relations	8	10	7	7	88%	70%
Court of Agrarian Relations	—	59	—	6	—	10%
Municipal Courts	948	796	48	38	5%	5%

Source: National Census and Statistics Office

uncontrolled pregnancies—the Philippines has one of the world's highest birthrates at 2.7 births per hundred women of child-bearing age per year—and widespread malnutrition, anemia, and disease exist among infants and their mothers. Women in government service and some other sectors do have paid maternity leave, but most women remain uncovered by such policies yet are vulnerable to state dictates about their private lives.

Muslim women are prohibited from getting abortions, but they can be divorced, though typically at the instigation of their husbands. To initiate a divorce, Muslim women must have the help of their male "guardian," usually their father or brother. Their husbands are also entitled to have up to four wives, but this is rare. Muslim Filipinas also have had much less access to education than their Christian counterparts, though this has changed in recent years with the advent of Arabic language primary schools and some colleges funded by Middle Eastern groups.

Is it any wonder, then, that though the society encourages marriage and procreation, many career-oriented women choose not to marry. In my sample of female deans, chairpersons, research directors, and university presidents, 25 percent were single.

While it is true that women control the purse strings in the family, doling out weekly allowances to their spouses, fewer than 30 percent of all families are above the very low poverty line. Thus, in most homes the purse is empty.

Crushing poverty has forced many women into prostitution to support their families. Historically, the bulk of the prostitution has been concentrated around the U.S. military bases: Clark Air Force Base and Subic Bay Naval Base. In recent years between eight and twelve thousand women were so employed. A more sinister and contemporary problem is tourism prostitution, which employs more than 100,000 in Manila alone [see selection 7.5].

Despite the fact that Filipinas excel in academic, commercial, and political life when given the opportunity, for many it is their attractiveness that determines their chances of success. In addition to the tawdrier forms of body-selling, like prostitution, beauty contests are everywhere. Unlike in the United States, there is rarely even a pretense of evaluating talent: being single, young, and sexy is all that counts. And count it does. For many middle and working class young women, such contests are rare chances for glamour and economic gain or access to those with power or money. Even Imelda Marcos, "the Rose of Tacloban," found a beauty contest to be her opportunity to transcend her once modest lifestyle and capture the attention of young politicians.

Women suffer not only from poverty but from outright economic and political discrimination. Those working for pay earn less than 60 percent of what men receive. Part of the disparity in pay reflects the fact that most women are concentrated in female-dominated occupations like teaching, nursing, secretarial work, and domestic help. (Thirty percent of all women working full-time for wages or salaries are employed as household helpers.) As in the rest of the world, jobs considered "women's work" are de-valued and paid far less than are men's jobs of comparable value, effort, and skill.

The statistical and legal data suggest that Philippine women have unusual opportunities for access to careers, but once in them they endure traditional pay disparities. For example, in 1980 in the Philippines 22 percent of the workers in the highest paying occupational sector, managerial and administrative work, were women (in contrast to 24 percent for the United States and 5.7 percent for Japan). Yet these women were clustered in the lowest paying positions of the managerial and administrative work sector (LouEllen Crawford and Nancy Sidener, "Women's Formal Education and Economic Growth: The Case of the Philippines," unpublished paper, 1984). Among professional and technical workers, men made an average of P2634 monthly compared with women who made P1522. Administrators, executives, and managers averaged P3839 for men and P2201 for women (National Census and Statistical Office, 2nd Quarter 1978). Part of the problem is also a reflection of the sexist assumptions written into the tax law. A married woman who is salaried is taxed more heavily than a man because her wages are considered supplementary.

Discrimination is also institutionalized in the Civil Code which considers women in the same category as the retarded and mentally deranged. Husbands legally control and administer the entire family's property. The husband also has a right to object to the wife's job if he can support the family and to be involved in any court suit affecting his wife. The wife has no such parallel rights. Other provisions of the Civil Code discriminate against women in terms of mixed marriages, freedom to choose one's residence, parental authority, legal separation, and widowhood.

Thus, while they may not have an agenda for change identical to their sisters in other nations, Filipinas like women everywhere face discrimination, political underrepresentation, economic disadvantage, treatment as sex objects, and the double pressures of domestic responsibilities and the necessity of outside employment.

Selection 6.4: Uses of the U.S. Military Bases in the Philippines

U.S. Foreign Interventions from its Military Bases
in the Philippines, 1900-1975

1900:	Philippines serves as staging area for U.S. military contingents sent to China to crush the Boxer Rebellion.
1918-1920:	Philippines serves as base for U.S. intervention in Siberia during the Russian civil war.
1927:	Philippines serves as base for protecting the "International Settlement" in Shanghai, China.
1950-1953:	Clark Air Base and Subic Naval Base play key logistical role in support of U.S. forces in the Korean war.
1954:	Plan drawn up to use bombers based at Clark Air Base to drop 3 tactical nuclear weapons on Viet Minh positions at Dienbienphu to aid France's colonial war. Plan not carried out.
1958:	Philippine bases used for clandestine supply drops to U.S.-backed right-wing rebels in Indonesia.
1958:	U.S. naval forces from Subic deployed to the Quemoy-Matsu area of China during crisis over the "off-shore islands."
1962:	Air Force units from Clark deployed to Thailand as show of force to back U.S.-allied rightists in neighboring Laos.
1965-1975:	Bases in Philippines play crucial logistical role during U.S. intervention in Vietnam, Laos, and Cambodia.
1971:	Naval force from Subic deployed to Bay of Bengal to support Washington's "tilt toward Pakistan" policy during the India-Pakistan-Bangladesh war.
1975:	Subic serves as staging area for U.S. military actions against Kampuchea during "Mayaguez" incident.

Source: William J. Pomeroy, "United States Military Bases in the Philippines," *Eastern World* vol. 29, no. 2, Feb. 1965, p. 7 (1900-1927); Roger Hilsman, *To Move A Nation* (Garden City, NJ: Doubleday, 1967), p. 369 (1958, Indonesia); Fred Greene, *United States Policy and the Security of Asia* (New York: McGraw Hill, 1968), p. 148 (1958, Quemoy-Matsu); Walden Bello, "Springboards for Intervention, Instruments for Nuclear War," *Southeast Asia Chronicle* no. 89, April 1983, p. 7 (all others).

Selection 6.5: U.S. Investment in the Philippines, Corporate Information Center

Editors' Introduction

The tables below are taken from a report prepared by the Corporate Information Center (now the Interfaith Center for Corporate Responsibility) of the National Council of Churches. The Center has investigated the social impact of corporations for church investors and others concerned about corporate social responsibility.

Tables 1 and 2 show that in 1971 U.S.-owned firms accounted for a substantial share of the sales, income, assets, and equity of the largest Philippine corporations, particularly in the manufacturing sector. Forty-seven of the top 200 Philippine corporations ranked by sales were U.S.-porations ranked by sales were U.S.-

owned. If one looks down the list of these 47 corporations (Table 3), one sees many of the largest U.S.-based multinationals: among them, the oil giants, Procter & Gamble, Del Monte, and Union Carbide.

Source: Corporate Information Center, "The Republic of the Philippines: American Corporations, Martial Law, and Underdevelopment," *Corporate Examiner*, Sept. 1973, pp. 3B, 3D. For the complete study, see Corporate Information Center, National Council of Churches of Christ in the USA, "The Philippines: American Corporations, Martial Law, and Underdevelopment," *IDOC*, International/North American Edition, No. 57, November 1973.

Table 1
Percentage of sales, income, assets and equity controlled by the 47 U.S. corporations ranked in the top 200 Philippine corporations
(Pesos in thousands—1971 data)

Group	Sales	Income	Assets	Equity
Top 200 corporations	19,588,292	1,249,831	20,353,433	8,488,785
47 U.S. corporations	5,755,228	452,486	5,702,907	2,581,102
U.S. firms' percentage of top 200 total	29.4%	36.2%	28.0%	30.4%

Source: **Business Day's 1000 Top Philippine Corporations,** Quezon City, Philippines, Enterprise Publications, Inc., 1971.

Table 2
Percentage of sales, income, assets and equity controlled by 35 U.S. manufacturing corporations ranked in the top 110 Philippine manufacturing corporations
(Pesos in thousands—1971 data)

Group	Sales	Income	Assets	Equity
110 Philippine corporations	10,723,372	592,373	10,305,830	4,319,764
35 U.S. corporations	3,605,047	278,753	3,552,295	1,596,352
U.S. firms' percentage of top 110 total	33.6%	47.1%	34.5%	37.0%

Table 3
47 largest U.S. corporations in the Philippines ranked by sales position among the top 200 corporations in the Philippines for 1971

Sales Rank	Name of Parent Corporation
3	Caltex Petroleum Corp.
4	A. Soriano Y Cia. (Atlas Consolidated)
5	Exxon Corp.
9	Mobil Oil Corp.
10	Exxon/Mobil
12	Granexport Corp.
17	Procter & Gamble Co.
18	Baker Commodities
31	Pepsico, Inc.
32	USI Philippines Inc.
33	Atlantic, Gulf & Pacific
37	Del Monte Corp.
38	General Milk Co.
45	Ford Motor Co.
46	Getty Oil Co.
49	International Harvester
52	Union Carbide Corp.
58	Goodyear Tire & Rubber
61	B.F. Goodrich Corp.
65	Honolulu Iron Works
67	A. Soriano Y Cia. (Bislig Bay Lumber Inc.)
69	Colgate-Palmolive Co.
70	Castle and Cooke, Inc.
73	Consolidated Dairy Products Co.
77	Firestone Tire & Rubber
78	A. Soriano Y. Cia. (Benguet Consolidated)

Table 3 (continued)
47 largest U.S. corporations in the
Philippines ranked by sales position among
the top 200 corporations in the Philippines for 1971

79	Theo. Davies Co.
85	CPC International, Inc.
90	Wilbur Ellis Co., Ltd.
107	Pillsbury Corp.
113	Georgia Pacific Corp.
118	Singer Corp.
123	Reynolds International
136	Philippine Rock Products Inc.
141	General Foods Corp.
152	Muller & Phipps (New York)
154	IBM Corp.
157	Warner Barnes & Co.
159	Weyerhaeuser, Inc.
170	Benguet Consolidated
171	Mead Johnson & Co.
174	Kimberly-Clark Corp.
175	American Wire & Cable Co., Inc.
178	Phelps-Dodge Corp.
186	Scott Paper Co.
188	Eastman Kodak Corp.
197	Hawaiian-Philippine Co.

Source: **Business Day's 1000 Top Philippine Corporations**, Quezon City, Philippines, Enterprise Publications, Inc., 1971; and "The Biggest American Companies in the Philippines," **Manila Chronicle**, June 18, 1971.

Selection 6.6: U.S. Commitments to the Philippines, Symington Committee Hearings

Editors' Introduction

In 1969, a U.S. Congressional subcommittee held hearings to examine the foreign commitments of the United States. Senate liberals worried about being drawn into another war like the one then raging in Vietnam, but they were concerned as well that U.S. allies were not doing enough to support that war. In the sessions on the Philippines, the subcommittee found that Philippine participation in the war effort (the dispatching of a civic action unit to Vietnam) had been secured by U.S. agreement to pay for the unit and by promises to supply additional military aid to Philippine President Ferdinand Marcos. In addition, Washington gave the Philippine government further payments, the precise destination of which—U.S. officials asserted—could not be determined. These revelations helped to fuel the protest movement in the Philippines.

Aside from the Vietnam question, the hearings provided more general illumination on the purposes of U.S. military aid to the Philippines. The following excerpts from the hearing transcript involve Sen. Stuart Symington of Missouri, the subcommittee chair; Sen. J. William Fulbright of Arkansas; Rear Admiral Draper L. Kauffman, commander of U.S. naval forces in the Philippines; Lt. Gen. Francis C. Gideon, commander of the 13th Air Force at Clark Air Base; James M. Wilson, Jr., deputy chief of mission at the U.S. Embassy in Manila; and Lt. Gen. Robert H. Warren, Deputy Assistant Secretary of Defense for Military Assistance and Sales. The document included in the transcript was submitted for the record by Col. Ernest W. Pate, commander of the 6th Air Division at Clark Air Base.

Source: U.S. Senate, Committee on Foreign Relations, Subcommittee on United States Security Agreements and Commitments Abroad, *United States Security Agreements and Commitments Abroad: The Republic of the Philippines,* Hearings, September-October 1969, pp. 60-61, 67-68, 161-62, 244-45.

SENATOR SYMINGTON. You said in your statement, Admiral, that it was agreed the chief problem was—I will read what you said—"The Board considers the principal threat to the Philippines to be Communist China with possible assistance from internal dissident groups."

What is the capacity from the military standpoint of the Red Chinese today in the Pacific to menace the Philippines from a military standpoint since this is a military board.

ADMIRAL KAUFFMAN. I would say at the moment, sir, very small.

SENATOR SYMINGTON. General, what would you say?

GENERAL GIDEON. Very small, very small.

SENATOR SYMINGTON. But you say it is the principal threat.

ADMIRAL KAUFFMAN. Of the threats that exist, I would say it is the principal threat; yes, sir.

SENATOR SYMINGTON. What you two are actually saying, militarily speaking, is there is no threat to the Philippines, are you not?

ADMIRAL KAUFFMAN. If, by the word "threat"—

SENATOR SYMINGTON. I am only using your word, not my word.

ADMIRAL KAUFFMAN. I think I was using it as a longer term implication perhaps, sir, than perhaps just right now.

SENATOR SYMINGTON. What do you mean exactly?

ADMIRAL KAUFFMAN. Well, I would say when the Chinese Communists have perfected the use of a nuclear weapon that the threat would increase.

SENATOR SYMINGTON. I do not want to labor it, but you have a fine air force in Formosa which the American taxpayer helped pay for. You have the U.S. Air Force in Okinawa. You have our air force in the Philippines, and you also have the 7th Fleet. So when you say that the principal threat to the Philippines is Communist China, without getting too syllogistic about it, what you are actually saying is that today there is no threat to the Philippines except an internal threat. Is that not a fair extrapolation?

ADMIRAL KAUFFMAN. Yes, sir, using the word "today."

SENATOR SYMINGTON. Thank you. . . .

SENATOR SYMINGTON. I think that's a very good answer. Let me put it like this and let us be frank about it. Under the circumstances, you heard Mr. Wilson's testimony, the truth of the matter is that the principal threat to the Government of the Philippines comes from the Filipinos who do not agree with the Government in the Philippines: is that not a fair statement?

ADMIRAL KAUFFMAN. I am loath to give a positive yes on that, sir, because it implies that I am seriously worried about the internal threat, and I am not. . . .

SENATOR FULBRIGHT. Maybe that is the point. We are not really there to protect the Philippines. We are there to serve our own purposes, to maintain a base for what we believe to be our forward protection against China or anybody else. That is our purpose.

ADMIRAL KAUFFMAN. Oh, yes, sir.

SENATOR FULBRIGHT. This rigamarole about protecting the Philippines is window dressing: is it not?

ADMIRAL KAUFFMAN. No, sir; I do not think it is window dressing. I think it is a mutual advantage or else we would probably have to pay rent, something like that, if there were no advantage to them.

I think they believe that it to be in their advantage from their own defense point of view, but I believe that we are there—and I am certainly speaking beyond my competence now—I believe we are there because these are very fine bases for the United States.

SENATOR FULBRIGHT. For our own purposes.

ADMIRAL KAUFFMAN. Yes, sir.

SENATOR FULBRIGHT. Well, to the extent that we believe there is a threat from China, I suppose that is justification.

MR. WILSON. May I add perhaps one word, Senator, to what Admiral Kauffman was saying. I think that there is no doubt whatsoever that [deleted] we [deleted] maintain those bases there to support what we consider to be our own interests.

One of those interests is the defense of the independence of the Philippines. If this were not so we would probably never have entered into a mutual defense treaty with them.

From the Filipino standpoint, I think those who have looked at this consider that having those bases there is a means of making it possible for the United States to operate in that part of the world and this is also in the Philippines interest. Indeed, President Marcos has said this also on several occasions, and so have a number of other leaders.

SENATOR FULBRIGHT. It is in the interest of President Marcos. But is it not inevitable that, because of our presence there, and with this purpose, we would always use our influence for the preservation of the status quo? We will always resist any serious change in political and social structure of the Philippine Government, which is very likely to be, in the long run, a detriment to the people of the Philippines.

This has been alleged and I think with much truth in Latin America, where we have the same policy. Wherever we have any kind of interest, why, we support the existing political and social structure. This has led time after time to revolt against it, as in Peru, and an alienation from the United States. I do not know how you get around this dilemma.

If you are there and you pledge to support the President of the Philippines, and suppose he were the most corrupt, along with his government and his party that you can imagine, and yet we really, by the nature of the situation, are committed to support him. We are committed to the stability of his government. We regard everything that threatens him as a threat to the security of the Philippines because we have to do business with him.

I am not saying that I know an answer or an alternative, as long as you feel we have to be there. I think it is a consequence of our presence there. We will always be a representative of a status quo, always in the position of preventing any change which, in effect, probably would mean improvement, when the present situation is not satisfactory, which it is not in most of these cases.

MR. WILSON. [Deleted.]

SENATOR FULBRIGHT. It is the same thing in Latin America. We run into it time and again where we are always aligned with the old crowd, in many cases the feudal crowd, which resists any change in the basic political and social structure of those countries, which are highly unsatisfactory to 90 percent of the people. . . .

Counterinsurgency

QUESTION NO. 5. Describe in detail, circumstances and contribution made by U.S. agencies to the Anti-Huk effort.

The following contributions were made by Clark Air Base authorities:

> a. In December 1967, a Joint State-Defense message authorized Clark Air Base to lend to the Philippine Constabulary two hundred M-16 rifles and 90,000 rounds of ammunition. This was to be done to assist in the on-going campaign against the Huk insurgents. The weapons were loaned from Air Force stocks currently at Clark Air

Base. It was specified that the rifles should be the newest in stock and in good condition. The necessary arrangements were made to provide 200 TCTO kits (Spring Guide Assembly Buffer) and the technical assistance to the PCs to perform modification. A directive to provide these rifles said that it was intended that the loan of rifles would be for an indefinite time and that they would be replaced when new rifles, purchased from MAP appropriated funds, were available from production.

b. In the Fall of 1968, Commanding General of the Philippine Constabulary made a request for 100 helmets and bulletproof vests to equip his PCs who were involved in searching for Huks in dense growth areas. The Base was able to deliver 100 helmets to the PC Hq at Camp Crame. Also in the Fall of 1968, the PCs requested some aerial photography of specific areas in the Zambales mountains. Three C-17 flights were dispatched from Clark Air Base and handheld cameras were used to take the photographs, which were turned over to the PCs.

c. Although the next items were not necessarily in direct support of the Anti-Huk effort, they were provided to the PCs in Oct of 1968. Preparation for the 4 Oct demonstration at the Clark Air Base Main Gate, the PCs were loaned 100 gas masks, 50 tear gas grenades and some illumination flares. The gas masks were later returned to Clark Air Base authorities.

d. The Philippine Constabulary requested helicopter support to aid in a raid of the Huks in the Bataan Province which took place on 10 Jan 1969. Clark Air Base provided one H-19 and crew at 0600 hours to furnish transportaion and air to ground communications for General Raval and General Zerrudo in connection with this encounter. The operation terminated at 0805 hours and the crew returned to Clark. It was reported in the newspapers that several Huks were killed in the raid.

e. On 16 Jan 1969, Hq 13th Air Force forwarded to PACAF a request from General Yan, Chief of Staff, Armed Forces of the Philippines, to perform some aerial photography coverage of some areas adjacent to the Clark Air Base reservation. The Philippine Constabulary required the coverage so that they could conduct raids in those areas. It had been reported that Huks were operating a Stalinist school in one of the areas to provide Communist Ideological Training to recruits. PACAF reconnaissance aircraft (two RF-4Cs from Kadena) flew approximately six sorties in covering these areas.

f. In the spring of 1969, General Zerrudo, 1st PC Zone asked for ammunition and tear gas to be used against Huks who were hidden in cane fields. Some 2000 rounds of .45 calibre ammunition and 24 tear gas grenades were given to the PCs. It was reported that this netted several Huks killed.

g. In May 1969, base guards at the PACAF Jungle Survival School Command Post, reported a firefight on the Clark Air Base reservation two miles to the west of Mount Dorst. Upon receiving this news, the Base Commander requested PC assistance and then provided transportation and a guide to the area of the firefight. Reconnaissance by the PC troops uncovered evidence of intruders but did not make contact with any Filipinos.

h. [Deleted.]

i. In Sep 1969, Major Gatan, requested C-Rations, .30 calibre ammunition and M-16 ammunition clips. Recently he had discovered a Stalinist School in a tunnel in the Tarlac area and suspected that a much larger tunnel operation was nearby. He wanted this equipment so that he could dispatch small three-man patrols to watch the activity in certain isolated areas for several days at a time. The Base was able to provide him with eight cases of C-Rations and no ammunition. . . .

SENATOR SYMINGTON. Yesterday we had testimony that the external threat to the Philippines was very little. Today we have testimony that the United States support of counterinsurgency is minimum. What, therefore, is the real purpose of this military assistance? Doesn't it come down to a *quid pro quo* for the bases and a means of contributing to the Filipino Government. There are figures from a House Committee that there are three and a half billion people in the world, and all but thirty-six million have received American aid. We are doing our best.

The question is how long can heavily taxed America take it? Isn't this really a means of keeping the Government satisfied? They know what the other countries are getting, and want their share also.

GENERAL WARREN. In my opinion, to a degree, yes, sir. But it is also to help the Filipino forces to physically protect U.S. Forces in the Philippines.

SENATOR SYMINGTON. From whom?

GENERAL WARREN. Internally, sir; to maintain internal security and stability and, thereby, make our own activities over there more secure.

SENATOR SYMINGTON. In other words, we are paying the Philippine Government to protect us from the Philippine people who do not agree with the policies of the Government or do not like Americans.

GENERAL WARREN. To a degree, yes, sir.

Selection 6.7: The CIA in the Philippines, James Burkholder Smith

Editors' Introduction

James Burkholder Smith served for 22 years as a covert action specialist in the clandestine services of the Central Intelligence Agency. Though disgruntled with the CIA when he retired, he nevertheless did not agree with former agents like Philip Agee who revealed names of CIA operatives; to Smith, Agee's action was a "dreadful betrayal." This continued loyalty to the CIA gives special credibility to Smith's memoirs, three extracts of which follow. The first adds to the account of the CIA role in the 1953 Philippine election described in selection 5.2. The second tells of CIA activities in Asia using Filipino operatives. And the third recounts covert involvement in the election of 1957, when, after Magsaysay's death, the CIA made an effort to assure the

defeat of Senator Claro M. Recto, a Philippine nationalist [on Recto, see next selection]. In its campaign against Recto the CIA played "dirty tricks," one of which is described here. Before this, in 1954, the CIA chief in Manila had discussed with the U.S. ambassador there a plan to assassinate Recto. Ultimately the scheme was rejected, on pragmatic rather than moral grounds, and the vial of poison that was to have been used was tossed into Manila Bay. (See Stephen Rosskamm Shalom, *The United States and the Philippines: A Study of Neocolonialism* [Philadelphia: ISHI, 1981], pp. 103-4.)

Source: James Burkholder Smith, *Portrait of a Cold Warrior*, New York: G. P. Putnam's Sons, 1976, pp. 109-10, 250-55, 279-80.

I learned about another maneuver of the Magsaysay men by accident—the way they split the Liberal Party. The day I moved into my house in Manila in 1958, my landlady appeared with a distinguished looking man. She introduced him as Senator Fernando Lopez, former president of the senate. I, of course, knew something about his political career. He had been vice-president under Quirino and had joined the Magsaysay team in the 1953 elections, and then later followed [Claro M.] Recto in breaking with the Magsaysay administration. I mentioned my meeting him to my Magsaysay-follower contact. He grinned.

"Your landlady has been Lopez's mistress for years. When you meet some of her children, after you've seen more of Lopez, you'll understand," he said. "Actually, it's hardly a secret anymore. As you found out, they go all sorts of places together quite openly. It wasn't always like that, though, but we knew about it and took advantage of it once when we wanted to lean on him a little bit.

"When he was vice-president and secretary of agriculture at the same time, I was working in the agriculture department and I found out he had a side room, next to his office, where the two of them spent a lot of afternoons. So I got some equipment from the [CIA] station and bugged the room. In fact, we discovered there was a bed in the room, so we bugged that too. Boy, we got some interesting recordings."

Vice-president Lopez broke with Quirino and agreed to run as vice-presidential candidate with Carlos P. Romulo, whose only claim to fame was having his picture taken wading ashore behind [General Douglas] MacArthur when the general kept his promise to return. But this ticket split the Liberal Party. As one of the Philippines' sugar barons from the southern island of Iloilo, Lopez not only controlled his home state but added a note of substance and money to the Romulo ticket. I didn't want to ask whether this move by Lopez was related to the recordings, but I did.

My friend grinned even more broadly. "I'm going to plead the Fifth Amendment," he replied.

The Romulo-Lopez ticket was approved by the acclamation of one thousand delegates to the Progressive/Democratic Party convention. . . . Their campaign was brief but if did have an effect on the Liberals Between those who followed Magsaysay into the Nationalist Party, and those who went with Romulo and Lopez, the Liberal Party leadership suffered important losses.

*   *   *

Magsaysay was the only really sure friend the United States and CIA could count on in Asia. . . .

When Magsaysay died [in a plane crash in March 1957], an elaborate structure of activities designed to help him turn the country into the showplace of democracy that [CIA head Allen] Dulles wanted came rather quickly apart. Not only was the station in Manila engaged in these efforts to support our man, but a large number of activities were being run from Manila to try to use Filipinos as our alter egos to spread democracy throughout the SEATO security area our Secretary of State had put together in Southeast Asia. It was believed that the Filipinos would be more readily accepted by Asians than Americans in roles as political advisers and liaison officers with local intelligence services.

The most venturesome enterprise was the so-called Freedom Company of the Philippines that was set up in 1954 by Ed Lansdale to help him establish the Diem regime in Vietnam. Magsaysay was the company's honorary president. The company was a mechanism to deploy Filipinos in Vietnam and possibly elsewhere, under cover of a public service organization having a contract with the host government. Freedom Company personnel helped write the constitution of Vietnam, trained the Vietnamese president's Guard Battalion, organized the Vietnamese Veterans Legion to tie in with one of Cord Meyer's schemes to use veterans groups internationally as an anti-Communist front, and ran the huge Operation Brotherhood activity.

Outside Vietnam, the Filipinos had less success, although they did get involved in Thailand and even got a toehold in Burma. Asians did not accept them as their own. They simply had been associated with Americans too long. As a Chinese told me in Singapore one time, "They have brown faces but they wear the same Hawaiian sports shirts the Americans do."

Back in Manila, the station tried to orchestrate the press of the capital and the provincial press to provide Magsaysay with a constant claque of support for his internal programs as well as his involvement in the anti-Communist crusade in Asia. They continued to supply him with the personal advice and comradely support in dealing with his problems that Ed Lansdale had established as a tradition when Magsaysay had been defense minister. They wrote his speeches too.

* * *

The election of 1957 turned into a four-man contest, and the station could not decide which one to support. Carlos Garcia was sixty years old when he succeeded Magsaysay. He was a Nacionalist, a Party hack from the small southern island of Bohol. His dark skin and, many said, his darker political past earned him the nickname "Black Charlie." His selection as vice-presidential candidate had been a sop to party regulars given by our people who never expected any plane crash and who knew that the office of vice-president of the Philippines was even less important than vice-president of the United States . . . . Magsaysay made Garcia foreign affairs secretary, which was, under the circumstances, a purely protocol post since all important decisions in the foreign affairs field were made between Magsaysay and his CIA station contacts. Consequently, no one from the station even knew Garcia when he took office.

The Magsaysay men pointed out at once that he was a crook who would return the country to all the evil ways that President Quirino had practiced. They were, of course, right. Garcia hadn't been in office six months before false bills of lading became standard at the Manila harbor, copra was being smuggled out of the southern islands in huge amounts, and a payoff system was put into effect for conducting any sort of transaction with the government. . . .

The Magsaysay men all resigned their government posts, and Manuel Manahan, who had proudly cleaned up Philippine Customs, which under Garcia quickly reverted again to a major cesspool of corruption, became their candidate for president on the Progressive Party ticket. . . .

Aurell [CIA chief in Manila] agreed that it would be the undoing of everything if Garcia won a full term in office, but decided that the Liberal ticket of old Liberal faithful Jose Yulo and young Diosdado Macapagal would have a better chance than the upstart third party. Nevertheless, he could not renege on the station's long-established suit, so he also agreed that some support be given to Manahan.

The fourth man in the race was Senator Claro M. Recto. Recto had broken completely with Magsaysay before the latter's death. The aftermath of this quarrel would be another of my headaches when I got to Manila. Recto took a nationalist stance which included opposing the close relationship between the United States and the Philippines and advocated dealing openly with the new power in Asia—Communist China.

The station's election operation was, therefore, more an effort to make sure that Recto was soundly defeated, so that the reputation of our principal SEATO ally not be sullied, than the positive effort that had been made four years earlier to elect our own president.

The results were what might have been expected. Garcia won a new full term as president. Yulo and Manahan split between them a total of more than 2,400,000 votes, enough to have elected either one or the other of them since Garcia got only 2,079,000 votes. Recto was ignominiously defeated. The "father of the Philippine constitution," as he liked to be known, gathered barely 400,000 ballots. Our friend Macapagal was elected vice-president, receiving over 100,000 more votes than Garcia. . . .

The station had helped Magsaysay fight this formidable opponent [Recto] every step of the way. He had been labeled a Chinese Communist stooge, an agent infiltrated into the Philippine Senate (shades of Senator Joe McCarthy), and, I discovered, he had been subjected to various dirty tricks. As I went through the files, I found something that absolutely astounded me. I saw a sealed envelope marked "Recto Campaign." I opened it and found it filled with condoms, marked "Courtesy of Claro M. Recto—the People's Friend." The condoms all had holes in them at the place they could least afford to have them.

I tried to find out what purpose the condoms had been supposed to serve. The best I could do was to learn that they were distributed to show how Recto would let you down.

Selection 6.8: Against U.S. Military Bases, Claro M. Recto

Editor's Introduction

Over his long political career, Claro M. Recto made the transition from a typical upper class politician to an outspoken nationalist. (For an account of Recto's career, see Renato Constantino, *The Making Of A Filipino*, Quezon City: Malaya Books, 1969.) Particularly in the last decade before his death in 1960, his nationalist credo had a profound influence on a whole generation of Filipinos. In the excerpts from two of his speeches that follow, he criticizes the U.S. military bases in the Philippines, first because they infringe on Philippine sovereignty and second because they serve as magnets for foreign—even nuclear—attack.

Over the years, the U.S. has had to make some concessions to nationalist objections: in 1959, Washington agreed to consult with Manila before emplacing long-range missiles in the Philippines or before using the bases for combat operations not related to mutual security; in 1966, the expiration date of the agreement was changed from 2046 to 1991. Recto's warnings about the bases serving as magnets for nuclear attack, however, has become more important than ever [see selection 8.6].

Source: Renato Constantino [ed.], *The Recto Reader*, Manila: Recto Memorial Foundation, 1965, pp. 96-97, 100-102.

The [Military Bases] Agreement purported to insure "the territorial integrity of the Philippines"; but by granting America extra-territorial rights in the bases, we surrendered to her the power, the jurisdiction, and the sovereignty of the Republic over portions of the national territory whose integrity is guaranteed by Article I of the Constitution. So the Agreement, instead of insuring our territorial integrity, accomplished the very opposite of its declared purpose with the impairment of our territorial integrity. The 99-year term, coupled with the fact that no stipulation for earlier termination of the same has been provided, has the same effect. Such an extremely long lease of territory is, for all practical intents and purposes, a perpetual lease tantamount to a grant in fee simple, an odious peace-time military occupation by a friendly country with immunity from our laws and our courts. A 99-year occupation of strategic areas of the national territory can never be justified.

— from "American Bases and National Freedom and Security," October 29, 1956

. . . American commentators candidly admit that the purpose of these bases is not our protection against, but our invitation to enemy attack in order to protect the people in the United States at the cost of the lives of our own people. I realize that this is a rather strong statement to make, and that a responsible representative of the people should not indulge in any speculation no matter how well-grounded. But I became convinced that it was no longer speculation when the military commentator of the *New York Times*, Hanson Baldwin, a trusted man in U.S. military circles, who has been writing in the *N.Y. Times* on military subjects for over 20 years, said in February 1957 (*N.Y. Times Weekly Review*, February 17, 1957) that the role of the U.S. overseas bases in the world—bases in the Philippines are among them—is to "act as magnets for enemy attacks, thus dispersing and weakening his threat to our (United States) cities and fixed installations." This he reiterated in a later article (*N.Y. Times Weekly Review*, August 18, 1957).

I am the first to admit that it is understandable that political and military leaders of the United States should devise ways and means of protecting the lives of their own people. If in a nuclear war they stand to lose 100 million in the first few hours of a concentrated enemy attack, it would be natural for them to try to minimize their casualties by diverting the attack. Overseas bases, like those in the Philippines, are precisely the diversionary objectives for such enemy attack on the United States.

That is the reason why I did not harbor any hatred, ill will, or resentment when I learned that the role assigned to U.S. overseas bases was to act as magnets for enemy attacks in order to disperse the attack on the American population.

What I deplore and condemn is the way we passively accept the role of magnets or decoys to draw enemy attacks away from the United States. . . .

—from "The Problem of Our National Physical Survival,
May 21, 1958

Selection 6.9: The Folklore of Colonialism, Lorenzo M. Tañada

Editors' Introduction

Lorenzo M. Tañada has been one of the leading Philippine nationalists for many decades. He served as the Solicitor General for the People's Court established to try war-time collaboration with the Japanese, was a member of the Senate for many years, and was involved in efforts to establish an alternative to the two dominant parties. Throughout the Marcos years he was known as "the grand old man

of the opposition." The following excerpts are from a commencement address Tañada delivered in May 1966.

Source: Lorenzo M. Tañada, "The Folklore of Colonialism," in *History of the Filipino People*, ed. Teodoro A. Agoncillo and Milagros C. Guerrero, Quezon City: R. P. Garcia Publishing Co., 1971, pp. 610-18.

The Myths We Live By. We have been living by illusions for such a long time that we seem not to have noticed the changing realities of our time. We belong to neither the advanced capitalist nor socialist camps. Our thinking and behavior, however, belie our real status—that we are a developing nation. Our habit of self-delusion has been a principal cause of our miseries. Many countries like our own have heroically resisted the incursions of metropolitan powers. Some have succeeded, while others are still fighting the pernicious hold of foreign interests. This determined struggle on their part has earned for them the respect of the nations of the world.

Because we have refused to recognize our real status, we have not only not resisted, we have even abetted foreign economic domination. We have been deluded into thinking that this is the correct road, because we are so anxious to establish affinity with an advanced power and because we believe any other road is unwise. We have been on this road for such a long time, yet we have not progressed. From this mistaken orientation have sprung all the myths that imprison us. We have lived on rhetoric and ignored reality. We pride ourselves so much on being the most westernized country in Asia that we actually sometimes tend to look down upon our fellow-Asians. We profess to have links with our brother Asians but we tend to look condescendingly on them because they do not speak English the way we do and have not adopted Western ways. This is the first of the myths we live by. . . .

The Myth of Identity of Interests. In the field of foreign relations, we have always proceeded on the assumption that America's interests are automatically ours also and vice-versa. We have followed her foreign policy closely and sometimes we have even outdone her. In Asia, our stock is low because we are regarded by our neighbors as America's obedient satellite. We are thus viewed with suspicion by fellow-Asians. In international conferences, we have always been identified with the American position. We have not recognized the communist countries not because we have studied this question ourselves and decided it would be bad for us but because we believed that by recognition we would be hurting America's cause, even if America itself has diplomatic, economic, and cultural relations with most of them. Thus we find our diplomatic maneuverability severely limited. We cannot trade with these countries, while many of the developing nations of Asia and Africa have found it profitable to do so.

Ever since the restoration of our independence, we have ignored the existence of the Soviet Union. This policy of non-recognition has grown out of a suspicion of communist intentions, out of a desire to please America and not out of any serious analysis of the objective situation. Hence, we have failed to develop our own experts on the Soviet Union. We have refused to seriously consider the position of the Soviet Union in world events, even after her amazing accomplishments in the realm of science and space.

From the inception of our independent life, Liberal and Nacionalista administrations have been guided by the myth of identity of interests into actions and policies that later proved detrimental to our country. We have subordinated even domestic policy to the demands of a foreign policy based largely on this myth that our interests are identical with those of the United States. But a cardinal principle of independent existence is that the foreign policy of a state should merely be a reflection of its domestic policy. Domestic policy is paramount and foreign policy is subordinate, or ought to be, to that policy. Domestic policy is based on our own needs and aspirations, not the needs, let alone aspirations, of our allies. Foreign policy must hence be a distinctly Filipino response to the world as we see it and not as others with their own biases and interests see it. Because it is only under an atmosphere of reduced tensions that we can carry on the building of our nation, the national interest would seem to require a foreign policy based on peaceful coexistence with all nations. But our foreign policy has in fact been just a bit more warlike than that as witness the proposal to send combat engineers to Vietnam. . . .

The Myth of American Benevolence. This is the myth of special relations. For so many years we have been acting as if we were special favorites of America. We feel especially privileged because we have "special relations" with America and America has a special place for us in her heart. Yet, this is not so; I even wonder if it has been so. Let us remind ourselves of the bitter start of the American intrusion into our shores. Even then, of course, words of great emotional appeal were used to disguise the truth. America had a "manifest destiny" to "civilize" us and teach us the ways of freedom and democracy. Later developments suggest that this was not so, that America had ambitions, too, in Asia, still has them, and that the Philippines was conquered by her to serve her own interests, certainly not those of our country. Similarly, America's attitude towards Philippine independence followed the dictates of her own self-interest. Her recognition of our independence became possible only as a result of the confluence of forces in America and these included the dairy industries, the sugar interests, American labor, etc., which wanted to deprive us of our preferred position in the American market because we were competing with their own interests. Self-interest beyond everything also dictated American withdrawal from the Philippines during the last war. The so-called "special relations" were weighted in her favor. When she returned after the war and gave us back the independence we had won from Spain and which she took from us by force and guile, what did "special relations" mean for us? Parity, Laurel-Langley [agreement], and bases agreement imposing extraterritorial rights for her.

Parity was imposed in exchange for war damage payments. Free trade was moreover guaranteed for a definite period. What did those signify? The perpetuation of our colonial type economy and the stifling relations with America are being invoked to give Americans more rights than Filipinos themselves in the case of retail trade nationalization and to demand the continuation of rights acquired under parity after 1974. Under Parity we have alienated huge tracts of the national patrimony to American corporations. Under Parity we have imported billions of pesos worth of duty-free American goods and exported to the United States less than a third in value of our export commodities. The influx of American goods has prevented industrialization. Professor George Taylor has observed, "It has to be admitted that the U.S. set up for its citizens monopolistic advantages. Through the American Chamber of Commerce and through the American embassy, the Americans can bring pressure to bear on a weak government and in some instances, this pressure may well make it more difficult for that government to carry out its reform."

The Myth of Foreign Investments. I hold no brief against foreign investments as long as those investments are reasonably controlled and made to serve our national interests. No Filipino who genuinely loves his country can be for foreign investments that would ultimately hand over the control of our economic life to foreigners. Loans are therefore to be preferred to direct investments for in the former case we remain in control of our resources and there is less danger of foreign influence on our policies. We should be on guard against a policy on foreign investments that has no well-defined safeguards. . . .

The Myth of Free Enterprise. The road to progress cannot be clear unless we shed yet another myth that dominates the thinking of our planners; that economic growth automatically means development and that development inevitably results in "democratizing" wealth through its equitable distribution. Surely each administration can show facts and figures attesting to the growth of the national product. But growth does not mean development. Nor does it mean that the poor will get a fuller meal or better homes or more adequate clothing or greater opportunity for education. When we talk of growth we should also talk of equitable distribution of the wealth of the land so that those who have been living for centuries under conditions of poverty will get their just rewards, so that those who work the land will not forever suffer from rural penury.

Tied up with this myth is the belief that democracy is synonomous with free enterprise. Complete free enterprise is not good for developing countries. Governments in these countries have to have some say in directing the development of their economies, otherwise domestic businesses could not compete on equal terms with foreign giants. Government direction for nationalistic purposes does not diminish our democracy for after all an essential goal of democracy is freedom from want.

Thus we cannot simply proceed with industrialization without revising our agricultural structure. Our entrepreneurs must realize that nationalism is not for the benefit of only a few Filipinos. Nationalism does not merely mean more profits for the few. Independence under democracy must have a meaning for all sectors of the population, not just one. To the masses it should mean higher standard of living, to the laborers, an assurance of employment at reasonable wages, to professionals, the attainment of proficiency in their respective lines of endeavor, to artists and intellectuals, the realization of creative talents. Once freed of the myths that imprison our minds, we shall clearly see what the struggle for economic emancipation entails. We shall see that it involves challenging many concepts and ideas, institutions and people and all the beneficiaries of the status quo.

Selection 6.10: The Growing Protest Movement, Philip Shabecoff

Editors' Introduction

The first three months of 1970 saw a massive wave of student demonstrations known as the First Quarter Storm. Student activism helped to politicize and radicalize other elements of the population as well. *New York Times* correspondent Philip Shabecoff filed a series of reports that graphically portrayed the growing discontent and protest. In one dispatch (March 8, 1970) he reported the story of a sick farm worker who appealed to his landlord for money to pay for an operation. "You should have died long ago anyway," the landlord told him. In the following article, Shabecoff gives a vivid picture of the situation in the urban slums.

Source: Philip Shabecoff, "Protest Movement in the Philippines Widening Rapidly," *New York Times*, March 12, 1970, p. 10.

Manila, March 4—The squatters in Barrio Magsaysay, a teeming, malodorous slum in Tondo District, a tough section of the capital, are skeptical of Government promises that they can keep the only homes they can afford.

The people—day laborers, the unemployed, ex-convicts, alcoholics—in the grim huddle of gray one-room hovels made of scrap have asked the Government repeatedly to give them title and it has said it would do so. They do not trust it, however, and they believe it is fully capable of turning their little plots over to speculators.

"That is why I support the student demonstrations," said Gloria Diang Sena, a mother of 10 who supplements her husband's meager wages as a laborer by selling fried bananas to her neighbors.

"The Government never kept its promises before," she said, brushing flies away from her wares on display beside the dirt-packed, garbage-strewn street. "Now the students are forcing the Government to keep their word. The Government doesn't care about poor people, so we have to speak up and demand our rights."

The recent spate of demonstrations, some violent, by the dissident students of Manila and their calls for reform are bringing to a boil the long-accumulated grievances of the 36 million people of the Philippines.

The demand for reform in a nation where political and economic power is concentrated in the hands of a tiny minority seems to be rapidly turning into a populist movement embracing workers, peasants, middle-class intellectuals, clergy and moderate students, as well as the radical revolutionary students.

In the wings, of course, is the outlawed Communist party of the Philippines and the armed guerillas of its New People's Army.

Early in February, responding to the agitation, President Ferdinand E. Marcos said that many of the students' grievances were legitimate but indicated that he thought Communist agitators were behind the violence. He said social inequities must be eliminated, jobs created, land reform continued and labor assisted if Communism was not to become a serious threat.

Critics insist, nevertheless, that thus far the Government's response to the protest movement has been largely defensive.

"The conditions in the country make it riper for upheaval than any other I have ever served in," said one foreign diplomat. "If there is not a major attempt at reform—and soon—I cannot see how threat of violent revolution can be avoided."

The average per capita income in the Philippines is $200 a year. But this figure does not describe the poverty in which the majority of the Filipino people live.

A widely used estimate has it that more than 50 per cent of all wealth in the country is owned by 5 per cent of the population. The median per capita income, therefore, is only about $50 a year. Taxation is regressive. The tax burden falls on the poor.

The means that the great mass of the Filipino people live in conditions almost as bad as the squatters of Barrio Magsaysay while a small minority enjoys a life of luxury in exclusive, heavily guarded communities such as Forbes Park near Manila or on the wealthy sugar haciendas of the island of Negros.

It is also an accepted fact here that political power is concentrated in the hands of this small, wealthy elite.

Raul Manglapus, a former Foreign Secretary and leader of the reformist Christian Social Movement, asserted that the two political parties—the Nationalist party of President Marcos and the opposition Liberal party— represent only the wealthy oligarchy.

"But the political system is corrupt," he said. "Only the two parties can count ballots and, since they are controlled by the economic blocs, the rest of the population is effectively shut out of representation in the Government."

The oligarchy also is accused of using its political power to concentrate ever more of the national wealth into its own hands.

Almost daily, the Manila newspapers carry articles of scandals in which friends and relatives of Government officials are awarded huge Government contracts or loans for economically worthless projects.

Meanwhile, small farmers are unable to get loans for seed and fertilizer from their local rural banks because the Government does not have enough money to distribute to these banks.

Crime and violence have been getting out of control. Political murders are almost daily occurrences. Politicians and businessmen hire professional gunmen for protection. In the hills of Central Luzon, Communist insurgents and Government forces intended to quell them outdo each other in acts of terrorism.

This was the general situation in the Philippines when President Marcos was elected to an unprecedented second term last November. He was expected to win, but not by the overwhelming two-million vote majority he achieved. Never before had reports of election fraud and vote manipulation been so prevalent.

Moreover, the Government spent a great deal of money before the election, with the result that the economy was severely set back and the peso weakened. Rising unemployment and soaring prices added to the burdens of the poor.

"We expected President Marcos to speak, to tell us he was going to reform the system," said a member of the moderate National Union of Students of the Philippines. "When the President remained silent, then we knew we would have to act ourselves."

Senator Benigno Aquino of the Liberal party asserted: "Marcos's big mistake was in crushing the opposition so overwhelmingly when he could simply have defeated us. We used to act as a buffer between the Government and all the protest in the country. Now the people are taking out all their problems directly on Malacañang [the Presidential Palace]."

The first protests were organized by moderate students in January with relatively moderate demands: that the President honor promises to improve education in the Philippines, that he pledge not to seek a third term of office, and that he take steps to see that all the people of the nation were fairly represented in a convention scheduled for June, 1971, to change the Constitution of the Philippines.

Since then, however, the base of the protest movement has greatly widened, especially after Government forces broke up a demonstration on Jan. 30 with a shooting spree that left six people dead.

The most articulate and conspicuous members of the protest movement are the radical left-wing students, loosely grouped in an organization called the Movement for a Democratic Philippines. The movement includes several allegedly Maoist groups in its ranks.

The left-wing extremists are calling for a violent overthrow of the existing political, economic and social structure of the Philippines, as the only remedy for the nation's deep malaise.

It is the radicals who are directing the wrath of the Manila mob against the United States Embassy. They call "American imperialism" the "No. 1 enemy of the Philippines and all mankind," in their manifestoes.

The Philippine Government and oligarchy, according to the radicals, are mere "puppets of American imperialism."

The anti-Americanism of the radicals seems to be striking a responsive chord among a wide segment of the people of the Philippines, where rising nationalistic feeling is accompanying the demand for reform.

The radicals, however, remain in the minority within the protest movement. The majority of students as well as other groups, such as the Christian Social Movement, are demanding sweeping basic reforms, particularly through the constitutional convention.

Other elements, including radical labor leaders and Roman Catholic clergy, are seeking to change the structure of Philippine society from the bottom through class confrontation.

For example, the Federation of Free Farmers, an agricultural union based on "radical Christian principles," wants to organize labor in the country so that it can oppose the moneyed interests in a nonviolent class struggle, according to its leader, Jeremias Montemayor.

Students and clergymen are moving into the fields to organize landless peasants and urge them to demand their rights.

What role the Communist party is playing in the spreading unrest is still unclear. The party was reformed in December, 1968, partly from the remains of the old Hukbalahap movement, the insurgent organization that threatened to take over the country in the early nineteen-fifties.

Some of the old Huks now are simply gangsters. But the reorganized party, whose chairman is said to be Amado Guerrero, is acknowledged to be a revitalized force, possibly receiving assistance from Peking.

The guerilla activities of the party, organized into the New People's Army, are slowly spreading through the country. The army is allegedly led by Bernabe Buscayno—more popularly known as "Commander Dante."

On the island of Negros, hungry sugar workers who have never even heard of the minimum wage law know that "the Communists are in the hills."

The radical students deny any affiliation with the Communist guerillas. But knowledgeable observers in Manila say there undoubtedly is at least some liaison between the two groups.

What comes next is uncertain. Certainly the protest will continue to expand and there will be more clashes between the students and their supporters on one side and Government authorities on the other.

If the Government does not make promised reforms, if it rigs next November's elections to the constitutional convention, then the protest movement could explode into something else. The word "revolution" is heard often in Manila these days. Fear also is expressed that a rightist reaction could lead to a military dictatorship.

Most Filipinos encountered over the last few weeks said that they were opposed to violence and that they hoped and expected that reforms would come without violence.

But there were many who felt the same way as Mrs. Diang Sena, the fried-banana seller of Barrio Magsaysay.

"I hate violence and fighting," she said. "A revolution would be a terrible thing for the Philippines. But I have 10 children to feed. Prices keep going up but not the money my husband brings home. If it takes a revolution to feed my children, then I say let's have it."

Ferdinand and Imelda Marcos

CHAPTER 7: MARTIAL LAW

Introduction

Three separate crises converged at the end of 1972: a crisis for Philippine President Ferdinand E. Marcos, a crisis for the Philippine supporters of the status quo, and a crisis for Washington. The result was the declaration of martial law in September 1972. This chapter will examine the impact of martial rule on the Philippine people, while the next chapter will focus on the external aspects.

Ferdinand Marcos had first been elected president in 1965. His presidency had been a typical one in many respects: great promises and few results. During the campaign, Marcos had declared that he opposed sending any Philippine units to Vietnam; no sooner had he been elected, however, than he urged the dispatch of a Philippine Civic Action Group. Social reform, particularly land reform, made no progress under Marcos, but Marcos himself had done very well: on a rather modest presidential salary, he became one of the largest taxpayers in the country.

In 1969, his consummate political skills and his ability to use the public treasury to advantage enabled Marcos to become the first Philippine president to be re-elected for a second term. According to a former official in the Reagan administration, W. Scott Thompson, a major source of Marcos's funds for the election came from manipulating U.S. government checks to its Filipino employees. The manipulation was acquiesced in by Washington after Marcos threatened to search U.S. naval vessels that might be carrying nuclear weapons, a prospect unacceptable to the Pentagon. The 1969 election was also characterized by unprecedented violence and widespread payoffs and fraud, not all but mostly in favor of Marcos's party.

The Philippine constitution, however, restricted the president to two terms in office, and thus by 1972 Marcos could see the impending twilight of his political career. For someone as committed to self-aggrandizement as Marcos, this presented a serious crisis.

Much more was threatened than Marcos personally, however. The nationalism and radicalism described in the previous section [see selections 6.8-6.10] was spreading rapidly. There was no imminent danger to the government, but the existence of civil liberties—for perhaps the first time in Philippine history—was allowing a broad-based challenge to the status quo to grow. The beneficiaries of the deeply inequitable social order saw a long-term threat to their positions and wealth.

The demands of the demonstrators were making their influence felt in the Congress and even in the Supreme Court. A treaty to normalize trade relations with Japan was stalled in the legislature and Senator Jose Diokno was heading an investigation into the operations of the multinational oil companies; in August 1972, the High Court issued two rulings—the Quasha and Lustevco decisions—that went sharply against U.S. business interests. Strikes were becoming more frequent and militant, and foreign firms were often targeted. Washington worried too about what it would be like negotiating revisions and extensions of the military bases agreement with a Congress susceptible to nationalist pressures.

In 1971, a Constitutional Convention was convened to revise the country's constitution. Barraged as it was by bribes from Marcos, the body was expected by many to allow Marcos to stay on in office. But Concon, as it was known, included a number of outspoken nationalists, and one U.S. analyst considered the outcome of Concon's deliberations to be unpredictable given the pressures that might be exerted by street demonstrations.

Then, on September 21, 1972, Marcos declared martial law, thereby responding at once to all three crises. To justify his action," Marcos alleged that there had had been an assassination attempt against his defense secretary. He then provided a more elaborate rationale for his martial law decree—that the government was threatened by conspiracy from the right and the left. Most observers dismissed his claims [see selection 7.1].

Marcos said he was going to root out corruption, but instead corruption became more centralized than ever before [see selection 7.2]. He claimed he was going to introduce dramatic reforms and establish a "New Society," but by the end of the decade, the poor were worse off than they had been in 1972 [see selection 7.3]. The centerpiece of Marcos's announced reforms was a land reform program, but its coverage excluded all landless rural workers, all tenant farmers working crops other than rice or corn, and all tenants on plots of less than 7 hectares (17 acres) [see selection 7.4]. And despite the desperate need for low-cost housing, the government undertook a massive project to build luxury hotels in an effort to promote tourism, a development strategy that has had serious social costs [see selection 7.5].

Marcos jailed his elite opponents and thousands of others; Amnesty International found widespread abuses of human rights, including the systematic use of torture against political prisoners [see selection 7.6]. Marcos closed down the Congress, arrested his opponents in the Concon, forced the country's judges to give him undated letters of resignation, and took over the media. Marcos ruled by decree and, through a series of rigged and manipulated referenda [see selection 7.7], he was able to consolidate his dictatorial hold on the country.

Opposition to Marcos took many forms. In the southern Philippines, long-term grievances of the Muslim minority were exacerbated by the declaration of martial law, and the Moro National Liberation Front launched guerilla warfare against the government [see selection 7.8]. Other national minorities found their tribal lands laid open to massive corporate exploitation and their disaffection often turned to resistance [see selection 7.9]. The New People's Army, the military arm of the Communist Party of the Philippines, though a rather minor force in 1972, grew rapidly after the imposition of martial law, its ranks swollen due to the depressed living conditions and the closing off of legal channels of dissent [see selection 7.10]. The National Democratic Front, formed in April 1973, brought together the Communist Party and others in a broad front that became the leading organized opposition on the left [see selection 7.11]. And the Catholic Church, particularly among its lower ranks, became progressively more disenchanted with the Marcos regime; radicalized priests and nuns worked increasingly on behalf of the poor and some even joined the guerillas in the hills [see selection 7.12].

In 1978, Marcos tried to deflect the growing opposition by holding elections to an Interim National Assembly. Neutral observers were agreed that Marcos used fraud to ensure the victory of his newly formed political party, the KBL. Opposition to Marcos continued to grow, with disaffection swelling even among the business community, long a supporter of Marcos but now feeling cut out from the fruits of his increasingly corrupt rule [see selection 7.2].

In January 1981, Marcos again attempted to preserve some credibility for his regime by announcing the formal lifting of martial law. But though martial law was lifted, all of Marcos's more than one thousand martial law decrees remained in force and Marcos retained the power to order arrests without charge, legislate by decree, and overrule the National Assembly [see selection 7.13]. Few Filipinos were fooled. Amnesty International reported a continuing pattern of systematic abuses of human rights [see selection 7.14]. Opposition continued to mount.

Selection 7.1: Martial Law, Staff Report for the U.S. Senate Foreign Relations Committee

Editors' Introduction

Marcos provided a number of justifications for his September 21, 1972 declaration of martial law. He claimed first that the Republic was in danger of being overthrown by leftist subversion. There was indeed an upsurge of radicalism in the period before martial law, as documented in the previous chapter, but few observers thought the government was in any immediate danger. There had been a murderous grenade attack on Marcos's political opponents in 1971; Marcos had accused the Communists of the deed, but the public was skeptical—Marcos, after all, stood the most to gain from killing off the leaders of the opposition party—and the perpetrators were never apprehended. In the weeks before the declaration of martial law, a series of bombings occurred in Manila, and on September 22 there was an alleged assassination attempt against defense minister Juan Ponce Enrile. As the *Wall Street Journal's* correspondent reported, however, it was "reasonably certain" that the attempt on Enrile had been "choreographed at Malacañang [the Presidential Palace], and the same probably holds true for the bombings." (After he defected from the Marcos government, Enrile acknowledged that the attack on him had been staged.)

With the argument regarding leftist subversion so dubious, Marcos then tried to justify martial law as a response to a rightist plot. In November 1972, the U.S. Senate Foreign Relations Committee sent a pair of staff members to investigate the situation, and following are excerpts from their report.

Source: Staff Report prepared for the use of the U.S. Senate Committee on Foreign Relations, *Korea and the Philippines: November 1972*, Committee Print, 93rd Congress, 1st session, February 18, 1973, pp. 1-2, 4, 31-33, 37, 41, 45-46. It should be noted that the notation "[Deleted.]" in the selection below appears in the original and indicates material removed at the suggestion of the Department of State, Department of Defense, or the CIA.

President Marcos signed Proclamation 1081, placing the Philippines under martial law, on September 21 and announced it on September 23. In his public statement at the time martial law was proclaimed, he said that the nation was "imperilled by the danger of a violent overthrow, insurrection and rebellion" justifying the imposition of martial law under Article VII of the Constitution. He went on to say that "there is no doubt in everybody's mind that a state of rebellion exists in the Philippines" and referred to the Supreme Court decision of December 11, 1971, in which such a finding had been made. He said that the danger had become graver since the Court's decision, the national and local governments had become paralyzed, the productive sectors of the economy had ground to a halt, the judiciary had become unable to administer justice, tensions and anxiety in Manila had reached a point where the citizens were compelled to stay at home, and lawlessness and criminality had escalated beyond the capability of the local police and civilian authorities. The President then referred to battles between Philippine government forces and "subversives" in a number of locations and to the activities of the Communist Party and the Maoist New People's Army in the Province of Isabela where "they are now in control of 33 municipalities out of 37." He also referred to the "violent disorder" in Mindanao and Sulu as a result of the activities of Muslim dissidents.

Proclamation 1081 began by referring to the threat from "lawless elements who are moved by a common or similar ideological conviction, design, strategy and goal and enjoying the active moral and material support of a foreign power . . . and (who) are actually staging, undertaking and waging an armed insurrection and rebellion . . . (to) supplant our existing political, social, economic and legal order with an entirely new one whose form of government . . . and whose political, social, economic, legal and moral precepts are based on the Marxist-Leninist-Maoist teachings and beliefs." Subsequent paragraphs referred to the New People's Army and other communist organizations. There was no mention in either the President's statement or in Proclamation 1081 of any threat from the right.

On September 19, two days before the proclamation was signed, an executive session of the Philippine National Security Council had been briefed on internal security. Security conditions were reportedly described at that meeting as between "normal" and "Internal Defense Condition No. 1" (the worst or most unstable security condition is No. 3).

One high Philippine government official told us that the real reason President Marcos had declared martial law was that he had uncovered a plot from the right to assassinate him and that the key figures in the plot were Vice President Lopez and Sergio Osmeña, Jr. (President Marcos's opponent in the last Presidential race who, at the time this report was written, was reported to be in hiding in the United States). . . .

That there were plots to assassinate high officials, including the President himself, seems clear. Certainly, the atmosphere in the Philippines was conducive to crimes of violence of all sorts. There had been a series of bombings of public buildings, demonstrations in which students had been killed and an increase in kidnappings. The insurgent strength on the left was growing, but we met no outside observer who considered it a real or near threat to the Government. Curiously, though, the incident that was supposed at the time martial law was declared to be the last straw—the attempt to kill the Secretary of Defense—was regarded as somewhat dubious by most observers. It was practically never mentioned to us by Philippine officials in discussing the reasons for martial law, and the few times it was mentioned it seemed to occur as an after-thought and to be accompanied by what appeared to be a certain embarrassment. [Deleted.] The fact of the matter is that the attempt against the Secretary of Defense occurred on the evening of September 22, the day before the declaration of martial law was announced but, as it turned out, the day after the declaration had been signed.

Was a rightist assassination plot really the reason martial law was declared? None of the foreign or Philippine observers to whom we talked alluded to the possibility of such a vast plot masterminded from the right. . . .

It was also suggested to us that because the Government's initial rationale involving a leftist plot had been greeted with such skepticism, the Government might now be seeking to justify its actions on grounds less likely to be rejected by liberal critics abroad. . . .

Since declaring martial law, President Marcos has put less emphasis on the threat from insurgent groups (which he claimed had led to his action) and on the measures to control that threat and more emphasis on the reforms necessary to build what he calls "the New Society," a phrase that is thrust into public consciousness by the government through all available media. . . .

Philippine officials said that President Marcos has long wanted to implement this elaborate program of reforms but that he had been prevented from doing so by a "corrupt Congress" and "irresponsible press." It is generally accepted in the Philippines that the few hundred wealthy families, referred to as the oligarchs, have dominated the economy and politics of the islands since the colonial period and that heretofore the Philippine Congress, bureaucracy and press have been dominated by them and operated primarily for their benefit.

Opposition figures, as well as many independent observers to whom we talked, pointed out that the government party has enjoyed a majority in both houses of the Philippine Congress and must therefore bear a considerable measure of responsibility for its performance. They also observed that the President has long been identified with the very interests he now criticizes. It is for these reasons, they said, that they were profoundly skeptical about the sincerity of the President's motives in proclaiming a "New Society," for they suspected that he had chosen the role of social revolutionary out of political expediency.

. . . how long will martial law be retained? President Marcos has said publicly that he hopes to lift it before the end of 1973 when his term as President expires. Most observers believe, however, that martial law will be retained for from 3 to 5 years. . . .

Taken in sum . . . the proposed new constitution is considered to be as favorable to the position of American investors as it could reasonably have been expected to be. It should not lead to any capital flight. In fact, we were told that there has been no capital flight since martial law was declared but, on the contrary, some capital inflow. Ford and GM are forging ahead with new plants, and a syndicate of 16 American banks (who are contributing $25 million), and 13 Japanese and European banks (who are contributing another $25 million), has recently established a Development Bank of the Philippines.

. . . U.S. authorities note that nowhere in the world are we able to use our military bases with less restrictions than we do in the Philippines. . . .

While the United States was vaguely critical of developments in Korea, it was altogether uncritical of what occurred in the Philippines. The distinction in American eyes appeared to be that while President Marcos's martial law measures were constitutional and deemed warranted (although not in terms of the alleged communist threat) those taken by President Park were unconstitutional and considered unnecessary. . . .

We found few, if any, Americans who took the position that the demise of individual rights and democratic institutions would adversely affect U.S. interests. In the first place, these democratic institutions were considered to be severely deficient. In the second place, whatever U.S. interests were—or are—they apparently are not thought to be related to the preservation of democratic processes. Even in the Philippines, our own colonial step-child and "showcase of democracy" in Asia, the United States appears to have adopted a new pragmatism, perhaps because there was no other choice, turning away from the evangelical hopes and assumptions with which it has tended to look at political evolution. Thus, U.S. officials appear prepared to accept that the strengthening of presidential authority will . . . enable President Marcos to introduce needed stability; that these objectives are in our interest; and that . . . military bases and a familiar government in the Philippines are more important than the preservation of democratic institutions which were imperfect at best.

At the same time, there is some apprehension on the part of American officials about the future. . . . [An official] in the Philippines stated that if President Marcos obtained the power he sought "the only alternative his opponents will have will be to go to the hills." It would be ironic indeed . . . if the constitutional changes made possible by President Marcos's declaration of martial law produced conditions which transformed the imagined threat into a reality or brought about greater political chaos than that which he supposedly acted to correct.

Selection 7.2: "Some Are Smarter Than Others," Anonymous

Editors' Introduction

Marcos's initial declaration of martial law had been met with enthusiasm by the Philippine business community. And many Filipinos no doubt wanted to believe Marcos's promise that he would root out the corruption that was endemic in Philippine society. It soon became evident, however, that martial law was going to centralize corruption in the hands of Marcos, his relatives, and cronies. By the late 1970s, there was a growing disenchantment with the Marcos regime by those business people who were not personally favored by the Philippine ruler.

When "First Lady" Imelda Marcos was asked why the president's relatives and friends had fared so well under martial law, she replied that "Some are smarter than others." This became the title of an underground study in Manila written and distributed by a group of business executives in 1979. Of course, the Marcoses' corruption was known by all who had their eyes open even before martial law was declared; but the magnitude of the thievery grew astronomically during the years of dictatorship. The full extent of the Marcoses' ill-gotten wealth began to be revealed only after their removal from power.

Source: "Some Are Smarter Than Others," mimeographed, Manila, 1979.

Purpose of Study

Our purpose in this short study is to present another indicator by which the performance of Mr. Marcos at reforming society can be judged.

It is the degree by which he, his family, and his friends have enriched themselves upon the proclamation of martial law.

It is from this angle that we offer *our* evaluation of the "new society."

The sociologist Fr. John Doherty came out with a book entitled *Interlocking Directorates* and presents the thesis that the country's major banks control the country's major corporations, and ultimately by this token, control the economy.

The present authors feel that Fr. Doherty has left out a major chunk of the controlling parties. In fact, we feel that Fr. Doherty has left out the biggest DIRECTOR of them all.

"Some Are Smarter Than Others" is an acceptance of Fr. Doherty's invitation to anyone to add any information or facts he may have missed or overlooked.

Scope of Study

... Of course, the biggest constraint that we faced in our research work was the constraint of martial law itself. Our access to information was severely limited due to conditions of information control and various degrees of repression. . . .

Roberto S. Benedicto

Roberto S. Benedicto is one of the closest personal friends of the President, being a classmate and fraternity brother of FM [Ferdinand Marcos] in the UP [University of the Philippines] Law School. He is an original fund raiser and crony.

Primitivo Mijares, a former presidential aide who defected in 1975 (and subsequently disappeared and was presumed dead) testified at U.S. congressional hearings held by Representative Daniel Fraser's subcommittee of the House Foreign Affairs Committee. In this testimony, Mijares singled out Benedicto as a front man for Marcos; "What Mr. Benedicto owns, Mr. Marcos owns." However, he could not furnish any documentary proof. In fact, some of Benedicto's enterprises are registered in the names of friends or associates, thereby making it difficult to prove even his ownership. It can be observed that prior to Marcos's ascent to power, Benedicto was not rich. Since then, however, he has come into the tightly-knit group of Marcos *nouveau riche*.

He is most popular for his direct involvement in the mismanagement of our sugar exports in 1974 and '75 that resulted in losses of $600m. He was formerly the head of the government-owned Philippine National Bank, which finances sugar operations and is currently the chairman of the Philippine Sugar Commission, the government institution that is the sole buyer of sugar from the farmers and consequently has a monopoly over Philippine exports of sugar. . . .

Benedicto also heads the National Sugar Trading Corporation. . . . In addition, he owns sugar lands and several new sugar mills, and his shipping line, Northern Lines, carries sugar to Japan. Benedicto was also a former ambassador to Japan.

Benedicto has controlling interests in Republic Planters Bank[1] and Royal Bank. He owns a local newspaper, the *Daily Express*. He also owns the largest TV and radio network in the country, which controls 3 of 5 channels. . . .

[There follows a listing of 10 Benedicto controlled companies.]

Eduardo and Ramon Cojuangco

The Cojuangcos come from the landed family whose traditional source of wealth is in its interests in banking and sugar in Central Luzon. Although some members of this family have lost political favor with the martial law regime, two members have been particularly successful not only in maintaining their traditional wealth but also expanding it through the political and financial ties they maintain with the first Couple.

These two are Eduardo "Danding" Cojuangco and Ramon C. Cojuangco.

Ramon C. Cojuangco, the president of PLDT [Philippine Long Distance Telephone], and who together with his brother-in-law Luis Tirso Rivilla owns United Amherst Leasing and Finance Corporation, maintains and furthers his financial status via the access he has with Imelda Marcos]. . . .

Eduardo Cojuangco, on the other hand, maintains his political leverage from Marcos himself. . . .[2]

He is now the biggest coconut landlord in the south, and he controls this industry together with [Defense Secretary Juan Ponce] Enrile, via the institutions of COCOFED, the Philippine Coconut Authority (PCA), and the United Coconut Planters Bank (UCPB). . . .

Danding was also the Chairman of the Philippine Racing Commission.

[There follows a listing of 11 Cojuangco controlled companies.]

Rodolfo Cuenca

. . . He has maintained a close personal friendship with FM, stemming from pre-martial law days. He was a fund raiser in the 1965 campaign and is a frequent golf partner of the president. In his varied ventures, it is widely accepted that he is a loyal front man of FM.

At 51, Rudy Cuenca heads an empire that got off the ground in 1966 when his original Cuenca Construction Company was awarded several large-scale construction jobs by the Marcos government. . . . [Cuenca's company became the Construction and Development Corporation of the Philippines, CDCP.]

In 1967, CDCP won the bidding for the completion of the North Luzon Expressway for P29M and the construction of the Manila South Expressway for P34M. After CDCP's success in the building of expressways it zoomed through other gigantic projects in the construction business, notably the San Juanico bridge connecting Leyte to Samar, the Pantabangan Dam, the Candaba viaduct, and other seemingly Herculian projects.

But by far, CDCP's most ambitious project is the new city or the Manila-Cavite Coastal Road and Reclamation Project . . . . In 1973, the quoted price of the project was P7.6 billion. . . .

Today, CDCP is the biggest local construction company and in 1977 was the country's 11th biggest corporation in terms of resources . . . . and the 14th largest in terms of fixed assets. . . .[3]

CDCP heads some 14 other companies in other sectors of the economy. . . .

[There follows a list of 17 Cuenca-controlled companies.]

Herminio Disini

The quick ascent of Herminio Disini is the most scandalous and most-talked-about in the group. Certainly this relative (he is married to Imelda's first cousin and personal physician, Dr. Inday Escolin, who was formerly the governess of the Marcos children) is "smarter than others." He is a close friend and frequent golfing partner of FM.

The Disini success story illustrates how "one of several close friends and relatives of the Marcoses have prospered as the President acquired power to issue governmental contracts and rewrite tax provisions by decrees" (*New York Times*, January 14, 1978). . . .

[Disini headed the small Philippine Tobacco Filters Corporation.] Then, on July 21, 1975 FM issued Presidential Decree 750 in order to "ensure fair competition in the local cigarette industry as well as to stimulate the development and growth of the local manufacturers of cigarette filter rods."

In the words of the *New York Times*, "the decree imposed a 100% duty on the imported raw materials of Mr. Disini's American and British owned competitor, Filtrone Philippines, Inc. and continued the usual 10% tariff on those used by Mr. Disini's company." Mr. Marcos issued the decree in 1975 after Filtrone had turned down an offer from Mr. Disini to buy it out, according to a former executive of Filtrone. The decree forced Filtrone to close its operations in the Philippines and left Mr. Disini with a near monopoly (in fact 75%) of the lucrative filter business. . . .

Now, Disini heads Herdis Management and Investment Corporation which controls some 30-odd enterprises, which altogether have assets of over P200M. . . .

A major Herdis subsidiary is Asia Industries, Inc. [AII] which was acquired in 1975 from its American owners. . . . AII is . . . the agent for Westinghouse, ITT, Peterbilt, Thermaking, and FMC Corporation . . . AII is the Philippine representative of Westinghouse Power System Company which brings us to the notorious Herdis-Westinghouse deal which a London publication, the *New Statesman*, called the "latest, probably the greatest nuclear bribe scandal."

For the Bataan Nuclear Power Project, two American companies presented their proposals: General Electric, in a "thoroughly documented proposal" with detailed costs and specifications for two 600 megawatt reactors amounting to $700M; and Westinghouse in nothing more than its standard advertising brochures, quoting a price of $500M for two reactors of the same megawatts. However, when Westinghouse presented its formal bid, the price increased to $1.2 billion for the two reactors.

A few months after this formal bid, the price again jumped, this time to $1.1 billion for just one 620 reactor. . . . This is the price at which the project was finally approved. . . .

Disini and several of his companies profited further from this deal. For "assistance in obtaining the contract and for implementation services," Mr. Disini stood to gain a commission and/or service fee estimated between $4 million to $35 million, according to *Time* Magazine. In addition, a year-old Disini company, Power Contractors, Inc. won the contract as chief subcontractor of civil works in the nuclear project. Technesphere Consultants Group, a Herdis company, will provide engineering and construction management. Still another Disini company, Summa Insurance [wrote a $10 million policy for the project, the] largest single policy ever written in the Philippines. The contract to install communications at the project site was won by ITT, of which AII is the Philippine agent. . . .[4]

[There follows a listing of 37 corporations in the Herdis group.[5]]

Manuel and Fred Elizalde

. . . [There follows a listing of 12 Elizalde-controlled companies.]

Juan Ponce Enrile

. . . After the initial Marcos victory, Enrile was awarded his first government post as Commissioner of Customs. He was subsequently appointed Secretary of Justice and later on as Secretary of National Defense. He lost badly in the Senatorial elections of 1971 but Mr. Marcos ignored the people's explicit rejection of Enrile as a worthy public servant and in turn reappointed him to the post of Secretary of National Defense. . . .

While most people know Enrile as the Minister of National Defense, this is only one of the pillars of Enrile's power. He has two other sources: virtual or almost complete control of the logging and coconut industries.

General [Romeo] Espino

General Romeo Espino is the present [1979] Chief-of-Staff of the Armed Forces of the Philippines. . . .

[There follows a listing of 11 Espino-controlled companies.]

Antonio D. Floirendo

Antonio D. Floirendo is a close personal friend of both FM and FL [the First Lady]. . . .

He got his big break in the early 1970s when he was awarded the lease of Davao Penal Colony land for his banana business . . . .Together with FM he owns, among other companies, Sucrest, the giant sugar refinery in the U.S. Sucrest is the sole refinery using the quota of raw sugar from the Philippines. . . .

[There follows a listing of 6 other Floirendo companies.]

The Marcos Family

Dr. Pacifico Marcos, the youngest brother of Ferdinand, is Chairman of the much-criticized Medicare Commission. . . .

Elizabeth Keon Marcos is the governor of Ilocos.[6]

[There follows a listing of 47 companies controlled by members of Ferdinand Marcos's family. This does not include Imelda Marcos's family, which is covered below.]

The Romualdez Family[7]

Benjamin "Kokoy" Romualdez is a brother of Imelda....Before Marcos took power he was generally unemployed and had no achievement to his name. However, he was formerly ambassador to Peking and at present is the governor of Leyte....[8]

Kokoy is presently the owner of the *Times Journal*, and under names of other people owns or controls other institutions. He controls the Philippine Trust Company....

[There follows a listing 10 companies controlled by Romualdez relatives and 69 other companies controlled by known fronts or business partners of Kokoy Romualdez.]

Ricardo Silverio

Ricardo C. Silverio is one of the closest friends of FM....

[There follows a listing of 21 Silverio-controlled firms.][9]

Luis Villafuerte

[Various conflicts of interest are described.] At present, Villafuerte is not only Minister of Trade but also a lawyer-consultant for around two dozen multinational corporations through Villafuerte, Zamora, and Associates....

[There follows a listing of 9 companies in which Villafuerte holds major interests.]

Conclusion

We have tried to show how Mr. Marcos has used martial law to enrich himself, the members of his immediate family, and his cronies.

Our lists were in no way complete, but we feel that we have presented enough data to make a case against Mr. Marcos's allegations that he has imposed martial law to reform the oligarchic structure of society.

What Mr. Marcos has actually done has been to perpetuate himself in political power and extend his control to corporate life and consequently enrich himself, his relatives, and his cronies.

In spite of his often repeated promises of reforming the oligarchic structure of society, Mr. Marcos's policy toward the traditional elite has in no way been consistent; he has been very selective with regard to whose wealth he chooses to "reform" in contrast to those whose wealth he chooses to fortify and extend. For example, Mr. Marcos had the military "sequester" all the corporations of the Jacintos but he has shown a lot of favor to the Elizaldes. These are two traditional families—the difference being that one is in active collaboration with him, while the other opposed him during his bid for reelection in 1969.

Marcos has created a new one out of his cronies. Disini, Cuenca, Silverio, and Villafuerte stand out as cronies who were formerly ordinary employees or small textile merchants but are now multi-millionaires who were able to become rich only upon the imposition of martial law.

Editors' Notes

1. In June 1983, Presidential Letter of Instruction 1330 voided penalties imposed by the Central Bank against Benedicto's Republic Planters Bank for failing to maintain adequate reserves.

2. Eduardo is the godfather to Ferdinand Marcos's son and grandson; Marcos is godfather to Eduardo's eldest son named Marcos.

3. In 1980, the government bailed out Cuenca's construction company when it was threatened with bankruptcy.

4. In 1980, Dr. Robert Pollard of the Washington-based Union of Concerned Scientists reported that the plant would not be safe, reliable, or economically rational. Specifically, he charged that the plant as designed could not meet post-Three Mile Island licensing standards in the United States. For discussion of the substantial safety risks involved, as well as the political and economic context, see Walden Bello, Peter Hayes, and Lyuba Zarsky, "'500-Mile Island': The Philippine Nuclear Reactor Deal," *Pacific Research* vol. 10, no. 1, first quarter 1979; Robert Pollard,

"More Facts on the Bataan Nuclear Plant" (1981), Third World Studies Program, University of the Philippines, Discussion Paper No. 22; Senator Lorenzo M. Tanada, "The Bataan Nuclear Power Plant: A Monument to Man's Folly, Pride, and Refusal to Admit Mistakes," Alliance of Concerned Teachers—Philippines, et al., 1983. In 1986, following the Chernobyl accident in the Soviet Union, the administration of Corazon Aquino announced that it would not go ahead with the plant.

5. Disini's mismanaged firms were bailed out by the government in the 1980s.

6. Marcos's son replaced his aunt in 1983 as governor of Ilocos Norte.

7. This is the family of Imelda Marcos who herself served as Minister of Human Settlements and Governor of Metro-Manila.

8. Kokoy served concurrently as governor of Leyte, ambassador to the United States, and member of the National Assembly.

9. Silverio's companies were since bailed out by the government.

Selection 7.3: Tables on Living Conditions under Martial Law

Editors' Introduction

As documented in selection 6.2 above, poverty and inequality were

pervasive aspects of life in the Philippines before martial law. But, as might be expected when strikes are illegal and the dictator is committed to nothing so much as the aggrandizement of his family and friends, these conditions grew even worse in the years after 1972.

Table 1 below demonstrates that the average monthly earnings of wage earners in the Philippines, after correcting for inflation, had declined some 20 percent over the course of the decade. In agriculture, the drop was 30 percent, and in commerce 40 percent.

Table 2 shows that both skilled and unskilled wage earners in Manila suffered sharp declines in their living standards, with the former earning in 1980 less than two-thirds what they did in 1972 and the latter about half.

Of course, with the oil price rises in 1973 and 1979, all non-petroleum exporting nations suffered economically in the 1970s. But the suffering in the Philippines was not uniformly distributed across the population. As Table 3 shows, the poor got a decreasing share of the national income from 1971 to 1981 while the rich increased their share. Indeed, in 1981, the top 10 percent of families received twice the income of the bottom 60 percent.

Table 4 indicates the priorities of the martial law government. The fraction of the national government budget spent on education decreased from about a quarter before martial law to less than a tenth by the end of the decade. It might be noted that the size of the armed forces of the Philippines more than doubled in this period.

Table 1
Index of real average monthly earnings of wage earners in the Philippines, in selected industries, 1972 = 100.

Year	All	Agriculture	Mfg	Commerce
1972	100	100	100	100
1973	87.4	77.2	97.6	77.5
1974	71.6	66.3	80.4	60.7
1975	75.1	76.7	83.7	58.4
1976	78.9	80.5	85.4	65.3
1977	72.9	62.4	81.2	62.4
1978	76.3	62.7	90.8	63.1
1979	80.8	70.4	84.3	67.8
1980	82.5	68.4	87.2	62.6

Source: National Economic and Development Authority, **Statistical Yearbook of the Philippines, 1979**, pp. 595-597 divided by CPI for Phil. p. 574; 1981, pp. 132-33 divided by CPI for Phil. Note: Agriculture, Manufacturing, and Commerce account for 75% of total employment.

Table 2
Real wage rates of laborers in industrial establishments in Manila and suburbs, 1972 = 100.

Year	Skilled Laborers	Unskilled Laborers
1972	100	100
1973	92.4	90.0
1974	75.6	72.6
1975	72.7	72.9
1976	71.2	72.3
1977	72.9	70.4
1978	76.1	68.4
1979	70.8	60.6
1980	63.7	53.4

Source: National Economic and Development Authority, **Statistical Yearbook of the Philippines, 1982.**
Note: After 1980, the Philippine government stopped publishing data on actual wages received, providing data on "legislated wage rates," which, given the widespread evasion of minimum wages, are essentially worthless.

Table 3
Percentage Share of Total Family Incomes of Different Income Groups

Year	Lowest 40%	Lowest 60%	Top 20%	Top 10%
1971	11.9	24.3	52.6	37.1
1978	10.3	22.3	57.7	41.4
1979	10.0	22.1	58.0	42.0
1980	9.7	21.8	57.4	40.9
1981	9.3	21.1	58.6	42.0

Source: Ellen H. Palanca, "Poverty and Inequality: Trends and Causes," **Philippines After 1972: A Multidisciplinary Perspective,** ed. Ramon C. Reyes, Budhi Papers [VI] (Quezon City: Ateneo de Manila University, School of Arts and Sciences, 1985), p. 109. 1975 data omitted because of serious problems with 1975 data collection.

Table 4

Budget of the Ministry of Education, Culture and Sports* as a Percent of the National Government Budget, 1970-1981.

Year	Percent
1970	24.97
1971	27.03
1972	26.23
1973	16.33
1974	17.18
1975	11.31
1976	7.51
1977	7.45
1978	11.14
1979	10.70
1980	9.01
1981	7.61

Source: National Economic and Development Authority, **Statistical Yearbook of the Philippines, 1984,** p. 501

* Originally the Department of Education, became the Department of Education and Culture in a 1972 reorganization.

Selection 7.4: Agrarian Reform in the Philippines, Rand Corporation

Editors' Introduction

Marcos called his martial law regime the "New Society" because, he asserted, the Philippines would at last be able to tackle some of its most persistent problems. In particular, Marcos declared that "Land reform is the only gauge for the success or failure of the New Society. If land reform fails, there is no New Society." Many observers were skeptical of Marcos's announced commitment to reform, given that he had not been a champion of social reform before 1972. And this skepticism proved war-

ranted, as was indicated by a 1977 seminar on land reform in the Philippines, sponsored by the Rand Corporation, a U.S. Air Force-funded think tank. Following is an extract from the report of that seminar, which brought together academics and U.S. government officials.

Source: Gerald C. Hickey and John L. Wilkinson, *Agrarian Reform in the Philippines*, Report of a Seminar, December 16-17, 1977 at the Rand Corporation, Washington, D.C., P-6194, Santa Monica, CA [?]: Rand Corporation, August 1978, pp. 3-15.

It was the consensus of the seminar that the present agrarian reform program in the Philippines is failing. Discussion and analysis focused on five interrelated reasons.

* As the program is presently structured, there is little likelihood that the current program will attain its goals of (1) effecting a more equitable distribution of land, and (2) stimulating an increase in agricultural production.

* Program implementation has been extremely slow.

* Many small landlords with holdings of less than 15 hectares have opposed the program.

* In many cases, tenants have demonstrated a reluctance to participate in the program.

* The Marcos government lacks the political will to push the program to a successful conclusion.

As the program is structured, the equity goal falls far short of bringing about any significant redistribution of land or income. . . . Only corn and rice lands have been affected, leaving the majority of the agricultural lands (including the large estates) outside the scope of the program. Further, since the program is applied to holdings in excess of seven hectares, only 520,000 of the total 914,000 corn and rice tenants are eligible to receive title. . . . In addition, other segments of the rural poor, such as the unemployed or landless farm laborers, do not benefit at all from the reform.

While the agrarian reform program places new burdens on both the small landlords and eligible tenants, other segments of the population, such as owners of large sugar, coconut, and banana estates, and urban property have remained totally unaffected. . . .

Another shortcoming of the agrarian reform program is that it has proceeded at a very slow pace. As of late 1977 . . . some 247,862 Certificates of Land Transfer (CLTs) had been printed for 520,000 tenants eligible to receive land. Only 130,000 of the CLTs have been distributed to villages, but a great many have not been given to the tenants because of legal barriers. Compensation has been paid by the Land Bank on 78,650 hectares for 41,614 tenants, who represent only 4.6 percent of the total number of tenants. Considering that the program has been in existence for five years, this is a low figure especially when it only represents about half the percentage of performance by Ngo Dinh Diem's land reform program in South Vietnam during the late 1950s—a program generally considered unsuccessful.

Considerable discussion during the seminar was focused on the roles of landlords and tenants and the relationships that exist between them. One reason the agrarian reform program is failing is that a great many of the small landlords oppose it. Also, a large number of tenants have been reluctant to participate in the program because of the way it is structured. . . .

Small holdings of less than fifteen hectares are now the predominant type of landholding in the rural areas. Unlike most of the large landlords of previous times, the small landlords have other occupations, such as civil servants, teachers, judges, surveyors, and army personnel. They have worked to accumulate some land as a supplementary source of income and as an important investment for retirement. In general, they have been opposed to the land transfer program because, in addition to losing future income from the rented land, they have had no guarantee that they will be compensated for land taken by the government. The government, however, has been careful in dealing with this opposition, and no small landlords have been jailed. . . .

Although the tenants are often portrayed as the benefactors of the agrarian reform, many of them have been unwilling to participate in the program. Significantly, seminar participants noted that some tenants have been jailed for their opposition to the program.

The primary reason for the tenants' attitude is that the added administrative responsibilities and financial burdens of becoming amortizing owners only serve to heighten their already deep-rooted uncertainty concerning the future. Most tenants are numbered among the rural poor in the Philippines and in normal times their survival is constantly being tested by capricious weather conditions, invasions of their crops by pests, and fluctuating prices. . . .

. . . A tenant receiving the average-size rice unit of 1.8 hectares assumes new financial obligations for amortization payments, taxes, farm cooperative dues, and other costs, amounting to around 1300 pesos annually. This is a staggering sum, given that the average yearly income of a tenant farmer in the relatively prosperous province of Nueva Ecija was estimated at some 1500 pesos in 1976.

One result of these burdens has been a great number of defaults (some claim a majority) on amortization payments. In this regard, infusions of credit by the government do not appear to have had a beneficial effect. In situations where the government has provided credit to new owners it has usually done so in an arbitrary and inefficient manner. . . . Many of the loan recipients were tenant farmers and sharecroppers who, with the increase of available credit, found that their rents were being raised by the landlords. In effect, much of the credit supplied actually became an income transfer from the government to the landlords. . . .

During the past four to five years, the government has made considerable investments in irrigation systems and infrastructural communal water systems, bringing irrigation to large areas. Without any personal investment, this has proven to be a windfall gain for landlords, who have seen an increase in the productivity of their lands. . . .

Uncertainty is also engendered by the growing fear among tenants that, as the government has become more concerned with rural development during the last five years, if they default on agrarian reform loans they can be jailed. There are cases, in fact, where the military have gone into villages and threatened the population with jail if they default. This has added to the uncertainty of the tenants to the point that they may fear to invest in their farms and take out loans for irrigation development, thus continuing the pattern of lack of water management. . . .

In the past few years it has been increasingly apparent that the Marcos government has lost interest in supporting agrarian reform. This has made even more tenants reluctant to participate in the program and has affected the self-image of some tenants who are amortizing owners. In a recent survey funded by AID [the U.S. Agency for International Development] and conducted by the Social Science Research Unit in the Bicol River basin region of southern Luzon, 50 percent of the farmers classified by the Department of Agrarian Reform (DAR) as landowners actually perceived themselves as share tenants or, at most, lessees. In their own eyes their status had not been altered by the program. . . .

Thus far, implementation of the agrarian reform program has been most successful in Central Luzon, where most of the 41,614 new amortizing owners . . . are located. Since this region has special characteristics, however, its success cannot be used to measure the potential performance in other regions of the Philippines. . . .

The observation was made during the seminar that if the agrarian reform program did result in a breakdown of the old patron-client relationship it might have the beneficial result of leaving the tenant free to participate in community organizations. It was pointed out, however, that agrarian reform came about through the declaration of martial law and that the idea of the peasant being free to participate in community decisionmaking is incompatible with martial law. The Samahang Nayon farmer associations illustrate this situation. While they were formed as part of the agrarian reform program, they function not as instruments of democratic decisionmaking, but of government control. . . .

Probably the most important reason the agrarian reform program in the Philippines is languishing is because there is no political will on the part of the Marcos government to see the program implemented to a successful conclusion. This appears to be directly related to at least one, unstated, political goal of the program—the attempt by Marcos to win the support of the peasantry by promising to give them land. When the agrarian reform was promulgated in 1972, however, Marcos failed to appreciate the fact that he would be dealing not with a group of large landowners, but a sizable number of small landlords. . . .

A successful agrarian reform program would undoubtedly benefit the rural poor, especially those with access to the land. Their lot has worsened, with landless farm laborers experiencing a 30 percent decline of real wages in the past 25 years. At the same time, the rural population is growing at the rate of 2 to 2.5 percent annually, which means that, since the agrarian reform began five years ago, an estimated one million new families have been formed in the rural areas. To this should be added the fact that, although the Philippines enjoys considerable natural resources, including access to good fishing areas, the nutritional standard is equal to that of Bangladesh, which is one of the world's lowest.

Selection 7.5: Tourism Promotion and Prostitution,
A. Lin Neumann

Editors' Introduction

A major aspect of the Philippine government's development strategy under martial law was tourism promotion. Economically, tourism could provide the country with a ready source of foreign exchange (though in fact much of it was used up on importing luxury goods for the tourists). More important from Marcos's perspective were the political benefits of tourism: luxurious accommodations and political stability generated good will among foreign business people and international bankers whose support the regime needed.

As part of the tourism promotion effort, Marcos sponsored the construction of 14 first-class hotels and a luxurious conference center in Manila at a cost of over $450 million, most of the financing coming from the government. The government spent some thirty to forty times as much on these facilities as it did on desperately needed public housing. Many of the new hotel rooms remained empty, requiring the government to bail out the private owners, often Marcos's relatives and cronies.

A different sort of impact of the government's promotion of tourism was the dramatic rise in prostitution, as described in the following article by journalist A. Lin Neumann. (For a fuller discussion of the tourism issue, see Linda Richter, *Land Reform and Tourism Development: Policy-Making in the Philippines,* Cambridge, MA: Schenkman, 1982.)

Source: A. Lin Neumann, "Scandal in Manila," *Ms.* February 1984, pp. 99-102.

Prostitution fueled by tourism in the Philippines involves at least 150,000 women by an estimate of the Liwayway Calalang, an official of the ministry of labor.

Of course tourism, the number three foreign-exchange earner for the Philippines, did not create prostitution. But the government's reliance on the travel trade as a quick fix for foreign exchange troubles and a shaky economy created the climate for an explosion in flesh-peddling as the Philippines—along with Thailand, South Korea, Taiwan, and other Asian nations—has become a center for everything from child prostitution to the well-publicized "sex-tours" favored by Japanese businessmen.

Before 1973 the Philippines was not much of a tourist spot. The combination of street crime and well-organized demonstrations against American imperialism and the Vietnam war created a less-than-friendly environment for a fun seeker. When President Ferdinand Marcos declared martial law on September 21, 1972, a lot of that changed. Criminals were rounded up and the political opposition jailed. In 1973 the Ministry of Tourism was established with former Marcos press agent Jose Aspiras in charge, and the number of visitors rapidly increased from less than 150,000 in 1971 to more than a million in 1980. A hotel-building boom occurred between 1974 and 1980, resulting in the construction of a dozen government-sponsored five-star emporiums. During the same period, the number of licensed cocktail lounges in Manila grew from 93 to 225. A cocktail lounge is understood, in Manila, Bangkok, and most of the tourist locales of Asia, to be a place where women are available, along with plenty of wine. They are licensed separately by municipal governments and constitute, along with massage parlors and go-go joints, the heart of the prostitution trade.

Sixty-six percent of all visitors to the Philippines in 1981 were male; 20 percent came from Japan and of the nearly 200,000 Japanese, 80 percent were male, according to figures released by the Philippine ministry of tourism. Americans also comprised 20 percent of the tourists but the proportion of men and women was more equal.

For Japanese men the main lure has been the sex tour. It's a very simple device. An agent in Japan puts together a package that include a "night-life tour" of Manila (or Taipei, or Seoul, or Bangkok). The cost of a night with a prostitute is included in the agent's fee. A tour operator in Manila takes over when the guests touch down, and generally everything is included—from buffet-style breakfasts in a five-star hotel to a stop at a "club." Everybody gets a piece of the action. Typically the woman costs about $60. She gets a little more than $5 of the fee, and the rest is divided between club owner, the tour guides, and the tour operator, with a few dollars thrown in for police protection. The hotel often gets $10 on top of that figure for a "joiner's fee," which allows the man to keep his guest in the room overnight. The women report that they are dependent for their living on cajoling tips out of their customers on top of the fee already paid. "Usually the Japanese will give us gifts or money but sometimes," joked one of the women, "it's TY only." ("TY" is Manila slang for "thank you.")

There is a lot of money in this system. Government figures show that the Japanese spend more than any other category of visitor—approximately $70 per day per visitor. Add in the cost of women, which is off the books and not counted in the $344 million earnings the government reported from tourism in 1980, and the figure nearly doubles.

Observers do not accuse the government of actually selling women, but little is done to curb the trade despite the nominal illegality of prostitution in the Philippines. "Well, I think, yes," said Calalang when asked if there was a relationship between tourism and prostitution. "If tourism is being promoted in the south, for example, the women will be there. They go where our tourism is promoted." Ben Abogadie, an officer in the Philippine Tourism Authority, a governmental promotional body, said the government was trying to promote other kinds of tourism but added, "Of course, we call this a country of beautiful women."

One way, presumably, to contact those beautiful women is to consult books like *Back Street of the World*, published by Freedom Nations Publishers of Tokyo. A sample: "When you meet a Filipina if you can say a few Tagalog words then her body and soul will be yours." *Playtown for Men*, another such guidebook, is illustrated with cartoons that advise the eager customer to steer clear of cabdrivers and instead consult the hotel bellhop for assistance in procuring women.

Professor Romeo Zarco of the University of the Philippines has made several studies of the prostitution problem. He is critical of the government's unwillingness to consider the social effects of tourism on the country, contending that the government refuses even to study the problem. "We are sometimes even called subversives," he said, "because we do not like tourism."

The seamiest scene in Manila now is the child-prostitution racket. Boys and girls, some as young as nine years old, can be found in the beer gardens or chatting with foreigners in shopping areas near the hotel district. A foreign male seated in one of the cruising areas will quickly be approached by a young boy—usually dressed in designer jeans and a well-tailored shirt—who will ask if he is looking for company and then produce a child and negotiate the price.

About a third of the children are girls, and the rest find their clients among gay men, mostly Europeans, who have received the word that Manila is a good place to find young boys. Many of the children reportedly have been sold into the business by parents in rural areas who, desperate for money, fall prey to the claims of recruiters that the children will be able to send money home. They can be seen not only in Manila but also at outlying tourist spots like Pagsanjan Falls—where some tour guides double as pimps.

There is a complicated system at work among the children that includes street gangs, foreign contacts, and police payoffs, and it is rumored to be headed by the son of a Manila politician. The situation is well known on the streets, but it has been kept out of the local press. A series on the phenomenon was slated to appear in a prominent Manila daily. It was killed, reportedly, after the First Lady made the editor aware of her displeasure with the first installment of the exposé.

This system of prostitution, especially the region-wide sex tours, has begun to draw fire from militant women networking in the Philippines, Japan, and elsewhere. In 1981, Zenko Suzuki, Prime Minister of Japan, then on a goodwill visit to the Philippines and Thailand, was confronted at several stops in Manila by women representing several church-related social justice organizations. "Your good intention of projecting an image of a friendly Japan is being destroyed by the Japanese male tourists who invade Asia in organized sex tours and degrade our women shamelessly," said the women in an open letter to Suzuki signed by 46 organizations. Thai women mounted a similar campaign.

The women's efforts were coordinated with the Asian Women's Association, based in Japan. The association has been lobbying for an end to the tours since about 1973 when a Korean women's group, now banned by the martial law government there, organized the first protests against the system. Women are finding one another in regional conferences and through journals such as "Asian Women's Liberation," the newsletter of the Japanese feminists.

The networks of women in the Philippines have become increasingly vocal following the protests lodged against the Suzuki visit. The Third World Movement Against the Exploitation of Women (TWMAEW), headquartered in Manila, hopes to become a region-wide coordinating body. A Filipina nun, Sister Soledad "Sol" Perpiñan, is credited with forming TWMAEW, whose aim is to be "an action-oriented, networking Women's Movement." Speaking in Manila, Sister Sol said, "We must take action to change an unjust economic structure. We will no longer allow the Japanese or any other nationality to invade our country and exploit our women." She further contends that the profits of the system are almost all repatriated to Japan. "The actual amount of money retained by the women is only one fifth to one tenth of what is paid as the prostitution fee—this is the structure of exploitation."

The members of TWMAEW are drawn mostly from the ranks of the religious and academe. Little organizing is done among the prostitutes themselves, but the issue is slowly cropping up in the consciousness of the politically active in Manila. It is rare that a forum on the oppression of, say, industrial workers, will not also mention the condition of women and the exploitation of prostitutes.

"We had been fighting against the tours but with little effect before Philippine and Thai women joined in the movement," said Sister Filo Hirota, a Japanese now working in Manila. A sympathetic chord has been stuck among Filipinas as a result of the protests both among women who are morally offended by the system and those who see the prostitution problem as one linked to the authoritarian government of the country. "The government is not only selling women to foreigners, but also the sovereignty of the nation itself," said Karina David, a sociologist at the University of the Philippines. "The problem of prostitution tourism will not be solved unless the present socioeconomic system that supports it is fundamentally changed."

Philippine government officials are reluctant to discuss the problem (they will not even acknowledge the existence of child prostitution), although it was pointed out that Japanese tours have declined significantly. "Sex tourism? It belongs to the past already," said Abogadie, "I don't think the ministry of tourism has done anything about prostitution," countered Professor Zarco, who noted, along with most observers, that the decline in sex tours has been the result of Japanese government pressure on Japanese tours, *not* diligence on the part of local Philippine officials.

Indeed, following the Suzuki visit and follow-up visits by Japanese tourism authorities in 1981, the tours were at least curtailed, if not halted.

The reaction to the Japanese had been building prior to the Suzuki visit. In November 1980, Takako Doi, a Japanese woman and a member of the Diet (Japan's Parliament), rose to the floor, denounced the sex tours, and called for an investigation. Philippine women, acting under the leadership of Sister Sol's organization (TWMAEW), issued a position paper on prostitution that called attention to the sex tours and sought to influence world opinion during the World Tourism Conference, a travel industry showpiece, held in Manila that fall. By the time Prime Minister Suzuki arrived in Manila in January, 1981, the movement was strong enough to gather a thousand supporters to protest the visit and dog his steps. Similar activities highlighted the visit of Suzuki to Thailand.

Upon his return to Japan, Suzuki "took measures," according to press reports, to counter the tours. At about the same time Jose Aspiras, Philippine Minister of Tourism, spoke out against the tours. The Japan Association of Travel Agents, a coordinating body, was pressured by the Japanese government to penalize member agencies that promote sex tours. Advertisements for the tours, which used to promote openly the sexual aspects of the voyage, have virtually disappeared from the Tokyo press. Japanese visits to the Philippines declined 26 percent from 1980 to 1981, and then dropped 17 percent in 1982. (More than 80 percent of Japanese visitors continue to be male, however.)

But as soon as the problem begins to recede in one place, it crops up in another: child prostitution in Manila is growing, and it is estimated that as many as 5,000 children are involved. Japanese sources point to the importation of Filipina "entertainers" into Japan by organized crime figures, and sources in the region report that the tour business, with women as an inducement, has increased in Indonesia and Sri Lanka.

Asian women were among participants from 24 countries who attended an unprecedented meeting last April in Rotterdam. Out of this 10-day meeting—organized by Kathleen Barry, author of *Female Sexual Slavery* (Prentice-Hall)—was formed the International Feminist Network Against Traffic in Women and Female Sexual Slavery to combat international trafficking of women and forced prostitution.

The mystique of the Asian woman—beautiful, obedient, available—combined with the poverty, underdevelopment, and authoritarian government of the Philippines, has obviously created a sex market. The ministry of labor in the Philippine could only tell this reporter that the First Lady of the country was personally concerned about each of the "girls" and that they are advised to guard their morals so that they won't be swept away by prostitution. It doesn't wash.

*   *   *

Lucinda [names have been fictionalized] is 16. She sits in a dingy open-air beer garden in the crowded "tourist belt" of Ermita, Manila. A light-skinned product of a liaison between her Filipina mother and a German tourist, Lucinda often acts as a "mamasan" to the young boys and girls she "introduces to foreigners." On the night we spoke, she had just gotten out of jail for "making trouble." She chain-smokes cigarettes, sniffs glue, and talks in a clipped manner. Lucinda is part of the burgeoning trade in child prostitutes. "I go with the men. I arrange for the others to go," she says matter-of-factly.

Loretta is 28. She works in a nightclub where the entertainment consists of approximately 200 women who sit on one side of the main room and wait to be chosen—by numbers pinned on their brightly colored party dresses—when the busloads of Japanese tourists arrive. Loretta supports two children from her $200 monthly earnings—far more, she notes, than she could earn working for the $3.50 a day factory wage. The children live with her grandparents in the province, a common arrangement for women in the "hospitality industry." "Of course, I hate this," Loretta says as we talk in the cramped home of a neighbor, "but there is no other way to make this much money."

Inday, 23, is a familiar sight along MH del Pilar Street, the main drag of the tourist belt. Dressed in a tight-fitting split skirt, she calls out to the men who cruise the avenue. She provides hospitality at a dark little pub famous for the photographs of foreign journalists that adorn the space above the bar. Once inside, the men can buy Inday and her co-workers "Ladies drinks" for about $3 a hit, of which the women receive $1.50. They can then negotiate for an evening's entertainment, pay the "bar fine" ($20 to $30), and take Inday back to their hotel. Inday has been at the bar for about three years. Perched on a bar stool in the pale afternoon light, she explains that she is three months pregnant and looking for an abortion (abortion, like divorce, is illegal in the Philippines). She tells a common tale: her father used to beat her; a boyfriend jilted her; a friend invited her to come to Manila from her home province of Bicol; she was hired as a waitress and only later discovered the duties expected of her. Her living depends on cajoling men into the bar. "I will leave here," she says hopefully, "if I can maybe save some money or meet someone who will marry me."

Cecile, a 14-year old, has been going with men for two years. She wears a T-shirt that says "I am a newly made Filipino—I am from God, the country, and the people." She ran away from a poor slum family to join a sister who works as a go-go dancer at a garish bar on del Pilar. "The men like small, young-looking brown girls," she said. "They don't like them when they are white." She is a leader among the children and carries the tattoo of one of the street gangs in the area. She had recently been in jail for several days. "Some drunk policemen—I know them, they had tried to rape me before—arrested me and took me to the station. They beat me," she explained, showing the bruises on her frail body to a couple of reporters. She feels that "when I am twenty-five, I will still be poor" and that she has nowhere to go. She drinks cough syrup to get high, and on nights when she has no customers, she sleeps in a city park.

Selection 7.6: 1975 Mission to the Philippines, Amnesty International

Editors' Introduction

Martial law, of course, means the suspension of many basic rights of the population. The following extract is taken from the conclusions and recommendations of a report on the Philippines by Amnesty International, based on a fact-finding mission it conducted to that country in late 1975. The International Commission of Jurists issued similar findings in 1977. Marcos responded to these reports with platitudes, and, indeed, because opposition to his rule grew stronger, human rights abuses intensified, as can be seen in a later Amnesty International report [selection 7.14].

Source: Amnesty International, *Report of an Amnesty International Mission to the Republic of the Philippines, 22 November-5 December 1975,* London: Amnesty International Publications, 1977, 2nd edition, pp. 13-19.

Conclusions and Recommendations to the Government of the Philippines

1. The mission found convincing evidence that the employment of torture was widespread. Of 107 prisoners interviewed, 71 informed the delegates that they had been tortured. . . .

2. The conclusion is unavoidable that torture of prisoners was part of a general approach to the treatment of suspects. This had the effect of intimidating all those arrested on suspicion of having committed political offenses . . . .

3. None of the prisoners interviewed had been convicted, although trial proceedings have begun for some of them. The mission asked the Judge Advocate General for transcripts of all proceedings against political offenders which had been concluded in the period of martial law since September 1972. None was made available to the mission. From this and other evidence, it appears probable to Amnesty International that not a single political prisoner detained under martial law had a trial which had been concluded. . . .

4. In cases of prisoners against whom trial proceedings had begun, the mission found that all known cases had been tainted by reliance on so-called evidence extracted from a number of prisoners by torture. The conclusion is unavoidable that in those cases the so-called evidence was literally tortured into existence. . . .

5. All the cases listed in this report are triable under martial law only by military commissions. These tribunals are staffed entirely by military officers, some of whom have had no legal training. The rules of procedure and evidence employed in trials before these tribunals are not those of civil or normal standards of justice, but instead follow the rules of procedure and evidence of military court martial. . . .

Moreover, under martial law, the appeals from these military tribunals end at the Department of National Defense. The power of presidential clemency is the only limitation on military authority.

6. The mission found that there was clearly a pattern of torture during the period of interrogation immediately following arrest. In many cases, the fact that a prisoner had been detained was concealed from his family and others.

The United Nations Standard Minimum Rules for the Treatment of Prisoners are applicable from the time of arrest and throughout the period of detention. . . .

7. The most effective safeguard for the arbitrary arrest, detention and ill-treatment of the citizen is the right to apply to the courts for the writ of *habeas corpus*.

Amnesty International *recommends* that the right of application for the writ of *habeas corpus*, denied under martial law, should be re-established without delay.

8. The mission found certain patterns of arrest and interrogation procedures. Typically, prisoners are arrested by military officers often belonging to different units. Following their arrest, they are taken out by particular units for interrogation. Thus, prisoners are taken to the offices of a particular unit or an interrogation center such as Metrocom-2, where they are tortured. They can then be taken by different units to other locations for further interrogation, often accompanied by torture. . . .

9. All forms of brutal treatment of prisoners are reprehensible. The government should issue instructions explicitly forbidding such torture as "Russian roulette," electric shock, the application of what the prisoners describe as "truth serum" and all other forms of brutal treatment. The government should state publicly the penalties for such offenses. . . .

10. The mission found that the system of amnesties for which prisoners could apply under martial law in effect deprived prisoners of their civil rights. The application forms (CAD form 72-11) required the prisoners to indicate which kind of offense they had committed, including elaboration of the alleged offenses. Most prisoners claimed that they had nothing to say which could incriminate them and were unable to meet these requirements. Many of these requirements were unacceptable to them, since they were in effect required to fabricate self-accusations. Moreover, of those prisoners in the detention centers visited who had applied for individual amnesties, very few applications were known to have been approved.

In the case of a number of prisoners held at Camp Olivas, the mission was given a copy of the instruction from the Secretary of National Defense granting amnesties to seven young detainees. When the mission inquired why those prisoners had not been released despite the instruction, the mission was informed that the order had been countermanded. The mission noted that no further appeal regarding amnesties was possible beyond the Department of National Defense.

Further, the mission requested a list of all political prisoners who had applied for individual amnesties to the amnesty commission, and as well as details of cases where amnesty had been granted. The list requested was not given to the mission. . . .

11. The mission found that the conditions for those detained in cell block

2 in Camp Bonifacio as "immigrant/deportation" cases were appalling by any standards. . . .

12. The mission had recommended to the Secretary of National Defense that all women held in detention who had young children should be released. This applied in particular to cases where both husband and wife were detained and the young child was also kept in prison. The following cases were known to the mission:

In 5th Constabulary Unit (5 CSU) stockade:
Jean Cacayorin Tayag (young child with relatives)
Milagros-Astorga Garcia (baby aged seven weeks, born in prison)
Amarylis Hilao (baby aged seven weeks, born in prison)
Zinayda Delica (child aged 3 years, with relatives)

In Camp Olivas female detention center:
Elita Ponce Quinto (child aged five months, born in prison)
Isabelita del Pilar Guillermo (child aged six months, born in prison)

The mission understood that there were administrative provisions for the release of women with young children where both husband and wife were detained, but the mission was unable to secure an adequate explanation for the continued detention of these women prisoners. . . .

14. The mission was deeply concerned by the cases of prisoners belonging to the Hilao family. Winifredo Hilao was subjected to extremely brutal torture. So was his brother-in-law, Romeo Enriquez. Winifredo's sisters, Josefina, aged 19, and Amarylis, aged 21, are also prisoners. His wife, Violeta Sevandal, is also a prisoner. His nephew, who was seven weeks old at the time of the mission visit, was in prison with Amarylis. The family firmly believe that their sister, Liliosa, who died while in detention, was killed by her interrogators during questioning. The mission was not convinced that sufficient investigations had been undertaken by the authorities to examine the allegation that Liliosa Hilao was murdered. . . .

15. . . .the mission had requested, and were promised by leading officials of the Department of National Defense, a list of all prisoners detained under martial law, together with details of the charges against each prisoner. The mission noted with regret that they were later told that the list was not forthcoming as promised, because matters of national security were said to be involved. Amnesty International respectfully requests that a complete list should be made publicly available.

Amnesty International publicly recognizes the spirit of open and constructive dialogue with which the government received the mission. It wishes to place on record its appreciation of the courtesy and assistance given to the mission by President Marcos and leading officials. It should be noted that when the AI delegates initially requested interviews with prisoners, they had not expected to find widespread evidence of torture. In allowing AI to have access to prisoners, the Philippine government had demonstrated to governments in other countries the need to allow delegates of independent international organizations to visit prisoners, in order to ensure that internationally recognized human rights of prisoners are protected.

However, it must be stated that although permission to visit prisoners was given by senior officials, the mission encountered problems in seeking interviews with specific prisoners. Furthermore there were difficulties in particular instances in securing confidentiality of interviews. Examples are given in the report.

It is to the credit of the Philippines government that in the past it has announced general amnesties with apparently partial application to limited numbers of political prisoners held without trial. It has conducted investigations into torture allegations, although these apparently failed to uncover the scale of torture, and it has allowed an Amnesty International mission access to interview specific prisoners. But it should be noted at the same time that the evidence of torture was overwhelming, and that it appears that torture was employed systematically in order to intimidate people arrested on suspicion.

Amnesty International wishes to emphasize that it has approached the problem of political imprisonment in the Philippines strictly on the basis of the treatment of prisoners according to due process of law and human rights. The Philippines government takes the position that most of the prisoners interviewed in the report allegedly have been connected with a communist underground movement, and that many allegedly were involved in attempts to commit rebellion or conspiracy to commit rebellion. . . .

Amnesty International is concerned that many of those interviewed who were charged with rebellion or conspiracy to commit rebellion have been tortured. Moreover none of the alleged offenses has been proven conclusively in open fair trials. AI, in accordance with its statute, works to abolish torture in all cases, and also works for prisoners of conscience who have been denied fair open trials. We do not wish to pre-judge the degree of truth in the government's allegations that the prisoners are guilty of attempts at rebellion or conspiracy to commit rebellion. We therefore urge the government to present the evidence in open fair trials. . . .

Selection 7.7: The Rigged Referendum of 1973, Primitivo Mijares

Editors' Introduction

To give his dictatorial rule the cover of legitimacy, Marcos sponsored various referenda. In January 1973, he convened citizen's assemblies in every village to vote on a new constitution and approve martial law. As all observers noted, many of the claimed 35,000 assemblies never met at all and the voting was by show of hands. Not surprisingly, Marcos was able to announce overwhelming support for his regime. In July 1973, the assemblies were convened again and they approved Marcos's remaining in office until he could complete his "reforms"—that is, indefinitely. According to Philippine military authorities, even 85 percent of the prisoners in military detention centers voted yes.

Primitivo Mijares served as head of Marcos's Media Advisory Council and as such was the chief press censor for the martial law government. In 1975 he defected to the United States. Mijares, in the words of a confidential telex to the State Department from the U.S. ambassador in Manila, "has performed many services for [the] martial law regime and undoubtedly has much inside knowledge that, if made public, could cause distress to [the] government of the Philippines." After charging that Marcos tried to bribe him to prevent his appearance before the U.S. Congress, Mijares gave testimony to the House Committee on International Affairs. In January 1977, Mijares mysteriously disappeared, never to reappear; a few months later, the beaten and stabbed body of his 15-year-old son turned up at a Manila funeral parlor.

The next reading is extracted from a memorandum Mijares submitted to the U.S. Congress that sheds further light on the first of the Marcos referenda.

Source: U.S. House Committee on International Relations, *Human Rights in South Korea and the Philippines: Implications for U.S. Policy*, Hearings, 94th Congress, 1st session, 1975, p. 474.

The New Constitution, on which President Marcos anchors the legality of his holding onto the presidency after Dec. 30, 1973 [the date his second presidential term would have expired had there been no declaration of martial law], and of his other acts, was not validly ratified by the Filipino people.

(1) Mr. Marcos issued on Jan. 17, 1973, a presidential proclamation (No. 1102) in which he declared that he considered the "overwhelming vote" of the people in the Jan. 10-15 referendum in favor of the New Constitution as a "ratification" of the said Charter. . . .

(2) Assuming that a referendum vote would have been a valid vote of ratification of the New Constitution, there could not have been such valid vote because there was no real referendum held on Jan. 10 to 15, 1973.

(3) The figures cited in Proclamation No. 1102—14,976,561 in favor and 743,869 against "approval" of the Constitution—as well as the figures on the other questions fielded in the referendum were manufactured by a group headed by the President's favorite brother-in-law, Gov. Benjamin Romualdez. I was a member of that group.

(4) The original three-man Commission on Elections was brought initially into the group, but it was excluded by Gov. Romualdez on the second day when the Commission members would not sanction what they called a "farce." This is the reason the chairman and one other "uncooperative" commissioner of the Elections Commission—Jaime N. Ferrer and Lino Patajo, respectively—were eased out of the poll body in April 1973.

(5) As early as Jan. 11, 1973, or on the second day of the referendum, when it became clear that the Commission on Elections would have no part in the conduct or results of the referendum, the group manufacturing the results had the voting figures readied for submission to the President. Secretary of Local Government Jose Rone was asked by Gov. Romualdez to handle the preparation of the official report to the President.

(6) Having heard instructions from President Marcos on the various questions which he wanted to address to the referendum, we knew exactly what he wanted us to report back to him as "the vote" of the people. . . .

Selection 7.8: The Muslim Insurgency, Lela Noble

Editors' Introduction

Muslims make up some five percent of the Philippine population. Located primarily in the southern Philippines, the long-standing grievances of the Muslims against the government erupted in open warfare following the declaration of martial law. Because the fighting took place far from Manila, it received relatively little press coverage; as a frontier war, the continuity of the central government was not in question. But the costs were real enough: thousands were killed, hundreds of thousands fled to neighboring Sabah (Malaysian territory which has been claimed by the Philippines), more than a million people were displaced.

In this next article, Lela Noble, who has done extensive field research in Muslim areas of the Philippines, describes the background to the conflict and events up to 1980. For the remaining years of Marcos's rule, the Muslim insurgency was relatively quiescent, though the underlying problems remained.

Source: Lela Noble, "The Philippines: Muslims Fight for an Independent State," *Southeast Asia Chronicle*, no. 75, October 1980, pp. 12-17.

The origins of the current fighting between Muslims and the predominantly Christian government go back approximately 400 years, when Spaniards discovered the islands they called the Philippines just as many of the islanders were being converted to and organized through Islam. Both the conversion and subsequent socio-political organization had occurred primarily in the southern islands, though seafaring Muslims had also made contacts and conversions in the north. The Spaniards managed to consolidate their control in the northern islands, converted the people there to Christianity, and conscripted them into their wars against the Muslims in the south. The Spaniards called the Muslims "Moros"—a term reflecting the historical context and hence the hatred involved in the struggle. The Spaniards had been fighting Moors for years. They were convinced that the only possible terms for coexistence with such infidels were conquest and conversion. The Muslims perceived the stakes accurately, and were determined to prevent the conquest which would inevitably destroy both their religion and the way of life it mandated. Hence Spaniards—aided by Filipino Christians—fought with Muslims intermittently for 300 years.

In 1898, the United States displaced Spain in the Philippines. American perceptions and policies were different; more importantly, American power was decisively greater than Spanish power. Most Muslims eventually capitulated to American military might. The American policy of integration—which replaced the Spanish policy of conversion—was less directly a threat, but nevertheless aroused the suspicions of many Muslims. Muslims saw land registration and education, for example, as threats to their way of life and hence to their religion. They avoided both whenever possible. Some Muslim leaders also explicitly opposed plans for Philippine independence which assumed the incorporation of Muslim areas into a Republic of the Philippines.

Their opposition was ignored, and after the independent republic was formed in 1946, increasing numbers of Muslims began to participate in its political and educational systems. They faced two fundamental problems in the new state. Partly because of their own earlier policy of withdrawal and because of continuing suspicions, Muslims were in fact comparatively disadvantaged. Muslims constituted only five percent of the Philippine population and were concentrated in the southern islands of Mindanao, Basilan, Sulu, and Tawi Tawi. While it is difficult to generalize, it is probably accurate to say that a smaller percentage of Muslims were educated and hence able to compete effectively in Philippine political and economic life. Many were very poor, and economic infrastructure was much less developed in their areas than in most Christian areas. Second, the government was sponsoring a program of migration which brought thousands of Christians into areas the Muslims regarded as theirs. The result was unending land disputes, which frequently ended in litigation and/or fighting. Since laws, courts, and the constabulary were generally controlled by Christians, Muslims felt doubly discriminated against. Moreover, the migration had political implications. As issues became more polarized and Christian majorities formed in more and more southern provinces, Muslim politicians felt increasingly threatened. Both Muslim and Christian politicians developed private armies.

Violence was particularly bad during the period preceding the 1971 elections. In both Lanao and Cotabato—two areas of mixed population in which Muslim-Christian balances were changing—rival bands were involved in several major incidents. The most publicized incidents were massacres of Muslims by Christian gangs with some connections with the Philippine Constabulary. Not surprisingly the massacres caught the attention of the Islamic World.

Full-scale fighting did not break out, however, until after Marcos's declaration of martial law in 1972. There were three reasons why martial law caused an escalation in the fighting: (1) the centralization of the regime left power almost exclusively in Christian hands; (2) by restricting the range of legitimate political activity, the regime left as options only the acceptance of the regime and its promises, or anti-regime revolutionary activity; and (3) the regime's moves to collect guns from civilians meant that compliance removed the potential for eventual resort to force.

In this context the Moro National Liberation Front, which had been formed in 1970, quickly emerged to lead the anti-government resistance. It was led by young men who were generally educated in universities in the Philippines or the Middle East. They were self-consciously Muslim rather than Maranao, Maguindanao, or Tausug, the major ethno-linguistic groups in Muslim Philippines; and they were committed to change in the distribution of wealth and power. Originally linked with older Muslim politicians, they quickly disassociated themselves from them—while conserving some of the benefits of their earlier connections. Most important of these were their contacts with Muslim leaders like Tun Mustapha, then chief minister of the Malaysian state of Sabah, and Libya's Muammar Qaddafi. These men provided money, arms, and refuge. Arms and supplies were channeled through Sabah; refugees fled there. Libya provided most of the money, and increasingly, a base from which the MNLF leadership could lobby other Muslim states, separately and through the Islamic Conference of Foreign Ministers.

In 1973, 1974, and probably the first half of 1975 the MNLF steadily improved its position, reaching a height of possibly 30,000 armed men. As it consolidated organizationally it also extended its control through significant areas of Mindanao and the Sulu Archipelago. It broadened its external base of support from people like Qaddafi and Tun Mustapha to all the states connected with the Islamic Conference. As a result, the MNLF could count on attention from the annual meeting of conference foreign ministers, who commissioned a "Committee of Four" and the organization's secretary general to keep them informed of developments and to oversee negotiations.

In late 1975 and 1976, however, the MNLF lost much of its momentum and at best held its own. Battlefield fatigue and government amnesty programs made "returning to the fold of the law," in government parlance, attractive. It is impossible to know how great the inroads were during this period, because government figures were not reliable—more were reported to have surrendered than the government had ever admitted were fighting—and because it was never clear who was and who was not part of the MNLF. The MNLF said most of those who surrendered were "bad elements," not their people. Nonetheless there were some who defected during this period who had held positions of leadership in the MNLF and whose loss mattered.

Also in 1975, Tun Mustapha fell from power in Sabah. His own aid to the MNLF and his willingness to use Sabah as a conduit for Libyan aid had been critical in sustaining the scope and intensity of the fighting. Aid from Sabah was drastically curtailed by late 1975. MNLF units henceforth had to depend mostly on weapons and ammunition captured in encounters with the Marcos military or bought from corrupt troopers. Consequently, resistance groups which had joined the MNLF primarily to secure their weapons supply had little incentive to remain loyal.

External connections did remain important for facilitating negotiations between the MNLF and the Marcos regime. Because of the implicit threat of an oil embargo, which Libya at times made explicit, the Islamic states had influence on the Marcos government. Thus Marcos had to consider negotiations on terms more favorable to the MNLF than he otherwise would have. The MNLF, then, benefited from having partisan and powerful mediators. Yet it also had to compromise its goals in exchange for that mediation: it reduced its demands from independence to autonomy for a meeting in Jeddah in 1975; and it probably made other concessions before and after a meeting in Tripoli in December 1976.

Nevertheless the MNLF had every reason to be satisfied with the ceasefire and preliminary agreement approved at Tripoli (through the joint efforts of Imelda Marcos and Qaddafi). While it originally demanded that 21 provinces be included in the Bangsa Moro State and was forced to settle for 13, eight of the 13 had Christian majorities. Moreover, the principles agreed to follow closely the MNLF's demands. Within the areas of the "Autonomy for the Muslims in the Southern Philippines," Muslims were to have the right to establish their own courts, schools, and administrative system. The Autonomy was to have a legislative assembly, executive council, special regional security forces, and economic and financial system. The ceasefire also allowed the Bangsa Moro Army to recoup and regroup, whatever the outcome of the negotiations to work out final details.

The Tripoli Agreement also benefited Marcos. The Philippine Armed Forces also badly needed a ceasefire. By approving an agreement which at first appeared to contain substantive concessions on his part, Marcos managed to reduce Islamic Conference pressure and even neutralize the Libyans, the MNLF's strongest supporters. Moreover, Marcos had the power to implement the agreement as he saw fit.

The Philippine government had insisted on a clause in the preliminary agreement that it would take "all necessary constitutional processes for the implementation of the entire Agreement." According to Philippine documents, it was understood by all parties that "constitutional processes" included a referendum and elections for public officials. Marcos announced immediately after the preliminary agreement was signed that a plebiscite was "under study," then twice postponed the date because of Muslim objections. Meanwhile the Tripoli meetings had reconvened and deadlocked, with each side blaming the other for the problems. Finally Imelda Marcos flew to Tripoli to work out another compromise. An exchange of cables between Marcos and Qaddafi produced the illusion of agreement, which quickly vanished when Marcos pushed ahead with the referendum over the protests of Qaddafi, the MNLF, and Islamic Conference representatives. The results of the referendum were similar to those of all votes held under the martial law regime. Marcos got what he wanted: opposition to the inclusion of certain provinces, opposition to the degree of autonomy presumably wanted by the MNLF, and support for his plan for two autonomous regions under central control.

Other gains for Marcos became evident only after several months. By holding out the possibility that the conflict might be settled by negotiation and then maneuvering carefully to nullify what he had agreed to, Marcos exacerbated already existing differences within the MNLF. Soon after negotiations finally broke down in April 1977, other Muslim leaders began to challenge both Misuari's leadership of the MNLF and the MNLF's role as representative of Muslims in the Philippines as a whole. There is now a three-way split among Muslims operating outside the Philippines. Personal rivalries are reinforced by differences in ethnic background, ideology and sources of support.

Nur Misuari is the original chairman of the MNLF's Central Committee. He was a member of a revolutionary group linked with the New People's Army (NPA) when he was a student at the University of the Philippines, and he remains more radical than either set of rivals. People associated with him, however, have consistently denied that he is a Marxist or affiliated in any way with Communist organizations. His radicalness is manifested in a militant nationalism which is defined primarily in terms of Islam and the experiences of Muslims within the Philippines, though MNLF spokesmen have tried to describe a "Moro" identity which would include sympathetic non-Muslims.

Misuari and his closest lieutenants are primarily Tausug and/or Samal from the Sulu area, and the headquarters of the MNLF's military command is in the Zamboanga area. But Misuari also has loyal allies among the Maguindanao of Cotabato and the Maranaos in the Lanao provinces. He is also generally admitted to have a stronger following among the younger, more committed, non-elite commanders of the MNLF than any of his competitors. Most of his external support has come from Libya, though he has also received aid from other states. He has recently paid particular attention to developing relations with Iran, the only state which has cut off oil deliveries to the Philippines.

Hashim Salamat is a former member of the MNLF Central Committee who publicly broke with Misuari in late 1977 for both ideological and personal reasons. Educated at Cairo University and connected with Muslim reformers in the Philippines, Salamat is generally seen as a more orthodox Muslim than Misuari and other MNLF leaders. According to Manila sources, his primary external support came from an Egyptian official later fired by Sadat for malfeasance. He also has contacts with, and perhaps support from, two private Muslim organizations, the World Islamic League and the World Islamic Conference. He has had support from some rebels in the field, particularly in the Cotabato area, and from some Cairo-based Filipino Muslims. Most of his supporters in the Cotabato area, however, have apparently decided to abandon military opposition to the regime in favor of a policy of cooperation.

The Bangsa Moro Liberation Organization is a Jeddah-based movement led by Rashid Lucman, Salipada Pendatun, and Macapanton Abbas. Lucman and Pendatun were both pre-martial law politicians—Lucman a Maranao, Pendatun a Maguindinaoan. Abbas served as the executive of Marcos's main civilian task force for the Muslim areas for two years after the declaration of martial law. These three men have worked primarily to secure their participation in any negotiations between the MNLF and the Philippine government. They claim that the BMLO preceded the MNLF (by their account the MNLF is a breakaway faction and Misuari a radical renegade) and that they represent traditional Muslim society. Jamil Lucman, Rashid's nephew, has sometimes been considered a pro-BMLO commander, but he has recently surrendered.

Quick to see the benefits of a divided MNLF, the Marcos regime has recognized the BMLO. Some observers in fact suspect that Marcos is secretly supporting it. Meanwhile Islamic organizations and states look with concern at the attention given to the BMLO because they fear that the divisions among Philippine Muslim groups will delay a settlement of the conflict.

Such attention as the BMLO has received from Muslims outside the Philippines seems to have been primarily a result of this concern, although it is conceivable that Saudi officials and others associated with private Muslim organizations have also been sympathetic to the group's conservatism. There were reports in August 1980, however, that the Saudis had ended their support and ordered the BMLO leadership to leave the country. Earlier efforts at getting U.S. support failed.

Thus far the foreign ministers of the Islamic Conference have recognized only Misuari's MNLF. But recent conference statements include pointed references to the need for "unity" among Muslim Filipinos—a tacit warning to Misuari. For his part, Misuari took the May 1980 meeting of the Islamic Conference to task for not providing enough support to the MNLF. He also reminded the Conference that the 1979 meeting had threatened to take the problem to the United Nations if the Marcos regime refused to negotiate further with the MNLF, and he recounted the unsuccessful efforts to arrange negotiations. Finally, he called for material assistance in the form of a "humanitarian fund." He did not go as far as he had at an April Islamic meeting in London, when he asked the Arab states to stop selling oil to the Philippines.

The communique issued at the end of the May Islamic Conference meeting underscored the limits of its diplomatic support. The conference charged that the Philippine government is continuing to violate Muslim rights, and it condemned the Marcos regime for its obstructionist tactics with regard to peace negotiations. But it did not support Misuari's more militant position. The statement made it clear that the foreign ministers would not support anything more than the regional autonomy provided for in the Tripoli Agreement and would not recommend sanctions stronger than an undefined "pressure." While the rivalry between competing factions clouds the international scene, at home Misuari apparently maintains the allegiance of most commanders in the field. It remains difficult to estimate how seriously the divisions and defections affect the MNLF: government figures are unreliable, and leaving the hills has short-term benefits and no lasting consequences. "Defectors" may simply be taking advantage of government-funded R & R leaves; they can return to the hills more easily than they left, and with new supplies.

The level of fighting continues to fluctuate, depending on weather, supplies, choice of tactics, and internal and external political needs.

Selection 7.9: National Minorities, Sally Swenson

Editors' Introduction

In the highlands of the Philippines live more than four million people, neither Christians nor Muslims, variously referred to as "tribal Filipinos," "cultural minorities," "ethnic minorities," or "national minorities." Of the many ethno-linguistic groups, the largest is the Igorots of northern Luzon, who number about half a million. These uplanders have been largely ignored in the political and social life of the country, so much so that Carlos Romulo, a prominent Philippine diplomat, could declare in 1968 that "the Igorots are not Filipinos." But although these indigenous national minorities have been ignored, their lands have not; they have been encroached upon by the Christian majority for many decades. For example, large tracts of what were once the ancestral lands of the Negritos have been appropriated for the U.S. military bases. But under conditions of martial law, corporate exploitation of tribal lands accelerated, further politicizing the minority peoples, as described in the following article.

Source: Sally Swenson [compiler], "The Philippines," *Background Documents prepared for the Conference on Native Resource Control and the Multinational Corporate Challenge: Aboriginal Rights in International Perspective,* Boston, MA: Anthropology Resource Center, 1982, pp. 36-38.

Indigenous people in the Philippines—called "tribal Filipinos" to distinguish them from the Philippine majority, which also descended from native peoples—include more than 4 million people, more than 40 ethnolinguistic groups, and over 12 percent of the national population. Many have retained a high degree of cultural, political and economic independence, often because they withdrew to isolated mountain areas to avoid Spanish and then U.S. colonial domination. Most tribal Filipinos subsist from *kaingin* or slash-and-burn farming; a sizeable number in northern Luzon have carved their steep mountain slopes into irrigated rice terraces.

Although tribal Filipinos have experienced the steady encroachment of land-hungry settlers and companies for over a century, the situation in the 1970s became especially intense and today threatens their survival as peoples. The land frontier had become exhausted in the mid-1960s; communities could no longer withdraw into further isolation. More significant, when martial law was declared in 1972, the regime of Ferdinand Marcos ushered in a new era of foreign-dominated and export-oriented development for the Philippines. Since they occupy areas rich with natural resources, tribal Filipinos are besieged by a growing number of corporations engaged in mining, logging, agribusiness and other export industries. To support these industries, the government is rushing the construction of massive dams and other infrastructure projects in ancestral areas. The military has moved in to relocate tribal Filipinos from the affected areas, to divide communities against one another, and to prevent their joining a growing national resistance.

The Invasion of PANAMIN

Much of Philippine law affecting tribal minorities is a legacy of colonial law formulated to facilitate economic exploitation after the U.S. takeover in 1901. Laws passed during the years of American rule granted private land titles to large owners, placed all undeclared land under state ownership, opened such land to "exploration, occupation and purchase by citizens of the United States and the Philippines," and banned traditional tribal use of huge areas covered by mining and logging concessions, public parks, forest reserves and other lands sold by the Philippine government to settlers or corporations. Much of this colonial law has been restated by the Marcos regime.

Government decisions regarding tribal Filipinos are enforced by the official agency known as PANAMIN (Presidential Assistant on National Minorities). Originally an effort to help tribal Filipinos, it is now the Marcos regime's primary instrument to move tribal Filipinos off their lands. Many PANAMIN board members are also directors of the companies encroaching on tribal lands. "Security" and relocation are the two most essential elements in PANAMIN's program. According to one leading army officer within the agency, "The purpose of PANAMIN is to check on the loyalty of national minorities. . . . Those minorities who pass our loyalty check are permitted to participate in the government's fight against subversive elements." The agency's enormous security budget is especially devoted to arming tribal communities against each other.

Relocation of tribal Filipinos to PANAMIN reservations is tied in with the agency's military role. The reservations are virtual armed camps, with guards and checkpoints and controlled entry and exit. The relocated tribal people—at least 2.5 million, PANAMIN claims—have found economic survival in the cramped, alien camps to be near impossible, while sickness and starvation are common. Aside from its military role, in fact, most of PANAMIN's attention has focused on enforcing "primitivism" on the reservations— refusing to provide even the simplest technologies necessary for the tribal people to be self-sufficient. The Marcos government hopes that by appearing "primitive," tribal Filipinos will become popular tourist attractions.

Tribal Land: Fuel For Corporate Development

The acceleration of logging, agribusiness and mining that has occurred in the past decade has deprived many tribal Filipinos of their land and livelihood. The Philippine government has used its claim over "public land" to integrate tribal areas into the export-oriented economy.

Logging is one activity that has proved extremely profitable in the Philippines. In 1979, forest products were one of the country's top export earners. Government development plans envision the "logging off" of all remaining forest—where the vast majority of the country's minority peoples live and farm—within the next 15 years. "Conservation" plans consist largely of controlling tribal farmers, not the logging companies; 400,000 families, approximately 2.4 million people, are to be moved and evidently employed as wage laborers on land cultivated by agribusiness corporations.

The Cellophil Resources Corporation, a logging company operating in the Abra province of northern Luzon, is a classic example of this process. Thousands of Tingguian people have lost lands included in the company's 200,000 hectare concession. The company's pulp and paper mill is rapidly destroying fishing, one of the Tingguians' main alternative sources of livelihood. The Tingguians, Kalingas, and others who dwell in the forested concession also face the loss of pasturelands for their water buffalo and the increased likelihood of erosion, landslides and floods. Cellophil has banned the cutting of trees for timber and discouraged the collecting of wood for fuel and rattan for handicrafts. Yet popular opposition to Cellophil has brought military harassment. Members of the tribal community have been arrested arbitrarily and detained without trial.

The encroachment of local and multinational agribusiness has produced a similar situation on the southern island of Mindanao, where the largest number of tribal Filipinos are located.

In the central Mindanao province of Bukidnon, the best known case of agribusiness landgrabbing is that of Del Monte Corporation's Philippine subsidiary, the Philippine Packing Corporation (Philpak). Established in 1926, Philpak steadily grew until by the 1970s it had become the largest food company in the Philippines and the top exporter of bananas and pineapples, two of the country's top ten foreign exchange earners. Encouraged by the Marcos regime's development priorities, Philpak decided to attempt to acquire 14,000 hectares owned largely by native Bukidnon. With the help of PANAMIN and Philippine troops, Philpak has now acquired more than half of this land. As in Luzon, resistance of native Mindanaoans to eviction has often been met with violence.

Poverty is the eventual result of corporate encroachment. Manobo people evicted from land taken by the Bukidnon Sugar Corporation (BUSCO) were finally relocated to an over-crowded PANAMIN reservation where they were forced to grow sugar for BUSCO. Others have settled for impoverished lives as plantation workers on their former tribal land.

The Dams Are Running After Us!

To attract the investment it desires, the Philippine government has made the development of hydroelectricity the foundation of its development program. With more than half its costs covered by loans from major development banks, the government plans to build at least 40 major dams during the next 20 years. Almost all the dams are planned for lands occupied by minorities and, as they will be built in wide valleys in otherwise mountainous regions, they threaten to submerge the best farm land of the affected communities. The watersheds of most of the country's major rivers, and the homes of more than 1.5 million people, may be affected.

The relationship of hydroelectric development to corporate expansion onto tribal Filipino land is exemplified by one of the first projects, the $70 million Pantabangan dam in the province of Nueva Ecija (Luzon). When authorized in 1969, the dam was the largest infrastructure project in the Philippines and the third largest in Asia. A joint project of the Philippine government and the U.S. Agency for International Development, Pantabangan was partially funded by a $34 million construction loan from the World Bank.

More than 9,000 people from the town of Pantabangan were displaced when their farmlands were flooded by the dam. Previously one of the highest in the country, the food production of the resettled villagers sharply declined. Their new land is poor, while the people have only squatters rights and thus see little interest in improving the land.

In displacing the villagers, the dam left them vulnerable to further exploitation. The National Irrigation Administration and the World Bank agreed in 1980 to establish a large agro-forestry project in the resettlement area. The people of Pantabangan fear this project; they know that it means the government will not recognize their petitions for ownership and cultivation rights to the land. Instead, the government wants to incorporate them into another "development" scheme—this time as laborers producing commercial crops.

A hydroelectric project to be built 25 kilometers from Manila in Luzon reveals a similar, if varied, process of exploitation. Funded partially by the World Bank and the Asian Development Bank, Kaliwa-Kanan will submerge 29,000 out of 50,000 hectares occupied by the Dumagat-Remontado people and non-native settlers. The government is now attempting to relocate seven barrios, containing 450 native families, claiming that the areas will be flooded by 1985.

Residents became suspicious of the government's attempts after learning from engineers in the site that the enormous dam will take from 12 to 18 years to complete. Dumagat-Remontado people have explained the discrepancy: from observing the recent growth in corporate ranching nearby, they believe they are being required to vacate the area so that others can make the most of it before the dam is built. A process of displacing tribal peoples is made clear by quite a few settlers, natives whose lands were flooded by other dams. As some of them put it, "We left our homes and moved here, but this dam is still running after us!"

The Chico Dam Victory

The $1 billion Chico River Basin Development Project could have become the biggest hydroelectric project in Southeast Asia. But the resistance of 90,000 Kalingas and their neighbors, the Bontocs, has prevented the construction of its four dams. The government's recently announced 10-year development plan does *not* include the Chico River project.

Like Pantabangan and Kaliwa-Kanan, these dams were not likely to hasten rural electrification or stimulate grass roots irrigation projects among the Kalingas and Bontocs. The actual beneficiaries would have been the foreign and national logging, mining, and agricultural companies that are rapidly acquiring land in northern Luzon.

Surveying began in February 1974, when Marcos instructed the National Power Corporation (NPC) to begin work on Chico II in Bontoc land. Native resistance was so strong that it made the work unsafe, and the NPC was forced to turn its attention to Chico IV in Kalinga territory. Because Kalinga society is more loosely organized than Bontoc, the government believed the Kalingas would prove more tractable. Units of the Philippine Constabulary (PC)—a paramilitary police force—accompanied the NPC as it set to work on Chico IV.

Although Kalinga resistance was sporadic, the opponents' dismantling of survey camps was disruptive enough to convince Marcos to withdraw the NPC and send in PANAMIN. The agency then began to divide the Kalinga, manipulating those villages not affected by the project. A delegation of Kalingas was invited to Manila and forced to sign blank sheets of paper which were then filled with an agreement to accept Chico IV in exchange for the cancellation of Chico II. PANAMIN organized armed militia units in villages which supported the agency, initiating inter-community hostilities which raged for several years. A series of PC battalions then replaced PANAMIN, and for years the situation resembled a foreign occupation. In 1980, a tribal leader active in the anti-dam movement was murdered on the steps of his home.

Kalingas and Bontocs opposed to the project, however, became more united. They used the *bodong*, or traditional peace pact, to weld their alliance. In 1976 the Kalingas sent Marcos a petition with 500 signatures protesting the occupation, and Kalinga and Bontoc leaders sent a letter to delegates at the World Bank-IMF conference held in Manila that year. In October, over 90 percent of the people in the threatened area boycotted a national referendum intended to affirm martial law.

The protests gradually grew more effective. Opposition expanded to include other peoples threatened by various types of development projects, while divisions among the Kalinga diminished with the withdrawal of PANAMIN. Perhaps most important, opponents of the dam found it easy to subvert construction efforts by controlling access to the rugged territory. These developments encouraged the World Bank, which had informally guaranteed funding for the project, to withdraw its support. The government's own decision to withdraw came soon after.

Other groups threatened by development projects have launched similar campaigns. They combine local disruption of construction with political appeals to the government and its funding sources. Many call not only for unity among all tribal Filipinos, but for solidarity with the mass of impoverished and powerless non-native Filipinos.

Yet tribal Filipinos are facing an uphill battle. Foreign support for the Marcos development program remains strong. Those involved in resisting Chico suspect that the government's "ceasefire" may be only a tactic designed to lower their guard. Many argue that in withdrawing funds from Chico, the World Bank simply distributed them to lesser known but equally destructive projects. Tribal Filipinos' rights to land and survival are still very much at stake.

Selection 7.10: Specific Characteristics of People's War in the Philippines, Amado Guerrero

Editors' Introduction

In late 1968, a group of young intellectuals broke from the Moscow-oriented Partido Komunista ng Pilipinas (PKP), charging that it was no longer interested in militantly challenging the status quo. They established the Communist Party of the Philippines (CPP) and, on March 29, 1969 they formed the New People's Army (NPA) as their military arm. Although a relatively minor force when Marcos declared martial law, by the end of the decade the NPA insurgency had become active in many parts of the country.

Armed struggle against domestic oppression and its external allies has a long history in the Philippines. During the period of Spanish rule, there were hundreds of uprisings against the colonial masters and their exactions, culminating in the nationwide Philippine Revolution of 1896. Under the United States, pacification of the islands was never complete, and armed revolts broke out on numerous occasions. Guerilla resistance

met the Japanese conquerors in World War II. And after the war, the peasants of Central Luzon were driven to take up arms in the Huk rebellion.

In its early years, the CPP identified closely with China and Maoism. As China moved to build ties to the governments of Southeast Asia, its support for the NPA, always more ideological than material, waned; and with Peking's growing rapprochement with the United States, the CPP no longer looked to China for inspiration. To U.S. officials, accustomed to attributing revolutions to foreign instigation, "one of the most troublesome aspects" of the Philippine insurgency has been that "there is no apparent external source of support" (*The Situation and Outlook in the Philippines,* Hearings before the Subcommittee on Asian and Pacific Affairs, House Foreign Affairs Committee, 98th Congress, 2nd session, September-October 1984, p. 191).

Amado Guerrero is the pseudonym of Jose Maria Sison, who was, until his arrest in 1977, leader of the

CPP. The following extract from a 1974 work shows an application of the theory of guerilla warfare to the special conditions of an archipelago and emphasizes a policy of self-reliance.

Source: Amado Guerrero, *Specific Characteristics of People's War in the Philippines* [1974], Oakland, CA: International Association of Filipino Patriots, 1979.

Ours is a national democratic revolution aimed at completing our struggle for national independence and giving substance to the democratic aspirations of our people. We have no course but to fight for national emancipation and social liberation against U.S. imperialism, feudalism and bureaucrat capitalism.

In a sense, our national democratic revolution is a continuation of the Philippine revolution that started in 1896. But this revolution has assumed new characteristics. It is of a new type. It is no longer part of the old bourgeois-capitalist revolution. It is part of the proletarian-socialist revolution which has emerged since the first global inter-imperialist war and the victory of the great socialist October Revolution. Though we are still fighting for a national-democratic revolution, this constitutes a preparation for carrying out a socialist revolution in our country. . . .

Between armed struggle and parliamentary struggle, the former is principal and the latter is secondary. Every genuine revolutionary knows that the chief component of the reactionary state is the reactionary army. The Filipino people are helpless without their own army. They cannot take a single step towards smashing the entire military-bureaucratic machine of the enemy without a people's army.

In carrying out a people's war, the Party builds the people's army as its main form of organization. . . .

Fighting in a Small Mountainous Archipelago

The Philippines is a small mountainous archipelago. It is made up of some 7,100 islands and islets with a total land area of 299,404 square kilometers or 115,600 square miles. The eleven largest islands . . . compose ninety-four percent of the total land area and also contain ninety-four percent of the total population of the country. Every one of these and many other islands have a mountainous terrain with fertile soil.

The importance of an island is not determined solely by its size. Population, forest area and mountainous terrain are more important considerations for our people's war, especially at the initial stage.

There are three outstanding characteristics of the Philippines in being an archipelago. First, our countryside is shredded into so many islands. Second, our two biggest islands, Luzon and Mindanao, are separated by such a clutter of islands as the Visayas. Third, our small country is separated by seas from other countries. From such characteristics arise problems that are very peculiar to our people's war.

On the one hand, it is true that our countryside is wide in relation to the cities. On the other hand, it is also true that we have to fight within narrow fronts because the entire country is small and its countryside is shredded. The war between us and the enemy easily assumes the characteristics of being intensive, ruthless and exceedingly fluid. While we have the widest possible space for the development of regular mobile forces in Luzon and Mindanao, these two islands are separated by hundreds of kilometers and by far smaller islands where the space immediately appears to be suitable only for guerilla forces throughout the course of people's war. The optimum condition for the emergence of regular mobile forces in the major Visayan islands will be provided by the prior development of regular mobile forces in Luzon and Mindanao.

Waging a people's war in an archipelagic country like ours is definitely an exceedingly difficult and complex problem for us. At this stage we are still trying to develop guerilla warfare on a nationwide scale, the central leadership has had to shift from one organizational arrangement to another so as to give ample attention to the regional Party and army organizations. This is only one manifestation of the problem. Armed propaganda teams and initial guerilla units scattered in far-flung areas are susceptible to being crushed by the enemy. This is another manifestation of the problem.

There is no doubt that fighting in an archipelagic country like ours is initially a big disadvantage for us. Since the central leadership has to position itself in some remote area in Luzon, there is no alternative now and even for a long time to come but to adopt and carry out the policy of centralized leadership and decentralized operations. We must distribute and develop throughout the country cadres who are of sufficiently high quality to find their own bearing and maintain initiative not only within periods as short as one or two months, periods of regular reporting, but also within periods as long as two or more years, in case the enemy chooses to concentrate on an island or a particular fighting front and blockade it.

The development of the central revolutionary base somewhere in Luzon will decisively favor and be favored by the development of many smaller bases in Luzon, Visayas and Mindanao. Thus, we have paid attention to the deployment of cadres for nationwide guerilla warfare. In a small country like the Philippines or more precisely in an island like Luzon, it would have been foolhardy for the central leadership to ensconce itself in one limited area, concentrate all the limited Party personnel and all efforts there and consequently invite the enemy to concentrate his own forces there. It would have been foolhardy to underestimate the enemy's ability to rapidly move and concentrate his forces in an island where communications are most developed.

The central leadership started the armed struggle where it best could by linking with Red fighters in the second district of Tarlac in early 1969. Soon, Party cadres were dispatched to the mountainous and hilly area of Isabela. Subsequently, what amounted to the main forces of the New People's Army vigorously grew here from early 1971 to the eve of the fascist martial rule. A few cadres trained here were dispatched for rural work in other regions. The first quarter storm of 1970 [student demonstrations] and the succeeding mass protest actions and mass organizing in Manila-Rizal and other urban centers in the country yielded the greatest number of cadres for the national expansion of the Party and the people's army in the rural areas. These cadres start raw but are enthusiastic, develop new Party cadres from the ranks of the local mass activists and Red fighters, and are tempered in the course of fierce revolutionary struggle.

We have already created seven regional Party and army organizations outside of Manila-Rizal. After strengthening them, especially those of Northwest, Northeast and Central Luzon, we can more confidently look forward to and take the step towards building the central revolutionary base in a favorable terrain that is better populated and more extensive than the east of the Cagayan River. It should be in an area far more difficult for the enemy to blockade. Necessarily, the central leadership would be able to maintain more immediate relations with the regional Party organizations in Luzon than with those in the Visayas and Mindanao. The latter could still be administered through a special organ of the Central Committee.

In the long run, the fact that our country is archipelagic will turn out to be a great advantage for us and a great disadvantage for the enemy. The enemy shall be forced to divide his attention and forces not only to the countryside but also to so many islands. Our great advantage will show when we shall have succeeded in developing guerilla warfare on a nationwide scale and when at least we shall have been on the threshold of waging regular mobile warfare in Luzon or in both Luzon and Mindanao.

We take the policy of a "few major islands first, then the other islands later." This is now well understood in the Visayas. In every island or in the specific part of an island that we choose to concentrate on, we must develop self-reliance; maintain our guerilla units within a radius that is limited at a given time to avoid dissipation of our efforts but wide enough for maneuver; and advance wave upon wave, always expanding on the basis of consolidation. Our bitter experience has shown that overextending our guerilla squads in the false hope of covering a wider area or attending to so many strategic points all at the same time result in shallow political work and are fatal for our squads. Among several guerilla squads, it is necessary to have some center of gravity or rallying point either for temporary retreat or for a concentrated operation against the enemy. At the same time, we should never lose sight of the necessity of fluidity, which often requires the shiftiness of such a center.

Each regional Party organization should see to it that at the present stage it develops only one, two or three armed fronts. The regional executive committee of the Party should be based in the main front. More guerilla bases and zones should arise only upon the consolidation of the few that could be sufficiently handled at one time. At present, it is not necessary to have an armed force in every province within a region. More often it is advisable for us to locate our armed force at an interprovincial border area for maximum effect because in the first place we do not have enough armed strength for every province.

The principle of self-reliance needs to be emphasized among all revolutionary forces on a nationwide scale. This is because our small country is cut off by seas from neighboring countries, particularly those friendly to our revolutionary cause. The Vietnamese, Cambodian and Laotian peoples are more fortunate than us in one sense because they share land borders with China, which serves as their powerful rear. Self-reliance can never be overemphasized among us. The basic needs of our people's war have to be provided for by the people's army and the broad masses of the people themselves. Our basic source of armaments is the battlefields. Our level of military technique and our ability in tactics and strategy will have to rise by our adhering strictly to the Marxist principle of advancing in stages and doing well at one stage to prepare for the next stage. The protractedness of our people's war is underscored by the archipelagic character of the country. . . .

From Small and Weak to Big and Strong

We must recognize the balance of forces between us and the enemy. This is the first requirement in waging either an entire war or a campaign or a single battle. As matters now stand, we are small and weak while the enemy is big and strong. There is no doubt that he is extremely superior to us militarily in such specific terms as number of troops, formations, equipment, technique, training, foreign assistance and supplies in general. It will take a protracted period of time for us to change this balance of forces in our favor. Thus, protractedness is a basic characteristic of our people's war. . . .

As matters now stand on a nationwide scale or even on the scale of every region, the New People's Army has no alternative but to be on the strategic defensive in opposition to the strategic offensive of an overweening enemy. But the content of our strategic defensive is the series of tactical offensives that we are capable of undertaking and winning. By winning battles of quick decision, we are bound to accumulate the strength to win bigger battles and campaigns to be able to move up to a higher stage of the war. To graduate from guerilla warfare to regular mobile warfare as the main form of our warfare, we have to exert a great deal of effort over a long period of time. We are still very much at the rudimentary and early substage of the strategic defensive.

We may state that in the long process of its growing from small and weak to big and strong, our people's army will have to undergo certain stages and substages. Having in mind a probable course of development whereby our forces are inferior now and will consequently become equal and finally superior to the enemy, we can tentatively define three strategic stages that our people's army will have to undergo.

It is now undergoing the first stage, the strategic defensive. Consequently, it shall undergo the second stage, the strategic stalemate, when our strength shall be more or less on an equal footing with the enemy's and our tug of war with the enemy over strategic towns, cities and larger areas shall become conspicuous. Finally, it shall undergo the third stage, the strategic offensive, when the enemy shall have been profoundly weakened and completely isolated and shall have been forced to go on the strategic defensive, a complete reversal of his position at the stage of our strategic defensive.

Selection 7.11: 10 Point Program, National Democratic Front

Editors' Introduction

On April 24, 1973, the Communist Party of the Philippines, underground organizations of workers, the urban poor, and youth, and Christians for National Liberation established the National Democratic Front (NDF). The "national democrats" or "nat-dems"—as the constituent organizations of the NDF and its other influenced organizations were referred to—became the leading force on the Philippine left.

On its founding, the NDF issued a 10-point program. This program was reaffirmed and elaborated on November 12, 1977. Following are excerpts from the 1977 elaboration.

Source: International Committee, National Democratic Front, *Philippines 1979: The Ten-Point Program of the National Democratic Front*, London: Philippines Research Group, 1979, pp. 19-42.

1. Unite all anti-imperialist and democratic forces to overthrow the U.S.-Marcos dictatorship and work for the establishment of a coalition government based on a truly democratic system of representation. . . .

Upon the overthrow of the U.S.-Marcos dictatorship, there should be a coalition government, a provisional revolutionary government with a united front character, to remove the anti-national and anti-democratic causes and results of the fascist dictatorship.

It shall be the task of the coalition government to draft and issue for ratification a new constitution on the basis of the national and democratic interests of the Filipino people.

The coalition government should recognize all the national and democratic forces that shall have caused the downfall of the fascist dictatorship and give them ample opportunity to participate in legal and peaceful political activities.

There should be no monopoly of political power by any class, party or group. The degree of participation in the government by any political force should be based on its effective role and record in the revolutionary struggle and on the people's approbation.

We always stand for the independence and initiative of the various political forces working for the overthrow of the fascist dictatorship.

The coalition government should allow the free interplay of national and democratic forces during and after election. Thus a truly democratic system of representation can develop and operate to the benefit of the people. Such a government should always be subject to the will of the people. . . .

A committee of civilian leaders highly respected by the people for their patriotism, civil libertarian stand and consistent opposition to fascism and puppetry should assume the reins of government. This committee should pave the way for genuinely popular, free and honest elections within a year's time from the overthrow of the fascist dictatorship. . . .

2. Expose and oppose U.S. imperialism as the mastermind behind the setting up of the fascist dictatorship, struggle for the nullification of all unequal treaties and arrangements with this imperialist power, and call for the nationalization of all its properties in the country. . . .

3. Fight for the reestablishment of all democratic rights of the people, such as freedom of speech, the press, assembly, association, movement, religious belief, and the right to due process. . . .

4. Gather all possible political and material support for the armed revolution and the underground against the U.S.-Marcos dictatorship. . . .

5. Support a genuine land reform program that can liberate the peasant masses from feudal and semi-feudal exploitation and raise agricultural production through cooperation. . . .

6. Improve the people's livelihood, guarantee the right to work and protect national capital against foreign monopoly capital . . . .

7. Promote a national, scientific and mass culture and combat imperialist, feudal and fascist culture. . . .

8. Support the national minorities, especially in Mindanao and the Mountain Provinces, in their struggle for self-determination and democracy. . . .

9. Punish, after public trial, the ringleaders of the Marcos fascist gang for their crimes against the people and confiscate all their ill-gotten wealth. . . .

10. Unite with all peoples fighting imperialism and all reaction, and seek their support for the Philippine revolutionary struggle. . . .

Selection 7.12: Church Opposition to Martial Law, Robert L. Youngblood

Editors' Introduction

For over three hundred years the Catholic Church was a major pillar of Spanish colonialism in the Philippines. Spain ruled, it was said, by using the Cross and the Sword. Under U.S. rule, the hated Spanish clergy were ejected from the archipelago and replaced by a new, Filipinized clergy. Some Filipinos followed a Filipino Catholic priest, Father Gregorio Aglipay, in breaking away from the Catholic Church and forming the nationalistic Philippine Independent Church, but a large majority of the population continued to identify with the Catholic Church, albeit in its new, Filipinized form.

Throughout the years of U.S. colonial rule and well into the post-independence period, the Catholic Church remained a powerful bulwark of the domestic status quo. In recent years, however, there developed among the lower ranks of the clergy a growing identification with the poor and their concerns; "liberation theology" began to take root, although it was not by any means the dominant ideology of the Church hierarchy. With eighty-five percent of the Philippine population Roman Catholic, the attitude of the Church to the Marcos regime took on considerable significance. The following account of Church opposition during the first half decade of martial law is excerpted from an article by Robert L. Youngblood, a political scientist at Arizona State University.

Source: Robert L. Youngblood, "Church Opposition to Martial Law in the Philippines," *Asian Survey*, vol. 18, no. 5, May 1978, pp. 505-20.

President Marcos's declaration of martial law on September 21, 1972 and subsequent inauguration of the "New Society" received a mixed reaction from some Christian groups as indicated by conflicting statements of support and opposition from relgious leaders and organizations throughout the country....

The Catholic hierarchy's initial reaction was restrained: applauding the President's reforms as essential but deploring human rights violations. As priests, nuns, and laypeople engaged in the social action work of the church began to be arrested and abuses of power (particularly by the military) were revealed, however, the church's position on martial law, while reflecting polarities within its organizational structure, has become more critical.

The elimination of institutionalized opposition by martial law left the Catholic Church as one of the few organizations able to challenge the policies of the government. Much of the church's power derives from the fact that 85% of the population professes Catholicism and from the existence of a nationwide structure of parishes where local priests (especially in the rural areas) are often key molders of public opinion. Despite the pervasiveness of the church, however, the Catholic hierarchy has not been united in its outlook toward martial law. The two major organizations of the church are the Association of Major Religious Superiors in the Philippines (AMRSP), representing 2,500 Catholic priests and 7,000 nuns, and the Catholic Bishops Conference of the Philippines (CBCP), composed of 76 Bishops. Of the two, the AMRSP has a younger, more social action-oriented membership that has typically been less inhibited about criticizing government programs and martial law abuses. And within the religious orders (as opposed to the diocesan priests) it has been foreign missionaries that have most often spoken out against the regime. Thus religious order priests and nuns and foreign missionaries have borne the brunt of government crackdowns that have included deportations, jailings, and the closing of church newspapers and radio stations.

In contrast, the CBCP is considered more conservative and contains some of the most powerful members of the church hierarchy. But even within the

Bishops Conference there are three identifiable divisions. The most conservative group, headed by Cardinal Rosales, has been the most supportive of the government's reforms and has generally couched criticism of the regime in moderate terms. This group of perhaps 15 bishops has been able to to control the conference and its executive board until quite recently by obtaining the support of the larger group of "moderate" bishops. The moderates like Cardinal Sin of Manila reserve the right to criticize specific injustices of the regime without attacking martial law in principle. The Cardinal, for example, has termed his archdiocese's policy as one of "critical collaboration" with the government rather than one of "critical opposition" adopted by more radical church elements. A third group, symbolized by Francisco Claver and estimated to include between 13 and 24 bishops, is considered liberal and has protested martial law in principle as well as spoken out against a wide array of abuses. These bishops tend to be younger, located in smaller dioceses, and more committed to the social action goals of the church. And finally, many of the social activists associated with both the AMRSP and CBCP appear to have been influenced by Latin American liberation theology.

The liberal-conservative dichotomy within the church's hierarchy has resulted in differences of opinion over the need for and the implementation of the reforms of the Marcos administration. Critics contend that many government programs such as land reform have failed and that the social costs of other policies threaten the traditional lifestyles of the peasants without much benefit to them. They note further that the Western model of development adopted by the regime has failed to liberate the poor so that they can realize their full potential as human beings. In short, the Western modernization model is dehumanizing, for it has not fundamentally reordered the socioeconomic system and the anticipated "trickle down" effects have been either too few or not forthcoming. Thus church liberals have protested the expansion of foreign plantations that encroach on peasant farm lands and the development of hydroelectric and other projects that dislocate communities from ancestral homes without just compensation, and have opposed the establishment of foreign enterprises that exploit cheap labor and often increase environmental problems. On the other side, supporters of the government within the church maintain that the best way to stall the downward spiral of poverty gripping the country is to accelerate modernization through additional foreign investments and government reforms. The alternative, they argue, is a leftist social revolution that will eventually undermine the stability and authority of the church. And perhaps more important, many church conservatives feel that the undue preoccupation of church activists with the governments' socioeconomic development strategies violates church-state separation in the Philippines.

At the heart of the church-state conflict from the activists' perspective is the immorality of martial law as manifested in heavy-handed government reform programs that do not adequately take into consideration the needs of the urban poor and peasant masses and the denial of basic human rights that have resulted in the detention of numerous critics of martial law since 1972.

While conservative elements within the church may disagree with liberals as to the morality of martial law and the methods by which the latter have opposed the regime, government jailings and deportations of activist priests and nuns and threats to legalize divorce and tax sectarian schools have tended to unite the church hierarchy. Thus the continued activities of liberal priests, nuns, and church workers have increasingly brought the Catholic Church into conflict with the government and the military on a number of issues in the past five years.

Religious Social Action vs. "Subversion"

An area of persistent irritation to the government has been the Catholic Church's social action program among rural peasants, wage earners, and urban squatters. Although the church has been active in organizing peasants through such organizations as the Federation of Free Farmers since the 1950s, its social action program was stepped up in the late 1960s and early 1970s to include more activities and more provinces. Increasing involvement with the problems of the poor by priests and nuns led them to intensify their criticism of the failures of government programs and, ironically, resulted in the communists branding church activists as part of the "clerico-fascist" enemies of the people. Rather than viewing church criticism as a positive step toward additional reforms, the government became defensive and tended to see religious social activists as "subversives" and tools of the communists. While a few priests and nuns had gone underground or were cooperating with the communists, the government has in many instances clearly overreacted to church liberals' concern for the poor. In this atmosphere, it is not surprising that with martial law a number of social action programs of the church came under attack and that certain priests and nuns were detained and/or deported for alleged subversive activities. . . .

Attempts by priests and nuns to assist peasants being dispossessed of their land or denied their rights as well as the association of church workers with anyone considered subversive by the military have met with opposition from the government. Arrests of church activists began immediately with the proclamation of martial law. In September 1972, a nun and eight priests, four of whom were Americans, were detained without charges, and in October 1972, two American priests, Bruno Hicks and John Peterson, were voluntarily deported for activities involving a church radio station on the island of Negros. Hicks and Peterson were accused of advocating rebellion over the radio, but they denied the charges once back in the U.S., saying the station was used as a forum for discussing and seeking solutions to peasant problems. The government's action was prompted by Hick's friendships with Maoists advocating land reform by force, his involvement with other activist groups, and his belief that the "real Christian message is to struggle against oppressive institutions". . . .

Activist priests and laypeople have also run afoul of the Marcos regime in assisting urban squatters and workers in their grievances. Beginning in January 1973, Fr. Jose Nacu, adviser and organizer for the Zone One Tondo Organization (ZOTO), a Manila squatter group, was detained several times for alleged links to the New People's Army (NPA), a Maoist group advocating the violent overthrow of the government, and eventually spent two years in jail without being formally charged. In November 1974, Archbishop Jaime Sin accompanied a delegation of squatters from the Tondo foreshore area to Malacañang for a meeting with the President over the eviction and demolition of their homes. Although Marcos temporarily suspended the eviction order and promised the squatters would be housed near their present places of work, church-state conflict over squatter problems continued and was heightened with the deportation in January 1976 of two Italian priests, Fr. Francis Alessi and Fr. Luigi Cocquino, on subversion charges. . . .

Church-state relations have also been strained over the government's policies toward wage-earners. Growing out of the rash of riots and strikes in the late 1960s and early 1970s, Marcos banned strikes "in vital industries" after martial law in General Order No. 5 to allay fears of foreign investors and to maintain exports in vital foreign exchange earning industries. And in November 1975, prompted by a strike at the Manila La Tondeña Distillery, Inc., over wages and hiring practices, Marcos issued Presidential Decree 823 prohibiting "strikes, picketing and lock-outs" and outlawing the participation of aliens in all trade union activities. The decree's banning of aliens was aimed at foreign priests who have played an active part in Philippine trade unionism and supported the demand of 700 casual laborers that they be hired permanently by La Tondeña rather than be laid-off and re-hired at regular intervals for less pay than permanent employees for the same work. The regime's move against church labor organizers and its January 1976 deportation of the two Italian priests for assisting squatters prompted sharp reactions from powerful elements in the Catholic hierarchy. The ban on strikes was protested by 3,000 priests and nuns, led by the Archbishop of Manila, at a mass at the Sta. Cruz Church, and after the deportation of the Italians, Cardinal Julio Rosales, president of the Catholic Bishops Conference, stated that the Catholic hierarchy would "do everything within its power" to see that foreign priests were not denied due process. The Vatican radio termed the expulsions a "witchhunt" and charged Marcos with "repression." While the government's public response to the church seemed conciliatory, immigration authorities went ahead with new, stricter regulations on foreign clergy in the Philippines that drew additional criticism from Cardinal Sin.

In addition to activities among peasants, squatters, and workers, church activists have disagreed with other martial law political and economic policies. Criticism of Marcos's periodic referendums, for example, began as early as 1974 when the CBCP suggested that any new referendum through the Citizens' Assemblies, where voting was open and reportedly subject to intimidation, be held in complete freedom to help eliminate the climate of fear pervading the country. By the third referendum in February 1975, liberal

Catholic church leaders were calling for a nation-wide boycott, denouncing the referendum as a "mockery of democracy" and a "Marcos gimmick to justify his unlawful stay in power," and again in October 1976 church activists were in the forefront of 5,000 demonstrators who clashed with the police over another referendum. In cooperation with the People's Assembly for Freedom (a newly formed anti-martial law body) and other groups, liberal elements of the church more recently called on Filipinos to boycott the December 1977 referendum on whether Marcos should stay on as President and Prime Minister after the interim Batasang Pambansa (National Legislature) is organized. Church liberals have also taken the government to task on individual economic programs such as the Chico dam project, which would dislocate Bontocs and Kalingas from ancestral lands, and the Lake Sebu hydroelectric project, which would destroy the homes and livelihood of the T'bolis, and have charged that PANAMIN, a government agency established to help cultural minorities, is being used to foster government policy at the expense of those it is supposed to protect. But perhaps the most persistent issue church activists have raised has been the regime's violation of human rights and the torture of political prisoners detained under martial law.

The Church and Political Prisoners

While church leaders agreed that Philippine society needed reform and urged the support of "worthwhile" government programs, they nevertheless indicated reservations from the beginning about the suppression of civil liberties and the violation of human rights. The Catholic hierarchy's initial reaction to reported abuses under martial law was restrained, with only a few liberal church leaders like Bishop Claver speaking out strongly. Following the arrest of priests, nuns, and laypeople engaged in the church's social action programs and continued reports of mysterious disappearances, arbitrary jailings, and the torture of political detainees, more church leaders began to raise questions and call for an accounting by the government. A nation-wide study commissioned by the AMRSP in September 1973 revealed widespread fear of criticizing the government and numerous violations of human rights, including the lack of "safeguards in matters of arrest, detention and trial." The reports of physical torture throughout the country prompted the AMRSP to establish a Task Force for Detainees (TDF) at its annual convention in January 1974. This action was followed in April by a statement from the Second Mindanao-Sulu Pastoral Conference deploring injustices under martial law such as the torture of detainees in violation of the United Nations' Declaration of Human Rights.

In a meeting with foreign correspondents in November 1974, Archbishop Sin of Manila stated flatly that "we cannot jail a man indefinitely and still call ourselves Christian" in expressing concern over "the indefinite detention of prisoners" against whom no formal charges have been filed. He also criticized the government for detaining prisoners for "subversion" without providing a definition of the term, and questioned the lack of a satisfactory government response to church protests over the murder of Marsman Alvarez, brother of a leading anti-Marcos critic now living in the United States, and the torture and shooting of Santiago Arce, a former official in the Federation of Free Farmers in Abra. . . .

In a speech on December 11, 1974, Marcos addressed the murders and other issues raised by Sin and activist church leaders. He claimed that arbitrary arrests were not occurring and that those detained had been charged, that prisoners were well treated and none had been tortured, that the Red Cross had found Manila prison camps exemplary (later denied by the Red Cross), and that the charges of torture in the cases of Alvarez and Arce were false. The AMRSP's political prisoner task force took issue with almost all of the points raised in the President's speech.

Church accusations of torture and abuse were strengthened by a prison hunger strike by Frs. Edicio de la Torre and Manuel Lahoz begun at Christmas-time, 1974. Beaten up himself, de la Torre claimed that torture was common in Camp Olivias, Pampanga, north of Manila. Prisoners had been subjected to beatings, sexual assault, electric shocks, cigarette burns, and various kinds of psychological intimidation. The priest's fast gained international attention, and prompted Archbishop Sin to request a joint church-military investigation of prison conditions. Although the assistance of a delegation recommended by the Archbishop was rejected, a subsequent investigation by military authorities revealed that indeed torture had taken place at the camp. This resulted in the Secretary of National Defense ordering 37 enlisted men dismissed from the military and having the officers bound over for pretrial hearings to determine whether courts-martial were required. . . .

Church-Government Relations: The Position of the Hierarchy

Government authoritarianism and the church's responsibility to protect human rights in teaching the Gospel have inevitably led to church-state conflict since the declaration of martial law. While the most powerful elements of the church hierarchy took a "wait and see" attitude, favoring the government's reforms, liberals within the church began questioning the need for martial law from the beginning. In September 1972, right after martial law was proclaimed, 16 bishops wrote Marcos voicing concern over the loss of fundamental rights and the possibility of repression. This was followed in October and November 1972 with letters to the President from Bishop Claver and the AMRSP also expressing alarm over government excesses. Yet the sharpest criticism from the church came in the wake of government raids on church institutions and the arrest of priests, nuns, and laypeople accused of subversion. The arrest of a priest, several sisters, and the padlocking of a church in Antique in July 1973 drew criticism from Jaime Sin, then Archbishop of Jaro, and Bishops Frondoza of Capiz and Fortich of Bacolod, while military raids at the convent of the Good Shepherd Sisters in Davao, St. Joseph's College in Quezon City, and Our Lady of the Holy Angels seminary in Novaliches in

September and October 1973 were challenged by a number of church groups. These raids plus other religious arrests (estimated at over 246 by the end of 1977) led to the formation in November 1973 of a Church-Military Liaison Committee (CMLC) to resolve differences over violations of martial law and arrests of church officials, with the military agreeing not to arrest any religious person or raid any religious institution without notifying the bishop or religious superior. The agreement was soon violated by additional arrests and raids without the knowledge or notification of religious authorities.

Perhaps the most celebrated violations of the CMLC agreement were military raids in June and August 1974. The first raid resulted in the arrest of Dante Simbulan, an arch-critic of Marcos, as well as the detention and/or deportation of several members of the Protestant National Council of Churches in the Philippines (NCCP). Along with capturing Simbulan, authorities claimed subversive literature was discovered, but critics felt the raid was in retaliation for criticism of martial law by Protestant clergy. Protestant expressions of concern over the raid were joined by requests from Cardinal Rosales and Archbishop Sin that Marcos see that cases, if any, against the Protestants were handled expeditiously. The August raid on the Sacred Heart Novitiate and San Jose Minor Seminary in Novaliches was carried out because of reports that Jose Maria Sison, head of the Communist Party of the Philippines, was hiding out there. Sison was not found, so instead the military arrested Fr. Jose Blanco, reportedly the secretary of a subversive organization (Kapisanang Sandigang Pilipino) and 20 of his students. They also detained Fr. Benigno Mayo, Jesuit superior in the Philippines, by mistake. Mayo, who was on his way to the seminary at the time of his arrest, was questioned and released without charges. The incident and subsequent claim in the government-controlled press that the raid had the sanction of the church resulted in Archbishop Sin's holding a vigil prayer for peace and justice in Manila Cathedral attended by an estimated crowd of 4,500 and the release of a letter drafted by the CBCP calling for the end of martial law. Although Marcos rejected the petition of the Bishops Conference, the government retracted claims of church approval and participation in the Novaliches raid.

The church hierarchy—especially the CBCP—has been most divided over the morality of martial law and most united in opposing government attacks on church officials, institutions, and policies. The strong letters of Bishops Claver and Nepomuceno in February and June 1973, respectively, asking Archbishop Alberto to put the question of martial law on the CBCP agenda for discussion was effectively side-stepped by the issuance of a moderate pastoral letter "On Evangelization and Development." The moderate position of the CBCP was also reflected in the July 1975 election of a conservative slate of officers led by Cardinal Rosales pledged to prayer rather than social action and in the CBCP's refusal to go along with religious liberals' boycotts of Marcos's referendums. Church activists received another blow in November 1976 when two visiting cardinals from the Vatican reprimanded bishops involved in social and political activities. Divisions within the CBCP have also been exacerbated by the regime. The government has asserted that there are clear links between the NPA and the church activists, and has threatened to tax church schools, step up the family planning program, and legalize divorce. To a certain extent, these moves have put the church on the defensive. A recent report of the CBCP claimed, for instance, that it was misleading to link the social action program of the Church "with Communists and subversive elements," and in December 1977 the Carmelite Fathers were constrained to explain that a Volkswagon registered to them but apprehended along with Jose Maria Sison had been sold the previous October. Most priests and nuns probably doubt the seriousness of the communist threat and no doubt oppose government reforms that would affect cherished church programs and policies, but the basic conservatism of the clergy coupled with the ability of the President to legislate by decree has tended to reinforce a cautious attitude toward opposing martial law.

Yet more recent crackdowns on dissident bishops, foreign missionaries, and church activists have worked to unite the church hierarchy. Cardinal Rosales, as indicated previously, spoke out sharply against the deportation of foreign priests engaged in social action work among squatters and workers. Equally, a spate of raids on religious institutions in November and December 1976, resulting in the closing of church radio stations in Mindanao, the arrest of a number of church workers, and the padlocking in Manila of *The Communicator* and *Signs of the Times*, two religious publications critical of martial law, drew united criticism from the church hierarchy. These actions and a government document listing 155 churchmen and laypeople, including four bishops, for arrest prompted 66 of 74 of the church's bishops to sign a strong statement against government interference in church evangelizing work. The pastoral letter is significant because most of the bishops who signed it usually support the government. The government's reaction was conciliatory with Marcos assuring the Papal Nuncio, Monsignor Bruno Torpigliani, that coordination with the church would be improved and with [Defense Minister] Enrile saying the regime was not anti-clerical. The government nevertheless commenced hearings in October 1977 to determine if 15 priests and nuns active in the administration of the AMRSP could be prosecuted and at the same time began presenting evidence against 14 former employees of the defunct *Communicator*. The sharp rebuttal of the government's charges by Fr. James Reuter, former editor of *The Communicator*, suggest that church-state conflict will continue at least until martial law is lifted.

Selection 7.13: On With the Circus, Civil Liberties Union of the Philippines

Editors' Introduction

By the end of the decade, opposition to the Marcos dictatorship had grown to include even significant portions of the business community and the clergy. In an effort to shore up his continued rule, Marcos decided to lift martial law cosmetically while retaining for himself all the essential martial law powers. The opposition was not fooled by the maneuver. On the eve of Marcos's January 1981 announcement lifting martial law, the Civil Liberties Union of the Philippines (CLUP) issued the statement below. The CLUP is an independent organization with a long history of outspoken criticism of violations of fundamental rights. The statement was signed by the CLUP board of commissioners: former Senator Jose W. Diokno (chair), Jose B. L. Reyes, and J. Antonio Araneta.

Source: Civil Liberties Union of the Philippines, "Tuloy Ang Ligaya [On With the Circus]," January 1, 1981, reprinted by Friends of the Filipino People, Washington, DC.

In view of the repeated promises of Mr. Marcos to lift martial law by January 31 and thus attain the long promised "normalization," can the Filipino people realistically expect that the democracy that martial law destroyed and the sovereignty it usurped will be restored at last?

The Civil Liberties Union of the Philippines [CLUP] believes that they cannot. Even if martial law were really lifted, normalization will only serve to institutionalize dictatorship as long as Mr. Marcos remains head of state.

"Normalization" Impossible While Mr. Marcos Remains

During the 8 years that he has ruled the country, Mr. Marcos has systematically created an all encompassing mechanism of personal power, control and coercion that will enable him to continue his one man rule with nominal restraint after he shall have lifted the formal, legalistic earmarks of martial rule.

Mr. Marcos affronts our people's intelligence by assuring them of normalization with the lifting of martial law. For the issue has gone far beyond martial law. Mr. Marcos may now restore all the freedoms he has buried these past 8 years—in fact, he may even dismantle the military altogether—but this will not restore democracy. And Mr. Marcos knows that.

To illustrate: Relinquishing his power to legislate and yielding this power to a slavish Batasan [Assembly], will not normalize the separation of powers mandated by a Constitution which he demolished 8 years ago. Debunking the military, confining it to barracks, while preserving the elaborate network of spies, informers and paramilitary groups which, because of martial law, he was able to create with massive, unaudited funds, will not reinstate the supremacy of civilian rule. Restoring the freedom of business while he retains absolute control over the funds and affairs of the nation's financial and investigative agencies will, simply, not mean a damn thing. Resurrecting press freedoms after making the media industry a monopoly of cronies and relatives, is a gesture of mock liberality.

The fact is that Mr. Marcos would be most unwise if he did not "dismantle" martial law. He has no need for it. Its continuation merely invites and focuses attention on the incompetence and corruption of his regime. He has used 8 years of martial law to build and perfect a pervasive infrastructure of personal power which he can dismantle only by stepping down, and leaving this country in peace.

Short of that, he fools no one—not even the U.S. government who, from the very start, has been in collusion with his regime. Together, Mr. Marcos and the U.S. government have obviously decided that it is time to deodorize their joint conspiracy against the Filipino people with the ultimate cosmetic: the removal, in name of the hated martial rule which, for 8 years, has enabled Mr. Marcos and American transnational corporations to ravage the economy and place the country under their complete control, while allowing the U.S. government to obtain a new bases agreement, unhampered by the vexatious queries which an independent Congress would at least have made possible.

Martial Law Will Remain Intact

But the truth is that Mr. Marcos is still playing his favorite sport of juggling with words, but leaving the people the same aches and pains: for his statements show that he will not even lift the substance of martial law—and the circus will go on.

Mr. Marcos himself has emphasized that martial law means using the military, rather than civilian authority, to enforce the law. . . . This will continue, Mr. Marcos has announced: for after martial law shall have been lifted, the military will not return to their barracks. They will stay where they are—which means they will stay in control.

Moreover, the military will now enforce two new "laws": the so-called National Security Code and the Public Order Law. . . . But no one, except Mr. Marcos and possibly the military, know what these new "laws" prescribe: they have not been published and not even the members of the Interim Batasan Pambansa [National Assembly] have been given copies. . . .

In short, after martial law shall have been "lifted," the constitutional protection against arbitrary arrests and unreasonable searches and seizures will remain suspended to the same extent it now is under martial law.

So, what is new?

Freedoms Not To Be Restored

Moreover, Mr. Marcos does not promise that freedom of speech and of the press will be restored—only that they will be "enhanced". . . .

Again, after martial law shall have been lifted, strikes, at least in vital industries, will continue to be prohibited, so labor will remain chained to low wages and inhuman working conditions.

Finally, city and town mayors will have the right to refuse permits for public meetings to "subversive" groups—but no one has defined what is a subversive group; so the right peacefully to assemble and petition for redress of grievances will remain chimerical.

In short, the same restrictions on individual freedom that are the hall-

marks of martial law will continue after martial law shall have been "lifted."
So, what is new?

Sovereignty Not To Be Restored

Moreover, sovereignty will not be restored to the people. The essence of sovereignty is that officials who run the government are responsible to, and may peacefully be changed by, the people; yet after martial law shall have been lifted, Mr. Marcos will still remain President-Prime Minister; his cabinet, which with a few exceptions, have been in office since 1965, will continue in office; and so will the interim Batasan which he selected in the "election" of April 7, 1978.

Not until May 2, 1984 are "elections" to be held—and even then, they will be held under a law that Mr. Marcos will promulgate through his "batasan," enforce through a military that he will keep out of their barracks, and supervise through a Comelec [Election Commission] he has totally appointed.

So, what is new?

A happy new year, Mr. Marcos. To put it familiarly, *Tuloy ang ligaya* [On with the circus].

Selection 7.14: 1981 Mission to the Philippines, Amnesty International

Editors' Introduction

Amnesty International sent another mission to the Philippines in November 1981, some 10 months after the "lifting" of martial law. The mission reported systematic violations of fundamental human rights—as had the 1975 Amnesty International mission [see selection 7.6 above]. No substantial differences were found in the human rights situation before and after the formal termination of martial rule. And, whereas the earlier mission reported just one claim of government murder, this mission reported serious allegations of numerous arbitrary killings and disappearances.

Source: Amnesty International, *Report of an Amnesty International Mission to the Republic of the Philippines, 11-28 November 1981*, London: Amnesty International Publications, 1982, pp. 10-14.

Chapter II: Conclusions and Recommendations

Amnesty International concludes from the evidence gathered during its mission to the Philippines in November 1981 that the security forces of the Philippines have systematically engaged in practices which violate fundamental human rights, including the right to life, the right to security of person and the right against arbitrary arrest and detention. Amnesty International has noted in this report the repeatedly stated commitment of the Government of the Philippines to uphold and protect human rights in accordance with the well-developed legal tradition of the country. Amnesty International believes that this development is to be dated from the introduction of martial law but has continued since its repeal.

Amnesty International is aware that elements of the opposition confronting the Government of the Philippines are armed and dedicated to the government's violent overthrow. This fact can in no way justify the type of practices attributed in this report to members of the security forces. Amnesty International is concerned that the government's failure to investigate promptly allegations of abuses of the type described in this report and to bring those responsible to justice will result in a further deterioration in the human rights situation. The Amnesty International delegation was deeply impressed by the common desire of those aggrieved parties who presented evidence of violations of human rights to obtain redress through legal channels. Their interest in testifying to the Amnesty International delegation often appeared as a last resort in an attempt to gain redress from the authorities. At the same time, the delegation also noted a growing cynicism in many quarters about the efficacy of redress through legal channels. Amnesty International has received reports of reprisals taken against people acting on behalf of the government who were alleged to have engaged in torture, abduction and killing. Amnesty International in no way condones such actions by any party. However, Amnesty International believes that they add urgency to the need for prompt measures to bring agents of the government within the framework of the law. . . .

2. Amnesty International is concerned that members of the armed forces and of authorized paramilitary groups such as the Integrated Civilian Home Defense Forces (ICHDF) have systematically violated the rights of prisoners including both civilians and captured armed opponents. This has happened sometimes in circumstances of armed conflict. While governments may in such circumstances derogate from certain provisions of international human rights instruments, they may not derogate from the provision against arbitrary deprivation of life or that against torture. This is spelled out in Article 4 of the International Covenant on Civil and Political Rights. Furthermore, Common Article 3 of the Geneva Convention, governing conflicts of a non-international character, prohibits *inter alia* torture or killing of prisoners whether civilian or combatant.

The Amnesty International delegation was presented with evidence on 49 cases in which serious allegations were made of abuses by members of the Armed Forces of the Philippines (AFP), the ICHDF, the Integrated National Police (INP) and irregular paramilitary units apparently operating with official sanction. These included allegation of:

- arbitrary killings;
- "disappearance";
- torture and other forms of ill-treatment;

- arbitrary arrest;
- incommunicado detention. . . .

3. The Amnesty International mission found that the procedures for filing complaints against members of the security forces and other personnel acting with official sanction were deficient. In those few cases where complaints have been investigated, the findings and recommendations resulting from such investigations were rarely announced. Persons wishing to make complaints were often deterred from doing so out of fear of reprisals or because of lack of confidence in the efficacy of doing so. Where investigations found grounds for recommending criminal or administrative action, these recommendations were not implemented. . . .

4. The Amnesty International delegation noted that an extensive array of procedural safeguards exist regulating the treatment of persons in the custody of the security forces. The delegation found that these had been systematically ignored with apparent impunity. In Amnesty International's experience, disregard for such safeguards by a government is often a precondition for torture and arbitrary killing. . . .

5. The Amnesty International delegation was disturbed to find that persons held in the custody of government agents were frequently reported to have signed statements waiving their Constitutional rights. The delegation found that such statements were usually reported to have been signed under some type of duress often including torture. . . .

6. The Amnesty International delegation found that intelligence units regularly took persons they arrested to secret places of detention ("safehouses") or held them incommunicado in special holding centers such as the Maximum Security Unit (MSU) at Fort Bonifacio, Manila, or in regular detention centers. During such detention, detainees were often tortured while under interrogation. . . .

7. Amnesty International is concerned at the continued suspension of the privilege of the writ of habeas corpus since the lifting of martial law and the introduction through Letter of Instruction (LOI) No. 1211 of 9 March 1982 of procedures giving military personnel discretion not to seek the authorization of the civil courts for arrests and detention. . . .

8. Amnesty International is concerned that the independence of the civil judiciary has been seriously threatened by acts taken by the government during martial law and since its lifting and that, despite the restoration to the jurisdiction of the civil courts of cases involving civilians on the lifting of martial law, the judiciary may be so undermined as to prevent its discharging its functions with the necessary independence. . . .

9. Amnesty International has received credible and repeated allegations that irregular paramilitary groups operating with official sanction have committed gross violations of human rights. These include paramilitary groups reported to have been recruited in the Integrated Civilian Home Defense Force (e.g. Rock Christ) and to have been designated Special Units of the Armed Forces of the Philippines (e.g. Lost Command).

U.S. military adviser and Philippine military officers examining weapons captured from Muslim guerillas.

CHAPTER 8: THE U.S.-MARCOS DICTATORSHIP

Introduction

Many opponents of the martial law regime condemned what they called "the U.S.-Marcos dictatorship." Originally a slogan of the left, this view became more widespread over the years as Philippine disenchantment with Marcos grew at the same time that U.S. support for the Marcos government increased.

Shortly before Marcos had imposed martial law, he had met secretly with U.S. Ambassador Henry Byroade and asked how Washington would react were he to take "stronger measures" to deal with the unrest sweeping the country. Byroade obtained from the State Department a confidential message for Marcos that promised the Philippine president U.S. support in the event of serious insurgency problems. The Nixon administration thus had given Marcos a blank check for authoritarian rule. (See Richard J. Kessler, "Marcos and the Americans," *Foreign Policy,* Summer 1986, p. 52.)

When martial law was declared in September 1972 the U.S. government expressed no disapproval; this contrasts with Washington's criticism, however vague, of martial law in South Korea the following month. For martial law in the Philippines did not just serve the needs of Marcos and his cronies, but of the U.S. as well.

First, U.S. officials saw events in the Philippines at the time against the backdrop of the all-consuming problem of Vietnam, where half a million U.S. troops had been unable to defeat an insurgency that was deeply rooted in the population. As the Nixon Administration struggled to extricate itself from the Indochinese quagmire, officials in Washington determined to apply what was for them the crucial lesson of this experience: that insurgencies must be defeated *before* they reach the level of Vietnam in 1965. The Philippines in 1972 was hardly at that level, but martial law could nip in the bud the growing radicalization that U.S. officials feared.

Beyond the general concern of ensuring that there be "no more Vietnams," U.S. officials had specific Philippine concerns that martial law could address. As discussed in chapter 6, demonstrators were in the streets, workers were increasingly on picket lines, and the Congress and the Supreme Court were moving in a nationalist direction. U.S. policy makers viewed with trepidation the impact that this upsurge of radicalism and nationalism would have on U.S. military bases and economic interests. Martial law eliminated this fear, at least for the time being.

Marcos moved quickly after his declaration of martial law to reassure the foreign business community. He issued a presidential decree overruling the Quasha decision (which had declared U.S. landholdings to be illegal) and he banned strikes, a move particularly gratifying to foreign investors who had been disturbed by the escalating labor militance. Foreign capital was warmly welcomed, as Marcos informed readers of the *New York Times* [see selection 8.1], and U.S. business interests in the Philippines indicated their support for martial law [see selection 8.2]. Despite the 1974 expiration of the Laurel-Langley Agreement, U.S. investment in the Philippines grew between 1973 and 1980, although this did not mean a corresponding increase in the well-being of Filipinos [see selections 8.3 and 8.4].

In 1976, Marcos began negotiations with the United States government on amending the military bases agreement. The chief sticking point involved the amount of military and economic aid that Washington would grant Marcos in return for access to the bases. In 1979, amendments to the military bases accord were formalized by means of an executive agreement, thereby bypassing the need for ratification by the U.S. Senate or by anyone in the Philippines other than Marcos. (When Jimmy Carter entered the White House in 1977, he had declared human rights the centerpiece of his foreign policy, but though there had been some criticisms of Marcos's serious human rights abuses initially, the criticisms were toned down when it came time to negotiate on the bases.) The amendments provided for some cosmetic changes—such as flying the Philippine flag over the bases—and promised Marcos the U.S. President's best efforts to secure half a billion dollars in aid over 5 years, an increase of 100 percent over previous aid levels. Most significantly, the amendments assured the United States of "unhampered" military operations. The bases were now valuable to the Pentagon for interventions as far away as the Persian Gulf [see selection 8.5] and Marcos evidently agreed that Washington did not have even to notify Manila regarding the presence of nuclear weapons on Philippine soil [see selection 8.6].

The United States government responded to martial law by increasing the level of military aid to the Philippines, particularly weaponry that could be used for counter-insurgency [see selection 8.7]. Economic aid was also increased, but most of it did not reach the needy [see selection 8.8]. Multilateral grants and loans, primarily through the World Bank and the International Monetary Fund, grew rapidly, and with them the interference of these institutions in Philippine economic life [see selection 8.9].

Within the United States there developed a broad-based movement in opposition to U.S. support for the Marcos dictatorship, at the head of which stood those who called for an end to U.S. intervention in the Philippines [see selection 8.10]. Through its political and educational efforts, this movement was able to make it increasingly difficult for the administration to get its Philippine military aid package through the Congress.

In January 1981, Marcos formally lifted martial law. The outgoing Carter Administration advised the Philippine opposition to accept Marcos's action as a "generous offer" and to forswear violence. The President-Elect, Ronald Reagan, had won election in part by attacking Carter for being too hostile to friendly authoritarian rulers. Reagan made the single exception to his rule of receiving no foreign leaders before his inauguration for Imelda Marcos and apparently advised against a too-hasty lifting of martial law [see selection 8.11].

Marcos ignored this advice and went ahead and announced the end of martial law. But, as noted in the previous chapter, Marcos retained for himself all the crucial instruments of dictatorship, so in fact martial law was lifted in name only. Amnesty International found a continuing pattern of gross human rights violations [see selection 7.14]. The view from Washington, however, was rather more optimistic: in August 1981, U.S. Vice President George Bush raised a toast to President Ferdinand Marcos, declaring "We love your adherence to democratic principle and to the democratic processes."

So the United States both in word and deed increased and strengthened its support for the Marcos dictatorship as opposition to the dictatorship reached new levels.

Selection 8.1: *New York Times* Advertisement, Philippine Government

Editors' Introduction

According to a U.S. oil executive quoted by *Business Week* (November 4, 1972, p. 42) shortly after the declaration of martial law, "Marcos says, 'We'll pass the laws you need—just tell us what you want.' " The following advertisement, placed in the business section of the *New York Times* by the Philippine government, provides further confirmation of the Marcos regime's solicitude for foreign capital.

Source: *New York Times,* July 28, 1974, p. 5F.

Seven Good Reasons Why You
Should Be Looking to the
Philippines. Now.

1. We've put our house in order. You can't afford to overlook the new Philippines in surveying your Asian prospect this year. For the authoritative government in Manila has put an end to political factionalism and social anarchy. Restored peace and order. Purged the bureaucracy of the inept and the corrupt. Freed economic policymaking from the constraints of extremist rhetoric. Result: The renewed optimism of 40 million people, and the resurgence of the national economy. . . .

2. Consider these investment opportunities. The government has just finished rationalizing the three major laws regulating foreign business operations in the Philippines. Foreign investment may now go into most sectors of the economy. There are attractive investment packages for you if you want to explore, develop and process mineral resources. There are just as magnificent opportunities in basic industry, finance, tourism, manufacturing, chemicals, engineering, commercial agriculture and export trading. . . .

Apart from the basic rights and guarantees written into the Constitution, the new incentives include: Unrestricted repatriation of earnings and investments. Tax exemptions and credits. Tax deductions for reinvestment and labor-training expenses. Accelerated depreciation. Carry-over of net operating loss incurred during the first ten years of operation. Easy entry for expatriate staff. Protection from government competition. Protection of patents and other proprietary rights.

Our corporate-tax incentives are rated as better than those offered by Indonesia, Singapore, South Korea, Australia and Japan. (This might be why close to $94 million came in from the United States alone during the first 11 months of 1973.) But the best incentive we offer may not be so easily quantifiable. It is the rationalization of economic policymaking, and the consequent certainty that economic expansion in the Philippines will from now on be by quantum jumps.

Doesn't that sound like an offer you can't refuse?

3. We like multinationals. Manila's natural charms as a regional business center have been enhanced by a special incentive package. The multinational company setting up its regional or area headquarters in the Philippines is now "exempt from all forms of local licenses, fees, dues, imposts or any other local taxes or burdens."

In Manila your expatriate-managers will enjoy Asia's lowest living costs among the most outgoing people in the Pacific. Many bungalows in the Makati area have swimming pools as standard equipment. A cook starts at $28; a maid at $14, and a first-class chauffeur at $52. Quick entry-and-exit clearances; income taxes limited to 15 percent of gross.

. . . Local staff? Clerks with a college education start at $35, a fourth of what they cost in Singapore. Accountants come for $67, executive secretaries for $148. Move your Asian headquarters to Manila and make your cost accountants happy.

4. The Pacific action is moving back to Bataan. The Philippines' first industrial estate is going up at Mariveles, a port town at the tip of historic Bataan peninsula, on the northwest coast of Manila Bay. . . .

The tax and incentives package for foreign investors at Bataan includes: Admission of 100 percent foreign-owned or controlled companies. Unrestricted employment of foreign personnel. Tax- and duty-free importation of capital equipment, spare parts, raw materials, and supplies. Exemption from export tax and payment of all municipal and provincial taxes.

Among the first ones into Bataan are Ford Philippines, which is setting up a $50-million car body stamping plant; Honda, British

Leyland and Winthrop Products, Inc. Can you afford to lag too far behind the competition?

5. Our labor force speaks your language. Whether you're talking electronic components, garments or car-manufacturing. National literacy was placed at 83.4 percent in 1973 (English is the medium of instruction), which brings the Philippines closest to the Japanese standard among all Asian countries. . . .

Recent Presidential decrees have simplified conciliation and arbitration of labor disputes (both strikes and lockouts are prohibited), lifted work restrictions on Sundays and holidays, liberalized the employment of women and children, and expanded the scope of the apprenticeship program.

Labor costs for the foreign company setting up plant in Manila could work out from 35 to 50 percent lower than they would be in either Hongkong or Singapore. . . .

6. The country is lovely. And loaded. Beneath the tropical landscapes of our 7,000 islands lies a wealth of natural resources. . . .

7. We sell seashells. As well as sugar, copper, plywood, copra, embroidered shirts, cam shafts, bananas, television tubes, handmade shoes and freshwater eels. And business is good. . . .

Selection 8.2: Telegram to President Marcos, American Chamber of Commerce of the Philippines

Editors' Introduction

U.S. investors in the Philippines, reported *Business Week* six weeks after the declaration of martial law (November 4, 1972, p. 42), "have become increasingly sanguine about their future." "On balance," declared the vice-president of the Ford Motor Co., "Marcos's actions have stabilized the situation." And the president of Mobil's Philippine subsidiary noted that the "reaction among businessmen is one of cautious optimism." The American Chamber of Commerce of the Philippines (ACCP) is the organized expression of U.S. business interests in the Philippines. The following document is the text of a telegram sent by the head of the ACCP to President Ferdinand Marcos on September 27, 1972, a few days after the declaration of martial law.

Source: Telegram reproduced in telegram of the same date from William Mitchell to W. S. Lowe, president of the Chamber of Commerce of the United States.

HIS EXCELLENCY

FERDINAND E. MARCOS
PRESIDENT OF THE REPUBLIC OF THE PHILIPPINES

THE AMERICAN CHAMBER OF COMMERCE WISHES YOU EVERY
SUCCESS IN YOUR ENDEAVORS TO RESTORE PEACE AND ORDER,
BUSINESS CONFIDENCE ECONOMIC GROWTH AND THE WELL
BEING OF THE FILIPINO PEOPLE AND NATION. WE ASSURE YOU OF
OUR CONFIDENCE AND COOPERATION IN ACHIEVING THESE OB-
JECTIVES. WE ARE COMMUNICATING THESE FEELINGS TO OUR
ASSOCIATES AND AFFILIATES IN THE UNITED STATES.

WILLIAM MITCHELL
PRESIDENT OF THE AMERICAN
CHAMBER OF COMMERCE IN THE PHILIPPINES

Selection 8.3: Foreign Investment in the Philippines, Charles W. Lindsey

Editors' Introduction

The following article, written for this volume, examines the role of foreign investment in the Philippine economy and its impact on Philippine development. Charles W. Lindsey is an associate professor of economics at Trinity College. (For more details and data, see Charles W. Lindsey, "In Search of Dynamism: Foreign Invest-ment in the Philippines Under Martial Law," *Pacific Affairs,* vol. 56, Fall 1983; and "The Philippine State and Transnational Investment," in *Transnational Corporations and the State,* ed. Robert B. Stauffer, Sydney: Transnational Corporations Research Project, University of Sydney, 1985.)

Historical Context

All Philippine presidents since 1946 have sought increased inflows of American capital and resisted nationalist-inspired legislation that would limit foreign investment. There was the persistent belief that, on its own, the Philippines did not have sufficient capital—nor, to a lesser extent, the technology and managerial skills—to develop its economy. Beyond these narrow economic considerations, however, was the larger political context. As former Philippine president Diosdado Macapagal put it, presidential candidates found it necessary "to obtain the support of the American government or at least not antagonize it in their bid for the Presidency."

Despite presidential support of foreign capital, however, Filipinization occurred in many sectors of the economy, though manufacturing remained relatively open to transnational corporations (TNCs). During the 1950s, foreign investment flowed into the Philippines in response to a strategy of import-substitution industrialization (i.e., producing goods formerly imported for the local market), but that policy reached its limit by the end of the decade. Other factors also contributed to a reduced flow of foreign investment during the 1960s and early 1970s: the ability to utilize local profits and loans for investment purposes, the rising tide of nationalist sentiment, and the approaching expiration of the Laurel-Langley Agreement and with it the privileged position of American capital in the Philippines.

During the late 1960s and early 1970s, small, but articulate and growing, groups of Filipinos took issue with the prevailing view and pointed to the openness of the Philippine economy as a reason for, rather than a solution to, the country's existing state of underdevelopment. The declaration of martial law in September 1972 brought this debate to a halt, as Marcos repressed the nationalists and welcomed foreign investment. In turn, Marcos received whole-hearted support from the foreign business community. As *Business International* authoritatively reported, "the overwhelming consensus of the foreign business community in the Philippines was that martial rule under President Marcos was the best thing that ever happened to the country."

Importance of Foreign Investment in the Philippine Economy

TNCs responded to the receptive climate of the martial law regime. Net equity capital flows turned significantly positive for the first time in a decade. Between 1973 and 1980 investment inflows exceeded withdrawals by $546 million; whereas between 1961 and 1972 equity withdrawals had exceeded inflows by $137 million. After 1980, however, the investment climate from the point of view of the TNCs deteriorated and the flows began to dry up.

The increased inflow does not appear to have resulted in foreign investment becoming relatively larger in the Philippine economy, although it does appear to have stopped a downward trend in the share of the economy that is foreign controlled. In 1948 (two years after independence), foreigners held at least 50 percent of the assets in the major non-agricultural sectors of the economy: manufacturing, commerce, electricity, and mining. By 1970 the share of foreign-owned equity had been virtually eliminated in electricity and fallen to around 40 percent in the other areas.

During the 1970s, the foreign-owned share of manufacturing declined even further to between 30 and 35 percent of the total, even though the majority of foreign investment inflow had been to this sector. The share of equity ownership, however, understates TNC influence and intrusion into the domestic economy. Licensing of technology and, particularly, of brand names is important in the Philippines with its exposure to, if not domination by, American consumer society. One preliminary study of only those products whose use could be identified with some part of the body found 800 consumer items with foreign brand names available in Philippine stores.

Traditional measures of monopoly do not always capture the power of TNCs. Consider the advertising industry, for example. One study traced the process by which advertising strategies for TNCs are developed within the TNCs' home country by TNC advertising firms. These strategies are then sent to the Philippines and implemented by subsidiaries of the TNC advertising firms, at times with some extension or adaptation to meet local conditions. The link with the parent TNCs provides the advertising subsidiaries an advantage over locally-owned advertising firms. At the same time, there is little done to stimulate the development of a domestic advertising industry.

Impact on Development

Although the need for additional resources from abroad has usually been the main justification given for foreign equity investment in the Philippines, the net flow of resources has been consistently outward since independence. In almost every year in the past two decades, the sum of repatriated capital and remitted profits exceeded the inflow of equity capital. If management fees, copyrights, and royalties are included (as alternative channels for getting profits out of the country), the outflow is even greater. There was also a net outflow during the 1949-1960 period.

The conclusion is inescapable: since independence (except for perhaps the early postwar reconstruction period), foreign equity investment has not made a positive contribution to aggregate savings and investment in the Philippines.

Foreign investment is purported to make a contribution to the economic development of Third World countries in a number of other ways, three of which will be touched on here.

First, TNCs are supposed to earn foreign exchange for the country. Research has shown, however, that both the older import-substitution and the newer export-oriented foreign investment in the Philippines have been and remain highly import dependent. This means that most inputs into the production process are imported; foreign exchange is used up, not saved. Moreover, a large majority of the TNCs in the Philippines produce only for the local market, and have generally not expanded into export operations. Therefore, they have generated relatively little foreign exchange. TNCs in mining and agriculture and those in export-oriented industries do contribute to foreign exchange earnings, but the import-dependent nature of the latter significantly limits the contribution.

Second, TNCs are championed as being a major source of new technology and of training for Filipinos. Certainly the Philippines is in no position to develop most of its own technology; interaction with the world economy is necessary. On the other hand, it is questionable how much advantage is gained from TNC investment. Ownership and control of technology provides TNCs with both power and profit; they are not going to give their technology away, and, in many cases, they are not even willing to sell significant elements of it. Some technology is being transferred to the Philippines, but the essential components of an indigenous technological base—the capacity for independent research, development, or production—have generally not been transferred.

Studies have shown that most TNCs in the Philippines (as in other Third World countries) engage locally in only the last stages of the production process: assembling, mixing, packaging. This requires relatively little sophisticated technology or trained personnel. The one bright spot is management training, but even here there is less than would be hoped for. Given the elementary nature of production processes, most aspiring Philippine executives choose marketing, personnel, and finance rather than production management.

Third, supporters of TNC investment claim that the inflow of foreign capital will result in a reduction of the high rates of unemployment and underemployment. Obviously, any firm setting up operations will provide some employment. However, in the Philippines, TNCs are not sufficiently numerous to impact significantly on overall employment levels. In addition, they tend to use capital-intensive methods, using relatively more equipment and machinery, and relatively less labor. In 1970, firms with at least 30 percent foreign equity were estimated to account for a little over one percent of total employment. An additional indirect stimulus to employment could occur if TNCs purchased their equipment or raw materials locally, but studies show that very little of this goes on.

Lastly, a brief comment is in order on the impact of TNCs in the agribusiness sector. Though Philippine law prohibits foreigners from owning land, agribusiness TNCs have engaged in extensive leasing of land or gone into joint ventures, often with a government corporation. The consequences of the very unequal power relationship between the TNCs and the people is stark. Examples abound of land speculation and the displacement of farmers, often with the connivance of the Bureau of Lands (in effect, stealing land from its rightful owners), or by outright intimidation. And small farmers who produce bananas for large TNCs have been forced to sign incomprehensible growers' agreements that ensure that the farmers have no control over the production process and that they must bear the brunt of the vicissitudes of the world market.

Conclusion

I have argued that the impact of foreign investment in the Philippines is largely negative. This does not mean that TNCs should necessarily be excluded from the country. Few in the Philippines have made such an argument. Rather, there is need for the potential gains to be more clearly specified and for efforts to be made to ensure that this potential is realized. TNCs unable or unwilling to assist should be excluded.

The problem is in part technical, but it is much more a social issue. Why has the government, both now and in the past, been so encouraging of foreign investment, and why has a large segment of the Filipino business community supported government efforts to attract outside capital? Part of the reason can be explained by the actions of the U.S. government and the historic dependence of the Philippines on the United States. But there are also internal reasons. Control of wealth in the Philippines is highly concentrated. Filipino capitalists have engaged in industrial activity, but—as with the TNCs—they have seldom gone beyond the final stages of manufacturing, for, given the security of their class position, they have not needed to. In addition, the link between economic and political power has made them attractive joint venture partners for foreign capital. In turn, Filipino capitalists can reap monopoly profits with little or no effort. The behavior of Marcos and his business associates—the "cronies"—is but an extreme example of the use of political power rather than entrepreneurial skills to amass wealth.

There are indeed exceptions to this characterization, but they are not sufficiently numerous to ensure that a successful industrialization process could occur. Nor, as I have tried to show, can TNCs accomplish the task. If genuine development is to take place in the Philippines, the criticisms by nationalists of TNCs in the Philippines and their call for self-reliance must broaden, and in some quarters has broadened, to an attack on the class structure and concentration of wealth and economic power that currently exists in the Philippines.

Selection 8.4: Philippine Women and Transnational Corporations, Sr. Mary Soledad Perpiñan, RGS

Editors' Introduction

Turning now from the macro-economic aspects of transnational corporations on Philippine development, the following article discusses the impact of transnationals on Filipino workers, particularly on women workers. The author is director of IBON, a research group popularizing socio-economic information on Philippine development, and of the Third World Movement Against the Exploitation of Women, both based in Manila.

Source: Sister Mary Soledad Perpiñan, RGS, "Women and Transnational Corporations: the Philippine Experience," in *Access to Justice,* ed. Harry M. Scoble and Laurie S. Wiseberg, London: Zed Books, 1985, pp. 162-72.

Case Study 1: BEPZ Women Workers

BEPZ (Bataan Export Processing Zone) is an industrial estate designed to promote export manufacturing principally through the attraction of overseas investment. It is a physically enclosed enclave consisting of standard factory buildings erected in advance of demand and of a variety of services and facilities for the occupants.

There are 58 export enterprises in BEPZ (as of January 1981) and the majority of these are units of transnational corporations. They enjoy the preferential treatment of: exemption from taxes and customs duties on exports and on imported machinery, raw materials and supplies; low rents (about P9 per square meter per month); full repatriation of foreign investment and profits at any time; and assistance from the Republic of the Philippines zone authority in recruiting labor and keeping it docile.

In 1979, there were 27,004 wage earners in BEPZ, of whom 90% were women. A total of P112 million went to salaries and wages that year, with an average annual pay per worker of P4,148 (or P17.28 daily, reckoned on a five-day working week). Included in this P112 million figure, however, are 6,827 non-factory workers including an unspecified number of administrative and technical personnel whose salaries, of course, are far above that of the common worker. The average wage of a factory worker actually ranges from P8 daily for casuals and apprentices to P13, with or without allowances.

In the same year, BEPZ factories realized a total production of $116.8 million. This means a gross earning of $5,789—or P42,528 (at the official rate of $1 to P7.3)—per employee. Even if the costs of raw materials, depreciation on machinery and equipment, rent, taxes and the average annual salary of P4,148 are deducted from this amount, a tidy sum is still left over for BEPZ participating capitalists, local or foreign.

Problem Areas

1) Wages are low—decidedly, since one of the most attractive features of BEPZ (or the Philippines, for that matter) for foreign investors is the low labor cost. As the Export Processing Zone Authority reported in 1978, one of the main reasons why Ford Philippines came to BEPZ is because of "the Philippines' inexpensive labor which is less than $2 daily as against Norway's $8 an hour."

2) Workers are kept docile and discouraged from unionizing.

3) Job insecurity is high. Lay-offs are frequent. Apprenticeship, which is paid less than the legal minimum wage, can extend for a year and even longer.

4) Workers' morale is very low. Workers suffer from lack of recreational and leisure-time activities, while there is an abnormally high percentage of women over men. Married female workers are discriminated against in employment, so abortions are frequent. Managers and supervisors take advantage of the very young working girls and exploit them sexually. The choice is to give in or lose one's livelihood. In BEPZ it is a common phenomenon to find unwanted babies strangled to death or otherwise done away with.

Other Problems

A survey of BEPZ workers conducted in August 1980 revealed rampant violation of their rights, such as: forced overtime, oppressive quota systems, union busting, absence of safety measures, and violation of minimum wage laws. . . .

Of all industries, electronics and garments have the largest proportion of women workers. It is therefore helpful to present two case studies of two relevant transnationals, TMX (electronics) and Triumph (garments), to particularize the plight and struggle of women industrial workers.

Electronics Industry

To avoid the rising wages occasioned by unionization and the growing labor shortage elsewhere in Southeast Asia, electronics firms have come to the Philippines. The country is the most attractive prospect in Asia because of a combination of factors: governmental incentives; a vast supply of young, relatively highly educated, cheap female labor; and a broad knowledge of English among the populace. However, only the labor-intensive and eye-straining assembly work has been relocated here. The initial and final testing stages, for example, are performed in the mother countries.

A study conducted by the RP [Republic of the Philippines] National Institute of Occupational Safety and Health reports that the third most dangerous industry, in terms of exposure to cancer-causing substances, is electronics. Throughout the production process, electronics workers in the Philippines are exposed to acids, solvents and gases which have various physically damaging effects, causing, for example, eye defects, cancer, lung disease, and liver and kidney troubles.

Meanwhile, the electronics industry remains one of the top non-traditional manufacturers of the Philippines, accounting for $138.19 million of exports. And the Philippines exports semiconductors to the United States, Japan, Western Europe, Canada, Singapore and Malaysia.

Case Study 2: TMX Philippines, Inc.

Address: Aurora Boulevard, Quezon City
Activity: Watch assembly
Status: Commercial operations began January 1978
Ownership: 100% American, wholly-owned subsidiary of TMX Limited
Net sales: P70,440,000; net income: P3,134,000
Market: Timex, Inc., Bermuda
Labor generation: 4,412 positions
Pay scale: Job 1 (line operator)—P13.95/day; Job 2 (line operator)—P14.45; Job 3 (inspector)—P15.15; Job 4 (jobmaster, assistant supervisor)—P15.65; allowance—P12.30/day.

Nana, a bespectacled 20 year old, has been working at TMX Philippines, Inc., for the past two years. Part of her earnings is sent home to her native province to augment her family's meager income. A portion is set aside to help her continue her studies. Most of the girls at TMX are students. She says, "It's very difficult; we get so tired!"

Soft Sell: Various incentives are given to the workers in order to increase productivity: on the annual awards night, prizes are given to the year's most outstanding operators on the basis of 100% attendance and performance. These operators usually have to maintain or even surpass their quotas in order to qualify. One award winner received a P100 gift certificate at Rustan's (a department store chain) and a plaque. Bonuses are also given to employees who do not avail themselves of their sick-leave and vacation privileges. As an extra incentive, raffles are held to determine the lucky employee who will be given the use of a Timex watch for nine months only. If the watch is lost, the worker is requested to pay the company its full value.

Hard Sell: The company also metes out "remedial actions" to workers who are unable to measure up to its standards. A dismissal threat awaits those who fail to meet their quota. Preventive suspension is the lot of an employee suspected of being a source of trouble.

Anti-Union Activities: Workers have grounds for believing that the company takes measures to spy on activities leading to the establishment of a union. Phones are tapped and workers are prevented from attending meetings by the enforcement of overtime work whenever the company gets wind of any such happening.

Lay-Offs: Approximately 1,500 workers of the TMX facility in Quezon City were laid off in 1980. Some 321 were dismissed. Workers have reason to attribute these measures to a move to make the Aurora Boulevard building merely a warehouse or an office and to concentrate on the newly inaugurated TMX plant in the Mactan Export Processing Zone.

Major Problems: Apart from low wages, Nana stated that the quota system is one of their major problems. "They continually increase our quota. It has come to a point that we have to utilize our break periods for working just to meet the minimum output. To make matters worse, if you do meet the quota, they raise it higher!"

Strike: Although such activity is banned by Presidential Decree 823, the TMX women workers went out on strike in late 1980 when management threatened them with another mass lay-off.

Filipino Garment Industry

The glowing reports about garment exports—ranked fourth in 1980 and worth $302.29 million—do not represent the net benefits to the country from this industry. About 56% of the exports' value is actually comprised of imported raw materials and only 44%—the value added thanks to the Filipino garment workers, mostly women—originates in the Philippines. In other words, for every $1 exported, according to the reports, only $.44 in fact constitutes export earnings.

Of these export earnings, about 30% are profits which may be repatriated to the headquarters company/mother country so that only 70% remains, from which wages and other local overhead expenses are paid. For every $1 of garment exports, therefore, the "net benefit" to the country (in terms of incomes that are paid to Filipinos and that remain in the country) is only about $.31.

This "net benefit" is wiped out entirely by the following; (1) low wages and harsh treatment of garment workers; (2) smuggling and transfer pricing through the "consignment system." The value of these two evils (which ultimately mean pure profit to the foreign companies) is estimated at twice the value of reported profits. And, for the 1972-78 period, this was placed at $296 million (P2.2 billion) or an average of $42 million (P303 million) per year. Profits are thus derived from two sources: (1) those from manufacturing, about 33%; (2) those from smuggling and intra-corporate transfer pricing, 67%. Meanwhile, the return on capital for every peso of compensation paid to garment workers in the Philippines has been increasing over the years. In 1974, it was a factor of 8.13. This means that a worker who received P8 a day in 1974 produced for the company P65/day in profits. For workers, it is a case of division. Each P8 gets subsequently divided into different items of expense (food, clothing, transport costs, etc.) among the members of the worker's family. For the company, it is a case of multiplication. Total profit is the product of P65 multiplied each day by the number of workers in the firm.

Case Study 3: Triumph International

Location: Food Terminal, Inc., Taguig, Metro Manila

Main office: Munich, West Germany

Branches:48 branches around the globe

Ownership:100% German capital; in March 1975, it began with an initial capitalization of $10 million

Products:Women's underwear, such as bras, girdles, panties, bikinis for export to Europe and Asian countries

Production:As of June 1979, a daily output of 10,500 pieces, 98% to Europe and 2% to the local market c/o Mondragon Industries

Net sales:P80,966,000 (1979); net income: P3.059 million

Work-force:95% female; 5% male

Workers' Complaints: Very high quotas are imposed on the workers (e.g. 450 pieces daily). With minimum compensation, they work under very strict conditions.

Bambi, a Triumph worker, said: "We are frequently watched by our supervisor. We are prevented from talking to each other and are always ordered to concentrate on our jobs. Whenever we commit mistakes in sewing, the bra is placed near our face and the supervisor sneers that it is as ugly as our face."

Each time complaints are voiced, management threatens the workers with preventive suspension and termination.

There are no safety devices in the work-place. The working conditions are so bad that there is a high rate of tuberculosis: three out of every 100 workers get TB.

Workers' Struggle: The genuine trade union PMTI [*Pagkakaisa ng mga Manggagawa sa Triumph International*] has led in the collective bargaining of Triumph workers. From the start, it has been militant in fighting for the workers' rights as indicated by the following PMTI actions:

1) The "Four Hour Strike" in July 1977, was to force management to comply with Presidential Decree 1123 and grant the workers a P60 increase in emergency allowance. Management conceded after negotiations, with military intervention, but retaliated by filing preventive suspensions against 56 workers and union officers.

2) The "Boycott of Management Memo" in August 1978 protested against a new lunch-break rotation among the workers of one shift and obtained the maintenance of the old schedule.

3) The "Boycott of Overtime" in October 1978 demanded an across-the-board increase of P1 daily, as provided by Presidential Decree 1389, and succeeded in obtaining a P.75 increase after two days of negotiation. However, management filed an unfair labor practices complaint against the union with the Ministry of Labor and Employment and pressured the union to accept an increase of only P.50.

4) The "Five Day Strike" took place during November-December 1978, in protest against the unbearable heat inside the factory and won the installation of an air-conditioning system. The brunt of management's ire fell on 71 officers and union members who were then placed under preventive suspension, which is tantamount to getting fired.

These examples of the Triumph workers' struggle prove the power of mass action as necessary to the enforcement of the law and of the Labor Code. . . .

Summing Up

. . . TNCs capitalize on the women's virtues of patience and tolerance, endurance and perseverance in work that is complex and minute, as well as repetitive and monotonous. This is particularly true of the electronics and garments industries. Management thinks it is to its advantage to have a vast majority of women in an enclave like BEPZ. As one of them put it, "We hire girls because they have less energy, are more disciplined, and are easier to control."

In Philippine society, there are built-in cultural distinctions between men's work and women's work and prejudiced assumptions that men can do better than women. As a rule, women are given fewer chances to acquire new skills and to take a more responsible role in production. For this reason, women workers are generally relegated to the lowest rung in management's ladder.

Wages: In the Philippines, as in the rest of the world, the female sector helps depress wage levels. As competitors for jobs, they swell the labor force and, because there are more potential workers to choose from, the TNCs can offer to pay less.

Even for the same work as men, women workers get lower wages: thus for the same work for which a man receives P296 per week, the female worker receives only P160 or 54%.

Doubly exploited: If both men and women are exploited by the capitalists (a workers' group estimated that in 1975 for every peso net output, a worker received P0.09 while the employer retained P0.91), women get doubly exploited. That same study reports that women workers not only have 7 hours and 16 minutes paid work but also face some 5 or more hours of unpaid labor at home each day of the work week!

Working conditions: Among the complaints of women workers are the imposition of heavy workloads in terms of quotas, intolerable heat in garment factories, and extreme cold in electronics firms.

Women workers are given only 15 minutes to eat their dinner outside factory premises and are also timed whenever they go to the rest room. There is also the rampant practice of forced overtime.

Job insecurity: Most female workers are hired on a temporary basis. In the BEPZ it is not unusual for workers to change jobs at least three times a year because of the short duration of work contracts. Avoidance of permanent workers is one way of avoiding payment of any fringe benefits and employer contributions—another tactic to increase profits.

Unionism: The high unemployment rate among women workers hampers to a large extent their attempts to get more benefits for themselves. Given their low level of educational attainment and the limited opportunities open to them, many production workers shy away from any real bargaining because the system works against them.

Presidential Decree 823, which bans strikes, prevents many workers from organizing for mass action. In the case of women, some still have the notion that unionism is men's prerogative.

Reduced benefits: Under martial law, Presidential Decree 148 introduced the following revisions affecting women workers:

1) Maternity leave with pay was reduced from six weeks to two weeks before, and from eight weeks to four weeks after, delivery.

2) In cases of medically certified illness due to delivery, the leave may be extended without pay in the absence of unused vacation and/or sick-leave credits.

3) Payment of maternity leave is limited to the first four deliveries, in line with the government's family planning program.

4) Setting up of special facilities for women, such as seats, separate lavatories and nurseries, is no longer required by law but left to the discretion of the Ministry of Labor and Employment (MOLE).

Meantime, inspection teams from MOLE do not really see to it that the Labor Code's prescribed standards of working conditions are followed by management.

5) Finally, Presidential Decree 1202, dated September 27, 1977, integrated maternity benefits into the Social Security system, in fact making it more difficult for workers to claim them.

Women in Agriculture

Since the majority of Filipinos live in the rural areas, it follows that most women are involved in agricultural work. They contribute about 21% of farm labor, or 36% of hired labor and 17% of unpaid family labor. They also devote much of their time to post-harvest activities. Hired female workers participate in almost all types of farm operations except land preparation and weeding.

Women peasants suffer mainly from the feudal exploitation of the entire peasant class. They are subjected to the exploitative landlord-tenant relationship, usury, price manipulation and obligatory menial service to the landlord: common abuses in rural Philippines.

Like women industrial workers female peasants also suffer discrimination. A comparison of wages of hired workers in rice production shows that males usually get higher pay except for harvesting and threshing (see Table).

Wage Payments of Workers for Rice Production
(in Pesos per Day per Person)

Activity	Male	Female
Land preparation	8.16	5.78
Transplanting and related tasks	9.43	8.72
Weeding	10.36	9.51
Other pre-harvest	—	3.28
Harvesting	12.86	14.32
Threshing	14.69	15.73
Other post-harvest	9.78	9.45

Source: Emmanuel Santiago, "Women in Agriculture: A Social Accounting of Female Workshare."

Although feudal oppression is more dominant and prevalent, the incursion of transnational corporations in the countryside has been very insidious. TNCs make their presence felt mainly through foreign investment in wood-based industries (logging, lumber), mining and processing plants, and agribusiness (corporate farms and plantations of fruit, coconut, sugar, etc.), as well as through infrastructural projects (dams, roads, etc.) financed by foreign loans or some government aid programs. In addition, some TNC products are practically forced into the hands of farmers, like farm inputs of fertilizers and pesticides, fungicides, etc., which are part and parcel of government credit programs.

With reference to the focus of this paper, rural women relate to TNCs as agricultural workers in foreign-owned agribusiness; as wives or family members of men engaged in wood-based, mining, and other TNC operations; or as members of communities affected by foreign-financed projects. Again we shall take case studies to put things across more concretely.

Case Study 4: Castle & Cooke in Mindanao

Castle & Cooke:43,700 employees; $36,500 sales per employee or total 1979 sales of $1.595 billion; profits of $700 per employee or total 1979 profits $30.1 million

RP operations: 100% American equity—Dole Philippines (DOLE-FIL) which began operations in 1963; 66% American equity—Standard Philippines Fruit Corporation (STANFILCO) which merged with Dole in May 1980

Location: General Santos and Davao

Activities: Growing and canning Dole pineapples, growing and exporting STANFILCO bananas

RP sales: DOLEFIL—P355,801,000; STANFILCO—P217,849,000 (both in 1979)

Nina's whole family is connected with Dole—her husband Alix and her three brothers. Her father used to work for Dole too, until he had to retire; he was given P3,000 ($405) severance pay.

The DOLEFIL hourly rates are as follows: cannery workers—P1.12, probationary; P1.36, under one year; P1.68, after one year; agricultural workers—P0.87, probationary; P1.11, under one year; P1.34, after one year.

Alix's first job was loading fruit. Now he loads fertilizer. His wage is P1.31 per hour (approximately 18 cents). Monthly take-home pay is P450. All Nina can buy out of his pay is rice and fish, a little milk for the four children, ages 2 to 6, occasionally some household items and clothing. "I have debts at all the grocery stores in Polomok." Her husband's pay is simply no enough, being far below the estimated monthly P1,555 that agricultural workers need to meet their basic requirements. Besides, things are more expensive at the work site than in General Santos some 15 kilometers away. To get to General Santos, workers have to pay P2.50 in fares—but lower- and middle-level executives pay half-fare while top management personnel are given free rides.

There are also differences in the kinds of housing they get. The superintendents are housed in a country-club estate called Kalsangi and they live in style: huge modern houses with lawns, a 9-hole golf course, tennis courts, a swimming pool, and restaurant. It costs them less than $4 a month to send their children to a company school with top-notch teachers. Unlike the workers, they are provided with water and electricity. All these bounties are subsidized by DOLEFIL. Here it is a case of social welfare for the rich!

Other victims: Dolly is Nina's neighbor. She has been working in the cannery for nine years, preparing pineapples for canning and shipping. The machines rotate so fast that Dolly has had several accidents. Work is particularly difficult during the night shift from 6 pm to 6 am.

Dolly and the other women workers feel frustrated about their condition. The union is weak and the people unorganized. And there are very important matters that concern the entire community: pineapple monoculture produces soil which cannot hold water and therefore erodes; and the chemicals used for the bananas have harmful effects on the workers' health—skin rashes, respiratory ailments—and cause ecological degradation.

Tess is a packer at TADECO, Tagum Agricultural Development Corporation, a contract-grower for United Brands (United Fruit) which exports RP "Chiquita" bananas to Japan through the Far East Fruit Co., Tokyo, and United Fruit, Japan.

Tess works in one of the ten packing houses of TADECO. She stands on her feet the whole working day, and gets P7 a day plus P110 per month living allowance, so that she can make about P300 a month. A third of this is sent to her family in the Visayas.

On Tess's leg is a large reddish, raw area, about 6 inches by 2 inches. The chemicals sprayed on bananas accidentally fell on her leg. There are many such accidents and allergic reactions.

Tess sleeps in a bunkhouse where 100 other women are packed like sardines. Unbelievably, 24 of them share one small room, sleeping in eight sets of three-tiered bunks.

Selection 8.5: Philippine Military Bases and the Middle East, Admiral Robert L. J. Long

Editors' Introduction

The uses to which U.S. bases in the Philippines have been put have changed with the changing emphases of United States military and foreign policy. Since 1950, the bases have played a major role as a source of supply and air support for U.S. forces in Korea. But by the mid-seventies, the Pentagon was referring to the Philippine bases as vital also for projecting military power into the Middle East. After the fall of the Shah of Iran in 1979, preserving the status quo in the Persian Gulf became a major preoccupation of U.S. policy makers, for Middle East oil resources have always been viewed by Washington as an economic and strategic prize of the first order. Carrier task forces from Subic Naval Base were sent to the Indian Ocean and Arabian Sea, with major deployments during the Iranian revolution, the 1979 North Yemen-South Yemen border war, and the Soviet intervention in Afghanistan. In February 1980, the Marcos government announced that it had agreed that U.S. bases could be used as staging areas for U.S. Marines bound for the Arabian Sea, and in April of that year Clark Air Base was used as a staging point for the abortive mission of U.S. Special Operations Forces who tried to free embassy hostages in Teheran. Today Subic and Clark supply U.S. forces, from the Korean peninsula to the Indian Ocean, and they serve as a potential jumping-off point for the Rapid Deployment Force to intervene in the Middle East. (See, more generally, Walden Bello, "Springboards for Intervention, Instruments

for Nuclear War," *Southeast Asia Chronicle*, no. 89, April 1983.)

The following excerpt is from the June 1983 Congressional testimony of Admiral Robert L. J. Long, then Commander-in-Chief of U.S. Naval forces in the Pacific. Long describes the U.S. military facilities in the Philippines and their mission.

Source: *United States-Philippine Relations and the New Base and Aid Agreement*, Hearings, Subcommittee on Asian and Pacific Affairs of the House Committee on Foreign Affairs, 98th Cong., 1st session, June 1983, pp. 7-12.

The U.S. has two major installations in the Philippines—Clark Air Base and Subic Naval Base which enable us to take advantage of the strategic location of the Philippines. We also operate several smaller supporting activities, such as San Miguel Naval Communications Station, Wallace Air Station and John Hay Air Base. Altogether, we estimate that the current replacement value of U.S. facilities at the bases would exceed two billion dollars.

Clark Air Base is the only major tactical operational Air Force installation remaining in the far west Pacific outside of Japan and Korea. Its 10,500 foot runway with parallel taxiway can be used by virtually all aircraft, including the largest military transports. It has 60,000 square yards of usable parking apron and 79,000 square feet of hangar space.

The major Air Force units located at Clark include a tactical fighter wing and a tactical airlift wing. The two tactical fighter squadrons, consisting of F4's, possess the only permanent all-weather air defense capability in the Philippines and are available for other contingencies. The C-130s of the tactical airlift squadron provide an airlift capability for the Pacific and Indian Ocean areas. Also based at Clark is headquarters, 13th Air Force which has command and control of Pacific Air Force operations in the western Pacific.

The Crow Valley Weapons Range at Clark is critical to maintaining the air combat readiness of U.S. Air Force, Navy, and Marine air units throughout the area. This range contains extensive bombing, gunnery and electronic warfare ranges, including simulated surface-to-air missile installations. These facilities, combined with extensive off-shore airspace and the availability of an aggressor training squadron, provide battlefield realism in preparing and training pilots for combat. Overall, the ranges at Clark are the best of their kind outside the United States, and contribute substantially to force readiness of air units in the western Pacific.

Clark is also a superb logistic support base. It can provide many forward operating locations with major aircraft maintenance and repair services, including rebuilding engines and issuing spare parts. It can store about 18 million gallons of jet fuel and has over a million square feet of storage areas for war readiness material. It can routinely handle more than 3,500 tons of cargo and 22,000 passengers daily. It serves as an important transfer point between airlift transportation systems and sealift systems at Manila and Subic Bay. Clark possesses the greatest capacity for movement of personnel and materiel in the western Pacific and is essential to the Pacific-Indian Ocean Airlift System.

Additionally, Clark is a hub for both North-South and East-West communications in the western Pacific. Its facilities and capabilities include a communications center, satellite terminals, an automatic switching center for global voice and teletype service, and high frequency radio facilities. It supports CINCPAC [Commander-in-Chief, Pacific] by providing voice and teletype alerting networks and Airborne Command Post support. Tactical units are also served by its facilities.

At Wallace Air Station, the U.S. Air Force provides a portion of the radar coverage for the air defense of the main Philippine Island, Luzon, as a key element in the air defense system. The Air Force also supports tactical air training from this site and provides air-to-air refueling assistance. Additionally, the Air Force launches and controls target drones from Wallace in support of the Pacific Air Force's Weapon System Evaluation Program.

John Hay Air Base is a rest and recreation center for personnel from all services. It plays an important role in maintaining their welfare and morale.

Turning to Navy facilities, the Subic Bay Naval complex is the largest naval installation outside the United States and its unique combination of ship, aircraft, and support facilities is essential to Seventh Fleet operations. One submarine and one cruiser are homeported at Subic, but Seventh Fleet carriers and their aircraft, surface combatants, submarines and support forces all use Subic Bay Naval Base extensively. It has three major wharves which can berth all ship types, including the Navy's largest carriers. Subic is invaluable to Seventh Fleet and Marine amphibious force readiness. Virtually every element of naval warfare is represented and can be exercised in the many operating areas in and around Subic Bay and in the Zambales Peninsula across from Subic. The Zambales ranges comprise one of the few remaining areas in the western Pacific where adequate terrain is available for amphibious training, ground maneuvers, and delivery of live ordnance by ships, aircraft, and field weapons. In fact, the Marines can use virtually every piece of equipment in their inventory in this area, including tanks. As principal users of these amphibious training areas, Marines from the Seventh Fleet Landing Force are often in port at Subic performing upkeep or on training duty. Additional training facilities are available at Binanga Bay and Tabones for air combat training.

The ship repair facility at Subic is the largest in the western Pacific and performs 65 percent of the ship repair work for the Seventh Fleet. It has drydock capabilities for all ships, except carriers and battleships. It has facilities for complete overhaul of most Navy ships. It can respond immediately to emergency repair requirements for ships at sea and in port. In constant operation 24 hours a day, 365 days a year, its labor costs are less than anywhere else in the Pacific.

The Navy Supply Depot is the largest U.S. naval supply depot overseas. It is in effect the "general store" for Seventh Fleet ships, aircraft, and units. It processes over 100,000 requisitions a month for everything from C-rations for a Marine patrol to a new five-inch gun barrel for a Seventh Fleet ship. The Depot's freight piers handle about 1,000 container vans per month, and the fuel department processes over one million barrels of fuel each month.

The Naval Magazine stores, repairs, and issues ammunition and explosives. Adequate storage is provided for significant amounts of ammunition.

Across the bay from the Naval Station is Naval Air Station, Cubi Point, the Navy's most active and densely populated overseas air station. The airfield can host 150-200 aircraft and averages about 15,000 landings or takeoffs per month, including practice operations. It receives some 800 tons of air freight and handles over 3,500 passengers each month. The Air Station also has comprehensive maintenance, repair, and other support facilities. It is the only overseas air station where aircraft can be off-loaded directly from the carriers, and one of only three with this capability that the Navy has in the world. The ability to directly off-load is advantageous for several reasons. For example, disabled aircraft which cannot fly off the carrier can be removed by crane and placed ashore at the air station where the required repairs can be made. Also, this capability enables airwings to more easily tailor their composition with the specific aircraft needed for a particular mission.

Cubi Point is the primary "home-away-from-home" for the Seventh Fleet's attack carrier striking force. The airfield is used by squadrons when their carriers are either in port or operating in nearby waters. It supports a patrol squadron flying P-3 Orion aircraft on antisubmarine warfare patrols over the South China Sea and the Indian Ocean, a fleet tactical support squadron which provides on-board delivery service to the carriers, and a fleet composite squadron which tows targets for surface and airborne gunnery exercises. Various Marine aircraft and helicopter squadrons, plus Navy helicopter detachments also use Cubi Point.

The naval communications station at San Miguel, about 25 miles from Subic, is one of the primary communications stations in the western Pacific and provides tactical communications support for the operating forces of the Seventh Fleet. Circuits at San Miguel link Subic with Navy ships and shore stations throughout the world. The facilities used to accomplish this task include two message centers, a microwave relay station, and a transmitter facility.

Clark and Subic provide U.S. operation forces with a wide variety of important services which significantly support our efforts in maintaining military capabilities in and adjacent to the region to support U.S. objectives. These capabilities include:

—A continuous air and naval presence in the western Pacific, with a capacity to extend the presence into the Indian Ocean. This includes our obligations under the Mutual Defense Treaty, for the defense of the Philippines.

—Air and naval capability to meet contingencies outside the western Pacific, such as in the Persian Gulf, Arabian Sea, East African waters and the Middle East.

—The ability to maintain a high state of readiness of U.S. operational forces in the Pacific.

—The ability to deploy and support U.S. forces rapidly anywhere in the western Pacific.

—Comprehensive support for all operating forces in the area, including communications, logistics, maintenance, training, and personnel requirements.

—Major war reserve materiel storage for a variety of contingencies.

Selection 8.6: The Amended Military Bases Agreement, *Malaya*

Editors' Introduction

In 1974, a U.S. diplomat in Manila told reporter Charles F. Thomson of the *Philadelphia Bulletin* that he preferred to negotiate about U.S. military bases with Mr. Marcos rather than with the nationalist-minded Congress that Marcos had recently abolished. The wisdom of this observation was confirmed by the 1979 amendments to the bases agreement. Earlier agreements, in 1959 and 1966, specified that the U.S. would consult with the Philippine government before emplacing long range missiles in the country and before using the bases for purposes not related to mutual security. The 1979 amendments gave the United States the right to "unhampered" military operations and, according to one of the members of the Philippine negotiat-

ing panel, Marcos agreed to allow the United States to store nuclear weapons in the Philippines without the need for prior consultation with or even notification of the Philippine government. There have been nuclear weapons stored in the Philippines for many years, but the privilege Marcos accorded the Pentagon is especially important now that technological developments (for example, the cruise missile) and U.S. strategic doctrine have blurred the line between conventional war, limited nuclear war, and all-out nuclear war. (See Walden Bello, "Springboards for Intervention, Instruments for Nuclear War," *Southeast Asia Chronicle,* no. 89, April 1983; John Miller, "Sea-Launched Cruise Missiles and the Philippines: Time To Act," *Philippine Research Bulletin,* vol. 1, no. 2-3, Fall/Spring 1984-85, pp. 13-14.)

The editorial printed below, from the opposition newspaper *Malaya*, summarizes some of the advantages secured by the United States in the 1979 amendments to the bases agreement.

Source: "RP-U.S. Pact Unsatisfactory," *Malaya* [Manila], April 2, 1985.

Former Vice-President Emmanuel Pelaez, who was a member of the Philippine panel that negotiated the RP-US [Republic of the Philippines-United States] bases agreement in 1979, has admitted the pact is inordinately in favor of the Americans.

He told a symposium sponsored by the Manindigan at the Ateneo law school last Friday that the bases agreement "is unsatisfactory, to say the least."

The one-time secretary of foreign affairs said the pact has no specific provision on whether the Americans could store nuclear weapons in their arsenal in Clark or Subic without informing the Philippine government.

According to him, the agreement allows the U.S. unhampered use of the two giant U.S. bases.

He said that when the question of storage of nuclear weapons came up during the negotiations, the American panel, led by then U.S. Ambassador Michael M. Armacost, told the Filipinos the question had been referred to President Marcos. The Filipino panelists were subsequently told by the Americans that Mr. Marcos had resolved the issue in favor of the U.S. government.

Pelaez disclosed the bases agreement expires in 1991 and should not be renewed because it is an "irritant." But should the Philippine government decide on an extension, the new agreement must be embodied in a treaty to be ratified by the Batasang Pambansa [Philippine National Assembly] and the U.S. Senate.

He also suggested that the matter of extension must also be submitted to the Filipino electorate in a plebiscite as a prerequisite to a new negotiation after 1991.

Pelaez' revelation that the bases pact is "unsatisfactory" to the Philippines and, therefore, "satisfactory" to the U.S. may explain why the American government has been sympathetic to the dictatorial Marcos government.

It was the same mistake that the American government committed in Iran and in Nicaragua. Will the Americans never learn?

For us in the Philippines, the lesson is that for our best interests, any foreign agreement should be negotiated by Filipino representatives carrying the mandate of the people and not just one man.

Selection 8.7: The Logistics of Repression, Walden Bello and Severina Rivera

Editors' Introduction

The next reading comes from a careful study of U.S. military aid to the Philippines in the years immediately following the declaration of martial law. The study documents the increase in military aid following martial law and the uses for which the aid was intended.

Source: Walden Bello and Severina Rivera, "The Logistics of Repression," in *The Logistics of Repression and Other Essays*, ed. Walden Bello and Severina Rivera, Washington, D.C.: Friends of the Filipino People, 1977, pp. 7-27.

Official Military Assistance

The Philippines has been a recipient country under the U.S. Military Assistance Program since 1947. Military aid, however, leaped spectacularly after the imposition of martial law in September 1972. It totalled $166.3 million in the four-year period (FY 1973-76) following martial law. This was 106 percent more than the total assistance of $80.8 million in the preceding four-year period (FY 1969-72). (See Table 1.) Military aid now averages $40 million a year, in contrast to the pre-martial law average of about $20 million. In FY 1976 the Philippines emerged as the ninth biggest recipient of military assistance out of 62 countries included in the program, up from sixteenth place in FY 1972.

The jump in military assistance was particularly sharp in FY 1973, a period which approximated the first year of martial law; total aid for that year ($45.3 million) more than doubled that of FY 1972 ($18.5 million). Although only $285 million worth of weapons and technical aid was proposed by the Pentagon during the Congressional appropriations hearings in June 1972— four months before martial law—the final figure for that year was about 60 percent greater. Increases of such a scale are not casually decreed, and the motivation behind the additional aid was quite obviously the need to gird the military effort that was necessary to impose Marcos's martial law decree after September 22, 1972. . . .

Arms Sales

Foreign military sales are not purely commercial transactions. They constitute an instrument of U.S. foreign policy. Under Secretary of State Philip Habib made this very clear before the House International Relations Committee on September 21, 1976:

> Let me emphasize that we do not sell arms unless there is a very substantial area of policy congruence—particularly security policy—between ourselves and the recipient. All of the nations which we are discussing today can meet that standard. . . .

Table 1
Official U.S. Military Assistance
to the Republic of the Philippines
(FY 1969—1977)
(in millions of dollars)

FY	MAP	FMSC	EDA	ST	MAAG	IMETP	Total
1969	17.7	—	0.6	—	2.3	n.a.	20.6
1970	15.0	—	0.6	—	1.7	0.9	18.2
1971	16.0	—	5.2	—	1.4	0.9	23.5
1972	12.9	—	1.4	1.8	1.3	1.1	18.5
Total	**61.6**	**—**	**7.8**	**1.8**	**6.7**	**2.9**	**80.8**
1973	15.9	—	4.3	22.8	1.5	0.8	45.3
1974	15.4	8.6	15.0	—	1.7	0.5	41.2
1975	19.1	14.0	1.3	—	1.9	0.5	36.8
1976	18.7	17.0	4.7	n.a.	1.9	0.7	43.0
Total	**69.1**	**39.6**	**25.3**	**22.8**	**7.0**	**2.5**	**166.3**
1977	19.6	20.0	3.0	—	(a)	0.6	43.2

MAP: Military Assistance Program
FMSC: Foreign Military Sales Credit
EDA: Excess Defense Articles
ST: Ship Transfers
MAAG: Military Assistance Advisory Group
IMETP: International Military Education and Training Program
n.a.: not available
(a) : included in MAP

The increase in the sale of arms to the Philippines after the imposition of martial law in September 1972 is particularly noticeable. In the four-year period following martial law, the U.S. government sold the Philippines $72.1 million in arms—or nine times the value of its purchases during the preceding 22-year period. . . . For FY 1977, the administration has approved the sale of $74.6 million worth of F-5E's and howitzers, putting the Philippines in the big league of arms purchasers internationally.

Commercial sales—private industry sales to foreign governments—are also controlled by the State Department, which supervises the export licensing of arms, ammunition, and military technology under the Munitions Control Act. That commercial sales are an instrument of U.S. foreign policy was admitted by a State Department representative before the Senate Foreign Assistance Subcommittee on June 18, 1975: "Even if it is not in the law we apply the same kind of policy considerations to commercial sales as we do to FMS [Foreign Military Sales] cases." As in the case of FMS sales, therefore, commercial sales to the Marcos government represent a quite conscious policy decision to prop up a dictator perceived as protecting U.S. interests at the expense of human rights. Since the imposition of martial law, commercial sales to Marcos, consisting chiefly of police weapons, rifles, and ammunition, have totalled $8.5 million, or more than four times the value of all commercial sales in the period 1950-72. Commercial sales in FY 1977 alone will total $5.6 million. . . .

U.S. Military Assistance and Counterinsurgency

. . . Admiral Thomas Moorer, then chairman of the Joint Chiefs of Staff, stated quite frankly during the congressional hearings on the 1974 military assistance proposal that:

> The security assistance program material . . . are designed to provide mobility, firepower, and communications—the three basic elements required to combat insurgency forces. We are providing helicopters and transport aircraft, machine guns, recoilless rifles, and other weapons, together with long-range communications equipment.

An examination of the types of technical assistance and weaponry reaching the Philippine Armed Forces during the last three years, would more than bear out Admiral Moorer's assertion. . . .

Proceeding to the heavy weapons systems supplied by the United States under the various aid and sales programs we find the concentration on counter-guerilla armaments:

* *The F-5E "Tiger II Fighter,"* according to the Defense Department spokesman Admiral Ray Peet, "was designed primarily for the international market—for countries such as Brazil and others which have insurgency problems . . . ." In FY 1977 eleven of these aircraft have been delivered to the Marcos regime under the FMS program.

* *The Bell HU-1 ["Huey"] helicopter*—a critical component of the helicopter-based anti-guerilla warfare in Vietnam—has been among the choice weapons grants to the Philippines. From FY 1973 to FY 1977 about 44 helicopters were transferred to the Philippine Army.

* *The M-113 APC [armed personnel carrier]* has been described by the standard references on weapons-systems as among the "most successful vehicles" in U.S. Army service, having "proved especially valuable in the special circumstances of the Vietnam War." Since the declaration of martial law about 80 of these vehicles have reached the Philippine Army. In addition, the Philippines has purchased V-150 "Commando" armored cars, a major weapon against street demonstrations and urban insurgency. In FY 1975 alone about 20 armored cars worth $2.1 million were received by Philippine internal security forces.

* *U.S.-supplied C-47 transport planes* convertible into gunships were observed in operation during the campaign against Muslim resistance groups on Jolo Island in early 1974. In FY 1973 and FY 1974 about 10 of these planes were

transferred to the Philippine Armed Forces under the MAP [Military Assistance Program] program. . . .

Civic action. One of the most publicized forms of extra-official military aid to the Marcos regime has been the "civic-action" activities conducted by U.S. Army Special Forces ("Green Beret") units in the Philippines. "Civic-action" is essentially a euphemism for ideological-support activities for counter-insurgent military operations—its character being exposed by the fact that it is carried out by military personnel rather than by civilian professionals. "Winning hearts and minds" through military civic action has traditionally been undertaken by U.S. base personnel in areas adjoining the bases, to which the "Communist insurgency," according to a Defense Department spokesman in the 1973 congressional hearings, "represents a . . . direct threat." Since 1970 U.S. civic-action projects began to acquire a more coordinated character and a nationwide scope. Before 1970 the formal policy on the use of U.S. personnel in the Philippines was enunciated by James Wilson, deputy chief of mission of the U.S. Embassy in Manila during the congressional hearings on the United States' base and security arrangements with the Philippines in 1969: "It is a well-established policy that U.S. military personnel are not authorized to participate in AFP operations of any kind." This "well-established" policy was reversed with the arrival of Special Forces teams from Okinawa who went to work "on a co-equal, integrated basis with the Armed Forces of the Philippines counterpart [civic-action] team." From October 1970 to May 1974 civic action activities embraced twelve provinces and had direct and indirect effects on some three million Filipinos.

Table 2
Dates and Areas of Special Forces Action Operations

Province	Date of Operation	Number of U.S. Personnel Involved
Western Samar	Oct. 1—Nov. 15, 1970	30
Albay	Jan. 25—March 17, 1971	48
Palawan	Jan. 20—March 17, 1972	39
Nueva Ecija and Nueva Vizcaya	May 9—June 28, 1972	38
Martial Law [Sept. 22, 1972]		
Zamboanga	Aug. 15—Sept. 30, 1972	41
Pampanga	Oct. 28—Dec. 13, 1972	41
Bataan and Zambales	Feb. 21—April 7, 1973	40
Capiz	April 10—May 25, 1973	39
Bohol	Oct. 15—Dec. 10, 1973	46
Northern Samar	March 15—May 5, 1974	49

According to a State Department statement regarding the Special Forces' area of operations, "As a general policy the presence of current insurgent/dissident activities or a recent history of such activities in the exercise area automatically eliminates the area from further consideration" for civic-action activities. An examination of the provinces where Special Forces have been deployed since the beginning of martial law reveals that the general policy was more the exception than the rule: five of the six provinces where Green Berets were assigned were clearly either insurgent areas or had a history of chronic insurgency.

Selection 8.8: Aid to the Philippines: Who Benefits? Jim Morrell

Editors' Introduction

A 1977 U.S. government study concluded that "After 30 years and $1.7 billion in U.S. economic assistance, concrete development advances are hard to identify" in the Philippines (*United States Development Assistance Programs in Pakistan, The Philippines, and Indonesia,* Staff Reports to the Subcommittee on Foreign Assistance of the Committee on Foreign Relations, U.S. Senate, Committee Print, 95th Congress, 1st session, February 1977, pp. 19-30). In 1979, the Center for International Policy in Washington, D.C. sent Jim Morrell to the Philippines to study the impact of U.S. aid projects. The Center is a non-profit educational and research organization. This next selection is taken from Morrell's study.

Source: Jim Morrell, "Aid to the Philippines: Who Benefits?" *International Policy Report,* vol. 5, no. 2, October 1979, pp. 1-8.

Is U.S. aid reaching the needy? To find the answer, our researcher visited aid projects in five provinces, consulted with senior aid officials, interviewed local residents, and analyzed aid documents. He found some bright spots, but many more examples of bureaucratic indifference to the poor. Here is his firsthand report.

Findings

1. Only 22 percent of U.S. aid is reaching the needy.
2. This amounts to less than a penny per person per day.
3. As many as 78 percent of preschool children are malnourished. Conditions for the poor have worsened since 1972. There are more desperately poor people in the Philippines today than at any time in its history.
4. The United States is responding to this urgent social and economic problem by increasing *military* aid by 138 percent. . . .

For most Americans the conditions in a country like the Philippines—the poverty, the crowding, the inadequate nutrition, the cruelly low incomes—are beyond imagining. The corn farmer in the economically-depressed Bicol area who gets a meager $240 for a year's harvest and must rely on planting root crops and tending water buffaloes; the fish vendor who earns $986 a year for his family of seven; young textile-mill workers making $1.76 for a hard eight-hour day—these might be people inhabiting a distant, unfathomable planet.

But they are real and so is the unjust economic system and unresponsive government that traps them in their poverty. The poorest 20 percent of the population only receives 3.9 percent of national income, the poorest 40 percent, 15 percent of national income. Rice and corn yields are only one-third those obtained in Japan, and as many as 40 to 45 percent of Philippine families are malnourished. Some 65 percent of the population lacks access to a clean water supply. Real wages have declined 12 percent since 1975 and, in the absence of social security or any effective government programs, population growth continues at 2.8 percent a year as parents create the only form of old-age insurance available—their children.

Since 1976 the United States has spent $1.8 billion in all forms of economic and military assistance to the Philippines, some of which has reached the poor. The Agency for International Development devoted 68 percent of its 1978 program to irrigation works, rural roads, safe water facilities, rural health centers and other projects to raise incomes and health standards of the poor.

However, the majority of U.S. aid to the Philippines is not even *intended* to help the poor. An agency-by-agency review of the total aid program suggests that only about 22 percent has gone into projects directly benefiting the poor. The rest went for tobacco loans, insurance for a Bank of America branch office, military aid to a country that the Pentagon says faces no external threat, rural electrification priced out of the reach of the rural poor, and balance-of-payments loans conditioned on the adoption of government policies that *reduce* real wages for the poor.

Unfortunately, in 1979 the Carter administration and Congress took few meaningful steps to reform the aid program to the Philippines. The only significant change was a 138 percent increase, from $31.8 million to $75.7 million, in military aid to a country that has already quadrupled in real terms its own military spending since 1972. In a country beset by urgent social and economic problems, the Carter administration is offering military solutions. . . .

The real U.S. interest lies in the future of the 46 million people of the Philippines, as they slowly grope for a solution to their internal political problems and move to develop the resources of their potentially bountiful islands. Americans can help most by pressing for an end to military aid and for a creative restructuring, without regard to bureaucratic prerogatives, of the entire range of U.S. economic programs to deliver aid directly to the needy.

A more humane, more sympathetic American policy could build on the Carter administration's early human rights activism which began to shift the

United States towards a neutral role in Philippine internal politics. The Carter administration abstained on six industrial loans in voting within the World Bank and Asian Development Bank because of Marcos's dismal human rights record. Using the controlled Philippine press Marcos tried to keep word of the new U.S. policy actions from reaching the Philippine population, but with only partial success. Congress also contributed to the pressure for improvement by cutting several million dollars in military aid. Another recent positive move is President Carter's decision to eliminate the PL-480 Title I concessional sales program for the Philippines, a program which provided a U.S. subsidy to the Philippine central bank.

Building from here, the United States could redirect its aid program to the Philippines. While many reforms are necessary, the following are vital if fundamental changes are to take place.

1. Quadruple the effectiveness of our total program by redirecting the money from military and financial aid to human-needs project aid.

2. Redirect aid for local projects to local social action committees and village associations whenever possible to avoid excessive identification with the government; alternatively channel more assistance directly to local governments (provincial, city, municipal) known to be led by development-oriented, uncorrupted officials.

3. Carefully monitor through on-site inspection all projects whose implementation is left to the Philippine government, such as those financed by the Eximbank, World Bank, or Asian Development Bank, in order to insure delivery of benefits to the poor.

4. Price all aid benefits, such as electricity, within reach of the poor through differential rate structures, adjustments of rate of return, longer project amortization periods, and other financial reforms.

5. Require consultation with those who will be affected by any given project during the feasibility stage and ensure their active participation thereafter.

6. Supplement fiscal and monetary performance criteria now imposed by the International Monetary Fund with income-redistributive criteria.

Poverty's Cruel Logic

The majority of Filipinos are trapped in permanent poverty, with only the slimmest opportunity to advance. The poverty is unnecessary. The people are ready to work, and need only an additional few hundred dollars a year per capita to escape malnutrition and disease.

Those most affected by malnutrition are the ones least capable of surviving it: infants and children. In four low-income communities studied, the caloric intake of adults was 81 percent of adequacy, the intake of infants aged one to three only 64 percent and of older children aged four to nine, only 69 percent. Such serious inadequacies threaten to cause permanent damage. A recent survey of the Tondo slum and squatter area of Manila reveals that 87 percent of the children had some clinical sign of malnutrition.

The cruel logic of survival under conditions of poverty gives the father priority at mealtime because he is the breadwinner, usually in a physically taxing occupation like farming. The mother is next, followed by the older children. The younger children are last. There is no choice if the family is to survive. Of the 6.8 million Filipino children aged four and under in 1975, the World Bank estimated that half were seriously malnourished. The Asian Development Bank places the figure at 78 percent.

Malnutrition leaves the most needy people easy prey to pneumonia, tuberculosis, and gastrointestinal infections, which are the three leading causes of death in the Philippines. In addition malaria is found in Mindanao and parts of Luzon, and schistosomiasis, a parasitic disease transmitted by an aquatic snail, in the Eastern Visayas and Mindanao.

Private medical care is for the urban well-to-do. Public health is grossly inadequate and overburdened; even urban clinics lack drugs and other supplies, while over 90 percent of rural health units lack adequate clinical equipment. Many lack electricity and potable water. Posts were vacant for 23 percent of the physicians and 46 percent of the nurses needed to staff the rural health centers. Salaries were half as large as in private practice. Half of the Filipino medical graduates going abroad for advanced training never return.

Overall, then, the economy has grown, and poverty has grown right along with it. In the late 1940s, the nutritional standard of the Philippines was comparable to that in neighboring Asian countries such as Malaysia, Taiwan, and even Japan. Today maldistribution of income, rapid population growth, and low yields have left the Philippines behind.

The Economy: Government Neglect

An overview of the economy shows that poverty is not an inescapable condition in the Philippines, as it is in some other Third World countries bereft of natural resources. Rather, poverty persists because the Philippine government has neglected or abdicated its responsibilities in every sphere.

It is here that the tragedy of an aid policy that diverts 78 percent of the money away from the poor becomes doubly apparent. Not only is American taxpayers' money wasted, it goes to support a government that has become the chief obstacle to progress.

Agriculture

In rice farming—

* Less than half of the total rice harvested area is irrigated; on non-irrigated rainfed areas, only one crop a year can be brought in. Up to 1.7 million hectares more could be irrigated.
* The government rice extension and credit program ("Masagana 99") provides seeds, fertilizer, and pesticides at skyrocketing prices, according to farmers interviewed for this report in Nueva Ecija province.

Note: Good weather, the introduction of high-yielding varieties of rice since the late 1960s, and the partial effectiveness of Masagana 99 has enabled the Philippines to attain rice self-sufficiency for three straight years. Production is expanding but overall yields are still only one-third of the land's potential.

In corn farming—

* The government extension program (Masaganang Maisan) has failed. Farmers in the Bicol area interviewed for this report said they didn't join it because they feared indebtedness. Membership in the program involved taking out a 500-peso ($67.57) loan, receiving 200 pesos ($27.03) in cash and the rest in seeds, pesticides and fertilizers. The price for fertilizer was higher than the market price.

In coconut farming—

* The majority of trees are overage.
* Replanting is not scheduled to begin until 1981.
* The government has neglected the farmers, although they provide a major revenue source through export duties. A typical coconut farming village in Quezon Province visited for this report was reachable only over miles of footpaths and bamboo suspension bridges. Just to ship their coconut products by water buffalo as far as the nearest dirt road costs the farmers 4 pesos (54 cents) a bag. They had no electric lights or running water.

Sugar farming on the other hand—

* Is an industry of large holdings and politically-connected landlords.
* Therefore the government's Philippine National Bank gave 78 percent of its loans to sugar producers.
* To help sugar growers in 1976 the government cut the growth of urgently needed credit to public-sector projects to 26 percent, half the amount planned, and placed a severe squeeze on credit to the private sector.
* Neither massive government aid to the sugar growers nor past prosperity ever trickled down to the workers. At the height of the sugar boom in 1974 when wholesale sugar sold for over 60 cents a pound, field workers earned less than a dollar a day. Today when it is selling for about 9 cents a pound, they earn slightly over a dollar.

Overall, agricultural production increased by 4.5 percent a year over the 1970s. Yields remain low because of inadequate irrigation, exposure to weather risks, inequitable and fragmented land-tenure arrangements, weak agricultural credit programs and ineffective extension programs.

Industry

Sluggish growth of domestic demand related to the poverty of the countryside has held the growth of industry to a relatively low 6 percent a year during the 1970s. World Bank and IMF economists point to structural underutilization of capacity and low rates of investment as major recurring problems. Government measures such as the investment incentives plan of the Board of

Investments have failed to stimulate or rationalize growth. The IMF reported that of more than 800 firms currently registered with the board, only 200 use its tax incentives because of their complexity and because benefits fall short of undeclared profits.

Institutionalized corruption is another problem. President Marcos's golfing partner Herminio Disini, head of the Herdis industrial conglomerate, reportedly received a multimillion dollar commission from Westinghouse in 1978 to facilitate approval of the nuclear power plant. In 1979 he reportedly delayed the decision and reopened the bidding on a diesel engine plant to throw the contract to his company.

Foreign businessmen say kickbacks to government officials are standard practice in contract awards; so-called "ten percenters" abound in economic development ministries. The bribe is automatically added onto the quoted price for foreign goods, thus adding to capital expenses and sapping the will to economize.

Government failure to provide elementary infrastructure support is a further obstacle. In all the factories four-hour electric power outages occur daily as the government shuts off the power to selected parts of the city because of insufficient fuel oil imports. Each day expensive machinery lies idle while the electricity is off, and the factory workers stand around collecting their pay.

Transport and Communications

It is only two years since the Manila South Road was completed as an all-weather artery to the Bicol area, and then only thanks to substantial Japanese aid. In the country as a whole, 50 percent of rural barrios (villages) are served by dirt roads which become impassable six months of the year, and another 20 percent are served by no roads at all, only footpaths.

In stark contrast is Metro Manila, where bumper-to-bumper traffic inches its way through major intersections and narrow streets. The snarled traffic burns up an estimated $200 million a year in imported gasoline. The traffic is not an annoyance, it is a major burden. In one survey private cars, owned by the middle class, accounted for 64 to 70 percent of the total traffic and buses only 4.5 percent, although the buses carried as many passengers as cars. The government has no plans to limit the cars. The cost of this misallocation of resources can be conservatively estimated at $3.25 billion over the last decade, some $2.25 billion for the cars and $1 billion for the gasoline they burned.

Resources exist, but the government misuses them. It lets the consumer tastes of middle- and upper-class buyers divert resources from the whole economy and, in the case of the cars in Manila, paralyze transportation in a city of six million. The tragic result is that lower-class poverty is growing even faster than upper-class wealth. The simultaneous increase of wealth and poverty is the great paradox of Philippine society today. Magnificent new office buildings and hotels jut into the sky, and in their shadows, miserable squatter communities and shacks spill out into the streets. The rich are increasing their wealth; the poor are increasing their numbers.

The Failure of Reform

Aside from the general state of the economy, the failure of two highly touted government programs illustrates the paucity of government will to alleviate growing poverty. One of these failures is the land reform program, and the other, tax reform. [For a discussion of the land reform program, see selection 7.4 above—Ed.]

Tax Reform

If the failure of the land reform is still only whispered about in aid circles, the failure of tax reform—the government's other great paper reform—is a staple topic of conversation at the closed-door executive board meetings of international financial institutions. "The momentum of fiscal reform appeared to have been slowing down," U.S. Executive Director Sam Cross said reprovingly at a February 1977 IMF executive board meeting. "Only by greatly increasing government revenues could expenditures be expanded without further aggravating an already serious foreign debt situation," he said. "In particular, no progress has been made in the important area of direct taxation." He called for a major effort to tax the rich.

An in-house IMF study ranked the Philippines 40th among 47 countries in taxes as a percentage of GNP during the period 1972-1976. Taxes accounted for 10.1 percent of GNP over the period. The study said the Philippines had made no progress in tax collection since 1969. Income taxes amounted to only 2.51 percent of GNP. Taxes on imports and exports provided most government revenue.

Considering this record of government abdication, the Japanese Executive Director Masanao Matsunaga complained of the "gap between promise and performance in tax reform and tax collection," while even a third-world representative, Alfredo Crespo, insisted that "changes in the tax system were urgently needed."

U.S. Foreign Aid: Small Leaven in a Large Mass

Against this backdrop of government neglect and unresponsiveness enters U.S. foreign aid. And the first fact to consider is how small this amount is relative to the need and to the Philippine government's own resources.

The $164 million in U.S. aid actually reaching the needy in 1978 amounted to $3.56 per capita, or less than a penny per person per day. It cannot even begin to substitute for effective mobilization of domestic resources in an economy that generates a gross national product of more than $23 billion.

Women and Philippine Poverty

Women in the Philippines bear the brunt of the country's unsolved problems. For example, they are the special victims of nutritional poverty. Although the caloric intake of low-income adults generally was 81 percent of adequacy in four communities surveyed, that of pregnant women was 64 percent and of lactating women only 46 percent.

Women also get the lowest wages. At a textile factory visited for this report, women workers were getting the minimum wage of $1.76 a day. Meanwhile for every yard of cloth selling at $1.89 the mill made 81 cents, and after depreciation the mill paid dividends of 25 percent. On top of this, the mill received a $5 million concessional loan from the World Bank-aided Development Bank of the Philippines.

Nevertheless, despite the high profit rate and the foreign aid subsidy, the millowner said he would not raise wages for his women workers until the minimum wage was raised. Thus the World Bank's aid bypassed these women workers.

Another aid agency, the International Monetary Fund, also failed to help them and may indeed have made matters worse. When the IMF granted the Philippines $189 million in May 1979, among the conditions it imposed was an incomes policy that would hold the line on wages. At the same time it pressed the government to raise the regulated prices of rice, canned milk, sugar, and bus and jeepney rides—all daily items of necessity. As a result, the women textile workers have seen their real wages decline since starting work at the factory.

Yet these women may be the lucky ones because at least they have jobs. Unemployment and underemployment are the lot of young women in the rural areas, many of whom therefore flee the poverty of the countryside for the squalor of Metro Manila, where some 350,000 have been forced for lack of a job into prostitution. Planeloads of Japanese men arrive at the airport where they are driven in busloads to one of the 14 luxury hotels built in the last few years with World Bank and Asian Development Bank aid, 20 percent of it provided by U.S. taxpayers. The hotel owners have the women waiting.

But some Filipino women are organizing in the Tondo slums and elsewhere. Trinidad Herrera is a leader of the Zone One Tenants Organizations in Manila. She was arrested and tortured with electric shock in 1977 and was only released after pressure from Vice President Mondale and the Canadian government. Amazingly, Trinidad Herrera several times earlier had been an honored guest at the presidential palace. But the capriciousness of martial law in the Philippines is such that the descent from presidential guest to torture victim was swift.

Selection 8.9: The International Monetary Fund in the Philippines, Walden Bello and Robin Broad

Editors' Introduction

Much of the "foreign aid" that the Philippines has received in recent years has come not bilaterally from the United States and other governments, but from multilateral agencies: the International Monetary Fund, the World Bank, and the Asian Development Bank. The next article discusses the impact of the first of these institutions on the Philippines.

Source: Walden Bello and Robin Broad, "20 Years of Intervention: the IMF in the Philippines," AMPO

[Tokyo], vol. 14, no. 3, 1982, pp. 28-31. For much more detail on the activities of these institutions, see Walden Bello, David Kinley, and Elaine Elinson, *Development Debacle: The World Bank in the Philippines,* San Francisco: Institute for Food and Development Policy/Philippine Solidarity Network, 1982; and Vivencio R. Jose [ed.], *Mortgaging the Future: The World Bank and the IMF in the Philippines,* Quezon City: Foundation for Nationalist Studies, 1982.

In early 1981, Gregorio Licaros was removed by President Ferdinand Marcos as Governor of the Central Bank of the Philippines. No official reason was given, although it was rumored that the grand old man of Philippine finance had been involved in shady financial deals.

Recently released confidential IMF documents, however, appear to confirm suspicions that Licaros' ouster resulted, at least partly, from strong pressure from the International Monetary Fund.

For long-time observers of the Philippine economy, the Licaros affair was not surprising. Among nationalists, the Fund and its sister institution, the World Bank, probably enjoy a notoriety worse than the CIA's. Because of their periodic interventions in economic policy-making and the harsh impact of these moves on living standards, the Fund and the Bank are seen as the chief engineers of the economic crisis now engulfing the nation.

The First Devaluation

It was 20 years ago, in 1962, that the Fund carried out its first decisive intervention. It forced the government of President Diosdado Macapagal to abolish foreign exchange controls on imports and devalue the peso by 50 percent relative to the dollar. Decontrol and devaluation were part of the IMF's strategy of "liberalization," which usually consists of lifting protectionist barriers to imports, abolishing nationalist controls on foreign investment, and depreciating "overvalued" currencies. The latter were regarded by the Fund as obstacles to the "free flow of capital and commodities"—that is, the unrestricted entry of foreign capital and goods into Third World economies.

The Fund was regarded as singularly fitted for its role as the vanguard of liberalization by the U.S. Government and U.S. corporations which stood to benefit the most from the strategy. Though the U.S. Government was the decisive voice in the IMF—controlling as it did over 21% of voting power— the image of the Fund as a multilateral institution composed of 140 member-nations provided a guise of neutrality and objectivity to its dictates. That this "democratic" structure could nonetheless produce policies with grave implications for the country could be inferred from the following 1971 study by a high-level panel of U.S. business and government officials:

> As the Filipinos deal more with International organizations like the IMF, World Bank, and Asian Development Bank (ADB), they will learn to address economic problems more realistically and accept the constraints on economic behavior that are required for participation in the international economic community.

The impact of the 1962 devaluation was severe. Between 1962 and 1964, Philippine workers saw their real wages decline by 10 percent. While big agricultural exporters such as the sugar landlords reaped windfall profits from the devaluation, the nascent Filipino entrepreneurial class found itself in a very precarious position, facing a 100 percent increase in the peso cost of their imported inputs and repayments of foreign loans. An estimated 1,500 Filipino entrepreneurs were forced into bankruptcy, and many of those who survived were pushed into joint ventures with American capital. The inevitable economic slowdown helped depress the growth of manufacturing from the 11-12 percent average annual growth of the 1950-57 period to a mere five percent annually during the sixties.

To counteract the IMF's abolition of import controls, desperate national manufacturers propelled the creation of a protectionist system of tariffs which effectively undermined the key objective of the IMF's liberalization strategy-the unrestricted entry of foreign goods into the domestic Philippine market. "Although the strict import restrictions prevailing in the 1950's were gradually decontrolled in the early 1960's," complained the World Bank, the IMF's sister agency, "they were replaced by a highly protected tariff system . . . policy reform in the 1960's did not alter the bias of the incentive system in favor of import substitution by national entrepreneurs."

Repeat Performance

The opportunity for a more dramatic intervention presented itself in late 1969, after Macapagal's successor, Ferdinand Marcos, "won" an unprecedented second term in the fraudulent elections held in November of that year. Marcos's costly electoral drive bankrupted the Philippine treasury, leaving the country with hardly any foreign exchange to cover the mounting trade deficit and service the external debt. Desperate, Marcos turned to the IMF for help. But, in return for granting a $37 million loan, the Fund demanded and got what it wanted: another drastic devaluation of the peso, this time by over 60 percent relative to the dollar.

As in 1962, the devaluation wrought havoc with Filipino entrepreneurs, who were suddenly faced with a more than 50 percent rise in the cost of repaying foreign loans and a more than 30 percent jump in the peso price of their imports. As Filipino businessmen teetered on the brink or fell into the abyss of bankruptcy, the World Bank congratulated Marcos for his "commendable display of political courage."

But the *quid pro quo* for the IMF loan went beyond devaluation. A "Consultative Group" of aid-giving countries and international agencies was created under the joint leadership of the IMF and the Bank. The key function of this body was revealed by the U.S. Treasury Department: " . . . the World Bank has sought to influence borrowers' policies indirectly through the mechanism of intergovernmental Consultative Groups on particular borrowing countries. Through these groups, the Bank attempts to rally other donors around its recommendations." In a key confidential memo, the IMF Managing Director delineated the complementary responsibilities of the Fund and the Bank in such bodies as the Philippine Consultative Group: " . . . the Bank is recognized as having primary responsibility for the composition and appropriateness of development programs and project evaluation, including development priorities." The IMF, on the other hand, "is recognized as having primary responsibility for exchange rates and restrictive systems, for adjustment of temporary balance-of-payments disequilibria, and for evaluating and assisting members to work out (*sic*) stabilization programs as a sound basis for economic advance."

Another condition for the loan was the installation of an IMF "resident officer" right in the Philippine Central Bank and the creation of a joint "Central Bank-IMF Commission" to overhaul the debt management policies of the government. According to one report, the IMF representative "sees reports, official figures and analysis for government agencies. Because of inter-agency secrecy, he probably has access to more documents than some high Central Bank officials."

The Central Bank-IMF Commission, for its part, went beyond sanitizing debt management: it pushed the government to allow foreign equity participation of up to 40 percent in local banks in line with its plan to double the capital base of the commercial banking system. This opportunity was promptly seized by nine international private banks, including some of the largest U.S. banks.

The IMF and Martial Law

The imposition of martial law on September 22, 1972, provided unprecedented opportunities for the IMF and the World Bank to fully restructure the Philippine economy along the lines desired by the liberalization strategy. While the World Bank presided over an ambitious strategy of "development from above, " the Fund assumed near total control over the Marcos regime's external economic policies.

Throughout the seventies, the Philippines was under one variety of IMF "stabilization program" or another, giving the country the distinction of being one of the very few nations to complete not just one but several IMF-imposed "cures." By mid-1980, the Philippines owed the IMF almost $1.6 billion, making it the Third World country most indebted to the agency and second only to the United Kingdom in overall indebtedness. The Fund's power, however, stemmed not only from its large share of the Philippine debt. Perhaps more important was the "good credit risk" status that it stamped on the regime. As one Bank report saw it, "The Government regards the IMF's role as essential not only for the large volume of resources provided, but also for the reassurance on economic management provided to private sources of finance." The IMF nod became increasingly important as the country's chronic balance-of-payments crisis went from bad to worse, necessitating huge infusions of foreign capital to cover the deficit.

The root cause of the worsening external economic position was the IMF-prescribed economic strategy itself. Beginning in the mid-seventies, the Fund and the World Bank threw the Philippines onto a path of economic liberalization and "export-led growth." That is, they deliberately did not base further economic growth on expanding the domestic market but hitched it to the demand of export markets in the advanced capitalist countries. This growth path was seen as a way to sustain continued growth while avoiding radical income redistribution, which was the only means of expanding the internal market. Developments in the late seventies, however, showed that export-led growth was, in fact, a suicidal strategy: the world prices for the Philippines' key exports, sugar and coconuts, declined drastically; the deepening international recession stopped the growth of export markets in the West; and because of the recession, the advanced capitalist countries began to erect tariff and non-tariff barriers against labor-intensive manufactured imports from the Third World.

With imports continuing to rise while export earnings were declining, the current account deficit widened steadily to $2 billion in 1980—a development that forced the Marcos regime to contract over $11 billion in loans from international banks to cover the yearly deficits. By 1981, the cost of servicing the external debt came to about $1.6 billion, forcing the regime to go deeper into debt simply in order to pay off installments of the already existing debt.

To many observers, it was obvious that the IMF-World Bank strategy of making the Philippines almost completely dependent on export markets was responsible for the disaster overtaking the economy. But the Fund and the World Bank proceeded to administer a cure that consisted of heavier doses of the disease of liberalization. The Fund took advantage of its power to dictate the Philippines' credit ratings in order to knock out, once and for all, the protectionist system and the ideology behind it.

The IMF had become impatient with Marcos's unfulfilled promise to dismantle the protective mechanisms sheltering the politically powerful national capitalists producing for the domestic market. The IMF-World Bank ultimatum delivered to the government during the Consultative Group meeting in December 1979 called for "restructuring of the economy and restructuring productive sectors of the economy." Industry Minister Roberto Ongpin tendered the government's capitulation:

> We are in agreement with the findings . . . that Philippine industry has suffered because of an overprotected system. We are determined to take the difficult and often painful decisions to dismantle some of the protective devices and thus to promote a free and competitive system.

The Fund could hardly conceal its pleasure, triumphantly announcing to the Group that "Further steps will be taken to reduce the level of protection in order to open import-substitution industries to the test of external competition."

Structural Adjustment

The main weapon for the destruction of the Philippines' protected industries was a $200 million Structural Adjustment loan from the World Bank. The carrot was a package of two IMF loans totaling $654 million, which was badly needed to carry the regime through its balance-of-payments difficulties. As a U.S. Treasury Department report explained, gaining "leverage" was the key consideration in the conjunction of the three loans:

> . . . The collaboration of other donors and the IMF is particularly important when it comes to influencing macro-level policy. Thus, structural adjustment loans are usually approved only when the borrower has negotiated an Extended Fund Facility agreement with the IMF, a factor which is producing increasingly close Bank/ Fund collaboration. Without the added weight and broader focus achieved through collaboration . . . the Bank's leverage over macro-level policy is limited.

The concerted pressure bore fruit: in January 1981, in what was billed as Phase I of the tariff reform, the government decreed drastic tariff reductions on 590 commodities. Dismantling protectionism, however, was not the only demand of the IMF and the World Bank. *The Fund demanded another round of devaluation.*

Under the "flexible" exchange rate system imposed by the Fund after the devastating devaluation of 1970, the peso had depreciated from 6.43 pesos to the dollar in 1970 to 6.78 pesos in 1973 to 7.50 pesos to the dollar in 1975. For the IMF, devaluation represented a "quick fix" to the Philippines' worsening external payments position in the late seventies: It would supposedly "cheapen" Philippine exports, resulting in a much greater volume of goods sold and thus more foreign exchange earnings.

But the Fund had another, more strategic objective in pushing devaluation: by raising the peso prices of raw materials, intermediate goods and machinery imports, monetary depreciation would help squeeze out the remaining "inefficient" Filipino producers. It was one more prong of the concerted offensive to totally denationalize Philippine industry in the name of efficiency.

The IMF Versus the Central Bank

The IMF plan, however, encountered opposition from several Filipino officials, including Central Bank Governor Gregorio Licaros. Licaros opposed the lowering of protective tariffs, and having helped implement the previous devaluations, he had also learned the bitter lesson that the so-called virtues of monetary depreciation were an illusion. He now argued that "relief" provided by another devaluation—an upsurge in foreign exchange earnings—would at best be temporary and superficial while the consequence—recession—would be severe.

The growing gulf between the Fund and Licaros is captured in a number of recently leaked IMF documents. An IMF mission in May 1980 recommended that, in order to achieve "external competitiveness" and "promote greater balance of payments adjustment . . . the authorities permit greater flexibility in the exchange rate". . . . The response from Licaros and his Central Bank team was disconcerting: "The Philippine representatives regarded the current level of the exchange rate as broadly appropriate. They pointed to the high growth of exports and stressed that there was no evidence as yet that domestic producers were becoming uncompetitive."

In August 1980, the World Bank added its voice to the IMF's call for devaluation, informing the Philippine government that "the foreign exchange accounts could be balanced by a moderate devaluation." Yet Licaros still dragged his feet.

The opportunity for the Fund and the technocrats to get rid of the stubborn Licaros emerged early in 1981, in the aftermath of the "Dewey Dee affair." After Dee, a Filipino-Chinese industrialist fled the country, leaving $100 million in bad debts, it was discovered that Licaros had been receiving kickbacks from Filipino-Chinese friends like Dee whenever the Central Bank approved their foreign exchange deals. The Licaros scandal was hushed up for fear of the impact on the Philippines' credit rating should it become widely known that the Central Bank Governor was not, after all, a model of bourgeois propriety. Yet it provided the excuse that the IMF, World Bank, and their technocrat allies within the Philippine Government needed to oust the Central Bank governor in early 1981.

With Licaros out of the way and replaced by a more flexible technocrat, the devaluation demanded by the IMF took place. By June 1981, the exchange rate had dropped from 7.5 pesos to the dollar to 7.9 pesos. By March 1982, it stood at 8.3 pesos to the dollar. The IMF was pleased, but it also made it clear to the new authorities that the currency had to be debauched even more to make up for Licaros' earlier stubbornness: "The staff would encourage the authorities to continue with their recent policies until the competitiveness lost during the past few years has been restored."

By 1981, the Fund and the World Bank stood at the pinnacle of their power in the Philippines. Not only had they virtually completed the liberalization of the Philippine economy and thus brought about its fuller integration into the world capitalist order, but they had also managed to install a cabinet of technocrats headed by Prime Minister Cesar Virata which amounted to no more than a group of front-men for the implementation of Bank and Fund-dictated policies. Yet it was a Pyrrhic victory, for in the process, major sectors of Philippine society have united in a determined nationalist movement to regain economic sovereignty.

Selection 8.10: Activities in the U.S., Campaign Against Military Intervention in the Philippines

Editors' Introduction

At the onset of martial law in the Philippines, Filipinos living in the United States who had been active in the Philippine student movement in the late 1960s and early 1970s formed organizations in opposition to martial law and U.S. support for it. First came the National Committee for the Restoration of Civil Liberties in the Philippines, then the Union of Democratic Filipinos. These two organizations paid special attention to the Filipino community in the U.S., as did a group called the Movement for a Free Philippines which, however, was more conservative in its orientation. In November 1973, church people, former Peace Corps volunteers in the Philippines, and anti-Vietnam war activists formed the Friends of the Filipino People to win support among the U.S. population as a whole for an end to U.S. aid to Marcos. Other anti-Marcos groups after this began to appear and in 1974 an alliance of many of these groups called the Anti-Martial Law Coalition was estab-

lished. In 1977, U.S. church leaders (both Protestant and Catholic) came together to form the Church Coalition for Human Rights in the Philippines. During these years a San Francisco paper, the *Philippine News,* with considerable circulation in the U.S. Filipino community, became increasingly militant against the Marcos dictatorship, operating from an anti-Communist position. Other, more left-wing, publications have included *Ang Katipunan, Philippines Information Bulletin, Pahayag,* and *Philippine Report,* the latter published by the Philippine Resource Center in California. The political thrust of these groups and journals centered around opposition to U.S. aid to Marcos, and as a result of their pressure Congress reduced the aid the Executive branch requested for Marcos more than once.

The Friends of the Filipino People and the Anti-Martial Law Coalition early on developed campaigns calling for the withdrawal of U.S. bases from the Philippines, parallel to their demands for an end to all U.S.

support for Marcos. But in January 1983, the U.S. anti-Marcos movement entered a new phase when a broad coalition was formed representing a number of organizations including the Church Coalition for Human Rights, Clergy and Laity Concerned, Friends of the Filipino People, Philippine Support Committee, Philippine Educational Support Committee, PAG-ASA, and the Movement for a Free Philippines. This coalition developed activities directly linking the call for an end to U.S. support for Marcos with a call for the removal of U.S. bases and nuclear weapons from the Philippines, under the heading of a Campaign Against Military Intervention in the Philippines. The following document is an account of the activities this group developed in 1983 and projected for 1984.

Source: Funding Proposal for the Campaign Against Military Intervention in the Philippines.

The primary motivation for United States support of the Marcos regime has nearly always been the U.S. desire to assure continued access to Subic Naval Base and Clark Air Force Base. These facilities house an array of nuclear-capable aircraft and vessels, as well as key military communications equipment, all of which serve as magnets of nuclear attack in the event of a superpower conflict. A concern for the basic human rights and survival of the Filipino people must therefore begin at home, in educating North Americans about the continuing role of U.S. military forces in determining present and future conditions in the Philippines. . . .

The campaign's strategy and objectives have been developed by a broad coalition of individuals and organizations, who have come together with the conviction that U.S. bases in the Philippines not only threaten the Filipino people, but also represent those aspects of U.S. foreign policy most harmful to our basic interests as a people and to the cause of peace: preoccupation with nuclear arms, tendencies toward military intervention in the Third World, and support for foreign dictatorships. The bases contribute neither to U.S. security nor to that of the Philippines and Southeast Asia, but instead foster a dangerous instability for all concerned.

As a result of U.S.-Philippines negotiations concluded on June 1 of this year, the two countries reached a new five-year agreement ensuring continued "unhampered military operations" for the U.S., in return for $900 million in U.S. assistance to the Marcos government. This represents an 80% increase in aid over the previous five-year period, and more than doubles the level of military assistance grants. The agreement thus seeks to lock the U.S. into five more years of support for the Marcos regime, a dictatorship which has been unanimously condemned by leading human rights organizations. . . .Under the current regime, the presence of U.S. nuclear weapons in the Philippines remains unchallenged, and U.S. troops retain the right to participate in "security activities" off the bases. Coinciding with the negotiations, the U.S. and Philippine forces conducted "Operation Balikatan (shoulder-to-shoulder) Tangent Flash," the largest combined military operation since World War II.

The primary aim of the Campaign Against Military Intervention in the Philippines is to challenge the new agreement and the continued presence of U.S. bases in the Philippines, particularly as Congress reviews the increased level of appropriations in the autumn of 1983 and spring of 1984. This period provides a key opportunity for locally-based public education about the effects of U.S. military presence in the Philippines, which has encouraged instability and widespread militarization throughout the country. Through a well-conceived congressional strategy, we hope to publicize and raise questions about the various issues involved in the renewal of the bases agreement, as well as mobilize opposition to the bases among church, human rights, disarmament, and other networks. The political situation in the Philippines has become increasingly polarized since the declaration of martial law in 1972, and the campaign will provide important opportunities for promoting a deeper understanding within the United States of the explosive conditions of Philippine society. More generally, the campaign will be engaged in educating North Americans about the overall effects of U.S. conventional and nuclear deployments in the Pacific and worldwide.

The campaign was formed in early 1983, as representatives from a number of Philippine support groups met in New York on January 8 to chart future plans. . . . Regional campaigns of CAMIP have been established in nine regions of the U.S. and Canada, involving a wide spectrum of local support.

Campaign Objectives

One of the campaign's main purposes is to strengthen North American support for the concerns of Filipino nationalists, who for decades have been raising questions about the presence of U.S. military bases on Philippine soil. . . .

In support of the goal of removal of U.S. bases from the Philippines, the campaign has five objectives:

1. No U.S. nuclear weapons in the Philippines.
2. No use of the Philippines as a "springboard of intervention" into other countries.
3. No counterinsurgency activities directed against the Filipino people, and no resettlement of Filipinos on the base perimeter.
4. No U.S. military aid to the Philippines.
5. A congressional investigation into the effects of the U.S. bases upon the human rights and social and economic conditions of the Filipino people.

Achievements to Date

. . . When the new bases agreement was signed on June 1, CAMIP simultaneously released a statement—signed by over 170 prominent religious labor academic, and governmental leaders—calling for the withdrawal of U.S. bases and nuclear weapons from the Philippines and emphasizing the close relationship of the bases to U.S. interventionary policy and Philippine human rights violations. As the most widely supported statement ever made on the issue, it signals a new awareness of the importance of challenging U.S. policy in the Philippines.

The campaign's major impact thus far has come through three very successful speaking tours. In June, CAMIP hosted the chairperson of the Civil Liberties Union of the Philippines, former Senator Jose W. Diokno, a most articulate spokesperson of Philippine nationalist concerns and a key figure in the Anti-Bases Coalition of the Philippines. Diokno addressed a range of media representatives, as well as church, congressional, human rights, and disarmament groups in San Francisco, Washington, D.C., New York, and Chicago. His visit greatly heightened the level of U.S. interest in current Philippine issues.

Because support for the Philippines has also been a key goal in our plans, two speakers were provided from the U.S. to the Philippines to strengthen educational efforts being conducted by medical and anti-nuclear groups there. . . .

In order to build on local interest generated by the Diokno tour and expand efforts in the nine regions that comprise the CAMIP network, the organizing kit was produced for the use of local activists in the Freeze campaign, the religious community, Philippine-related groups, etc. As part of the kit, a speakers' bureau has been developed to encourage local forums on the bases. A petition drive, emphasizing the connections between anti-nuclear concerns and the Philippines bases, also assists organizing efforts on the local level. The drive is being coordinated by the Church Coalition for Human Rights in the Philippines.

Future Plans

With developments in Congress as a focus for action, the key period for the campaign's educational work is in late 1983 and early 1984. While there was never any expectation of influencing the negotiations process itself, there are important opportunities to raise our opposition to the new agreement and to the continued presence of U.S. bases in the Philippines through congressional proposals related to the increased appropriations requested by the Reagan Administration. Support from church, disarmament, human rights, and Philippine-related organizations is crucial to this effort, and therefore all congressional work is being closely coupled with strengthening the distribution of CAMIP resources to church networks and such organizations as the Freeze campaign, promoting the petition drive and use of organizers' kits, etc. Action and education within local church and governmental bodies (diocesan justice and peace councils, city councils, councils of churches, etc.) will increase the impact of our congressional work.

Already this past spring, the campaign initiated the circulation of two "Dear Colleague" letters in the House. The first, circulated by Rep. James Jeffords, called for no increase in the level of assistance given by the U.S. to the

Philippine government in return for the bases. The second letter, circulated by Rep. Ted Weiss, asked the Subcommittee on Military Installations and Facilities of the Armed Services Committee to call hearings on the U.S. bases and their military and political implications. The letter declares that any storage of nuclear weapons at Clark or Subic "would violate our understandings with the Filipino people."

In addition, two members of the CAMIP Coordinating Committee have testified in Congress: Earl Martin of the Mennonite Central Committee before the Subcommittee on Foreign Operations of the Appropriations Committee and Dante Simbulan of the Church Coalition for Human Rights in the Philippines before the Subcommittee on Asian and Pacific Affairs of the Foreign Affairs Committee. We plan to exert influence in additional hearings planned by these committees, as well as in the hearings of Rep. Ron Dellums' Subcommittee on Military Installations and Facilities. Particularly critical, of course, is the appropriations process. While CAMIP supports a cut-off of all military aid to the Philippines, it will also be important to support sound proposals developed in Congress which would reduce in any way the level of assistance given to the Marcos government. . . .

Press conferences and aggressive media work will be a vital component of the overall congressional strategy. We are providing articles on particular aspects of the bases issue to sympathetic publications, and information on some of the particularly abhorrent activities encouraged or caused by the bases' presence (sexual exploitation of Filipino women/prostitution, U.S. involvement in counterinsurgency efforts, resettlement and harassment of Filipino residents on the base perimeters, etc.) will be provided to important national columnists. In order to give maximum publicity to the congressional hearings, important testimony can be reproduced for wide distribution among campaign supporters and endorsers.

At key points in our congressional work—as determined by the timetable established by Congress—CAMIP will plan a National Lobby Day and appropriate vigils or rallies in perhaps 3-4 cities nationwide. A postcard campaign, based on a specific congressional proposal, will also be initiated at a strategic time, either in autumn 1983 or early 1984. Action alert networks will be established by regional campaigns. In order to give maximum publicity to the Congressional hearings, important testimony can be reproduced for wide distribution among campaign supporters. Finally, an "Action Notes" series can update supporters about current developments in campaign strategy.

Selection 8.11: Reagan's Advice, Steve Psinakis

Editors' Introduction

Steve Psinakis is related by marriage to the Lopez family, a wealthy clan whose members were forced into exile by martial law and most of whose assets ended up in the hands of Marcos and his cronies. The Philippine government accused Psinakis and others of responsibility for bombings in Manila; Psinakis charged that Marcos headed a terrorist regime. In December 1980, Imelda Marcos and Psinakis met in New York City. The following is from Psinakis' account of their meeting, not disputed by Imelda Marcos. The late Senator Benigno Aquino, Jr., who also met with Imelda Marcos in December of 1980, told a similar story.

Source: Steve Psinakis, *Two "Terrorists" Meet*, San Francisco: Alchemy Books, 1981, p. 100.

[Imelda Marcos said to me:] "Steve, the President [Ferdinand Marcos] has decided to lift martial law next month. He is very sincere about it, and he has already made an announcement. You know, last week I met with President-elect Reagan and Mr. Bush; they both expressed their friendship and support for the Philippines and for the President. They realize what an important ally we are to the U.S. and how important our country is to the security of the U.S. interests in the region. Reagan is quite different from Carter. I told Reagan—please, Steve, keep this to yourself—that the President plans to lift martial law next month and he told me not to act hastily. He said the stability and security of our country is vital to the U.S., and we should not rush into any changes which might affect the stability of the Philippines. He practically told me not to lift martial law yet, but the President has made up his mind. He will do it next month."

Imelda's remark about Reagan had a clear purpose. I had anticipated it because Imelda had told Ninoy [Benigno Aquino, Jr.] the same thing, and Ninoy had mentioned it to me the previous day.

Opposition leader Benigno Aquino, Jr., assassinated August 21, 1983.

CHAPTER 9: THE GATHERING STORM

Introduction

In August 1983, the most prominent leader of the opposition to Marcos, former Senator Benigno Aquino Jr., returned from exile in the United States. On his arrival at the Manila airport Aquino was killed while in the custody of the Marcos military. Almost at once it became a common belief in the Philippines that elements in the military high command, if not Marcos himself, were responsible for the murder. A little over a year later an official investigation went a long way toward confirming this belief, implicating Marcos's chief of staff, General Fabian Ver, and other military officials in the murder [see selection 9.1]. Completely destroying the credibility of Marcos's rule, the Aquino assassination triggered demonstrations bringing millions into the streets, betokening a deeper crisis for the Philippine dictatorship than it had ever faced before.

A decade of martial law had not solved the age-old problems of the Filipino people: their poverty and their lack of sovereignty in their own land. On the contrary it had aggravated them. Consequently, underneath the repressive policies of the dictatorship, stimulated by them in fact, a massive groundswell of popular unrest had been building. Aquino's killing became the catalyst for this swelling force, turning unrest into active opposition, throwing forward a popular resistance of unprecedented dimensions and diversity that was to bring the Marcos dictatorship to its end.

Contributing to the explosive growth of the political opposition were the economic effects of the assassination. These were immediate, tangible, and dramatic. Even before August 1983 falling prices for Philippine raw material exports and corruption and gross mismanagement by the Marcos dictatorship had brought the Philippine economy to the brink of ruin; the Aquino assassination pushed it over that brink. There was a massive flight of capital from the Philippines and by October 1983 it was evident that the economy of the country was "all but officially bankrupt" [see selection 9.2].

The assassination greatly accelerated the opposition of the working people in the cities and the countryside to the Marcos regime [see selections 9.3 and 9.4]. But while this opposition was intensified, it was not new. The poor had been a source of active opposition to the dictatorship from its first days because of the hardships it brought them. For ten years their resistance had been led very largely by those on the left of center in Philippine political life and by the more liberal forces in the Church. A staff report of the U.S. Senate Foreign Relations Committee described the new element, the change, that the Aquino murder brought to Philippine politics, warning that it "galvanized the political center of Philippine society—the business community, the Catholic faithful, the middle class which until recent years had grown in numbers and prospered." The Aquino assassination moved the center in both the political and religious life of the country into active opposition to the Marcos government. The massive street demonstrations that followed Aquino's murder were now more than ever before marked by the participation of the middle class, the church, even some of the business elite.

The heightened opposition to the dictatorship brought with it a new wave of nationalist feeling that was reflected in a wider and more intense opposition to U.S. military bases in the Philippines. These were now regarded even more sharply as a source of U.S. support for the dictator and a symbol of the nation's flawed sovereignty [see selections 9.5 and 9.6].

Finally, the Aquino assassination stimulated a militant and nation-wide movement of Philippine women [see selection 9.7]; it crystallized a loose grouping of reform-minded officers in the Philippine armed forces united by their desire to rid the military of the corrupting influence of the Marcos dictatorship [see selection 9.8]; and it encouraged the growth of the communist-led New People's Army [see selection 9.9].

To this rapid and many-sided growth of popular resistance the dictatorship responded with an increase in repression and terror [see selection 9.10]. But it seemed largely ineffective. The opposition continued to grow.

Bringing the brutality of the Philippine dictatorship to television screens in millions of U.S. homes, the Aquino assassination had a pronounced effect upon domestic opposition to Washington's support for Marcos, broadening that opposition considerably and bringing into it additional forces representing the mainstream of U.S. political life. This was particularly to be noted in the U.S. Filipino community where an organization called the Ninoy Aquino Movement brought into play many middle class and professional Filipinos who had formerly been silent. The change in the attitude of the U.S. media was also significant. When Marcos first established martial law, the U.S. media was generally favorable to the Philippine dictatorship. While there was a gradual erosion in this attitude over the years, with the Aquino assassination the U.S. media almost unanimously turned against the Philippine regime. Thus the efforts of the early opponents of U.S. support for the Marcos dictatorship [see selection 8.10] gained new adherents with a corresponding effect upon Congressional opinion. Legislators on Capitol Hill increasingly challenged White House requests for aid to Marcos.

As a result of the growth of Philippine opposition to Marcos (and its echo in U.S. public opinion), members of the Reagan administration and of Congress began to sense that Marcos was losing control. From the beginning the U.S. government had given the Philippine dictatorship support because it regarded Marcos as the guarantor of the status quo in the Philippines. Reports of Marcos's failing health had raised concerns among some policy makers that his regime could not last. And now with the unrest in the aftermath of the Aquino assassination, Marcos seemed increasingly unable to guarantee the "stability" Washington saw as necessary to protect its military and economic interests in the Philippines. As a result, U.S. policies toward that country began to change—in two ways.

First, a posture of intervention that had combined ever-increasing military and economic aid with unqualified support for the dictatorship shifted toward a more active and critical intervention in Philippine affairs. While the policy of aid continued, it became linked to pressure upon Marcos for various reforms [see selection 9.11]. In this way the conservative Reagan administration moved closer to liberals like Representative Stephen J. Solarz of Brooklyn, who had been advocating the linkage of aid to reforms for some time.

In the second place, Washington's Philippine policy became increasingly differentiated and ambivalent. The Reagan administration seemed to speak with two voices concerning the Philippines. George D. Moffett III in the *Christian Science Monitor* (February 18, 1986) explained this peculiarity in the following way:

> Behind the consensus for reform were differing views within the Reagan Administration on the Philippine crisis. At one end of the spectrum was the White House, where support for Marcos was strongest. At the other end were mid-level policy analysts at the State and Defense Departments and in the intelligence community who, months before the Aquino assassination, became concerned about the durability of the Marcos regime.

As the crisis deepened, the split in the administration deepened, with Reagan holding tight to Marcos until the force of events tore the dictator from his embrace [see selection 10.4], even while those in the administration representing the opposite view were developing connections with some of Marcos's political and military critics who would eventually dislodge him [see selections 9.11 and 9.15]. It must be emphasized, however, that representatives of both points of view within the administration wanted the same thing: security for U.S. interests in the Philippines. Reagan thought this could best be achieved by supporting Marcos; the others by encouraging a replacement for Marcos who would be of the moderate elite, friendly to the U.S.

The escalation of U.S. intervention in Philippine affairs that took place after the Aquino killing was first seen in the military field, and especially in U.S. pressure for Philippine military reform. Like the reform elements in the Philippine Armed Forces, the Pentagon wanted to see the Philippine military purged of Marcos-inspired corruption. The Pentagon, however, laid emphasis on this reform as a means of "professionalizing" the Philippine military, so to make it a more effective counter-insurgency force. Senator John Kerry (Democrat of Massachusetts) reported after a visit to the Philippines in April 1985 that "a little more than a year ago, the U.S. Embassy in Manila began to view the insurgency of the New People's Army with a "sense of urgency" believing "that the NPA could be in a position to contend for power in a few years. . . ." Evidently the Embassy communicated this "sense of urgency" to Washington, for in October 1984, Assistant Secretary of Defense Richard Armitage came before Congress with a call for reform in the Philippine military, citing its failures in the face of NPA growth. Armitage also advised Congress that the Defense Department was aware of "a solid cadre of competent, patriotic officers in the AFP [Armed Forces of the Philippines] who have the determination to institute the necessary reforms."

But the pressure for professionalization, while the chief manifestation of increasing U.S. intervention in Philippine military affairs, was not the only one. In 1984 instances of what appeared to be covert U.S. military intervention against the NPA came to light [see selection 9.12]. Then, in 1985, according to a report in the *New York Times* of October 27, the number of U.S. military advisers assigned to the Philippine armed forces was increased substantially.

U.S. officials in Manila told Senator Kerry on his spring 1985 visit that President Marcos stood in the way of U.S. proposals for Philippine military reform. But, they reported, Defense Minister Juan Ponce Enrile and Deputy Chief of Staff General Fidel Ramos were sympathetic in their response [see selection 9.13]. Besides amplifying on the support of Ramos and Enrile for military reform, Kerry's account suggested U.S. connections with these two military leaders.

Marcos's negative attitude was not surprising, perhaps, since one of the main reform proposals called for the dismissal of General Ver and some twenty "over-staying" Philippine generals. The Pentagon regarded these high officers as corrupt and ineffective. They were, however, Marcos's base of support in the Philippine military.

In the spring of 1985, as it became clear that U.S. pressure on Marcos for military reform was getting nowhere, the escalation of U.S. intervention in Philippine affairs was carried over from the military to the political arena. Now Washington urged political reform on Marcos, and in particular the holding of an early presidential election. (Marcos had, at this time, scheduled local elections for the spring of 1986, and presidential elections for 1987.) In May 1985, William Casey, head of the CIA, visited Marcos in Malacañang Palace to press for an early presidential election. When Casey's visit seemed lacking in result, President Reagan in October dispatched his close friend, Senator Paul Laxalt, to Marcos with the same request, and in addition bearing a letter that came directly from Reagan. A fanfare of publicity accompanied Laxalt's mission in order to maximize its effect both in the Philippines and in the United States.

Marcos's resistance to military reform may have suggested that additional pressure was advisable. But the chief motivation for escalating U.S. intervention in the field of Philippine politics may well have sprung from an increasing concern on the part of the administration about Philippine political developments that was similar to its military anxieties. Here, too, the influence of the left seemed to be showing signs of rapid growth.

In July 1985, a special national intelligence estimate, prepared by the CIA, the Defense Intelligence Agency, and the State Department, warned that growing left-wing and communist influence in Philippine political parties and local administrations might reach dangerous proportions in the next year and a half (in other words, in the period before the scheduled presidential elections) [see selection 9.14]. Seen in this context, an early presidential election might serve as a pre-emptive move to counter the expanding political influence of the left before it assumed threatening proportions.

On the U.S. side the pressure for an early presidential election was a demand upon which both those members of the Reagan administration who favored Marcos and those who did not could agree. The former saw the election as an opportunity to refurbish Marcos's credibility; the latter, as an opportunity to replace him with a moderate alternative.

Of all the reforms pressed on Marcos by Washington, an early election was the easiest for him to concede. The economic reform most desired by Washington was the break-up of the crony-held monopolies in the sugar and coconut industries that restricted the free play of foreign and Filipino capital in those fields. Marcos had resisted this reform for the same reason that he rebuffed the dismissal of the "over-staying" generals: these economic and military cronies were his crucial base of support. By agreeing to an early election, Marcos may have thought it possible both to deflect the mounting U.S. pressure on him, and to come out on top with a new "popular mandate" by means of the fraud and violence that had served him so well in previous elections. Here he underestimated the breadth, depth, and passion of the popular opposition to his rule that had by now developed. It was to be the fatal miscalculation of his political career. On November 3, on a David Brinkley show before a U.S. television audience (a format Senator Laxalt had suggested) Marcos announced that he would hold an early presidential election in January 1986, later postponed to February. Because of the short notice, Filipinos referred to this as the "snap" election.

The Aquino assassination thus triggered a new stage in the popular opposition to the Marcos regime. It further stimulated left-wing opponents and widened their influence. More important still it brought into active opposition the middle forces in Philippine political life, where they took their place alongside those who for years had energetically opposed the dictatorship. The result was that the dictatorship was left in virtual isolation, stripped of all but its hard-core of political support and its cronies in the military and the economy.

In these changing circumstances, the Reagan administration did not abandon the traditional goal of U.S. policy in the Philippines, namely the preservation of a Philippine status quo advantageous to U.S. military and economic interests, however disadvantageous it might be to Filipinos. But now, to preserve U.S. interests, it had to press Marcos for reform. One wing of the administration led by President Reagan expected that Marcos, by adopting a posture of reform, could ride out the storm. Another, more realistic, wing of the administration, despairing of Marcos, sought to develop contacts with the Philippine political and military elite so as to keep the post-Marcos political situation as much as possible out of the hands of the Philippine people. As it turned out, neither wing of the administration had its way. In what became the final crisis of the Marcos regime it proved impossible to save Marcos or to keep the Filipino people out of the picture.

Selection 9.1: Majority Report, Agrava Commission

Editors' Introduction

The massive public outcry at the killing of former Senator Aquino on August 21, 1983, forced President Marcos to appoint a special committee to investigate the assassination. But this did little to calm the popular outrage, for all the panel members were known to be Marcos loyalists. Finally, public pressure became so intense that the panel members themselves resigned, citing the widespread doubts as to their impartiality. A new five-member commission was selected, headed by Corazon Agrava, a former appellate judge.

In October 1984, the commission issued two separate reports: a minority report by Agrava alone, and a majority report, released the following day, by the other four commission members. Both reports rejected the contention of the military that Aquino had been killed by a lone gunman hired by the Communists. Both reports found that Aquino's assassination was the result of a military conspiracy. The majority charged that the conspiracy involved a civ-ilian and 25 military officers, including the chief of staff, General Fabian Ver, a cousin and close friend of Marcos's; excerpts from this majority report are reprinted below. The minority report implicated a single general and six soldiers.

Marcos denounced the authors of the majority report, and remanded the entire matter to a court previously responsible only for handling minor corruption cases and run by his appointees. In December 1985, after the disappearance of numerous witnesses and the exclusion of much evidence and testimony, the court found all those named by the majority and minority reports innocent, and found that Aquino had been killed by the lone communist gunman—the conclusion unanimously rejected by the Agrava Commission. The verdict was greeted with derision in the Philippines and skepticism worldwide, even from the Reagan administration.

Source: *Philippine News* [San Francisco], October 31-November 6, 1984, special supplement.

II. CONCLUSION

It is against the background of the facts above detailed that We now address Ourselves to the principle questions which it is this Board's mission to answer.

FIRST. Who was it who shot and killed ex-Senator Benigno Aquino, Jr.? Where was he shot? Was it Rolando Galman who did it, in the manner described in the common narratives of the AVSECOM [Aviation Security Command] witnesses, or was it somebody else?

SECOND. What was the weapon used in the slaying of Senator Aquino? Was it the Smith and Wesson .357 Magnum revolver, bearing Serial No. K919079, marked Exhibit 65 in these proceedings?

THIRD. Is the ubiquitous hand of the NPA/CPP perceivable in the events that unfolded at the tarmac at noon of that tragic day, August 21, 1983?

FOURTH. On the other hand, if negative answers should be dictated by the evidence, then who was the killer, and how and why did he do it?

FIFTH. In any event, whichever it was who performed the dastardly execution, was he acting alone or in conspiracy with others; and, in the affirmative case, who are the co-conspirators?

Answers to these queries have been given by Maj. Gen. Prospero A. Olivas, the Chief Investigating Officer designated by the Chief of Staff to direct and oversee the official police inquiry into the Aquino assassination . . . .

[Olivas concluded that Galman killed Aquino with a Smith & Wesson .357 on orders of the New People's Army or the Communist Party of the Philippines (NPA/CPP).] . . .

We cannot accept this version of the killings. We have carefully analyzed the testimonial bases of the military versions as against testimonies of other witnesses and other related physical evidence presented before us, and find that there is irreconcilable contradiction between these two sets of proof leaving Us no alternative except to reject the former. . . .

Thus, the auditory and the visual proofs at hand clearly and unmistakably prove that all the military men who regaled Us with the story of how Galman had supposedly shot Senator Aquino are shown to have been lying, deliberately and in cooperation and confederation with each other. . . .

Expert testimony, therefore, contradicts and mandates rejection of the Olivas theory that Senator Aquino was shot with a .357 Magnum. On the contrary, the scientific evidence proves that it was a .38 or a .45 caliber that killed Senator Aquino. . . .

We, therefore, reject the hypothesis advanced by Gen. Olivas, adopted by every other responsible military officer including the Chief of Staff, that it was Rolando Galman who assassinated Senator Benigno Aquino, Jr., using a Smith & Wesson .357 Magnum revolver. Indeed, We find that the evidence satisfactorily proves that the version of the military witnesses as to the manner by which Galman was supposed to have shot Senator Aquino is entirely false, and these witnesses conspired and confederated together to narrate this untruthful version to Us and thus mislead Us. The evidence of the physical facts, auditory and visual, sufficiently establishes the actual occurrences on the tarmac on that fateful day of August 21, 1983. We declare as lacking in basis, and in fact contradicted by scientific proof of the most persuasive character, the theory that the murder weapon was the .357 Magnum revolver identified as such by the military investigators, the proofs on the contrary indicating that it was either a .38 or .45 caliber pistol that did the nefarious job.

The next question which We will now resolve, the third in Our list, is whether or not the insidious machinations of the NPA/CPP figured in the assassination of Senator Aquino, as strongly urged by the military . . . .

The major obstruction to the acceptance of the theory that "GALMAN was under instructions by the New People's Army when he committed the dastardly crime" of assassinating Senator Aquino . . . is, *firstly*, the fact that, in reality, Galman did not commit "the dastardly crime." *Secondly,* the proofs upon which the theory is made to depend . . . are, in so far as they purport to establish a link between Galman and the NPA, either outright hearsay or baseless opinion, or both, and will therefore have to be rejected out of hand as bereft of probative force. *Thirdly,* although concededly Galman's criminal record is quite unprepossessing, it includes no charge involving acts of subversion and thus negates any communist connection. . . .

If it was not Rolando Galman who killed Senator Aquino, the evidence to this effect being undeserving of credit—because contrary to the physical fact, and it was not [a] .357 Magnum revolver that slew him, as persuasively proven by scientific evidence, and Galman was not an NPA or subversive or otherwise acting under instructions of the NPA/CPP—We now address ourselves to Our last two questions, to wit: if not Galman, then who was the killer, and how and why did he do it; was he acting alone or in conspiracy with others; and if so, who are his co-conspirators?

The evidence presented before us reveals a string of events and circumstances indicating that the assassination of ex-Senator Aquino was a criminal plot among many persons. We cannot accept the view that the assassination was the work of a single gunman, working clandestinely, moving and positioning himself at various places in the tarmac and other premises of the MIA [Manila International Airport] without the knowledge and consent of the numerous military personnel in the area who were then enforcing strict security controls and safeguards and "sanitizing" the area and had in fact been doing so since early morning of that day. . . .

Whoever was the assassin, Galman or another person, he was able to shoot Aquino only by cover [of] special arrangements of certain officers of the security forces. If it was Galman, additional arrangements were made to ensure his immediate death and silence. If it was not Galman, then Galman was used as a decoy/scapegoat to hide the identity of the real assassin. . . .

The involvement of various levels of military personnel, particularly ranking officers of the AVSECOM and units assigned to the operations of the MIA, leads to the conclusion that the principals in the conspiracy were persons who could exercise official authority or powerful influence over the involved military personnel. . . .

No other person was in a position to shoot Senator Aquino at the stairway except his escorts themselves. It was therefore no other than one of his escorts who actually killed him. . . .

. . . Senator Aquino was shot behind the head as he reached the bottom of the service stairs attached to the airbridge of Bay 8; he was not shot by Rolando Galman who was never at the stairway; it was in fact only the soldiers in the staircase with Senator Aquino who could have shot him . . . .

We now address ourselves to the final questions: who are the other persons who are involved in this conspiracy, either as principals, upon the theory that the act of one is the act of all, or as accessories, for attempting to hide the corpus of the evidence? . . .

We are also satisfied that the evidence proves the complicity of Gen. Fabian C. Ver in this tragic affair, in attempting, like Gen. Olivas, to cover up the crime, or hide the corpus or effects of the crime. . . .

    1. . . . a. Ver at first denied any "monitoring" of Aquino's activities in the USA. It was only after intensive questioning that he finally admitted to "following up" Aquino['s] movements in America. He had to admit he was being regularly informed of the messages from the Philippine Consul General in New York, and, later, from the Philippine Ambassador in Singapore. Those messages leave no doubt about the close monitoring of Senator Aquino's activities. . . .

    2. The evidence shows the military authorities knew that Aquino was coming via CAL [China Airline] CI-811. Yet Ver denied awareness of this fact. . . .

With respect to Col. Arturo Custodio, "Galman could not have moved around and remained in the tarmac or the airport building except with the knowledge and consent of the AVSECOM officers and men engaged in the operations at the time. Col. Arturo Custodio is the link between Galman and the AVSECOM. Galman was his personal friend. He and Hermilo Gosuico were the ones who picked up Rolando Galman from his house at Bagong Silang, San Miguel, Bulacan, on August 17, 1983." [Quoting from the report of the Board's counsel.] . . .

In the light of all the foregoing considerations, We find the following to be indictable for the premeditated killing of Senator Benigno S. Aquino, Jr., and Rolando Galman at the MIA on August 21, 1983:

    1. General Fabian C. Ver [Chief of Staff, Armed Forces of the Philippines]

    2. Maj. Gen. Prospero A. Olivas

    3. Brig. Gen. Luther Custodio [head of Aviation Security Command]

    4. Col. Arturo Custodio. . . .

    [and 21 other military personnel and a civilian]

III. EPILOGUE

We close our Report with a candid and honest exhortation to our people to demonstrate sobriety and to remain calm while pursuing with vigor and tenacity our firm resolve to see that justice is done to former Senator Benigno S. Aquino Jr. and the Filipino people.

    To be sure, there are forces around us that will use this report to discredit our traditionally revered institutions as they have unscrupulously done with the valid grievances that we have always articulated. We hope and pray that the Filipino people are able to recognize and resist the subtle entrapment that these forces have so carefully designated in order that, in their naivete, the people will find themselves unwittingly supporting these forces' objectives to destabilize our country and to fall prey to an intolerable political ideology.

This ideology is antithetical to the Filipino people's traditional love of freedom, justice and adherence to democratic ideals. . . .

More than any other event in contemporary Philippine history, the killing of the late former Senator Aquino has brought into sharper focus the ills pervading Philippine society. It was the concretization of the horror that has been haunting this country for decades, routinely manifested by the breakdown of peace and order, economic instability, graft and corruption, and an increasing number of abusive elements in what are otherwise noble institutions in our country—the military and law enforcement agencies. We are, however, convinced that, by and large, the great majority of the officers and men of these institutions have remained decent and honorable, dedicated to their noble mission in the service of our country and people. . . .

A tragedy like that which happened on August 21, 1983, and the crisis that followed, would have normally caused the resignation of the Chief of the Armed Forces in a country where public office is viewed with highest esteem and respect and where the moral responsibilities of public officials transcend all other considerations.

We anticipate that there will be those who, because of their prejudices, will express dissatisfaction over our conclusions. To them, we can only say that we did what the law mandated, using as basis nothing but the evidence, and, invoking as guide in our search for truth in the Aquino assassination, nothing but our conscience.

Selection 9.2: Post-Assassination Economic Crisis, Gerald Sussman, David O'Connor, and Charles W. Lindsey

Editors' Introduction

The Philippine economy all but collapsed after the assassination of Benigno Aquino. The deep economic crisis brought with it wider unemployment, lower wages, higher prices —more hunger and misery for the working population of the country. Nor was hardship limited to the working poor; the middle class also suffered economically. On a different plane the wealthy business elite, except for the narrow circle of Marcos's cronies, were affected negatively by the rapacity and corruption of the regime.

Following are excerpts from an article by three U.S. academics written in 1984, shortly after Aquino's assassination.

Source: Gerald Sussman, David O'Connor, and Charles W. Lindsey, "The Philippines, 1984: The Political Economy of a Dying Dictatorship," *Philippine Research Bulletin,* Summer 1984, Friends of the Filipino People, Durham, North Carolina.

Introduction

The shock of the assassination [of former Philippine Senator Benigno Aquino] and local political reaction have focused world attention on the Philippines and put the regime under the greatest scrutiny since Marcos assumed power in 1965. Reluctance on the part of international banks to renew loans and the threats of transnational firms to withdraw their investments have also made transparent the dependent nature of the Philippine economy. Reeling under a $26 billion debt, rocked by scandals involving government financial misman-agement and cronyism, and subjected to International Monetary Fund (IMF)-dictated policies, the economy is in shambles. . . .

Economic Deterioration

Underlying the escalating political tensions are the less understood but more fundamental anxieties aroused by the Philippine economic situation. At the time of the Aquino assassination, the economy was purportedly showing favorable signs after weathering a prolonged recession. Prices of some export commodities were beginning to turn up and the government was speaking of a recovery phase. In reality, however, the economy was in quite fragile shape. The assassination had the effect of bringing events to a head. Subsequent attempts of the Marcos regime to cope with the situation, while at the same time maintaining itself in the good graces of the International Monetary Fund (IMF) and international banking community, impacted harshly on the already depressed domestic economy.

During the 1970s, real gross national product (GNP) officially grew at an average rate of about 6.6 percent per annum. In the 1980s, however, the economy slid, with real GNP growing at only 4.7 percent in 1980, 3.6 percent in 1981, and 2.8 percent in 1982. The decline worsened in 1983 to an estimated 1.4 percent, a rate lower than that of the population growth. For 1984, a 6.8 percent real decline in GNP is forecast. [The 1984 GNP decline was 5.3 percent—eds.]

As prices of primary products fell dramatically after 1979, often by more than 50 percent, Filipinos increasingly felt the effects in reduced wages and rising unemployment. Conservative estimates are that unemployment increas-ed to 19 percent in 1983 (according to the government Development Academy of the Philippines). At present [1984], it stands at almost one-fourth of the labor force.

The economic crisis has also been exacerbated by official cronyism: that is, Marcos's bailout of unstable companies managed by his business and "old boy" networks. After business magnate Dewey Dee fled the country in 1981 with debts of an estimated P700 million, more than 80 firms became virtually insolvent, and several investment houses were forced to close their doors. The government responded with emergency loan funds and, in some cases, con-verted existing loans to equity. However, the condition of many of the firms did not improve appreciably, and for some it got worse. In fact, the govern-ment Philippine National Bank, the largest commercial bank in the country, has been heavily involved in the bailout of faltering firms, and is now itself faced with the possibility of financial collapse.

This occurred while the government was instituting a World Bank-funded restructuring of the manufacturing sector, dismantling the existing tariff wall in order to encourage a program based on export promotion. The World Bank loans were to tide the Philippines over what was hoped to be a transitional period, as new industries replaced many of the older, "import-substituting" ones that were not expected to survive, and until exports caught up with imports. The timing of such restructuring could not have been worse.

Imports rose while exports fell. In 1982 the current account deficit was equivalent to 8.5 percent of GNP. The Philippines (the sixth largest recipient of World Bank funds) had incurred rapidly increasing amounts of foreign currency debt during the 1970s. As the current account deficit grew, the country began to incur difficulties in meeting debt servicing obligations. By early 1983, the Philippine economy was in a precarious situation; one headline announced that "Emergency Aid from IMF, World Bank Helped the Philippines Avert Default." To keep the government from going under, the IMF agreed in February 1983 to a $543 million emergency loan. This was followed by a $300 million loan from the World Bank, and another loan of the same amount from major New York banks with significant interests in the Philippines. The New York banks proclaimed "Manila's return to grace" and momentarily prevented the Philippines from being cast as "Asia's only Latin American debtor."

The price of reprieve, however, required the Philippines to agree to stringent conditions imposed by the IMF, including limiting its balance of payments deficit for 1983 to $598 million—about half the 1982 figure of $1.14 billion. By mid-1983, however, it had already reached $562 million. In an effort to limit the deficit for the rest of the year, the government devalued the peso by 7.3 percent to P11 to the U.S. dollar (on top of a 10.3 percent fall that had already occurred during 1983), cut the projected government budget of P9.4 billion by P1 billion, and ended subsidies on petroleum products. These measures reinforced the already depressed state of the economy.

Economic Hemophilia: Rx-Debt Addiction

By October 1983, it was obvious that these measures had not stopped the hemorrhaging and that the reaction to the Aquino murder had intensified the situation. The balance of payments deficit during the third quarter of 1983 alone (July-September) was $780 million, bringing the total for the year to $1342 million. On October 5, in an attempt to stem the tide, the government again devalued the peso, this time by 21.4 percent (from P11 to P14:$1). Furthermore, the IMF is suggesting that a devaluation to at least P18:$1 will be needed in the near future.

The descent continues. By the middle of October the balance of payments deficit had swelled to over $2 billion, and the international reserves of the country had fallen by another $1 billion to $430 million, less than the value of one month's imports. Later, it was reported that during October reserves hit a low of $290 million. On October 17, it was announced that the government could no longer meet its debt obligations and was asking for a 90-day moratorium on principal payments, with interest payments to continue. (The government has already requested and obtained two extensions of the debt moratorium.) Propped up only through foreign bailouts, the Philippine economy is all but officially bankrupt.

Rather than dealing with the basic inequities and corruption of its economy, or altering the structure of ownership of production or the pattern of income distribution, the Marcos government has fostered dependence on foreign assistance and in the process has become the proverbial debt junkie. Gradually, it built up its dependence on an external stimulant in order to maintain high rates of economic growth. Ever larger doses of foreign exchange became needed to achieve the same effect, as more and more of the new money was simply consumed in payments for the old.

Making matters worse, the Marcos regime had for some time been hiding the seriousness of the situation. First, the Central Bank had been understating the size of the foreign debt; in mid-October 1983, it revised the figure upward by some $7-$8 billion to $25.6 billion. Also the composition of the debt had been shifting, so that the short-term portion had grown to about 40 percent of the total. This increased the cost of servicing the debt. In 1982 debt-service was more than one-half export earnings.

In addition, the Central Bank had been drastically overstating the size of its foreign exchange reserves in order to maintain the confidence of international bankers. "Corrections" made in the first two weeks in October amounted to $600 million of the reported $1 billion decline in reserves during that period. Once the scandal became public, the Philippine Central Bank governor, Jaime Laya, was forced to resign, reportedly at the insistence of an embarrassed IMF.

Confronted with the glaring irregularities in the Philippine Central Bank's bookkeeping procedures and the rampant dishonesty of its officials, the IMF was understandably concerned that a seal of good housekeeping for the Marcos regime at the moment would strain beyond repair its own credibility in the eyes of foreign bankers. Undoubtedly, there will be a short-term resolution of the Philippine debt crisis. Negotiations on the rescheduling of some $9 billion of the Philippine debt and $3.3 billion of new loans should resume once the IMF and Marcos reach agreement on a new standby credit, which is expected to total $650 million. The IMF will extract further concessions from Marcos in exchange for any new money lent. The cost will be a new austerity program, demanded and overseen by the IMF, which will further depress the growth of the economy; in other words, the price of a resolution of the immediate debt crisis is certain to be the deepening of the overall economic crisis.

For its part, the U.S. government has also become involved in the current debt crisis, thus far providing the Philippines with "short-term, stopgap support" of $320 million. The U.S. Treasury Department is reportedly preparing additional bridge financing of about $150 million, an amount equivalent to the first two tranches of the proposed IMF standby arrangement.

Thus, although the Reagan administration has recently kept a lower profile publicly toward the Marcos regime, it is privately undertaking economic measures to keep it afloat. One reason is that about $4 billion of the Philippine commercial bank debt, almost one-fourth, is held by the nine largest U.S. banks.

In the meantime, the Marcos government has placed severe restrictions on imports and the use of foreign exchange, and has limited the expansion of domestic credit. It has also taken several measures to attract more foreign investment in the hope of increasing foreign currency inflows, as well as present a more favorable image to international capital. Throughout the crisis, it has appealed to subsidiaries of transnational corporations and domestic capitalists in joint ventures with foreigners to use their influence to get the transnationals to provide credits and to invest more in their Philippine operations. To make such activity more attractive, Marcos signed a presidential decree, effective for one year beginning December 4, 1983, which, reminiscent of the unpopular "parity amendment" that was attached to the postwar constitution for U.S. economic assistance, allows foreign investment in local companies to rise from a previous limit of 40 percent to 100 percent. Should transnationals be lured by such a seductive, though politically unstable, investment climate, they will enjoy acquisition opportunities of local firms at virtually giveaway prices.

Toward a Political Economic Prognosis

Rather than investing, a number of major transnationals in the Philippines have been disinvesting over the recent past. Mobil Oil has sold off its Philippine operations and Ford Motor Company plans to do the same. American Can has decided to withdraw from a joint venture that would have made food beverage cans in the Philippines. Signetics, the U.S.-based semiconductor manufacturing subsidiary of the Dutch transnational Philips, has closed down its Philippine assembly plant, transferring operations to plants in South Korea and Thailand. . . .

Already the standard of living of ordinary Filipinos has been deeply affected by the current economic crisis, not only in growing unemployment, but also by depressed real wages. During 1982 they declined by 5.7 percent, and the fall continued in 1983. The P10 increase in the minimum wage in 1983 was largely offset by inflation, currently running above 35 percent. Moreover, published consumer reports indicate that the cost of living has risen beyond official estimates. In the eight weeks after the Aquino murder, the price of white sugar increased by 38 percent; salt was up 100 percent; cooking oil, 100 percent; chicken, 75 percent; pork, 66 percent; tomatoes, 100 percent; onions, 66 percent; and garlic, 100 percent. In November 1983, there were also reports of shortages of rice and cooking oil. There are indications that 1984 will be worse, as the government has already decontrolled the prices of a long list of basic food stuffs, such as rice and eggs, in keeping with the IMF demands for tougher austerity measures.

Since the onset of the country's economic decline, the Philippine business community has grown considerably more critical of the Marcos government, particularly against the bailing out of bankrupt firms owned by friends of the President. These complaints, however, were mild in comparison with their more virulent attacks since August 21: in rallies, marches and demonstrations, public speeches, media articles and, in general, in demands that Marcos dramat-ically change his policies and/or step down. The President has responded to the business sector by alternatively cajoling and berating its leading represen-tatives.

Selection 9.3: Growth of the Labor Movement, Karin Aguilar-San Juan

Editors' Introduction

The following article describes work-ing conditions of Philippine labor in the eighties and the explosion of labor organization and militancy that were key components in the popular resis-tance that led to Marcos's overthrow.

The Philippine Workers Sup-port Committee, referred to in the article, is an organization formed in April 1984 of U.S. trade unionists who support the efforts of Filipino labor.

Source: Karin Aguilar-San Juan, "Labor Movement Sparks Philippine Resistance," *Resist Newsletter*, Som-erville, MA, January 1986.

Poverty and hunger are forcing Filipinos into rebellion. Last September, 10,000 farmers and their families marched peacefully into the town plaza of Escalante, Negros, drawing attention to the stark contrast between their lives, and the lives of the sugar *hacenderos*. Near the end of their 3-day long demon-stration, they barricaded a portion of the major road leading out of the city, and linked arms in front of the public market. They were met by two firetrucks and para-military forces under the orders of a powerful local sugar baron. Soldiers hit the protesters with blasts from the waterhoses, and threw two cannisters of tear gas before unleashing a volley of gunshots into the crowd.

When it was over, 27 civilians were killed (most from shots in the back), 21 were charged with inciting sedition. . . . A respected human rights organiza-tion in the Philippines, the Task Force Detainees, calls the Escalante Massacre the worst attack by the military since Marcos declared martial law in 1972.

Except for the depravity of the killings, what happened in Escalante probably did not shock many Filipinos. Negros has been submerged in famine since early this year. A 40 percent drop in this year's sugar crop, combined with plummeting world sugar prices, has brought massive unemployment to the local economy. By September, over 350,000 laborers and farmhands had lost their jobs, and one child was dying every day from starvation.

Even when times were good in Negros, they were not much better. Cane-cutting in the scorching sun earned an adult laborer 20 pesos for a day's work, or $1.08. Teenagers and young children who worked in the harvest were rewarded 5 pesos for eight hour's toil, or about 25 cents.

Now, even some planters are on the brink. Dissident sugar growers blame the government for mismanagement and corruption, but labor organizers point out that the problem has much deeper roots. The development of the cash-crop economy, they say, is skewed, not to meet the food needs of the people, but to accommodate power-hungry Filipino businessmen and profit-seeking foreign corporations.

This sort of hardship is fertile soil for revolution. For the Marcos regime, there could be nothing more frightening than the growing involvement of the NPA guerillas with the plight of the hungry farmers. The easiest way to undermine the farmers' legitimate protest, from the government's point of view, is to blame the armed rebels for wielding a corrupting influence over the countryside. But, even though anyone who tries to organize the farmers is branded a "communist," says Roberto Ortaliz, president of the National Federation of Sugar Workers (NFSW), "there is no time to study communism." There is only time enough to decide how to best serve the liberation movement, whether as a labor activist, a church worker, a feminist, or a professional.

Union Organizing

Ortaliz was one of three Filipino trade union representatives invited by the Philippine Workers Support Committee to tour the United States this fall [1985]. He spoke to labor groups, human rights organizations, anti-intervention activists, the church community, and the local media to inform them of the current situation facing his country, and to garner support for the activities of the Kilusang Mayo Uno (May First Movement) or KMU, the largest anti-Marcos union center.

A native of Negros Occidental province, where over half of the country's sugar is produced, Ortaliz' first involvement in the community began when, at 19, he became a Catholic lay leader. He served the church for 17 years before he joined the workers in the canefields as an organizer for the NFSW.

In 1984, Ortaliz was elected Secretary-General of the 500,000 member KMU. He explained the origin of his organization this way: Militant trade unionism in the Philippines began in the 1900s, as part of the movement for independence from the United States. Up through the 1950s, however, unions did not have much influence. In the 1960s and 70s, the Marcos government kept wages low and banned union activities, specifically to attract foreign corporate investment to the Export Processing Zones. As a result of low wages and increasing military repression of unionism, worker militancy was rekindled.

In 1977, the government established the Trade Union Congress of the Philippines (TUCP), with support from the AFL-CIO. Its purpose was to co-opt the labor movement. The TUCP is tagged a "yellow" union because of its sweetheart ties to the Marcos regime.

Three years later, eight union federations (including the NFSW) formed the KMU as an alternative vehicle by which the workers would be able to express both economic and political demands.

The potential for union growth in the Philippines has, perhaps, never been greater. The Filipino labor force numbers some 21 million. For those who have jobs, there is a glaring discrepancy between actual income, and what it costs to feed a family. The minimum wage, set by the Ministry of Labor, stands at $3 a day. The cost of living is three times this amount. To top it off, since few companies in the cities bother to comply with the legal minimum, the average Filipino worker brings home about $1 a day.

Eight million Filipinos are unemployed. Most of these are women. The only options available to a woman who cannot find a job—besides finding common cause with the armed resistance—are for her to join with the ranks of prostitutes who entertain tourists and U.S. servicemen, to go overseas to look for work as a domestic, or to become a mail-order bride and find a husband living abroad. The government solution is to boost the sex and tourism industries by legalizing prostitution.

Trade unions, however, are not enough of a vehicle for women who want to raise political questions about sexual exploitation. Women workers have formed autonomous organizations throughout the country to address the specific circumstances they face as women: wage discrimination, sexual harassment and abuse in the workplace (the "lie down or be laid off" policy), pornography, tourism, and institutionalized prostitution. In the Export Processing Zones, where most of the assembly work in textiles and electronics is done by young women, organized labor depends on the participation of women, even at decision-making levels.

GABRIELA, a coalition of middle-class oriented women's groups sums up the causes of women's oppression in four very loaded terms: feudalism, patriarchy, colonialism, and U.S. imperialism. The politicization process of working women qua feminists has the potential of becoming a forceful form of resistance within the labor movement and outside of it, as the sources of class and gender oppression in the Philippines are, as these women assert, closely intertwined [see selection 9.7].

In any case, the nature of revolution in the Philippines—as elsewhere—has meant that solidarity among various social and political groupings is essential. Ortaliz cited a recent "sympathy strike" in which 29,000 Export Processing Zone workers walked off the shop floor in support of a group of union activists who were being harassed by management. In 1984, a strike by the transport union on the island of Cebu forced daily business to a halt, but only because it drew the support of most other economic sectors. Twice this year, workers were able to paralyze the entire island of Mindanao, including the operations of the 120 foreign-owned corporations housed there. Ortaliz said that plans are underway to stage a nationwide people's strike in the next couple of years.

With each passing strike or demonstration, labor activists are meeting up with increased government violence and military abuse. From January to June 1985, 38 workers were killed in strike dispersals, 8 are missing and presumed dead, 355 were arrested, and 50 remain in political detention. Since September, between 50 and 70 workers have been killed by the military or paramilitary in rallies and demonstrations. . . .

Against many odds, the Filipino labor movement may well be currently the fastest growing in the world. Marcos, and the United States, have much to fear if this growth continues. Their counter-insurgency plans aim to smother the "collective imagination" of the working poor. . . .

According to the *San Francisco Examiner* (7/21/85), at least $3 million in U.S. taxpayers' money is being directly applied to programs designed to destroy the urban labor movement in the Philippines.

Through the National Endowment for Democracy Act, Congress allots funds through the U.S. Information Agency to the National Endowment for Democracy (NED). The NED, a private organization based in Washington, then distributes the money to the U.S. Chambers of Commerce, the AFL-CIO, and other beneficiaries. The Free Trade Union Institute, an entity created by the AFL-CIO for work in "troubled" areas, channels the cash to Latin America, Africa, and Asia. Finally, the Asian American Free Labor Institute (AAFLI) appropriates part of the finances for the Philippines. The money has helped individuals win elections for management positions in the TUCP, and keeps several radio stations and labor publications in operation. . . .

Selection 9.4: Hunger in the Countryside, Kathy McAfee

Editors' Introduction

The great and enduring problem of Philippine society has been the poverty and landlessness of the majority of the population who live in the countryside. In the last days of the Marcos dictatorship conditions of life in many rural areas became truly desperate. The result was the increasing support the rural population gave to grassroots organizations of all sorts: the National Sugar Workers' Union, Basic Christian Communities, and farmers' cooperatives. This rural misery was as well a key factor in the dramatic growth of the New People's Army [see selection 9.9]. In June 1985, the KMP or National Peasant Union was founded.

The article below describes the crisis in the countryside and the efforts of the rural poor to meet it. The author works with Oxfam America, a private international relief organization.

Source: Kathy McAfee, "The Philippines: A Harvest of Anger," *Facts for Action* [An Oxfam America Educational Publication], #15, Boston, October 1985.

Why are we farmers who work so hard still poor? Why is it that those who own our land do not work? That is what we have been asking and that is why my son became an organizer. We farmers have to unite, so that we can control the land, and share it among those who work. That is the only way we can have real liberty.

As he walks home at dusk from the small plot he farms, Lino Mangubat's [his name has been changed to protect him and his family] face is furrowed and tired. But his gaze is direct and his voice does not hide the anger he feels when he explains why 40 years of unceasing labor on the land have left him still hungry and poor.

"These government programs have stolen our land! They are crushing us farmers to the ground!" he says, as he scrapes the mud of the fields from his feet.

The programs that have angered Mr. Mangubat are the result of agricultural policies adopted by the Philippine government to increase food production. They are part of an international "green revolution" backed by advice and financing from the United States and international development agencies.

In theory, green revolution programs are supposed to help poor farmers like Lino Mangubat. But in reality, they have contributed to making him— and millions of other Filipino peasants—even poorer. Fertile and rich in resources, the Philippines has the potential for producing more than enough food for its population of 54 million. Instead, hunger is spreading, fueling an explosive cycle of discontent, repression, and rebellion.

Farmers Work Harder, Grow Poorer

Lino Mangubat and his family raise rice and sweet potatoes on the lowland plains of the province of Zamboanga del Sur. They live in a tiny, two-room house of thatch and bamboo. Their possessions are few: a change of clothes, some plates, pots and spoons, thin reed mats for sleeping, a water buffalo for plowing, simple farm tools, a few chickens, and one old radio.

Like most peasants in Zamboanga, they must struggle to survive, especially during the "hungry season" from December to March. By then most families have little rice left, and must subsist on thin rice gruel, wild roots or cassava, and immature bananas. Weakened by hunger, many people succumb to pneumonia and dysentery.

In the past, the Mangubat family farmed two hectares (about five acres) of rented land. They were able to grow enough rice for their own consumption and to pay the rent—one quarter of their harvest. In good years they had a small surplus to sell. Now the Mangubats work longer and harder at farming, but they do not produce enough rice to pay their debts.

Mr. Mangubat traces the problem to 1980, when he and many of his neighbors agreed to join a government-sponsored farm loan program, Masagana 99 (M99). The loan program, along with a related land reform program, are the twin foundations of the rural development strategy introduced by President Marcos after he declared martial law in the Philippines in 1972. (Although martial law was lifted in 1981, Marcos retained his decree-making powers.)

M99 was designed to increase total rice production through the use of green revolution technology: chemical fertilizers, insecticides, mechanized irrigation, and new, high-yielding varieties of rice. It was part of an effort to modernize Philippine agriculture along capitalist lines by inducing farmers to grow crops for sale and not just for subsistence.

M99 was planned with the aid of the World Bank and the U.S. government, and was promoted to farmers with the help of a New York advertising agency. To encourage the planting of hybrid M99 rice, government extension agents collected and burned local stocks of traditional rice seeds. They predicted that the new seeds would yield 99 sacks of rice per hectare, more than double what local farmers had been getting from native varieties grown without fertilizer.

Seeds of Failure

Mr. Mangubat's M99 loan consisted of cash to cover the increased cost of irrigation required by the hybrid rice. He was also given part of his loan in-kind: the new seeds, plus three sacks of fertilizer and several gallons of pesticides, which all loan recipients were required to use.

"The hybrid rice did grow faster," Mr. Mangubat explains, "but so did the weeds." The new farming methods required so much more labor that the family could plant only half their usual land area.

The Mangubat's total harvest from one hectare was just 39 sacks. This was about equal to their previous harvest from two hectares, just enough to cover living expenses and the land rent. Mr. Mangubat took on extra work as a carpenter, but he still could not repay the entire loan, and had to take out a second loan from a private lender to prepare for the next planting.

Worse, the intensive cultivation quickly exhausted the Mangubats' land. Now rice will barely grow there without the application of large amounts of fertilizer. Fertilizer prices increased 126 percent in the four years after Mr. Mangubat joined the M99 program. During the same time, the price he and other farmers got for their rice went up only 62 percent.

There is no way for the Mangubats to cut their living costs: their meals are already meager. Their main source of income is the rice they grow, but they cannot produce more rice without going deeper into debt and risking the loss of their remaining land.

Other farmers in the Philippines face the same grim dilemma. During the first four years of the M99 program, the real income of the average peasant family declined substantially, according to the World Bank's own studies. Seventy-three percent of the farmers who received M99 loans were unable to repay them.

"These programs have only helped to destroy the fertility of our soil and make our lives harder," Mr. Mangubat declares. "The only ones who have gotten anything out of M99 are the companies that sell us the fertilizer and pesticides."

Hunger Amid Bountiful Harvests

From the viewpoint of the Philippine government, the M99 program has been a great success. In some areas, irrigation of fast-growing, hybrid rice has permitted two yearly harvests instead of one. About 80 percent of Philippine rice land is now planted with high-yielding varieties.

In many cases, better-off landowners who can afford the costs of green revolution technology have taken over land that poor peasants can no longer afford to farm. Total rice production has increased by about 40 percent, and from 1977 through 1982 the country even exported rice.

But increased rice production has not meant that most Filipinos eat better. Surveys by the Philippine Ministry of Agriculture showed that the average yearly grain consumption per person decreased from 358 to 305 pounds during the first nine years of martial law. Consumption of protein-rich foods, already low, decreased even more.

Other government surveys have found that 69 percent of all Filipino children are under weight for their age because they do not get enough to eat, and that the average Filipino's diet provides insufficient amounts of every important nutrient except niacin.

The second pillar of the Marcos agricultural policy, land reform, has had similarly dismal results for poor farmers. Initiated by presidential decree in 1972, Marcos's land reform program was designed with U.S. government advice. Marcos proclaimed that by helping tenant farmers to buy the plots they till, land reform would "emancipate the Filipino farmer from bondage to the soil."

But the Marcos land reform plan was a token measure which, even if carried out completely, would apply to only 13.7 percent of the country's farm land. Many categories of land, particularly land planted in export crops, were exempted.

Only 396,000 of the estimated seven million Filipino tenant farmers are eligible to become landowners under the program. According to figures published by the Philippines Ministry of Agrarian Reform, after 10 years of land reform, fewer than one percent of the eligible farmers had actually obtained titles to the land they were tilling.

Agribusiness Bonanza

The main beneficiaries of the Marcos government's land and farming policies have been agribusiness and forestry corporations, which expanded rapidly during the 1970s. Entire villages have been uprooted to make way for logging concessions, cattle ranches, and the planting of bananas, pineapple, sugar cane, and rubber and palm oil trees. By 1980, an estimated 45 percent of the country's cultivated land was being used for these and other export crops.

The United States imports about 350 million tons of sugar, 315 million tons of coconut oil, 95 million tons of canned pineapple, and 22 million gallons of fruit juice yearly from the Philippines. The Philippines also exports about $80 million worth of fish and $100 million worth of bananas every year, mostly to Japan. While the average Filipino consumes only about 89 percent of the calories needed for adequate nutrition, the country exports about 800 calories per person per day in the form of coconut oil alone.

Many export plantations in the Philippines are American-owned, for example, the 56,000-acre Del Monte pineapple plantation on the island of Mindanao. Massey-Ferguson, the North American farm machinery company, recently acquired 12,000 acres to grow yellow corn, used mainly as food for animals and targetted by the Philippine government as a top-priority export. Other plantations and food processing plants are controlled by European, Australian, or Japanese corporations, or, in the sugar and coconut industries, by members of the Filipino elite.

Since the declaration of martial law, the full weight of the Philippine government has been placed on the side of agribusiness. In 1979, Agricultural Minister Arturo Tanco promised members of the American Chamber of Commerce in the Philippines that their ventures in the growing and marketing of agricultural products would continue to "be rewarded" by his government. "What you have done in sugar, coconut products, and rubber you can do in other agribusiness areas," Tanco said.

The Philippine constitution limits the amount of land a foreign individual or corporation may own to 2,530 acres. Marcos has helped foreign investors circumvent this restriction by granting them long-term leases on large tracts of land. A 1984 presidential decree gave to anyone who invested more than $75,000 the same rights as citizens of the Philippines to own land and remove its resources.

The export of food from the Philippines is likely to increase as a result of a new government plan, the Balanced Agro-Industrial (BAID) Strategy, adopted in 1984. The BAID plan calls for increased export of "nontraditional" food products such as mangos, papayas, citrus fruits, cacao, feed grain, and shellfish.

BAID offers tax breaks and other generous incentives to foreign investors. It includes a plan for reclassifying government-owned land to make it available for logging and export crop production, even though much of this land now is being used by peasants for subsistence farming. The hill and mountain areas to be reclassified include some of the last refuges of tribal minorities in the Philippines.

The expansion of agribusiness has already deprived many thousands of Filipino families of their homes and of the ability to grow food for themselves. There is very little undeveloped land remaining on the islands, so rural families who lose their land have nowhere else to go. Nevertheless, peasants found "squatting" on land granted to agribusiness—even land they have farmed for many generations—are often evicted at gunpoint by the military.

Peasants Call for Justice

Hard-pressed by the rising cost of farming, or facing the loss of their land, Filipino peasants are calling for change. In October 1984, on the twelfth anniversary of the Marcos Land Reform Proclamation, hundreds of thousands of peasants gathered at peaceful protest rallies throughout the islands.

Lino Mangubat and his wife were among 3,000 farmers and fishermen who assembled in the town of Dinas, Zamboanga del Sur. Many of the farmers who came to Dinas that day had risen before dawn to walk from their homes in distant villages. Most were barefoot, or wearing only simple rubber sandals, straw hats, and clean but tattered clothes.

As the marchers arrived at the rally site, the town's small sports field, they were surrounded by jeeps full of armed soldiers. Many of the peasants drew bandanas over their faces to avoid being recognized by the military. A similar demonstration in Dinas the previous month had ended with the arrest of all those who had addressed the crowd.

Despite the menacing presence of the military, the demonstrators carefully unfurled hand-lettered banners and signs that read: "Bring down food prices!", "Disarm the death squads!", "Food, not militarization!", and "We need *real* land reform!"

One by one, representatives of local farmers and fishermen's associations came forward to speak. "The big crocodiles are grabbing all our land," the president of the province-wide peasants association said. "Around here, the crocodiles are the rubber companies, the logging companies, and the mining companies. But Marcos is the biggest crocodile of them all. If we depend on him, we'll never have land of our own."

A missionary priest from New Zealand, watching from a distance, remarked: "I've been here five years, so I can understand their desperation. From parish records I've found that 70 percent of the deaths here are of children aged six or under. That has to do with landlessness. Seventy-two percent of the people own no land. Their diet consists of little but corn, and not enough of that."

As in Latin America, religious people in the Philippines have established Christian Base Communities where peasants and urban poor people meet to read scripture and discuss its application to their own problems. The consciousness-raising that takes place in these Bible study groups has inspired many poor Filipinos to organize for better living conditions.

Even when they have the backing of the church, it is an act of courage for peasants like the Mangubats to attend a rally, pursue a court case against eviction, or join a village farmers association. In the Philippines, whenever a person speaks out against the government, or takes an action that may be interpreted by the government as a challenge to its control, he or she risks arrest, torture, or assassination.

Blood in the Fields

A 1984 mission by the Geneva-based International Commission of Jurists found evidence of "widespread abuses of human rights by military and security forces, including extra-judicial killings, massacres, 'burnings', arbitrary arrests and torture . . . prevalent throughout rural areas of the Philippines." Amnesty International's 1985 Annual Report cited a "consistent pattern of gross violations" of human rights in the Philippines.

In Zamboanga del Sur, during eight months preceding the Dinas rally, at least 48 people died at the hands of government troops or secret paramilitary groups. These deaths were documented by the church-sponsored Philippine human rights organization, Task Force Detainees, during a fact-finding tour of the province.

In Zamboanga and other regions of the Southern Philippines, paramilitary terrorist groups are becoming increasingly active. These groups claim to be motivated by a sort of fundamentalist Christianity. They are known, however, for carrying out brutal executions, sometimes hacking people to death with machetes.

Amnesty International and other human rights organizations have condemned the common practice of extra-judicial killings by Philippine armed forces, known to Filipinos as "salvagings." Frequently workers and peasants are abducted on their way home from meetings or picket lines by men in uniform. Their mutilated bodies are left in conspicuous places as warnings to others.

Among other people "salvaged" have been doctors who treated people in rural areas where government control has been challenged by rebel movements, students who worked for the release of political prisoners, and church lay workers. According to the Washington-based Church Coalition for Human Rights in the Philippines, seven priests were assassinated in 1984-85. The most notorious case of "salvaging" was the airport murder of moderate opposition leader Benigno Aquino in 1983.

The Philippine government also uses legal repression to stifle opposition. Hundreds of peasants, labor organizers, and political leaders have been jailed under statutes such as Presidential Decree 1834, enacted just before the lifting of martial law and still in effect. It establishes penalties of long-term imprisonment for actions that threaten or "undermine people's faith in" the government, including being present at an anti-government meeting, creating or displaying "seditious" art, or "spreading false rumors or gossip."

Rural communities which have made organizing gains often face another type of repression. Village residents are ordered by the military to dismantle their homes and move to sites along roadsides or in towns where they can be watched more closely. This practice has been used most often on the southern island of Mindanao.

Philippine military spokesmen say the purpose of such forced moves is to bring isolated villages closer to services such as electricity, and to give the villagers greater "security." But the real purpose of the military in most cases appears to be to prevent peasant involvement with an armed rebel movement, the New People's Army (NPA).

Opponents of the government refer to the forced moving of civilians as "hamletting." The term is derived from the tactic used by the U.S. Army in South Vietnam, where peasants were required to live in "strategic hamlets" to prevent contact between them and anti-government guerillas.

Critics of "hamletting" say it is also used to remove peasants from land coveted by agribusiness, and to break up peasant organizations which might achieve too much economic or political independence. A peasant woman from Leyte, the home province of First Lady Imelda Marcos, described the experience of her village to Oxfam America staff members in October 1984:

> The soldiers came and told us we must stay away from the land behind our village because Imelda's family wanted to put a cattle ranch there. Until then we had been using that land to grow abaca (hemp).

> Then one day they came again when my neighbor was cutting wood on that land. They didn't give any warning. They killed him with a machine gun. They came to my house and strafed it. I was the only one hurt.

She lifted her skirt to show the scar on her thigh left by the bullet.

> They made us lie face down while they cooked and ate all the rice I had left. They used pieces of my house for the cooking fire. After that they made everyone in our village move into town, near their barracks.

> After we got there, their officer wanted us all to sign a paper saying that we were surrendering, and that we were NPAs (members of the New People's Army). We refused to sign because all we wanted was to keep our land.

> The next day the soldiers came back with a man from the newspaper. The officer asked us how many of us needed rice, so we all raised our hands. After that there was a picture in the newspaper of us with our hands raised. Under the picture it said that all these people who were NPAs have surrendered.

"We still can't go back to our fields," she concluded, "but now we will never surrender."

Toward Sustainable Agriculture

Increasing alienation from the government, along with the failure of its agricultural programs, is causing Filipino peasants to look in other directions for help in growing food crops. One promising approach is regenerative agriculture: nonchemical farming methods and simple technologies that use local skills and materials. . . .

In the Bicol region, where coconuts are the main crop and yearly family income averages only $330, tenant farmers have formed the Bicol Coconut Planters Association (BCPAI). BCPAI members plant small plots of sugar cane among their other crops. With the help of Oxfam America, they have built a mill to crush the cane and process its juice into cakes of hardened molasses, called sangkaka.

The machine that crushes the cane is powered by water buffalo; the molasses-making process uses coconut husks for fuel. Thus the mill needs no imported inputs except an occasional can of axle grease. BCPAI runs the mill as a cooperative; members keep some of the sangkaka for home use and sell the surplus. This way they raise their families' nutritional level as well as their income. (In the Philippines, where many people cannot get enough food to supply the minimum needed calories, consumption of this sugar product can improve their diet.) . . .

Empowerment for Survival

For peasants in the Philippines, economic self-help and political organizing go hand-in-hand. For income-generating projects like the BCPAI molasses mill to work, farmers need to share labor, information, and sometimes land, so they have to be well-organized.

Organized peasants are better able to win reductions in interest rates and land rents, as farmers in the Bicol region have done. At the same time, projects that raise rural families' incomes make them less vulnerable to economic retaliation by local landlords and moneylenders, and thus help them in their struggle for empowerment.

The movement of organized peasants is gaining momentum across the Philippines, propelled by economic crisis and the increasing militarization of the countryside. There are 33 provincial peasant associations and hundreds of local ones. In June 1985, a National Peasant Union, the KMP, was founded to take the place of the Federation of Free Farmers, a nationwide peasant organization crushed by the martial law regime in the early 1970s.

Workers on export plantations, where pay is less than $1 a day, are joining unions like the National Federation of Sugar Workers. The NFSW represents many of the 400,000 canefield and refinery workers on the island of Negros, where the sugar industry is collapsing and hunger is widespread. With the aid of a grant from Oxfam America, the NFSW is organizing laid-off workers to plant food crops on idle land loaned by sugar planters.

These peasant and farmworkers' organizations are making full use of the limited civil liberties still allowed in the Philippines. They are running training courses for farmers and organizers, publishing journals, and holding forums and demonstrations for economic reform and relief from hunger.

But in the Philippines, freedom granted by day is often denied by night. The number of death squad assassinations of peasant and labor activists is on the rise. Even elected officials who have shown sympathy for the peasant movement have been "salvaged," and many of the movement's middle-class supporters have gone into hiding or exile for fear of their lives. If the space for legal reform continues to grow smaller, the remaining legal opposition groups may be driven underground, and the peasants' struggle for economic survival could be reduced to a military question.

Selection 9.5: Declaration, 1983 International Conference on Peace and Removal of Foreign Bases

Editors' Introduction

The touchstone of the Philippine nationalism that became more intense and pervasive after the Aquino assassination was the question of the U.S. military bases. To more and more Filipinos it was becoming apparent that U.S. support for the Marcos dictatorship was motivated in large measure by concern for these bases. It was this perception that brought the Marcos dictatorship, U.S. support for that dictatorship, and U.S. bases all into the central focus of a growing nationalist consciousness.

In October 1983, an International Conference on Peace and Removal of Foreign Bases was held in Quezon City by the Anti-Bases Coalition of the Philippines. Taking place in the midst of the militant currents of resistance set in motion by the Aquino assassination, the conference was a high point in the nationalist and anti-bases movement in the Philip-

pines. It was attended by Filipinos from different walks of life and representatives from Palau, Guam, and Japan in the Pacific; Greece, Spain, and West Germany in Europe; and Canada and the United States (including the American Indian Movement) in North America. The final declaration of the conference, printed below, explicitly stated a position on the bases that was non-aligned and anti-nuclear, identifying itself with the movement for a nuclear-free Pacific.

The Declaration was read at a demonstration held during the conference in front of the U.S. Embassy in Manila by former Senator Jose W. Diokno, one of the Philippines' most consistent and principled nationalists, and conference chairperson.

Source: Declaration of the 1983 International Conference on Peace and the Removal of Foreign Bases.

WE, the participants in the 1983 International Conference on General Disarmament, World Peace and Removal of all Foreign Military Bases held in Quezon City, Philippines, on October 24 to 26, 1983, coming from North America, Europe, Asia and the Pacific,

REFLECTING UPON the consequences of the arms race, the proliferation of nuclear weapons, and the presence of foreign bases on the peoples of the world, particularly those in Third World countries in Asia and the Pacific,

HEREBY DECLARE THAT:

1. The arms race is a scourge to humanity. This is particularly true with respect to developing and deploying newer and deadlier nuclear weapons such as the Tomahawk and the SS-20. These weapons have increased not security but insecurity. The desire of the super-powers to keep pace with one another has led to a tragic waste of human life and material resources, and can end only in a war that could extinguish human, animal and plant life as we know it today on this planet.

2. The renewed tensions between the super-powers has led to the abandonment of the strategy of mutual deterrence, and the adoption of the strategies of first strike capability. This has caused them to deploy nuclear and other weapons, ready for immediate use in their own and other countries, and to establish military bases in foreign countries, test each other's will particularly in Third World countries of the Middle East and Asia. The tragic probability is that war, not of its own choosing or making, may break out in a Third World country, which will destroy it and ultimately the rest of the world.

3. We reject the concept of armed peace or nuclear deterrence and its corollaries like "nuclear war can be limited, controlled and won," "rapid deployment forces" and "first strike capability," and plans to use outer space for launching nuclear attacks. Even on the assumption that no nation would deliberately start a nuclear war, armed peace creates grave risks of such a war by accident, mistake, a misreading of the intentions or misinterpretation of the acts of a presumed enemy.

4. Armed peace is in fact war by governments on their own people. It requires governments to consume tremendous resources, manpower, time, capital and creativity in making or acquiring weapons of destruction, that soon become outmoded or obsolete and require continuous replacement. These expenditures have deprived the peoples of the world of a higher standard of living, and produced world tensions that have lowered the quality of life. They lead to the spread of militarism and the oppression of minorities, as the examples of the American Indian people and Third World communities in the United States and of the indigenous, ethnic minorities in other countries show. In the Third World particularly, as illustrated by the Philippines, more has been spent in the last decade on the military than on education and health. Had expenditures been devoted to human needs, there would be less hunger, disease, poverty and exploitation than exist today.

5. Foreign military bases are means of offense, not defense. In the Third World, they are instruments of imperialism and domination, not equality and justice among nations. The cases of Guam,

Micronesia and the Philippines clearly illustrate this. Because of U.S. military bases, the people of Guam have been kept ignorant of their right to self-determination and prevented from exercising it; and the efforts of the people of Palau and Micronesia to exercise that right have been manipulated and frustrated. In the Philippines, military bases were imposed upon the people as a condition of the recognition of their independence, though there was no external threat to the nation's security. They continue though no such threat exists today. In the 60s, the vague threat cited was the People's Republic of China; today it is the USSR. But the one admitted purpose that has not changed is that the bases serve to project U.S. military power into the Indian Ocean and the Middle East to protect and to "control the sea lanes . . . to the rich resources of the East Indies." That was said in 1969. Today, they serve, as the Commander of Clark Air Base said in January 1983, to "provide the punch to protect our (U.S.) trade initiatives and economic interests."

6. Foreign military bases do not deter aggression, they provoke it. The presence of military bases of one super-power in a country leads to the establishment of similar bases by the other super-power in a neighboring country. Thus, U.S. naval and air bases in Subic and Clark Air Base in the Philippines have led to the use by the USSR of naval and air bases in Cam Ranh Bay and Danang in Vietnam.

7. Foreign military bases lead to the militarization of the societies of both the host country and the country operating the bases. The pretext for such bases is mutual defense. This requires that arms be supplied to the host country and this, in turn, requires increased development and production of arms by the dominant country. As a result, the temptation is great in other countries to solve political, economic and social problems by military repression rather than by democratic dialogue and consensus. In Japan, for example, military spending has increased greatly and the military mentality is becoming dominant because of the pressure of the U.S. government on the Japanese government to share the burdens of the domination of Asia. In the Philippines, in the early 70s, there was a clamor for reform, nationalist in character, that demanded among other things the dismantling of the U.S. bases. To quell these demands, martial law was imposed. After martial law, U.S. military and economic aid more than doubled. Martial law resulted in the total dismantling of the institutions of democracy in the Philippines—an independent Judiciary, a freely elected Legislature, a free press, and freedom of assembly and expression. They have resulted in unjustified arrests, torture, unexplained disappearances and extra-legal executions, the most prominent and one of the more recent being the assassination of the opposition leader, Senator Benigno S. Aquino, Jr., while under custody of the military.

8. Foreign military bases prevent independent economic development of Third World countries which host such bases. Such development requires changes—often fundamental—in political, economic and social structures. These changes are opposed by those in power in the host country, and they are supported by the foreign power having bases there. As a result, foreign military bases inevitably support the status quo. Guam and the Philippines are cases in point. In the Philippines, the status quo has been characterized by an outmoded and archaic free wheeling capitalist system, functioning within the context of an equally outmoded and archaic free trade and free enterprise ideology. This system has perpetuated a social order marked by extreme concentration of wealth and a political economy that is grossly underdeveloped and dependent on the United States.

Prior to martial law, Congress and an ongoing Constitutional Convention were in distinct and irreversible process of overhauling the socio-economic system. Such a process required a package of fundamental changes being demanded by a rising nationalist and anti-imperialist movement.

The changes clearly called for the dismantlement not only of U.S. economic and financial monopoly in the Philippines, but also of the military bases.

As mentioned, this challenge could be met, and aborted, only by dismantling the institutions of political democracy through which the reformist and nationalist movements were voicing and accomplishing their demands.

9. Foreign military bases distort the social and cultural values of the host country. This distortion is particularly virulent in the Third World. Foreign bases foster smuggling, drug abuse, and the exploitation of women and children. They create a psychology of import-oriented consumerism that is not only wasteful and inappropriate for the Third World but which also deepens their economic dependence.

10. The arms race, nuclear weapons and foreign military bases violate the moral sense of humanity. They are condemned by the religious of the world and by all peace-loving peoples.

IN THE LIGHT of these conclusions, We resolve:

1. To maximize our individual and collective efforts for general disarmament, and particularly for the total abolition of nuclear weapons.

2. As steps towards such goals, to call for: (a) the immediate ban of all nuclear testing, particularly in Micronesia and the South Pacific; [a ban on] the production of nuclear weapons; and the denuclearization of Asia and the Pacific; (b) the immediate dismantling of all foreign military bases in Asia and the Pacific and the recall of all foreign troops to their homeland, in order to achieve a nuclear free, self-determined and non-aligned Asia and Pacific.

3. To call on the super powers categorically and unequivocally to abandon the preventive strategy of first strike.

4. To engage in educational campaigns, beginning in the home and the school, concerning the immorality, the risks and consequences of nuclear weapons, the arms race, foreign military bases, militarism and imperialism.

5. To encourage the creation and growth of peace movements in Asia and the Pacific, and establish closer and better coordination of efforts among peace movements all over the world.

6. To associate ourselves with the cause of the people of Guam, Palau, Micronesia, New Caledonia, Tahiti, other South Pacific countries, the Philippines and all other oppressed peoples of the world.

UNANIMOUSLY APPROVED AND ADOPTED this 26th day of October 1983, at Quezon City, Philippines.

—Jose W. Diokno, Conference Chairperson

Selection 9.6: The Convenors' Statement

Editors' Introduction

On December 26, 1984, at a meeting in the home of Corazon Aquino, wife of the assassinated Benigno Aquino, Jr., a statement of political principles was signed by the three convenors of the meeting, Corazon Aquino, Jaime Ongpin, prominent business executive, and former Senator Lorenzo Tañada. (Hence the document became known as the Convenors' Statement.) The statement was signed as well by nine leaders of the opposition to Marcos, all of whom were regarded as possible presidential candidates in the next election. These were Jose Diokno, Raul Manglapus (though still in the U.S. at the time), Ambrosio Padilla, Ramon Mitra, Jovito Salonga, Rafael Salas, Aquilino Pimentel, Jr., Teofisto Guingona, and Agapito Aquino, brother of Benigno Aquino. Only two such potential candidates refused to sign: former Senator

Salvador Laurel, Chair of UNIDO, the largest coalition of opposition parties, and Vice-Chair Eva Estrada Kalaw.

While the document is interesting as a general statement of principles, its call for the removal of U.S. bases from the Philippines is especially noteworthy. The fact that the great majority of outstanding opposition leaders of moderate political persuasion signed this statement indicates the growth of nationalist sentiment against the foreign military presence. The document also serves to correct the impression that might arise from public statements of the Reagan administration, namely that it has been only the Communists and the NPA in the Philippines who want to see the bases go.

Source: *Philippine News* [San Francisco], January 2-8, 1985.

Whereas, it has become imperative and a duty that all who are opposed to the Marcos authoritarian regime join forces to restore the freedom and sovereignty of the Filipino people; and

Whereas, all of us are united under a common cause, guided by the following fundamental convictions, values and objectives:

1. Respect for freedom of conscience and religion.

This means that freedom of religion and conscience will be respected and protected and no one will be excluded from active participation in the life of the nation because of one's beliefs.

2. Belief in the inalienable dignity of the individual human person.

This means that every human being has certain inalienable rights which the State cannot deprive him of; that the object of socio-economic development is human development; and that the State exists for the people and not the individual for the State.

Thus,

2.1—the Bill of Rights enshrined in our 1935 Constitution which guarantees, among others, due process, free speech, the right of information, free press, freedom of assembly, freedom to be secure from unreasonable searches and seizures, freedom of movement and to decide one's domicile, must obtain not merely in our statute books and jurisprudence but in the very conduct of government and its officials and the latter's interaction with the citizenry;

2.2—violators of human rights will be subject to immediate prosecution; and

2.3—general and unconditional amnesty will be granted to all political detainees and all suspected political offenders.

3. Belief in developing the fullness of our nationhood and in the supremacy of national interest.

This means belief in the promotion of love of country and of culture and an affirmation that in no case should national interest be sacrificed to foreign interests and that the Filipino must be the sole determinant of the nation's political, economic and cultural life and the principal beneficiary of the national patrimony.

Thus, the freedom of the nation from any form of economic, cultural, and political domination or interference by the government of any foreign power or by any international institution or group will be safeguarded.

A self-determined and self-reliant course of economic, cultural, social, technological, and political development will be pursued in order to enhance higher income for all, an expanding domestic market, appropriate basic industries, effective technology, the use of Filipino creativity and resourcefulness, equity in the use of resources and in the distribution of the fruits of development. All economic and financial agreements will be periodically and openly reviewed to the end that the welfare of our people will not be sacrificed to satisfy foreign economic and financial interests whether they be governmental entities or transnational corporations.

An educational system will be established which provides opportunity of education for all and which will promote our national identity, desirable values, critical thinking, creativity, scientific research, the development of technology and responsible citizenship.

The Philippines will seek to actively cooperate with its neighbors to make ASEAN [Association of Southeast Asian Nations], in particular, and Southeast Asia, in general, a zone of freedom and peace, free of all nuclear weapons and free from the domination of all foreign powers. As a consequence, foreign military bases on Philippine territory must be removed.

4. Belief that ownership of the principal means of production must be diffused and income equitably distributed to promote development, alleviate poverty and ensure the rational utilization of resources.

This means that ownership is stewardship; that material wealth is not just for the welfare of the owner but also for the welfare of all; that the accumulation of profit must not ignore the requirements of social justice; that ostentatious display of wealth is to be deplored; and that the use of resources must be for the benefit of all, especially the underprivileged.

Thus,

4.1—Social structures that perpetuate the oppression of the poor and the dispossessed will be eliminated;

4.2—Effective cooperatives will be encouraged;

4.3—Free trade unionism will be encouraged and the right to organize, to picket, and to strike will be vigourously protected; and

4.4—An effective land reform program truly beneficial to the underprivileged will be vigorously and honestly pursued.

5. Belief in free, honest and orderly elections. This means that free and honest elections will be assured and safeguarded. Thus, there will be vigorous resistance to all forms of authoritarianism.

Thus,

5.1—The formulation and popular ratification of a new Constitution, within eighteen months after the new leadership is in place will be accomplished.

5.2—The new Constitution will provide for:

5.2.1—New institutions that will lodge the power to decide as close to the people as possible.

5.2.2—representation for all sectors and classes of society in order to monitor the performance of government.

5.2.3—a government elected by direct vote of the people, with specific tenures.

5.2.4—an independent, capable and honest judiciary.

5.2.5—an adequate system of checks and balances and of public accountability.

5.2.6—the supremacy of civilian over military authority.

Belief in a pluralistic society. This means that the new leadership will be committed to respect the freedom of all non-violent philosophies and programs; to trust the capacity of the people to freely choose what is best for them and to honor their choice, even if it is not ours.

The Communist Party will be legalized.

All groups who, given the prevailing oppressive conditions, have resorted to armed struggle, will be given an opportunity to integrate themselves within the context of the post-Marcos societal/governmental framework. Thus, the new leadership group will, within a reasonable period, undertake negotiations with the leadership of the armed struggle to the end that obstacles to unity may be peacefully resolved.

7. Belief that leadership means service to our people and accountability to them.

This means that commitment to service is working *with* and *for* the people, especially the poor and oppressed.

To this end,

7.1—An effective system of recall of any elective/appointive public official will be provided for, paving the way for an earlier replacement or reaffirmation of the people's confidence in the said public official.

7.2—The social cancer of graft and corruption, public and private, will be addressed so that there will be a truly just system of public service.

Therefore, we the undersigned, hereby bind ourselves and resolve to unite our strength in order to achieve the foregoing principles and objectives as soon as possible.

Selection 9.7: "A Woman's Place is in the Struggle," Brenda J. Stoltzfus

Editors' Introduction

Women have always been a significant force within the Philippine opposition, but—except for the short-lived organization MAKIBAKA before martial law—it was not until recent years that women began to organize as women. In response to the fraudulent parliamentary elections of 1978, Concerned Women of the Philippines was formed, an organization primarily of middle-to-upper class women united around a moderate opposition program. This was followed by organizations of women professionals, youth, urban poor, peasant, and urban workers: PILIPINA, Center for Women's Resources, Third World Movement Against the Exploitation of Women, KALAYAAN, SAMAKANA, SAMAKA, MAKASAMA, KMK, BAGONG PILIPINAS.

With the assassination of Benigno Aquino, there was an upsurge in women's political activity. An all women's protest demonstration against the Marcos regime was held; a new militant women's organization—WOMB (Women for the Ouster of Marcos and Boycott)—was established; and coalitions and congresses of women's organizations began to form. The most significant of these coalitions was the militant General Assembly Binding Women for Reforms, Integrity, Equality, Leadership, and Action—GABRIELA—founded in March 1984.

GABRIELA's membership primer stated its four major principles:

One, the women of GABRIELA are united and determined to restore democracy. They join forces with men in opposing, at whatever cost, the dictatorial rule imposed upon the entire Filipino people.

Two, as part of the nation's productive force, the women of GABRIELA adhere to actively and decisively work for the attainment of a genuinely sovereign and independent Philippines where women will be true and equal partners of men in developing and preserving national patrimony.

Three, recognizing the strength of the majority of the Filipino people, the women of GABRIELA believe that it is their primary responsibility to enhance the development of women in the grassroots and oppose any moves that dehumanize our less privileged sisters. We resolve to support the struggles of women workers, peasants, and urban poor settlers to attain their economic well being.

Four, national liberation is incomplete without women's liberation. The women of GABRIELA are determined to advance the women's movement that seeks to eliminate all forms that oppress women, particularly structures which relegate women to an inferior and lower-status position and restrict women to fully and actively participate in all spheres of endeavor.

What follows is an account by a U.S. feminist of activities sponsored by GABRIELA on the first anniversary of its birth. Brenda Stoltzfus works for the Mennonite Central Committee, a church organization doing justice and human rights work in the Philippines.

Source: Brenda J. Stoltzfus, "A Woman's Place is in the Struggle," March 30, 1985.

Gabriela Silang was a Filipina General in the revolution against Spanish colonialism in the Philippines. She is a heroine to many. Last year an umbrella women's organization was formed, taking her name which stands for: General Assembly Binding Women for Reforms, Integrity, Equality, Leadership and Action. GABRIELA brings together various women's organizations from all over the Philippines. March 1-8, 1985, GABRIELA organized a women's week in Manila which marked the end of the UN decade on women and celebrated the first anniversary of the organization. Living in Manila, I was able to attend many of the events and would like to share some glimpses of the week and the women's movement here with women elsewhere.

The final event remains foremost in my mind not only because it is most recent. More importantly, because I, as a feminist in the USA, never had to face what women here faced on March 8, and face repeatedly. The final event was a march to Mendiola. Mendiola is the bridge to Malacañang, the Presidential Palace. Marching to Mendiola has become a symbolic statement of protest against the abuses of the present government and has been the scene of several violent dispersals with tear gas, truncheons, and water cannons. This march was unique. The marchers were all women. Women from all sectors of society, joining the struggle for justice as Filipino people with their struggle for justice as women.

Malacañang was prepared as usual. As we approached the bridge, we saw the water cannons behind the barbed wire. On a side street were the truncheon bearers. Something about them was different. The truncheons were carried by women. They were anti-riot policewomen. Rows and rows of women wearing helmets and carrying shields and truncheons. Obviously a psychological ploy. "Divide and rule"? If the rally had to be violently dispersed, it would be women beating women. There were a few rows of men at the back of the ranks. Reinforcements? In case the women could not handle the job? Several rallyists negotiated with the police while the rest gathered in front of the barbed wire for a presentation of songs, drama, and speeches. A large circle of women around the outside kept men out.

It was a peaceful demonstration and a peaceful dispersal. Yet, the threat of violence sent chills through me. Not because the visible threat looked so horrifying, though it was formidable. Rather, I was well aware of what the Marcos dictatorship is capable. I had heard the stories. Most recently, the stories about and from women. Women who had been salvaged (summarily executed), detained, tortured, raped. . . . One event of the week was "A Tribute to Women Martyrs." An evening of stories, pictures, and songs in memory of women who had been killed by the military, or had disappeared, which generally means the same. Strong women were recognized and remembered. Liza Balando was a Rubberworld union organizer who refused to remain silent about the workers' situation. She was shot on May 1, 1971 at a rally. Jennifer (Jing Jing) Carino, a tribal woman who did political work while taking care of her child alone, was violently killed at 26 along with her child. And Nilda, who began her political work at 9 years old, was killed by the military at 13.

One speaker, Fely Aquino, a lawyer who hears many stories from her clients, clearly and articulately connected the perpetuation of militarization to a patriarchal ideology of women as threats to public order. To quote loosely, "Torture and sexual violence against women cuts across all class lines. Sexual violence is seen as the key to controlling women political prisoners. Women who take control of their lives by political activism are often targets. Torture is essentially structural, done by a regime which needs to stay in power unchallenged." Women are challenging that regime and are punished for it. Women

political detainees routinely suffer sexual violence as a part of their interrogation, and rape is used to obtain information from the woman herself or from a
husband, father, or son who is forced to watch. I sat listening to a woman give
hints for survival in prison and tell of a horrifying investigation by the NBI
[Philippine National Bureau of Investigation]. I listened to a little girl sing a
song in honor of her mother who is in prison. I listened to another tell of four
years in solitary confinement. I wanted to weep and cry out my rage that such
things should or could happen. I wanted to weep my shame for what my
county does here. I wanted to find some way of joining the struggle to end
such abuse.

A banner on display during the week read: "A Woman's Place is in the
Struggle." This paraphrase of the saying we all know too well illustrates the
way Filipino women have integrated their struggles. The struggle against
male domination, the struggle of the Filipino people against a U.S.-backed
dictatorship, and the struggle of poor people against the structures which keep
them poor are both separate and unified struggles. Fe Arriola spoke of this
integration in the conference opening address,

> Women do not form an isolated category that can be placed apart
> from society as a whole. Women are distributed across the class
> spectrum, and it is this, their different class positions, rather than
> their shared sex that finally determines their basic and varied politi-
> cal allegiances. Thus there can be no single women's movement in
> the Philippines united solely on the basis of gender, to the negation
> of class. The women's movement must first take up the needs of the
> most oppressed and exploited among us. Thus the struggle for the
> freedom of all women is inseparable from the struggle of the
> working classes and from global struggles of peoples the world
> over fighting racism and imperialism.

Women of GABRIELA point to the U.S.-Marcos dictatorship, as the
government here is commonly referred to, as their principle enemy. An
example of why this is the case is the current economic conditions. The high
inflation, high peso-dollar exchange rate, and ever-increasing foreign debts
have resulted in greater poverty. As in other countries, statistics generally fail
to identify those who suffer the most. Women and children. The Philippine
economy is closely tied to the U.S. through multinational corporations, a
corrupt government which the U.S. continues to support monetarily and
militarily, and the IMF [International Monetary Fund]. Hence, Filipino
women work against their own subjugation by working to dismantle the
present regime.

The women's movement here actually emerged as women became politically active and involved in the general protest movements. A few women
began banding together during Martial Rule which began in 1972. Two
months after the assassination of Sen. Benigno S. Aquino on August 21, 1983,
several grass-roots organizations held an all-women's rally to protest the
Marcos regime. Soon after, several women's groups with a political orienta-

tion took shape and, in March 1984, GABRIELA was formed as a coalition of the various politically active women's organizations throughout the country.

A blatant manifestation of the oppression of women and the exploitation of Filipino people is the immense problem of prostitution. Several symposiums addressed the problem, identifying root causes and connections, and searching for responses. Some of the root causes named were: economic deterioration; internal neocolonial attitudes of men and women; government acceptance and encouragement; the presence of the U.S. bases; and the tourist industry. The two largest naval and air force bases outside the U.S. are in the Philippines. Women from poor rural areas flock to Manila, Olongapo (site of the naval base), and Angeles (site of the air force base) in search of work. With the economy growing steadily worse, work is usually not to be found. Prostitution is the only alternative. These women who are victims of poverty resulting largely from foreign domination end up in cities where much of the economy revolves around a "Flesh Trade" catering to foreigners. The problem is economic and political rather than moral. The struggle of the Filipino people as a whole and the liberation of women go hand in hand.

As I listened, observed, and participated in the events of the week, I remembered the rhetoric I so often heard in the States. The rhetoric of Sisterhood. In one workshop I attended, the ideology of bonds between women automatically transcending "First World"-"Third World" injustice was in question. "First World" women are also the oppressors. The connections with other "Third World" women were more clear. Connections with women in Latin American countries, for example, who have also suffered under militaristic states supported by the U.S. Yet, even as I was aware of my identity as oppressor, I was also aware of the all-too-familiar themes I heard. Unequal pay for equal work. Poor women suffering the most. Women treated as sexual objects. The dichotomy of images: Virgin Mary or Cursed Eve. And, women internalizing the ideal of becoming a housewife with no other options.

I have a friend here in Manila. She is ten years old. Her family is quite poor. They have no house, but she is able to go to school, unlike some of the children in her community. Each time I see her, each time she hugs me, each time she smiles and waves good-bye, I wonder about her future . . .

Selection 9.8: The Military Reform Movement, Marites Danguilan-Vitug

Editors' Introduction

In the following selection Philippine journalist Marites Danguilan-Vitug gives an account of a loose grouping of reform-minded officers of the Phi-

lippine military that was established in February 1985, a few months after the release of the report of the Agrava Commission implicating General Ver in the Aquino assassination. The network seems to have had the double aim of purging the Philippine military of corruption and cronyism and of improving combat effectiveness against the New People's Army.

Two features emerge from this account: the sympathetic attention Defense Minister Enrile and Acting Chief of Staff Fidel Ramos evidently gave this group from the beginning; and the encouragement the group gave to questioning orders from above when necessary, rather than blindly following them. These features were to become significant later [see selections 10.6 and 10.7 below].

Source: Marites Danguilan-Vitug, "Young Philippine Officers Press for Reform in the Military," *Christian Science Monitor*, May 8, 1986, pp. 15-16.

The Philippine military is facing a strong demand for change from its young officers. The armed forces have become unsettled by the erosion of the military's credibility, alleged internal corruption, charges of mismanagement of resources, and a system of promotion the officers call "unfair."

Col. Hernani Figueroa, the leader of the reform group, said Tuesday that the movement had no intention of undermining the government, committing unlawful acts, or doing anything to subvert the military's chain of command.

The reform movement was designed by several colonels in February to work peaceful and legally for change. They say they want the armed forces cleansed of "undesirables," enforcement of a merit system of promotion, imposition of a "high standard of discipline," and restoration of camaraderie.

Leaders of the movement say it was started by a group of graduates from the Philippine Military Academy, the premier military institution in the country. They claim that they have already reached reservists and enlisted men not only in metropolitan Manila but also in other provinces.

Esteem for the Philippine military sank low after October 1984, when a Fact-Finding Board accused the chief of staff, Gen. Fabian Ver, and other officers and men of participating in the 1983 assassination of opposition leader Benigno Aquino Jr. Morale among the Army officers also suffered.

Leaders of the movement who met with acting chief of staff Lt. Gen. Fidel Ramos on April 20 say they were promised action. In return, they assured General Ramos they would not sanction a *coup d'etat* and would abide by the military chain of command. Ramos has temporarily taken over from General Ver, who is accused as an accessory in the Aquino murder and is currently on leave while on trial.

Defense Minister Juan Ponce Enrile told reporters Monday that the movement "does not intend to undermine society, government, or [the] presidency." Mr. Enrile said he and Ramos have discussed the activities of the group with President Ferdinand Marcos. So far, however, there has been no response from the President.

"We are not politically motivated," one Navy officer says. "We do not want to be involved in a power struggle. All we seek are reforms in the military."

Some civilians welcome the concept of the reform movement. "It's good that men in the military are concerned about the welfare of the country," says businessman Jose Concepcion. "We need professional soldiers."

Other civilians, however, fear the movement could be used as a vehicle to seize government power.

Some high-ranking military officers also fear the movement will stage a coup within the military if an unpopular chief of staff is installed, one military officer says.

But members of the movement deny the possibility of a coup within the military.

"We merely want to return the AFP [Armed Forces of the Philippines] to the center. It has been pushed to the right. . . . And it is very repressive," one Air Force intelligence officer says.

It is difficult to assess the strength of the reform movement. Its leaders want to keep the membership "loose" and the organization "unstructured," and plan to remain unidentified. Their reason: They don't want to be squashed by those affected by the movement—namely high-ranking officers who have benefited from the way the AFP has been run in terms of wealth and promotion.

The leaders of the movement say they do not gauge their success in terms of numbers.

"We'd rather have 50 committed men than a thousand who are not," a colonel says.

For them, an indicator of effectiveness would be an improvement in morale—which could then be translated into combat effectiveness.

At present, the military is perceived to be losing ground in both combat effectiveness and the propaganda battle.

Recently, the underground National Democratic Front—an umbrella organization composed of communists and other left-wing groups—held its first press conference. A week later, rebel priest Conrado Balweg, who is sought by the military, was interviewed by journalists in the mountains of Luzon Island, northern Philippines.

Official statistics show that the majority of the combat initiatives come from the guerillas.

The movement's main activities are meetings and "education sessions."

Usually, the members discuss current issues and the role of the AFP, and reassess the response of the entire military organization to present national problems, as well as their individual responses.

"We look inward. It is self-criticism, in a way," one officer says.

Supporters say the movement is in the "awareness stage," where officers and men discuss the "unhealthy" state of affairs of the armed forces. Men are encouraged to question not only what they perceive to be irregularities but also orders which traditionally are always obeyed.

"An order is no longer an order. We want it explained," says an army officer.

So far, they say, two generals have attended their meetings "to listen."

Selection 9.9: The Growth of the New People's Army, U.S. Senate Intelligence Committee

Editor's Introduction

In November 1985 the Staff of the Senate Select Committee on Intelligence issued a report on the situation in the Philippines. Printed below are excerpts from this report that have to do with the growth of the New People's Army. While the report saw the poverty in the countryside in large part responsible for this growth, it also laid considerable blame on the Marcos government. Marcos's loss of credibility following the Aquino assassination and military abuses against civilians, according to the report, had brought recruits to the New People's Army.

Source: Committee Print, *The Philippines: A Situation Report*, Staff Report to the Senate Select Committee on Intelligence, U.S. Senate, November 1, 1985, pp. 1, 4, 5, 7, 8.

Executive Summary

The United States has major political and strategic interests at stake in the Philippines. As the former colonial power, the United States is probably identified more closely with the Philippines than with any other Asian country. In addition, the United States maintains major air and naval facilities at Clark Field and Subic Bay. The post-1975 Soviet military presence in Vietnam has given the two bases a new importance as the southern anchor of American power in Asia. From Clark and Subic, U.S. naval and air operations extend westward as far as the Persian Gulf.

American interests are imperiled by a rapidly growing Communist insurgency that threatens the 20-year rule of Ferdinand Marcos and aims to install a Marxist, anti-U.S. regime. U.S. concern is shared by Manila's Southeast Asian neighbors, who see Philippine stability and the U.S. bases as crucial to the overall security of the region.

The Communist-led New People's Army (NPA) has grown from a minor presence in the 1970s to a number now estimated at over 30,000 armed *regular and irregular guerillas*. [*Regulars* are members of full-time, mobile guerilla units. *Irregulars* are part-time fighters who stay close to their home villages.]

The NPA in conjunction with the Communist Party of the Philippines (CPP) *controls or is contesting control* of settlements inhabited by at least 10 million people. The military initiative clearly rests with the NPA. It has supplied its guerillas almost entirely with weapons captured, and occasionally purchased, from the Philippine Armed Forces.

The recent rapid growth of the CPP/NPA is attributable to its skillful exploitation of a growing catalog of popular grievances against the Marcos regime.

Political and economic power are monopolized at the top by a small oligarchy, while at the bottom the mass of Filipinos live in poverty without real input into the political process. A few favored Marcos cronies have been given control of large agricultural and industrial monopolies that dominate the economy. They retain their favored position by demonstrations of loyalty to the President and financial support for his political machine. Political corruption and human rights abuses, particularly by the Armed Forces, have fueled popular resentment. The 1983 assassination of President Marcos's strongest political opponent, which the Agrava Commission concluded was committed by Philippine military personnel, greatly hastened the decline in popular support for the regime while stimulating recruitment for the NPA. . . .

The Insurgency

The origins of the present insurgency can be traced to 1968 when a group of Maoist students left the University of the Philippines and linked up with the remnants of a Huk guerilla band to form the New People's Army. Their objective was an armed revolution using a "peoples war" strategy developed and implemented by Mao Tse-tung. They suffered a number of setbacks at the hands of the Philippine Armed Forces in the 1970s and remained little more than an irritant throughout most of the decade. During this period the Government's attention was focused on a Muslim insurgency in the south. Meanwhile, the NPA learned by trial and error and gradually strengthened its organizational base. By the 1980s, they were entrenched on all major islands and operating in most provinces.

The NPA insurgency differs from that of the Huks in a number of respects. Whereas the Huks were geographically concentrated in central Luzon, the NPA has established itself throughout the Philippines. The Huks' appeal was based on age-old agrarian problems. The roots and causes of the NPA insurgency are more varied, including economic deprivation, social injustice, Government corruption and abuse of power, and the decrepitude of existing public institutions. Consequently, the NPA has already become a far more formidable force than the Huks ever were.

In the 2 years since the Aquino assassination, the NPA has expanded so rapidly that it now poses a credible threat to the survival of the Philippine Government. From a total force of a few thousand armed guerillas in 1980, the NPA has grown to probably over 15,000 regulars and a somewhat larger number of part-time irregulars. These forces are fighting on as many as 60 fronts around the country, including occasional company level (200-300 men) operations. Some level of NPA activity now exists in almost all of the country's 73 provinces.

The NPA is the military arm of the Communist Party of the Philippines, which has an estimated membership of at least 30,000. The party controls or is contesting control of settlements inhabited by at least 10 million people—out of a total population of 53 million. In some areas, notably in Davao on the island of Mindanao, the party has begun to establish a significant presence in the cities.

Communist long-term efforts to politicize the rural population against the Government are increasingly paying dividends. New guerilla fronts are being formed regularly, and the number of villages falling under Communist control has escalated rapidly since mid-1983. In southern Mindanao, for example, where the CPP/NPA is very active, conservative estimates indicate the Communists have more than doubled the number of villages they control since the Aquino assassination in 1983.

The level of insurgent activity nationwide has been increasing steadily over the last decade, with the most dramatic growth occurring since 1980. Last year, a vast majority of the more than 5,000 violent incidents were initiated by the NPA. Even discounting the 1,300 ballot box snatchings that occurred during elections in 1984, there were 9 times as many violent incidents in 1984 than 10 years earlier and 50 percent more than in 1983.

NPA units nationwide now routinely attack Government forces. These include 100- to 300-man assaults on poorly defended armed forces garrisons and economic and strategic targets. Despite recent Government sweep operations in Mindanao and northern Luzon, the NPA—not the armed forces—still initiates most of the military actions. Many NPA attacks on military outposts are intended to acquire weapons. By the end of 1983 the NPA claimed to have obtained 20,000 weapons, including machineguns and grenade launchers, in this fashion. Each year the number of weapons captured has increased. In the first 5 months of 1985, the NPA captured more than in all of 1984. . . .

Soviet Interest

The CPP/NPA is an indigenous Philippine movement. At the beginning in the 1960s, it received ideological inspiration plus some training, political, and material support from the People's Republic of China. However, by 1975, the Maoist strategy of relying on armed struggle to create revolutionary conditions in the countryside had proven ineffective. Further, Hanoi's postwar alliance with the USSR and the permanent presence of Soviet forces in Vietnam caused China to focus on improving its relations with the non-Communist governments of Southeast Asia. Assistance to Communist insurgencies, including the NPA, was terminated. In 1976 an NPA leader stated flatly that "we are not Maoists." With the Chinese connection severed, the NPA relied almost entirely on weapons captured from Philippine Government forces. This has remained true up to the present.

Until the late 1970s, there was apparently no significant contact between Moscow and the CPP. By the end of the decade, ties were established between unions affiliated with the Soviet-controlled World Federation of Trade Unions and the CPP/NPA's labor front, the Kilusang Mayo Uno. There is no convincing evidence that the Soviet Union has provided funding for the CPP. Some external funding for CPP front groups has apparently come from leftist and social democratic organizations, particularly in Europe. However, the CPP/NPA is still essentially supplied and financed from domestic sources. . . .

[T]he CPP/NPA is very much a home grown movement and its leadership will probably be hesitant to become dependent on the USSR for arms and funding if it can avoid doing so.

Selection 9.10: Increasing Terror,
Sr. Mariani C. Dimaranan, CFIC

Editors' Introduction

The Marcos dictatorship responded to the growth of popular resistance following the Aquino assassination with increased repression. The following excerpts from a report by Sister Mariani Dimaranan, chairperson of Task Force Detainees, indicate that there were increases in the number of arrests, extra-judicial killings, and disappearances beginning in 1983. Reports of the Task Force Detainees on the civil rights abuses of

the Marcos regime have been widely regarded as credible and authoritative.

Source: Sister Mariani C. Dimaranan, CFIC, "The Human Rights Situation and Social Consequences of the Crisis in the Philippines," a paper presented at the Conference on the Political and Economic Crisis in the Philippines, October 4-6, 1985, sponsored by the Transnational Institute, Amsterdam, The Netherlands.

A survey of the human rights situation in the Philippines in the last two-and-a-half years defines these new trends: 1. There has been an alarming increase in cases of political arrest and detention, torture, extra-judicial killings (also called "salvaging" in the Philippines), and kidnapings and disappearances; 2. there has been a growing tendency to victimize not only peasants, workers, urban poor residents, youth and students, but also a growing number of journalists, clergymen, intellectuals, professionals, and businessmen; and 3. there has been a marked increase in human rights violations related to the counter-insurgency program of the Marcos government directed against New People's Army (NPA) guerillas and their sympathizers, particularly in the countryside.

Some figures are significant and in order.

Arrest and detention: According to Task Force Detainees reports, a total of 11,270 persons have been arrested and detained for political reasons from 1977 to 1983. Unofficial reports say that at least 70,000 people have been arrested and detained since martial law was imposed in September 1972. TFD has documented that from 1977 to June this year, a total of 17,723 persons have been arrested and detained.

TFD data show that in 1983, 2,088 persons were arrested and detained. In 1984, 3,038 persons were arrested and detained, or an increase of 48 percent from the previous year total. [Based on incomplete reports; see Table 1 for more complete data—eds.]

The most common causes of arrest noted in fact-finding mission reports were suspicion of the detainee's membership in the New People's Army or his knowledge of or support for the rebels.

From January to June this year, 2,351 were confirmed arrested. A total of 547 persons remain in various prisons in the country, excluding those held in secret military safehouses, at the end of last June.

Torture: In two separate reports issued in 1976 and 1982, Amnesty International focused on the Philippines and came out with strong indictments of the Marcos government for employing torture and other forms of maltreatment on political detainees.

In 1983, at least 644 cases of torture were confirmed. There were 449 other torture cases reported in 1984. In the first half of this year, partial reports (no figures for Luzon, the Philippines' biggest island), TFD listed 341 cases of torture.

A TFD report described several favorite and common methods of torture used by the Philippine military: the "water cure," the "telephone" in which the ears of the victim or detainee are simultaneously hit with the hands thus causing the rupture of eardrums in some cases; the "wet submarine" in which the victim's head is submerged in water, often in a toilet bowl with feces; Russian roulette in which a single dud bullet is placed in a revolver and then pointed at the victim's head to scare him; and electrocution, usually applied on the victim's private parts and genitals. Other forms of torture are sexual abuse, beatings, the use of handcuffs and manacles on political prisoners, and other actions causing indignities and mental and emotional dislocation. . . .

Extra-judicial Killings: This is often called "salvaging" in the Philippine media, quite contrary to the literal meaning of the word which is to save or to rescue. The term now refers to the secret liquidation or execution of a person without any judicial sanction whatsoever. The "salvaged" victim disappears after being arrested by security and military forces, and is later found dead some days later, his body bearing evidence of torture.

TFDP has documented a total of 2,255 cases of extra-judicial killings from 1973 to June 1985. Of this total, 321 cases were reported in 1981; 210 cases in 1982; 369 cases in 1983; 557 cases in 1984; and 219 cases for the first half of this year. . . .

Disappearances: TFDP has noted a big number of cases of involuntary disappearances in the last several years. This may be an indication that with the growing strength of the anti-dictatorship movement, the government has been finding it more difficult to justify political arrests and detentions. In typical cases of disappearances, the victims are arrested without witnesses and never found again. Those arrested are sometimes held "incommunicado" in military "safehouses" and may later reappear in detention centers. In other instances, the victims are summarily executed in secret and their bodies never found.

TFDP has documented 334 disappearances from 1977 to 1983. Our reports listed 42 cases in 1982; 145 cases in 1983; 137 cases (partial and with incomplete figures for Mindanao) in 1984 [see Table 3 for more complete data—eds.]. For the first six months of 1985, we have already documented 110 cases of disappearances.

Table 1
Number of Arrests from 1977—June 1985

Year	Metro-Manila	Luzon	Visayas	Mindanao	Total
1977	414	345	214	378	1,351
1978	320	202	193	905	1,620
1979	265	183	111	1,402	1,961
1980	170	125	141	526	962
1981	52	304	255	766	1,377
1982	226	795	76	814	1,911
1983	185	152	108	1,643	2,088
1984	599	375	403	2,725	4,102
June 1985	482	253	448	1,168	2,351
Total	**2,713**	**2,734**	**1,949**	**10,327**	**17,723**

Source: TFD

Table 2
Salvaging (1973—June 1985)

Year	Metro-Manila	Luzon	Visayas	Mindanao	Total
1973	—	1	—	—	1
1974	—	—	—	—	—
1975	—	11	—	—	11
1976	—	16	—	—	16
1977	—	24	21	6	51
1978	1	25	44	16	86
1979	—	56	38	102	196
1980	—	45	36	137	218
1981	—	65	28	228	321
1982	—	46	28	136	210
1983	1	62	41	265	369
1984	—	128	61	368	557
June 1985	5	33	46	135	219
Total	**7**	**512**	**343**	**1,393**	**2,255**

Source: TFD

Table 3
Disappearance (1974—June 1985)

Year	Metro-Manila	Luzon	Visayas	Mindanao	Total
1974	—	—	—	1	1
1975	1	4	—	—	5
1976	2	33	—	—	35
1977	2	11	—	3	16
1978	1	3	4	2	10
1979	2	12	—	34	48
1980	2	17	—	—	19
1981	—	88	—	45	53
1982	—	16	2	24	42
1983	2	13	15	115	145
1984	7	22	24	97	150
June 1985	3	23	18	66	110
Total	22	162	63	387	634

Source: TFD

Selection 9.11: U.S. Policy Toward Marcos, National Security Study Directive

Editors' Introduction

In November 1984 a National Security Council Study Directive signalled that the Reagan administration was moving from a policy of increasing aid coupled with wholehearted support for the Marcos dictatorship to a policy of increasing aid coupled with pressure for economic, military, and political reforms.

The directive gave official sanction to the development of contacts with "those Filipinos who have been on the cutting edge of moderate reform or change," that is to say moderate critics and opponents of the Marcos regime.

Emphasizing the importance of "the way we convey our policy messages to the government leadership," the opposition, the Church, and the business community," the directive suggested that the desirability of reform could be urged upon Marcos by a high level emissary or by a presidential letter. (As it turned out, both of these methods were used, first with CIA chief Casey's visit in May 1985, then the letter from the White House delivered by the President's close friend Senator Laxalt in October of the same year.)

The document below was leaked to Dr. Walden Bello of the Philippine Support Committee, and released at a press conference in Washington, D.C., on March 12, 1985.

Source: *Philippine News*, April 3-9, 1985.

The United States has extremely important *interests* in the Philippines:

* Politically, because the U.S. nurtured the independence and democratic institutions of our former colony, the Philippines must be a stable, democratically oriented ally. A radicalized Philippines would destabilize the whole region.

* Strategically, continued unhampered access to our bases at Subic and Clark is of prime importance because of the expanded Soviet and Vietnamese threat in the region. Fall-back positions would be much more expensive and less satisfactory.

* A strong ASEAN [Association of Southeast Asian Nations] that includes a healthy Philippines allied to the U.S. is a buffer to communist presence in Southeast Asia and a model of what economic freedom and democratic progress can accomplish.

* Economically, we benefit from a strong investment and trade position.

Political and economic developments in the Philippines threaten these interests. Long-standing political and economic problems came to a head following the Aquino assassination in August 1983, which destroyed most of the political credibility the 19-year old Marcos Government enjoyed and exacerbated a shaky financial situation. A positive political dynamic in the direction of greater openness has developed in the wake of the Aquino assassination, but many question whether President Marcos can or will allow sufficient revitalization of democratic institutions to prevent a full-scale polarization of Philippine society.

Meanwhile, although the Philippines is likely to overcome the current financial crisis with considerable outside help, medium-term economic prospects are quite gloomy and in the absence of major structural economic reform the longer term outlook does not permit such optimism. At the same time, the communist New People's Army, taking advantage of the depressed economy, the weaknesses of the Philippine military and its abuse of civilians, popular fear and resentment of the military, and the government's inability to deliver economic and social development programs, has continued to expand significantly. This threat will doubtless continue to grow in the absence of progress toward credible democratic institutions, military reform including the curbing of abuse, and basic economic reform. Absent political and economic stability, continued steady progress toward an insurgent communist take-over is a distinct possibility in the mid-to-long term, and possibly sooner.

However, reforms are likely in the short run to weaken some bases of support for the current government, which will resist many of them. While President Marcos at this stage is part of the problem he is also necessarily part of the solution. We need to be able to work with him and to try to influence him through a well-orchestrated policy of incentives and disincentives to set the stage for peaceful and eventual transition to a successor government whenever that takes place. Marcos, for his part, will try to use us to remain in power indefinitely.

U.S. Goals

Politically, the U.S. wants a strong, stable, democratically oriented, pro-U.S. Philippines. However, without a healthy economy, the Philippines cannot achieve political stability. Thus, specific U.S. *economic* goals remain:

* To strengthen the Philippine economy through our multilateral and bilateral assistance programs;

* To move the Philippine economy toward a free market orientation;

* To maintain and expand current levels of trade and investment (U.S. exports: $1.8 billion; imports: $2 billion; direct investment: $1.3 billion);

* To contribute to lifting the Philippine economy from its currently projected negative growth rates in 1984 and 1985.

Our security and defense goals are to maintain U.S. military presence, and to fulfill treaty obligations and commitments made operational through our naval and air bases at Subic and Clark. Through military assistance and training provided the Philippines Armed Forces our objectives are:

* To assist in maintaining internal defense and conventional deterrence capability;

* To continue to support military civic and social action activities;

* To assist in defeating the ongoing insurgency.

Strong people/cultural relationships and broad existing institutional ties over many years assist us in achieving all our goals.

Premises Underlying U.S. Policy

The U.S. does not want to remove Marcos from power to destabilize the GOP [Government of the Philippines]. Rather, we are urging revitalization of democratic institutions, dismantling "crony" monopoly capitalism and allowing the economy to respond to free market forces, and restoring professional, apolitical leadership to the Philippine military to deal with the growing communist insurgency. These efforts are meant to stabilize while strengthening institutions which will eventually provide for a peaceful transition.

Our approach assumes that our interests in the Philippines are worth a high-priority and costly effort to preserve. At the same time, and although we have important influence and leverage vis-a-vis the Philippines, we cannot take the lead in reforming the Philippine system; the Filipinos must do this themselves. Our influence is most effective when it is exercised in support of efforts that have already developed within the Philippines.

We must pursue a comprehensive approach to the triad of challenges affecting our interests because the problems themselves are interlinked. This will require:

* A more open economic system that ends or substantially alters "crony capitalism" and agricultural monopolies;

* A more open political system that offers a credible promise of democratic reform;

* An effective military capable of carrying the fight to the communist insurgency while controlling abuses of its own power.

Our assets include not only the economic and military assistance that we are able to provide but also the respect and sympathy that we continue to enjoy with most segments of the Philippine population. Our support is one of Marcos's largest remaining strengths. Our assets, particularly at the people-to-people level, could be lost if we come to be seen as favoring a continuation of the Marcos regime to the exclusion of other democratic alternatives.

U.S. policy during the current crisis has included aid and other measures tailored to respond to the crisis in ways that have underlined U.S. resolve to be of assistance. Our active public and private diplomacy has been aimed at demonstrating to the Philippine public that we stand with them in their time of troubles, but that we are encouraging the basic reforms necessary to the survival of their democratic institutions.

We have adjusted our policy to the evolutionary internal political dynamics at work, an approach which has achieved some success. Through public and private statements, we have:

* Sought to support those Filipinos who have been on the cutting edge of moderate reform or change;

* Influenced positive decisions and movement on such issues as the need for a new presidential succession formula, a credible investigation of the Aquino assassination, and the beginning of institution building through an acceptable parliamentary election.

Specific Short to Medium Term Goals

1984 to 1987, that is, from the 1984 parliamentary election to the 1987 presidential election, may be a major transition period. Changes are already underway: new political forces are mobilizing; the first signs of economic response to austerity measures are being seen; the military, following the Agrava Board revelations, is looking inward. In order for the Philippines to remain politically and economically stable, and for its military to be able to contain the growth of the insurgency, the following high priority changes are required. U.S. policies must be linked to progress in all of them.

Political

* Institutional change in preparation for the 1986 local election and the 1987 presidential election.

* Reform of the Commission on Elections (COMELEC), the key to the control of election fraud.

* A new election law which *at least* offers the same guarantees as the election law which applied to the 1984 parliamentary election.

* Legalization of NAMFREL (National Citizens' Movement for Free Elections).

* Amendment or reform of presidential decree-making powers.

* Changes in the media—particularly television but also radio and print—to permit opposition access.

Financial, Economic and Development

* Adherence to the IMF Program.

* Significant reduction of government interference in agricultural production and marketing; an end to monopoly capitalism.

* Policy reforms in rural credit.

* Continuation of import liberalization.

* A diminished role for public enterprises in financial and industrial activities or improvement in their performance, including accountability.

* Significant tax reform to reduce distortions.

Military

* Restoration of professional, apolitical leadership in the Armed Forces in order to deal with the NPA threat.

* Improvement in dealing with military abuse.

* Improved training.

* More military equipment in logistics, communication, and basic military needs.

The Consensus Approach: Quid Pro Quo

The basic consensus *quid pro quo* approach begins with the tacit understanding by the Philippine leadership that the political and economic liberalization trend currently underway will continue, and continued U.S. assistance is linked to this trend. . . .

In the Philippine cultural context, the way we convey our policy messages to the government leadership, the opposition, the Church, and the business community is almost as important as the policy.

An effective, low key approach involves no special efforts at communication other than the normal—an occasional presidential letter, regular visits by administration officials, close Embassy contact, and regular one-on-one meetings between President Marcos and Ambassador Bosworth. This has the advantage of moving issues along one at a time in ways that clearly spell out U.S. intentions. Occasional high level meetings, particularly with President Marcos, would be geared to making sure our messages are received, understood, and placed in the appropriate policy context. This mode is appropriate for expressing U.S. support for initiatives needed to move the Philippines successfully through the transition period such as strengthened/reformed election bodies (NAMFREL and COMELEC), a stronger independent judiciary, and revitalized rural development efforts.

A presidential letter would be key to setting the stage for linking increases in economic, military, and financial assistance to major reform. The same message could be sent by a high level emissary such as Secretary Shultz or NSC Director McFarlane. A third option would be to ask one of several private sector leaders known to Philippine leadership (a "wisemen's mission") to carry the message. This would be particularly advisable if a high level trade/aid/investment initiative effort is made. . . .

Selection 9.12: Special Operations Forces Activities in the Philippines, U.S. Air Force

Editors' Introduction

Pressure for military reform was not the only form of escalation of U.S. intervention in Philippine military affairs after August 1983. In 1985 the number of U.S. advisers to the Philippine military was increased markedly. In July 1985 evidence was made public of what appeared to be covert military activity against the NPA by the U.S. In that month the *Fort Walton Beach Log,* a newspaper printed in a town adjacent to the Florida headquarters of the U.S. Air Force's Special Operations Forces worldwide, published a document that it had obtained through the Federal Freedom of Information Act. This document, marked "confidential," revealed that in the previous year and a half two Special Operations Forces planes had been shot at and damaged while on "low altitude training missions." The paper noted that these missions were flown over northern Luzon in areas of NPA activity. Since these planes were designed for reconnaissance activity, it is possible that whoever shot at them could not distinguish between a reconnaissance and a training mission.

Only a month before this story appeared in the Florida paper, Professor Roland Simbulan of the University of the Philippines in Manila, an authority on the U.S. bases, pointed out the presence of U.S. Special Operations Forces in the Philippines and warned that these could be used for covert military intervention in Philippine affairs. Professor Simbulan's statement caused a stir in the Philippine press and was answered by the U.S. Embassy in a denial of his contention that these forces might be used for intervention in the Philippines.

Source: Photocopy obtained through the Freedom of Information Act.

PHILIPPINES: USAF MC-130 HIT BY SMALL ARMS FIRE

At approximately 2035, 22 May 1985, a USAF MC-130 aircraft assigned to the 1st Special Operations Squadron (SOS), Clark AB, was hit by small arms fire during a routine low-level, terrain-following mission over northern Luzon in Cagayan Province, about 18 miles south of Ballesteros and 180 miles northeast of Clark AB.

The aircraft was heading southeast at 220 knots at an altitude of about 500 feet. Three rounds penetrated the aircraft causing extensive damage. One round penetrated the cowling under the oil supply system of the MR 4 engine, causing the loss of that engine. Another round entered the area behind the right main wheel well and penetrated the refueling manifold line causing an intense fire that melted portions of the aircraft skin on the right side of the cargo bay. A third round entered the upper cargo door and traveled into the vertical stabilizer. There were no injuries to the ten man crew and the aircraft successfully recovered at Clark AB. Damage is estimated at $250,000.

[CLASSIFIED]

On 5 February 84 another USAF MC-130 was hit by two rounds of small arms fire while on a routine low-altitude training mission in northern Luzon. Investigations by U.S. and Philippine agencies failed to identify the perpetrators of the first incident. It is likely that the perpetrators of this latest incident will also remain unidentified because the area of the incident is remote, mountainous and heavily forested.

Affected commanders and HQ MAC officials have been briefed.

SPECIAL HANDLING REQUIRED (APR 124-4)

REPRODUCTION NOT AUTHORIZED

DISSEMINATION AND ACCESS TO THE INFORMATION IN THIS ITEM IS BEING LIMITED TO PRECLUDE DISCLOSURE ON OTHER THAN A NEED-TO-KNOW BASIS

CLASSIFIED BY: MULTIPLE SOURCES

DECLASSIFY ON: OADR

NOT RELEASABLE TO FOREIGN NATIONALS

Selection 9.13: The Difficulties of Military Reform, Senator John Kerry

Editors' Introduction

On his visit to the Philippines in April 1985, Massachusetts Senator John Kerry had interviews with U.S. Ambassador Bosworth, chief of the JUSMAG General Teddy Allen, Subic Base Commander Admiral Edwin Kohn, Philippine Defense Minister Juan Ponce Enrile, and Deputy Chief of Staff Fidel Ramos. Kerry's report on his trip indicated the difficulties the Defense Department was having in promoting military reform in the Philippines. Marcos evidently turned a deaf ear to any suggestion of removing Ver and the overstaying generals. Enrile and Ramos, on the other hand, while sympathetic to many of the proposed reforms, implied that without Marcos's assent it would be impossible to rejuvenate the top military leadership, and they showed themselves, as Senator Kerry perceived it, to be blind to the need for checking military abuses against civilians.

Source: *Congressional Record*, Senate, 99th Cong., 1st sess., August 1, 1985, pp. S10624-S10625.

———

U.S. officials believe that the Armed Forces of the Philippines is failing to bring the insurgency under control. As one U.S. military officer declared in a meeting with me, "We've got an ineffective armed forces and an insurgency that's growing day by day." A specialist on the insurgency pointed out that the NPA is taking over the countryside with such speed that time is running out on the Philippine government. This official agreed with the estimate given by Assistant Secretary of Defense Armitage that the NPA could be as strong as the government militarily within three to five years but thought it might happen even sooner.

U.S. officials said they believe that acting Chief of Staff General Fidel Ramos and Minister of Defense Juan Ponce Enrile have finally recognized that major changes must be made in the AFP to increase its effectiveness. They noted that it has been only in the past several months that the Embassy has been able to conduct realistic discussions with them on the seriousness of the problem.

Other Embassy officials warned, however, that it is unclear whether these officials are capable of turning the deteriorating situation around. They observed that Enrile and Ramos are constrained in their ability to initiate personnel changes by the fact that most of the commanding generals of the AFP are loyal to General Fabian Ver, the former Chief of Staff. Ver, who is very close to President Marcos, is now on trial for his alleged involvement in the assassination of opposition leader Benigno Aquino in August 1983. Nevertheless, a statement pledging "unwavering loyalty" to Ver was signed by 63 Generals and flag officers, signifying Ver's continued domination of the military.

Of the 90 active duty generals in the AFP today, 30 are past retirement age, but have been kept on active duty by President Marcos. Most of these "overstaying generals" are considered political appointees whose main function is to protect the interests of Marcos and Ver in the military.

Both Defense Minister Enrile and Gen. Ramos told me they emphatically oppose the extension of active duty for these "overstaying generals" (even though Ramos himself also falls into this category). But they implied that they cannot do anything about the problem without the support of President Marcos. Marcos himself has publicly declared his intention to reinstate Ver as

Chief of Staff if he is acquitted of the charges in the Aquino assassination, thus creating the impression among Filipinos that the outcome of the trial is a foregone conclusion. Most Americans and Filipinos with whom I talked expect Ver to be acquitted and to be reinstated by Marcos. That would be a serious blow to the chances for genuine reform of the AFP.

In our meeting, Enrile seemed to be arguing that the NPA problem is manageable without any major changes in organization or policy by the AFP. He emphasized that the NPA had little chance of winning without advancing from guerilla warfare to main force warfare, and suggested that the NPA would be "lucky" to reach the stage of strategic stalemate within five to ten years. The Defense Minister also asserted that the AFP has already reversed the initiative on the battlefield. The NPA took the initiative in seventy percent of the contacts in 1984, he said, but the AFP has taken the initiative in sixty percent of the contacts so far this year. He said the AFP should be "alarmed" only if the NPA starts using artillery against it.

This view is a good deal more optimistic about the main trends in the conflict than that of U.S. officials in Manila. Even more disturbing, however, was the refusal of Enrile and Ramos to acknowledge that the AFP has a serious problem with abuses of civilians. He [Enrile] attributed reports of "salvaging" to "propaganda by radical anti-government groups." He also claimed that the AFP had investigated several cases in which such killings by AFP personnel had been alleged by human rights groups and had found no evidence to support the allegations.

U.S. Embassy officials indicated that the AFP and the Ministry of Defense are well aware that "salvaging" is continuing, however, and that they know the U.S. Embassy is also aware of it. The refusal of Enrile and Ramos to admit frankly in conversation with me that extrajudicial killings are a serious problem and to discuss the ways in which they intend to tackle it suggested to me that the government has not yet decided to firmly address the issue.

Enrile and Ramos have agreed to reforms in the previous AFP procurement system which will eliminate the systematic graft and corruption which previously surrounded the purchase of military equipment by the AFP. They have also agreed to the reorientation of procurement away from modern weapon systems like the F-16 fighter plane and toward enhancing force readiness through the purchase of basic items like trucks and communications equipment, and to the establishment of an effective operations and maintenance system. In addition, they have set up centers for the retraining of troops whose performance in the field has been particularly poor. But on the critical problem of military abuses and extrajudicial killings, U.S. officials say, the leadership of the AFP has yet to propose any concrete actions.

Selection 9.14: The Special National Intelligence Estimate, Nayan Chanda

Editors' Introduction

The Far Eastern Economic Review of October 31, 1985 carried a report by its Washington correspondent, Nayan Chanda, of a special national intelligence estimate (SNIE) of July of that year. The report was especially noteworthy because of one feature: it predicted a military growth of left-wing influence in Philippine political parties and local administrations that might reach threatening proportions in the next 18 months (that is, before the scheduled presidential election of 1987) unless somehow checked. While the report echoed the standard warnings about the growth of the NPA, its emphasis seemed to place the growth of left-wing *political* influence as an even more immediate threat. Indeed, according to Chanda, certain administration officials confidentially acknowledged that the military threat might have been overblown in order to attract attention to the gravity of the Philippine situation.

Giving public voice to the concerns of the SNIE report, on December 5, 1985, James A. Kelly, Deputy Assistant Secretary of Defense for East Asia and the Pacific, International Security Affairs, told the Subcommittee on Military Construction of the House Armed Services Committee that it was not only a victory of the Communist New People's Army that threatened U.S. bases in the Philippines. Kelly asserted that "even a leftist coalition government dominated by Communists" would pose an identical threat.

The SNIE report therefore may help to explain the motivation behind the administration's pressure on Marcos for an early election; elections could stabilize Philippine politics before left-wing influence could grow any greater.

Source: Nayan Chanda, "Dear Mr. President. . . ," *Far Eastern Economic Review,* October 31, 1985, pp. 16-17.

After nearly two years of unsuccessful behind-the-scenes effort to persuade Philippine President Ferdinand Marcos to reform his administration, the U.S. despatched a high level emissary to Manila on October 13 with a tough message. Well-placed sources told the *Far Eastern Economic Review* that the visit was intended to be as much of a signal to the country's opposition forces and reformist elements in the military as a warning to Marcos.

President Reagan's decision to send Sen. Paul Laxalt, chairman of the Republican Party and a close friend of the president, as a personal envoy to convey his concerns to Marcos came in the wake of a special national intelligence estimate (SNIE) which warned of the seriousness of the communist insurgency in the Philippines. The Laxalt mission also sought to end public assertions by Marcos that despite criticism by some U.S. officials, Marcos enjoyed Reagan's support. . . .

The idea of sending a presidential envoy to Manila goes back to January. According to a draft of a national security directive signed by Reagan at the time and leaked to the press, "a presidential letter would be the key to setting the stage for linking increases in economic, military and financial assistance to major reforms."

The grave conclusions of the July SNIE of the Philippine insurgency and the recommendations of a panel of interagency experts and academics which met in late July under the auspices of the National Defense University seem to have given additional impetus to high level intervention. The fact that Marcos had not only side-stepped past U.S. advice on reforms but was claiming to enjoy Reagan's support made a publicized visit by a Reagan emissary seem necessary to counter the impression.

A key element in the high level appraisal was the completion of the Philippine insurgency SNIE, prepared by the CIA, the Defense Intelligence Agency (DIA) and the State Department after several months of work. Sources said the SNIE drew a grim picture of NPA growth in recent years and concluded that if the present trend continues, within three to five years the NPA would be able to fight the Armed Forces of the Philippines to a stalemate and grab political power. . . .

Some administration sources privately admit that in the past some concerned U.S. agencies have tended to overemphasize the threat from the NPA "in order to bring the Philippines up on the agenda" of senior policy makers who tend to focus on problems only when they demand urgent attention. But the latest SNIE raised the possibility not so much of a military victory by the guerillas as the chances of their eventual political victory.

The SNIE noted increasing infiltration of political parties and accommodation with local administrations as leading to the CPP's emergence as the dominant political force in the not too distant future. It warned that unless action was taken within 18 months to halt the trend—by sharply curbing rising unemployment, poverty and military abuses among the civilian populace—the insurgency might reach the point when it would be irreversible.

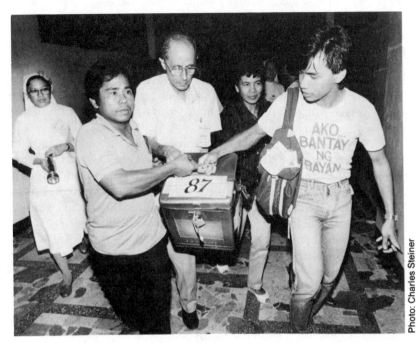

Photo: Charles Steiner

Philippine citizens protecting a ballot box during the February 1986 "snap" election.

CHAPTER 10: MARCOS'S FINAL CRISIS

Introduction

The final crisis of the Marcos regime was marked by two crucial episodes—a presidential election and a military revolt. While the United States government and the Philippine political and military elite had a hand in shaping both of these crises, it was the intervention of the Philippine people that proved decisive in each case, tipping the scales against the Marcos dictatorship and sealing its defeat.

Looking toward the election, Corazon (Cory) Aquino, widow of the murdered Senator, and Salvador "Doy" Laurel were the two favorites in the field of opposition candidates. While both were members of the Philippine social and economic elite, Laurel had been a supporter of Marcos until 1980 and, in further contrast to Cory Aquino, had been one of the two outstanding potential presidential candidates who had refused to sign the Convenors' statement of December 1984 which called for the removal of U.S. bases [see selection 9.6]. Aquino's sincerity and courage, her freedom from past association with Marcos, and her strong identification with the many victims of the regime as one of the most prominent among them made her the most popular candidate. As head of the opposition UNIDO party, however, Laurel had the best political machine. After some hesitation on Laurel's part as he held out for the presidential slot, and upon the urging of the Catholic primate of Manila, Cardinal Jaime Sin, a united ticket was arranged with Aquino as the presidential candidate and Laurel her vice-presidential running-mate. Classified documents obtained by Walden Bello of the U.S.-based Philippine Support Committee and later made public in the *New Statesman* of February 21, 1986, revealed that State Department officials had also met in Manila with backers of Aquino and Laurel to recommend a united ticket that would be anticommunist and refrain from opposing the U.S. bases.

Declaring his interest in a free and fair election, President Reagan appointed Richard Lugar, head of the Senate Foreign Relations Committee, to lead a commission to monitor the vote in the Philippines. While President Marcos had earlier invited such foreign monitors, during the course of the campaign he suddenly adopted a nationalist stance and denounced U.S. meddling in Philippine affairs. Many noted the hypocrisy of his position given that he had been the chief beneficiary of U.S. intervention for two decades. Moreover, in the course of the campaign, Marcos accused Aquino of being dominated by Communists, a charge with special appeal to President Reagan, his chief sponsor in Washington.

Other themes of the Marcos campaign were his greater experience (Aquino responded by acknowledging her inexperience at corruption and dictatorship) and that a woman's place was in the bedroom. For her part, Aquino pledged to release all political prisoners, to negotiate with the New

People's Army, and to institute economic and social reforms [see selection 10.1]. On the other hand, Aquino declared that U.S. bases could remain until 1991 (when current agreements end), after which time she would keep her options open. She also announced that there would be no Communists in her cabinet.

Philippine Communists and BAYAN, a leading left-wing nationalist organization, urged boycott of the election. BAYAN asserted that free elections were impossible under Marcos and that the Aquino program did not go far enough in economic and social reform and in defense of national sovereignty [see selection 10.2].

KAAKBAY, a prominent nationalist organization to the left of center, while acknowledging the hand of the U.S. government in calling the election, urged participation, declaring the removal of the Marcos dictatorship to be the first step on the road to Philippine independence [see selection 10.3].

On voting day and the days of vote-counting immediately after, it became obvious that Filipinos were not allowing either the U.S. initiation of the election or the possibility of fraud and violence by Marcos keep them from the polls. Instead, in great numbers, they were taking the electoral process into their own hands in a passionate attempt to bring down the Marcos dictatorship. They watched the polls at considerable risk of physical attack from Marcos's goons. With their bodies they guarded the ballot boxes from theft and tampering. Their effort to protect the vote reached a climax when a group of computer operators (mainly women) working for COMELEC, the official election body, courageously walked off the job, saying that the count was being falsified. (Members of the reform movement in the Philippine army then came forward to protect these computer operators from physical harm.)

A citizens' poll-watching group called NAMFREL, headed by an anti-Marcos businessman, Jose Concepcion, Jr., declared Aquino the winner by its count. COMELEC and the Philippine National Assembly, dominated by the Marcos party, claimed a Marcos victory.

At a press conference in Washington, President Reagan declared the Philippine election to be a sign of a healthy two-party system, spoke of the possibility of fraud on both sides, and reminded the public of the importance of the U.S. bases in the Philippines [see selection 10.4]. The President announced that he was sending the State Department trouble-shooter Philip Habib to the Philippines to look into the situation and make a report. A White House spokesperson urged Aquino to compromise with Marcos and to keep her followers off the streets. Leslie Gelb, the *New York Times'* well-connected Washington correspondent, reported that Habib's mission was actually to attempt to fashion some sort of compromise.

Reagan's press conference remarks contradicted the findings of Senator Lugar's commission which reported evidence of massive fraud on the part of Marcos. Reagan's stand was consonant with the views of those, like his chief of staff Donald Regan, who in the closing days of the campaign had let it be known that they considered the distancing from Marcos to have gone too far.

Even if Marcos won by massive fraud, Regan had declared, the U.S. would have to work with him. "There are a lot of governments elected by fraud," he observed. Reagan's press conference comments caused consternation among State Department officials, however, and they were able to get the President to reverse himself after some delay. The administration was adamant, however, in opposing the growing moves in Congress to cut off aid to Marcos.

Corazon Aquino reacted with asperity to President Reagan's initial statement and announced her intention to realize the victory she believed was rightfully hers. She promised to topple Marcos from power with a program of non-violent resistance, urging economic boycotts of crony businesses and a one-day nation-wide general strike as a first step.

In an unprecedented move the Catholic bishops of the Philippines denounced the fraud and violence of the Marcos campaign and urged the Catholic faithful to support a campaign of non-violent resistance to right the electoral wrong [see selection 10.5].

For his part, Marcos stood pat, proclaiming himself the rightful winner and setting his inauguration ceremonies for February 25. Aquino announced that she would have her inauguration the same day.

On February 22, however, before the inauguration ceremonies could take place, Marcos's Defense Minister Juan Ponce Enrile and Deputy Chief of Staff General Fidel Ramos gathered a handful of reformist troops around their headquarters in Camp Aguinaldo and Camp Crame and announced that they were no longer loyal to Marcos. They called upon the President to resign from office because of election fraud.

Both men declared they took the step they did in self-defense because they had learned that President Marcos planned to arrest them. Marcos countered by saying that he had uncovered a plot by the reformist military to storm Malacañang Palace and carry out a coup d'etat. The later testimony of Captain Robles, a leading reformist officer, tended to confirm both claims [see selection 10.6].

At this juncture the people of Manila once again took affairs in their own hands and, on the urging of Cardinal Sin and Corazon Aquino's brother-in-law, filled the streets around Camp Crame and Camp Aguinaldo. So it was that when Marcos sent troops, tanks, and guns to put down Enrile and Ramos, these forces would have had to fire on thousands of civilians, with nuns and priests trained in non-violence prominent among them, ringing the rebel headquarters. This the Marcos troops refused to do.

The confrontation on February 23 between the unarmed civilians and the troops of Marcos was the turning point of the last crisis of the Marcos regime [see selection 10.7]. It gave Enrile and Ramos time to lobby key officers of the Marcos military and win them to the side of the revolt. The next morning helicopters sent to attack Camp Crame defected to the rebels. Later that day rebel forces took over the Marcos television station, and again thousands of civilians thronged the streets to protect them from attack. On the third day—as commanders formerly loyal to Marcos deserted him, as the people of Manila continued their vigil in the streets, and as rebel helicopters flew over Malacañang—it was becoming clear that Ferdinand Marcos's occupancy of the palace was drawing to a close. In desperation he called President Reagan's friend Senator Laxalt, and Laxalt advised him to step down.

That evening two U.S. helicopters carried Marcos and his family and entourage from Malacañang Palace to Clark Air Field, and from there two U.S. air force jets carried them to Hawaii. General Teddy Allen, chief of the Joint U.S. Military Advisory Group (JUSMAG) in the Philippines, escorted the Marcos party, which included, as baggage, crates holding millions of freshly printed Philippine pesos and Pampers boxes loaded with Imelda Marcos's jewelry. Corazon Aquino thus became the undisputed president of the Philippines.

Did the U.S. government have any part in the uprising of Enrile and Ramos? The evidence is difficult to evaluate because it is ambivalent and contradictory. The overthrow of Marcos was so enthusiastically received world-wide that U.S. officials may have been inclined to inflate the U.S. role in this critical event, even going so far as to picture President Reagan entering the scene at the last minute as the savior of Philippine democracy. And on February 25, 1986, the Associated Press urgently informed its subscribing editors that "we are recasting the U.S.-Philippine story to focus on the American role" in Marcos's resignation and questions about his ultimate destination. Years of U.S. support to the Marcos dictatorship were thus to be hypocritically dismissed. On the other hand, those on the left in the United States and elsewhere may have been inclined to overestimate the role of United States intervention, reducing the last crisis of the Marcos regime to an episode controlled by the CIA, the U.S. Embassy, and the U.S. military in the Philippines. Finally, Enrile and his supporters may have wished to underplay the role of the United States in their uprising (aided by denials from the U.S.) so as to preserve a more nationalistic image.

With these cautions in mind, let us review some of the evidence of U.S. involvement in the February events.

Senator Dave Durenberger, the head of the Senate Intelligence Committee, stated publicly in late 1985 that the CIA had failed to organize an alternative to the Sandinistas when Somoza fell in Nicaragua, but that the same mistake would not be made in the Philippines. According to the *Far Eastern Economic Review* of March 6, 1986, before the revolt took place:

> the U.S. Embassy, which had been augmented by dozens of officers with some Philippine expertise, was engaged in intense secret contacts with the opposition, Marcos ruling party, and the military in an effort to bring about a reconciliation of the two political groups, without Marcos.

Such activity may have had the effect of preparing the ground for the coup. Asked about the U.S. role in the revolt itself, Senators Lugar and Alfonse D'Amato (Republican of New York) gave similar answers to the press. Lugar said that the visit of President Reagan's emissary Philip Habib was not coincidental with the uprising, but "was a cause and effect" relationship, adding "I suspect that immediately upon his [Habib's] departure various people knew where we stood and accelerated events" (*Boston Globe*, February 24, 1986). D'Amato said, "There are things, obviously, that we are doing behind the scenes that can and should be done. Obviously we've encouraged the military to take a certain posture and activity and we've seen two high ranking officials have done that" (*Boston Herald*, February 24, 1986). Neither Lugar nor D'Amato, however, gave any specifics. Defense Minister Enrile met with Philip Habib before the uprising and spoke with the U.S. Ambassador Stephen Bosworth and Kiyosha Sumiya, the Japanese Ambassador (*Newsweek*, March 3, 1986). In the *Wall Street Journal* of March 3 a Manila correspondent wrote that the U.S. Embassy notified reporters about the Enrile-Ramos press conference that announced their rebellion, so as to help ensure publicity. Some Philippine officers claimed that U.S. officials gave them valuable information on the disposition and activities of troops loyal to Marcos during the revolt.

On the other hand, Washington issued an official denial that it had actively encouraged the military defection (*Wall Street Journal*, February 24, 1986). There is also the testimony of Renato Cayetano, an extremely close friend of Enrile's. Cayetano told one of the editors of this book that he was sent by Enrile to U.S. Ambassador Bosworth shortly after Enrile and Ramos established themselves at Camp Aguinaldo. Cayetano urgently asked for U.S. help but was told by Bosworth that there was nothing that the United States could do. Two days later Washington threatened to cut off military aid to Marcos if he attacked the rebels, but this came after Marcos had already launched (unsuccessful) attacks against Camps Aguinaldo and Crame, and well after the crucial first day when the rebels were especially vulnerable because the people's power throngs hadn't yet materialized. According to statements made by some of the reformist military officers, they believe that the United States deserted them in their hour of need.

There were reports in the press, confirmed by Defense Secretary Caspar Weinberger, that the U.S. allowed rebel helicopters to refuel and load ammunition at Clark Air Base (*Washington Post*, March 3, 1986). The helicopters *were* permitted to refuel (though this was already after the military balance had swung decisively against Marcos), but the ammunition came from Philippine Air Force stocks at Clark, the Philippine base commander having already defected to the rebel side.

There is no doubt that the military uprising had, in part, an effect that was advantageous to U.S. supporters of the status quo in the Philippines. Immediately after the election Aquino had announced a program to topple Marcos, a program that included economic boycott of crony businesses and a one-day general strike led by a labor movement containing elements of left-wing leadership. Should such a scenario have been run through and should such a strike have played a role in bringing down Marcos, Aquino would have been indebted to the Philippine labor movement. As a result of the military uprising, Aquino was instead indebted, in good part, to the conservative military leaders, Enrile and Ramos, who then received leading positions in her government.

But to argue that the outcome was partially advantageous to the Reagan administration does not lead to the conclusion that the whole uprising was scripted by Washington. In fact, it is likely that the evidence of Washington's relation to the uprising is ambivalent and contradictory precisely because the Reagan administration's policy towards the Marcos dictatorship was contradictory and ambivalent right up to the moment that popular intervention in the streets of Manila finished it off. Even discounting events such as Reagan's February 11 press conference—which certainly does not lend itself to any mechanical and one-sided interpretation—too much of what occurred between February 22 and February 25 seemed impossible to predict or control, and was, moreover, in its essential determinant, contrary to what Washington desired, by its own testimony. The Reagan administration had expressed its aversion to the Philippine people taking to the streets—that is, to popular participation in the crucial Philippine decision making process. But the telling irony of the February events is that the military coup could not have succeeded without the very intervention of the "people in the streets" that Washington wished to avoid.

Before the February days, U.S. intervention stimulated two lines of Philippine development—with pressure for political reform, which led to the early election, and with pressure for military professionalization, which encouraged the reformist officers. It was the intersection of these two lines of development in the military uprising which threw its support to Aquino that provided the possibility of Marcos's downfall in this last crisis. It was the intervention of the Philippine people themselves, however, that was finally decisive, turning this possibility into an actuality. It was the hundreds of thousands of Filipinos in the streets of Manila that prevented Marcos from crushing this uprising in cold blood, that took his officers and troops away from him, that guaranteed his ruin. Therefore, Aquino came to office indebted above all to the people of the Philippines.

Selection 10.1: Program of Social Reform, Corazon Aquino

Editors' Introduction

The selection below is from a speech delivered by Corazon Aquino at Davao City, Mindanao, on January 16 in the course of her election campaign. It outlines her program of reform on eight social issues: land reform, labor laws and the conditions of labor, housing, rights of Muslim and tribal minorities, medical services and public health, teachers' conditions and education, the question of insurgency, and women's rights.

Source: Mimeographed text of speech.

What will be my priorities?

Necessarily, my list of priorities is tentative. It will be finalized after I have heard more from you and from all sectors of the Filipino people. As I look at our nation today, however, I see the following as my priorities:

First, efficient utilization and equitable sharing of the ownership and benefits of land. . . .

The two essential goals of land reform are greater productivity and equitable sharing of the benefits and ownership of the land. These two goals can conflict with each other. But together we will seek viable systems of land reform suited to the particular exigencies dictated not only by the quality of the soil, the nature of the produce, and the agricultural inputs demanded, but above all by the needs of the small farmers, landless workers, and communities of tribal Filipinos whose lives and whose personal dignity depend on their just share in the abundance of the land.

For long-time settlers and share tenants, land-to-the-tiller must become a reality, instead of an empty slogan.

For the growing number of landless workers, resettlement schemes and cooperative forms of farming can be introduced.

And for the island of Mindanao as a whole, the conservation of our forests and other natural resources against illegal loggers and other exploiters must start now. . . .

My friends, this is the land policy I propose to pursue. And while I announce it here in Mindanao, I also intend to apply the same general policy to other parts of our nation. You will probably ask me: Will I also apply it to my family's Hacienda Luisita? My answer is yes; although sugar land is not covered by the land reform law, I shall sit down with my family to explore how the twin goals of maximum productivity and dispersal of ownership and benefits can be exemplified for the rest of the nation in Hacienda Luisita.

My second major concern is the problem of labor. Our nation has an abundant supply of workers willing to labor hard at the task of ensuring the productivity of land and of generating the engines of industry. Workers comprise 30% of the population. To this day, however, a large proportion of the working force of the nation are broken victims of the avarice of individuals and of an oppressive social structure and hostile labor laws. Our workers continue to clamor for relief from their sufferings. They continue to clamor for fair remuneration, decent working conditions, meaningful participation in the decision processes of business and industry, and respect for their right to protect themselves through concerted action. But whenever workers seek to organize and press for legitimate demands, they are subjected to harassment, intimidation and violent dispersal by goons, by the police, or by the military. Union busting is a common occurrence, and, often times, happens with the direct participation of the very government agencies which are supposed to protect workers. Moreover, to the detriment of the working man, government intervention by the Ministry of Labor and Employment and by the courts in the settling of labor disputes has only delayed instead of speeding up the settlement of disputes.

I pledge to work for the repeal of repressive laws and for the dismantling of economic structures which keep workers in a state of quasi-slavery. A liberated and properly motivated working force can be trusted to be able to take care of its best interest and the best interest of the nation as a whole. Moreover, I also take this opportunity to repeat what I said to the business community of Manila. I believe that, on the whole, the effective solution to the problem of the laboring poor should lie in the proper understanding of the partnership between labor and capital in the task of creating wealth, an understanding which should naturally lead to the equitable sharing of the benefits created. Finally I add that the partnership between labor and capital should aim beyond mere sharing of material wealth; it must also aim at the total human development of individuals and communities.

My third concern is housing. Land problems, labor problems, and housing problems are intimately related. Because of the irrational use of land, many of you, in search for work, have been driven to the cities where you have been reduced to the status of squatters. Cities have become over-populated because rural folk looking for work have flocked to urban centers. Much of the housing problem here and in other parts of our nation will be solved if the rational use of lands can attract the teeming city population back to the rural areas. The major thrust of my solution to the housing problem will be the creation of work opportunities and self-contained communities outside the crowded urban centers. As I said in my speech on the economy, I "shall stimulate investments primarily in labor-intensive, rural-based, and small- and medium-scale agricultural enterprises" and I "shall postpone capital intensive, urban-based industrial projects". . . .

My fourth concern are our Muslim brothers and our Tribal Minorities. For decades they have been neglected. Historically, they have been deprived of their ancestral lands, and their rights to security and cultural integrity have been ignored. They have been marginalized from our economic, political, and cultural life. The Marcos regime has alienated them even more than in the past.

For our Muslim brethren therefore, within the context of greater decentralization, my government will encourage and assist them to develop as autonomously as possible, not, however, apart from the Republic, but as strong, able, and progressive partners in nation building.

For the tribal Minorities both of the South and of the North, my government will respect their right to preserve their identity, traditions, language, cultural heritage, customary laws, and ancestral domains, to the end that these people will have the same rights as other citizens to participate on an equal basis in the life of the nation.

My fifth concern will be adequate health care. As a mother, I am particularly appalled to know that 80% of the school children of our nation are malnourished. Unsafe water causes many of the diseases prevalent in the country. The Ministry of Health, in its 1986 report, has admitted that diseases associated with underdevelopment, such as tuberculosis, malaria, schistosomiasis, diarrhea, and communicable diseases, have persisted in the country. Tuberculosis is still the second leading cause of death in the country. Malaria is endemic in 70 out of 75 provinces. It is a disgrace, for instance, that with all the hooplah about the City of Man, within a thirty minute drive from Malacañang, in the municipality of Montalban, malaria is still a dreaded scourge.

All of this is compounded by the fact that medical facilities are concentrated in the urban areas and by the fact that the cost of medicine here is said to be the highest in Asia. And as if this were not punishment enough for the poor, funds for health care are channeled to specialized and underutilized medical centers built primarily to satisfy the vanity of the powerful. This is another manifestation of a major vice of the present administration; it engages in a deceitful showcase approach to social services and achieves mere pretentious posturing while at the same time robbing the poor of the services they are entitled to. . . .

Mr. Marcos today spends millions of pesos to support the Office of Media Affairs for purposes of deception and propaganda; my government will put an end to deception and use much of this money instead for health education. Proper health education is the foundation of people participation in health programs. And only when people participate in the care of their own health can we make meaningful progress in preventive and promotive programs.

My government will also make medical and para-medical schools focus on a system of medical training which will motivate doctors, nurses, and other health workers to attend to the health needs of the population even at their own personal sacrifice. . . .

My sixth major concern is education. . . .

Quality depends more than on any factor, upon the teacher. Unhappy and discontented teachers cannot be expected to teach effectively. Therefore, we must before all else restore teachers to their honored place and give them back their self-respect. With the looted state of our economy, I am sure they will understand if I do not promise them the moon. But I promise that their economic welfare and their other concerns will have highest priority in my government. Moreover, my government will recognize their right to unionize and even to go on strike. Even more important, however, I ask them to be partners in the task of re-building the youth of our land and to be honored leaders once more in our communities.

Second, we must restore education to the priority in the budget and in cabinet concerns which it had before Mr. Marcos twenty years ago. For I believe that the foundation of a stable and prosperous society is a well educated and productive populace. We must break the burden of unaffordable costs and make education accessible to the majority of our people.

Third, we must make education an instrument of formation and liberation and not of indoctrination. . . .

My seventh concern is the problem of insurgency. . . .

Together we must face the problem of insurgency. The insurgents, like you and me, are also Filipinos. They are our brothers and sisters. Like you and me, they have minds and hearts fashioned by our common Almighty Father. Many of them believe they have just causes but they have given up on the capacity of the Marcos regime to give relief to their just grievances.

The social and economic reforms I propose will go a long way towards solving the insurgency problem. Beyond social and economic reforms, however, should you elect me President, I will, as I have repeatedly promised, immediately declare a cease-fire with the rebels and release political prisoners and thereafter enter into dialogue with the insurgents in order to afford the new administration the opportunity to immediately redress their legitimate grievances. On the other hand, the criminals among them who merely prey on helpless citizens will be dealt with as they deserve. I ask you to trust me that I will be fair and just.

As for the Armed Forces of the Republic, it is admitted that the military has been demoralized and dishonored by the Marcos regime. I assure you, however, that there are among the military a restlessness and a desire for the restoration of the honor and prestige which the profession once possessed but which years of dictatorship have tarnished and debilitated. There is in fact among many in the military a sense of shame that an honorable establishment which took so long to nurture has within the brief span of Mr. Marcos's regime been transformed into an object of mockery and hatred. The military ideal has been tragically tarnished by Mr. Marcos. My leadership will lend support to the restoration and revitalization of the military ideal. The soldiers are demoralized because the leadership of the military, at the expense of military professionalism, has capitulated to the blandishments of a President who uses the misplaced loyalty of some of the military to perpetuate himself in power. As a first step, therefore, in the restoration of the morale of the military, I shall upon assumption of office set in motion a process of immediately retiring all overstaying generals. . . .

Finally, let me speak of my eighth concern which is especially dear to me because I am a woman. . . . I know for a fact that Davao City is home to Gilda Narciso[1] whose example of courage and love of country is an inspiration to men and women alike. I am proud of her and of women like her. I am convinced that we women have an indispensable role to play in the rebuilding of our nation. Our motherly instinct impels us to protect our land, our home, our family, our community. It is a natural impulse God has gifted us with, and this gift is at once a moral responsibility. Hence, it is with pride and joy that I also welcome the courage of Leticia Ramos Shahani[2] who, in defiance of family sentiment and political party pressure, has shown us an example of principled life placed at the service of a suffering people. I am confident that there are thousands of other Leticia Shahanis and of Gilda Narcisos and that standing together they can withstand the destructive rapacity of male chauvinism which even now characterizes the campaign techniques of the presidential team of the other side.

Let me conclude by summarizing my social position for you here in Mindanao and for other Filipinos in our nation. . . .

In substance, I have eight major social concerns. I stand for efficient land use and equitable distribution of ownership of land. I pledge to rid the statute books of oppressive labor laws and I shall create for the Filipino worker an economic atmosphere which will give a just share of the fruits of his labor as well as opportunities for total human development. I will work for an integrated solution to the critical housing problem. I will attend to the clamor of our Muslim brethren and our Tribal Minorities for recognition of their autonomy rights long neglected by past governments. I will make medical services adequate and affordable by every Filipino and not just a showcase of imposing architecture and shining instruments which are of minimal usefulness especially to the poor. I will improve the lot of teachers and make education enhance personal dignity and respond to national goals and I will free it of the enslaving instruments instituted by an authoritarian regime. The problem of insurgency will be given the total attention it deserves and I shall quickly act to establish peace and order. I will harness the special talent of Filipino womanhood not only for the protection of the rights of women but also for the upliftment of men.

Editors' Notes

1. Gilda Narciso is a Philippine church worker arrested in March 1983 and raped by the Marcos military. After her release in September 1983, she devoted herself to a campaign against military abuse, and, in particular, the rape of women prisoners.

2. Leticia Ramos Shahani, a Philippine diplomat and assistant secretary general for Social Development and Humanitarian Affairs of the United Nations, resigned from the foreign service on January 6, 1986 to endorse Aquino. Her brother, Fidel Ramos, was at the time deputy chief of staff of the Philippine armed forces. She has been named deputy foreign minister in the new Aquino government.

Selection 10.2: Call for Boycott, BAYAN

Editors' Introduction

In the spring of 1985 the New Patriotic Federation or BAYAN (from the acronym of the Tagalog name Bagong Alyansang Makabayan) was formed bringing together a large number of opposition organizations. Initially conceived as a coalition of national democrats, social democrats, liberals, and independent leftists, internal disagreements resulted in BAYAN's becoming essentially a federation of national democratic organizations [see selection 7.11 for a discussion of the national democrats]. The combined membership of all of BAYAN's constituent organizations came to some two and a half million. Its program called for popular democracy, national sovereignty, people's welfare and economic development, national unity, and international solidarity.

In January 1986, after much internal debate, BAYAN called on the people of the Philippines to boycott the upcoming snap presidential election. BAYAN gave two basic reasons for this stand: the impossibility of a free and honest election under the Marcos dictatorship, and Aquino's refusal to include BAYAN's demands for reform in her campaign platform. As a result of the boycott decision, some of BAYAN's most prominent leaders took leaves of absence from the organization to campaign for Aquino. BAYAN's boycott appeal is printed below.

Source: BAYAN, "Persevere in Correct Struggles, Boycott the Sham Snap Election!"

We, in the Bagong Alyansang Makabayan unite with the Filipino people in fighting to oust Marcos.

We affirm that:

the ouster of Marcos is part of the people's struggle for genuine freedom and democracy, but this alone shall not solve the people's problems;

a truly fair, free and clean election will result in the ouster of Marcos; under which condition, it is only logical for the people to take to the polls and unite with the opposition on this basis.

We believe, however, that:

the coming snap election is not going to be fair, free and clean: Marcos refuses to resign and to concede electoral reforms, precisely, to ensure his "victory" at the polls; he will undoubtedly employ the entire state machinery to again rig and terrorize the election for a "fresh mandate" to continue his rule;

if there is any force that can restrain Marcos from committing massive fraud and terror, it is his U.S. imperialist patron: the U.S. being the single dominant force in Philippine politics, the decisive voice in all Philippine presidential elections;

the "vote" of the U.S. remains firmly cast for Marcos: the U.S. badly needs the tested fascist hand of Marcos to continually protect its strategic interests in the country against a rapidly advancing nationalist and democratic movement; the U.S. cannot afford to dislodge the well-entrenched Marcos clique at a time when it must intensify its "counter-insurgency" program in the country;

U.S.'s foremost concern in the Philippines is not democratization, but the maintenance and consolidation of its client fascist dictatorship: while it has thus been supposedly pressing for reforms, the U.S. has actually increasingly beefed up the regime's arsenal of repression with various forms of financial and logistical aid, and while it is supposedly pressing for a clean and honest election today, the U.S. actually does nothing substantial to stop Marcos from manipulating and terrorizing his way to another "mandate"; the U.S. has not even raised a finger over Marcos's refusal to resign and the pervading climate of state terrorism.

There is no sense believing, therefore, that the snap election shall lead to the ouster of Marcos from power. In truth, it shall only fortify the U.S.-backed Marcos dictatorship.

We maintain that:

aside from its utter inutility in ousting Marcos, the snap election does not promise meaningful changes in Philippine society, too; the program of the opposition does not even reflect the people's aspiration for basic social changes which will deliver them from poverty and oppression;

because the snap election shall not result in the ouster of Marcos, the most that can be gained from it is the opportunity to advance further the anti-dictatorship struggle; for which matter, it is necessary to focus the electoral campaign on the people's basic nationalist and democratic demands which shall serve to further isolate the dictatorship and raise the political consciousness of the citizenry;

unless the electoral campaign can be transformed into a militant forum for advancing the anti-dictatorship struggle, the snap election shall be entirely meaningless.

In pursuit of a meaningful campaign in this meaningless election, BAYAN has negotiated for the inclusion of the following in the opposition's platform:

—the people's basic nationalist demands to immediately remove all U.S. military installations in the country;

—abrogate or repeal all unequal treaties and agreements, laws and decrees that impair the nation's sovereignty;

—repudiate all foreign loans that did not benefit the people and service valid foreign debts on the basis of the nation's ability to pay;

—nationalize all basic and strategic industries; and re-orient Philippine education to serve the nation's interests;

—the people's basic democratic demands for genuine land reform in accordance with the principle of land to the tillers;

—the dismantling of all private monopolies, both foreign and local;

—the repudiation of Marcos's 1973 Constitution and all his repressive and anti-people laws and decrees;

—the establishment of a democratic coalition government that is truly representative of all sectors and classes of Philippine society;

—the immediate and unconditional release of all political prisoners;

—the investigation of human rights violations, the prosecution of the perpetrators and the indemnification of all victims of political repression;

—the promotion of the rights of the Bangsa Moro and Cordillera peoples to self-determination;

—and the recognition of all political groups and forces, which have been struggling against the U.S.-backed Marcos dictatorship.

But since the electoral opposition has refused to campaign on the basis of the people's urgent nationalist and democratic demands, participation in the snap election has become a total exercise in futility.

In view of the foregoing, the Bagong Alyansang Makabayan deems that the people are left with no other principled option but to boycott the snap election.

Boycott means the rejection of the sham electoral scheme of the U.S.-backed Marcos dictatorship to prolong its rule.

Boycott means the rejection of a meaningless electoral campaign that does not respond to the people's basic demands.

Boycott expresses the people's determination to struggle against the U.S.-backed Marcos dictatorship, relying not on sham elections, but perservering mainly in direct combative forms of mass struggles.

If we have to go against the tide in this particular struggle, so be it. But the course of history shall eventually vindicate our principled position.

Freedom and democracy are won not through sham electoral contests but through actual battles between the mighty force of a united people and the forces of oppression.

Selection 10.3: Support for Aquino, KAAKBAY

Editors' Introduction

KAAKBAY is a nationalist organization to the left of center led by former Senator Jose W. Diokno. In the statement printed below it threw its support to Aquino, as did most opposition organizations that were not heavily influenced by the national democrats. While stressing the importance of an Aquino victory, KAAKBAY declared the February election to be "neither the sum total nor the culmination" of the Philippine strug-gle for freedom and drew attention to major reforms that would have to be fought for after an Aquino victory.

It should be noted that in the course of the election campaign, Aquino changed her position on the bases. In the Convenors' Statement of 1984 [see selection 9.6], Aquino had called for the removal of foreign bases; during the course of the campaign she said that the bases could remain until 1991 after which time she would keep her options open.

This change occurred after the
KAAKBAY document was issued.
Source: "KAAKBAY Supports

Cory Aquino's Quest for Freedom
and Democracy," December 9, 1985.

Because Mr. Marcos likes to play games with his American sponsors and with the Filipino people, we will never know whether the snap presidential election will ever be held until it is actually held. It is part of the tragedy of our nation that our people must live with a president who cynically uses democratic processes like elections and structures like the legislature and the judicial system merely as props in a personal shadow-play.

But to every challenge we must rise, even when the opponent appears as if he is just making fools out of all of us. Every chance that we get to unseat the dictator, we must seize, even when the odds are heavily in his favor. Our nation was formed in the womb of a struggle, and therefore surrender should never be part of our national vocabulary. But let us be clear about the nature of this struggle.

Our people face two opponents at the same time: *U.S. Imperialism and the Marcos Dictatorship.* The coming presidential election is just one more arena in this continuing struggle to establish a free and democratic society in our land. It is neither the sum total nor the culmination of this long struggle.

It is in this light that KAAKBAY throws its support behind the presidential candidacy of Mrs. Cory Aquino, a Filipino who, at this time, best personifies our collective contempt for and rejection of a dictator who has destroyed our country, reduced our people to degrading poverty, and mortgaged the future of our children.

To many, Cory Aquino is also the perfect embodiment of our people's exasperation with the guile and insincerity of many professional *politicos.* For us in KAAKBAY, however, what has encouraged us most is her recent unequivocal statement of her commitment to some crucial demands that we and many other cause-oriented organizations have long been articulating in the streets and other public forums, namely:

—the unconditional removal of all U.S. military installations in the Philippines not later than the expiration of the Military Bases Agreement in 1991.

—the release of all prisoners and the grant of general amnesty to those charged with political offenses under the Marcos regime.

—the drafting of a new Constitution to replace the present Marcos Constitution.

These commitments give us reason to expect that a new government, led by someone like Cory Aquino, may also have the will to stand up to tremendous pressure from the U.S. government, should she get elected, so that other equally vital demands of our people may be addressed, such as:

—the restoration of all the fundamental rights of labor and the raising of wages to a level above the poverty line.

—the proclamation of a genuine land reform program and the grant of full support to our small farmers and small and medium-sized producers.

—the repeal of all repressive decrees.

—the investigation of all the crimes of the Marcos regime, especially those of its corrupt cronies and abusive soldiers.

—the rejection of continued dictation of Philippine economic policy by the IMF and the World Bank.

—the immediate renegotiation of the country's external debt, including the cancellation of a portion of this debt, so that the long-term development of our economy and the welfare of the poorest of our people are not sacrificed in the name of debt-repayment.

—the conduct of Philippine foreign policy exclusively from a national interest point of view, and the rejection of all U.S. attempts to determine the types of alliances we can make as a nation.

Implicit in all these demands is the simple analysis that the two principal opponents of the Filipino people today are American imperialism and the dictatorial regime of Ferdinand Marcos. Their defeat is the key to the attainment of genuine national independence and sovereignty, popular democracy and real development.

Selection 10.4: Statement on the Philippine Elections, President Ronald Reagan

Editors' Introduction

If Reagan's initial reaction to the Philippine election meant anything, it was evidently that the President was determined to hold on to Marcos even after most of his administration had given up on the Philippine dictator. Marcos was pleased with Reagan's initial statement and interpreted it, correctly it would seem, as an endorsement of his re-election. Others in Reagan's administration, however, very quickly reached the President and four days later he declared

that Marcos's party had been responsible for the fraud. The selection below is taken from Reagan's presidential press conference of February 11. Since Reagan had said the same thing the day before, it is clear that this statement was not a slip of the tongue.

It should be recorded that soon after "people's power" had carried the Enrile-Ramos revolt to victory, statements appeared in the U.S. press complimenting Reagan on his skill in getting rid of Marcos and restoring

democracy to the Philippines.   *Presidential Documents,* Feb. 17, 1986,
Source: *Weekly Compilation of*   vol. 22, no. 7, pp. 211-12, 218.

Q. Mr. President, the observers you sent to the Philippines have just returned with reports that they witnessed fraud and violence. Doesn't this undermine the credibility of the election and strengthen the hand of the Communist insurgence on the island?

The President. Well, Mike [Mike Putzel, Associated Press], I am not going to comment on this process, just as they are not going to render an official report, until the counting has finally been finished. I don't think it would be proper to do so. Yes, they told me in just an interim few remarks and made it plain that they're not going to issue the official report yet. But they told me that there was the appearance of fraud and yet, at the same time, said that they didn't have any hard evidence beyond that general appearance.

So, we're going to wait. We're neutral. And we then hope to have the same relationship with the people of the Philippines that we've had for all these historic years.

Q. If I may follow up, sir, did what they tell you give you concern about the credibility there and what the impact will be for U.S. interests in the Philippines?

The President. Well, I think that we're concerned about the violence that was evident there and the possibility of fraud, although it could have been that all of that was occurring on both sides. But at the same time, we're encouraged by the fact that it is evident that there is a two-party system in the Philippines and a pluralism that I think would benefit their people. And we're glad to see that particular thing happen, and we'll wait until we hear the outcome. . . .

Q. Mr. President, are the two U.S. bases in the Philippines of paramount importance when you consider U.S. policy for the Philippines? Or would you put the future of those bases at some risk if it meant standing up for democracy?

The President. One cannot minimize the importance of those bases, not only to us but to the Western World and certainly to the Philippines themselves. If you look at the basing now of the blue-ocean navy that the Soviet [sic] has built, which is bigger than ours, and how they have placed themselves to be able to intercept the 16 chokepoints in the world. There are 16 passages in the world, sea passages, through which most of the supplies and the raw material and so forth reaches not only ourselves but our allies in the Western World. And obviously, the plan in case of any kind of hostilities calls for intercepting and closing those 16 chokepoints. And we have to have bases that we can send forces to reopen those channels. And I don't know of any that's more important than the bases on the Philippines.

Selection 10.5: Post Election Statement,
Catholic Bishops' Conference of the Philippines

Editors' Introduction

After the Aquino assassination the center forces in Philippine politics moved into a more active opposition to the Marcos dictatorship. The same process took place in the Catholic Church of the Philippines, and the election statement of the Catholic Bishops' Conference represented its culmination.

The statement had another significance, however. It gave expression to the Church's advocacy of non-violent resistance as a method of struggle against the dictatorship. In a Boston interview of June 1986, Cardinal Jaime Sin, Archbishop of Manila, said that the Church had turned to the teaching and practice of non-violence in 1985. To promote an understanding of this method of op-

position, Cardinal Sin secured the help of Jean and Hildegard Goss-Mayr, both associated with the International Fellowship of Reconciliation. In 1985 these two held 40 to 50 classes on non-violent resistance in 30 provinces in the Philippines. "That work helped to prepare for the training of half a million poll-watchers who were ready to give their lives to protect the ballot boxes after Ferdinand Marcos called the 'snap election' for February" (*Boston Globe*, June 1, 1986). Furthermore it certainly influenced the behavior of millions in the streets of Manila later on [see selection 10.7].

Source: Catholic Bishops' Conference of the Philippines, "Post Election Statement," Claretian Publications.

Introduction

The people have spoken. Or have tried to. Despite the obstacles thrown in the way of their speaking freely, we, the bishops, believe that on the basis of our assessment as pastors of the recently concluded polls, what they attempted to say is clear enough.

The Conduct of the Polls

In our considered judgment, the polls were unparalleled in the fraudulence of their conduct. And we condemn especially the following modes of fraudulence and irregularities.

1. The systematic disenfranchisement of voters. The sheer scrambling of the voters' lists made it impossible for vast numbers of our people to express their proper preference of candidates.

2. The widespread and massive vote-buying. The vote-buyers in their cynical exploiting of the people's poverty and deep, if mis-

guided, sense of *utang na loob* [gratitude] deprived a great many of any real freedom of choice.

3. The deliberate tampering with the election returns. The votes of the people, even when already duly expressed and counted, were altered to register choices other than their own.

4. Intimidation, harassment, terrorism and murder. These made naked fear the decisive factor in people not participating in the polls or making their final choice. These and many other irregularities point to a criminal use of power to thwart the sovereign will of the people. Yet, despite these evil acts, we are morally certain the people's real will for change has been truly manifested.

Government Based on the Polls

According to moral principles, a government that assumes or retains power through fraudulent means has no moral basis. For such an access to power is tantamount to a forcible seizure and cannot command the allegiance of the citizenry. The most we can say then, about such a government, is that it is a government in possession of power. But admitting that, we hasten to add: because of *that* very fact, that same government itself has the obligation to right the wrong it is founded on. It must respect the mandate of the people. This is precondition for any reconciliation.

Response in Faith

If such a government does not of itself freely correct the evil it has inflicted on the people, then it is our serious moral obligation as a people to make it do so.

We are not going to effect the change we seek by doing nothing, by sheer apathy. If we did nothing we would be party to our own destruction as a people. We would be jointly guilty with the perpetrators of the wrong we want righted.

Neither do we advocate a bloody, violent means of righting this wrong. If we did, we would be sanctioning the enormous sin of fratricidal strife. Killing to achieve justice is not within the purview of our Christian vision in our present context.

The way indicated to us now is the way of nonviolent struggle for justice.

This means active resistance of evil by peaceful means—in the manner of Christ. And its one end for now is that the will of the people be done through ways and means proper to the Gospel.

We therefore ask every loyal member of the Church, every community of the faithful, to form their judgment about the February 7 polls. And if in faith they see things as we the bishops do, we must come together and discern what appropriate actions to take that will be according to the mind of Christ. In a creative, imaginative way, under the guidance of Christ's Spirit, let us pray together, reason together, decide together, act together, always to the end that the truth prevail, that the will of the people be fully respected.

Conclusion

These last few days have given us shining examples of the non-violent struggle for justice we advocate here:

* The thousands of NAMFREL workers and volunteers who risked their very lives to ensure clean and honest elections;

* The COMELEC computer technicians who refused to degrade themselves by participating in election frauds;

* The poll officials—registrars, teachers, government workers—who did their duty without fear or favor;

* The millions of ordinary voters who kept the sanctity of their ballot untarnished, their dignity intact;

* Radios Veritas [Catholic radio station] and fearless press people who spoke and reported the truth at all times.

Men and women of conscience, all. We cannot commend them highly enough.

There are thousands of their kind among government officials in the Batasan, the military, the COMELEC, among millions of our people who in the face of overwhelming odds voted and acted as their conscience dictated. Are there other men and women of conscience who will stand up like them and courageously confess their Christianity?

Now is the time to speak up. Now is the time to repair the wrong. The wrong was systematically organized. So must its correction be. But as in the election itself, that depends fully on the people, on what they are willing and ready to do. We, the bishops, stand in solidarity with them in the common discernment for the good of the nation. But we insist: Our acting must always be according to the Gospel of Christ, that is, in a peaceful, non-violent way.

May He, the Lord of Justice, the Lord of Peace, be with us in our striving for that good. And may the Blessed Virgin Mary, the Queen of Peace, and patroness of our country, assist us in this time of need.

Selection 10.6: Interview with Captain Rex Robles, Alan Berlow

Editors' Introduction

On Saturday, February 28, 1986, National Public Radio broadcast an interview conducted by Alan Berlow in Manila with Captain Rex Robles of the Philippine Navy, a key figure in the reform movement in the Philippine military. Robles told of two post-election plans that had been discussed by the reformists. The first, to carry out a palace coup against President Marcos, was discarded in favor of the second, to initiate five regional military uprisings that would eventually converge on Manila. These regional revolts were to have taken place on Saturday, February 28, two days after the nationwide general strike projected by Corazon Aquino.

According to Captain Robles, Marcos got wind of the first plan, the palace coup, and on Saturday February 21 gave orders to arrest Enrile, Ramos, and the reformist officers. When Robles and the reformists were informed of Marcos's arrest plans, the improvised uprisings at Camps Aguinaldo and Crame took place with the participation of Ramos and Enrile.

Robles mentions the cooperation of Clark Air Field, but gives no indication of any U.S. participation in the planning of the uprising that took place February 21 or the one that was projected for February 28. The fact of the matter seems to be that while the Reagan administration wholeheartedly encouraged the Philippine military reform movement, its attitude toward the military revolt sponsored by this movement was ambiguous until its success was guaranteed. Then Washington became unanimous in support.

Source: Tape of broadcast by National Public Radio, "All Things Considered," Feb. 28, 1986.

The rebellion that led to the downfall of Ferdinand Marcos earlier this week took place in a very confined area of Manila: for practical purposes, at two military bases, a television station, and in the streets surrounding them. But there was another rebellion on the drawing boards which would have thrown the Philippines into a more protracted war in at least five different provinces of the country.

Captain Rex Robles is a leader of the Reform the Armed Forces Movement, a group that had been pushing Marcos for the last year to clean up his notoriously corrupt and ineffective armed forces. When Marcos was proclaimed president, the group decided it had to stage a revolt.

[Capt. Robles:] *It's a plan to—we call it—liberate certain areas— actually to take over certain military camps in certain parts of the country, certain regions we call it.*

Robles said the plan was to rebel today, the 28th of February. The strategy was this: Marcos would be inaugurated on Tuesday [Feb. 25], Cory Aquino's planned general strike and boycott would begin Wednesday, and then the reformers would force the country to make a critical choice.

[Capt. Robles:] *We feel that by coming out two or three days afterwards we get the maximum impact for such a—you know—it's actually a propaganda piece: daring the people to side with us or to side with Marcos's government.*

Robles said the plan was to engage loyalists—that is pro-Marcos forces— in more rural areas, liberate these areas, and then move to Manila and the armed forces headquarters at Camp Aguinaldo. As it turned out, the rebellion started at Aguinaldo. Why?

The main reason is that Marcos's defense minister, Juan Ponce Enrile, and his vice chief of staff, Fidel Ramos, joined the reformers. But by the time they joined, the reformers plan had been scuttled.

Getting Enrile and Ramos on board, however, was no easy matter. The reformers had been working on both for months. Robles said he knew Enrile was sympathetic to the reformers' ideas of cleaning up the military. Enrile's personal security guard of 150 men was actively involved with the reform movement and it subsequently played a major role in the rebellion.

But after a meeting with Enrile last Friday night [Feb. 21], he had made no commitment to the reformers. So they decided to go ahead without him.

The final plan, agreed on last Friday, was to revolt in one week. That's what would have happened today.

But on Saturday morning pressure began to build on Ramos, Enrile, and the reformers. Robles got his first hint that something was about to happen from an intelligence officer, Colonel Gallileo Kintanan, who had been monitoring activities of the reformists.

Robles said Kintanan, who was by no means a personal friend, called at 7 a.m., started to talk about the reform movement, and then began telling him a strange and seemingly irrelevant story.

[Capt. Robles:] *And then he did a very strange thing, he started to tell me about his trip to Baguio. He said, "I'm going off and see my wife. My wife's living in Baguio—whatever, she's a teacher, and so forth." I said, "What's all this at 7 o'clock in the morning? My breakfast is getting cold." He says, "You know I think I plan to go up at 12 o'clock noon time today. Twelve o'clock." And I said was he trying to tell me something?*

Kintanan's suggestion that noon was somehow a critical time began to make sense as the morning progressed. Robles said the reformers began getting tips that Enrile, Ramos, and the reformers were about to be arrested.

Robles then got information, which he was able to verify, that fifteen men, including five associated with the reform movement, had been arrested. Finally, Robles got a call from a source at Malacañang, the presidential palace, saying soldiers were on their way to pick him up.

Robles stayed at Camp Aguinaldo until 3:30 when he was sent to make contacts with reporters and the U.S. and Japanese governments to let them know what was happening. He missed being arrested by about thirty minutes.

As he was leaving Aguinaldo, Enrile and then Ramos arrived. Enrile brought 300 armed reformist troops. Within the next two hours, Enrile and Ramos agreed to make a stand at Aguinaldo. That night they announced the rebellion at a press conference, and tens of thousands of Filipinos surrounded the camp to protect them from an invasion.

As this latest plan was agreed on, Marcos was discovering plots of his own. He went on television to announce that he'd uncovered a plot to assassinate him and his wife and to overthrow the government. Marcos paraded before the cameras a handful of soldiers involved in these plots.

Robles says three of the men picked up were associated with the reform movement. And he says the alleged plot to stage a coup d'etat at the presidential palace had been discussed by the reformers, but was rejected.

Over the next two days the world watched a military stand-off between the two sides. When the rebels moved from Camp Aguinaldo to neighboring Camp Crame, Marcos brought in tanks, then helicopters.

But an even more critical event was Marcos's decision to send fighter planes swooping in over Camp Crame.

According to Robles, sources at the presidential palace told him that Marcos ordered the planes to strafe and bomb Camp Crame and Robles said *that* order was a fatal mistake. The pilots recognized that with tens of thousands of civilians surrounding Camp Crame massive casualties would be unavoidable. So the pilots defected to Clark Air Field, the U.S. air base.

[Capt. Robles:] *When five jets flew out of Basa—Basa Air Base—and they were ordered to strafe and bomb that fateful Monday morning— remember, all those helicopters and airplanes—they were loaded with just enough fuel to reach Clark Air Base, where they radioed urgently to land because they ran short of fuel. And it's a great technicality because they had to land and they could no longer be serviced because it was a foreign base. And any actions by the United States would be interpreted as partisan. And of course they couldn't touch the airplanes and it worked to our advantage.*

In all, 11 F-5's defected to Clark Air Field. Robles's account is of no small interest for Americans. In his speech on national security two days ago, President Reagan saluted the "remarkable restraint shown by both sides in the Philippines to prevent bloodshed during these last tense days."

If Robles's account is accurate, and Marcos's orders had been carried out, thousands of civilians could have died in an air attack on Camp Crame.

Robles insists that the order to bomb Camp Crame led to Marcos's loss of his air force. Without the air force, Robles said, Marcos had no chance of winning if a full scale war broke out.

Within 24 hours, Marcos fled to the same U.S. air base, Clark Air Field, and then to the United States.

Selection 10.7: The Confrontation of February 23, John Burgess

Editors' Introduction

At the crucial moment of the first confrontation on February 23, the Marcos military refused to obey orders and use the force necessary to put down Enrile and Ramos. In effect the soldiers and officers of the army of Marcos were affirming their iden- tity as Filipinos. Their refusal to obey Marcos's orders seemed to de- clare before the world their recogni- tion that the sovereign will of the nation was represented by the people who faced them in the streets rather than by the tyrant in Malacañang Palace.

How did this development come about? Many years of effort and sacrifice by many Filipino oppositionists, illustrious and unknown, helped make it possible to reach this moment of heightened consciousness, giving thousands the strength to face the troops, giving the troops the ability to see themselves in those who faced them, forging a unity of purpose in the destruction of the dictatorship. In addition, it is obvious that the nonviolent resistance practiced by the people, clergy and laity alike, permit-ted the troops to share in the popular mood. The people's nonviolent opposition enabled the military to see Marcos's orders as clearly immoral, and to understand, therefore, the need to disobey them.

Below is an account of the confrontation between civilians and troops at Camp Aguinaldo that took place on February 23.

Source: John Burgess, "Praying Crowd Halts Marcos Tank Column," *Washington Post,* Feb. 24, 1986, pp. A1, A17.

Manila, February 24 (Monday)—The choice given to the Philippine marines manning two tanks stopped on Ortigas Avenue Sunday afternoon, as tensions first began to build, was simple. If they wanted to reach their objective, they would have to roll over the crowd that was enveloping them.

In its ranks were Catholic nuns reciting the words "Hail Mary, full of grace . . . ." There were priests with heads bowed in prayer and young women offering orchids to any soldier who would take them.

So the marines bluffed. Over and over, they fired up their tanks' mammoth diesel engines and edged forward. Shouts of "Sit down! Sit down!" would ring out. People would drop to the pavement and the tanks would stop. Applause and cries of rapture would go up at this new victory.

In the end, after four hours, the tanks and the armored column of about 1,000 marines they were leading went back to their barracks, having unexpectedly met with a remarkable display of citizen activism by supporters of opposition leader, Corazon Aquino.

In the early hours of Monday morning, troops came back elsewhere, according to widespread reports, using tear gas and truncheons against crowds. But those troops also failed in their mission.

The withdrawal of the military in the confrontation on Sunday brought jubilation.

"Liberation day!" declared a young man surveying the scene with others from atop a bus.

The danger to the crowd was probably not as high as it might have seemed. From the start it was clear that the marines, many of whom had been flown to Manila only days ago from duty fighting Communist insurgents on Mindanao Island, did not have their hearts in the task. Many flashed the *laban* (fight!) hand signal of the opposition.

The crowd treated them not with contempt but as errant brothers they hoped would return to the fold.

"We are all Filipinos—there is no fight here," shouted one man as a column of marines weighted down with M60 machine guns and a bazooka passed by.

The marines left Ft. Bonifacio, a major military base in Manila, in early afternoon. Their mission, officers said, was to proceed to Camp Aguinaldo, the Defense Ministry headquarters where military rebels who support Aquino's claim to the presidency were in control.

Their tracked vehicles chewed up soft pavement as they rumbled across the city through light Sunday traffic on Epifanio de los Santos Avenue. Crowds of people watched from overpasses and sidewalks.

At the intersection with Ortigas Avenue, about one mile from the camp, Aquino supporters had blocked passage with about two dozen commandeered buses. As the crowd of about 20,000 looked on, the marines turned off the avenue and crashed through a wooden fence, entering a vacant lot of about 10 acres in an apparent effort to skirt the barrier. Two tanks broke through a wall at the field's far side and entered Ortigas Avenue. The crowd closed in and that was as far as the soldiers got.

The marine commandant, Brig. Gen. Artemio Tadiar, dressed in a camouflage jump suit, waded into the crowd around the tanks and tried to work out passage with a businessman who had emerged as a spokesman. "If we can't clear this and it gets dark, there will be trouble," he told reporters later.

The crowd's spirits were high and the general drew applause when he climbed atop a tank to address them with a loudspeaker.

"Let us just move," he pleaded.

"No! No!" the crowd responded.

He tried again. "We want to go on quietly and I want to assure you there'll be no trouble." That appeal also was rejected.

Women moved among the soldiers, giving out purple orchids. A marine packing an M16 rifle stuck one in his shoulder harness. Sandwiches were passed forward by the crowd and given to the marines.

"Look at the faces of the soldiers. They are not the faces of people we want to fight," said Freddie Aldeguer, a salesman for a pharmaceutical company.

The first sign of victory for the crowd came when the tanks lurched back through the hole in the wall about 4:45 p.m. and rejoined the rest of the force in the field. "It seems we cannot go forward without hurting someone," a colonel said.

People began feeling bolder. Ignoring gestures of admonition, women strode into the field to deliver marigolds to sheepish soldiers.

When a helicopter set down in the center, they rushed toward it and chanted, "Cory! Cory!" at the men who got out.

A colonel said there would be no violence from the soldiers. "We told them not to follow unlawful orders," he said. "Killing people is unauthorized. That's why we didn't push through. Some of us have relatives in the opposition. Some of us have relatives in the mountains," a reference to the Communist insurgency.

The gathering acquired even more of a fiesta atmosphere as dusk approached. A family posed for a photo against an armored car. Two men volunteered to a reporter that the Filipino people would welcome U.S. intervention.

The marines began leaving as darkness fell. The buses were removed and the crowd parted. The tanks, armored cars, personnel carriers, jeeps and trucks picked their way through amid applause.

People grabbed the hands of soldiers walking out, often drawing warm smiles in return, and joined the convoy in a victory march as it rolled back toward Ft. Bonifacio.

It is unclear why the order to withdraw was given. President Ferdinand Marcos said tonight he gave it after the rebels pleaded with him not to use force. But to the crowd, the victory was all theirs.

Photo: Charles Steiner

Which way for the Acquino administration: combatting guerillas . . .

Photo: Charles Steiner

. . . or combatting poverty?

CHAPTER 11: THE FUTURE

Introduction

The significance of the new administration of Corazon Aquino for the Philippine people is not so much its accomplishments—though these have been considerable—as the possibilities that have been opened up.

In ending the dictatorship of Ferdinand Marcos and the repressive decrees of that dictatorship, Aquino has unleashed social forces and encouraged popular movements seeking to restructure Philippine society in the direction of greater sovereignty and social justice.

But the forces for change do not hold the field alone. Even discounting the remaining Marcos loyalists—whose unrepentant association with the former dictator discredits them in the public eye—there are many advocates of the status quo. Some of these are part of the new government, reflecting Aquino's personal political ambivalence as well as the broad spectrum that came together in February 1986 to oust Marcos.

On the question of democratic rights, however, Aquino moved decisively. Her second act as president was to restore the writ of habeas corpus [see selection 11.1]. Courts were freed from political interference and the newly unshackled press bloomed as more than twenty papers appeared daily on Manila's newsstands. A commission was established to investigate those responsible for human rights abuses under the Marcos dictatorship. The repressive labor laws of the Marcos era were repealed. And another commission was appointed to write a new constitution.

Aquino also kept her campaign pledge on releasing Marcos's political prisoners. She freed over four hundred individuals charged with subversion, including—after brief hesitation and over the objections of the military and the U.S. government—Jose Maria Sison, the founder of the Communist Party of the Philippines, and Bernabe Buscayno, the former leader of the New People's Army. In addition, many who were detained by Marcos as common criminals but were in fact political prisoners are being released on a case-by-case basis.

The military represents the right-wing in Aquino's administration. Juan Ponce Enrile and Fidel Ramos obtained their positions in the new government not by their long-standing opposition to the dictatorship but by their last-minute defection from the Marcos camp. As the Minister of National Defense in Marcos's decaying regime, Enrile's prospects had not looked very bright, but his eleventh-hour rebellion allowed him to secure for himself the powerful defense portfolio in the new government. In what may have reflected Aquino's wariness, however, the new chief of staff, Ramos, was to report directly to the president rather than to Enrile. And when Ramos recommended that one of the generals implicated by the Agrava Commission in the assassination of her husband be appointed the new head of the National Police, President Aquino refused the recommendation. Aquino has retired many of Marcos's "over-staying" generals, a step in the direction of increased professionalization of the military, but with little impact on its rightist orientation.

Enrile let it be known that he and the armed forces expect a significant role in the new government. He publicly raised the possibility of a coup to counter left-wing influence in the Cabinet. "The moment they start subverting the goals of the government and undermine the stability of the government," he told reporters, "then I assure you the military will not just sit on its butt and let the government be subverted." Tellingly, Enrile did not indicate how he would determine that such subversion had occurred nor whether he would allow Aquino to judge her own government's stability (*New York Times,* April 25, 1986, p. A2). Enrile has spoken out for an uncompromising military policy towards the New People's Army and has objected strenuously to investigations of human rights abuses on the part of the military [see selection 11.2]. He also has called for the retention of the U.S. military bases and for an economic policy based on private enterprise.

Vice-president of the new government, and concurrently Foreign Minister, is Salvador Laurel. In addition, a number of other cabinet positions are held by Laurel loyalists, who, like Laurel, only broke with Marcos in the latter years of martial law. With his well-oiled political machine, UNIDO, and his well-known political ambitions, Laurel is a force to be reckoned with. Along with Ramos and Enrile, he is a U.S. favorite in the cabinet; Filipinos consider the United States their "closest friend," Laurel declared.

When opposition leaders issued the Convenors' statement in 1984 [see selection 9.6], Laurel refused to sign, objecting to the provisions on the U.S. military bases and on the release of political prisoners. During the snap election campaign, Aquino essentially adopted UNIDO's ambiguous stand on the bases, but she stuck with her position on the detainees.

Aquino's cautious attitude toward Laurel is indicated by her selecting Aquilino Pimentel, the leader of her political party, PDP-Laban, as Minister of Local Government. In this position he has a decisive voice in the appointment of officers-in-charge, those who are given authority over provinces, municipalities, and cities on a temporary basis until new elections can be held. Laurel accuses Pimentel of favoring PDP-Laban members for these positions over UNIDO members. Politically, PDP-Laban represents younger reformists, while UNIDO is a traditional elite party.

Key economic positions in the cabinet were given to prominent business figures, dubbed the "Makati Mafia" (Makati is the business district of Manila). The new Minister of Finance is Jaime Ongpin, the former head of the largest mining company in the country, Benguet Consolidated. Ongpin had been a leading business critic of Marcos, although it has recently come to light that Marcos cronies secretly owned Benguet. The Ministry of Trade and Industry was given to Jose Concepcion Jr., head of the nation's largest flour mill and chair of NAMFREL, the organization that fought to keep the February election clean. Jose Fernandez has been retained as Governor of the Central Bank; he had served in this post under Marcos and was well respected in international financial circles.

Ongpin's economic program is what one would expect from a leading member of the business community: dismantle the crony monopolies, restore business confidence, encourage free enterprise through "privatization" of as much of the economy as possible, and improve the climate for foreign investment [see selection 11.3]. Other economic policy-makers, notably Solita Monsod, the director of the National Economic and Development Authority (NEDA), have suggested that the country ought to consider selective repudiation of some of the $26 billion debt with which Marcos burdened them. Ongpin has been adamant, however, that all debts will be repaid. On the other hand, NEDA agrees with the Makati Mafia on the importance of the privatization of the economy. Years of Marcos's personal domination of key sectors of the economy have discredited in the eyes of many Filipinos the notion of social ownership of the means of production; in fact, however, rather than creating an all-powerful public sector, Marcos had allowed his private circle of friends and relatives to loot the public coffers.

A different economic agenda is favored by the militant labor organization KMU, which has as little faith in Ongpin's free market capitalism as it had in Marcos's crony capitalism [see selection 11.4]. The new minister of labor, Augusto Sanchez, was appointed by Aquino with the strong backing of the KMU and he has urged that improving the living standards of workers be a top priority of the government. Sanchez's appointment was opposed by the American Chamber of Commerce in the Philippines, the Philippine business community, and the right-wing labor organization TUCP. (TUCP was set up by the Marcos regime and received funding from the United States government [see selection 9.3]; it supported Marcos's repressive labor legislation and only moved to disassociate itself from the dictator in late 1985. In the snap election, one faction of the TUCP backed Marcos and the other stayed neutral.) Sanchez and some other like-minded officials find themselves up against formidable opposition, for Ongpin's priorities are shared by Washington and the International Monetary Fund. According to the *Christian Science Monitor* (May 8, 1986), the U.S. Embassy has already served notice on Aquino that U.S. aid could be jeopardized by such actions as "Aquino's May 1 Labor Day declaration of lenient policies toward labor unions and strikers, which might scare away new foreign investors" and the serious consideration given at two Cabinet meetings to selective repudiation of the debt. Aquino has reduced the prices of gasoline, and some food necessities, but as of yet the economic program of the government has not been clearly defined.

The most pressing issue of social and economic justice facing the country is the question of land reform. Where Ongpin and others want to stress the free market and foreign capital, the largest peasant organization in the country, the KMP, has called for "genuine land reform" [see selection 11.5]. Long promised, but never realized, land reform to the KMP has to consist of more than the cosmetic pronouncements of Marcos and his predecessors.

As on economic policy in general, the Aquino administration has yet to chart a firm course on the land question. But, unlike in the Marcos years, government policy is not a process isolated from popular pressures, and the peasant and labor organizations will have the chance to press Aquino and the more conservative elements of her cabinet for thorough-going reforms.

In the present open political environment there is opportunity for the left to make its influence felt. The claims by the military and the Marcos loyalists that Aquino's is a communist government are ludicrous, but there is no doubt that the left is in a position to exert pressure for change. Some members of Aquino's administration before their appointment had long been identified with nationalist and cause-oriented organizations: Joker Arroyo and Rene Saguisag, Aquino's executive secretary and presidential spokesperson, respectively, had been prominent human rights lawyers; Dr. Mita Pardo de Tavera, the new Minister of Social Services and Development, was a pioneer in community-based health care. And former Senator Jose Diokno and Sister Mariani Dimaranan were made human rights commissioners. Individuals such as these are likely to be sensitive to popular pressures.

For its part, the left has responded to the post-Marcos political dispensation with a flowering of new ideas, approaches, and organizations. The Communist Party of the Philippines (CPP) has undertaken a self-criticism of its boycott position during the election [see selection 11.6], made changes in its top leadership, permitted more vigorous internal debate, and agreed to enter into negotiations with the government for a cease-fire in the countryside. Jose Maria Sison, the former leader and founder of the Communist Party of the Philippines, is heading up efforts to establish Partido ng Bayan (People's Party) which will contest elections. An unprecedented Political Party of Women is being set up as well. Others have begun a group called Volunteers for Popular Democracy. And an organization of independent Marxists, BISIG, has formed, putting forward a Philippine vision of socialism and calling for a broad coalition of all progressive forces in the country [see selection 11.7].

Advocates of change are not alone in being able to pressure the Aquino government. And of those forces inclined to defend the status quo, perhaps the most powerful is the U.S. government.

Washington's goals are the same as they have been for nearly a century: to maintain what it sees as U.S. military and economic interests and to oppose any popular movements that might undermine those interests. The current agenda of the Reagan administration is parallel to that of Enrile's: deal militarily, not by negotiations, with the NPA; exclude leftist influence from the government; preserve U.S. military bases after 1991; and encourage an economic program of free enterprise with a substantial role for foreign capital.

U.S. officials have made clear that the retention of base rights is of fundamental importance [see selection 11.8]. They are hopeful that U.S. economic leverage will be adequate to ensure these rights—some, like Senate majority leader Robert Dole want to explicitly condition U.S. aid on continued access to the bases; others consider that the implicit leverage will be sufficient.

Washington cannot be altogether sanguine on this score, however. Aquino has stated that the bases could remain until 1991 and that after that she would keep her options open. But the Aquino government is known to include many opponents of the bases (recall that Aquino and Ongpin both signed the Convenors' statement [selection 9.6] opposing the bases). And a number of recent statements from Aquino and others undermine some of the leading arguments in favor of the bases. Aquino has declared that the Philippines would not face an external threat if the bases were removed (*Christian Science Monitor*, 25 July 1986, p. 1); Vice-President and Foreign Minister Salvador Laurel has suggested that the bases make the Philippines a nuclear target (*Malaya*, 11 April 1986); and Deputy Foreign Minister Leticia Shahani has indicated that the Philippines is set to re-examine its policy on the storage of nuclear weapons at U.S. bases and the presence of nuclear-armed ships in the region (*Manila Bulletin*, 18 March 1986).

The nuclear issue may well be the weak link in the case for retaining the U.S. bases. Without the right to store and transport nuclear weapons, the bases are considerably less valuable to the Pentagon, for whom the integration of nuclear and conventional forces is an important component of its politico-military posture. And anti-nuclear sentiment is growing apace in the Philippines. In the aftermath of the Chernobyl disaster, the Aquino government decided to cease work on the Westinghouse nuclear power plant—a Marcos-era boondoggle, involving major U.S. financial participation [see selection 7.2].

While the people of the Philippines may regard the removal of Marcos as opening the door to a better life, the Pentagon looks on it as opening the door to an effective campaign against the NPA. An essential element of Washington's strategy for retaining the bases in the post-Marcos era is to press the Aquino government to adopt an iron-fist approach to the NPA, in order to make the military suppression of the communist insurgency that government's top priority. The probable effect of such a policy would be to put right-wing military leaders like Enrile, determined champions of the status quo, in a dominant position in the government. An all-out offensive against the NPA, as desired by the Pentagon, would serve to diminish and sidetrack efforts for social reform (including base removal), if not to brand and suppress advocates of such reform as subversive. Previously the U.S. supported the Philippine military's efforts against the NPA in order to keep Marcos in power. Now, with Marcos gone, U.S. support for military confrontation with the NPA may well tend to counteract the democratic gains made by Filipinos when they overthrew Marcos and to block their further advance.

Defense Secretary Caspar Weinberger—the first U.S. cabinet officer to visit the post-Marcos Philippines—stressed the importance of military aid to Aquino. On April 21, the *Christian Science Monitor* reported that "under pressure from Washington," Aquino was putting "a limit on her turn-the-other-cheek policy toward the communist insurgents." In May it was confirmed that the Pentagon was sending a team of advisers to train Philippine military personnel in counter-insurgency (*Malaya*, 7 May 1986). Fighting between the Armed Forces and the NPA is still going on—as one might expect given NPA suspicions of the army, the continued activities of local warlords and the Civilian Home Defense Forces (which Aquino pledged to disband but—under military pressure—has not yet done), and Enrile's policy of taking the military initiative whenever communist targets present themselves (*Newsweek*, 5 May 1986, p. 39). The Heritage Foundation—a think-tank closely identified with the Reagan administration—has published a blueprint for U.S. intervention to help defeat the NPA. Negotiations don't figure in their scenario [see selection 11.9].

Despite objections from Philippine military leadership and Washington, President Aquino is going ahead with the negotiations for a cease-fire. She appointed as the government's representatives to the talks Jose Diokno and Ramon Mitra. Mitra is a landowner who serves as Minister of Agriculture; both he and Diokno signed the Convenors' Statement [see selection 9.6], have spent time in Marcos's jails, and are acceptable negotiating partners to the NPA, which had refused to negotiate with the military. (Because of ill-health, Diokno was replaced by Teofisto Guingona, another signer of the Convenors' Statement.) Having overcome objections to a cease-fire in its own ranks, the NPA is preparing to enter such negotiations. However, the opposition of U.S. officials and the Philippine military headed by Enrile to Aquino's policy of cease-fire is likely to make pursuit of that goal difficult.

One final element that must be factored into the Philippine political process in the post-Marcos era is the effect of U.S. public opinion on Washington's Philippine policy. Just as U.S. opinion was not undivided at the turn of the century, when imperialists and anti-imperialists clashed over U.S. Philippine policy, nor during the years of martial law, when voices were raised against Washington's policy of supporting the Marcos dictatorship, so today there are those who oppose the efforts of the U.S. military and corporate elite to promote their strategic and economic interests at the expense of self-determination and social justice for Filipinos [see selection 11.10]. In opposing their government's intervention, U.S. citizens can help Filipinos as they struggle to decide the future course of their society, free from outside interference. In doing so, people in the United States will also be helping to secure a future of peace and democratic development for their own country.

Selection 11.1: Proclamation Number 2, President Corazon Aquino

Editors' Introduction

The outstanding contribution of the Aquino government thus far has been its effort to restore civil rights to Philippine society, particularly in re-

establishing freedom to speak, write, and organize without repressive hindrance. Especially symbolic in this regard is her Proclamation Number 2 restoring the writ of habeas corpus in order to prevent arbitrary arrest and detention. When Ferdinand Marcos first suspended habeas corpus in August 1971 over a year before his declaration of martial law it was a clear indication to many of the road he was to take in the erection of military dictatorship. Similarly President Aquino's restoration of habeas corpus in March 1986 has given hope to Filipinos that it is a first step on the road her government must travel if it is to realize its self-declared ideals of "justice, liberty, and freedom for all."

As Aquino's proclamation indicates, when, in January 1981, Marcos nominally did away with martial law, he quickly moved to suspend the writ of habeas corpus once again.

All observers agree that the Aquino government's restoration of civil liberties has had more effect in Manila and other urban centers than in the country-side, where the Philippine military and landlords' private armies still tend to hold sway.

It is important, however, that Aquino's measures to restore civil rights have already provided a "democratic space" which the people of the Philippines are using to organize themselves for the improvement of their lives and society. And President Aquino has explicitly urged Filipinos to make use of this democratic space. In a speech accompanying Proclamation Number 2, she said:

"I call on all of you to organize at the grassroots level, in your communities and villages, by interest group, by sector—build people's organizations to turn the spontaneous birth of our people's power into more permanent structures for meaningful participation of the citizenry in the shaping of our nation's future. *Mag organisa kayo para hindi maging ningas-kogon ang ating People's Power.* [Organize so that our People's Power will not be short-lived.] Through these organized groups you will be in a better position to participate and contribute to ensuring that the freedom we have won is not compromised, that the revolution will not be stolen by those who lurk in the shadows waiting for the slightest chance to do so."

Source: Mimeographed text of proclamation.

PROCLAIMING THE LIFTING OF THE SUSPENSION OF THE PRIVILEGE OF THE WRIT OF HABEAS CORPUS THROUGHOUT THE PHILIPPINES

WHEREAS, the then President Ferdinand E. Marcos, issuing Proclamation No. 2045 dated 17 January 1981 and Proclamation No. 2045-A dated 23 July 1983, suspended the privilege of the writ of habeas corpus in the two autonomous regions of Mindanao and in all other places with respect to persons detained "for all cases involving the crimes of insurrection, rebellion, subversion, conspiracy or proposal to commit such crimes, sedition, conspiracy to commit sedition, inciting to sedition, and for all other crimes or offenses committed by them in furtherance or on the occasion thereof, or incident thereto, or in connection therewith, such as but not limited to offenses involving economic sabotage, illegal assemblies, illegal associations, tumults and other disturbances of public order, unlawful use of means of publication and unlawful utterances, and alarms and scandals, or with respect to any person whose arrest or detention was, in the judgment of the President, required by public safety as a means to repel or quell the rebellion in the country";

WHEREAS, the proclamations and decrees mentioned and all the related decrees, instructions, orders and rules were not warranted by the requirements of public safety since the existing rebellion could have been contained by government sincerity at reforms, by peaceful negotiations and reconciliation, and by steadfast devotion to the rule of law;

WHEREAS, instead of serving its purpose of suppressing the rebellion and other threats to national security, the suspension of the privilege of the writ of habeas corpus drove many to the hills and fanned the conspiracy to overthrow the government by violence and force; and

WHEREAS, the Filipino people have established a new government bound to the ideals of genuine liberty and freedom for all;

NOW, THEREFORE, I, CORAZON C. AQUINO, President of the Philippines, by virtue of the powers vested in me by the Constitution and the Filipino people, do hereby revoke Proclamations No. 2045 and 2045-A, and do hereby lift the suspension of the privilege of the writ of habeas corpus so that this guardian of liberty and freedom may be available to all.

IN WITNESS WHEREOF, I have hereunto set my hand and caused the seal of the Republic of the Philippines to be affixed to this proclamation.

DONE in the City of Manila this 2nd day of March, in the year of Our Lord, nineteen hundred and eighty-six.

Selection 11.2: The Philippine Armed Forces, James B. Goodno

Editors' Introduction

On the Op-Ed page of the *New York Times* of July 30, 1986, Victor Gotbaum, a leader of the American Federation of State, County, and Municipal Employees, urged the Democratic Party to repudiate support for the right-wing military in the Third World. "Throughout the developing world, the military is a constant threat. When it rules it is brutal and destructive. When it is finally forced to leave, it manages to hover around the ruins, a threat to return."

As the people of the Philippines struggle to move beyond the disaster of the Marcos dictatorship, they are confronted by a right-wing military leadership and apparatus left over from the former regime. Juan Ponce Enrile, Marcos's Defense Minister, and Navy Captain Rex Robles of the Reform the Armed Forces Movement (RAM) may have taken prominent parts in the military revolt that helped to topple Marcos [see selection 10.6]. The Philippine military may now be called the *New* Armed

Forces of the Philippines. But the military leadership is still permeated with the right-wing ideology of the Marcos dictatorship that labels all efforts at social change "subversive" and worthy of repression. Indicative of the "unreformed" character of the Philippine military leadership is its militant opposition to President Aquino's policies of cease-fire and reconciliation with the New People's Army, as is explained in the following article by James B. Goodno, the Manila correspondent for *In These Times* (a Chicago-based socialist newspaper) and other publications.

Source: James B. Goodno, "General Machinations Mark Aquino's Army," *In These Times,* May 21-27, 1986, p. 9.

Various forces pose a threat to this country's emergent movement for peace and a broad democracy, but the gravest danger does not now come from those sources most commonly cited—the far left or Marcos's supporters—but from the leaders of the military.

The new government's military men, most of them holdovers from the old regime, are vehement anti-communists who lack democratic credentials. Defense Minister Juan Ponce Enrile, Gen. Fidel Ramos and the senior leaders of the Reform the Armed Forces Movement (RAM) perhaps strengthened their standing when they abandoned the fading Marcos dictatorship for Corazon Aquino. Their revolt was motivated largely by Marcos's failure to contain the growing communist-led insurgency. They are now waging an aggressive campaign, both verbal and military, against the Communist Party of the Philippines (CPP) and the organizations under it—the National Democratic Front (NDF) and the New People's Army (NPA).

The military group forms the most cohesive block within the ruling coalition and state apparatus. Though Aquino's power rests on popular support and approval, it is still unclear if that support is organized and active enough to withstand opposition from the army. Through Enrile, the military has one voice in the cabinet. But because of the military's central role in the final anti-Marcos revolt that voice is exceptionally loud and influential.

Psychological warfare is the military's favored strategy. As it did under Marcos, the military command is using propaganda—some based on fact, some not—to smear the left and enhance the reputation of what is now being called the New Armed Forces of the Philippines (NAFP). Propaganda has made it difficult to discern the truth in recent military reports. But the struggle is more than a war of words. In some areas fighting has reached unprecedented levels.

Some government officials blame the military for delays in calling a cease-fire and accuse them of stalling other policies that might aid a political settlement. Many of these same officials, however, offer only a confused plan for dealing with the insurgency.

"The government has been moving too slowly on this," said Political Affairs Minister Antonio Cuenco, who also belongs to a committee on reconciliation and peace efforts. "We've met resistance from the military. They think the Communists are out to dismantle the government. I don't think this is true anymore."

Anti-Cease-Fire Litany

Speaking shortly after Aquino came to power, Navy Capt. Rex Robles, an Enrile confidant and RAM leader, said a cease-fire would play into the hands of the Communists who would use it to consolidate their position and prepare them for future military struggles. This reasoning was repeated countless times by others in the military and eventually found its way into Aquino's speeches.

Instead of a cease-fire, Robles said, the government should launch an all-out drive against rebels in the hills by deploying government troop units in search-and-destroy missions. Military patrols in rebel-influenced zones continued unabated between the February 25 overthrow of Marcos and the recent outbreak of serious fighting in parts of northern Luzon.

After months of opposing the cease-fire, Enrile recently said he is open to negotiating if both the NAFP and the NPA identify the location of their forces and agree to stay put during the cease-fire. Enrile's apparent turnabout came after the military consolidated its position in the new government. Aquino has now come to accept key elements of the military's position on the NPA.

"The time for peace has come," Aquino said during an April 20 address to graduating seniors at the University of the Philippines in Quezon City. "But I have no illusions that peace will come easily. For to the Communist true believer the road to victory bristles with arms and resounds with combat."

Aquino's Mind Reading

Aquino expressed her hopes for a cease-fire after holding the rebels alone responsible for the ongoing fighting. She said that during the proposed cease-fire "the armed forces will maintain their defensive posture. I am sure the Communist leadership can read my mind as well as I believe I can read theirs. They will use the cease-fire to consolidate their position, recruit and recoup the losses of the preemptive February revolution."

It wasn't long after Aquino came to power that the military began accusing the NPA of violating a non-existent cease-fire. When Aquino first seemed to be on the verge of ordering a cease-fire, shortly before the March 22 commencement at the Philippine Military Academy, the military escalated its anti-Communist propaganda campaign. The top brass attended a mid-March cabinet meeting. They brought classified documents and a classified slide-show purporting to expose NPA atrocities. Witnesses say the presentation resembled one used during the Marcos years.

Around the same time, some RAM members accused several cabinet ministers of having "Communist leanings." The targets were ministers who had been vocal foes of military abuses during the Marcos years. RAM leaders muzzled the charges, but only after they received wide play in the local media. Similar charges have since been thrown at independent and church-supported human rights advocates.

"We believe that the wild claims of the military were intended to malign the names of human-rights advocates and institutions, which had the courage to expose continuing military abuses," said Father Luciano Pili, executive-secretary of the Luzon Secretariat of Social Action. "It is lamentable that the military has chosen to attempt a cover-up by using the old Marcos trick of playing up the Red Bogey."

Ramos is at the forefront of the military's new image campaign. He has appeared before civic and business clubs in Metro Manila to discuss military reform, the "communist threat" and the primacy of civilian rule. During these appearances Ramos consistently opposes human-rights investigations that focus only on the military. He advocates a plan to grant amnesty to men in uniform in return for amnesty for rebels.

The military apparently fears the investigation being conducted by the presidential committee headed by former Sen. Jose Diokno. Several "heroes" of the February revolt may be called before his committee. The RAM member most often cited in connection with human rights abuses is Col. Rodolfo Aguinaldo, currently the Philippine Constabulary (PC) provincial commander in Cagayan. Aguinaldo stands accused of torturing several political prisoners.

Current top military officers long served the dictatorship. Enrile was martial law administrator before he became Marcos's defense minister. Ramos headed the PC for the final years of Marcos's reign and acted as chief-of-staff of the old AFP for one year. During his term as head of the PC it earned a sorry reputation for human rights abuses. Most of the RAM members knew no other commander-in-chief than Marcos until recently. They were at the forefront of counterinsurgency campaigns against the NPA and the Islamic-oriented Moro National Liberation Front in the '70s before many of the senior reformists gravitated to the security and intelligence detachments at the [defense] ministry and PC headquarters.

Election Provided a Smoke Screen

Three reasons are most often given for the revolt of the military, which had long served as a primary pillar for Marcos's rule. The former dictator's inability to halt the growing insurgency is the most commonly cited reason. The other two are related. One was AFP corruption, which prevented junior officers from advancing to the top echelons of the military. The other is the stranglehold Marcos, his wife Imelda and his Chief-of-Staff Gen. Fabian C. Ver had on the military. The trio's stranglehold kept Enrile and Ramos on the fringes of power.

Robles said RAM knew Marcos was a counterinsurgency failure well before their revolt. He said RAM expected an eventual triumph of the insurgents if Marcos remained in power. RAM began organizing for a revolt before the election campaign. It used the campaign to extend its organization under the guise of preparing to safeguard the ballots. According to Robles the motivation was counterinsurgency effectiveness and anti-Communism.

Less charitable critics of the military didn't grant them that idealistic, if distorted, motivation. They see the revolt and the aborted coup as part of a pure power-grab by Enrile.

"The military rebels were preserving their own power." said Randy Echanis, a recently released political prisoner tagged by the military as CPP chief in Cagayan. Echanis was arrested and detained by members of Enrile's security group. "Enrile has bigger ambitions. He had to distance himself from Marcos. So the idea was not to side with the people, but to preserve the group. And the group was able to sneak into the government."

By revolting, the military showed its willingness to intervene in the nation's political life. The possibility of a coup is mentioned by many if Aquino should fail to establish a stable government or if the left becomes too strong in her administration.

Some observers believe Aquino's failure to launch an all-out peace offensive stems from her fear of the military as much as from her acceptance of the military's view of the NPA. They suggest that Aquino is worried about the impact of a second military revolt on the country's development. At any rate, the military has been able to manipulate developments in the country and slow the march toward peace. In allowing itself to be distracted, Aquino's government has played into the hands of those—the militarists in the armed forces and on the left—who only see a military solution to the nation's problems.

Selection 11.3: Ongpin's Vision, Paul A. Gigot

Editors' Introduction

While there is considerable support for President Aquino's efforts to restore civil rights and erase the corruption of the Marcos dictatorship, within the ranks of her government and its supporters there is disagreement on economic policies.

Aquino's new finance minister is Jaime V. Ongpin, whose economic program is "to privatize everything" and depend heavily on foreign investment. While this program may represent the views of many of the business elite, it puts him at loggerheads with union and peasant organi-

zations like the KMU and the KMP, whose outlook on economic reform is quite different [see selections 11.4 and 11.5]. Ongpin, for example, would throw agriculture completely open to private enterprise, which includes of course powerful foreign agribusinesses. The KMP, on the other hand, would nationalize land presently owned by these foreign firms. But the KMU and KMP represent that type of grassroots organization whose support President Aquino believes to be necessary if her government is to resist pressure from right-wingers who want to turn back the thrust of people's power [see introduction to selection 11.1].

Such is the dilemma of the Aquino government.

Source: Paul A. Gigot, "Manila's Economic Revolutionary," *Wall Street Journal*, 5 March 1986, p. 32.

Manila—As a private businessman three years ago, Jaime V. Ongpin attacked a government bailout of a Ferdinand Marcos crony as "the most obscene, brazen and disgraceful misallocation of taxpayers' money in the history of the Philippines." It didn't matter that the bailout was ordered by his older brother, Roberto, then a cabinet minister.

Today, Mr. Ongpin is the new Philippine finance minister, but he still isn't talking in euphemistic terms. Asked about negotiations with the International Monetary Fund, Mr. Ongpin says, "Now that [the IMF] isn't dealing with a bunch of thieves, we hope we won't be treated like a bunch of thieves."

Both comments are vintage Ongpin: candid, principled but loaded with tart derision for what the meddling Marcoses wrought for the Philippine economy. The comments also symbolize the freshest economic thinking to blow through the Philippines in at least 20 years, and maybe ever. As President Corazon Aquino's main economic adviser, Mr. Ongpin will lead the attack on a Marcos legacy that had turned the Philippines into something of a feudal economy, where favors from the throne often determined who would succeed in business. And as a (classical) liberal, Mr. Ongpin hopes to achieve this by sweeping away both government interference and monopolies, by liberating small capitalists and farmers, and by purging any hint of Marcos-style cronyism.

"First of all you dismantle all of this crony structure," the 47-year old Mr. Ongpin told a handful of reporters over lunch yesterday. "I think government should get out of business completely. Privatize everything . . . . I don't think you need any fancy bag of tricks. All you need to do is say, 'Here's the set of rules. It applies to everybody, fairly, equitably.' I am philosophically committed to the absolute minimum of government interference."

Putting all of this into practice, unfortunately, may take a revolution on the order of last week's at Camp Crame. The Marcos regime gave government interference a bad name, but it also created political forces that won't always, if ever, agree to liberal reform. Some of those forces sit with Mr. Ongpin in President Aquino's new cabinet, a motley and fragile political coalition if ever there was one. Protectionists also lurk here, as everywhere. And there is the left, waiting to make hay if Mr. Ongpin and his allies stumble. The U.S., the IMF, the creditor banks and, especially, most Filipinos will want to see that they don't.

If anyone has to lead these battles, however, it's hard to imagine a better general than Mr. Ongpin. Indeed, friends at Harvard (M.B.A. '62) called him "the general," says his former roommate, because Jaime Ongpin was strong-willed even then. His Jesuit training also made him idealistic, friends say, and he remains so. One prominent Filipino recalls having dinner at the Ongpins' home last year and asserting that Filipinos really did need an authoritarian ruler, to impose order. A heated argument ensued (Mr. Ongpin's wife, Maribel, is said to be as strong-minded as Jaime), and the man says he hasn't been invited back.

For almost 20 years Mr. Ongpin avoided politics, climbing the ladder at a big Philippine mining company, Benguet Corp., rising to president. As the Marcos years lumbered on, however, Mr. Ongpin grew increasingly critical— and vocal. His public blast at his brother marked the first major attack on the Marcos government from the Philippine middle and business classes. His work for the opposition increased until, last week, Mr. Ongpin found himself sleeping on the floor of Camp Crame with the rebels, hoping loyalist soldiers wouldn't attack. "I was never so frightened in my life." he says.

This record of dissent has given him credibility with President Aquino, whose own economic views are unclear, if not unformed. He helped write her major economic policy speeches before last month's election, for example, and Filipinos say he has had significant influence in Mrs. Aquino's choice of other economic advisers. Every one of them shares much of Mr. Ongpin's free-market philosophy.

Mr. Ongpin will need this credibility, because he is certain to face some wrenching political battles. Mostly Roman Catholics, Filipino politicians have long stressed "social justice," often assuming that government action is the only way to achieve it. This view has several supporters in the Aquino cabinet, especially the influential local governments minister, Aquilino Pimentel, a self-professed socialist. Mrs. Aquino herself has also sometimes expressed a vague populism that, if given any rein, could derail market reforms. Mr. Ongpin, for his part, is optimistic, claiming that only one cabinet member is really a statist and that he isn't handling an economic portfolio.

Another threat could come from business nationalists. Throughout the Marcos years, many Filipinos built inefficient business empires behind high tariffs; effective rates of protection remain more than 40%, far higher than anywhere else in East Asia. Mr. Ongpin wants to dismantle those trade barriers, saying that "philosophically, I don't believe in protection, period." Instead, he wants to make local businesses more efficient and export-competitive. That view is bound to irk many businessmen, however, and a few have already started griping to the newly free press. Mrs. Aquino's new minister of industry, Jose Concepcion, has wavered from a free-trade stand and his brother, Raul, is among the loudest protectionists.

Mr. Ongpin says the best compromise may be to tell the inefficient that, OK, "we'll buy you a little time. But the minute the economy gets back on its feet . . . that's it." The Aquino government has already asked for, and been granted, a 60-day delay in its current import-liberalization program with the IMF.

The IMF will be a target of economic nationalists for other reasons, too. Because it distrusted the Marcos government, the IMF in 1984 imposed on

Manila the toughest austerity package it has ever signed anywhere. Many Filipinos now chafe at the terms, especially because service on the country's $27 billion foreign debt continues to eat up some 50% of exports. That austerity and falling commodity prices have caused gross national product to sink nearly 10% over the past two years.

Mr. Ongpin wants some IMF relief (thus his comment about thieves), but he doesn't favor any Peruvian-style militancy. "We don't intend to do anything unilaterally," he says. "I don't blame the IMF for what they did. If I were in their shoes, I would have been tougher." His job of selling the IMF accord will be made even more difficult, however, by Mr. Marcos's spending raid on the treasury during the last campaign; sources say Mr. Marcos may have exceeded IMF money-supply targets by as much as $500 million. A new period of austerity will be required to mop up all that inflationary credit.

Mr. Ongpin already has had to expend political capital in this IMF debate. Last week he fought to have Marcos's Central Bank governor, Jose Fernandez, retained by Mrs. Aquino because, Mr. Ongpin says, he's competent and wasn't personally tainted with mismanagement. As the symbol of austerity, however, Mr. Fernandez is anathema to many businessmen, and a few have already taken to picketing Mrs. Aquino's headquarters in protest.

For all these potential dangers, however, the sense of economic optimism in Manila today is tangible. Though the Aquino government hasn't done much of anything yet, the Philippine peso has already firmed and the Central Bank says gold and dollar transfers (in return for pesos) are at record levels. The stock market, a dog for years, has perked up. Demand is already picking up in some of Manila's main housing developments, too, as Filipino expatriates begin to return home. Mr. Ongpin figures there may be as much as $10 billion in Philippine flight capital abroad, waiting to return.

"Our priority is to convince Filipinos to invest in their own country," says Mr. Ongpin, "and we're confident that if we achieve that, the foreign investors will follow."

Indeed, Mr. Ongpin isn't even that eager to take advantage of the "mini-Marshall Plan" in aid for Manila now being talked about in Washington and Tokyo. "I would actually be inclined to start very modestly," he says. "The problems here are too severe and too complex to assume they can be solved by throwing huge amounts of money at them."

He says he wants to solve the economy's structural problems first— dismantle the farm monopolies, make the tax system fairer, implement a land reform based on the successful (and not confiscatory) Malaysian model. And when the aid money does flow, he says, "I would like all of this made available to the private sector"—as equity capital for farmers, perhaps. He doesn't, Mr. Ongpin stresses, want the aid channeled through a government agency that might abuse it for political gain.

"I haven't the slightest doubt in my mind," he says, "that if you just create the right climate, and make sure you're fair . . ." He pauses: "I guess it's the invisible hand. It'll work."

Selection 11.4: Position on Job Creation, KMU

Editors' Introduction

In its program for job creation in the post-Marcos era, the left-wing labor federation KMU recommends a number of government interventions to provide more jobs and develop the national economy, including: state subsidy for small farmers, prohibition of 100 percent repatriation of

multinational corporate profits, Filipinization of ownership in key industries, genuine land reform, government financing to establish heavy industry, selective repudiation of foreign debts.

Source: "KMU Position on Job-Creation," mimeographed, Manila, n.d.

1. The country is basically a backward, non-industrialized economy that is easily affected by external pressures, especially from the world capitalist market. A majority of the labor force continues to be absorbed by agriculture which remains largely backward and does not employ a significant amount of modern technology. Industry has remained stagnant especially in recent years, and the backlog in employment is filled up mainly by the commerce and service sectors. The country possesses practically no heavy industries to manufacture capital and intermediate goods necessary to supply industrial firms. Instead, we rely mainly on importing capital and intermediate goods to feed our industries, nearly all of which are light consumer industries in nature and oriented toward the world market. Our exports continue to meet stiff competition abroad and have to cope with the rising protectionism among the more advanced capitalist countries. Thus, the country is trapped in a vicious cycle of underdevelopment where we are forced to export all we can, import in order to survive, and meanwhile remaining backward and non-industrialized basically.

This situation, the KMU believes, is the root cause of unemployment and underemployment in the country. The task of the government, therefore, is not only to come up with short-term, patch-up solutions to the problem but to pursue a long-term program for genuine industrialization that will essentially restructure the Philippine economy. By this, we mean the expansion of local industry, with the domestic market, not the world market, as its base. This is what the KMU basically means when we call for nationalist industrialization.

2. This does not mean to say, however, that the KMU is not open to short-term solutions to the problem of unemployment and underemployment. On the contrary, we do realize the urgency of immediately instituting measures that will, somehow alleviate the problem.

Towards this, we propose the following:

a) State subsidy for small-scale business. At a time when the industrial sector has remained largely stagnant, the small-scale businesses have the best potential of generating immediate employment.

Government, therefore, must lend greater financial assistance to those firms. The private sector can help by contributing to a common fund for such a program.

b) provision for reinvestment of profits of big companies. One factor that has contributed to the problems of backwardness and unemployment is the policy of the past regime concerning the full repatriation of profits by multinationals. Thus, instead of contributing to national development, these multinationals tend to milk the country of much needed dollars that could otherwise be useful in generating employment. It goes without saying then that such policy must be corrected. A law must be provided that will ensure reinvestment of at least thirty (30%) to fifty percent (50%) of profit by big companies, partly or wholly owned by multinationals.

3. Short term solutions to the problems of unemployment and underemployment, however, will not work unless accompanied by a comprehensive long-term program for national industrialization to cure the ills of backwardness and underdevelopment. To do this, government will have to take the initiative.

As history has shown, the dominant elements in the private sector cannot be relied upon to fully develop the industrial potential of the country. These elements find it more profitable to deal with the world capitalist market rather than assist in building an industrial base for the country. Considering that, it is the task of government to intervene on the people's behalf to effect a program for the expansion of industry and attain genuine national development.

The following measures will facilitate such:

a) the Filipinization of basic industries. By basic industries, we mean those that produce capital and intermediate goods and play a key role in serving the needs of industry. These include such sectors as mining, transportation, communication, electricity, gas, steel and chemical manufacturing, and others. The point here is to ensure that these industries will be genuinely responsive to the domestic needs of the economy and to the cause of national development. This can only be if they are wholly owned by Filipinos and not by foreigners, as most of them are presently.

b) genuine land reform to cover all agricultural lands. A program of genuine land reform will help raise per capita income in the rural areas and create the base for the development of the domestic market and the expansion and dispersal of industry. Genuine land reform in itself is a means towards the equitable distribution of wealth.

c) setting up heavy and light industries. The structure of our industry is such that it has practically no heavy industries, and is completely dominated by light industries producing consumption goods and semi-processed products for the world market. This is because the dominant elements in the private sector find it cheaper to directly import their industrial needs rather than produce it locally. Government should fill in the gap by financing the setting up of strategic heavy industries. The country must be able to produce its own cars, tractors, machines for industry, and fertilizers.

d) regional dispersal of industries. Because of the backward state of the economy, the country is unevenly developed and industry is concentrated almost totally in the cities and major towns. A program of genuine land reform will create the necessary base, but will not necessarily lead to the dispersal of industry since the private sector will most likely find it more profitable to operate in the urban areas where there already exists a relatively developed market. Government should lend its hand in this respect.

e) selective repudiation of onerous debts incurred by the previous regime and pegging the debt service ratio to a level of ten percent (10%) of exports. It is impossible to finance the huge foreign debts inherited from the past regime and at the same time pursue an ambitious program for industrialization. As a compromise between total repudiation and total acceptance of the regime's onerous obligations, we propose a policy of selective repudiation and the pegging of the debt service ratio to a level of ten percent (10%) of exports.

g) expansion of trade with the socialist bloc. As it is, trade with the socialist countries accounts for a miniscule three percent (3%) of total trade. And yet it is the socialist bloc that constitutes an alternative supply of capital and intermediate goods necessary to fuel industrial growth. The socialist countries can also be an alternative market for our export goods, and where we can easily avail of barter trade. What we propose basically is that the government undertake steps to balance trade with East and West, as in the case of India which has been able to develop by doing so and is in fact regarded now as [one of the more] industrialized countries in the world, yet able to maintain its non-aligned status.

These measures will obviously require the heavy interference of government in the economy, but we believe that there is nothing to fear about that. During the past regime, government interference was bad because its ultimate objective was to loot the economy and reinforce the general status quo of backwardness that characterizes the Philippine economy.

What we propose is that government interfere in order to remedy the ills of the economy. There will be no danger of corruption as long as there is an effective system of checks and balances. Likewise, it is suggested that where government intervenes, it sets the example in implementing profit-sharing as a matter of policy and in recognizing workers' rights. Whatever profit government earns in such an endeavor should be used to further the industrialization program and expand social services. That, in the long run, would be the more meaningful approach to profit-sharing.

Selection 11.5: Program for Genuine Land Reform, Union of Philippine Peasants

Editors' Introduction

The KMP, or Union of Philippine Peasants, was organized in June 1985. A year later it put forward an extensive program for land reform excerpts from which are printed below.

The heart of the KMP program is free distribution of land to landless tenant farmers and farm workers. Other features include: reduction of land rents where immediate distribution is not possible, abolition of usury, improvement of farm workers' wages and conditions, protection of the lands of tribal minorities, encouragement of cooperatives, selective compensation of former landlords, nationalization of lands owned by multinational agribusinesses.

Source: Kilusang Magbubukid ng Pilipinas, National Council, "Program for Genuine Land Reform in the Philippines," June 1986, mimeographed, Quezon City, pp. 4-9, 11-13.

Chapter III. Peasant Direction of Their Own Destiny: Pre-requisite for Genuine Land Reform

The government should recognize the right of the peasants to direct the path of their development as the main pre-requisite in the success of any well-meaning effort to alleviate them from poverty and suffering....

Chapter IV. General Objectives

For land reform to be genuine, it has to totally abolish the feudal system in the Philippines and fulfill the long-standing peasant demand for land. Towards this end, a genuine land reform program should provide for:

Section A

The free distribution of land to the actual tillers who have little or no land. This should be the central objective of the program. It is the embodiment of the age-old aspiration of the Filipino peasant.

1. Landlordism has resulted from the historical dispossession of the tillers of the soil dating as far back to the massive acquisition of lands under the *encomienda* system [landed estates] of colonial times followed by wholesale landgrabbing aided by a series of land laws which discriminated against the poor and unschooled occupants of the land in favor of the wealthy and the knowledgeable.

2. The peasants have more than paid for the land already after so many decades of paying exorbitant land rent, usurious debts and other onerous exactions by the landlords. The landlords, for their part, have been living in luxury on the basis of exorbitant rents, and have not reinvested their earnings significantly into agriculture or industry.

3. The vast majority of peasants cannot afford to pay for the expropriated lands because their incomes are not even enough for them to subsist on. Past land reform programs have failed to redistribute land simply because the peasants were required to pay for the land. Marcos's land reform program was a sham not only because of its very limited scope but also because it required the would-be beneficiaries to make installment payments for the land which were so exorbitant that they could not even make good their initial installments.

4. No amount of government assistance could significantly raise the income of peasants nor could it induce them to produce more until they come to own the lands they till. And this could only be possible if the lands, which remain concentrated in the hands of a few landlords, are expropriated and equitably distributed to the landless tillers for free.

5. It is therefore, only just, moral, as well as practical that land be distributed to the actual tillers at no cost to the latter, without prejudice to possible compensation arrangements between the government and the landlords.

Section B

The reduction of land rent in areas where free land distribution cannot yet be immediately implemented. . . .

Section C

The abolition of usury and other feudal evils. . . .

4. Usury may be diminished through the concerted action of peasants demanding lower interest rates both from formal and informal sources of credit, and through agricultural cooperation. In the long run, usury shall be eliminated when the peasants control their land and other means in production, a genuine program for agro-industrialization is implemented, and agricultural cooperation is fostered.

Section D

The promotion of all forms of agricultural cooperation such as simple exchange of labor, mutual aid, and cooperatives.

1. Land distribution should be complemented by agricultural cooperation if it is to succeed in increasing production and productivity as well as raising the incomes of peasants.

2. Through cooperation, the peasants can cope with production, processing, marketing, and credit in an organized way.

Section E

The increase in wages and improvement in the working and living conditions of farmworkers. . . .

2. Legislated wage rates and benefits for agricultural wage earners are not only pitifully inadequate, these are almost always violated by their employers. The protection of the rights of farmworkers should constantly be upheld and more effective measures should be undertaken in dealing with exploitative employers.

3. Women farmworkers are exploited on two counts: as wage earners and by virtue of their sex. They bear the brunt of discrimination in wages, employment opportunities and the absence of benefits such as maternity leaves, health care services, and day-care services for their children. This results in the extreme marginalization of women farmworkers. Discrimination and oppression of women farmworkers must be eradicated. There must be explicit legislative provisions on the rights of women peasants and farmworkers to just wages, equal pay for equal work, equal rights in determining the number of children, priority to employment opportunities, security of tenure, better working and living conditions, and protection from sexual harassment at the workplace.

4. Child labor is a rampant reality in the countryside as a result of poverty and the absence of restrictions on this exploitative practice. Child labor should be abolished and the rights of children to adequate food and nutrition, recreation, and education should be upheld.

Section F

The systematic resettlement of landless peasants in public lands and the protection of homestead rights of small settlers without violating the prior rights of the original inhabitants. . . .

Section G

The protection of the ancestral land rights of indigenous minorities against unjust encroachment. . . .

Section H

The optimum and efficient use of land resources towards meeting the needs of agricultural production and national industrialization, while recognizing the importance of a healthy ecology and environment. . . .

Chapter V. Coverage of the Land Reform Program

As a matter of government policy, genuine land reform should be applied to all croplands and for the benefit of the entire agricultural labor force. Specifically, it includes the following lands:

(a) all tenanted private agricultural lands, regardless of crop;
(b) all *haciendas* and plantations regardless of crop and land tenure arrangement;

(c) idle, abandoned, and foreclosed lands suited for agriculture; and,

(d) public lands and/or government and military reservations and ranches suited for agriculture.

Chapter VI. Particular Policies for Genuine Land Reform

Section A. On Free Distribution and Related Programs. . . .

8. In general, selected compensation shall be undertaken by the government to the previous owners of the expropriated lands. Compensation for landlords can take the following forms:

(a) cash payments on the land;

(b) government bonds and securities;

(c) opportunities for investment, entrepreneurship, or employment in preferred areas of agriculture and industry.

9. Outright confiscation of ill-gotten lands, especially those owned by Marcos and his cronies, or those found out to have been acquired through deceit, fraud, intimidation and violence, shall be undertaken.

10. Landlords who are not despotic and abusive shall not only be compensated, but will also be permitted to retain a portion of their landholdings, without violating the prior rights of the tenants on those lands, provided they render the land productive and maintain its productivity. Tenancy will not be permitted in the retained landholdings.

11. As a general policy, rich peasants who have surplus lands which are rented out to tenants, shall be persuaded to eventually sell their excess land to the government for redistribution to tenants. The same policies on compensation and possible retention as stated in Article 8 of this section shall apply to the rural middle class, the teachers, professionals and the like who own small tenanted landholdings. . . .

13. Corporate farms and plantations run by wage labor shall be confiscated if found to be Marcos or crony-owned, or proven to have been acquired through deceit, intimidation, and violence. Plantations and corporate farms foreclosed by banking institutions shall also be expropriated, without prejudice to possible compensation arrangements between the government and the banks, provided the transactions are free from manipulation and fraud. . . .

15. Plantations owned and controlled by transnationals shall be nationalized. Their being in control of thousands of hectares of agricultural lands is a direct transgression of the national patrimony of the Filipino people. These plantations can be managed according to the aforementioned categories. . . .

Section B. On Rent Reduction

1. As a matter of policy, the reduction of land rent in tenanted lands should be pursued only as the initial step towards the eventual free distribution of these lands to the tenant peasants. . . .

Section C. On Promoting Agricultural Cooperation

1. Simple forms of agricultural cooperation such as labor exchange and mutual aid should be promoted and encouraged among the peasantry to cut down on production expenses, increase productivity, preclude dependence on usurers and advance the general welfare. . . .

Selection 11.6: Self-Criticism, *Ang Bayan*

Editors' Introduction

In the weeks that followed the ouster of Marcos, intense self-criticism took place within all the organizations that had boycotted the election. In May 1986, the Communist Party of the Philippines published the reassessment printed below. The Party acknowledged that although it had been, along with the National Democratic Front, in the forefront of the struggle against the dictatorship for years, when the final blow against the Marcos regime was struck—both in the snap election and the people's power outpouring that enabled the military revolt to succeed—they were *as an organization* caught standing on the sidelines. Significantly, the Party declared not just that it made errors in judgment, but that greater internal democratization was needed. The ultimate import of this statement cannot easily be judged; after all the CPP remains an illegal organization and as such much of its internal workings are secret. It does seem, however, that the CPP has replaced its general secretary and chairperson—the two top positions in the party—and that it now permits the publication of a dissident journal within its ranks. It has also agreed to begin cease-fire talks with the Aquino government.

Source: Central Committee of the Communist Party of the Philippines, "Party Conducts Assessment, Says Boycott Policy Was Wrong," *Ang Bayan*, May 1986, pp. 1-3.

For more than 17 of the 20 years that the Marcos fascist puppet regime was in power, the Communist Party of the Philippines (reestablished in December 1968) had played a leading role in our people's anti-fascist, anti-imperialist and anti-feudal struggles.

In all those 17 years, the Party and the revolutionary forces that it leads have contributed tremendously to exposing, isolating and weakening the regime, leading to its eventual downfall.

Yet, where the people saw in the February 7 snap presidential election a chance to deliver a crippling blow on the Marcos regime, a memorandum by the Executive Committee of the Party Central Committee (EC-CC) saw it merely as "a noisy and empty political battle" among factions in the ruling classes.

And when the aroused and militant people moved spontaneously but resolutely to oust the hated regime last February 22-25, the Party and its forces were not there to lead them. In large measure the Party and its forces were on the sidelines, unable to lead or influence the hundreds of thousands of people who moved with amazing speed and decisiveness to overthrow the regime.

This was because of the Party's official policy enunciated by the EC-CC to launch an active and vigorous boycott campaign vis-a-vis the election, a policy that was based—as the events showed—on an incorrect reading of the political situation.

A recent assessment conducted by the Political Bureau (Politburo) of the Central Committee characterized the boycott policy as a major political blunder.

Roots of the Error

As evaluated by the Politburo, the boycott policy erred in its overall assessment of the political situation at the time of the snap election, in its understanding and application of the Party's tactics against the U.S.-Marcos fascist dictatorship, and in its understanding and application of the Marxist-Leninist organizational principle of democratic centralism.

In the main, the political assessment on which the boycott was based mechanically analyzed the various political forces with regard to their basic class standpoint and subjective intentions. It paid little or no attention to the objective positioning of each of the political forces in motion and in interaction with the others.

Thus it failed to grasp the essence of the whole situation that was in flux at that time.

The assessment had earlier described this period as the setting for an important political battle with a tremendous impact on the people and on the major political forces. But when this came initially in the form of the snap election, the assessment underpinning the boycott policy belittled it as nothing but a noisy but meaningless interfactional contest among the ruling classes. Specifically, the assessment:

1. Did not correctly understand the character and operation of U.S. policy toward the Marcos regime. It overestimated U.S. capacity to impose its subjective will on local politics and misread the U.S. dilemma over the conflicting needs it had to simultaneously attend to. It failed to appreciate the possible effects on U.S. policy of local developments over which the U.S. did not have full control.

2. Underestimated the bourgeois reformists' capabilities and determination to engage the Marcos regime in a decisive contest for state power.

3. Ignored the fact that the Marcos clique had become extremely isolated and its capacity to rule was fast eroding. It failed to look more deeply into the contradictions developing within the Armed Forces of the Philippines.

4. Above all these misread the people's deep anti-fascist sentiments and readiness to go beyond the confines of the electoral process in their determination to end the fascist dictatorship.

As practice subsequently showed, the snap election was not just "a noisy and empty political battle." The election and the major events it unleashed constituted the climax of the people's long-drawn struggle against the Marcos regime. During and after the snap election, the historically determined central political struggle was the showdown over the very existence and continuance of fascist rule. The snap election became the main channel of largescale mobilization and deployment of the masses for the decisive battle to overthrow the dictatorship.

This being the case, it was tactically necessary for the revolutionary forces to participate critically in the snap election in order to effectively combine and make use of all forms of struggle, march at the head of the politically active masses, and maintain flexibility and an active position in the face of the fast-changing situation. Only by doing so could the revolutionary forces have maximized their political and military capability and reaped the optimum gains for the revolution under the prevailing circumstances.

The boycott policy forfeited all these.

As regards understanding and applying the party's tactics against the U.S.-Marcos dictatorship, the boycott policy failed to give commensurate political value to the anti-fascist struggle that assumed primacy during and after the snap election. The anti-fascist struggle united the various levels of revolutionary, democratic and anti-Marcos sentiments during and after the election, and created a mass force capable of toppling the regime.

The boycott policy not only failed to give enough value to the question of reaching and mobilizing the majority of the people. It directly and openly went against the desire of the broad masses to pursue the anti-fascist struggle by means of critically participating in the snap election.

More specifically, the boycott policy concentrated on addressing and consolidating the advanced section of the people, or the revolutionary forces, at a time when the people were already gearing for a decisive battle with the fascist regime.

This showed an insufficient understanding of the tasks of political leadership during such a time, as well as a lack of appreciation of the current level of mass participation in revolutionary struggles, and confusion regarding the actual needs of the revolutionary armed struggle.

The Party leadership is now encouraging leading Party organs which have not yet done so to sum up their experiences regarding the boycott policy. The results of the different studies and summing ups will be circulated within the Party, to develop a common understanding of the lessons from the boycott campaign.

Likewise, a general summing-up will be conducted of the Party's experiences in the struggle against the U.S.-Marcos dictatorship. At the same time, steps will be taken to strengthen the Party's ideological foundation and raise the theoretical knowledge of the entire Party.

Steps are being taken to encourage and develop the democratic spirit and democratic way of doing things in the Party. To this end, forums and channels will be created for the full expression within the Party of the various ideas and views on significant questions so as to arrive at a unified understanding and stand.

The Future is Bright

While we missed out on important political as well as military opportunities and suffered other negative effects as a result of our erroneous boycott policy, the fact remains that the events of last February represented a great victory for our people and for their struggle towards genuine national freedom and democracy.

The Party and its forces are intact, and these are now in the process of strengthening their ranks for new tasks in the post-Marcos period which is highly conducive to the heightened and more extensive politicization of our people.

While the Party perseveres in strengthening itself ideologically, politically and organizationally, while it looks inward from time to time and learns both from its negative as well as positive experiences, it will continue reaping the people's wholehearted support.

The future is bright for the party, for the entire national democratic movement, for the revolution, and for the entire Filipino people.

Selection 11.7: A Philippine Vision of Socialism, BISIG

Editors' Introduction

The flush of victory over Marcos led to a proliferation of new groupings on the Philippine left. One of these is a new socialist organization known by the acronym BISIG.

BISIG's program is defined in two documents. One, "The Present Political Situation and the Tasks of Filipino Socialists," sees the ouster of Marcos as a great victory for the Philippine people, but warns of the limits of the revolution: "the daily lives of ordinary people have not improved to a significant degree." BISIG calls for defending and advancing the gains of the February revolution by forming a broad united front of all progressive forces in the country. "If democracy is to become real," states

BISIG, the people must "relentlessly apply pressures from below." The second document, "A Philippine Vision of Socialism," had initially been drafted in the closing days of the Marcos regime by a group of individuals then calling themselves the "Independent Caucus"; it subsequently became one of BISIG's founding documents. The excerpts below show something of the long-range goals of some Philippine socialists. Although BISIG has just a few hundred members at this time, its intellectual influence on the Philippine left is considerable.

Source: Independent Caucus, "A Philippine Vision of Socialism," mimeographed, September 1985.

This document is a preliminary attempt to conceptualize the principles and guide-posts of a Philippine socialism that would not be a mere copy of foreign models but would be based on a critique of existing socialist states and a creative application of the socialist ideology to the Philippine reality. Our people's struggle to bring about a fundamental restructuring of our society must be fueled by a clear vision of the society we desire. The crystallization of this vision, however, must take place within the struggle itself in order that it can serve as a primary instrument for mobilizing people to participate in the process of transformation.

Economic Progress

Capitalism thrives on exploitation. Its logic is that of profit. Its morality is that of self-interest. Socialism, on the other hand, stresses the cooperative rather than the selfish nature of human beings by eliminating the conditions that promote the self-centered lust for property.

. . . a socialist society must be based on social ownership of the means of social production. . . .

Social ownership of the means of social production does not mean absolutely no form of private property or the caricature of people having to borrow each other's toothbrush. Objects of consumption properly belong to the personal and private sphere. . . .

In the process of building a socialist Philippines, a large amount of redistribution will have to be undertaken. This includes, for example, the redistribution of private property that has been used, not for personal enjoyment, but for the oppression and exploitation of the majority. In fact, the goal of socialism is to enable everyone to have access to more personal property such as food, housing, clothing, books, leisure.

Democratic Economic Planning. Philippine socialism means the creating of a society where the people, not a few property owners, own and manage the economic affairs of the country. In such a society, production will be basically oriented to need, not to market demands. This can only be accomplished through rational social planning.

A planned economy requires the identification of basic needs that must be met, and an efficient distribution system. These can only be achieved through the effective participation of people in the determination of national goals. It is crucial, therefore, that a planned economy be the result of decisions popularly participated in by all sectors of society. This is the only way through which real needs can be arrived at, people can be motivated to act collectively, and sacrifices can be made based on rational choice. A planned economy must also ensure a wide and even dispersal of industries in the countryside in order to create work opportunities for a vast number of our people and avoid centralization of development in only selected areas.

Workers' Control. Economic planning, if it is not to degenerate into the control of a bureaucracy, must be based on the direct producers' control over decision-making. Under capitalism, control is purely in the hands of the owners of the means of social production. Philippine socialism, on the other hand, must emphasize the need for producers to get the greatest share of the surplus. Thus, social profit must not be expropriated by the state.

While a percentage of the social profits must be contributed to the state in the form of taxes, the rest must be at the disposal of the workers. These funds can be used either to modernize the tools of production or as a social fund for collective services or individual bonuses. Workers must also have control over both the organization and technology of production to avoid becoming slaves to these.

Ownership, like control, does not automatically refer to national ownership. Emphasis can be given to a variety of forms—cooperative, factory, municipal, or regional ownership—each with autonomous workers' councils which will make specific decisions but within the broad guidelines laid down by the regional or national bodies.

It is important to strike a viable balance between nationalization and private property especially during the stage of social reconstruction. All monopolies must be nationalized. However, in the case of individual enterprises, the informal business sector, and petty commodity producers, the state must encourage cooperatives rather than resort to the imposition of socialized systems. People should understand and accept the socialist system because it responds to their own aspirations and not because the state decrees it.

Philippine socialism must also avoid the over-centralized systems of some present-day socialist states. Instead, it must strive towards a system where the means of production and social services are owned and managed by communities of direct producers within the broad guidelines provided by the state. In addition, to ensure a vibrant, self-propelling economy, a market system may be retained for as long as no monopolies arise. In this regard, the economy should encourage healthy competition between production units and factories in order to improve the products, create new product lines, and provide incentives to innovate.

Development of the Domestic Economy. Under capitalism, especially when it is dependent, the economy always responds to the logic of the world capitalist market. Since Filipino capitalists do not have to rely on the local market, they feel no pressure to increase the buying capacity of workers. In fact, any attempt to control capital generally leads to its flight because capital knows no nationality.

In contrast, a socialist system, being under the control of the people, produces the strongest pressures to develop the domestic economy because production is sensitive to local needs rather than to [world] market demands. The very survival of the economy therefore heavily depends upon the improvement of the purchasing capacity of the local consumers which also necessarily entails the improvement of the standard of living of the masses.

. . . A socialist state must also guard against the uncritical adoption of capitalist technology. While the instruments may be neutral, these are part of a technological system designed for the exploitation and control of workers.

Furthermore, technology that leads to the wanton destruction of natural resources must be avoided. A socialist science and technology must always be conscious of the need for technology that does not alienate, but rather enhances the humanity of the worker. Such a technology must therefore be at the control of the people.

Preservation of the Environment. Economic development in a socialist society can be sustained only through a stable and adequate resource base. Hence, the conservation of natural resources and the maintenance of ecological balance must be integral parts of a Philippine socialism.

People's Democracy

While recognizing the limitations of democracy in a capitalist order, we must also deplore the depoliticization that has taken place in many socialist countries where a small bureaucracy has effectively paralyzed the masses and simply rules in their name.

Popular Power. The propaganda against socialist states has always been that the party would dictate policy. Socialism in the Philippines will encourage the presence of multiple parties, each one with its own perspective on the correct path towards socialism. After all, an agreement on the basic goals does not automatically mean total agreement on the process of attaining such goals.

Unlike the much misunderstood and sometimes abused concept of the vanguard party, socialism in the Philippines will encourage the interplay of forces and perspectives on socialism, each aspiring for the vanguard role. The vanguard role, therefore, is not one that is bestowed on any party or political force. It is a role that is dependent upon the support of the majority for a party's policies and programs. With each of the parties vying and aspiring for the vanguard role, it is then necessary to have regular elections to validate policies and programs and to feel the real pulse of the people. It must be made clear, however, that while no single party can automatically lay claim to possess the correct road to socialism, all parties and forces agree on basic socialist goals.

. . . However, while one of the competing socialist parties may even openly espouse some non-socialist perspectives, this will be allowed only for as long as there is neither foreign nor armed intervention. . . .

The only antidote to any form of dictation, whether by military or by bureaucracy, is a politicized, well-informed, organized and armed citizenry. Communities and sectors must be organized into popular and autonomous bodies, not into front organizations that are controlled by either a political party or the state. This will ensure that power resides in the hands of the majority. The experience in some countries has been the depoliticization of the masses after the attainment of socialist victory.

Dissent. The experience of some socialist states has shown that a socialist system does not automatically result in greater human rights. Philippine socialism must therefore ensure the full flowering of equal rights and freedoms. One of the basic requirements is the full guarantee of the right to dissent.

The freedom to criticize must be guaranteed not only in the law but in fact. The right to free speech, to assembly, to demonstrate against the government must be protected at all times. But the actual guarantee of these rights can only come from an organized and politicized people and from the existence of a multi-party system.

Religion. Earlier socialists denounced the institutionalized church as a bastion of reaction. The antagonism between the church and socialists derives from the role religion, especially in the past, was made to play—that of the source of conservatism because people were taught to entrust their destinies to a supernatural being. But in recent years, a section of the Church has eloquently spoken of a slice of heaven that must be aspired for in the temporal world and must be actively sought in the here and now. Philippine socialism recognizes that religion can be a potent force for progress.

The freedom to worship as well as the freedom not to worship therefore must be upheld. . . .

Human and Personal Development. Philippine socialism must be directed towards the ultimate fulfillment of the full potential of every Filipino. There must be a constant check to ensure that material welfare is not substituted for human development. The subordination of the individual to the state, the regimentation of life, the loss of a sense of humor, the imposition of a puritanical lifestyle or a "proletarian" culture, the death of affection and romantic love, the break-up of the family, are *not* outcomes of socialism. And they ought not to be. In fact, socialism is aimed at the fullest development of each individual. In the final analysis, the process towards full socialism requires a parallel growth of human and economic development.

The Family. As the basic unit of society, the family plays a crucial role in the socialist order. Economic progress and political freedom under socialism will allow each family to develop mutually enriching relations unencumbered by the pressures of poverty and oppression. Special emphasis will be placed on maintaining and enhancing the strength of family ties since it is through the experience of the beauty of shared privileges and responsibilities that the workings of socialism can be born, nurtured and developed.

Women. While socialism as a political-economic system does not directly confront the issue of gender oppression, a socialist structure is better able to handle this reality. The elimination of private ownership of the means of social production and democratic economic planning create the bases for gender equality in both economic and political spheres. Socialists, however, must confront the private/public contradiction that relegates the woman to the domestic sphere, reduces her work to a biological and therefore insignificant category (as against the economic and significant category) and subordinates her being and her activity at work and in society at large.

The double burden of home and work lies at the core of female oppression. Unless socialists confront this issue, women's liberation will remain the partial vision and piecemeal reality that it has largely been in existing socialist societies. The logic of female degradation is manifested in sexual discrimination, prostitution and the exploitation of women.

Socialists must seek to end these forms of female oppression. As the feminist struggle conjoins with the socialist struggle, women can move from a position of weakness to a position of equality and strength—not in theory but in the concrete—by acting and struggling. Socialists must support socialist feminists as they confront their class and gender oppression together and as they call for transformed structures at home and in the workplace for the full liberation of women.

Cultural Minorities. For centuries, Philippine cultural minorities have insisted upon retaining their own culture and traditions. They have confronted a variety of oppressors: foreign, Filipino Christians, as well as their own indigenous elites. But they have struggled for the right to their ancestral lands and to determine their own future. Their quest for self-determination is an articulation of the aspiration to liberate themselves from their oppressors. A socialist society must therefore honor the right of ethnic communities to retain their cultural identity and to insist on self-determination. It must take the necessary steps to encourage the development of their cultures as legacies to the nation.

National Sovereignty

. . . socialism will pursue a foreign policy that best serves the interests of the majority of our people. It will abrogate all unequal treaties with the United States and negotiate new treaties, not with the posture of a mendicant, but from the proud and principled standpoint of a people who have won their freedom.

While upholding our people's interests as the primordial basis of foreign policy, Philippine socialism also adheres to the principles of international working class solidarity. . . .

Independent and Principled Foreign Policy. Socialist internationalism should never degenerate into flunkeyism, that is, the tendency to follow blindly the leadership of another socialist state. . . .

. . . no foreign military bases must be allowed on Philippine territory. The U.S. bases agreement must be unilaterally abrogated. . . .

Economic Relations Based on the National Interest. . . . A socialist Philippines does not mean autarky or isolation from the world economy. Rather, it is participation on the basis of conscious recognition of the national interest and not of a specific class. The necessity for foreign investment and aid must therefore be assessed based on the minimum we cannot do without rather than the maximum we can get. . . .

Selection 11.8: U.S. Bases Post-Marcos, Gaston J. Sigur, Jr.

Editors' Introduction

Following is the testimony of Gaston J. Sigur, Jr., the U.S. Assistant Secretary of State for East Asian and Pacific Affairs before the Subcommittees on Sea Power and Force Projection and on Military Construction of the Senate Armed Services Committee on April 10, 1986. Sigur emphasizes the importance that Washington attaches to the military bases in the Philippines. "No one should underestimate our resolve to...preserve our access to the facilities at Subic and Clark through 1991 and beyond. . . ." In addition to enabling the Pentagon to project power, the bases serve—according to Sigur—to offset the Soviet military presence at Cam Ranh Bay. In fact, however, Soviet facilities in Vietnam are much less substantial than the U.S. bases in the Philippines, and in Southeast Asia the U.S. naval advantage over the USSR is overwhelming. If Washington were genuinely interested in the Philippine bases only to balance the Soviet presence, then one would expect the U.S. to embrace suggestions for the neutralization of the Southeast Asian region; these the U.S. has consistently rejected.

Sigur states that U.S. aid to the Philippines is intended to refurbish the armed forces and to provide them with the means to defeat the New People's Army. Less than two months after Sigur's testimony another top U.S. official—Assistant Secretary of Defense Richard Armitage—appeared before the Senate Foreign Relations Committee. Despite optimistic statements coming from Manila regarding the Aquino government's efforts to obtain a cease-fire. Armitage grimly warned that "at the end of the day, military action will be required to defeat the insurgency."

Source: U.S. Department of State, Bureau of Public Affairs, "U.S. Security Interests in the Philippines," *Current Policy*, no. 815, Washington, DC: April 1986.

I appreciate the interest of your respective subcommittees in the Philippines, and I welcome the opportunity to discuss with you vital U.S. security interests in that country. One of the hallmarks of our Philippine policy during the past several years has been the close consultation between the executive and legislative branches regarding the formulation and implementation of our Philippine policy objectives. The recent dramatic changes in the Philippines that produced a return to democracy and the election of a popular new leader are eloquent testimony to the value of the bipartisan approach. When the U.S. Government speaks with one voice, that voice is heard abroad and the effectiveness of our foreign policy is enhanced.

I intend to continue this tradition of close consultation and look forward to a productive dialogue with you and the members of your subcommittees regarding the security aspects of our Philippine relations.

U.S. Security Interests

U.S. security interests in the Philippines stem from three agreements signed with the Philippine Government in the years immediately following its independence in 1946. These agreements concern military bases, security assistance, and mutual defense. The first of these agreements was the basing accord signed in March 1947. It marked the beginning of our defense relationship with the modern Philippines and has been the focus of our defense policy there ever since.

The military basing agreement was amended in 1966 to shorten the term of our basing agreement in the Philippines from 99 to 25 years. A further amendment in 1979 specified that the bases at Subic and Clark became Philippine bases encompassing U.S. defense facilities and also provided for regular 5-year reviews of the agreement. At the expiration of the original 25-year agreement period in 1991, the basing agreement's term becomes indefinite. Thereafter, either side has the option to terminate the agreement on 1 year's notice. This provision is quite similar to those in our security treaties with NATO, Japan, and Korea. It is, therefore, a misapprehension that the agreement automatically terminates in 1991.

While our basing agreement has been amended many times during the past four decades, the fundamental import of our facilities at Subic Bay and Clark Air Base to our defense posture in Asia has remained constant. The location of these two facilities, in close proximity to each other, and their combined capabilities place them among the most important military establishments we maintain anywhere in the world. Essentially, these facilities:

* Guarantee the external security of the Philippines and represent our most significant contribution to the U.S.-Philippines mutual defense pact;
* Support our wide-ranging commitments all along the Asian littoral, including our security commitments in Korea, Japan, and Thailand and important national interests in the Persian Gulf—the geostrategic location of the Philippines is unsurpassed with regard to meeting these vital national security commitments; and
* Offset the expanding Soviet military presence at Cam Ranh Bay and, as a consequence, preserve the stability of Southeast Asia by securing the vital South China sealanes against the ever-increasing Soviet threat.

The facilities at Subic and Clark have also helped to preserve a stable regional environment which has permitted East Asian states to avoid diverting excessive amounts of scarce resources to military efforts and to concentrate instead on economic development which is crucial to long-term stability. Possible locations other than our present facilities exist but would be much more expensive and considerably less effective in terms of contributing to regional peace and prosperity.

Future of the U.S. Security Relationship

Seven Philippine administrations, including the present government, and eight American presidents have supported close defense ties between the United States and the Philippines and have attested to the importance of the facilities at Subic and Clark in serving our mutual interests. We look forward to a continuation of this close security relationship with the new democratic government in the Philippines headed by President Aquino. Her position with respect to U.S. facilities has been consistent. She has pledged to uphold the current agreement until 1991 and to keep her options open for the post-1991 period. Both sides will have the opportunity to look closely at bases issues during the next 5-year review scheduled for 1988.

We believe the importance of the bases to the security of the Philippines is well understood by Filipinos. Recent, reputable public opinion surveys point to acceptance of the bases by the majority of the Filipino people. This high approval level represents a fundamental recognition by Filipinos that U.S. access to the facilities benefits their country. Economic factors may also influence this approval, as the U.S. facilities are the second largest employer in the Philippines and contribute an estimated $350 million to the Philippine economy each year.

We also note that the Philippines' ASEAN [Association of South East Asian Nations] neighbors, as well as Japan, Korea, and other key states in the region, have expressed their strong support for our continued presence at Subic and Clark. These countries have a keen appreciation of the direct contribution our facilities make to regional security.

In view of this widespread support and because there are no other attractive locations, we have no plans to relocate our facilities from the Philippines. As a great power, we must, of course, plan for contingencies. Evaluations of other possible locations are a regular feature of our strategic planning. Prudence demands it. But no one should underestimate our resolve to maintain our defense and mutual security arrangements with the Republic of the Philippines and to preserve our access to the facilities at Subic and Clark through 1991 and beyond—with the continued cooperation and support of the Filipino people.

Because we have close ties with the Philippines, we are concerned about the threat posed by the communist insurgency. Measures to improve the security of our facilities at Subic and Clark have been undertaken and will continue. We have also targeted our security assistance program to support Philippine efforts to counteract the internal threat they face. The twin objectives of our aid are:

First, to help restore professionalism to the "new" Armed Forces of the Philippines; and

Second, to provide the armed forces with the means to fight the communist New People's Army.

The coming to power of the Aquino government has dealt a political blow to the communist insurgents. The principal target of their propaganda—

former President Marcos—is now gone, as is the "crony" military leadership which so demoralized the Philippine Armed Forces. Reform of the military has taken a big step forward with the forced retirement of many "extendee" generals and colonels and their replacement by professionally qualified officers.

The efforts of the communists to organize a boycott of the recent presidential election were a dismal failure, repudiated by Filipinos even more emphatically than during the 1984 National Assembly election. President Aquino is considering several new approaches to dealing with the communist insurgents, including a possible amnesty and a cease-fire.

However, in order to be successful, the government's program against the insurgents should also include economic and political reforms which promote an effective system of justice that punishes wrongdoers down to the village level, including errant military personnel who violate the human rights of civilians. A close, coordinated relationship between civilian and military authorities in an anti-insurgency strategy will be required—the type of plan that Defense Minister Enrile and [Armed Forces Chief of Staff] General Ramos are now proposing to the civilian leadership. Although great difficulties remain, there exists now the vital element that previously was lacking in the Philippines anti-insurgency struggle—a credible government.

U.S. security assistance can play an important role in support of Philippine Government efforts to enhance its counterinsurgency capabilities. Following recent visits to Manila of senior U.S. officials—including myself—to consult with President Aquino and senior members of her government on Philippine needs and priorities, we are now working on a proposal to increase the level of our economic and security assistance to deal with these deep problems. We expect to consult with the Congress shortly on the details of our expanded assistance program.

Conclusion

In conclusion, our facilities at Subic and Clark continue to play an indispensable role in contributing to the stability of the region. They support our strategy of forward deployment in Asia and provide a secure foundation which makes possible the pursuit of our larger political and economic interests in this key part of the globe.

Our bilateral relationship with the Philippines, which is crucial to maintaining U.S. facilities, is excellent. We are impressed with the skillful leadership of President Aquino and the team she has assembled to carry out her policies. We look forward to working with the Aquino government, as appropriate, in helping to find solutions to the formidable challenges facing her country. There are occasional problems, of course, and there will be others in the future. But with good will they can be worked out to the full satisfaction of both sides.

We believe that the prospects for continued, unhampered access to Subic and Clark are very good. Access to our facilities is best preserved, we maintain, by supporting broader U.S. interests in the Philippines—particularly a healthy free market economy and the development of democratic institutions.

Selection 11.9: The Communist Threat to Reviving Democracy in the Philippines, Richard D. Fisher, Jr.

Editors' Introduction

The Heritage Foundation is a conservative, Washington-based think-tank that has been very influential with the Reagan administration. In January 1984, the Foundation published a backgrounder on "The Key Role of U.S. Bases in the Philippines," by A. James Gregor, arguing that the U.S. had to back Marcos even against the moderate opposition because the latter were anti-bases. On February 25, 1986, the same day Marcos fled his country in disgrace, the Foundation published another study on the Philippines, this one by Martin L. Lasater and Richard D. Fisher, Jr. After noting the widespread election fraud, the authors concluded that the U.S. should not cut off aid to Marcos but instead should seek to diffuse the crisis by bringing about a reconciliation between the Marcos and Aquino factions.

Both of these studies reflected the thinking of the Reagan administration, backing the dictatorship to protect U.S. interests. The excerpt below from an April 1986 Heritage Foundation backgrounder is indicative of the military approach the Reagan administration would like to take to the insurgency problem in the post-Marcos era. The author suggests accelerated U.S. military aid to Manila, aid to the police, and an increased propaganda effort.

The "information" campaign is to include continued funding for "free trade unions" [see selection 9.3 and the introduction to this chapter for a description of the labor organization, TUCP, that Washington has been supporting] and exposing Soviet assistance to the Communist Party of the Philippines. In fact, the evidence for such assistance is exceedingly thin. The Heritage Foundation backgrounder (in a section not printed here) is apparently satisfied with evidence like: "Noncommunist Philippine labor leaders strongly suspect the CPP is receiving Soviet money through the KMU." Other right-wing ideologues who see the Soviet genie behind the CPP point to such telling facts as that the CPP, like the USSR, opposes U.S. intervention in Nicaragua. (Leif Rosenberger, "Philippine Communism and the Soviet Union," *Survey*, Spring 1985, p. 137.) Rosenberger's claims are well refuted by Prof. David Rosenberg in the U.S. Information Agency's publication *Problems of Communism*, July-Aug. 1985, pp. 84-87. Most official U.S. sources agree with the statement in the Senate Intelligence Committee study [see selection 9.9] that there "is no convincing evidence that the Soviet Union has provided funding for the CPP."

Source: Richard D. Fisher, Jr., "The Communist Threat to Reviv-

ing Democracy in the Philippines,"   ton, DC, no. 45, April 23, 1986, pp.
Backgrounder, Asian Studies Center,   1, 11-12.
The Heritage Foundation, Washing-

Introduction

Philippine President Corazon Aquino has an opportunity to rebuild Philippine democracy. The major obstacle she faces probably is the Communist Party of the Philippines (CPP). It continues to wage its so-called people's war, which has cost the lives of over 250 Filipinos since the end of February. The CPP is active in all of the nation's 73 provinces and controls up to 20 percent of the population through "shadow governments." These "governments" maintain their hold over local citizens through a combination of promised reforms and selected terrorism. To make matters worse, until the election, the ranks of the CPP's guerilla arm, the New People's Army (NPA), was growing by 50 percent a year. It can now engage 200- to 300-man government military units in the countryside.

The CPP's urban action arm, the National Democratic Front (NDF), foments unrest in the cities to complement the NPA's military action. Recent demonstrations in a provincial capital on Panay were coordinated with rural NPA attacks. The CPP, meanwhile, has infiltrated the powerful Philippine Catholic Church and receives international support from Western Europe, Australia, the U.S., Canada, and the Soviet bloc.

The CPP's vision of the Philippines' future resembles the repressive societies of Vietnam and Nicaragua. Totalitarian control would extend to all spheres of Philippine society. A CPP regime in Manila almost surely would mean that the U.S. would lose its access to vital Philippine military bases. . . .

How Washington Can Help

It is clearly in U.S. interests in Asia to ensure that Manila is able to defeat the CPP threat to Philippine democracy. The Aquino government is beginning a process of military reform and is developing a comprehensive counterinsurgency strategy. Washington should provide material and other assistance to counter the local and international dimension of the CPP threat. The Administration should accelerate delivery of $55 million in military assistance allocated for FY 1986. If the Administration believes that more aid is needed this year, Congress should approve supplemental requests and should fund the FY 1987 request of $100 million.

Military aid should be designed to promote professionalism and the Philippine military's ability to counter the NPA. This can be accomplished by providing supplies such as uniforms and boots, which improve the soldiers' self-image and reduce the likelihood of stealing from peasants. The AFP also needs spare parts for inoperative trucks, helicopters, and troop transport ships. If NPA activity increases in the future, additional transport and communications equipment will be required. In addition, the Administration should consider aid to improve the capability of Manila's police forces, as it is in El Salvador. The U.S. should also consider helping to fund amnesty and rehabilitation programs that Manila may launch to entice rebels to surrender.

To help the Aquino government bolster its credibility and strengthen democracy, the U.S. should urge Manila to hold local elections soon and provide aid to stimulate economic growth in the countryside. This will help eliminate the political and economic grievances that feed CPP propaganda. Finance Minister Jamie Ongpin seems to favor stimulating private sector investment and growth, especially in agriculture. U.S. economic assistance can help Manila diversify Philippine farming away from such traditional crops as sugar and coconuts for which demand has been declining for several years. The NPA is strong in areas where these crops dominate the local economy, such as Negros and Mindanao.

The U.S. should increase its information effort to help counter increased CPP attempts to inflame Filipino nationalism by attacking U.S. influence in the Philippines. Additional funds should be allocated for student scholarships. For FY 1986, only $293,000 was allocated for 21 new and continuing students by the Fulbright scholarship program. The National Endowment for Democracy should continue to fully fund the Philippine program of the AFL-CIO's Asian-American Free Labor Institute. This program has successfully enabled Filipinos to create free trade unions in Negros and Mindanao, where the communist-controlled KMU is strong.

In addition, the U.S. should increase its efforts to expose the CPP's international supporters, especially Soviet attempts to assist the CPP. The U.S. should share such information with Manila and allied governments to facilitate interdiction of the CPP's international support network.

Selection 11.10: Letting Go, B. David Williams

Editors' Introduction

The murder of Benigno Aquino and the massive popular upheavals it unleashed brought the horror and corruption of the Marcos dictatorship to the attention of millions in the United States. In these circumstances the continued U.S. support for that dictatorship threw new light on U.S. policy towards the Philippines. It became clear to many that—on the evidence of the Marcos years, at least—the long-standing popular belief in U.S. generosity and benevolence towards the Philippines had no basis in fact. Only a pre-occupation with U.S. economic and military privileges in the Philippines, to the exclusion of any concern for the welfare of most Filipinos, could explain the U.S. embrace of Marcos.

So it is that in the United States today, at the end of the Marcos era, there appears to be developing a much wider and deeper understanding of the need for a change in U.S. policy towards the Philippines. Indicative of this new understanding is a study guide on the Philippines prepared for use in mainstream U.S.

churches. The excerpt printed below from the summary section of this document makes a strong case for an end to the historic pattern of U.S. intervention. If present policies are allowed to continue, it warns, the result could be outright U.S. military intervention with horrendous human consequences. "We must *not* allow that to happen."

The study guide calls upon the United States to respect the right of the Philippine people to reject U.S. bases after 1991.

To fill out the picture, however, it is necessary to add that there are currently those in the United States and elsewhere who believe that an even more assertive stand should be taken on the issue. Declaring that U.S. bases in the Philippines "exist solely to promote U.S. participation in nuclear war and wars of foreign intervention in Asia and the Mideast," the Friends of the Filipino People at a 1986 national conference called for their immediate dismantling. So did, in a similar gathering, the Alliance for Philippine Concerns, a San Francisco-based coalition of some 48 organizations composed primarily of Filipinos living in the United States, Canada, and Mexico.

Source: B. David Williams "The Philippines at a Crossroad: A Background Study Paper for the U.S. Churches," *Ecumenical Perspectives,* Occasional Papers on International Affairs, International Affairs Commission, National Council of Churches of Christ in the USA, New York: 1986, pp. 43-44.

How can we adequately express our consolation and caring, our practical, active concern for the Filipino people? The present crisis challenges and judges us.

"What must we do?" This is a good American question, and there are indeed urgent things to be done. We must *do,* yet we must go beyond doing to ask how the Philippines and some other regional crisis situations concretely reflect *who we have become.* Our own selfhood is at stake as well as the selfhood of Filipinos, our own liberation is bound up with theirs.

As for *doing,* will we stop our insistence upon military solutions for the long-standing unrest? Will we withdraw our support from the elitist elements which are essentially anti-democratic?

Why did it take us so long to express our outrage and disgust at the consistent, blatant violations of human rights? Why do we still call Ferdinand Marcos "our good friend and ally," and give him costly favored treatment?

Will our intervention in the Philippines become more direct? Unfortunately, history says it probably will. Some of our high officials recently inferred that there are circumstances in which we might undertake direct military intervention. Such a dreadful mistake would kill many, many people. We must *not* allow that to happen.

The Philippines is not "something that we could lose"—it does not belong to us. Filipinos are not simple-minded people incapable of resisting "foreign" ideologies—they are a gifted people with minds and values of their own, a people who love democracy! Filipino Nationalism is not a sinister force—let us affirm with Filipinos, "yes, it is good to love one's country and to insist upon the sovereignty of one's country, to struggle for one's selfhood."

Will we have the grace to leave the question of U.S. bases in the Philippines to Filipinos? If in 1991 they decide not to renew the agreement, will we respect that choice?

Going to a deeper level: the current crisis is not a new question, nor is it a partisan issue. U.S. direct involvement in the Philippines has now spanned sixteen U.S. presidencies. What are the deep attitudes and values that are betraying us there? What is it that we need to change in ourselves? Have we spawned a "national security culture" that will in the end alienate many, devour us, and take many with us? Of whom, really, are we afraid?

What prophetic call should be sounding forth from the U.S. churches concerning this our crisis of culture?

With deep gratitude for the countless ties and enduring special bonds we have with the Filipino people, and in contrition for serious mistakes in the Philippines, let us *LET GO!* . . .

POSTSCRIPT

In the few months since this volume was completed, there have been a great many new developments in the Philippines. Most of these have been along the lines of the trends we described earlier in the book. But nothing that has occurred has been decisive enough—in our view—to allow us to answer the crucial question of where the Aquino administration is ultimately heading. Some of the positive trends we identified in chapter 11 have continued, but so too have some of the negative trends.

The most significant political development has been the signing of a sixty-day cease-fire between the New People's Army (NPA), and the Aquino government. The truce was not easily arrived at. On the eve of a cease-fire agreement at the end of September, the military announced the arrest of a top Communist Party leader; given that his capture "appears to have been possible only because he came to Manila in connection with the negotiations and because the military shadowed a bodyguard who accompanied the Communist negotiators" (*New York Times*, 5 Oct. 1986), many concluded that this represented an effort on the part of the armed forces—who made no secret of their opposition to a cease-fire—to scuttle the truce talks.

Negotiations resumed and were again on the verge of completion in mid-November when the head of the KMU, the militant labor union organization, was murdered. Elements of the military connected to Defense Minister Juan Ponce Enrile were widely suspected of the crime and the left responded with the largest political demonstration the country had seen since February.

Enrile meanwhile had been seeking to portray himself as the Philippines' only hope against communism. He had held a series of anti-communist rallies around the country, in which he attacked Aquino's alleged weakness in the face of the red threat. The audience for these rallies was made up largely of former Marcos supporters. The latter had tried to mount a coup against Aquino in early July, but the effort fizzled (as even Enrile had astutely opposed the move so closely identified with the thoroughly discredited former dictator).

On November 23, Enrile and his supporters in the military sought to engineer their own coup. The armed forces chief of staff, General Fidel Ramos, however, remained loyal to Aquino and blocked Enrile's effort. Enrile was promptly removed from the Cabinet, and replaced by General Rafael Ileto, a U.S.-trained career officer, who had fought against the Huks in the 1950s, but who had opposed Marcos's declaration of martial law. This did not signify, however, the end of the armed forces' right-wing influence on Philippine politics. Ramos himself had delivered a list of military demands to

Aquino shortly before Enrile's coup attempt. Ramos in fact shared Enrile's program—opposition to the leftist members of Aquino's cabinet and to a cease-fire—while opposing Enrile's megalomania. Indicative of the military's continued impact, Aquino has replaced Local Governments Minister Pimentel and Labor Minister Sanchez. On the other hand, Pimentel remains an Aquino adviser and Joker Arroyo, Aquino's Executive Secretary who has been especially anathma to the military, retains his post.

More significantly, Aquino rejected the military's position on the cease-fire talks, and in early December an agreement was reached with the guerillas establishing a sixty-day cessation of hostilities. Both sides agreed to begin discussions to try to resolve the issues underlying the rebellion: the questions of land reform, human rights, social justice, and national sovereignty. No one expects any quick resolution of these matters, but many expect that the cease-fire can be extended, and there is reason to hope that these root issues can be dealt with in the political rather than the military sphere. The Communist Party and other elements of the left have made clear their intention to fully participate in the political arena; this will be more likely if the Communist Party is legalized, now a possibility. The armed forces, for its part, may well try to undermine the cease-fire just as it attempted to sabotage the negotiations.

The economic program of the Aquino administration continues along the lines described in chapter 11: that is, a strong commitment to the free market and to foreign capital. Philippine government advertisements in the U.S. press courting foreign investment are reminiscent of those of the Marcos years and some of the government's policies go beyond anything enacted by Marcos: for example, some foreign investors are offered the opportunity to acquire Philippine citizenship. Unlike the situation under Marcos, however, under Aquino unions and strikes are legal and political debate is unfettered, providing at least the potential for checking the power of capitalists, domestic and foreign.

Obviously, the economy was left a shambles by Marcos, and no program of economic recovery will be easy. However, a free enterprise model—as we indicated in chapter 11—puts the burden of the recovery on the urban and rural poor. And Aquino's programs to help deal with poverty and unemployment have been moving at a snail's pace. By December only 8 percent of the government's job-creating public-works projects for the year were completed.

The most distressing aspect of Aquino's program to those concerned with economic and social justice is the total lack of progress on the issue of land reform. Aquino's own lands—which were to be the first on which genuine land reform was to be enacted—remain untouched. Humanitarian aid programs have mitigated some of the starvation that was rampant in the sugar-growing areas of the country, as has the illegal use of land by peasants encouraged by the NPA. But malnutrition continues to afflict 70 percent of the children on the island of Negros. A demonstration of more than 20,000 farmers converged on Manila in October calling for land redistribution.

The Constitutional Commission appointed by Aquino completed its draft of a new constitution in October. The document is to be voted on in a referendum on February 2. Under the terms of the constitution, Aquino will remain president until the next presidential election scheduled for 1992 (which is why Enrile and the Marcos loyalists oppose the document); local and congressional elections are to be held in May 1987. The constitution restores a presidential system of government, contains a bill of rights, establishes a human rights commission, and places checks on authoritarian rule. The constitution also condemns abortion (a provision engendering little public dissent).

Many nationalists consider the economic provisions of the new constitution to be wholly unsatisfactory, permitting as they do a preponderant role for foreign capital. The KMU, claiming that the interests of labor have been slighted, has decided to campaign against ratification of the constitution.

On the issue of foreign military bases and nuclear weapons, the Constitutional Commission came up with a formulation somewhere in between what the United States wanted and what the anti-bases activists hoped for.

The constitution provides that U.S. military bases may remain until 1991 but that any future bases agreement with the U.S. must have treaty status and be approved by both the Philippine and U.S. Senate. Moreover, the Philippine legislature is given the right to submit any such treaty to a national plebiscite. This assures that any bases agreement will be the subject of widespread public debate, both in the Philippines and in the United States, which is in marked contrast to the previous military bases agreement, whose terms were adjusted every few years subject only to the whim of the Philippine dictator and the U.S. executive. U.S. Senator Robert Dole, reflecting conservative and military opinion, has already publicly complained about an arrangement that gives the Filipino people input, thus turning the matter into "an explosive domestic political issue."

The constitution further provides that the Philippines shall be nuclear free, "consistent with the national interest." This is a substantial loophole—there are a number of countries where similar provisions have inconvenienced the Pentagon not a whit—but it gives the anti-nuclear movement an opening to raise the question of what really is in the Philippine national interest.

While critical of the serious weaknesses in the bases and nuclear provisions, the Nuclear Free Philippines Coalition, a grouping of Filipino anti-nuclear organizations, has called for a "yes" vote on the constitution because it will necessarily put the bases and nuclear issues on the public agenda. In the United States, too, anti-intervention activists hope to be able to use the constitutional provisions to force a real debate on the bases and on the broader issues of what constitutes genuine security.

Although the United States government still worries about Aquino's reliability and her commitment to U.S. goals, it continues to give her public support. It does so not because it has any moral objections to dictators like

Marcos, but because she seems to offer the best hope for preventing a further growth in both the political and military strength of the left, which would endanger the status quo, including the U.S. military bases. While Enrile may be useful as pressure upon Aquino for the resumption of the counter-insurgency war, realists in Washington appear to understand that such a war would best be waged under the nominal leadership of the popular Aquino, serving as figurehead for the Philippine military, her significance for necessary social reform much diminished. Thus, the U.S. publicly opposed Enrile's November coup and reiterated its support for Aquino's government. But at the same time, Washington is doing everything it can—albeit discreetly—to try to minimize the role of the left in Philippine politics, to support the right-wing military, and to push Aquino toward an all-out war on the insurgency.

In September, just before Aquino's trip to the United States, unnamed White House sources urged Aquino to stop seeking conciliation with the communist rebels. Prominent right-wing figures—retired General Singlaub of the Nicaraguan contra support movement and the World Anti-Communist League, former CIA officials, and others—have been meeting with Ramos and other Philippine military leaders. Before the recent revelations regarding the White House-orchestrated covert operations network, these visits might have been dismissed as merely private undertakings, but now their official sponsorship seems more likely. Reagan has ordered the Pentagon to send a Navy hospital ship *Mercy* to the Philippines in early 1987; the ship was designed solely for the purpose of providing emergency surgical care to war casualties. "I can't predict what the situation would be as far as the Communist insurgency in the Philippines in the early part of next year" and "whether they will have combat casualties that we might assist in treating," said a Pentagon spokesperson (*Pacific Stars and Stripes,* 20 Sept. 1986).

Indeed, no one can predict what the situation will be, but to U.S. officials and the Philippine military a counter-insurgency war represents their most favored option. As the *Far Eastern Economic Review* reported (18 Dec. 1986), "Senior military sources say the 250,000-man armed forces can continue to handle the military threat posed by the NPA, but they say the prospect of a full-blooded political assault on which the Left now seems to have embarked is more insidious and worrisome."

SUGGESTED ADDITIONAL READINGS

The following list of suggested readings omits sources which have been excerpted in this book.

General

Agoncillo, Teodoro A. *A Short History of the Philippines*. New York: Mentor Books, 1969.

Agoncillo, Teodoro A. *Filipino Nationalism, 1872-1970*. Quezon City: R. P. Garcia Publishing Co., 1974.

Bunge, Frederica M. (ed.) *Philippines: A Country Study*. Foreign Area Studies, The American University. Washington, DC: U.S. Government Printing Office, 1984.

Constantino, Renato. *Neocolonial Identity and Counter-Consciousness: Essays on Cultural Decolonization*. White Plains, NY: M. E. Sharpe, 1978.

Corpuz, Onofre D. *The Philippines*. Englewood Cliffs, NJ: Prentice-Hall, 1965.

Steinberg, David Joel. *The Philippines: A Singular and A Plural Place*. Boulder, CO: Westview Press, 1982.

Wernstedt, Frederick L., and J. E. Spencer. *The Philippine Island World: A Physical, Cultural, and Regional Geography*. Berkeley: University of California Press, 1978 (reprint).

Chapter 1: Conquest

Agoncillo, Teodoro A. *Revolt of the Masses: The Story of Bonifacio and the Katipunan*. Quezon City: University of the Philippines, 1956.

Agoncillo, Teodoro A. *Malolos: The Crisis of the Republic*. Quezon City: University of the Philippines, 1960.

Beisner, Robert L. *Twelve Against Empire: The Anti-Imperialists, 1898-1900*. New York: McGraw-Hill, 1968.

Blount, James H. *The American Occupation of the Philippines, 1898-1912*. New York: Oriole Editions, 1973 (reprint of 1912 ed.) [by a colonial official].

Constantino, Renato. *The History of the Philippines: From the Spanish Coloniza-tion to the Second World War*. New York: Monthly Review Press, 1975.

Francisco, Luzviminda Bartolome, and Jonathan Shepard Fast. *Conspiracy for Empire: Big Business, Corruption and the Politics of Imperialism in America, 1876-1907*. Quezon City: Foundation for Nationalist Studies, 1985.

Gates, John Morgan. *Schoolbooks and Krags: The United States Army in the Philippines, 1898-1902.* Westport, CT: Greenwood Press, 1973.

Gatewood, Willard B., Jr. *Black Americans and the White Man's Burden, 1898-1903.* Urbana: University of Illinois Press, 1975.

Ileto, Reynaldo Clemena. *Pasyon and Revolution: Popular Movements in the Philippines, 1840-1910.* Quezon City: Ateneo de Manila University Press, 1979.

LaFeber, Walter. *The New Empire: An Interpretation of American Expansion, 1860-1898.* Ithaca, NY: Cornell University Press, 1963.

Majul, Cesar A. *The Political and Constitutional Ideas of the Philippine Revolution.* Quezon City: University of the Philippines Press, rev. ed., 1967.

May, Glenn A. "Why the United States Won the Philippine-American War, 1899-1902," *Pacific Historical Review,* vol. 52, no. 4, 1983.

Miller, Stuart Creighton. *Benevolent Assimilation: The American Conquest of the Philippines, 1899-1903.* New Haven: Yale University Press, 1982.

Schirmer, Daniel B. *Republic or Empire: American Resistance to the Philippine War.* Cambridge, MA: Schenkman, 1972.

Schumacher, John N. *The Propaganda Movement, 1880-1895: The Creators of a Filipino Consciousness, the Makers of the Revolution.* Manila: Solidaridad Publishing House, 1973.

Stanley, Peter W. (ed.). *Reappraising An Empire: New Perspectives on Philippine-American History.* Cambridge, MA: Harvard University Press, 1984.

Storey, Moorfield, and Marcial P. Lichauco. *The Conquest of the Philippines by the United States, 1898-1925.* New York: G. P. Putnam's Sons, 1926.

Sturtevant, David. *Popular Uprisings in the Philippines, 1840-1940.* Ithaca, NY: Cornell University Press, 1976.

Thomson, James C., Jr.; Peter W. Stanley; and John Curtis Perry. *Sentimental Imperialists: The American Experience in East Asia.* New York: Harper & Row, 1981.

Welch, Richard E., Jr. *Response to Imperialism: The United States and the Philippine-American War, 1899-1902.* Chapel Hill, NC: University of North Carolina Press, 1979.

Wolff, Leon. *Little Brown Brother.* Garden City, NY: Doubleday & Co., 1961.

Chapter 2: Colonization

[see also Blount, Constantino, and Stanley in chap. 1 above]

Bulosan, Carlos. *America Is In the Heart*. Seattle: University of Washington Press, 1973 [autobiography of Philippine poet in the Philippines and the U.S.].

Constantino, Renato. *The Making Of A Filipino: A Story of Philippine Colonial Politics*. Quezon City: Malaya Books, 1969 [biography of Recto].

Forbes, W. Cameron. *The Philippine Islands*. Cambridge, MA: Harvard University Press, revised edition, 1945 [by a U.S. colonial official].

Freer, William B. *The Philippine Experiences of an American Teacher*. New York: Charles Scribner's Sons, 1906.

Friend, Theodore. *Between Two Empires: The Ordeal of the Philippines, 1929-1946*. New Haven: Yale University Press, 1965.

Harrison, Francis Burton. *The Cornerstone of Philippine Independence: A Narrative of Seven Years*. New York: The Century Co., 1922 [by a colonial official].

Hayden, Joseph Ralston. *The Philippines: A Study in National Development*. New York: Macmillan, 1942.

Kirk, Grayson L. *Philippine Independence: Motives, Problems, and Prospects*. New York: Farrar & Rinehart, 1936.

Lasker, Bruno. *Filipino Immigration*. New York: Arno Press, 1969 (reprint of 1931 ed.).

May, Glenn Anthony. *Social Engineering in the Philippines: The Aims, Execution, and Impact of American Colonial Policy, 1900-1913*. Westport, CT: Greenwood Press, 1980.

Owen, Norman G. (ed.). *Compadre Colonialism: Philippine-American Relations, 1898-1946*. Center for South and Southeast Asian Studies, University of Michigan, Michigan Papers on South and Southeast Asia no. 3, Ann Arbor, 1970.

Pomeroy, William J. *American Neocolonialism: Its Origins in the Philippines and Asia*. New York: International Publishers, 1970.

Quezon, Manuel. *The Good Fight*. New York: D. Appleton-Century, 1946 [autobiography of Philippine leader].

Salamanca, Bonifacio S. *The Filipino Reaction to American Rule, 1901-1913*. Norwich, CT: The Shoe String Press, 1968.

Stanley, Peter W. *A Nation in the Making: The Philippines and the United States, 1899-1921*. Cambridge, MA: Harvard University Press, 1974.

Taft, William H. "Civil Government in the Philippines," in *The Philippines*. New York: The Outlook Co., 1902 [by a colonial official].

Worcester, Dean C. *The Philippines Past and Present*, 2 vols. New York: Macmillan, 1914 [by U.S. colonial official].

Chapter 3: War, Collaboration, and Resistance

[see also Constantino and Friend in chap. 2 above]

Abaya, Hernando J. *Betrayal in the Philippines*. New York: A. A. Wyn Co., 1946.

Agoncillo, Teodoro A. *The Fateful Years: Japan's Adventure in the Philippines, 1941-1945*, 2 vols. Quezon City: R. P. Garcia Publishing Co., 1974.

Constantino, Renato, and Constantino, Letizia R. *The Philippines: The Continuing Past*. Quezon City: Foundation for Nationalist Studies, 1978.

James, D. Clayton. *The Years of MacArthur* vol. 2, *1941-1945*. Boston: Houghton Mifflin, 1975.

Petillo, Carol M. "Douglas MacArthur and Manuel Quezon: A Note on An Imperial Bond," *Pacific Historical Review*, vol. 48, no. 1, Feb. 1979.

Recto, Claro M. *Three Years of Enemy Occupation: The Issue of Political Collaboration in the Philippines*. Manila: People's Publishers, 1946.

Shalom, Stephen Rosskamm. *The United States and the Philippines: A Study of Neocolonialism*. Philadelphia: Institute for the Study of Human Issues, 1981.

Chapter 4: Independence with Strings

[see also Friend in chap. 2; and Abaya, Constantino, and Shalom in chap. 3 above]

Edgerton, Ronald K. "General Douglas MacArthur and the American Military Impact in the Philippines," *Philippine Studies*, vol. 25, 4th quarter, 1977.

Grunder, Garel A., and William Livezey. *The Philippines and the United States*. Norman: University of Oklahoma Press, 1951.

McCoy, Alfred W. "The Philippines: Independence Without Decolonization," in *Asia: The Winning of Independence*, ed. Robin Jeffrey, New York: St. Martin's, 1981.

Shalom, Stephen R[osskamm]. "Philippine Acceptance of the Bell Trade Act of 1946: A Study of Manipulatory Democracy," *Pacific Historical Review*, vol. 49, no. 3, August 1980.

Ventura, Mamerto S. *United States-Philippine Cooperation and Cross Purposes*. Quezon City: Philippines Publications, 1974.

Chapter 5: Suppression of the Huks

[see also Constantino and Shalom in chap. 3 above]

Abueva, Jose V. *Ramon Magsaysay: A Political Biography*. Manila: Solidaridad Publishing House, 1971.

Kerkvliet, Benedict J. *The Huk Rebellion: A Study of Peasant Revolt in the Philippines.* Berkeley: University of California Press, 1977.

Lachica, Eduardo. *Huk: Philippine Agrarian Society in Revolt.* New York: Praeger, 1971.

Lansdale, Edward G. *In the Midst of Wars: An American's Mission in Southeast Asia.* New York: Harper & Row, 1972 [by CIA operative].

Scaff, Alvin H. *The Philippine Answer to Communism.* Stanford: Stanford University Press, 1955.

Starner, Francis L. *Magsaysay and the Philippine Peasantry: The Agrarian Impact on Philippine Politics, 1953-1956.* Berkeley: University of California Press, 1961.

Taruc, Luis. *He Who Rides the Tiger.* New York: Praeger, 1967.

Chapter 6: The Philippine Republic to 1972: Elite Democracy and Neocolonialism

[see also Stanley in chap. 1; Constantino in chap. 2; and Constantino and Shalom in chap. 3 above]

Center for Strategic and International Studies. *U.S.-Philippine Economic Relations.* Georgetown University, Special Report Series no. 12, Washington, DC, 1971.

Constantino, Renato (ed.). *M.A.N.'s Goal: The Democratic Filipino Society.* Quezon City: Malaya Books, 1969 [program of the Movement for the Advancement of Nationalism].

Corporate Information Center, National Council of Churches of Christ in the USA. "The Philippines: American Corporations, Martial Law, and Underdevelopment," *IDOC*, International/North American Edition, no. 57, November 1973.

Feder, Ernest. *Peverse Development.* Quezon City: Foundation for Nationalist Studies, 1983 [on Philippine rural development].

Golay, Frank H. *The Philippines: Public Policy and National Economic Development.* Ithaca, NY: Cornell University Paperbacks, 1968.

Golay, Frank H. (ed.). *The United States and the Philippines.* Englewood Cliffs, NJ: Prentice-Hall, 1966.

Guerrero, Amado. *Philippine Society and Revolution.* Hong Kong: Ta Kung Pao, 1971 [CPP classic].

Hart, Donn V. *Compadrinazgo: Ritual Kinship in the Philippines.* DeKalb: Northern Illinois University Press, 1977.

Hollnsteiner, Mary R. *The Dynamics of Power in a Philippine Municipality.* Quezon City: Community Development Research Council, University of the Philippines, 1963.

Hollnsteiner, Mary R. *The Filipino Woman: Her Role and Status in Philippine Society.* Quezon City: Institute of Philippine Culture, 1976.

Kaut, Charles. "Utang Na Loob: A System of Contractual Obligations Among Tagalogs," *Southwestern Journal of Anthropology*, vol. 17, no. 3, 1961.

Kerkvliet, Benedict J. (ed.). *Political Change in the Philippines: Studies of Local Politics Preceding Martial Law.* Honolulu: University Press of Hawaii, 1974.

Lacaba, Jose F. *Days of Disquiet, Nights of Rage: The First Quarter Storm and Related Events.* Manila: Salinlahi Publishing House, 1982.

Lande, Carl H. *Leaders, Factions, and Parties: The Structure of Philippine Politics.* Southeast Asian Studies, Yale University, Monograph Series no. 6, New Haven, 1965.

Lichauco, Alejandro. "The Lichauco Paper: Imperialism in the Philippines," *Monthly Review*, vol. 25, no. 3, July-August 1973.

Lynch, Frank, and Alfonso de Guzman II (eds.). *Four Readings on Philippine Values.* Quezon City: Ateneo de Manila University Press, Institute of Philippine Culture, fourth revised edition, 1973.

Meyer, Milton. *A Diplomatic History of the Philippine Republic.* Honolulu: University of Hawaii Press, 1965.

Owen, Norman G. (ed.). *The Philippine Economy and the United States: Studies in Past and Present Interactions.* Center for South and Southeast Asian Studies, University of Michigan, Michigan Papers on South and Southeast Asia no. 22, Ann Arbor, 1983.

Rojas-Aleta, Isabel; Teresita L. Silva; and Christine P. Eleazar. *A Profile of Filipino Women: Their Status and Role.* Manila: Philippine Business for Social Progress, 1978.

Taylor, George E. *The Philippines and the United States: Problems of Partnership.* New York: Praeger, 1964.

Wolters, Willem. *Politics, Patronage and Class Conflict in Central Luzon.* The Hague: Institute of Social Studies, 1983.

Wurfel, David. "The Philippines," in *Government and Politics of Southeast Asia*, ed. George M. Kahin, Ithaca: Cornell University Press, 1965, 2nd ed.

Chapter 7: Martial Law

[see also Shalom in chap. 3; and Feder, Guerrero, and Wolters in chap. 6 above]

Aguilar, Delia. "Filipino Women in the National Liberation Struggle," *Women's Studies International Forum*, vol. 5, nos. 3-4, 1982.

Anti-Slavery Society. *The Philippines: Authoritarian Government, Multinationals and Ancestral Lands.* London: Anti-Slavery Society, Indigenous Peoples and Development Series, Report no. 1, 1983.

Aquino, Belinda A. (ed.). *Cronies and Enemies: The Current Philippine Scene.* Philippine Studies Program, University of Hawaii, Occasional Paper no. 5, Honolulu, 1982.

Baumgartner, Joseph (ed.). "The Cultural Minorities of the Philippines," *Philippine Quarterly of Culture and Society* [Cebu City], vol. 2, nos. 1-2, 1974; vol. 5, nos. 1-2, 1977.

Bello, Walden; Peter Hayes; and Lyuba Zarsky. "'500-Mile Island': The Philippine Nuclear Reactor Deal," *Pacific Research*, vol. 10, no. 1, first quarter 1979.

Canoy, Reuben R. *The Counterfeit Revolution: Martial Law in the Philippines.* Manila: Philippines Edition Publishing, 1980.

Cheetham, Russell J., et al. *The Philippines: Priorities and Prospects for Development.* Baltimore: Johns Hopkins University Press, 1976.

Claver, Bishop Francisco F., S.J. *The Stones Will Cry Out: Grassroots Pastorals.* Maryknoll, NY: Orbis Books, 1978.

de la Torre, Edicio. *Taking Root, Touching Ground: Theological and Political Reflections on the Philippine Struggle.* Manila: Socio-Pastoral Institute, 1986.

Gaspar, Karl. *How Long? Prison Reflections from the Philippines.* Maryknoll, NY: Orbis Books, 1986.

George, T. J. S. *Revolt in Mindanao: The Rise of Islam in Philippine Politics.* Kuala Lumpur: Oxford University Press, 1980.

Gowing, Peter Gordon. *Muslim Filipinos: Heritage and Horizon.* Quezon City: New Day Publishers, 1979.

Jocano, F. Landa. *Slum As A Way of Life.* Quezon City: University of the Philippines Press, 1975.

Khan, Azizur Rahman. "Growth and Inequality in the Rural Philippines," in *Poverty and Landlessness in Rural Asia.* Geneva: International Labour Office, 1977.

Lande, Carl H. "Philippine Prospects After Martial Law," *Foreign Affairs*, vol. 59, no. 5, 1981.

Lawson, Don. *Marcos and the Philippines.* New York: Franklin Watts, 1984.

Ledesma, Antonio J., S.J.; Perla Q. Makil; and Virginia A. Miralao (eds.). *Second View from the Paddy: More Empirical Studies of Philippine Rice Farming and Tenancy.* Quezon City: Ateneo de Manila University, Institute of Philippine Culture, 1983.

Majul, Cesar Adib. *The Contemporary Muslim Movement in the Philippines.* Berkeley: Mizan Press, 1985.

Manglapus, Raul. *Philippines: The Silenced Democracy.* Maryknoll, NY: Orbis Books, 1976.

Marcos, Ferdinand E. *The Democratic Revolution in the Philippines*. Englewood Cliffs, NJ: Prentice-Hall International, 1974.

McLennan, Marshall S. *The Central Luzon Plain: Land and Society on the Inland Frontier*. Quezon City: Alemar-Phoenix Publishing House, 1980.

McCoy, Alfred W. *Priests on Trial*. New York: Penguin, 1984 [1982 trial of Fathers Gore and O'Brien].

Mijares, Primitivo. *The Conjugal Dictatorship of Ferdinand and Imelda Marcos I*. San Francisco: Union Square Publications, 1976.

Nemenzo, Francisco. "Rectification Process in the Philippine Communist Movement," in *Armed Communist Movements in Southeast Asia*, ed. Lim Joo-Jock with Vani S. New York: St. Martin's Press, 1984.

Noble, Lela Garner. "The Moro National Liberation Front in the Philippines," *Pacific Affairs*, vol. 49, no. 3, 1976.

Permanent Peoples' Tribunal Session on the Philippines. *Philippines: Repression and Resistance*. London: KSP Komite ng Sambayanang, Pilipino, 1981.

Pomeroy, William J. *An American Made Tragedy: Neocolonialism and Dictatorship in the Philippines*. New York: International Publishers, 1974.

Richter, Linda K. *Land Reform and Tourism Development: Policy-Making in the Philippines*. Cambridge, MA: Schenkman, 1982.

Rocamora, Joel, et al. "Tribal People and the Marcos Regime: Cultural Genocide in the Philippines," *Southeast Asia Chronicle* (special issue), no. 67, October 1979.

Rosenberg, David A. (ed.). *Marcos and Martial Law in the Philippines*. Ithaca, NY: Cornell University Press, 1979.

Rutten, Rosanne. *Women Workers of Hacienda Milagros: Wage Labor and Household Subsistence on a Philippine Sugarcane Plantation*. Amsterdam: University of Amsterdam, Department of South and Southeast Asian Studies, Publication no. 30, 1982.

Scott, William Henry. *On the Cordillera: A Look at the People and Cultures of the Mountain Province*. Manila: MCS, 1969.

Third World Studies Center. *Marxism in the Philippines: Marx Centennial Lectures*. Quezon City: Third World Studies Center, University of the Philippines, 1984.

Wery, Rene, et al. *Population, Employment, and Poverty in the Philippines*. Geneva: International Labour Office, 1977.

Wurfel, David. "Martial Law in the Philippines: The Methods of Regime Survival," *Pacific Affairs*, vol. 50, no. 1, Spring 1977.

Chapter 8: "The U.S. Marcos Dictatorship"

[see also Shalom in chap. 3; Feder and Owen in chap. 6; and Rosenberg in chap. 7 above]

Bello, Walden. "Springboards for Intervention, Instruments for Nuclear War," *Southeast Asia Chronicle*, no. 89, April 1983 [on the U.S. bases].

Bello, Walden; David Kinley; and Elaine Elinson. *Development Debacle: The World Bank in the Philippines*. San Francisco: Institute for Food and Development Policy/Philippine Solidarity Network, 1982.

Buss, Claude A. *The United States and the Philippines: Background for Policy*. Washington, DC: American Enterprise Institute, 1977.

Emmanuel, Jorge. *The Immediate and Long Term Consequences of Nuclear War in the Philippines*. Durham, NC: Friends of the Filipino People, 1983.

Fuentes, Annette, and Barbara Ehrenreich. *Women in the Global Factory*. Boston: South End Press, 1983.

Jose, Vivencio R. (ed.). *Mortgaging the Future: The World Bank and the IMF in the Philippines*. Quezon City: Foundation for Nationalist Studies, 1982.

Kessler, Richard J. "Marcos and the Americans," *Foreign Policy*, no. 63, Summer 1986.

Lindsey, Charles W. "In Search of Dynamism: Foreign Investment in the Philippines Under Martial Law," *Pacific Affairs*, vol. 56, no. 2, Fall 1983.

Lindsey, Charles W. "The Philippine State and Transnational Investment," in *Transnational Corporations and the State*, ed. Robert B. Stauffer, Sydney: Transnational Corporations Research Project, University of Sydney, 1985.

Miller, John. "Sea-Launched Cruise Missiles and the Philippines: Time To Act," *Philippine Research Bulletin*, vol. 1, no. 2-3, Fall/Spring 1984-85.

Paez, Patricia Ann. *The Bases Factor: Realpolitik of RP-US Relations*. Manila: Center for Strategic and International Studies of the Philippines, 1985.

Poole, Fred, and Max Vanzi. *Revolution in the Philippines: The United States in a Hall of Cracked Mirrors*. New York: McGraw-Hill, 1984.

Pringle, Robert. *Indonesia and the Philippines: American Interests in Island Southeast Asia*. New York: Columbia University Press, 1980.

Simbulan, Roland. *The Bases of Our Insecurity: A Study of the U.S. Bases in the Philippines*. Metro Manila: BALAI Fellowship, Inc., second edition, 1985.

Stauffer, Robert B. "The Manila-Washington Connection: Continuities in the Transnational Political Economy of Philippine Development," *Philippine Social Sciences and Humanities Review*, vol. 47, nos. 1-4, January-December 1983.

Thompson, W. Scott. *Unequal Partners: Philippine and Thai Relations with the United States, 1965-75*. Lexington, MA: D.C. Heath & Co., 1975.

Villegas, Edberto M. *Studies in Philippine Political Economy*. Manila: Silangan, 1983.

Yoshihara, Kunio. *Philippine Industrialization: Foreign and Domestic Capital*. Singapore: Oxford University Press, 1985.

Youngblood, Robert L. "Philippine-American Relations Under the 'New Society,' " *Pacific Affairs*, vol. 50, no. 1, Spring 1977.

Chapter 9: The Gathering Storm

[see also Wolters in chap. 6; Gaspar, Nemenzo, and de la Torre in chap. 7; and Poole & Vanzi in chap. 8 above]

Aquino, Benigno S., Jr. *A Garrison State in the Make and Other Speeches*. Metro Manila: Benigno S. Aquino, Jr. Foundation, 1985.

Bello, Walden. "Edging Toward the Quagmire: The United States and the Philippine Crisis," *World Policy Journal*, vol. 3, no. 1, Winter 1985-86.

Doherty, John F. *The Philippine Urban Poor*. Philippine Studies Program, University of Hawaii, Occasional Paper no. 8, Honolulu, 1985.

Gregor, A. James. *Crisis in the Philippines: A Threat to U.S. Interests*. Washington, DC: Ethics and Public Policy Center, 1984.

Hill, Gerald N. and Kathleen Thompson Hill with Steve Psinakis. *Aquino Assassination: The True Story and Analysis of the Assassination of Philippine Senator Benigno S. Aquino, Jr*. Sonomia, CA: Hilltop Publishing, 1983.

Lawyers Committee for Human Rights. *"Salvaging" Democracy: Human Rights in the Philippines*. New York: Lawyers Committee for Human Rights, 1985.

Magno, Alexander R. (ed.). *Nation in Crisis: The University Inquires into the Present*. Quezon City: University of the Philippines Press, 1984.

May, R. J., and Francisco Nemenzo (eds.). *The Philippines After Marcos*. London: Croom, Helm, 1984.

Munro, Ross H. "The New Khmer Rouge," *Commentary*, vol. 80, no. 6, December 1985 [attack on NPA].

Niksch, Larry A., and Marjorie Niehaus. *The Internal Situation in the Philippines: Current Trends and Future Prospects*. (Report No. 81-21F.) Washington, DC: Congressional Research Service, Library of Congress, 1981.

Rosenberg, David A. "Letter," *Problems of Communism*, July-Aug. 1985 [on NPA and the USSR].

Rosenberger, Leif. "Philippine Communism and the Soviet Union," *Survey*, no. 124, Spring 1985 [by Defense Dept. official].

San Juan, E. *Crisis in the Philippines: The Making of a Revolution*. South Hadley, MA; Bergin & Garvey, 1986.

Solarz, Stephen J. "Last Chance for the Philippines," *New Republic*, April 8, 1985 [by key U.S. member of congress].

Sullivan, William H. "Living Without Marcos," *Foreign Policy*, no. 53, Winter 1983-84 [by former U.S. official].

Chapter 10: Marcos's Final Crisis

Constantino, Letizia R. *The Snap Revolution: A Post-Mortem.* Quezon City: Karrel, Inc., 1986.

Fenton, James. "The Snap Revolution," *Granta*, no. 18, (New York: Penguin, 1986).

Laxalt, Senator Paul. "My Conversations with Ferdinand Marcos," *Policy Review*, no. 37, Summer 1986.

Mamot, Patricio R. *People Power: Profile of Filipino Heroism.* Quezon City: New Day Publishers, 1986.

Manila, Quijano de. *The Quartet of the Tiger Moon: Scenes from the People-Power Apocalypse.* Manila [?]: The Book Stop, Inc., 1986.

Mercado, Monia (ed.). *People Power: The Philippine Revolution of 1986.* San Francisco: Ignatius Press, 1986.

Project 28 Days, Ltd. *Bayan Ko! Images of the Philippine Revolt.* Hong Kong: Project 28 Days, Ltd., 1986.

Shaplen, Robert. "From Marcos to Aquino," *New Yorker*, August 25, 1986 and September 1, 1986.

Chapter 11: The Future

[see also Shaplen in chap. 10 above]

Aguilar-San Juan, Karin. "Living in the Post-Marcos Era," *Dollars & Sense*, no. 118, July-August 1986.

Albinales, P. N. "The Post-Marcos Regime, the Non-Bourgeois Opposition, and the Prospects of a Philippine October," *Kasarinlan* [Third World Studies Center, University of the Philippines], vol. 1, no. 4, 2nd quarter 1986.

Alliance for Philippine Concerns. *The Case for a Nuclear Free Philippines: A Proposal for a Non-Nuclear Provision in the Philippine Constitution.* San Francisco: Alliance for Philippine Concerns, July 1986.

"Aquino Welcomes Foreign Investors," *Washington Post*, Sept. 17, 1986, pp. A20-21; *New York Times*, Sept. 19, 1986, pp. A21-23.

Bello, Walden. "Reflections on a New Era in the Philippines," *Christianity and Crisis*, April 7, 1986.

Clines, Francis X. "Putting It Together," *New York Times Magazine*, April 27, 1986.

Landé, Carl H. (ed.). *Experts Assess U.S.-Philippine Relations: A Six-Month Review of President Aauino's Government*. Washington, DC: The Washington Institute Press, forthcoming.

Landé, Carl H., and Richard Hooley. "Acquino Takes Charge," *Foreign Affairs*, vol. 64, summer 1986.

Lichauco, Alejandro. *Towards A New Economic Order and the Conquest of Mass Poverty*. Quezon City: SPP, 1986.

A Letter of Concern from U.S. Missioners in the Philippines to the Christian Churches of the United States. Davao City: July 1986 [distributed in the U.S. by the Church Coalition for Human Rights in the Philippines, 110 Maryland Ave., N.E., Washington, DC 20002].

Magno, Jose P., Jr., and A. James Gregor. "Insurgency and Counter-insurgency in the Philippines," *Asian Survey*, vol. 26, no. 5, May 1986.

Mydans, Seth. "Dilemma of A Priest in the Philippines," *New York Times Magazine*, Sept. 14, 1986.

Olalia, Rolando M. "Give Filipinos 'A Genuine Choice,'" *Philippine News* [San Francisco], November 19-25, 1986 [speech by KMU leader before his assassination].

Porter, Gareth. "Firm Steps in a New Direction," *Christianity and Crisis*, April 7, 1986.

Porter, Gareth. *The Politics of Counterinsurgency in the Philippines: The Military and Non-Military Options*. Philippine Studies Center, University of Hawaii, Occasional Paper no. 9, Honolulu, forthcoming.

Tadem, Eduardo C. "Lessons for the Philippine Left," *Kasarinlan* [Third World Studies Center, University of the Philippines], vol. 1, no. 4, 2nd quarter 1986.

Tarr, Peter. "Can Aquino Revive A Plundered Land?" *The Nation*, April 19, 1986.

Villegas, Bernardo M., et al. *The Philippines at the Crossroads: Some Visions for the Nation*. Manila[?]: Center for Research and Communication, 1986.

INDEX

417